ALLEN DULLES

ALLEN DULLES
MASTER OF SPIES

James Srodes

Since 1947
REGNERY
PUBLISHING, INC.
An Eagle Publishing Company • Washington, DC

Library of Congress Cataloging-in-Publication Data

Srodes, James.
    Allen Dulles : master of spies / James Srodes.
         p.   cm.
    Includes bibliographical references (p.   ) and index.
    ISBN 0-89526-314-9 (alk. paper)
    1. Dulles, Allen Welsh, 1893–1969. 2. Spies—United States—Biography. 3. United States. Central Intelligence Agency—Officials and employees—Biography. 4. Intelligence service—United States—History—20th century. 5. Espionage, American—History—20th century. I. Title.
E748.D87S68 1999
973.9'092—dc21
[B]
                                          99-19401
                                              CIP

Published in the United States by
Regnery Publishing, Inc.
An Eagle Publishing Company
One Massachusetts Avenue, NW
Washington, DC 20001

Distributed to the trade by
National Book Network
4720-A Boston Way
Lanham, MD 20706

Designed by Marci Hecht
Set in Minion
Printed on acid-free paper
Manufactured in the United States of America

10 9 8 7 6 5 4 3 2 1

Books are available in quantity for promotional or premium use. Write to Director of Special Sales, Regnery Publishing, Inc., One Massachusetts Avenue, NW, Washington, DC 20001, for information on discounts and terms or call (202) 216-0600.

CONTENTS

TO CECILE

WITH ALL LOVE AND DEVOTION

CHAPTER ONE

Allen Welsh Dulles (1893–1969)

"I've Got a Secret."

ALLEN DULLES LOVED TO attend dinner parties with his old friends among the Washington elite. Even in retirement the old spymaster and his wife Clover were happy ornaments whenever there was a Georgetown gathering of the powerful and well positioned. Dulles enjoyed the cocktail hour and appreciated the good food and wine that followed. But most of all, he relished conversation. Chalmers Roberts, the *Washington Post*'s star political reporter and a frequent social companion of the Dulleses, recalls, "Allen gave the impression of being a gregarious type. He was full of jollity. With his hearty laugh, his tweed coat, and his love of the martini, he cut quite a figure. But he never left any doubt that he was always looking for information rather than giving it out. He was very good at giving you tidbits in order to draw what he wanted from you."[1]

Dulles especially enjoyed the moment at these affairs when someone would try to put him on the spot with an embarrassing question. He came to call these incidents "I've Got a Secret," after the popular television quiz show. Late in the evening, a self-appointed questioner often asked, in a voice loud enough to silence the other dinner guests, "Now, Mr. Dulles, we all want to know what *you* think about this matter." The topic often was the crisis of the day, some tension along the Berlin Wall, or a fresh outburst against the West by Nehru or Castro. In later years, attempts to lure him into indiscreet criticism about the Vietnam War were the most popular gambit. Within the Georgetown enclave of mandarins of high politics, there was a tradesman's envy of anyone who held a bigger inventory of inside information. Allen Dulles was correctly judged by most to hold more secrets than anyone. There was the delicious possibility that if he could be coaxed into some leak it would be an instant prize for the nonstop gossip mill of the city. It might even turn into a scandal and boost the status of the salon where it occurred.

What did Dulles think? While the others leaned forward in their seats, Dulles, savoring the moment, would take his time to stoke and relight the crusty old pipe that was as much his trademark as his professorial bow ties. He absorbed the attention. Once the pipe was drawing to his satisfaction, he would fix his pale blue eyes on his interrogator. The tutorial was about to start.

One of his favorite opening lines was, "You know, my brother Foster and I ran into a similar situation when we worked for President Wilson at the Paris Peace Conference in nineteen-hundred and nineteen." The anecdote could run as long as half an hour, but no one grew bored. He had long perfected the ability to appear to confide dark revelations. His tales had the taste of crucial current events cast against dramatic history. World figures such as Anthony Eden, Jan Masaryk, Franklin Roosevelt, and Winston Churchill paraded through the story line. He had been one of the first American officials to interview Adolf Hitler in 1933, and he had actively plotted with German aristocrats to assassinate the Nazi despot during World War II. One of his funnier anecdotes was about how he bypassed a chance to meet Lenin just before the Bolshevik leader left Switzerland in 1917 to capture the Russian Revolution. Instead, Dulles said, he had insisted on keeping a tennis date with a beautiful blonde. And then there was the time Khrushchev told him they both read the same daily intelligence reports; but were they Russian or American reports? His stories usually ended with a punch line that drew appreciative laughter around the table.

At that point, Dulles would glance at his watch. "Is that the time? My goodness, Clover, we must be going." Amid hasty good-byes and gracious thanks, the couple would sweep out of the room. Those left behind basked in an afterglow, feeling they had been present at a rare inside look into the workings of high affairs. Only later, sometimes the next day, it dawned on everyone that Allen Dulles had once more managed to avoid answering the direct question put to him.

Even in an open democracy, intelligence is the first ingredient of the policies that guide both diplomacy and war. During his life, Allen Dulles gathered and kept secrets for a greater length of time than any man of his day. For more than fifty years he was one of the constant forces in the hesitant march by the U.S. government to create a system to generate information to serve the secret needs of decision-makers. Other actors came and went during the twenty-year drama that saw the dismantling of our World War I spy apparatus and the creation of the one that served us in World War II. Only Allen Dulles was there from the opening line to the final curtain. His imprint is also firmly visible on the uniquely American intelligence *process* that has evolved since the end of World War II. In shaping the Central Intelligence Agency (CIA), he took that espionage service from the gentleman's game it had been since the nineteenth century and propelled it into the space age. At that point official espionage ceased to be the sometimes plaything of privileged dilettantes, and became the indispensable tool of strategic thinking for a democracy.

The mystery and controversy over the life of Allen Dulles persist even to this day. His life remains one of the few topics that can lead to a heated dinner table argument in many capitals of the world, Washington, D.C., included. There is often a feigned confusion between Allen Dulles and his brother, John Foster Dulles. It is a plausible enough ploy, but one that is usually disingenuous. Foster Dulles was secretary of state for President Eisenhower at the same time Allen Dulles was building the CIA. Both men bore a strong family resemblance; they both dressed in the uniform of Wall Street attorneys, which is what they were when they were not engaged in the broader arena of world affairs; and they were partners in the policy objectives of President Eisenhower. But as their sister, Eleanor Lansing Dulles, shrewdly observed, "It was easier to notice the similarities when they were apart. When you looked at them close together, you noticed the differences."

First, Allen Dulles was a far more complex personality than his brother. He shunned the front rank of history but hungered for power and the accompanying celebrity. He was a driven man who worked single-mindedly at a pace that damaged his own private life and wore out those who served him. Yet he played at a genial casualness, a gentleman's ease that made those who did not look closely conclude he was a lightweight in a heavyweight's job. One of his undisputed strengths was his sense of moral certainty and his reputation for incisive honesty, and yet his private life was marred by blatant sexual escapades. At the time, his affairs merely added weight to the belief among his critics that he was a frivolous man.

In the popular histories of our just ending century, Allen Dulles rates only a footnote as a character who was on the stage during most of the 1950s but who had entered a deserved exile by the early 1960s. Yet an astonishing number of those who dominate our history of the past hundred years had a high regard for

Allen Dulles. Many looked to him for guidance and insights into the most pressing problems of war, peace, and survival that engaged them then and still engage us now. Allen Dulles never laid claim to being the father of either modern American intelligence or the CIA. Nevertheless, most of his early life and all of his later years were devoted to honing and positioning this country's main intelligence weapon.

A moment's reflection on the more than fifty-year career of Allen Dulles—from fledgling intelligence agent in 1916 to public defender of his agency's beleaguered reputation at his death in 1969—prompts one to argue that he can certainly lay claim to two very important achievements that set him apart for history's consideration.

First, consider that intelligence drives the world of nations as we know it. When defined as seeking out "the intentions and capabilities" of other governments, intelligence becomes the raw ingredient of any foreign policy. This is true no matter whether kings or committees direct those strategies. What one does not know, one cannot consider. Absent the perfect universe of total knowledge, what policymakers are told by their intelligence providers takes on a weight beyond the raw facts themselves.

So while Allen Dulles did not "invent" America's intelligence system, he was one of its earliest midwives, first as an active agent in World War I, then as a planner and designer in the gray testing time between the wars, and again as the most productive generator of intelligence for the Office of Strategic Services (OSS), that romantic secret spy agency of World War II.

Dulles was not merely a "gentleman spy," as one early biographer dismissed him. He transcended the mechanics of espionage technique and became one of the most important voices in the debate on the conduct of the war with the Axis powers and on what our strategy should be after the war. As OSS station chief in

Bern, Switzerland, during World War II, Dulles is justly credited with developing unrivaled sources of intelligence within the highest levels of the Third Reich. His intelligence network included all of the often competing resistance groups in France, Italy, the Balkans, and Eastern Europe; in return he sent back into the war zone invaluable resources of arms, equipment, money, and information gathered elsewhere. The result was an output of intelligence "product" and "interpretation" that at times dwarfed the amount produced by all of the other OSS stations combined. In value, the information Dulles produced and sent to Washington and London became the dominant witness to what was happening inside Nazi-held Europe. Dulles thus became a compelling voice inside Allied war councils. But his was not the only voice. Dulles operated under the handicap of being isolated thousands of miles from Washington, which allowed others to discount or dismiss his views when they disagreed with their own. Yet even British intelligence officials, whose own goals and strategies were often at odds with those of Dulles, have since freely conceded that his contribution was the most important single force in the Allied intelligence effort. Sir Kenneth W. D. Strong, who served as General Eisenhower's wartime intelligence aide and dominated Britain's spy services for twenty-five years, thereafter judged Allen Dulles the "greatest intelligence officer who ever lived."

Dulles's second claim to eminence lies with his influence in shaping America's postwar foreign policy. While America's leaders were quick to scrap the OSS and retire its senior officials once the fighting stopped, Allen Dulles was preserved for future use. He had sharp and well-defined opinions about what America's goals should be in the Cold War that came after open-armed conflict had ceased, and they were opinions that changed history.

Allen Dulles's private life and public career have as many detractors as devotees. Much of the argument over the man's worth centers on a paradox built into the CIA. America, the peace-seeker and sower of democracy, rightly stands blamed for committing all manner of mayhem around the world nominally in the cause of universal freedom and in its own national interest. First as the CIA's deputy director for operations, and then as director of Central Intelligence, Allen Dulles gave American presidents a new weapon—an Alexander's sword to cut through the insoluble stalemates that confound diplomats and block generals from resorting to all-out war. By more closely merging intelligence gathering and assessment with covert operations and paramilitary intrusions than had been attempted before, the Dulles CIA provided the presidency with a liberating device that was satisfyingly direct. Covert action stops just short of the horrors of modern armed combat, which is made all the more unthinkable with the threat of nuclear weapons. No president from Harry Truman onward has been able put that weapon aside.

Allen Dulles is praised among those who were intimately involved in America's Cold War conflict, but some now wonder whether the agency he shaped has become as much a part of the problem as it was a solution. The questions he addressed nearly fifty years ago are as current as today's hot public debate about whether we even need a CIA in this post–Cold War world. We would not be Americans if we did not have two minds about whether clandestine spying and covert force are fit tactics for the kind of nation we hold ourselves to be. It does not seem as important as it might that the agency proved to be both a potent force against our enemies and a protector of our friends. There is in our national character a self-absorbed strain that makes us shrink from the hostilities of the world even when our own security is threatened. We want to be universally admired as a people while as a nation we are kept safe from the world fray. Allen Dulles knew that the choice was not a simple trade-off between morality and safety.

This story is about how Dulles came to that viewpoint and how our present intelligence service evolved over more than a century of experimentation and testing. After watching other approaches fail through two world wars, Dulles knew what he wanted to do when he got his chance. He had been preparing for such a task all his life. We live with the legacy of that life today, three decades after his death.

ALLEN WELSH DULLES was born at 3:00 AM on April 23, 1893, to a family that was neither wealthy nor especially advantaged. Other histories of his family have portrayed the Dulleses as pompous pretenders to Gilded Age aristocracy, or as dried-up Presbyterian messianics. These portraits are not true. The Dulleses of Watertown, New York, were eminent but not rich. They invested a level of energy in their careers that is remarkable even in today's hectic times, but they enjoyed life's simpler pleasures to the fullest.

The father, Allen Macy Dulles, was a third-generation Presbyterian minister and a self-propelled rising star in the progressive movement within the Protestant clergy. The mother was Edith Foster Dulles, the daughter of a former secretary of state, a match to her driven, outspoken husband. Between them, the minister and his wife managed to build two significant careers devoted to the service of others. At the same time they raised five children (two sons, three daughters) who were themselves remarkable characters for their time; three of them would go on to have spectacular public lives of their own.

There were, however, key differences between the Dulleses and other notable nineteenth-century American families. An enlarged portrait of several generations of the Dulles clan reveals a level of eminence—three secretaries of state and other holders of important positions in diplomacy, government, the law, and the church—that places them among such monumental historical names as the Adamses, the Lees, and the Roosevelts. Yet during his life, the Reverend Allen Macy Dulles never earned more than $3,500 a year (roughly $30,000 a year in today's money), and the broader family fortunes did not reach significant prosperity until well after most of the five children were young adults.

To dig deeper into the early years of young Allen Dulles, one turns to that most valuable of biographical records, the "Line-a-Day" diary that Allen Macy and Edith Dulles kept during most of their married lives. The Dulleses took a leather-covered plain notebook and dated each page with 1 of the 365 days of the year. In tiny script, one or the other would write a one-sentence description of that date's events, year after year, for more than forty years. Each page marked the ebb and flow of family life across the years. There emerges a sense of enormous energy being expended as those lines reveal remarks about the weather, trips, social events, and the minister's sermon topics. Other family recollections and interviews reinforce the same sense that the Dulles family was in constant motion. Adults and children alike were always busy doing something, striving, learning, working. Even on the long summer vacations the family took together, there was never an idle moment. Dulles family life was comfortable and secure, but it was robust to the point of being somewhat spartan. A Dulles plunged ahead. A Dulles did not dwell on the past.

This explains Allen Macy Dulles's terse notation on the birth of his second son, "Allen Welsh Dulles born 3 AM." It would not be until July that the diary, again in the father's hand, notes, "E. [Edith] takes Allie to Philadelphia to see about leg." Allie Dulles, as he was called, had been born with a clubfoot. Such malformations were easily correctable by surgery in those days, but there was still something jarring about it. More than the commonplace belief that birth defects were some sort of curse, Edith and her husband had been much worried about their decision to have a third child. When eldest son John Foster Dulles was born in January 1888, and, fifteen months later, when daughter Margaret was delivered, the births were so difficult as to be life-threatening to both mother and children. Edith's doctor warned her that the infections associated with childbirth in those days had so weakened her that she must postpone the decision to have more children for at least five years. That meant giving up the physical intimacies that were very much a part of their married life. Their resolve lasted little more than three years.

After Allie's troubled birth, the minister and his wife continued a sexually active marriage despite the increasing toll it took on Edith. In 1895 a second daughter, Eleanor, was born. She was, by her own description, "a tough little nut" who was afflicted with weakened eyesight. She compensated for her poor vision by becoming a sharp judge of character. She also shared Allen's adventurous spirit, and it would take her every bit as far in the world of history-making affairs as her two elder brothers. The baby of the family, Nataline, was born in 1898. That event apparently marked a final change in the parents' relations. The Reverend Dulles built a larger house, a colonnaded manse on Mullins Street in Watertown, New York, that included a separate study on the third floor where he spent considerable time. There he found refuge for his heavy burden of theological studies and writing. Edith, although she kept up a breathless round of good works and lengthy travel, suffered increasingly from debilitating headaches and bouts of melancholy that often left her bedridden. Depression would haunt later generations of Dulles offspring.

Eleanor Dulles remarked later, "I remember asking Mother about the gap in the births of Foster and Margaret and then of Allen, who was born four years later. She said about how ill she had been for months after each of them had been born, and what the doctor had said. Then she added, 'It was hard on your father,' and that was the closest I came to talking about sex with her. There were, of course, no birth control devices that worked very well in those days."

Allen Dulles was influenced throughout his life by the solitary personalities of so many in his family. Outsiders often mistook this aloofness as a sign of clannishness. Yet the Dulleses were socially adept and convivial company; Allen was especially lighthearted and charming. And there was a robust sexuality that ran through most of their lives. Yet there was a point beyond which non-Dulleses could not penetrate, an inner recess where others, be they lovers, wives, or friends, could not go. It was not easy to be a Dulles, harder still to love one. It was difficult to be a child of Allen and Edith Dulles, harder still to be a grandchild.

FAMILY HISTORY SPECULATES that the original Dulleses may have been named Douglas and been part of the Scots transplantation into Northern Ireland during the time of the Tudors. The first of the line to arrive in America was a Joseph Dulles, who arrived in Charleston, South Carolina, during the Revolutionary War. He undertook stints as a soldier and storekeeper before marrying a wealthy land-owning widow. The two children from this marriage both gravitated northward. The son, also Joseph Dulles, went to Yale and became a minister. The daughter, Elizabeth, married Langdon Cheves, a South Carolinian who was sent to Congress and then stayed on in Washington as president of the short-lived Bank of the United States.

John Welsh Dulles, Joseph's son, also a Presbyterian minister, answered the call of missionary work that had so gripped the American Protestant churches of that time. The Reverend John Dulles and his wife went to India to preach at a mission in Madras and stayed there for years before health problems drove them home to Philadelphia. His wife, Harriet Lathrop Winslow, had income of her own, which helped this Reverend Dulles ascend into the hierarchy of the Presbyterian Missions Board. He became something of a celebrity for his memoirs of his work in India and his tours of the Holy Land. Meanwhile, an uncle earned a tour as U.S. ambassador to the Court of St. James in London for his charitable largesse to political causes. The Dulleses, in short, were a solid, pious family of notable accomplishment. Since the Presbyterian church was such an important part of the family's identity, it was only natural that later generations of Dulles sons were educated at Princeton College, which was founded by Presbyterians.

When it was his turn, Allen Macy Dulles graduated with honors from both the undergraduate college and the seminary. But he was no bookish, diffident vicar. He played on the school's undefeated varsity football team when the sport was a national scandal for its violence and danger. Princeton's Tigers were noted for their fierce play and for the spirited coaching of one of the upperclassmen, a friend of Allen's named Thomas Woodrow Wilson, the future president. The Dulleses had a knack for making friends early with those who would later prove important to their careers.

Edith Foster Dulles was a nineteenth-century portrait of a dutiful wife, a loving mother, and a tireless worker for disadvantaged women in whatever town her husband's calling took them. But Paris—glorious, gilded, liberating City of Lights—was where her heart lay from her first encounter with it as the teenage daughter of a diplomat. The amount of travel Edith managed during her life was extraordinary, such as the necessary trips with her husband to various church-related conferences. Then, too, Allie had to be taken often in his early years to the New York City surgeons who straightened his clubfoot and worked to rebuild his withered left leg. Also there was an increasing cycle of spur-of-the-moment visits to Philadelphia to visit her husband's family, and to Washington, D.C., where her own father's fortunes were based and where, in time, her sons Foster and Allen would be drawn as well. And there was always Paris. As we will see, the Dulles family's stays in France and the rest of Europe were perhaps more formative for the later public career of Allen Dulles than the time he spent at the primitive public schools of Watertown and Auburn, New York.

Among the forceful characters in Allie's family, perhaps the most important was Edith's father, General John Watson Foster. As much as any person, Grandfather Foster shaped the minds and the outlook of grandsons Allie and Foster and set their careers along the path that he himself had followed quite by accident.

General Foster—he prized that title above others—was one of the genetic keys to the fierce ambitions of the Dulles clan. He also established the family's proprietorial claims on the U.S. State Department and on the diplomatic careers that were viewed as something of a Dulles birthright. If the Dulles progeny got their energy and sense of mission from their parents, they got the grit and vision they needed from this grandfather. The Dulles passion for education and travel was greatly compounded by General Foster's conviction—also passed on through his daughter—that one could not travel too much or learn enough.

By the time Allie became aware of his grandfather, General Foster had already worked through several careers—lawyer, soldier, editor, politician, diplomat—all culminating in a brief lame-duck term as secretary of state in 1892, in the waning days of the administration of President Benjamin Harrison. Foster was one of those Americans of the Gilded Age who won advancement and place in the world beyond the wildest dreams of his youth. But what set him apart from his contemporaries was that his vision of the future stretched beyond the curve of sight of others of his day.

General Foster was the third son of a pioneer into the Indiana region in the early 1800s who had prospered as a grist mill operator. The young man was accorded a first-rate education. He was the valedictorian of his class of 1855 at Indiana University, and his stint at Harvard Law School was followed by a year of reading law with Algernon Sullivan, an established attorney in Cincinnati. When the Civil War broke out, he joined the Indiana Volunteers and, through the prevailing system of choosing officers, was elected to the rank of major. He had what the British call "a good war." He had never been in robust health—he was thin, taciturn, with delicate skin that would redden painfully if exposed too long to the sun—yet, oddly, he was one of those who thrived and actually enjoyed the privations of military campaigning. Foster became an officer who was not only popular with the soldiers but also able to command them with skill in the chaos of a skirmish. He managed to transfer from the infantry to command a cavalry brigade and won commendation repeatedly for bravery and skill in the bloody battles at Fort Donelson and Shiloh. The friendships he formed with two other rising stars—Ulysses Grant and William Tecumseh Sherman—would prove invaluable in later life.[2]

Foster returned to Evansville, Indiana, where he edited the local newspaper and participated in the rowdy politics of that brawling time. In the 1872 presidential campaign, President Grant's tolerance of the corruption of his inner circle nearly cost him reelection. Yet despite the thousand faults and worries that beset Grant, General Foster, who was chairman of the Indiana Republican Party, stuck loyally to his wartime commander. Through his newspaper's fiery editorials and his own personal campaigning, Foster won credit in Washington for leading the upset win in Indiana for Grant, who carried all but six states and polled 800,000 votes more than his nearest rival. In 1873 Grant rewarded his old friend by naming him minister to Mexico. Foster would later recall that he had wanted the envoy's job in Switzerland because it was a quiet, out-of-the-way place where his inexperience would cause no harm.

The Mexican posting, by contrast, was a sensitive one. The United States had leaned heavily on the French government to remove its suzerainty over Mexico but had not assured the succeeding governments of Benito Juarez and Porfirio Diaz that the United States was a benevolent neighbor. Although a more polished and seasoned diplomat might have made more sense as the choice for ambassador to Mexico, Grant believed Foster would be as quick a study of the task as he had been of military command. And indeed, in the seven years the Fosters spent in Mexico, he insisted that his family mingle freely among the leading Mexican families, joined his children in learning Spanish, and sent Edith and Eleanor to a school for the young daughters of Mexican government officials. While Mexican wariness of its neighbor to the north would remain for another hundred years, Foster did win a number of commercial agreements that eased tensions.

The seven-year tour of duty in Mexico was the first of nearly thirty years of assignments that took Foster and his family far away from Indiana forever. The next stop was an appointment by President Rutherford B. Hayes in 1880, as minister to the court of Russian Czar Alexander II. By then, daughter Edith, seventeen, was keeping a diary that recorded the lavish life of the Imperial Court, the glittering dances, and the moonlight races of horse-drawn troikas across the frozen wastes outside St. Petersburg. Edith was observant enough to notice the explosive pressures building up in Russian society, even from the protected safety of the American Legation. Years later, in a memoir crafted from her diaries for her grandchildren, she would recall, "It is hard to exaggerate the oppression, the cruelty of the Russian system of government, the ignorance in which the people were kept, the espionage to which all were subjected."[3] General Foster too learned his first lessons about intelligence operations from the czar's dreaded *Okhrana* secret police.

The family headed home from St. Petersburg to Washington in the spring of 1881 but paused for a lengthy stay in Paris, the first of many long visits that would lie wrapped as a treasure in Edith's heart. Mary Foster ensured that Edith and Eleanor continued regular schooling during the long visit there. The family also made friends with many wealthy Americans who had sought culture and relief from boredom by living abroad. The Fosters with their two lovely teenage daughters were immediately welcomed into the lavish apartments along the Champs Elysées that were home to the Yankee expatriates.

Edith's diary for the 1881 stay in Paris records one of the regular Sunday soirées where she met a confident, athletic young Princeton seminarian named Allen Macy Dulles. She recorded his name as "Mr. Dunis" with a question mark after it and thought little more about him. Some of the matchmakers among the ladies of the American clique in Paris invited them both to teas during that summer interlude before both were to return home. With her head still swirling from visions of the Russian court, of nights at the opera in Paris, Edith was not much interested in any young man at that moment. Allen Macy Dulles, however, was smitten at once and laid a dogged siege for Edith's affections that lasted six years.

AFTER MARRYING IN 1886, the couple moved to a congregation in Watertown, New York. This bustling trading center north of Syracuse served the prosperous dairy farms of the area and was a popular gateway for families who used the Thousand Islands lake region as a vacation resort from the heat of the cities. Allie was squeezed in by the two older children, Foster and Margaret, and his two younger sisters, Eleanor and Nataline. No surprise then that Allie had problems finding his place in the ranks. His weakened leg was the least of his handicaps. Sister Eleanor recalls, "As children we were not allowed to tease my brother about his leg.

That's about all. It never slowed him down as a boy, as I recall. He was always active, running about, as I remember him. He was my closest brother, remember. Foster and Margaret both were much older by the time I came along, so Allen was my friend and the one I followed around, so I would have noticed if he had been slowed down. He wasn't. But we just didn't talk about it." Since Allie himself as a young boy was not above using the leg as a real or imagined excuse for sympathy, the family's deliberately impassive posture stemmed in part from an attempt to toughen the boy to the rigors of life.

The young Dulles children were hardly oppressed by any fair measure and were more uninhibited than most. It is never easy to be a minister's child. But the Dulleses approached their family obligations in a matter-of-fact manner. They were the supporting cast for their father's churchly duties and so worshipped and participated in hymn singing and Bible studies.

"I think we looked forward to Sundays," recalled eldest sister Margaret Dulles Edwards. "Every Sunday morning as our family grew up, we five children, led by my mother, walked sedately up the church aisle and took our places in the next-to-the-front pew. And each of us was equipped—this was my father's idea—with a pencil and notebook. We were to take notes on the sermon. Of course for the younger ones, my two little sisters, this didn't amount to very much. But for my brother, Foster, and myself, and for Allie, it was a very serious undertaking. We felt we were reporters on our father's sermon.

"And then at Sunday dinner our notes were brought forth, and we discussed the sermon. And my father always said that if our notes were not good and clear, he must have preached a very poor sermon. He always took the blame on himself. So that made us very eager—because we loved our father—very eager to make our notes as accurate as possible. I think it was very interesting training."[4]

Allen Macy Dulles, because of his scholarly bent, was punctilious about words and their usage. As a result, the children grew up with a healthy caution about what they said and wrote. In adulthood, this caution rendered some of their public utterances pedantic but never imprecise. As adults, the children's main remembrance was of a loving father whose approval they all eagerly sought and who was not stinting in his praise and encouragement. If he required more of his children, they were willing enough to try to meet his expectations.

The education offered by the Watertown public schools was of indifferent quality—at least Edith Dulles thought so. Much of what Foster and the other children would remember so fondly about their education was the large amount of reading, learning, and reciting they were encouraged to do at home. Foster and Allen particularly thrilled at the histories of ancient Greece and Rome; both read Gibbon's *Decline and Fall of the Roman Empire* at early ages. They also read *Pilgrim's Progress* and *Paradise Lost* as well as the more accessible poetry of Keats, Shelley, and the Brownings. It was routine on a Sunday for each of the children to learn a new poem, a chapter from the Bible, or several verses of a hymn. Foster, at one time in his youth, had memorized the entire Gospel of Saint John. More arcane studies of Greek and Latin were provided by special tutors for each child's individual needs.

Foster Dulles quickly developed the prodigy's odd mixture of shy reserve and off-putting self-confidence that brought strangers up short on first meeting. Perhaps because the place of the dutiful son was already so ably filled, young Allie was the charming rascal of the family, insofar as rascality was tolerated in the Dulles household. Schoolwork came less easily to Allie than it did to Foster, and there is evidence that he tried to gloss over his shortcomings by adopting a careless attitude, to appear that he was not really trying. This earned him numerous sessions in his father's study, where, as Eleanor, another frequent visitor, recalls, "Father would very patiently explain where you had done wrong and what you must do to do better. And he would explain it to you so there was no uncertainty."

Because of the distance in years between himself and his older siblings, Allie benefited from the increasing preoccupation of his parents with outside interests by being more on his own. He was also thrown more often into the company of Eleanor, who from the early years was herself struggling mightily to carve out her own identity.

"Allen was an important figure in my life," Eleanor would write in her memoirs seventy years later. "He helped me with various land and water ventures. He even tutored me in ancient history when I began to consider college entrance examinations. I found him companionable and saw some of the charm for which he was well known in later years. Ours was a fluctuating relationship. It ranged all the way from dislike and anger to a passionate desire for approval. My changing moods and his strong reactions to them continued throughout our lives and added pain and pleasure. His charm was irresistible and his intensity of rage was occasionally overwhelming, though not many people saw his tougher side. I know that there were months in our later years when I stayed out of his orbit to avoid the stress and furor that he stirred in me. Once he stormed when I parked too close to the door; another time he accused me of 'blowing the cover' of one of his CIA agents—I didn't. His ability and his skill in handling people were real to me over the years."[5]

Allie was one of those boys who escaped the awkward-looking period as he grew from young boy to young man. Photographs of him as a boy show an angelic, cheerful face made striking by his blue-gray eyes. He would grow to nearly six feet tall and would always be somewhat less bulky than Foster; both men would be athletes. Allen also shared with Foster, and Eleanor, the broad fore-head of the Dulleses, but he inherited his Grandfather Foster's elongated jawline and jutting chin. As a young man he would appear older than his years; in later life his firm chin and clipped mustache would give him even more authority. He kept his athletic build most of his life because of an enormous and constant need to be active; his physical energy and stamina became as much his personality as the booming laugh and merry sense of humor.

Life in the main was good for the Dulles children, far more so than for most children in that well-to-do part of nineteenth-century America. There were plenty of interests besides Bible studies and hymn singing. Both the Clinton Street and Mullins Street parsonages in Watertown had plenty of horses, ponies, and other pets. Edith and Allen Macy organized parties, picnics, sporting events, and concerts to draw the young people of the congregation closer to the church, and their own children were both bait and beneficiaries. In short, the Dulles family routine was a mix of group ritual and individual freedom.

"We were like a pride of lions," Eleanor summed up. The description is apt. It calls to mind a sleepy sunny afternoon with complacent but watchful parents gazing on as their cubs wrestle in mock struggles that prepare for the tougher battles of survival. While there was not the money to elevate the family to the haughty levels of America's elite, it was also true that, in the words of one of John Foster Dulles's biographers, "to the outsiders the Dulleses were a formidable and unusual family, just a bit larger than life, full of spirit and character."[6]

Allie's family circle expanded in other ways. In 1890 Edith's sister Eleanor Foster married Robert Lansing, the son of Dulles neighbors whom she had met on a visit to Watertown. Bert Lansing, as he was called, practiced law with his father and was ambitiously active in the Democratic Party machine of his part of New York. He would not stay a local lawyer for long.

During the period between the late 1880s and early 1890s, General Foster drew so many special assignments as a diplomat that House Speaker Chauncey Depew quipped he was the "handyman of the Department of State." Among the reforms he actively promoted within the U.S. foreign service was to expand the use of military and commercial attachés (then common only among the major European powers) as gatherers of intelligence for the secretaries of state and war. General Foster also had considerable vision in spotting the onrushing horror of modern warfare in an industrial age. He was one of the earliest American foreign policy figures to advocate the use of international arbitration courts to settle specific disputes between nations and to urge the kind of permanent international forum for peace that ultimately evolved into the United Nations.

In 1893, the year Allie was born, General Foster wound up his career as the State Department's man-of-all-work. He finished the final months of the Harrison administration as secretary of state, during which time he brokered U.S. interests in the coup organized by American planters against the Hawaiian royal family. At the same time, he recruited son-in-law Bert Lansing to help him prepare America's case for the country's first venture into an international arbitration court to settle a dispute between the U.S. government, the British, and the Russians over rights in the Bering Sea. He and Lansing went to Paris to argue the case. Then, freed from his obligations to government life, he and his wife embarked on a world tour. They journeyed through Italy, Syria, Egypt, India, and on to the Far East, with long stops along the way where General Foster's rank and reputation made him something of a celebrity.

The trip brought an unexpected dividend. Almost as soon as they had arrived home, General Foster was commissioned by the Chinese Imperial Government to go to Japan and sue to end the devastating war over which nation would rule Korea. Although

Japan was only a tenth the size of China, it had destroyed the Peking government's armies and navy in the early months of 1894. General Foster's taciturn formality and his punctilious attention to fairness won effusive praise from both governments. The Treaty of Simonoseki that was signed in 1895 was hailed as a model of peacemaking, and both sides felt they had done the best they could under the circumstances. The Japanese had triumphed in their first foray into modern warfare. China's premier Li Huan Chang considered his nation lucky to have survived the onslaught and gave credit to John Watson Foster for preserving the Manchu Imperial throne. General Foster received the profound compliment of being asked to represent both the Japanese and Chinese governments in future dealings in international disputes. While he confessed he was fascinated by the dynamic Japanese rush toward modernity, he stuck with the Chinese and a lucrative legal relationship that lasted until the revolution of 1911.

General Foster returned to Washington from Japan in June 1895 to resume his private law practice. Bert Lansing, in the meantime, was commuting between Watertown and Washington, establishing a reputation as a legal expert on arbitration proceedings between governments and claimants on a wide variety of trade and legal matters. Between then and 1914, it was said, Lansing served on more international arbitrations than any other living American.[7]

Lansing introduced his father-in-law and the rest of the Dulleses to the Henderson Harbor area of Lake Ontario at about the time he married Eleanor. Lansing and General Foster shared a love of fishing for the feisty small-mouth black bass that ruled the local waters there. Both had also been drawn to the solitary woods of beech trees and the dark-watered arc of the coastline. There were dozens of isolated tiny islands nearby where boats could be pulled onto the gravel shores; they were ideal for nature rambles and for the lavish noonday dinners of fresh-caught fish that became a tradition.

The rural lakeside area of Henderson Harbor was roughly twenty-six miles from Watertown and a summertime paradise. Nearby there were prosperous farms and the cottages of the local fishermen and captains of the small trading sloops that sailed to Canada and among the islands. Later each of the Foster-Dulles family branches would build houses or cottages along the harbor shore. The headquarters of the compound was "Underbluff," a large red clapboard house with a vast circular porch that reached out to the water's edge. It featured a huge living room, the focal point of family activity.

But Henderson Harbor, as the compound has since been known, became more than a vacation retreat. Edith would bundle the family off to Underbluff as soon as school was out each summer. Life at Henderson Harbor was strenuous even by the standards of the time. A windmill pulled water from the lake as far as the house; the kitchen had a hand pump. A wood-burning stove had to be brought out from home for cooking and to heat Underbluff. Bedding, crockery, and other furniture were also brought out in a horse-drawn wagon each season, even a portable tin tub for Saturday night bathing. The only real concession to leisure was that the family ate its breakfast and dinner meals at the home of a nearby farm family that hired out tables to vacationers. On special occasions there would be "shore dinners," cookouts where chops and freshly caught bass would be grilled over open fires and wolfed down along with corn and other vegetables fresh from local gardens and topped off with the seasonal local fruits in pies.

During much of this time, the little lakeside community became a virtual State Department vacation resort, for either General Foster or Lansing was serving in some official capacity at the State Department or was involved in some major international dispute. There passed before the children's eyes a never-ending procession of famous and colorful personages. American political figures including future President William Howard Taft regularly sought Foster's advice there. Li Huan Chang, the foreign minister to the Manchu throne, and other Chinese dignitaries came for extended visits. They arrived in the formal tail-coated attire of the West, but switched to colorful and more comfortable silk robes and slippers when they climbed into the sturdy fishing smacks with Foster and Lansing for the deadly serious business of pursuing the wily black bass along the rock-bound coastline.

The fishing expeditions quickly became a firm ritual, and the makeup of the boat parties fixed by custom. There was a local guide in each of the two skiffs that were usually used. Lansing would be in one, General Foster in the other. A Chinese guest or some other dignitary could go along, but no more than three adults were taken on board. That left room amidships for the picnic baskets and tackle and one of the boys. Foster would go with his grandfather, Allie with Uncle Bert. Eleanor recalls that she was sometimes permitted to go along if there was room, but she was judged too fidgety to be a true dedicated fisherman.

"The competition was really serious," Allen Dulles noted later. Talking was strictly frowned upon while the actual fishing was going on, in part because of the taciturn natures of the local guides and General Foster. Dulles recalled that, as a boy, the code of silence added to the manly seriousness of the competition.

During the long lunch stops General Foster and Uncle Bert would begin to discuss the great events that engaged them. When there were foreign visitors or other dignitaries along, high policy would be debated with young Foster and Allie as an avid audience. The boys were already competing with the adults for the big city newspapers that arrived by mail, the *Times* and the *Tribune* from New York City, and opinion journals such as *Outlook, Harper's,* and *The Atlantic Monthly*. The Chinese visitors became especially avid fishing companions, and Li Huan Chang enjoyed telling dignitaries from Washington that he had once offered General Foster a high position in the Imperial Court, making him a virtual viceroy, but that the offer had been politely refused. The general reportedly begged to be allowed to return home because, as the story goes, "I have a firm appointment to take my seven-year-old grandson on his first fishing trip." Months later, a photograph arrived in Peking of a jubilant Foster Dulles hoisting a bass that was nearly as tall as the boy himself.

The talk around these outdoor dinners and the living room at night was not merely recreational banter. The world was steadily becoming an extraordinarily dangerous place. Miracles in communications, shipping, and railroads had shrunk the world so that neighboring nations felt abrasively rubbed by each other's ambitions. War had become so lethal on a mass scale that statesmen were terrified, even as they ordered up larger engines of destruction. Men such as General Foster, who had survived the industrialized carnage of the Civil War, shuddered as they looked at the devastation wrought during the Sino-Japanese War, the war between France and Prussia, and the later war between Japan and Russia.

At Henderson Harbor the debate centered on how to overcome the roadblocks to the first international conferences on world peace. Some mechanism had to be found whereby nations could attempt impartial reconciliation and agreement before disputes boiled over. The flickering of a world rule of law could be seen at the First Hague Conference on world peace in 1899, when more than two dozen nations gathered. This first attempt at world order set the stage for the larger Second Hague Conference in 1907, with President Theodore Roosevelt as the moving force.

The discussions were always held in the full view and hearing of the Dulles boys. Often enough, some visitor would break the flow of a particularly spirited debate to pose a teasing question to young Foster, and later on to Allie. The lads were hardly embarrassed or shy about speaking up.

Allen Dulles noted later: "Through that we learned how to talk to people like Li Huan Chang and the other Chinese and to the ambassadors and others. And so, even in those early days we began to get a good deal of talk about the world at large…. We'd keep abreast of it…."

Early in 1902, eight-year-old Allie scored something of a triumph of his own with his grandfather. The boy's pity had been aroused by the bitter struggle the Boer settlers were waging against Britain for control of South Africa. Allie was inspired by the debate he heard around him and astonished everyone by producing a five thousand–word pamphlet that angrily sided with the Afrikaners.

"The Boers want peace but England has to have the gold and so she goes around fighting all the little countries, but she never dares to fight either China or Russia. All the people that have their independence should like to see the Boers win for England is trying to take it from the Boers," Allie concluded. "I hope the Boers will win for the Boers are in the wright [*sic*] and the British are in the wrong in the war."[8]

The booklet demonstrated the flaws of the Watertown school system's teaching of spelling. But it also showed in Allie a precocious ability to marshal facts and a keen sense of argument: "All this talk about the Boers having slaves is not true for the Boers have not had any slaves since 1832, for a Boer captain told me so. America cannot say anything about the slavery for the Americans let men have slaves in the Phiipens [*sic*] now."

Amused and proud, General Foster ordered two hundred copies printed privately, and he circulated copies around official Washington among his friends. In an unsigned preface to the little booklet, his grandfather reported, "Two months ago [Allie] determined to write a history of the war with the avowed purpose of sending the money which he should receive from its sale to the Boer Relief Committee for the benefit of these sufferers. Since that time he has industriously gathered his facts, and day after day for nearly two months he has written out what he has read and heard together with his own opinions and conclusions. It is needless to say to one who reads this volume that throughout his labors the author has been entirely free from suggestion or correction in regard to subject, language or arrangement."

To the family's surprise, Allie's little pamphlet began to get a wide reading around Washington, and General Foster had to order a second printing. An enterprising newspaperman picked up the story, and soon the article, childish misspellings and all, was being reprinted in newspapers across the United States. It was the kind of light feature that newspapers still love today, and it gave the pervasive anti-British sentiment of many editorial writers the peg they needed to sound off once again on the unpopular war England was waging for control of southern Africa. At fifty cents a copy, young Allie was able to send more than a hundred dollars to the refugee relief organization, and hundreds more would be donated in his name before public interest dwindled and his celebrity faded. Only brother Foster held back his praise, churlishly calling the book "a wrong-headed and infantile effort."

The story about the booklet and other family tales of Allie's youth draw a picture of a high-spirited, bright boy trying very hard to push his way into a place within a family where roles and obligations were pretty rigidly defined and where the preferred places were already taken. Allie did his best within his powers. He sought attention that merited praise if possible, but attention at almost any cost. One day, he and Foster found an injured crow at Henderson Harbor, and Allie fashioned a splint that fixed its broken wing and tended the bird until it recovered. Allie tamed the bird and taught it to sit solemnly on his shoulder without moving. It was his delight to provoke stifled laughter from the family and visitors on Sundays, when Reverend Dulles would lead the community of vacationing residents in outdoor services and the bird would alight on Allie's shoulder and appear to listen to the sermon. Of course Allie then had to push his luck. One Sunday he waited until the congregation had been seated in the Watertown church before he made his entrance down the center aisle with the solemn crow on his shoulder. Punishment was meted out to Allie; banishment was imposed on the bird.

The Allie that emerges from the family's collective memory was given to the dramatic gesture, and, as he got older, he fancied a more romantic image of himself. Eleanor remembers him walking through the woods both at home and at the compound, declaiming lines in Greek; occasionally he would affect a limp to add to the Byronic impersonation. Most of the time, however, he more closely resembled Booth Tarkington's immortal lad of high spirits, Penrod Schofield, or Peck's *Bad Boy*, than he did one of the languid Regency poets.

While Allen Macy Dulles and Edith traveled a great deal early in their marriage, the first major family expedition abroad occurred in the summer of 1903. Fifteen-year-old Foster was to graduate from high school the next summer and wanted to go to Princeton. Edith decided it was time to round off the rough edges of the somewhat patchwork education he and Margaret had received. She recalled the trip: "I made a visit to Washington early in that year and my Father told me that he would give me money to take the two oldest children to Europe. He had realized from his own experience the importance of learning French when young and also knew that it could not be done in this country, so he proposed that I take the two children to Switzerland for the summer.

I shall never forget the delight and excitement of the children when I broke the news to them. Our joy was marred only by the disappointment of Allen, who being so much younger had to be left alone."[9]

In fact, young Allie pitched a memorable tantrum. He was outraged that just because he was not quite ten he would be excluded, especially since Foster was the clear beneficiary of the trip. Indeed, more than sixty years later, Dulles compiled some handwritten notes for a potential autobiography project. On a page headed "Sketch of my life and its points of decision," Dulles listed setbacks that still rankled: "Being left at home when the other two went abroad. A summer trip. Was left at home with the two youngers [sic] when I was almost 10."[10]

In 1904 Reverend Dulles uprooted the family and moved to Auburn, New York, when he was offered a chair of Theology and Apologetics at the Presbyterian Seminary there. He was also offered the pastorate at the Second Presbyterian Church. The professorship alone paid $3,500 a year (he had scrimped along on $3,000 in Watertown), and he was also allowed to hire one of the more promising seminarians from each class to serve as an assistant. Reverend Dulles also found teaching to be more congenial, and the seminary provided him with a publishing bully-pulpit that increased his prominence in the church hierarchy. Allie soon discovered the joys of being the oldest boy in the house. With Foster off to Princeton in 1904 and Margaret gone to Bryn Mawr two years later, Allie was relieved of the pressure to compete with his two older siblings; his parents too were preoccupied to a greater extent with their own careers by now. Eleanor has noted that Allie's temper began to improve and his tantrums disappeared. By all accounts he quickly fit in with the gang of boys of the neighborhood and did well enough, but not spectacularly, in school. He became more interested in sports, mastering golf and tennis and doing well enough to win friends and some important self-esteem. He made a fitful early teenage attempt at a mustache but was laughed out of it. Photographs of that time show the teenage Allie as tall and slender with a longer oval face than Foster's.

Foster's graduation as class valedictorian from Princeton in 1908 was all the excuse Edith needed for another family excursion to Paris; a $600 prize for a dissertation was burning a hole in the graduate's pocket, and he wanted to study for a year with philosopher Henri Bergson, the future Nobel laureate at the Sorbonne. The family sailed in August and spent the summer in Lausanne with an artist and his family who helped them improve their French. By October they had leased an apartment in Paris owned by an American heiress who wintered in Rome; it was furnished and fully staffed, and the family hired a French-speaking companion to sightsee with them and hone their conversational French. They settled in for a winter of work and pleasure. Foster and Margaret took classes at the Sorbonne while Allie was enrolled in the Ecole Alsacienne, where he studied French and prepped for history and math and the sciences with an eye to his Princeton entrance examination two years away. A report from the school in the family papers showed that he made good progress, especially in picking up the foreign language.

Instead of returning in the spring as planned, Edith was stricken with a series of illnesses that made it impossible to travel. Besides, she did not want to go back to Auburn so soon. It was not until late in the summer of 1909, after Allie had successfully taken the entrance examination for Princeton, that the Dulleses sailed for Auburn. The next year passed quickly. Foster stayed in Washington with his grandparents; he had decided to study law at George Washington University. Allie was about to fly the nest. He would enter Princeton in September 1910.

PRINCETON TURNED OUT to be a happy place for Allen Dulles. He was more at home there than Foster had been six years earlier. He also profited more from the experience than had his older brother.

Only two years separated Foster Dulles's graduation from Princeton in 1908 and Allie's arrival. But in that time the college, the boys there, and America had all undergone dramatic change. Foster's class had been firmly rooted in the nineteenth century. During Allie's four years there, Princeton and the world took a last deep breath and then plunged headlong into the twentieth century.

The personification of that force for change—for the Dulles brothers and for a growing number of Americans—was Woodrow Wilson, Princeton Class of '79. After a frustrating career as a history professor at Bryn Mawr and Wesleyan, Wilson had returned to his alma mater in 1890, eleven years after his graduation, to teach jurisprudence and political economy. But he had larger ambitions. Wilson had an uncanny ability to articulate beliefs that resonated deeply with his audience. In 1902, two years before Foster's arrival as a freshman, Wilson accepted an offer to become Princeton's president. He demanded, and got, full powers over faculty appointments. Then he pushed through an ambitious reorganization plan to remodel Princeton along the lines of the great English universities. He hired fifty young, talented teachers to act as tutors and required that the unmarried men live in the same quadrangle dormitories as the undergraduates. He also mandated a total overhaul of the college's curriculum to include a broader offering of engineering and physical sciences, but set against an emphasis on the liberal arts. To pay for this revolution, Wilson took his considerable speaking skills on the road to address powerful alumni clubs in major cities across America. He also courted the recent converts to institutional generosity among the nation's corporate chieftains. Men like Andrew Carnegie, J. P. Morgan, and Andrew Mellon were actively recruited and feted at Princeton.

Wilson freely used the contacts of former President Grover
Cleveland, who had retired to the village of Princeton and whose
son was an undergraduate protégé of Wilson's.

The years the Dulles brothers attended Princeton spanned
the glory years of Wilson's tenure there. He was accessible to the
students and regularly appeared in the lecture hall, where his
dynamic discourses on ethics and government frequently moved
his hearers to standing ovations. By the time Allie began his freshman year in 1910, Wilson's imprint was firmly fixed on Princeton,
but the reputation of Wilson the man had run out its string at the
university. Wilson was nimbly leaping upward onto the national
political stage just a few steps ahead of a group of disillusioned and
angry university trustees who wanted to fire him for making the
college too secular.

Today's image of Woodrow Wilson is a faded one, tinged
with sadly unrealized good intentions. Wilson is treated by many
as a well-meaning explorer who ventured too far into uncharted
territories and who perished alone because others could not share
his vision and follow. It takes effort to recall what a self-propelled
meteor Wilson was on the American skyline, or how one prime
object of Wilson's lifelong quest was his own personal advancement. But in that quest to satisfy his ambition, Wilson sounded a
theme that long outlived his political successes and frustrations.
Wilson used morals to test the validity of all questions of public
affairs, foreign or domestic. It was not enough for America to be
strong; America must be in the right. It was not enough for government to work for the public good; it must make people better
than they were. There was nothing among humanity's problems
that a government could not solve if that government consisted of
a cadre of sound-thinking, morally upright men who dealt with
each other's differences in an open and honest manner. More than
any president since, Wilson gave America the moral compass it
follows today.

Allie was marginally less straitened financially than Foster had been, although he competed for the same cash prizes for essays as his brother had. Allen Macy Dulles's book, *The Living Church*, had sold respectably, and there was extra money now from both the Auburn seminary and the church. With Foster living in Washington and Margaret (who had dropped out of Bryn Mawr and returned home to Auburn) no longer in college, the family budget was more stable than it had been in memory. There was a difference in the attitudes of Allie's classmates as well. They were much more creatures of the exciting new century than their older brothers had been—and better off financially. Most on average would spend around $900 for their room, board, tuition, books, and expenses for the thirty-six–week year, although some of the better heeled could spend twice that much if they brought their own automobiles for weekend outings to the New Jersey beaches or New York City. Still, it was not a particularly elitist group. More than a third of the 350 graduates in Allie's class worked at summertime and holiday jobs to pay all or part of their way through the college. Four in ten had graduated from a public high school, and another two had left public education for a last year at some preparatory school in order to qualify for Princeton's difficult entrance examinations.

Allie was not interested in being a campus hero on the playing field, nor did he participate in the regular outbreaks of fistfights that erupted between the upperclassmen and freshmen. But neither was he prepared to be a "poler," a serious studier. Early on, he demonstrated a taste for appearing to coast through his responsibilities rather than own up that he had to work harder than his elder brother. He joined the Whig Society debate and discussion group as well as Princeton's Law Club and its Municipal Club, which helped students prepare for careers in those professions. He just as quickly accepted the invitation, when it came, to be a junior class member of the Cap and Gown eating club, one of the more posh Patterson Avenue cliques, which boasted a grand three-story mock Tudor hall for a clubhouse. Foster, during his time there, had led a protest against the exclusivity of the eating club system; he would always remain his own fraternity—another early difference between Foster the "poler" and Allen the joiner.

Like most of his classmates, Allie affected a sporty sophistication that may have reached beyond actual experience. One of the features of the Princeton yearbook was a composite profile; the Class of '14 noted that tennis was the favorite sport, followed by baseball and football. The Princetonians claimed to prefer brunettes with blue eyes over blondes, and they liked girls named Helen, Dorothy, Mary, and Ruth. Those on the prowl for dates and girlfriends hunted on the campuses of Smith and Vassar, although a few opted for Wellesley or Bryn Mawr.

More than any previous class, the Class of '14 generally admitted to dancing the one-step; a shrinking minority of just twenty-three out of ninety-four considered dancing "morally wrong." Those who admitted to playing cards and to having actually kissed girls were also in the majority. The class had scandalized some of the older faculty when their graduation ball had featured a professional dance team from New York City that exhibited the sultry intricacies of that hot new dance, the tango.[11]

Allie listed himself as being five-feet, eleven-inches tall, a "Presbyterian, a Republican, a Whig Literary Society member." He expressed a preference for French, and tennis was his favorite recreation. Class and family photographs of the time show an attractive, slender youth with a broad forehead and elongated jaw. He was an inch or two taller than most of his classmates. He favored the newly fashionable soft shirt collars but still kept his pocketwatch in his coat pocket with a button and chain affixed to his lapel, in the fashion of his Uncle Bert. He spent many weekends in New York City, where he affected a sophisticated taste for musical comedies that was based more on his imagination than on his stay in Paris. He even got into trouble a couple of times when these champagne weekends proved too exhilarating.

During his final year, 1913–1914, Allie buckled down. Real life was just around the corner, and much depended on his graduating from Princeton with some sort of distinction. By all accounts he concentrated on studies and even attempted a difficult dissertation on philosophy and science in competition for the school's highest essay prizes. His diligence paid off. He was graduated ninth in his department's ranking of ninety-four, achieving high honors, a *cum laude* for his degree. He also won the Class of 1869 essay contest and walked off with $500 in cash from another prize in philosophy for an essay on "The Practical Value of Ethical Theory." Like Foster, Allie was elected to Phi Beta Kappa.

Something else happened to Allie in that senior spring of 1914. Princeton was visited by one of its most charismatic young alumni. Sam Higgenbotham was a Presbyterian missionary who ran the Ewing Christian College in Allahabad, India. The school's focus was on training Indian farmers in the latest agricultural methods, but it had an inexhaustible need for instructors in all areas of learning, in basic English most of all. The two men warmed to each other, and Higgenbotham offered Allie a post at the school as an English instructor at a nominal sum of money. The deal was that Higgenbotham would pay for Allie's passage out to India and a stipend of $500. If he stayed a second year, there would be another $500, and the school would pay his passage back. With the prize money already in hand, Allie decided at least to give the first year a try and pay his way home if he must.

Two weeks after graduation, Allie boarded the Lloyd's liner *Hamburg* for France on his way to India. Paris in the last weekend of June 1914 was hot, and tourists crowded from everywhere, almost as if the world sensed it had one last fling at a summer holiday and would never have another. American college students, the vanguard of the newly affluent middle class, had flocked abroad for the obligatory bicycle tours of the cathedrals and museums of the Continent. Allen Dulles was not surprised to bump into any number of Princetonians who were "doing Paris" before moving on, as he was, to someplace even more exotic.

"I recall vividly that I was enjoying the beauties of the boulevards of Paris at the moment the extras appeared on the streets announcing the assassination of Franz Ferdinand at Sarajevo," Dulles recalled years later in an interview. "The time is fixed in my mind in part because several of my classmates of the Princeton class of 1914 and I had just attended the annual running of the Grand Prix at Longchamps."[12] He confessed that he had paid little attention to the murder of the crown prince and his blonde wife Princess Sophie because of the excitement of his own adventure.

Nor did the assassination mean much at the time back home in America. At least one newspaper was of the opinion that, "to the world, or to a nation, an archduke more or less makes little difference." The *New York Sun*, for another, felt the killing might remove one of the sources of potential war in Europe.[13]

Six days later, on July 4, Allen traveled by train to Trieste. From there he sailed to India, arriving on July 20. Another three days brought him to Allahabad, a crowded town of about 180,000 at the junction of the Ganges and Jumna Rivers. Here was the Ewing Christian College run by Sam Higgenbotham. The school was a rambling affair of clay brick one-story buildings built around a tree-shaded central courtyard. Allahabad was high enough in the hills to be cool even in summer, and during the dry season classes were taught outside in the courtyard. Allen was assigned a sparsely furnished room in the adjoining quarters for the dozen or so other bachelor faculty and staff. But the position included a personal servant, whom he paid $2.50 per month to make innumerable cups of tea on demand and to see to Allen's clothes. The servant also served as a local guide during Allen's frequent excursions to nearby fortresses and temples. Allen's quick humor made him new friends among the younger faculty members, who were themselves recent graduates of American and British universities. Some of his letters home must have reflected a suspect enjoyment, for several letters from sister Eleanor earnestly warned him against the luxury of servants.

Higgenbotham put Allen to teaching English to a class of about three dozen Indians who were there to learn the skills of modern agriculture. Most of the men were older than Allen. The course consisted in the main of rote exercises with verb forms and sentence structures and wading through huge tracts of Shakespeare and some of the better known poets. Not surprisingly, it was pretty heavy going.

Toward the end of the first term, Allen confessed his frustration in a letter to his Aunt Eleanor: "I don't think I am very much of a success as an English teacher. I am enjoying it but I don't know much more about English syntax than they do." He must have been of some use, for later he added that Sam had offered to keep him on for the second year, but Allen had decided against it.[14]

Allen slogged on for the rest of his promised year. He immersed himself in the ferment of India and its early bid for independence from the British Raj. One of the more organized centers of the independence movement was in Allahabad. Allen regularly went with some of his pupils to the clandestine meetings of various rival factions who were in constant dispute over how to win separation. During his spare hours at the school, he swapped extra tutoring in English for lessons in Hindi and acquired a working familiarity with that difficult tongue. He even studied Sanskrit.

Among the centers of protest in Allahabad was the home of a prominent lawyer, Motilal Nehru, and Allen soon was introduced to his children, including eldest son Jawaharlal and a daughter, Vijaya Lakshmi. In later reminiscences with his family, Allen judged the son, who had just returned from Harrow and Cambridge, a stiff fellow. The sister, Vijaya Lakshmi, still in her early teens, was something else. With a fierceness that Allen found charming, the schoolgirl argued passionately that independence for India meant little if at the same time Indian women were not freed from the restraints and discrimination applied by traditional society. It sounded just like the kind of thing his sister Eleanor had picked up at Bryn Mawr. The young friends would meet again many years later when Vijaya Lakshmi Pandit arrived in New York in 1953 to become the first woman president of the United Nations General Assembly. The fabled Allen Dulles collection of friends who would become world leaders had just begun to grow beyond its Princeton origins.

As the second term began in early 1915, it became obvious to Allen that he must return home at the end of it. Too much was going on, both in a world at war and within his own family. He did not want to be left out. But what to do? Rather than apprentice himself to some bank or business, he decided to go back to Princeton as much for the time to figure out his future as for the graduate degree he would pursue. Early that spring, he applied and was quickly accepted for the term that began in September.

On March 15, 1915, Allen left Allahabad for Calcutta and from there sailed in leisurely stages to Penang, Singapore, Canton, and Hong Kong before arriving in Peking on May 8. There he taught English at a school run by the YMCA for a few weeks before traveling by rail across Korea and sailing to Japan for a two-week visit of U.S. legations. On July 4, just a year after he had left Paris, he voyaged across the Pacific for home. The option of retracing his journey west through Europe and back across the Atlantic had been shut off. On May 7 a German submarine torpedoed the British Cunard liner *Lusitania* off the coast of Ireland. Of the 1,198 who drowned in the sinking, 128 were American nationals. One of the direct effects of the tragedy was the abrupt elevation of Robert Lansing to secretary of state for President Woodrow Wilson. Even though he had been yearning for advancement, no one was more surprised than Uncle Bert himself.

CHAPTER TWO

1915–1917

"Germany must not be permitted to win this war."
—*Robert Lansing*

IT IS POSSIBLE THAT had the Republicans retained control of the White House in the years before and during World War I, Robert Lansing would have continued to ply the trade of the Washington lawyer who represented occasional foreign clients. He had become one of the founders of the *American Journal of International Law* and remained on its editorial board until his death in 1928. It seemed he was not destined to advance beyond that.

But Woodrow Wilson's election in 1912 changed all that. The new president was willing to use his political patronage, and the State Department was as much part of the spoils system as any other agency. Wilson intended to be his own foreign service, conceding that he might turn for help to the ubiquitous and wily Colonel Edwin House, a wealthy Texas political fixer. So Wilson was happy to fill the State Department with worthy men who had helped his cause. One of his more politically popular first appointments was that of William Jennings Bryan to be secretary of state.

Bryan was a pacifist and a populist who fought without success to restore the balance between rural, farming America and the sprawling cities and huge corporations. He was also intellectually lazy and had little head for administrative detail. Wilson gave a number of choice diplomatic appointments to old Princeton loyalists, and Bryan filled the rest of the department with cronies from all parts of the hinterlands. It was no surprise, then, that the old State, War, and Navy Building next to the White House was in chaos through most of 1913.

In his first post-election bid for the administrative post of assistant secretary of state, Lansing missed out despite the warm support of a New York senator and a successful interview with Bryan himself. There just wasn't room. But a year later, an even better job opened up, and Lansing secured the nomination to be counselor of the State Department, the number two post, just below that of secretary. The equivalent today would be undersecretary of state. On April 1, 1914, Robert Lansing took the counselor's oath of office at the State Department. The beginning of World War I in Europe was less than ninety days away.

During that first year of his career at State, Lansing won wide public praise for his quick assumption of the administrative reins that had been neglected by the feckless Bryan. At fifty, Bert Lansing looked every bit the competent diplomat. His gray hair contrasted with a handsome and usually tanned face. He was something of a dandy in dress, and while he was shy and somewhat diffident on formal occasions, he could unbend and be genuinely amusing in more relaxed situations. The Washington press corps, dismayed by Bryan's clumsiness, took Lansing's appointment as a reform move to put the department back on a professional basis.

In his splendid isolation, Wilson never bothered to examine Lansing's background or attitudes. Between his own intuitions and Colonel House's canny political advice, he felt in control. What he wanted at that moment was a good technical adviser on the law of nations; he could figure out the moral implications and political ramifications on his own. He might have had second thoughts about having a man like Lansing had he bothered to read his many lengthy articles on the rule of law among nations.

Robert Lansing dissented sharply from his father-in-law's (and Wilson's) cherished belief that moral rules of conduct could be imposed upon sovereign nations with no more force than moral suasion. He reasoned that if a nation is truly sovereign, then only a greater physical force can change its course; questions of right or wrong were on the margin. In these beliefs, Lansing was on an inevitable collision course with the president he sought to serve. Wilson not only believed that a standard of morality should inform the affairs of nations, he also believed it *must* be the cornerstone of any future system of agreements to enable nations to live together in peace and justice.

Historian Daniel M. Smith summed up Lansing's argument that "to feel that the foreign policy of a nation is based on unselfish motives, is a fallacious assumption, and to base a foreign policy on it is a grave error. In essence a nation deals with its own people in a civilized manner and with other nations in a savage way, with the basic assumption underlying international relations being the presumption of violence and physical force. To Lansing, a policy which denied or repudiated facts, or which was based on an impractical theory or objective, was a menace to the best conduct of foreign affairs. 'Idealism which cannot be harmonized with sound common sense is worse than useless.'"[1]

This dichotomy between idealism and hard political reality sharply marks the division between General Foster and Wilson, on the one hand, and Lansing on the—and a key difference in the attitudes of Allen Dulles and his brother. Perhaps because Foster had spent more time with his grandfather and worked more closely with Wilson he proved the more evangelical of the two brothers. Allen, because his Uncle Bert would later plunge him into a harsher arena at a younger age, would develop the colder eye of the two.

In the months that counted down to American involvement in the war, Lansing was pressed to develop his own sources of intelligence for authoritative information. There was also a great urgency to learn what the intelligence services of the Central Powers and the Allies were up to inside the United States, for it was obvious from the start of the war that the Europeans were well ahead in the use of propaganda agents, saboteurs, and sophisticated gatherers of the most sensitive information within the government. Spies and the threat of spies became part of a national psychosis that would persist long after the war had ended.

The Germans had the most elaborate spy apparatus in the United States in the early days of the war. Supplied by funds and directions from Count Johann von Bernstorff, the ambassador to Washington, agents kept a close watch on American ports and signaled the sailing dates of merchant ships suspected of carrying war material to Britain. Other German agents bribed journalists and planted stories that discredited the British. Attempts to bribe public officials were routine, and many were believed to be successful. Among the more successful agents was Franz von Papen, a military attaché who later would briefly become Germany's chancellor and earn the dubious distinction of maneuvering Adolf Hitler into power after the Nazis had failed at the ballot box. Von Papen was accredited both in Washington and to the Huerta government in Mexico City. He played a major role in the plot to build an anti-U.S. alliance with various Latin American countries; one key objective was to win a German and Japanese military presence in Mexico.

While the British were just as active, they had less manpower on the ground at the opening of the war. They also had more territory to cover since their security concerns included the United States and Canada, a reluctant ally in the war from the start. The British actively shared with Lansing the information their agents gathered on topics of vital interest such as the steady evolution of American public opinion and the operations of German and other enemy agents inside the United States. After German agents blew up an ammunition train unloading at a pier in New York harbor, Sir William Wiseman, the British Secret Intelligence Service's representative in Washington, and Captain Guy Gaunt, the naval attaché in New York, took the unusual step of hiring the Pinkerton Detective Agency to assign operatives to every major American port from Maine to Seattle from the early months of 1915 onward. Other operatives were directed to infiltrate labor unions, including the International Workers of the World, while others kept watch on groups with ties to Irish or pro-German interests.[2]

Lansing had few resources of his own at the start of the war. Information passed to the State Department from other departments or private persons was logged in by one elderly and rather junior clerk, but there was no systematic review or dissemination. As he recalled in his memoirs, "The Secret Service of the Department of State was an organization of slow growth during the period when this country was neutral. Prior to that time the Department had no Secret Service. It was found necessary for the Department to conduct some investigations of a highly confidential character and for this purpose a few operatives of other departments were detailed to it. Agents were also employed in other countries, which necessitated an office in the Department to issue instructions to them and to digest and analyze their reports without going through the regular channels of departmental correspondence."[3]

Even the security of the department's communications with its embassies and consulates abroad was something of a joke. In his memoirs on the development of the American Black Chamber code service, Herbert O. Yardley, who developed the earliest ciphers for the war, recalls that in the evening the Code Room

became "a loafing-place" where Lansing and other senior diplomats would drop by after official social functions for a check on
the latest traffic and to exchange gossip and reminiscences. He
described Lansing as "immaculately dressed, gray hair, a short
mustache, and the blank face of a faro dealer. In a deuces-wild
poker game, I mused, he should hold his own...."[4]

It became increasingly clear that Germany had little to gain
by courting American neutrality, especially since it was judged a
physical impossibility for the United States to intervene militarily
with any force. Early in his appointment as counselor, Lansing
wrote a memorandum that must have jarred Wilson:

> Germany must not be permitted to win this war and to
> break even, though to prevent it this country is forced
> to take an active part. This ultimate necessity must be
> constantly in our minds in all our controversies with
> the belligerents. American public opinion must be pre-
> pared for the time, which may come, when we will have
> to cast aside our neutrality and become one of the
> champions of democracy.
>
> We must in fact risk everything rather than leave
> the way open for a new combination of powers,
> stronger and more dangerous to liberty than the Central
> Powers are today.[5]

The sinking of the Lusitania had effectively destroyed Bryan's
effort to keep Wilson and America neutral. On June 8, 1915, he
tendered his resignation to President Wilson. Lansing's succession
to the Wilson cabinet was not automatic by any means. While the
president recognized Lansing's skills as an expert on diplomatic
legal matters, he was annoyed when Lansing sometimes doodled
during the lengthy cabinet sessions during which Wilson weighed

and often delayed decisions. The president's first thought was to turn to two of his closest cabinet friends, Treasury Secretary William Gibbs McAdoo and Agriculture Secretary David F. Houston. Houston was later quoted as saying he brought up Lansing's name at this point in the conversation. Wilson, he said, "remarked that Lansing would not do, that he was not a big enough man, did not have enough imagination, and would not sufficiently vigorously combat or question his [Wilson's] views, and that he was lacking in initiative."[6] In light of the bitter conflicts that would estrange Lansing and Wilson over the next five years, that judgment has a certain irony. The remarkable intervention of Colonel House himself convinced Wilson to nominate Lansing.

House did not want any rivals for Wilson's ear and made the same mistaken judgment about the counselor's pedestrian facade: "[T]he most important thing is to get a man with not too many ideas of his own, and one that will be entirely guided by you without unnecessary argument, and this, it seems to me, you would find in Lansing. I only met him once and then for a few minutes only, and while his mentality did not impress me unduly, at the same time, I hope that you have found him able enough to answer the purpose indicated."[7] With the press supporting Lansing's succession, Wilson yielded. He recalled the sad lament of William Seward, the secretary of state during the Civil War, that he was "nothing but Abe Lincoln's little clerk." Wilson joked, "All I want is a good clerk, and [Lansing is] a good clerk."[8]

Others made the same error. *The Nation* said that Lansing "has earned his position fairly and will adorn it," but its editors added that "every president has to be, in the big matters, his own secretary of state and Mr. Wilson will undoubtedly continue to determine for himself the main features of our foreign policy." Count von Bernstorff messaged Berlin, "Since Wilson decides *everything*, any interview with Lansing is a mere matter of form."[9]

Colonel House exacted a price for his sponsorship. Frank K. Polk, a New York lawyer and close friend of House's, was appointed counselor with strict orders to report any important information from within the department. Lansing fretted about Polk's ties to House but finally turned necessity to an advantage. Since Polk was so interested in information to report to his master, Lansing put him in charge of the department's fledgling intelligence operations with the specific task of coordinating the flow of information from the Secret Service of the Treasury, the Army G-2 (military intelligence), the Justice Department's Bureau of Investigation, and other agencies that regularly collected foreign intelligence. Polk also formalized relations with Sir William Wiseman's intelligence operations at the British Embassy.

DURING THE FAMILY'S August 1915 reunion in Henderson Harbor, Allen Dulles greeted the exciting happenings during his absence with a mix of pride in his Uncle Bert's new job and of anxiety to get in on the dramatic times. The life of a diplomat lured him, but first he had to gain entrance to the caste. Allen dropped the notion of pursuing graduate studies in philosophy and switched instead to Princeton's masters degree course in international law. By all accounts, he became something of a "poler" during that graduate year. Nevertheless, he was not so much a recluse as to be immune to the frenzy over a possible war with Mexico that swept America the next spring and led him and a large group of his Princeton classmates to join the 16th Regiment of the New Jersey National Guard. Allen and his roommates went down to Trenton to enlist and were duly sworn in, although it is unknown whether he was given more than a cursory physical examination.

Back at Princeton, Allen put the insights he had gained abroad to good use both in academic papers and public articles. Throughout the winter and spring, he had been writing articles, or what today might more accurately be called op-ed pieces, for the *New York Tribune* on foreign affairs based on his travels and law studies at Princeton. The pieces themselves show no particular flash of insight; many reflected the views of his own family circle. Their importance today lies in how many he wrote, how seriously they were taken by the *Tribune* and its readers, and how they must have built Allen's confidence in his own abilities and station. In one piece, on the question of India's loyalty to the empire, Dulles noted the bravery of Indian troops on the Western Front but also reported the intense resentment among Indians at home to their lack of power about their own government and the discrimination they faced when they tried to emigrate within the empire.[10]

Allen sat for the Foreign Service examination in May 1916. On May 18 Frank Polk notified him by telegram, "You have been appointed a secretary of Embassy or Legation of class five in the diplomatic service. It is desired that you report at the Department of State at an early date. You will receive instructions here for about two weeks and should be ready to proceed shortly thereafter to the post in the foreign service to which you will be assigned."[11] A few days later, the New Jersey National Guard notified him that his regiment was being called to active duty on the Mexican border. Although he would collect his masters in law, there would not be time to attend the graduation ceremonies.

"I really wasn't sure what I should do," Dulles later recalled. "I decided to leave it up to the National Guard and if they really needed me, I would not use the excuse of my appointment to the foreign service to get out of going. But they must have decided that they had enough for they said I should go ahead to Washington and that is what I did." On June 3 the U.S. Embassy in Vienna received word that its newly minted grade five clerk would sail on the 17th. Ambassador Frederic C. Penfield telegraphed back, "Assignment Dulles pleases me."

Allen Dulles was not to be an ordinary clerk, grade five, stamping passports and sipping tea at receptions. He was going to Vienna to become one of his uncle's new cadre of diplomat-intelligence officers in the embassy there. One of the special tasks he drew was to lure Austria out of its alliance with Germany and to negotiate a separate peace. If it was successful, the mission could change the course of the war; indeed, America might not have to enter the conflict at all.

On May 22, 1916, Allen Dulles took the oath of allegiance to the United States and received his commission. It was a point of honor with him that he had successfully qualified for the Foreign Service through the open examination on his own and without any influence from his uncle. By coincidence Secretary Lansing had suffered a temporary collapse from overwork and was confined to his house in Watertown during most of May. Consequently, Allen received his appointment and his first assignment from the hands of Frank Polk, the counselor of state and acting secretary. For Allen, it was the best of both worlds. Being Bert Lansing's nephew made his path within the diplomatic world infinitely smoother, but he was also seen as one of Frank Polk's protégés. That brought a double benefit because Polk was now running the State Department's rapidly developing intelligence service. As with everything from shipbuilding to armaments-making, official Washington was in a frenzy to catch up and painfully aware that its methods of gathering information about the world were stuck in the previous century. In earlier times Allen might have expected to slave for several years shuffling papers in one of the cavernous rooms of the State, War, and Navy building next to the White House. But now, raw as he was, he was needed in an important posting overseas, and in a hurry.

As a neutral, the United States still maintained embassies in both Berlin and Vienna as well as in the capitals of the Allied powers.

In John Watson Foster's time, the embassies of the more socially
fashionable capitals of Europe had been plumy postings for the
political faithful of incumbent presidents. But the war ended the
nature of American embassy life as a sleepy backwater. Scores of
thousands of Americans abroad were trapped without travel documents or funds to get home. Hundreds of thousands more displaced refugees of other nationalities viewed getting to the United
States as a life-or-death goal. It seemed the mobs of desperate persons demanding visas and other assistance would never diminish.
In the meantime, the stepped-up burden of sensitive diplomatic
consultation and full-time intelligence gathering ran the diplomatic service ragged. Telegram archives of the time bulge with
frantic cables to Washington from traumatized ambassadors who
warned that their staffs were breaking down under the strain.

The U.S. Embassy in Vienna was just such a post under siege.
Ambassador Frederic Courtland Penfield was a dour man of sixty-
one who had been a pro-Wilson newspaperman and had had the
good fortune to marry a wealthy wife. His reward from the president in 1913 was to be sent to that unparalleled capital of music,
art, and imperial (if slightly faded) glamour. But Penfield was
clearly out of his depth once Austria-Hungary joined forces with
the kaiser. Before Allen's arrival, he had only a counselor and three
clerk-secretaries to handle the staggering volume of people who
lined up each day to plead for passports, visas, and validation of
citizenship based on often questionable claims. The embassy could
not even respond to the growing demands for military information and political intelligence from within the Habsburg court.
Even after Allen arrived, there was no military attaché, and the
naval attaché was a junior officer.

Polk summoned Allen to Washington so quickly that Dulles
had scant time to outfit himself with the regalia of cutaway coat,
striped trousers, and formal evening wear that were required of the

junior diplomatic corps secretary and to be briefed by his now-recovered uncle. On June 17 he embarked on the *Philadelphia*, sharing a "splendid upper room" with James Cabell Bruce, the older brother of his Princeton classmate David K. E. Bruce. James, a recent law school graduate, had just turned down his father's invitation to join his law practice. Instead, he was bound for London to learn the international banking business. During the voyage the two young college grads amused themselves by dancing and flirting with all the pretty girls they could find on board.[12]

The two young Americans enjoyed themselves in the nightlife of wartime London, but there was serious work for Allen during the daytime. There were important confidential documents and messages to deliver to Walter Hines Page, the American ambassador to the Court of St. James. Allen would also have to pass through Paris on his way to Vienna, and that meant he had to arrange the visas and permits necessary to travel across the English Channel through the British Foreign Office. Here the biographer runs into tantalizing hints that the British spy services may have had their first contacts with the young diplomatic secretary. There are even unconfirmed assertions that Dulles may have met with intelligence officers from MI6, the British foreign spy service, and indeed may have undergone some rudimentary training in basic spycraft before he set off for his highly charged posting. If Allen Dulles did have such a relationship with British intelligence officials, it hardly would have been unique, even so early in the history of World War I. The American government, through both private citizens and official representatives, had for months been eagerly soliciting whatever tutoring it could scrape together from the British on the techniques and objectives of information-gathering. While many European nations, Germany particularly, had long had secret services and police agencies, the modern system of coordinated intelligence collection, and, most important, of coordinated intelligence analysis, was still in its infancy.

Still, it was pretty primitive stuff, the spy business. As late as 1907, a study authorized by Britain's recently established Committee on Imperial Defence discovered not a single intelligence agent in British service was anywhere on the continent of Europe. After some embarrassing starts, the committee formally created a British national intelligence service in 1909. Its functions were to be divided into two distinct areas of coverage—home and abroad. The first section, coverage of Britain's internal security, at first was given the designation MO5, later to be known as MI5. The foreign section was known as MI6.

The British managed in a few short years to create an intelligence service of enormous size, complexity, and extraordinary productivity with far greater successes than those of its rivals or even of its allies. One positive notion was common among the men who directed those early spy services; they recognized that individuality—and sometimes even eccentricity—can have value in service to the nation. T. E. Lawrence is the example that comes to mind of a man totally unfit for the strictures of high military command but who may have been the greatest guerrilla force leader of all time. As we will see, that same belief filtered into the attitudes of Allen Dulles and others who later were the architects of U.S. spy services.[13]

The British intelligence establishment resembled a fractious three-horse race during the war and even afterward. In addition to MI5 and MI6, the Royal Navy appointed one of its own spy heroes as director of Naval Intelligence in 1914. Vice Admiral Reginald "Blinker" Hall had in 1909 been captain of a cadet-training ship and on his own initiative carried out a clandestine mission to photograph the German strategic port of Kiel. He also benefitted in stature by being in favor with young Winston Churchill, then the first sea lord.

No innovation of Hall's was more productive than Room 40, the band of code-breakers assembled in the Admiralty under the cryptographic wizard Alastir Denniston. Not long after the start of the war in 1914, the Room 40 team had broken the code used by the Imperial German navy to communicate both with its ships at sea and with naval attachés in the embassies abroad. Within a year or two after that, Room 40 had broken into and was reading nearly all of the German codes, either by the direct method of stealing the cipher books or by the painstaking method of working through the possible combinations of letters and numbers that masked the true message. This triumph had tremendous impact on the Allied conduct of the war, particularly during the darkest days. But perhaps the biggest British code breakthrough, as we shall see later, would have its greatest impact on America and its decision to join the war on the Allied side.

Undoubtedly, the British spy services might have been quite happy to take a few days in mid-1916 to run an American diplomatic clerk named Allen Dulles through a short course on espionage procedures and to give him a list of friendly contacts in Vienna. Such aid would have been part of a broader strategy to draw Washington into a closer alliance, and in those early days there was a premium on soliciting information not only from American officials but also from the large number of Yanks who were passing through London on their way behind the lines of war under the guise of the numerous peace and war relief organizations. These groups provided some of the characters who would play a larger role in the structure of American intelligence a generation—and a world war—later.

But did the British actually formally brief Allen Dulles in 1916 on some of the simple mechanics of spycraft and how to get in touch with MI6 operatives in Vienna? One important source who ought to know says yes, but there is no further corroboration. William Samuel Stephenson, a Canadian, was nominally a captain in the Royal Flying Corps, but he had been personally recruited for special tasks by Admiral Hall, the navy spy chief. It was not unusual for wounded officers, such as Stephenson and William Wiseman, to be seconded to spy work under the cover that they were doing light duty at home while they recovered from their injuries. Much later, in 1940, Stephenson would turn up with the pseudonym "Intrepid" and orders from Winston Churchill to go to New York to hasten America's entrance into the Second World War. Stephenson and his helpers also conspired to train the early recruits for America's first wartime independent spy service, the Coordinator of Information, later the OSS.

But in 1916 it appears that Stephenson was already busy briefing fledgling American spies. One of them, he later claimed, was William J. Donovan, who in his own right is called the father of modern U.S. intelligence practice. Born in 1883, ten years before Allen Dulles, Donovan was an ambitious attorney and National Guard officer from Buffalo, New York, whose political connections had won him a curious assignment from the Rockefeller Foundation—to glean information about the famine that was decimating Poland, caught as it was between the armies of the kaiser and the czar. He arrived in London just two months before Allen Dulles received the necessary British visas to travel on through neutral Scandinavia to Poland.

But the British blocked his way. So Donovan turned to Herbert Hoover, then just forty-two but already something of a legend in London and abroad. A self-made millionaire in mine engineering, Hoover had by 1916 helped more than 120,000 Americans who had been caught by the war away from home to get back to the United States. He now headed a relief organization that fed and cared for more than ten million Belgians whose homes were part of the war's battlefield. Hoover promptly hired Donovan to go to Belgium and oversee the distribution of the huge shipments of food and clothing that U.S. church and charity groups were sending over. The Poland mission is not mentioned again.

As the unconfirmed story has it, Donovan met with Stephenson just before he left for the Continent. A biographer of Stephenson[14] and two who studied Donovan's life say there are quotes from Donovan's private notes that recall his meeting in early April 1916 over dinner at Brown's Hotel with the twenty-year-old Stephenson. "I felt an old man," Donovan wrote, "wickedly well-fed, against this skinny kid. But when he started to talk, I paid attention. I had asked a couple of routine questions. His answers were concise and perceptive." The topic of this important dinner conversation was "German military and psychological weaknesses." The Donovan biography is cautious about confirming that the purpose of the meeting was an official briefing. But it does add, "as an American official on famine relief service in Belgium Donovan was in a position to render British Intelligence services of great importance—a fact that would not have escaped the officials whose duty it was to keep an eye on foreigners on British ships and in London hotels."[15] This biography also quotes a response by the CIA in 1981 that Donovan "probably" received "military intelligence" training by the British "during World War I."

Nigel West, the British intelligence writer, goes further in his history of MI6. Donovan, he says, went from London directly to Liège, Belgium, where Cardinal Mercier, the Catholic bishop there, put him to work as a courier to gather intelligence reports throughout the network known as *The White Lady*, the most successful of the operations conducted by MI6 during the First World War.[16]

There is more than a controversy about sources here. British writers tend to give more credence to the Donovan-Stephenson 1916 meeting because it gives weight to the notion of America's dependency on Britain as a spycraft instructor. Not surprisingly, loyalists to the Donovan tale repudiate such a notion. Not only are there no documents that can verify such a meeting, at least one Donovan biographer uses the travel records of both men to argue that such a meeting could not have taken place.[17]

There are plenty of other questions whose answers still lie buried. Was Herbert Hoover, who would later use Allen Dulles's intelligence skills throughout his own presidency, aware of what Donovan was up to? Did he approve? Was part of Hoover's mission for the American Relief Committee the task of inserting Americans into the German territories to perform intelligence work?

It is a matter of record that Donovan did reach Holland in April and received German permission to enter Belgium to carry out the work of Hoover's group. And it is also true that he found time to journey both to Liège and to the city of Louvain, which the German army had sacked in a particularly brutal fashion. From there he embarked on a bewildering series of trips through Germany, Austria, Holland, and then to Sweden, without ever attempting to go to Poland. It is asserted that Donovan's final task was to gather important information about German troop dispositions and supply lines just before the British launched their summer offensive on the Somme. It is also a fact that late in June, just as the Allied attack was about to begin, Donovan's relief work was canceled, and he was ordered by Washington to return to Buffalo and take command of his cavalry regiment for service in Mexico. His ship returning home passed the *Philadelphia* bearing Allen Dulles and James Bruce on their way over.

Numerous sources, both British and American, report conversations with Stephenson after World War II in which he asserted that in those early months he not only helped brief Donovan but also met Dulles and numerous other American pupils of British tutelage. Many of these same sources, however, warn about the lack of accessible document confirmation. Worse, in the final years of his life, the old Canadian hero was not above gilding his own yarns.

But there can be no doubt that an active intelligence sharing was going on between Lansing's fledgling intelligence department and the various British services even before American entry into the conflict. More importantly, at this early episode Allen Dulles was introduced at a very young age to an extremely high level of sophisticated intelligence work. From the summer of 1916 through the next fifty-three years, Allen Dulles would be an active gatherer and analyzer of intelligence in his country's interests.

ALLEN ARRIVED IN VIENNA on July 7 and plunged immediately into the overtime task of dealing with frenzied visa applicants and helping Ambassador Penfield catch up on his huge backlog of official correspondence. Allen, as low man on the seniority ladder, often found himself opening the embassy's offices first thing in the morning and closing up late at night. Then he faced learning German vocabulary at night to prepare for a weekly tutoring session. The frenzied workload borne by the tiny six-man staff of clerks became even worse as the summer wore on into autumn. Finally, Penfield was forced to open the offices seven days a week to handle the public traffic. Still, the diplomatic community kept an unbroken schedule of parties, balls, and official social functions that provided Allen with a hectic, but exhilarating, introduction into diplomatic life. He found a small two-room apartment near the embassy and quickly made friends with the second secretary, Frederic Dolbeare, a Harvard man who would remain a lifelong friend. The thirtyish Dolbeare was something of a bon vivant and the proud owner of a motorcycle and sidecar. He quickly initiated the younger man into the delights of Vienna's splendid public gardens, where wine and Strauss waltzes flowed late into the night, war or no. Because Austria had shifted to daylight savings time, there was plenty of light for a quick game of tennis at one of the outdoor courts before relaxing at a pleasant outdoor restaurant or a wine garden.

Allen found he enjoyed even the routine work of foreign service, and he moved up the promotion ladder with amazing speed, in part because he was given increasing responsibilities that required higher rank. By August he had been promoted to a fourth-class clerkship, and by October had climbed to the third-class rank, which meant that his salary had rocketed from $1,200 to $1,500 per year.

A bit of good luck occurred in mid-autumn, 1916. Emperor Franz Josef, who had ascended the throne in 1848 in the midst of the radical revolutions shaking Europe, had died on November 22, worn out at eighty-six. For sixty-eight years he had presided over a patchwork quilt of an empire that was both resolutely polyglot and seething with resentments. The funeral signaled the start of a frantic bid by the Americans to lure Austria back to the sidelines of the war. Advisers to the hastily crowned successor, the dead emperor's nephew Charles I, worried that the belated entrance of Italy into the war on the side of the Allies threatened that Austria would lose its vital seaport possessions on the Adriatic and that the eastern parts of the empire would be overrun by the Russians. Moreover, the thirty-year-old Charles was known to have liberal inclinations and even to approve of Wilson's writings about democracy, which he had read with interest. Perhaps a transition to a British-style constitutional monarchy might be a way for Charles to preserve the restive people under his dominion. But Charles had a far greater fear—crossing his cousin Wilhelm II of Germany.

Any approaches had to be most carefully concealed and conducted on the most unofficial levels, and this led to the first hurdle within the embassy, for Ambassador Penfield disapproved of such radical and risky departures from the formal business of diplomacy. Penfield believed his job was confined to expressing official statements of intention and exchanging views only at the highest and most authoritative levels. But Dolbeare and Dulles had different marching orders and few scruples about taking informal soundings among the young Austrian nobility who were confidants of the new emperor. One of them was particularly amusing and lighthearted—

Prince Maximilian of the Hohenlohe family, which had holdings in Austria, Carinthia, and Hungary, and ties to a former prime minister of the kaiser's Germany. Young Prince Max played an important and controversial role in Allen Dulles's spy career during World War I and then again in World War II, but for the moment, he was a charming friend who was happy to carry messages in and out of the royal court as long as he did not get into any trouble.

President Wilson continued to stall while he pursued various schemes to force the combatants to a conference table, where he would be the influential presiding force. And he clung to the public wish for "peace without victory," a phrase that made Lansing rage with anger and caused even the loyal Colonel House to despair privately.

Lansing had written in an internal memorandum on the mediation schemes:

> I am most unhappy over the situation, because on no account must we range ourselves even indirectly on the side of Germany. The amazing thing to me is that the president does not see this. In fact he does not seem to grasp the full significance of this war or the principles at issue. I have talked it over with him, but the violation of American rights by both sides seems to interest him more than the vital interests as I see them. That German imperialistic ambitions threaten free institutions everywhere apparently has not sunk very deeply into his mind. For six months I have talked about the struggle between Autocracy and Democracy, but I do not see that I have made any great impression....
>
> I only hope that the president will adopt the true policy which is "Join the Allies as soon as possible and crush the German Autocrats." If he takes drastic mea-

sures against Great Britain, he will never be forgiven; if
he attempts to mediate now, he will commit a grave
error, because I am sure nothing will come of it, and I
hope nothing will. As to my own position, I will never
sign an ultimatum to Great Britain. I will act in favor of
mediation though with great reluctance, but I would
not do it if I thought it would amount to anything.[18]

Lansing did not handle Wilson as skillfully as he thought,
certainly not as well as House did. On several occasions he pushed
the president too hard and had to backpedal and apologize. By
early 1917 he was effectively banished from Wilson's councils
because his remarks at an impromptu press conference gave the
impression that American intervention on the side of the Allies
was a certainty. For several weeks in early 1917, his letters to
Wilson received no response.

Lansing's fall from power and his subsequent disgrace two
years later provided lessons that were indelibly stamped on Allen
and Foster's characters as men who advised later presidents. The
lesson was a stark one, and apparently it must be learned afresh by
succeeding advisers to every chief executive. A president can be
counseled, argued with, and even nagged. But not even the most
exalted or powerful within his inner circle can force a president to
act against his will, however ill-considered his decisions might be.
Those who accuse the Dulles brothers of occasionally allowing the
presidents they served to plunge headlong into misadventures
need to remember how deeply they reacted to the disaster that
befell their Uncle Bert when he stepped beyond the limits of influence granted him by Woodrow Wilson.

As it appeared ever more likely that the United States would
enter the war, the determination of refugees and expatriate
Americans alike to get out of Europe threatened to swamp the

main diplomatic posts in Rome, Berlin, Paris, London, and, of course, Vienna. Moreover, it was increasingly alarming to the senior Washington officials who had been working on preparations for the eventuality of war that their grip on events in the Balkans and Eastern Europe was virtually nonexistent. Penfield remained a roadblock. He resisted efforts by Lansing to send him the manpower to undertake the new vital tasks on the grounds that it reflected badly on his ability to conduct the embassy's affairs. The strain began to tell. First, the counselor of the embassy, Penfield's second in command, collapsed from overwork. Others of the clerks went down in a succession of colds, fevers, and general collapses, due in part to having to work weeks on end without a break on a diet of diminishing nourishment and under the increased hostility of the local spy and police agencies. The ambassador was not a particularly bad man. He was, however, a product of another time and simply could not adjust. When, in the first week of January, Allen was stricken with a high fever that affected the already vulnerable joints of his legs and feet, Mr. and Mrs. Penfield took the young clerk into their personal quarters and nursed him back to recovery; the ambassador even sent a cable over the diplomatic wire to Allen's family in Watertown so they would not worry.[19] Yet at the same time, Penfield could be obtuse, and Allen, in those early days, had not mastered control of the prickly Dulles pride. When the ambassador gave him a suit to be cleaned, the young man retorted, "I may be your third secretary, but I am not your valet."[20]

Allen did not hesitate to upbraid his ambassador in private correspondence bitterly critical of Penfield's refusal to put the embassy formally into the task of intelligence gathering. This refusal was especially galling to Allen and Fred Dolbeare since they had achieved some minor success in making contact with sources within the Czech and Hungarian circles of power based in Vienna.

One particular friend who confided in Allen was Dr. Heinrich Lammasch, tutor to Emperor Charles when he was a youth, and still an influential adviser with strong liberal leanings.[21] "We have plenty of work at the Embassy connected with the 'peace' proposals but very little prospect of it as far as one can see," Allen wrote to his mother after his recovery in early January. In a letter to his grandfather, Allen referred to a detailed list of complaints about Penfield that he had earlier sent to Lansing, who had shown the letter to General Foster. "He is a man for whom I can feel no respect. If I were writing on that subject now, I would express myself rather more bitterly than in that letter to Uncle Bert...."[22]

Lansing was more successful on another front. Just days before Wilson would ask for the declaration of war, Lansing borrowed John Foster Dulles from the Sullivan & Cromwell law firm and sent him on a secret trip. Foster was to secure from the governments of the most strategic of the Central American countries promises to support the U.S. war effort and to assist in the efforts to keep the vital sea lanes of the Panama Canal and the Straits of Florida secure from German naval incursion. In the early part of 1916, Foster's involvement in the crossover world of business and government moved him closer into Lansing's orbit. Whatever hesitancy he may have had about this, there is little doubt that a close relationship between the State Department and the senior partners of Sullivan & Cromwell suited all the parties very well. William Cromwell and most of the senior partners had been supporters of Woodrow Wilson, particularly of his efforts to keep the United States out of the war while furthering the trading fortunes of the firm's larger corporate and shipping clients. Moreover, Cromwell had been instrumental in arranging financing when Theodore Roosevelt snatched the Panama Canal project away from its French developers, and he had remained a potent political power in the region ever since. Questions of conflicts of interest

rarely arose in a time when the interests of commerce and government were so closely allied. The law firm was lucky to have the talented, hard-working, twenty-eight-year-old lawyer on its staff
with a direct family pipeline to Washington. The government was
lucky to be able to call, without charge, on a skilled young envoy
whose foreign credentials could be ratified by some of the biggest
names in American international business and banking.[23]

Lansing wanted more than goodwill. He did not want the
region to become a safe haven for enemy agents or a staging base
for attacks on the vital Panama Canal or shipping lanes of the
Caribbean. He wanted serious efforts by those governments to
keep the region secure. While the diplomatic status of the young
Foster would have assured his prompt reception in most of the
capitals, he also carried with him a potent agenda of business and
banking matters that concerned many of the French and British
banking clients of Sullivan & Cromwell, bankers who held the
bonds of these governments. It was a one-two punch that the
Central Americans could not withstand, nor did many even try. In
Nicaragua, President Chamorro greeted his friend Foster and
immediately severed relations with Germany. They then spent the
visit working out the refinancing of his government's foreign
debts on more favorable terms. In Costa Rica, Foster urged, and
won, U.S. recognition of the local tyrant who until that moment
had run a regime considered hostile in Washington. There, too, he
conducted a survey of the bond situation for his foreign clients.
Panama was more difficult because an election was already under
way, but both announced candidates were considered equally corrupt thugs. Foster convinced a group of pro-canal business interests to support a third nominee. On his way back to Washington
in May, he also won declarations of war from both Panama and
Cuba the only two Latin American nations to join the Allied
cause.

It was a triumph for the young lawyer, but an arduous trip. He contracted a severe case of malaria, and the heavy doses of quinine damaged his eyes. Even though he recovered, convalescing at the Foster-Lansing home in Washington that summer, his eyesight was permanently weakened and, during moments of fatigue, would cause excessive tearing. That summer, Foster applied for officer's training in the army but was rejected because of his poor eyesight. Later, he won a reserve commission in the Signal Corps as a captain and was assigned to the economic section of the intelligence department of the army's General Staff. His wife Janet soon joined him in Washington.[24]

IN THE MEANTIME, war came to America. After all the arduous tugging on both sides, to get into the struggle or to keep out, the immediate causes of America's entrance in that dreadful slaughter are almost laughable to recount. In January, "Blinker" Hall's Royal Navy code-breakers in Room 40 of the Admiralty in London had intercepted and cracked a telegram from Arthur Zimmermann, the kaiser's foreign secretary, to the German ambassador in Mexico City. The message confirmed that submarine attacks would resume on February 1, 1917. Zimmermann said Berlin would try to keep America neutral, but failing that, it would undertake an alliance with Mexico and, with the proposed assistance of the Japanese, Germany would take the war to the United States on its home territory. There was a promise to help Mexico "regain by conquest her lost territory in Texas, Arizona, and New Mexico."[25]

London hesitated about a month before making the incendiary telegram public while the British found a way to do so without tipping the Germans that their code had been broken. The solution was for Lansing and Polk's intelligence agents to pry copies of the message sent to Ambassador von Bernstorff's Washington embassy out of Western Union's confidential files and to ensure an unquestioned reception in the press by leaking confidential copies of the message to trusted journalists.

The notion that Germany and Mexico could mount a land war across the Rio Grande made about as much sense as had the foolish American border expedition in 1916 after Pancho Villa. But the American people were in an illogical mood; the national ego had been bruised by the Carranza government. The Zimmermann telegram, Lansing noted in his *Memoirs,* created "a profound impression" among the outraged people. But even more than that, it was a bombshell whose impact jolted America to a degree that not even "Blinker" Hall and Ambassador Page could have dreamed of. At this point the hapless Zimmermann compounded the blunder. Despite the prompting of a Hearst newspaper correspondent in Berlin who doubled as a German agent, Zimmermann not only refused to deny that the telegram was accurate, he also tried feebly to justify it.

Submarine attacks on merchant vessels and death lists of Americans continued daily through March 1917. On March 18 three American merchantmen were sunk in a single day with appalling casualties. On March 19 the czar of Russia abdicated, and Lansing and House renewed their argument that the Allies were now free of the taint of any absolutist governments. The issues were clear. Wilson's duty lay in leading a crusade for the democratic nations to final triumph. On March 21 Wilson called Congress back early from its Easter recess for a session on April 2.

His evening address to the joint session in the House chamber, jammed with senators and cabinet members, resplendent in the uniforms of the military and the frock coats of the diplomats, was all the more dramatic because the rest of the world waited outside. It may have been Woodrow Wilson's greatest moment. As so often with his sermons and lectures at Princeton, the president began with quiet solemnity by asking Congress to recognize that

Germany was already waging war against the United States. He said that the German government was an autocracy and, as such, the natural enemy of liberty, and that the Germans were waging a war against mankind. "The world must be made safe for democracy," he sold, and his audience understood what he meant.

As historian Dumas Malone described the speech, "Wilson asked not only for war but also for a profound revolution in the foreign policy of the United States: from nonentanglement in European politics and neutrality, to collective security and participation in world politics in support of freedom and peace against tyranny and aggression."[26] A morose Wilson had a darker view as he sat back at the White House that night. He confided to a secretary that his speech "was a message of death for our young men." Then he burst into tears.

The Senate voted the war resolution on April 4; the House, on April 6. Wilson signed the declaration on April 7.

CHAPTER THREE

1917–1920

"It has to do with intelligence."
—*Allen Dulles*

AMERICA'S ENTRY INTO THE WAR found Allen angling for a transfer from the Vienna embassy. During the early part of 1917, Allen had taken on the chore of establishing a new transmittal route for the embassy's communications. Previously, the diplomatic pouch, mail, and newspapers had to journey all the way to Berlin before traveling out through one of the still-neutral Baltic ports. Sometimes a month would go by before German authorities would clear communications in or out of Vienna. As an alternate route, Allen drew the weekly chore of an arduous two-day train trek to Bern. The train journey went over the Ailberg Mountains, through the Swiss Tyrol region, and then to Zurich before the traveler took a local trolley to Bern, the capital of resolutely neutral Switzerland. He often had to manage as many as two dozen of the bulky leather pouches and argue their way through border checkpoints while keeping a constant vigil on their security. He noted to his mother that the Swiss capital "is quite waked up by the war as it is the diplomatic and spy center. A good many of the old resorts are entirely deserted, so they say, while Zurich and Geneva flourish—the one being the German and the other the French center for Switzerland."

On April 12, five days after Wilson signed the declaration of war, Ambassador Penfield and Allen were summoned to Paris to confer with the senior American diplomats gathered there in the offices of William Graves Sharp, the recently appointed U.S. ambassador to France. They received fairly abrupt orders: to close the Vienna embassy and move its personnel and records to safe territory as soon as possible. Then Penfield was to go home to the United States. The intelligence and diplomatic operations were to be shifted to the U.S. Legation in Bern. With the shutdown of the U.S. embassies in Berlin and other embassies within the Central Powers group, Bern would inherit the job of looking after American interests in Central Europe and the Balkans. Fred Dolbeare was already in Bern as a second secretary and writing Allen about the fun he had working for a minister who did not actively interfere in his work. Two days before the Paris trip, Allen cabled Washington asking to be transferred to Bern, and approval was waiting for him when he arrived in Paris. He rushed back to Vienna to pack and arrived in Bern on April 23. He was able to rent a tiny but expensive room in the back regions of the posh Palace Bellevue Hotel, a large structure and one of the landmarks of Bern. It also had the advantages of being within walking distance of the legation and a social magnet for the congeries of international refugees, diplomats, and spies who had jammed into the Swiss capital for the war. He reported for duty to Alfred Donegan, the legation's counselor, the next day.[1]

Life in the Bern legation was more chaotic than in Vienna. Being a legation, not a full embassy, the Bern staff was considerably smaller. The historical excuse had been that since there were American consuls in most of the other main cities of Switzerland, a full embassy was not needed. Besides one military attaché and one commercial specialist, Donegan had only Hugh Wilson, Fred Dolbeare, and Dulles actually to attend to the business of the legation. Worse, most of the legation staff were new boys. Nearly all had less than a year in the Foreign Service, and all of them had transferred to Bern in the last few weeks before the United States declared war. The legation's minister, a Georgia newspaper publisher and Wilson political crony, Pleasant Stovall, was aptly named but had even fewer of the skills needed to run a crucial wartime diplomatic and espionage post than had Penfield in Vienna. Stovall's singular advantage, it turned out, was staying out of the way of his staff.

According to Dulles's reminiscences, his first day on the job showed how confused matters were. Working his way through the crowd of official visitors and refugees, he managed to reach Donegan's office, where the harried official shook his hand perfunctorily and said, "I don't know exactly what your duties will end up being, why don't you take over intelligence for the time being?" A later arrival was Robert Murphy, a recently appointed junior clerk just out from Washington. Murphy was sworn in as a clerk on April 23, in Washington, the same day Allen arrived in Bern, and he followed within two weeks. "I was rushed to Europe and tossed into international politics before I had firsthand knowledge of any foreign country, indeed, with very little knowledge of any sort," he recalled. Murphy would go on to become a senior career diplomat, an intelligence expert, and an undersecretary of state; he would also play a major role in one of Allen Dulles's more important OSS exploits. But for the moment, as the most recent arrival he was lumbered with the tedious job of being the legation's code specialist.

Murphy recalled: "After a few months I suffered my first disillusionment with our foreign service organization when I learned that some of my encoding and decoding probably had been wasted motion. The Germans rather disdainfully returned a State Department code book that had been used by the American consulate in

Leipzig, thus hinting broadly that they had keys to all our codes. The Germans were way ahead of us in cryptography. It was child's play for the German Black Chamber to break our simple book codes of that period. Moreover, most Americans had never even heard of security in the Bern Legation; certainly they did not practice it. Foreign employees had the run of the Legation and it would have been comparatively easy for some of them to get hold of our code books."[2] Minister Stovall, to Murphy's unsparing eye, was "a monument to the dignity of his office."

Yet out of chaos came the opportunity for these schoolboys to turn themselves into spies. "I am one of the many cogs in the wheel and I cannot tell you much what I do, except that it has to do with intelligence!" Allen wrote home. Truthfully, that could be said of Fred Dolbeare, Murphy, and the other clerks, too. But Allen landed a special brief to keep watch over and establish communications lines into the Central European and Balkan countries now sealed off from contact with the United States by the war. He continued fitful attempts to revive the secret talks between the White House and the Austrian emperor. He also was busy meeting with myriad dissident groups within the tottering Austrian empire who circulated in Switzerland seeking money and political support for their schemes. Lenin and his Bolsheviks were based in Zurich; there were also colonies of Hungarians and Czechs grouped around Edvard Benes and Jan Masaryk, and Allen established contact with them all. These contacts lasted him through another world war.

He outlined a typical day to his mother: "On weekdays I am up by 7:30, breakfast in my own room, read the morning papers, one French, *Le Journal de Geneve,* and one German, *Die Zurcher Zeitung.* I make it a point to be in the Legation by 9:00 as I am absolutely overwhelmed by work which I can't find time to do. I leave the office a little before 1:00, walk back to the hotel about a half a mile away, have lunch generally with work that keeps me in touch with both the French and British here. Passport matters of these countries are now entirely under the control of the military authorities which means efficiency. We are now flooded with Americans of doubtful loyalty and citizenship who have come and are still coming every day from Germany and Austria, not to be speaking of those from Turkey."

The Germans had stepped up their previously successful campaign to insert agents into the United States, and they specialized in forged or stolen documents to win the needed visas for entry from besieged legations such as the one at Bern. Close questioning and unmasking of these spies became a skill and particular pleasure for Allen. As the American involvement in the war gathered force, the spy game in Bern became more dangerous. "I shall close this unusually dull letter by saying in a tantalizing way that the past week has been full of incidents of more than usual interest. Certainly *new* experiences but which I cannot now divulge in confidence even. Someday I shall come back and tell all about the various unmentionable happenings," he hinted in a letter to his father. In an earlier note he recounted how one of the legation clerks had been assaulted on a Saturday night by someone with "a *German* German accent," as opposed to the Bern accent. The laugh was that the American clerk had been a successful lightweight prize fighter and the assailant was left unconscious on the pavement. Danger or no, Allen was having the time of his life.

"Bern is *the diplomatic* and *spy* center," he exulted to his mother. His boyish pride poking through the facade of the twenty-four-year-old diplomat, he added that he had been gathering reports on Austro-Hungarian affairs: "Also I now hobnob with all sorts of outlandish people, Czechs, Yugoslavs, Albanians, Montenegrins, Ukrainians.... There is a chance to do as much here as if one were shooting personally a whole regiment of Bosche [*sic*]."

Among the longer-term visitors was his old friend Prince Max von Hohenlohe.

In a note to his family later that summer, Allen described a typical official trip to Zurich:

I had an appointment with a Pole for 9 PM. He brought in a long and interesting memorandum on internal conditions in Poland and the Central Powers. Then he made some very sensational charges against a fellow Pole who has always been considered very pro-Ally in sympathy and had been on intimate terms with our allies and ourselves. Such incidents are occurring continually and it is very difficult to get the truth of such cases. Refugees from oppressed countries are always singularly jealous of fellow countrymen in a like position and very given to suspect each of their motives and activities. After my Pole had left, at the Minister's request, I saw the counselor of our Allied Legation who had a very delicate commission of inquiry about America's relations with Bulgaria. As he tried to dodge around the questions he wanted to find an answer for, and as I was all the time trying to find out what he was really trying to find out and why, we had an interesting quarter of an hour of it.

In the afternoon I spent some time working on a long report which had been sent in from a private service in regard to some German plans for the commercial and political domination of Switzerland of which the first steps might be to try to prevent American grain which is still long overdue from arriving in the country. Then the Legation had a call from Elliott Wordsworth, the second in command in the Red Cross, who is here on a tour of inspection. I tried to be of assistance to him

in an interview which he gave to the chief Bern newspaper and which was rendered difficult by the fact that
Wordsworth knew no German and the reporter knew
no English. I am ashamed to say that while my reading
German is clear, I'm still not a great success as speaking
goes.

Then I was just able to finish up some routine
work and then left to catch a 7:00 train for Geneva where
I am spending Sunday with Dr. George Herron, an
American writer and professor who is one of our most
influential Americans in Switzerland. I arrived at his
house at about 11:15 PM, and found there two Yugoslavs.
Our southern Slav friends stayed for an hour during
which we discussed the future of Serbia, the coming conference of the Yugoslavs in Rome to which our friends
were going the next morning, and the fallacy of the
American belief that the Hungarians, the most reac-
tionary people in Europe, were really a liberty-loving
race. The real objective of my journey here was to get
into touch with some Czechs who are working here for
Bohemian independence and who are in close touch
with Czechs who come out of Austria. Dr. Herron has
arranged tonight a gathering of a dozen or so of Geneva's
leading citizens who make his house quite an intellectual
center. The Genevaise are very much worried over the
food situation.[3]

It may have been an exhausting schedule, but Allen apparently thrived both on the physical demand of the extra hours and
travel involved and on the intellectual challenge of meeting so
many diverse personalities and weeding through the unfamiliar territories of their special motives. In May, he wrote to Grandfather

Foster to thank him for the gift of a substantial sum of money. The general had set up a trust fund as part of his estate to give the hefty sum of $20,000 to each of his grandchildren upon his death. But he had given Foster and Janet Dulles their inheritance when they married after a whirlwind courtship in 1912, and, while the amount given to Allen was not specified, it clearly was meant to make him financially able to carry the extra expenses of the diplomat's life, which scarcely could be covered by a $2,000 annual salary and travel expenses reimbursed at five cents a mile.

Dear Grandpapa, The last pouch brought me your letter telling of the generous allowance you had made for me. I shall try to make good use of your gift. However, what will be of more value to me in life is your example; the principles which have guided you, and the high objects you have always kept foremost.... I try to work hard and get as much done as possible. When I left Austria I was pretty well tired out—the nervous strain of the work there affected us all. But now I feel quite fit. Some of my recent experiences have been rather trying.... Mr. Stovall, my present chief, is very pleasant, and has been especially kind to me. I should add, however, that one fails to see the sparks of genius.

I become more and more convinced that the future peace of Europe rests on separating Austria from Germany. If the latter, even though beaten, is able to realize its idea of a "Middle European" union, under the leadership of Germany, it will be possible to defy the rest of the world even more successfully at a future date.... There is a growing party in Austria which would welcome a severance from Germany. It is not now strong [enough] to control Austrian policy, but it would be, I feel sure, if Germany even partially defeated, losses [*sic*] the prestige which she now has. I am so glad that it has been American policy to help along this movement in Austria, by refusing to sever relations and by differentiating its treatment of Austria from that of Germany.

The surest way to defeat this policy, and to throw Austria into the arms of Germany is to carry out the policy of the Entente… which is to strip it of its anti-Germany elements, alienate it, by humiliating it, and force a weakened Austria and Hungary, joined to a weakened Germany (but will still be the power in central Europe) to try, in making common cause, to win back their losses. Austria and Hungary are entirely different from Germany, and so many of both peoples dislike the Germans, as I know from personal experience. They are not a menace to the world peace as Germany is, and, I am afraid, will continue to be, until a new generation of Germans, under different leaders and teachers, and with a different philosophy of life comes along.[4]

Life was not all clandestine meetings and deep thinking, however. One gets an impression from other letters to friends and relatives that strenuous physical exercise, especially long mountain walks and steep climbing, were something of a release for Allen after the stresses of legation life. Bern is situated on the steep terraces up from the horseshoe bend of the Aare River as it snakes through the Bernese Alps, or Oberland. The Jungfrau at 12,000 feet and other high mountain peaks look down upon it. It was a matter of no more than an hour in a borrowed automobile to reach some spectacular vantage point. For all its medieval architecture and arcaded streets, Bern was much more than a provincial capital and the seat of the Swiss federal government; it was a major world focal point. Artists on the run from the war sparked a theater and music hall revival. Food was scarce until the American aid

shipments started to arrive regularly in 1918, but there was plenty
of money floating around for those quick enough to grab it. And
money bought comforts, even scarce ones.

Allen apparently made the most of the area's recreational
facilities, including the attractive young ladies from the staid local
community, from refugee families, and from among the pool of
Swiss girls who flocked to the embassies to work as secretaries,
stenographers, and clerks. When romance palled, there were lively
golfing weekends for those who did not hike. Allen reported home
that he had shot the tough golfing course at Aigle in eighty-six, so
his athletic skills were pretty well honed. And Allen certainly did
not have to go far for entertainment. A lively international set of
young diplomats, military attachés, and swells quickly formed, and
the Palace Bellevue Hotel, with its nightly jazz band dances, became
the place where the young of all nations came to play. In addition
to Fred Dolbeare and Bob Murphy, Allen's closest friend in Bern
was Robert Craigie, a second secretary at the British Embassy.

Craigie was to be yet another of the long-term Dulles friends
whose life would crisscross his with unusual coincidence in future
decades. That summer of 1917, Craigie and Dulles became a formidable tennis partnership and made the rounds of the various
charity tournaments in Zurich, Geneva, and Bern. They also developed a taste for champagne, pretty girls, and various harmless high
jinks at the Palace Bellevue, including taking over the drums during the hotel band's performances, a stunt that earned them an
eventual caution from the hotel's management. While Craigie did
not have a direct intelligence brief, he did become something of a
liaison with Dulles and the U.S. Legation. It was a relationship that
became very deeply personal after Craigie fell in love with, and
ultimately married, one of Pleasant Stovall's daughters. Allen
Dulles was the best man at the wedding.[5]

One factor in the Dulles-Craigie popularity in Swiss sporting
circles was the steady supply of American-made tennis balls that

brother Foster conscientiously included during the tennis season as part of the American shipment of food relief aid to the Swiss people. Late in 1917 Foster had been recruited out of military uniform to go to work for Vance McCormick, the chairman of the War Trade Board. The board, whose members included the secretaries of state, treasury, agriculture, and commerce, supervised American trade to ensure that no goods slipped through to aid Germany. Foster Dulles was liaison between the board and the War Department, and he quickly made a specialty of negotiating complex trade agreements with the European nations that were still neutral in the war and still eager to trade with America. As the demands of supplying the U.S. military establishment on the Western Front soared beyond the abilities of the home economy to provide, Foster found himself swapping American cotton and petroleum products for European mules, horses, and foodstuffs for the troops arriving by boatloads in France. He soon developed a reputation as solid as Allen's in this new area of government law.

That winter of 1917–1918 brought to Bern another set of diplomatic newcomers—the representatives of the Bolshevik government, who now demanded control of the old czarist embassy. The situation was equally fluid and perilous. The czar had been an ally; it was clear that the triumphant Lenin was not. There were hints that he might actually take the Russians out of the war altogether—a potential disaster for the beleaguered Allies on the Western Front. Allen and his colleagues had their hands full just keeping track of the changes. In a letter to Foster, which noted in passing the arrival of more tennis balls, Allen sounded a concern that eventually vexes anyone responsible for ordering the flow of information that any intelligence operation produces.

> At present I am busy trying to develop a political information service for Austria, Hungary and the Balkans.... The sources of political information are outside the

enemy press which we cover carefully; there are many
political exiles who follow events closely, very closely in
their country of origin. In every different question there
are specialists with whom we keep in touch. The Poles,
loyal Romanians and Russians are great sources of information. The problem is not so much to collect a volume
of material. I have more memoranda to read than I can
get through in my branch of the work. But I have to be
able to weigh the material and judge the reliability of the
informant and then to put a great mass of material in
shape for the information of the Department.[6]

Not all of his efforts were successful. Sometimes the ham-
handedness of the American diplomatic and intelligence effort
would not be overcome. Other times, Allen and his colleagues simply fell down on the job. One of his most glaring gaffes, perhaps
the best known of the Allen Dulles yarns about this time in Bern,
had to do with his narrowly missing what might have been a critical interview with Lenin, who was heading off to take control of
the Russian Revolution in 1917. It was a story that Dulles himself
repeated countless times as a cautionary tale to successive classes
of CIA trainees.

    One version has Dulles and Craigie in hot pursuit of two
blonde and spectacularly buxom Swiss twin sisters who had agreed
to a weekend rendezvous at a country inn. Dulles's own version
had him about to close the legation offices early for a Friday afternoon tennis date—with a girlfriend—when the telephone rang.
The caller identified himself as Lenin, then known to the
Americans as the leader of a ragged band of revolutionaries who
plotted and wrote revolutionary tracts from their base in Zurich.
The caller was in a high state of excitement and demanded to
speak to someone in authority; Dulles told him to call back the

next day since the office had closed. Lenin reportedly insisted on speaking to someone who could take an important message and negotiate with him. Dulles was adamant. Whatever it was could keep overnight, and he firmly hung up the telephone. That weekend, the punch line to the story goes, Lenin boarded the famous sealed train that carried him and his conspirators across Germany, to the famous arrival in St. Petersburg's Finland Station, where his destiny awaited. The moral Dulles drew for generations of CIA trainees who heard the story was, never refuse to see anyone or listen to anything, however improbable.

Dulles and the other Americans also had frequent run-ins with Herbert Field, an officious Quaker Bostonian who was in charge of one of the more important refugee relief groups based in Zurich. Field fancied himself a private intelligence operative and succeeded in denouncing as a German spy one of the more effective sources of German information that the Americans were running. His son, Noel Field, would be a crucial liaison during World War II with the communist exile groups Dulles needed for anti-Nazi resistance groups inside Germany. Later he would be a major figure in the Alger Hiss Soviet spy case. These links underscore that Allen Dulles's spy career was firmly rooted in these early days in Switzerland.

Nor did Dulles have to wait until World War II to become used to the spy's dark world of betrayal and violence. One of the émigré sources Dulles came to rely upon was Jan Masaryk, the Czech leader then in exile. According to British and other sources, a Czech girl who was employed at the U.S. Legation had been allowed access to the room where the new American codes were housed. The British brought evidence to Dulles that she was informing both Masaryk and the Germans, and they insisted that she be handed over to them to be liquidated. According to the story, Dulles took her to dinner one night and then walked her to a point where he handed her over to two British agents; she disappeared forever.[7]

Back in Washington, Robert Lansing attempted to strengthen his control over the intelligence system he was building for President Wilson. Among his official correspondence with Wilson is the first formal proposal that the diverse flows of U.S. intelligence information be gathered and analyzed in one location before being presented to the chief executive. On April 8, 1917, two days after Wilson signed the war declaration, Lansing sent the following letter:

My dear Mr. President: There is one matter of very great importance which it seems to me ought to be decided at once, and that is the coordination of the secret service work of this Government, of which the secret service office of the Department of State has been for eight or nine months the "Clearing house" [sic] or at least the depository of information gathered from various sources....

I am not courting additional responsibilities but I do feel that the central office of secret information of all sorts should be in the State Department because this is a time when the safety of the state is threatened from without and because the head of the service must confer constantly with the Embassies of the Allied powers and with the missions of certain Latin American countries, and because it is only by a thoroughly experienced and trustworthy man who is expert in international matters and to whom the Department archives are open, that the information gathered can be properly valued.

I believe that on the nucleus already formed in this Department a very efficient organization can be built up....[8]

Thus we come to one of the first plans on record for setting up a central intelligence agency—within the State Department—and in fact it soon came to be. It would remain for William Donovan to create a totally separate paramilitary spy service for wartime service and for Allen Dulles to establish the intelligence culture and the form of the final product decades later. But in the never-ending debate over credit, Robert Lansing deserves a solid mention. Wilson was all for the consolidation of power in central authorities. And in truth, the country's intelligence needs had changed forever with the declaration of war.

In responding to Lansing's proposal for a "clearinghouse," Wilson probably was more shrewd than his secretary of state. A formally created special organization for intelligence coordination at that time would have been upsetting to more than just the agents of Justice and Treasury; General Pershing, for one, would never have allowed his G-2 military intelligence chief, General Dennis E. Nolan, to participate. Instead, Wilson allowed Lansing and Polk quietly and informally to channel the flow of military and law enforcement material into the State Department's Bureau of Secret Intelligence, also known as U-1, which was an off-the-books adjunct to the Division of Information. The two men picked a young clerk named Leland Harrison "to take charge of the collection and examination of all information of a secret nature coming into the Department from various sources and also to direct the work of the agents specially employed for that purpose."[9] Another building block in Allen Dulles's career was put in place, for Harrison was to head the U.S. Legation in Bern while Dulles was OSS station chief there during World War II.

Allen and his young colleagues in Bern drew increasing amounts of raw data and tutorial help from the Swiss intelligence service, which was by far the best organized and most productive of all the European spy groups of that time. The Swiss were driven by a fanatical commitment to their own national independence and neutrality, and, being the ultimate pragmatists, they divided their intelligence service neatly between the warring parties. One branch of the service did business with the Germans and Austrians, while another shared information and trade craft with the Allies. Since most adult Swiss males were military reservists, the large number of ordinary business travelers and journalists became instant intelligence agents throughout Europe; indeed, since Switzerland was a neutral nation, active-duty Swiss military staff officers were welcomed observers on both sides of the battle lines. Moreover, the Swiss quickly developed a code-breaking skill that rivaled that of the British Room 40 wizards, and the government's huge wireless stations perched on Alpine peaks were able to snatch messages out of the air from nearly every country in Europe.

Dulles learned more than the technical and professional side of the spy trade from the Swiss. His personal contacts with the senior colonel in charge of the service, a man named Sonderegger who "in civil life is the manager of an export house at Herisau," and other officers of the service taught by example how tough-minded the intelligence professional must be and how his only loyalty must be to his nation's security. The Americans became the beneficiaries of much of this shared intelligence. The flow of information out of the U.S. Legation in Bern to Allied headquarters in Paris and on to Washington became truly staggering in volume, in the importance of specific information, and in the time lines of the intelligence.

In one roundup report for September 1917, Dulles and his colleagues were able to give detailed reports on German troop movements by train to the Western Front, including the names of regiments, the number of troops, and their destination; the information was no more than one week old, and much of it was within three days of the events. In the same file, the Americans included the debriefing of a German officer who had deserted with a list of divisions being massed near Cologne for an attack in Champagne; the locations of new German batteries in the Ypres salient were also listed, and a confidential agent in Lausanne reported the date of a planned large German air bombing of a French railyard near the Swiss border. Perhaps the most important news of that one file was the location of a secret new factory and training base for the manufacture of a new generation of the Zeppelin bombing dirigibles that had so terrified London.

In addition to his spying, Allen was learning other more formally diplomatic skills and was marked within the Foreign Service as one of the young men of promise. During this time, Allen made friends with a young Christian Herter, who was working with Ellis Dresel, the State Department's expert on German politics. Herter would go on to be undersecretary of state for the last three years of Foster Dulles's secretaryship and would succeed him for the remainder of the Eisenhower administration.

In a Christmas 1917 letter home, Allen wrote, "Bern now is the center for organizations representing every nationality and sect and scheme. Most turn most willingly to the Americans as being the people with honest interests and the most disinterestedness as well as having the best-lined purse. We have various sects of Russians and Poles, Ukrainians, Lithuanians, all variations of Slavs and Czechs, recalcitrant and liberal Germans and Austrians, all turn to us for assistance and we use them to secure information and to help keep current on the various tendencies and movements. We are busy with rumors and stories of military attacks of the Germans, of the political projects of the Central Powers and their allies, of peace feelers from the Germans and Austrians. This all comes in the daily work; we have to sift and investigate and get at all the truths. It all is a liberal education."[10]

After the Armistice, he accompanied Dresel to Berlin for the preliminary talks with the distraught Germans who had been left in control of the government after the kaiser had fled and many of his minions had resigned. By this time he had won his spurs as a talented diplomat. U.S. ambassadors at other posts coveted his skill at getting sensitive tasks done deftly. His work with the Czech and Polish exile groups had earned him first claim on senior undersecretary positions in the American legations that were to be opened in Warsaw and Prague. Instead, Dresel recruited him to be assistant head of the Department of Current Political and Economic Correspondence for the U.S. delegation to the Peace Conference in Paris. The section was to be the nexus of the American participation in the historic parley that would follow any armistice. Dresel's office was to serve as both a secretariat and communications center, but more importantly, it was to coordinate all the intelligence that would flow into the delegation from the other delegations and sources. The problem would not be to get information, it would be how to manage the information, the pleas, the accusations, the plans, and the bargains that would be directed at Woodrow Wilson, the man who for a few short moments of history held the destiny of the world in his hand.

The statesmen who rushed to Paris in the autumn of 1918 were united by only one common goal: A European peace must be made an inevitable result of whatever agreement was reached. The world as it was known then could never stand such a war again. The French and British both were adamant that German militarism, whatever tunic clothed it, must never again set out on a march of conquest. What is remarkable about the Paris meeting is not its naiveté but its vision. Leaders from sixty-five nations faced not only the collapse of the old world order, but also future threats that were only dimly foreshadowed. In that light, it is a marvel that the delegates did as well as they did in such a short time. The lesson of the Treaty of Versailles is not its manifest failures. Rather, the Paris Peace Conference of 1918–1919 was a kind of baccalaureate for the diplomats of our century. The problems they wrestled with then for the first time would persist even after the carnage of World War II and on into the long Cold War after that. It can be argued that the most intractable and dangerous of the problems that still threaten us today trace their causes to the hatreds and fears that the Versailles diplomats were the first to confront.

The eight months that encompassed the arrival of the first delegations in late November of 1918 until the treaty was formally signed on June 28, 1919, gave both Allen and Foster Dulles credentials and acquaintances of the first rank in American foreign affairs. They met and earned the respect and often the friendship of other rising diplomats who would mature into world leaders over the next half century. Both were extraordinarily young for the responsibilities they took on; Allen was twenty-five, and Foster would celebrate his thirtieth birthday in Paris. Older men before and afterward never had the opportunities for responsibility and experience that would be thrust upon what might be called the Class of 1918. The seasoning of statecraft gained at Paris would lift the careers of other men too, such as Herbert Hoover, George Marshall, Bernard Baruch, Adolph Berle, Christian Herter, journalist Walter Lippmann, and historian Samuel Eliot Morison, along with the Dulles brothers, for the next fifty years of American history. Statesmen such as Andre Tardieu and Louis Loucher of France and John Maynard Keynes, Anthony Eden, and Harold Nicolson of Britain dated their first acquaintance with the brothers Dulles from the months they spent in Paris together in these early days.

ALLEN ARRIVED IN PARIS a few weeks after the Armistice was announced. He was assigned the rank of a second secretary of legation and attached in December to the American Commission to Negotiate Peace. His working assignment was under Ellis

Dresel in an office called the Department of Current Political and Economic Correspondence. In reality, Dresel was to oversee the State Department's intelligence efforts at the conference, both the public and the more covert variety. Allen wrote to Hugh Wilson, a friend who was the first secretary in the Bern legation, "Ellis and I receive all incoming mail, telegraphs and letters and are responsible to see that action is taken."[11]

The intelligence services of the major powers were already busy trying to tap each other's telephones in the various delegation offices around Paris. The communications center set up by the Americans at their headquarters at the Hotel Crillon had to be made secure, while at the same time providing a link to the equally elaborate telephone network maintained by General Pershing's staff and the troops at the front. Back in Washington, to be sure, State Department agents had been monitoring telegraphic traffic abroad and, through cooperation with the International Telephone Company, they now had taps on trans-Atlantic telephone traffic too.

Dresel and his secretariat had other duties. As the department's expert on German matters, Dresel was given responsibility for keeping contact with both the governments of the defeated Central Powers and the various competing power groups within those countries. He was the first of the Americans at Paris to warn that Germany must not be punished beyond the point that it could serve as an adequate bulwark for the rest of Western Europe against the ambitions of the Bolshevik leaders in Moscow. Allen became a much relied-upon aide. He was detailed, because of his past experience, to handling the correspondence and communications dealing with Austria-Hungary. Because of his friendship with Edvard Benes and Tomas Masaryk, Allen also became the focal point for the often conflicting émigré groups who demanded that a Czechoslovakian nation be carved out of the old empire.

The rush of duties from preliminary meetings to logistical tasks kept Allen on the run. There was no time for more than a glimpse of his sister Eleanor, who had paid her own way to Paris well ahead of Pershing and his troops. Using her skills as a social economist, she prowled the shell-wrecked slums of Paris for a relief agency trying to help the destitute. But once the Americans arrived in force, her group was peremptorily shut down by the Red Cross. Refusing to go home, Eleanor transferred to a Quaker relief organization that assisted French rural villagers in rebuilding their farms and homes. She found herself working in the region of the Marne between Chateau Thierry and Belleau Woods, where some of the heaviest American casualties of the war were suffered and where the landscape had been scoured of all life. She worked with young Quaker women and young American men who had been conscientious objectors to build temporary shelters and then, later, to begin the task of economic and social reconstruction that was beyond the resources of the French government. For the next year Eleanor's economic education confronted the practical tasks of getting a war-shattered society to function again so that its citizens could resume their lives.

Foster too was on his way to Paris, despite a frank reluctance on the part of Uncle Bert. Lansing by now must have felt he would be surrounded by family obligations in Paris. "Foster, don't ask me to take you, I just can't," he said in exasperation to his nephew. "I'm having enough trouble with the president on who is going and I just can't take you along."

Early in the war, President Wilson had the wisdom to see that the U.S. government lacked adequate information about the most serious issues it would confront in Europe after the war. American ignorance of ethnic politics went so far that the most basic maps of the continent's borders and important resources simply did not exist. Wilson created a special advisory group, "The Commission of Inquiry." It quickly became known as "The Inquiry," and the press called it Wilson's "brain trust." Under Colonel House's direction, the group was made up of historians, geographers, economists, and other experts on world affairs. Also ordered to Paris were many of the key war industry advisers such as Herbert Hoover, Vance McCormick, and Bernard Baruch, and bankers such as Norman Davis and Thomas Lamont. The whole entourage would accompany Wilson on the liner *George Washington* and serve as his human encyclopedia at the conference. The group also was to frame the specific tasks of the League for Peace that the president insisted upon. With typical Wilsonian confidence, the president told his advisers not to bother him with the details of the issues he would confront. "Just tell me what is right, and I will fight for it," he said.

McCormick and Baruch wanted Foster Dulles. The young lawyer had impressed them with his capacity for mastering huge amounts of information. They also prized Foster's ability to win friends among the tetchy neutral negotiators on complex financial and trade matters during the war. Most of all, Foster was developing a reputation for being able to devise plausible legal arguments to justify more pragmatically motivated compromises. They knew, too, for it was no secret, that William Cromwell, the white-maned senior partner of Foster's law firm, was an ardent Francophile with extremely potent contacts within the Clemenceau government and the Belgian royal family. Cromwell would be in Paris, having set up in an opulent apartment there. He had arrived to hand out hundreds of thousands of dollars in aid funds that he had raised among his U.S. clients. Wilson, it turned out, was aware of the good job the young lawyer had done for McCormick and viewed him as something of a Princeton protégé. So Foster joined the delegation on board the *George Washington*. Janet followed in March 1919. On the voyage over, Foster played bridge with Franklin Roosevelt, the assistant navy secretary, and his wife Eleanor, while Uncle Bert vainly tried to win the president's agreement to let him handle the negotiations.

In all, there were roughly four hundred Americans coming to the conference from various directions; roughly ninety were civilians, while the others were in the military or diplomatic services. Buried within the listing of the forty staff members for The Inquiry was a counterintelligence and cryptographic team made up from military intelligence and Leland Harrison's operatives from the State Department. By now both the army and navy had elevated their intelligence duties to general staff rank, and Polk had managed to institutionalize within the State Department most of the wartime spy, code, and analysis sections that he had built up. Coming to Paris, then, was the first real effort whereby, as one commentator has noted, "strategic national intelligence could be put in the service of American foreign policy."[12]

Colonel Ralph Van Deman was in charge of setting up the U.S. Peace Commission's internal security system and its counterespionage capability. Herbert Yardley, now an army major, ran a cryptological section that secured the communications the American delegates used internally and worked on cracking the codes of the other foreign delegations in Paris. The whole apparatus was plugged into Dresel's operation, where he additionally had the resources of the Foreign Service's young legation secretaries; these were sent all over Europe during the conference for firsthand information-gathering.

The Inquiry had set up a formal liaison with the Political Intelligence Office of the British Foreign Office, thanks to the good offices of William Wiseman, MI6's man in America. But the fledgling Yankee spies won admiration from both the French and British services for the way they came up to speed in developing their own contacts and the spirit that they brought to the darker side of the game. Allen Dulles and a subsequent OSS and CIA compatriot, Whitney H. Shepardson, shuttled between Dresel and Van Deman to ensure that the information gathered was delivered to Wilson and the other commissioners. It should come as no surprise to find the names of men who were with Allen Dulles in Paris in the subsequent history of this country's spy services; the Peace Conference was where they learned their craft.[13]

The Paris negotiations sent the careers of Allen and Foster Dulles rocketing, but it also marked the eclipse of Robert Lansing's career as secretary of state. If President Wilson could have had his way, he would not have brought Lansing to Paris at all. That was not a realistic option, however, since all the other foreign ministers of the great powers would be members of their official Peace Conference commissions. Indeed, there is much controversy even today over whether Wilson should have stayed home in Washington and exercised his potent moral veto over the outcome, thereby leaving the dirty business of diplomatic horse trading to Lansing and Colonel House. That is what both of those two men had devoutly desired.

Lansing believed that he would be going as the head of the American delegation or, at the worst, in tandem with House. House presumably would be tied up with the more immediate task of disarming the Germans. Thus Lansing would inherit the challenge that was really interesting to him, brokering the precise language of the peace agreement and the arbitration of all the tangled disputes. It would have been a lawyer's dream. Disappointed and alarmed at the president's decision, Lansing made the first of a series of serious mistakes. His downfall would be engraved in the minds of Allen and Foster Dulles, a lesson on how to survive with the presidents one serves.

Both Lansing and House privately dated the decline of their personal influence with Wilson from the rebukes they received at that time. In fact, Lansing did not have that far to fall in the president's estimation. Nor was House as cherished an adviser to Wilson as he thought.

Vance McCormick, Foster Dulles's boss, took his own risk and called on Wilson not to go. Wilson's response was a plaintive cry, "Who can head the Commission if I do not go? Lansing is not big enough. House won't do. Taft and Root are not in sympathy with our plans. I must go."[14]

That act was both heroic and petulant. Woodrow Wilson was sixty-three and had never been in robust health. Various circulatory and neurological ailments made him susceptible to exhaustion, and his doctors had worried he would never live out his first term in the White House, let alone the current one. Yet Wilson was no coward. And despite the obstruction of a malignant ego, he believed passionately in the cause of peace and justice. He can even be forgiven him for seeing his homeland as mankind's best hope for the future. There were plenty of men who viewed the Paris negotiations as a quixotic and self-aggrandizing junket, and plenty more who rejoiced in the president's final failure and downfall. But none was more ennobled by that failure than Wilson, the flawed dreamer who set the United States on a course in the world from which it has not varied to this day.

Even Wilson was stunned by the wave of adulation that crashed about him when the *George Washington* docked at Brest on December 13, 1918. His parade between the Arc de Triomphe and the Place de la Concorde in Paris the next day was a triumphal entry never matched before or since as a throng of two million crushed around his carriage. Eleanor Dulles, who had denied herself the Paris celebration on Armistice Day, had come up from her village near the Marne and talked her way into the Lansing suite at the Crillon to await Uncle Bert and Aunt Eleanor. She watched the parade hoisted on the shoulders of one of the young military officers attached to the U.S. delegation. Then she luxuriated in a hot bath in Lansing's tub, used up all his fresh towels, and was fast asleep in his bed when the family finally was shown into its rooms.

Later she would recall that she did this a number of times when the privations of the war zone became too much. And only later did she realize that she had never asked her uncle if she might and that he had never commented on this presumption; he merely moved his things into his wife's quarters until she was gone again.

Wilson hit Paris ready to go to work at once. But England's David Lloyd George, France's Georges Clemenceau, and Italy's Vittorio Emanuele Orlando were not prepared to come to terms so quickly. For much of the rest of December, Wilson was diverted to lengthy, arduous tours of Britain and Italy, each as wildly adulatory as the other, but increasingly frustrating for the American president, who wanted to win peace quickly and go home in triumph. The Europeans, for their part, were not so sure they wanted Wilson's ideas, let alone his leadership.

The lobby of the Crillon Hotel became a literal global marketplace where the colorfully robed T. E. Lawrence campaigned for Arab nationhood even as Jewish leaders caucused for a Zionist homeland. Indian maharajahs and revolutionaries plotted against each other and the British. And the Chinese and Japanese sought sanctions against the other. Business was transacted as well, as South American governments sought new financing from international bankers who had come to count the profit from the penalties exacted from the Central Powers. But everything came to a halt each time Wilson and his entourage swept in or out of the Crillon. The spring and summer of 1919 brought American tourists flooding over in far greater numbers than had come five years before. The idle and curious were mixed with those moved to work for one of the many relief organizations coping with the devastation in Belgium and France and the threat of starvation in other parts of Europe. All found time to crowd outside the Crillon to see the sights and cheer Wilson to the sky whenever he emerged to return to his residence.

One of the fortunate who was able to wangle entrance to the hotel lobby was a twenty-five-year-old New Yorker who had come with her brother to work at one of the YMCA canteens for the soldiers. Martha Clover Todd looked very much the lively American flapper, with her hair in an auburn bob and a shapely athletic form that drew the servicemen in droves to her counter at the canteen. But Clover was more than a carefree tourist; the constant parade of wounded past her canteen post and the serious high purpose of the Paris Conference had sparked something in her. The Todds had a cousin from Baltimore on the commission staff, and it was on his pass that Clover caught her first sight of Wilson, smiling and wan, as he passed through the delirious throng one January afternoon.

In a letter back home to her mother, Clover reported, "It was well worth it in interest. First the bell rang four times and then the elevator came down laden with dignitaries and finally the president. I'm so glad to have seen him here. You know he is a tremendous hero with the peoples of the allied countries. It was quite thrilling to see him and to hear how all the people cheered him and shouted his name." There is no mention of whether she noticed either of the Dulles brothers doing convoy duty ahead of Wilson. Perhaps she was distracted by the young officer with whom her cousin had fixed her up on a luncheon date. A family story tells that this luncheon date had been with Allen but that it had been broken because another girl had complained that both the Dulles brothers were too engrossed in the conference to be any fun. In any event, within eighteen months she would be married to Allen.

By then Allen was surely worth an admiring glance. He was no longer the wiseacre schoolboy. The sheer crush of work and the darker side of the intelligence game had matured him in a hurry. He had stopped signing his letters "Allie" even to his mother, and family members had tactfully altered their salutations to him in all but the most intimate correspondence. He had adopted the trim, close-cut mustache that he would wear all his life, and his suits, while well within the guidelines for a young diplomat, still had the shaped waist jacket and high starched collar of the dandy. He had not yet come to wearing glasses as Foster had been forced to by his injured eye, but he had begun to affect the pipe that would be another of his hallmarks. Allen kept his light brown hair in a fairly close but natural cut that, with his high forehead and elongated jawline, gave him a somewhat stiff and formal appearance—not a bad thing for a rising young diplomat. Not that Allen had turned into a "poler." Despite the almost nonstop demands of Dresel's office, there was plenty of time to sample the gaiety that was returning to Paris. There were formal social occasions where young diplomats could unbend even when their bosses were going through the rituals. General Pershing, it seemed, had an eye for the ladies and threw a number of dances, which began at 10:00 PM and to which the young staffers were invited. There were several Princeton old-boys reunions, and there seemed to be a nonstop flow of friends who managed to pass through Paris on some military or political business. Allen's room, Number 471, adjoining Foster's office in the back regions of the Crillon, became something of a caravan stop for the visitors. In addition to the prospect of temporary shelter, the room boasted its own private bath and, even more rare, a private telephone.

Foster had found a berth as an adviser to Norman Davis, a New York banker who was a U.S. representative to the group of conferees meeting on the reparations issue. He also found himself drawing assignments from McCormick and Baruch, who were on various committees arguing over economic and trade issues. Thomas Lamont, another banker representing the Morgan interests, was part of the Peace Commission's negotiating team, and he began to rely on Foster for help as well. The reparations group was one of the permanent committees formed by the Big Ten (the heads of government and foreign ministers of the United States, Britain, France, Italy, and Japan) in an attempt to come to some sort of agreement on these key treaty issues. From the start, there was disagreement over more than just how much money should be exacted from Germany and the other foes. One point of disagreement was whether the reparations should be a straightforward penalty or the money tied to specific damages caused by the war. Davis, arguing that "enslaving one generation is enough," wanted a limit of $30 billion imposed on Germany. The British advisers demanded $90 billion. The French, remembering that Bismarck had exacted $1 billion to withdraw his troops in 1874, said that they would take nothing less than $200 billion plus the coal mines of the Saar and the return of Alsace-Lorraine.

In the weeks that followed, both Allen and Foster probably spent more time directly with Wilson than did their uncle. The two were involved in virtually every matter that concerned the conference. For the first time since they had sailed out of Henderson Harbor on their lazy boyhood excursions, Foster and Allen were in a partnership that fit so naturally it seemed to benefit both men equally. They found enormous pleasure in working together; their minds seemed to click as a single entity. And because they both worked harder than many of their colleagues, they spent long hours together, and in so doing, they were drawn together as friends, choosing to take many of their meals together at the hotel or in some quiet cafe. Allen, by the early spring, was doing extra duty as the senior staff person on the special commission to draw the boundaries for Czechoslovakia and on the panel that dealt with the broader political issues involved in carving out the new nations of Central Europe. Both brothers were also on the secretariat for the Steering Committee of the Council of Ten that had to pull the precise language of the treaty together. According to Foster's meticulous appointment records, he and Allen would often meet alone to decide agendas for the senior negotiators on one or another of the committees. After the treaty with Germany was signed in June, there still were separate treaties to be drafted and reparations argued over with Austria, Bulgaria, Turkey, and the other defeated nations. The Dulleses traveled frequently to London for meetings of the Supreme Economic Council, which the victors had set up to oversee the new trade and banking order for Europe.[15]

Paris and the treaty offered the chance of a lifetime for both brothers. In later years Allen would remember the excitement the two of them felt as they sat directly behind Wilson in one of the gilded conference rooms, passing notes forward to aid their president in his increasingly desperate fight. Allen reported to his mother breathlessly, "I hardly agree with your belief that we have played a small part in the war and therefore should let the other nations settle the peace. As a matter of fact we played the decisive part in the war and very possibly shall do the same as far as peace is concerned…." He went on to describe attending a conference with Wilson on Czechoslovakia and then added a homely note: "Foster and I have adjoining rooms in the Crillon and are as comfortable as hotel life can make it. Our offices are also in the hotel. We often take our meals here and as often as we can afford it we go out. The price of meals in the good restaurants is something out of sight. From time to time we eat with Aunt and Uncle Bert."[16]

In mid-February, Wilson sailed for home thinking he had won firm agreement to include the establishment of a League of Nations as an integral covenant of the treaty. He had not reckoned on Senator Henry Cabot Lodge, however. Combining with disaffected western state Democrats, the Republicans forced a stalemate on a number of key budget bills having to do with funds for the government and the military. An emergency session was called by the president, and the opponents to the treaty began to fulminate in earnest. On March 4 Lodge introduced a resolution signed by thirty-nine senators, more than enough to declare that the league provision in the treaty "in the form now proposed" would not be acceptable to the Senate.

Worse, from Wilson's point of view, was that when he returned to Paris on March 14, he found that Lansing, as the leading U.S. representative on the Council of Ten, had agreed with the French, British, and other nations to push ahead on a military and political treaty agreement that severed the question of the league and held it back for later debate and negotiations. This was the old two treaties idea that Wilson had spurned all along; there must be only one treaty, and that must include a league. Lansing for his part argued that conditions were changing rapidly in Europe, too fast for the Paris Conference to take it all in. Struggles for power in most of the newly liberated territories of Eastern Europe threatened to plunge the continent into a free-for-all of civil war. Further east, the Bolshevik regime that had seized control of Russia had wasted no time in fomenting revolution in the adjoining lands; a communist uprising had actually seized control in Hungary.

Allen Dulles suddenly found himself drafting a lengthy memorandum on using the former Prussian provinces of Latvia, Lithuania, and Estonia as "bulwarks against Bolshevism." Dresel circulated his own memos within the U.S. delegation, arguing that if the treaty were not soon signed, the United States should sign its own mutual defense pact with the German government and assure it of support in any conflict with a Soviet aggressor.

At this point the Dulles brothers, Lansing, and the rest of the American delegation saw the brittle hardness of Wilson's determination. His fixation on the league issue and his estrangement from many of his own commissioners led Wilson to rely more and more on the tentative agreements worked out at the junior staff level agenda conferences. Other issues crowded into the conference room, but Wilson was coldly dismissive of them, willing to sacrifice often-stated principles and engage in the clandestine horse trading he so despised in order to put the league back on the agenda and back into the treaty as Covenant One. More and more he relied on Allen, Foster, and the other young aides to provide the details he needed to make a point. Whatever they recommended was suitable no matter how complex the issue or how painful the consequences might be. Everyone had a claim to one colony or another of the old German possessions abroad. There was the Ottoman Empire to break up and distribute. Japan was making claims on Chinese provinces as a matter of right. National boundaries that were first drawn on hotel stationery forced the resettlement of millions of people. Wilson cared little, just as long as what he wanted was secure. Key elements of the Fourteen Points, such as open access to the sea lanes for all nations, were simply dropped. In April the president's health began to fail, and he wavered between episodes of forced immobility and frenzies of activity. His anger at Lansing's perceived perfidy was further irritated by evidence that a nephew of Colonel House, Gordon Auchincloss, had used his position on the commission staff to leak items to the press that were critical of the president. His isolation grew daily. Once he left Paris, Wilson would never see House again.[17]

Finally, the Treaty of Versailles was completed and signed. The stunned German delegates, who had been locked out of the deliberations, were led past lines of wounded soldiers into the Great Hall of Mirrors. The room was choked with symbolism and doubts. It was five years to the day after the murder of the Austrian archduke and his wife. A glum Lloyd George predicted the treaty was "all a great pity. We shall have to do the same thing all over again in twenty-five years at three times the cost."

The major participants began to flee Paris at once, though there remained an enormously detailed set of agreements on borders, arms, trade, and nationalities—thirty-five separate committees in all—that would have to be worked out for the final act of the drama; the Treaty of Sevres would be signed in August 1920. Wilson left the night of the Versailles Treaty signing to begin his fateful campaign across the United States to generate one of his patented tidal waves of public support that would overcome all opposition in the Senate. Uncle Bert and Aunt Eleanor began to break camp, too. Janet would join them, and even Eleanor was headed back to Henderson Harbor for a summer's recuperation. Foster, who now had been absent from his lawyer's job for two and a half years, was uncertain what path to take; he even applied to have his Army Intelligence Corps commission transferred to the regular army and asked that he be sent to artillery officer's school.

Allen kept getting more responsibility. He continued to negotiate on the details of the next peace treaty on the assembly line after the German pact. Frank Polk, who arrived from Washington to replace Lansing, appointed Allen chairman of the staff steering committee, which had to wrestle with the gritty details so blithely tossed about in the Versailles document. The old Habsburg grouping was in many ways harder to come to terms with because so many huge pieces of it had already gone into new nations—Yugoslavia, Hungary, Czechoslovakia—and each one of them was hardly organized; all were divisive and in angry moods. The Italians had successfully gained the Tyrol and control over 200,000 ethnic Austrians, who were outraged. The Serbs hated being linked with the Croats, and so it went. In a letter to Hugh Wilson, an old friend who was now the first secretary in the Bern legation, Allen complained, "The tendency which has hit the Conference of reopening and reversing decisions repeatedly only results in persuading the little nations that are waiting to feed upon Austria and Hungary that the Conference does not know its own mind and that they had best take matters into their own

hands.... [T]he future will probably show the necessity of a recon-
sideration of a good many of the decisions taken in Paris."[18]

By midsummer, Allen's steering committee job made him
heir to a range of negotiating responsibilities that stretched from
the Balkans to the Baltic. In an almost continual commute between
Paris and London, he found himself working out agreements,
boundary lines, and concessions with the likes of Jan Padarewski of
Poland and Edvard Benes of the new republic in Czechoslovakia.
He wrote one of the final memos on the Danzig Corridor and other
compromises that sought to deny Germany the ability to threaten
any of its neighbors ever again. At the same time, he and Dresel
were increasingly faced with the added problem of denying the
reach of the Bolsheviks, who were exporting their revolution to
every country that concerned the Paris diplomats. At one point,
Allen was offered the first secretary's job of the new U.S. Embassy
in Prague; Dresel talked him out of it, offering instead to take him
to Berlin once the final round of treaties was completed that
autumn.

It was heady stuff. An envious State Department friend wrote
Allen in September that he was being called "the Universal Expert"
back home. Foster, too, had built an impressive reputation, especially on the reparations and finance issues. But he kept an eye on
his career as well. During the summer, Foster had organized
lunches at the Ritz for William Cromwell and senior U.S. conference advisers such as Thomas Lamont and George Sheldon, both
of whom represented the Morgan banking interests. Often
Norman Davis and Vance McCormick were included. On one
occasion, he had pulled off a coup by bringing together his law
firm boss with his Uncle Bert, the Chinese minister of foreign
affairs, and the American ambassador to France. Cromwell was
impressed with the younger man's energy and his ability to win the
confidence of powerful clients.

Foster was anxious to return to New York when the Lansings and Cromwell had gone home in July, but Wilson himself had intervened and asked him to stay as a personal favor. Cromwell was even more impressed by just how important Foster had become in the continuing debate over the issues of high finance that would dominate the European scene long after the conference had ended. The Paris Peace Conference would conclude before Christmas in 1919, but the continuing Reparations Committee would not actually settle all the damage claims until 1921, and it proved to be a boon to American banks and law firms that was never forgotten. The reparations compromise also helped the Big Four leaders get their work done in time and still give a restive world public the impression that enormous sums of money would soon begin to flow into the coffers of the victorious Allies. For that, Foster was one of the Americans awarded the Legion of Honor by the French at a Bastille Day ceremony. Foster and Allen went on a drinking spree that ended in Montmartre at dawn the next day. On August 28 Foster sailed for England for a brief golfing holiday with U.S. Ambassador John W. Davis, the future presidential candidate. Then he returned to his career in law, a career unlike anything he might have imagined when he passed the bar exam in 1912.

A damp, cold autumn descended on Paris. Allen became more anxious to conclude the projects he was working on and get off to Berlin with Dresel, where the intrigues of intelligence beckoned. There was little profit in being the last of the American commission left to turn out the lights in the Crillon offices. Besides, the painfully constructed compromises and artificial agreements that had constituted much of the nation-building of the conference threatened to come unstuck even before the final gavel fell.

In a letter to a friend back in Washington, Allen confided that dire economic conditions and civil unrest were spreading from

Warsaw to Vienna. The new Czech nation tottered from a corruption scandal, and Hungary still reeled from its Leninist coup.

"To add to this pleasant picture," Allen continued, "all is not well in Yugoslavia. The Croats are at best a flighty people who can't stand adversity or pursue a definite policy.... [T]he Serbs have not always shown the greatest tact in the world.... [T]he [Romanian] hold on Transylvania was never too secure and now they have gone far towards alienating even Romanians in the province....

"Clemenceau, in his inimitable way, made a very true and striking statement in the Council the other day—'What an ungrateful task it is to release peoples from oppression so that they can oppress others,'" he added.[19]

Yet Allen was by no means converted to the isolationism that would become so popular back home. Writing to John Hughes, a veteran of Pershing's staff who had returned home, he observed:

> Our efforts over here do not seem to have found very much favor with the Senate. The result is to leave matters in a very embarrassing situation. Just at the crucial moment we will probably have to relax our participation in European affairs which may result in the formation of a European policy which it may be difficult to influence when we do come in later. As I feel pretty confident we will do when the personal struggle in Washington dies down a bit. We are a strange and disappointing country as far as foreign affairs are concerned. Just as we get everything where we want it, we leave the whole show to its own devices which certainly will not be ours.[20]

Allen also prophetically worried that the carefully constructed network of new nations that he had played so large a part in build-

ing in Eastern Europe and the Balkans would not jell. To his friend
Alexander Kirk at the State Department he confided:

> While all these frontiers in Central Europe were quite
> conscientiously drawn and can, for the most part, be jus-
> tified on ethnic and moral grounds, I am afraid that they
> have failed to take sufficiently into account economic
> necessity and also the fact that you can't distribute people
> the way you can vegetables.... I hope to leave for Berlin
> with Ellis [Dresel] within the next two weeks, a sadder
> but a wiser man after a year of the Peace Conference. In
> case you people stage another Peace Conference, I shall
> have a little book all prepared with good advice and sug-
> gestions of mistakes not to be repeated.[21]

Even though Allen had the distaste for Germans common at
that time, he was keen to get to Berlin and begin the task of setting
up American intelligence lines inside the former capital of the
kaiser. He told his old Princeton roommate John Colt that dealing
with the Germans "will be most difficult and unpleasant, not to say
delicate. Luckily the personnel of the mission which is being sent in
contains some of my very best friends [Fred Dolbeare and Chris
Herter were to be among them] which will make the going easier."[22]
Yet the Dresel mission did not leave Paris before Christmas as
planned and was still stuck in the Crillon in mid-January 1920, distracted by another problem that had intruded on the weary
Allies—Soviet Russia.

Now in the winter of 1919–1920, the president reached
across the Atlantic to set his diplomats off on another ill-fated task.
William Allen White, the midwestern newspaper editor and
adored iconoclast, had been named to head a peace conference on
the Turkish island town of Prinkipo to which all the participants

in the Russian civil war, and other disputants in the region, were invited to sit down and come to terms. It also was an attempt to bring some Western pressure to bear on the combatants to agree to some kind of peace and particularly to lean on the Bolsheviks to stop stirring up revolts in the new nations being chartered in Paris.

Allen was soon working on the preparations for the Prinkipo Conference and, not for the first time, was in direct conflict with the State Department's in-house specialists on Russian affairs. Not that Allen Dulles cared much. He had done his staff work for his bosses, and they had been cool to Prinkipo, especially when Wilson became immobilized by illness and immured in a darkened room at the White House. When Allen finally headed off to Berlin in late January 1920 it was with a light heart. It was back to the kind of work he loved—spycraft.

CHAPTER FOUR

1920–1926

"We felt a great adventure had really begun."
—*Clover Dulles*

BY JANUARY 1920 most of Allen Dulles's fellow intelligence officers had returned to private lives or idled at the ornate headquarters for the State, War, and Navy departments in Washington. But
Allen and his mentor Ellis Dresel were finally in Berlin watching
the German public recoil in revulsion from the politicians who
had signed the Versailles Treaty. As they watched, German society
degenerated into anarchy. It was a hectic time to be planting
agents and penetrating the profusion of political parties.

Allen was kept working full out. U.S. intelligence operations
were primitive with limited resources and manpower and much
ground to cover. Dresel and his staff could do little more than
introduce themselves to the various political factions and garner
names, telephone numbers, and subscriptions to the competing
propaganda newspapers. Nor could they solely concentrate on
Berlin. Other parts of Germany were on the boil. There was a
need for constant liaison with Hugh Wilson and his thinly staffed
embassy in Warsaw and with the other U.S. legations throughout
Eastern Europe and the Balkans. While large parts of Western
Europe had been hideously damaged by the war, there was even

less of an economic and social infrastructure east of the Elbe River, and the closer to the borders with the new Soviet Union, the greater the desolation became. Unlike past years, American relief faltered in its task, and no other victorious nation could take up the slack.

Berlin, wracked by poverty and suddenly freed from Prussian constraints, sank into an orgy of violent political strife and vice. The communist *Spartakist* rebellion staged in the city in 1919 had been crushed by the still-armed but uncontrolled bands of troops known as the *Frei Korps*. Munich and other major cities similarly had become the focus of a tug-of-war between right-wing militarists and socialists.

One force that brought all Germans together was that they detested the reparations demands of the Allies.[1] Yet the Americans were quick enough to sense that Germany's drift was to the right, not the left. Scarcely had a right-wing *putsch* led by Wolfgang Kapp been contained in Berlin in late March than Allen was off to Munich, "where," he wrote to his father, "I spent four days last week interviewing the leading government people to find out what the situation was in Bavaria. I rather liked Munich...."[2] Field Marshal Eric von Ludendorff had just returned there from exile in Sweden to rally a movement of like-minded officers and aristocrats around him; some months later his aides would recruit the recently demobilized infantryman Adolf Hitler as an agitator and organizer among the disaffected soldiers who crowded Bavaria.

In the same letter to Reverend Dulles, Allen noted, "Foster arrived in Berlin this morning from Cologne after having visited most of central Europe...." The plan was for the brothers to leave Berlin at the end of April, get in two weeks of golf and holiday time in England, and then sail home together in mid-May; Allen had applied for and won two months' leave. After four years of almost nonstop work, the young man had earned a rest, and even

Dresel could not deny him that. Allen was curious to see his older brother and learn if there was a reason for his impromptu visit.

FOSTER'S STAR HAD RISEN quickly since his return to New York in August 1919. He continued to be in the forefront of the forces that pushed the committee to adopt a harder line on German reparations payments. In this, he was in direct opposition to his British colleague John Maynard Keynes, who foresaw the seeds of a future war if the vanquished nation was kept destitute. Foster, who agreed with Keynes about Germany's inability to pay, nevertheless took the line advanced by Bernard Baruch and other bankers that if Germany could not pay it should borrow the money and work the debt off later. The lenders, not surprisingly, would be the New York and London banks who stood to reap millions in loan fees and interest. Foster's credentials came from his new status as a partner at Sullivan & Cromwell, a promotion that propelled him over the heads of a number of more senior associates. What is more, William Cromwell had moved back to Paris to pursue his charities, and Foster was designated as the older man's roving emissary to push the business interests of American clients in a European market that had been closed to them since 1914. Foster's client lists read like a directory of U.S. corporate might: Babcock & Wilcox, General Electric, International Nickel, and a host of mining, railroad, and banking firms that were all in a rush to reconstruct the new peacetime world.

Foster's ability to rise so far and so fast just seven years out of law school lies in the then-blurred dividing line between government service and private enterprise. While he was busy pursuing the needs of the firm's clients abroad, he also served as the legal counsel to the U.S. government corporation that made export financing loans to American firms that wanted to sell their products overseas; an unprecedented $400 million in these short-term loans were made to commodities and machinery exporters, most of them clients of Cromwell's practice.[3]

Arriving in Berlin in the midst of the Kapp *putsch*, Foster pushed his way past the frontier guards and spent the week roaming the barricades at night with Allen to watch the brawls and gunfights. In the daylight hours they roamed the empty official hallways of the government ministries, looking for contacts. One of the figures most helpful to the New York lawyer was a Brooklyn-born German economist whose full name was Hjalmar Horace Greeley Schacht. A member of the German Democratic Party in 1920, Schacht urged the Dulles brothers to do all they could to draw American capital into Germany. Only economic growth, he argued, would enable Germany's well-intentioned middle class to become strong enough to thwart the forces arrayed against it on the right and left. Schacht, to the Dulleses' embarrassment, would become one of the leading architects of the fantasy economic underpinnings of Adolf Hitler's brand of national socialism. He would later be tried, though acquitted, at the Nuremberg war crimes trials at the end of World War II.

Foster had an important reason for wanting to spend some time with his younger brother. Allen had developed an extraordinary reputation in Foreign Service circles for his ability to amass huge amounts of information and to develop acquaintances at all levels of European life. The brothers had found they enjoyed working with each other; their minds seemed to share a synchronization of thought that made problem-solving stimulating and satisfying. Foster had come to respect his younger brother's enormous energy and ability, and the old sibling friction had dissolved into close intimacy. Perhaps it was time for Allen to leave the Foreign Service and come to work with Foster and Sullivan & Cromwell in handling the foreign business affairs of the firm's growing list of clients. Perhaps the younger brother could work out a transfer back to State Department duties in Washington and get a law degree; a job at Sullivan & Cromwell would be guaranteed. Allen was interested but noncommittal.

There was an even more immediate reason why Allen might want to consider leaving the Foreign Service. On February 11, 1920, a furious Woodrow Wilson wrote to Robert Lansing, "While we were still in Paris, I felt, and have felt increasingly ever since, that you accepted my guidance and direction on questions with which I had to instruct you only with increasing reluctance….

"I must say that it would relieve me of embarrassment, Mr. Secretary, the embarrassment of feeling your reluctance and divergence of judgment, if you would give your present office up and afford me an opportunity to select someone whose mind would more willingly go along with mine." Lansing had been sacked.

In his own memoirs of the time, he conceded, "The President was right in his impression that, 'while we were still in Paris,' I had accepted his guidance and direction with reluctance. It was as correct… that as early as January 1919, I was conscious that he was no longer disposed to welcome my advice in matters pertaining to the peace negotiations at Paris."4

The depth of the Lansing-Wilson estrangement was made embarrassingly clear in August 1919 during grueling hearings by Henry Cabot Lodge and the Senate Foreign Relations Committee. In two days of questioning, Lansing was unable to provide details of the reasoning behind many of the agreements the president had made on behalf of the full peace commission. Secret treaties and agreements were revealed. Lansing denied any role in their making or even knowledge of their existence. In his own private papers, Lansing deliberately chose to appear ignorant rather than make public the seriousness of his disagreement with Wilson and thereby hand the president's foes a weapon. But there was betrayal seen in his pose, and the secretary's much cherished reputation for rectitude was ruined forever. In the end, Wilson's enemies used Lansing's deception to injure gravely both master and man.

Lansing's ordeal in August was bad enough. It was an embarrassment to someone with as strong an ego as Lansing's to have to admit that he had been intentionally barred from the president's councils. Some anti-Wilson newspapers carried the two days of testimony in virtual verbatim transcript. "'I Do Not Know,' Most Frequent Answer to Questions of Inquisitors," one headline trumpeted.[5]

The hearing was a tremendous humiliation, but worse was to come. Congress had recessed for the summer, and, in September, President Wilson had embarked on his last fateful campaign by rail across the United States to win public support that would silence his Senate critics. Yet the Republican opposition continued to hold antitreaty hearings in a rump session of its own. With the president away, Lansing had left town for the sanctuary of Henderson Harbor and his family. On September 12 Senator Lodge scheduled testimony from William C. Bullitt, one of the young staff of the Russian section from the Peace Conference, who had been outraged over the refusal to come to terms with the Bolsheviks while they were making terms for the Central Powers. Bullitt had been to Moscow on a mission to feel out Lenin as to what it would take to bring him to terms with the Western powers—in short, whether anything could be done to get him to drop his movement's rhetoric about spreading the communist revolution to their nations. When Bullitt had come back to Paris with responses that Wilson and the other Big Four found too vague to deal with, he had resigned in a fury. But before leaving Paris he held a final private conversation with Lansing. The harassed and resentful secretary, who shared some of the anger of the outraged youth, may have tried to soothe Bullitt's temper by revealing some of his own unhappiness. He certainly considered the conversation to be a private, off-the-record talk.

Bullitt, whose hatred of Woodrow Wilson would become a lifelong mania, later told others he felt such scorn for Lansing's refusal to resign in protest that he did not feel bound to honor any confidence the secretary had uttered on the subject. According to one newspaper account, Bullitt told the fascinated senators that during the chat, Lansing "had stated his own objections to the Treaty and had expressed fear that if the American people fully realized the large number of League Commissions in which the United States would have to participate, approval might be withheld.... When Bullitt appeared on September 12... he testified rather freely from well-prepared notes about his confidential conversation with Lansing. According to Bullitt, the secretary considered that... the League of Nations at present is entirely useless. The great powers have simply... arranged the world to suit themselves."[6]

Lansing was stricken with remorse and anger; his anxiety was all the more heated because he could not flatly deny ever having expressed the feelings quoted by Bullitt. He could only argue weakly that the young man had deliberately distorted and exaggerated his depth of opposition to the treaty. Eleanor Dulles remembers being taken along on two successive days as Lansing traveled from Underbluff by carriage to the nearest telephone in a country store some miles away. She recalls how he frantically tried to talk personally to Wilson, who was deep into the Middle West on his campaign tour. But each time his way was blocked on the line either by Joseph Tumulty, the press secretary, or by Edith Wilson, the president's wife. Finally, on September 16, Lansing sent a telegram to the Wilson campaign train that tried to place the blame for the damage on Bullitt's bitter betrayal. But he finally admitted that there was more than a grain of truth in the testimony.

Wilson in the meantime was making dozens of impassioned and exhausting extemporaneous speeches every day, traveling hundreds of miles across the country to urge anyone who would hear him that they must continue to back him, one more time, in this final struggle for peace. On September 26, after a speech in Pueblo, Colorado, where the strain was plain for all to see, Wilson became seriously ill in his train compartment, and the tour was canceled. On October 2, he suffered a paralyzing stroke. If Wilson had kept his health, Lansing would have been fired as soon as the campaign tour ended. But the president remained partially paralyzed and often not alert to his surroundings. He was isolated in his room in the White House for two months, with only Tumulty, Mrs. Wilson, and the doctors deciding what business could be brought before him. This gave Lansing a reprieve. As the country's secretary of state, he was the chief officer of the Wilson cabinet and as such had to try manfully to work out a compromise that would set aside the sections of the Versailles Treaty that Lodge and his allies found most objectionable, in return for prompt ratification of the basic treaty. But the Republicans smelled more than a treaty victory; they sensed a return to full power in Washington. In January 1920 Wilson had sent messages to the Democratic Party leadership that he wanted that autumn's presidential election to be a referendum on the treaty and especially on the league covenant. There were even a few feelers about Wilson's being willing to run for a third term if his health returned; the Republicans could not believe their luck.

Lansing's final mistake, at least the one for which he was formally fired, was that he had held a number of cabinet meetings in the White House, a traditional prerogative of the president. There was worse. In those meetings, and in private conferences with Tumulty and the doctors, Lansing raised questions about whether the president might be too ill to continue in office and, if so, who should make that official determination, and at what point the vice president, a quiet cipher named Thomas Marshall, should be formally notified to take over. Later, Lansing argued that he had taken both actions with the full knowledge and consent of the president's close aides, Tumulty included, and that they had led him to believe in the final months of 1919 that Wilson was unlikely to recover.

Yet Wilson did recover. At least he regained enough strength and alertness to reassert day-to-day command over White House affairs. Not surprisingly, among the first pieces of bad news brought up by Edith Wilson was that the secretary of state had been trying to usurp the powers of the presidency. Actually, some historians, including David Smith, have argued that Lansing's publicly announced cabinet meetings during October and November probably forestalled Lodge and other Wilson foes from demanding a congressional probe of Wilson's disabilities. In any event, the league membership treaty was voted down in the Senate.

Lansing's public disgrace was not the only shock awaiting Allen Dulles when he returned to America. So much had changed by that late spring of 1920; he had left the country six years earlier, and, except for the two terms spent back at Princeton in graduate school, he had missed the transformation of the nation that the stimulus of war had brought about. He had gone away a boy, leaving behind a nation on the brink of greatness; he returned a man who had matured under the most adverse circumstances and who was secure in his own successes. He found others of his contemporaries had moved up the ladder, too. Young Franklin Roosevelt, the family friend who had been undersecretary of the navy during the war, was on the verge of following his own presidential aspirations. Roosevelt and others had tried to lure the universally popular Herbert Hoover into accepting the Democratic nomination for the 1920 campaign. It was a bid to prevent Wilson from embarrassing himself, but more, it was a last effort to rescue U.S. participation in the league. Hoover, however, demurred, and Roosevelt ended up accepting the party's nomination for vice president with the obscure James M. Cox leading the ticket. They were swamped by

Warren Harding and Calvin Coolidge, and the eight-year Democratic interruption of Republican power over the White House was
at an end.

Despite the rough handling Robert Lansing had received
from Wilson, the president still claimed an emotional loyalty from
Allen that lasted all his life. As he summed up in a speech at Yale on
Wilson forty years later, Dulles argued: "Some historians have criticized Wilson for being too inflexible in his beliefs, too quick to act
on slogans, too sure that he had a guaranteed position. There is no
doubt some justice in these criticisms. Basically, however, Wilson
was right in his major beliefs—and, indeed, these have been largely
accepted as American policy: a deep concern for the freedom and
independence of people everywhere; and, at the same time, commitment to an international body as the best hope for peace in
troubled times. From the depth of his spiritual convictions, Wilson
realized in his own day—and reminds us in ours—that national
policy like life itself needs a sense of direction and high purpose."[7]
This was the testament of Allen Dulles as much as of Wilson.

When Allen presented himself at the State, War, and Navy
building in May 1920, he found his masters more interested in what
he knew about Turkey and Persia than the more dramatic conflict
in Berlin. The emergence of petroleum as a vitally strategic resource
was a spur in Washington's side to become more of a participant in
the global arena. Oil, gasoline, and other petroleum products had
assumed an enormous importance during the war that no general
or economist could have predicted in 1914. While airplanes, tanks,
and automobiles had been exciting innovations in the war arsenal,
the conversion of much of the world's navies from coal-fired power
to fuel oil made petroleum crucial to all the great powers.

America's vast oil resources in the western states were still
some years from discovery and development. Besides, the U.S.
Navy needed handy oil reserves around the world if it was to be

an all-ocean force. The rich oil fields of Persia and other parts of
the old Turkish Empire beckoned to American oilmen. It was as
important for America to stake its claim to a share in these easily
exploitable supplies as it was to ensure that other powers—
Britain, surely, but also the new competitor, the Soviet Union—
not be in a position to control Middle Eastern oil supplies and
thus wield enormous military advantage. Allen had worked both
on the Paris Conference formal treaty of peace with Turkey and
also on the daily planning sessions for the failed Prinkipo
Conference. While the details of a Turkish peace were not quite
settled, representatives of Britain, France, and Russia were all busy
in Constantinople trying to bribe, bargain, and otherwise secure
the lion's share of the Turkish National Oil Company's undeveloped leases as well as properties that would be secured from the
newly installed shah of Persia.

The United States was a member of a special tripartite Allied
Commission, which, with France and Britain, kept watchful oversight of the Turkish government; warships of all three nations
rode at anchor in the Bosporus lest anyone doubt who was in
charge. But America was far from being an equal competitor for
Turkish and Persian petroleum reserves. The U.S. commissioner
was a tough-spoken admiral named Mark Bristol who hated the
British worse than he had hated the Germans. His outspoken
rudeness had ruined any attempt at an effective Allied mandate of
Turkey, and, in retaliation, the French and British were determined to cut the United States out of any bargaining for oil.

ALLEN HAD ARRIVED HOME with Foster in New York on the
Adriatic on May 12, 1920, and after a brief reunion with his parents in Watertown he journeyed to Washington to report to his
new bosses at the State Department and for a reunion with
Christian Herter and other veterans of Paris. He was drawn into

the department's debate over what to do about Turkey, and it soon developed that his background information on Turkish issues brought him into the center of that debate. Because of Turkey's borders with Russia, an American presence began to assume a new importance; hundreds of Russian refugees were interned in camps, and White Russian counterrevolutionaries plotted in the crowded coffee shops of Constantinople.

Dresel must have gotten wind of what was up, for scarcely had Allen begun his leave and returned to help the family move to Henderson Harbor for the summer than telegrams began arriving at the department from Berlin reminding them that "Dulles must be sent back immediately upon expiration of leave." But wheels were in motion in another direction in Washington. While Allen was sailing around the familiar islands of Lake Ontario (Foster had let him borrow his boat), he was appointed to a second-class rank in the Foreign Service; in mid-July, his leave was extended through August, "for personal reasons." An alarmed Dresel cabled with increasing urgency: "I trust, however, that if these personal reasons are no longer applicable he will be immediately reassigned here. I think the Department must realize that we are over a series of vol-canoes and that the political situation here looks more than ever ominous...." Allen in the meantime was in the enviable position of having other legation chiefs bidding for his services; Hugh Wilson, in Warsaw, where a civil war brewed, had no compunction about trying to steal Allen from his old mentor. He cabled with high drama: "There is no work here for a second-rate man, and unless I can have someone of Dulles' caliber I should prefer no addition to staff. But in that event, the Department must realize I cannot keep up the pace much longer."[8]

While Washington pondered what action to take in Turkey, Allen enjoyed his social popularity at home. His network of Foreign Service friends had their own family circles, and most had summer homes to which attractive eligible bachelors were always welcome. After a few weeks reveling in the waters of Henderson Harbor, he accepted the invitation to join friends at a lakeside resort further north in the Thousand Islands. There, one July afternoon, he was introduced to a young lady visiting from New York City named Martha Clover Todd.

Clover (a family surname) was just a month older than Allen and forbade him to joke about it. She had a healthy, energetic beauty that combined with a mind drawn to the mysterious and exotic. She had light auburn hair, clear fair skin, and blue eyes set above high cheekbones. Her face was charming when she laughed and heart-stoppingly pretty in repose. She was, to those who remembered her at the time, the golden American girl of those days. She was an adventurous free spirit who was given to long periods of introspection. She was about five-feet, seven-inches tall and kept a trim figure by being an avid horsewoman. But she was not at all an athletic hearty like Allen or others of his family. The golf and tennis triumphs were happily left to him. Clover's preference was to wander and explore some wooded trail with a quiet companion or, preferably, alone. Her abiding passion was travel, which she enjoyed both for the physical excursion and the intellectual quest. In addition to the trip to work in the canteen in Paris and the later tour through France and Italy, Clover had undertaken a fairly ambitious exploration of Aztec ruins in southern Mexico and Guatemala earlier in the spring of 1920. She remembered Allen's reputation as one of the bright young men at the State Department and was pleased that he was not the stuffed shirt she had been warned about. She was also more impressed by his quick mind and ready humor than his aggressive athleticism. They fell instantly in love, and Allen later joked that he had shown enormous restraint and had not proposed marriage until the third day of the visit. She accepted at once.

Allen found a wife who both admired the man he had become and wanted to share in the exciting life he planned to pursue. She would bring to him what he lacked, a good and loving companion who accepted him, flaws and all. Clover saw ahead a life of excitement and movement with a man who adored her. The attraction of Allen Dulles was all the more pronounced because her life had largely been conventional to the point of suffocation. Her mother's family was a wealthy Baltimore clan that originally made its fortune making the steel for the Union's first ironclad, the *Monitor* of Civil War fame. More recent generations had gone on to found banks and play a major role in the organization of Johns Hopkins University.

But Clover carried an unhappy inheritance to her marriage. The Todds had a history of chronic depression that, according to family letters kept in the Dulles collection at Princeton, they sought to alleviate through travel. Her mother, too, suffered so severely that Clover and her two brothers often had to stay with relatives for extended periods of their childhood; one of the boys later committed suicide.

Her father, Henry Todd, was a leading scholar at Columbia in the origins of the Romance languages. He was also something of a pedant and a stuffed shirt. One of his hobbyhorses was a campaign to forbid immigrants to the United States to adopt "Americanized" names such as Washington or Smith and thereby assimilate into the culture. It was a family joke that on hearing the name of his prospective son-in-law, Professor Todd went to Columbia University's library catalogue to see what he could learn. He found Allen's name and a citation to *A History of the Boer War*, which had been published in 1902. There was no mention that the author had been eight at the time. "The family must be intellectual," he reported back to his wife and daughter. "Perhaps he is all right, but is Allen an old man?"

With the announcement of the engagement in August came the news that the State Department had appointed him as the first secretary to Admiral Bristol in Constantinople. His orders were to work on getting a peace treaty signed with the Turks, to help American oil interests (particularly Rockefeller's Standard Oil) to secure concessions held by the Turkish National Oil Company. He was also to keep a watch on the Russian border with Persia and Turkey. Allen immediately went to Washington to begin the round of briefings he needed to prepare for the post. On October 16 Reverend Allen Macy Dulles and most of the family gathered at Woodlands, the estate of one of the Gilman relatives of the Todds in Baltimore. There he performed the marriage service for Clover and Allen.[9]

Clover and Allen Dulles sailed off on their first voyage as a married couple on November 5, 1920, on the *S.S. Olympic,* which took them to Cherbourg. From there they took an overnight ferry to Southampton and then went on to London by train. For the moment at least, Clover and Allen felt they had plenty of money. In Berlin he had lived on $2,000 a year, but his promotion to first-class rank and the cost-of-living supplement for enduring in a hardship post such as Constantinople boosted his total salary to $3,625 per year, a not inconsiderable sum for those days. On the Monday after their arrival in London, the young couple went shopping, Clover to the big department stores of Oxford Street, Allen to "his tailors," who specialized in outfitting young diplomats headed for foreign postings. The next day Clover reported in a letter to her mother that they were guests at a U.S. Embassy lunch to honor Lady Astor, the American-born celebrity who had become a member of the House of Commons. One night, the Dulleses were taken to dinner at the Ritz Hotel by Allen's old comrade from the Peace Conference days, Harold Nicolson, the diplomat, biographer, and dues-paid member of the Bloomsbury set. "Allen and Mr. Nicolson had a whole year's time to cover in their conversation and they sat at the dinner table until 10:30," Clover reported. It was the first of many similarly long-winded dinners in their forty-nine–year marriage.

The dinner with Nicolson, as with the earlier round of meetings between Allen and the British foreign affairs specialists at Whitehall, was very important business. There were friendly reunions with old Paris hands and with Robert Craigie, his chum from Bern. But there was also a crucial meeting with Sir John Tilley, the Foreign Office undersecretary responsible for Turkey and the Middle East. To outsiders, much of diplomacy appears to be boring ritual. In reality, the truly important business of bargaining, conceding, and coming to mutually agreeable terms depends on these slow rituals. While each side wants to win, no serious diplomat wants his adversary to fail too badly; that is how deals get broken.

Allen's job was a delicate one. Without in any way undercutting his new boss, Admiral Bristol, he had to smooth ruffled British feelings so that American oil producers and other commercial interests could have fair access to the vast but collapsed Ottoman Empire that was now up for grabs. America's position in Turkey was an awkward byproduct of the reluctant role the United States had played in the First World War. President Wilson had purposely evaded becoming an "Ally," and the United States had not gone to war with every one of the Central Powers. By failing to join the League of Nations, the United States was reduced to observer status on, or had been left off of, many of the working commissions that dealt out concessions and administered banking and financial affairs in Turkey and elsewhere. The question of who would give out, as well as get, the prospective oil leases being staked out was just one of the vexing problems in which Washington wanted a voice.

In his handwritten memorandum to the foreign secretary, Lord David Balfour, Sir James Tilley reported meeting with a "Mr. Dullas [*sic*] who was going to Constantinople... to act as a sort of peacemaker between the British and American High Commissioners and to bring about greater harmony.

"Mr. Dullas [*sic*] thought I would be interested to hear something of the state of feelings in the State Department about affairs in Turkey," Tilley recounted. "They could not help feeling there that we had veered a very long way round since the time when we would have welcomed American cooperation. This was perhaps resultant from the way the U.S. had treated us over the Treaty. He personally realized that they were responsible for much of the trouble in the Near East by the delay they had caused."

With deliberate expressions of his own conciliatory feelings, Allen worked toward his point: The United States wanted full membership on the financial commission that oversaw export and import licenses and, of course, oil leases. Sir James could not resist complaining about the behavior of the U.S. Senate in flatly refusing to ratify the Versailles Treaty or even to send a representative to the Reparations Commission, which had become the overall machinery for imposing the Allied will on the vanquished nations. It appeared to the British that the Americans wanted to cherry pick the commissions and the concessions that attracted their business leaders, and let the hard work of making the peace fall on European backs. Yet in the end, Tilley saw no reason why American diplomats should not sit on the financial panel, and he promised closer relations between the British representatives in Constantinople and the Americans. Young Mr. Dulles, he judged at the end, "is animated by the best intentions of making things work smoothly...." It also helped in Sir James's eyes that Allen had a close acquaintance with the current British high commissioner from their days together in Bern.[10]

It was something of a triumph for Allen, and Clover shared in the lift it gave him. "Many of the people have been to Constantinople and all envy us being able to go there. Allen has had a talk with a great many people and I believe he wishes he could stay longer here for interviews. But at all events, we leave Saturday morning for Calais...." She added, closing her letter to her mother, "Allen is just as much of a dear as ever...."[11]

The four-day trip took them through Switzerland to Milan, Venice, on to Trieste, Belgrade, and Sophia until, at two o'clock on the fifth morning, the train reached the outskirts of Constantinople. Clover was agog about everything from the deep blue brocade of the upholstery on the luxury-class train (one-way fare for them both cost nearly $1,100) to the culinary changes as the train left the influence of French chefs. "We felt a great adventure had really begun," she wrote her father. To her mother, she described their arrival on the morning of the fifth day. "As to the hour of our arrival, no one could tell us but we were told we must leave the train no matter at what time of night it might be so we prepared the bags and lay down to sleep half dressed. Shortly before 2:00 we were up and saw the lights of the city.... I was thrilled by the glimpses we had of silent mysterious houses in the blackness, beneath a sky full of brilliant stars."[12]

They were met at the train by Lamott Belin, a third secretary at the U.S. Embassy and a member of the Du Pont family. Despite the formal posting, no housing had been organized for Allen and Clover, and so they spent Christmas and the first half of January 1921 as the guests of Belin and his wife, beginning a lifetime friendship between the two couples.

Constantinople had been overcrowded for centuries, but the upheavals of wars all around had choked the city beyond endurance. Even in the Pera, the quarter reserved for foreigners, Clover found the "narrow pavements quite inadequate to the mass of people surging back and forth, chiefly Europeans but with a liberal sprinkling of Turks, Greeks, Priests, Sikhs, Russians and great bear cubs, interesting characters of all sorts." It was in this teeming ghetto that they finally found a ramshackle house that became their joy. One entered from a doorway that faced on a street, the Rue d'Sera Selvi, and then proceeded down a narrow alley to a small courtyard where the two-story wooden house was nestled into the back of the buildings that fronted on the street one block over. The house had two bedrooms and a living room upstairs that overlooked a small garden and gave a breathtaking view of the Bosporus. Wisteria vines and roses climbed the back wall of the house and shaded the garden during the late afternoons. The bath, a maid's room, and another room were on the ground floor, and the kitchen was below. It cost them $138 a month, a pretty steep sum.

Allen was immediately pressed into service and won the turbulent Admiral Bristol's confidence. The young married couple also made something of a splash in the exotically cosmopolitan society of the city. Within a few days of arriving in town, Allen wrote his father:

> The situation here is the most confused I have ever had anything to do with. Constantinople, while nominally Turkish, according to the unratified peace treaty, is policed and practically controlled by the Allies who themselves have no very clear idea of their respective functions. Meanwhile, the Turks here have no control over the Turks of Anatolia who are in revolt against the Allies and the Constantinople government. All the way, the Bolshevists are making headway in the Caucasus and have, apparently, control of Armenia. Constantinople itself is just beginning to clear itself of the mass of

[White Russian] refugees who are sent to starve elsewhere as there are plenty of starving people here without them.... So far we have been here three evenings
and have been to three big dinners and last night a
dance that lasted until 4:00. In fact we have been much
too gay to suit my tastes or Clover's but as newcomers
we have to go the rounds.[13]

If anything united the Allies, it was the certainty that the
Bolsheviks had eyes on the established rich oil fields of Persia and
Bessarabia—and that Russia must not have what it wanted. There
was no secret about this. American and British troops were in
Siberia and elsewhere, ostensibly keeping the peace and protecting
a division of Czech soldiers who were guarding the trans-Siberian
railroad. It also was no secret that a leading White Russian commander who was headquartered in Constantinople, Baron Piotr
Nikolayevich Wrangel, was pro-American. His father had been the
czar's last governor of Alaska and a famous explorer of what was
now the American part of the Arctic. The baron and his wife made
friends with Clover, who organized a group of diplomatic corps
wives to go daily to the Russian refugee camps to deliver supplies
and conduct classes in everything from crafts to English. Among
the vast profusion of medals, plaques, and citations that Allen
Dulles housed in his family's collection at the Mudd Library at
Princeton, there is a large silver medal awarded to Clover by the
baron and baroness for her "selfless service." Later in life, Clover
would say that she was never happier or felt more alive than during
those chaotic days in Constantinople. But life was not unalloyed
bliss, by any means. The city was hideously expensive; Allen judged
it "more so than in London or Paris and almost as bad as New
York," and after a sharp shock they had to set a budget on the
amounts they could subscribe to the various society charities and
limit their ball-going to the ones made mandatory by politics.

Constantinople society also provided Clover and Allen with a lifelong friend and Allen with a lifelong intelligence contact. Bertha Carp was the daughter of an Austrian-born Jewish merchant of the city who had died at the outbreak of the war in 1914. She was left without money, but she was well educated, fluent in at least six languages, and well connected within that Byzantine web of highly placed families whose alliances crossed ethnic and religious boundaries with ease. One of those contacts was Henry Morgenthau, the American ambassador to Turkey early in the war. Morgenthau hired her, as her first job description stated, "as a type-writing machine operator," but her first jobs were to help him establish safe communications lines with the varied, and often contentious, sects of Jews in the city. By 1920 Betty Carp, as she became known, had become an indispensable figure of the U.S. Embassy staff, so much so that Morgenthau had helped her acquire American citizenship as a protection. Betty soon became the "fixer" for the American diplomats in Constantinople, and she would still be on the job more than forty years and a thousand grateful American diplomats later. Shorter than five feet, she was a dark, plain, exuberant woman with the fierce energy of a hummingbird. Betty could round up a scarce apartment or arrange a meeting with a spy with equal ease. There was no one in Istanbul, as the city became renamed, that she did not know or who did not know her. She was a confessor to unhappy embassy wives and a discreet booster of diplomatic careers. Over the next five decades, her contacts spread across the Middle East, and she became something of an institutional treasure for the scores of U.S. diplomats she served.

Betty Carp also fell in love with Allen Dulles. She became one of a long line of women whose intense and long-lasting affection for Allen Dulles occasionally lapsed into love affairs but more often persisted as loyal friendships. In her later years, after his death in 1969, she often boasted of her love for Allen in a lighthearted way, sometimes even asserting that the child she had adopted was really his "love child"; this was a chronological impossibility but was often taken at face value by credulous newcomers to Istanbul, and has become institutionalized in the Dulles sexual mythology.

Now is as good a time as any to confront the fact that Allen Dulles pursued a number of romantic liaisons outside his marriage, although it is unlikely that Betty Carp was one of them. Indeed, one retired American diplomat who visited her just days before her death in 1975 says privately that Betty conceded her relationship with Allen was platonic but nonetheless genuinely intense. It remains that Allen all his life was drawn to attractive women, and many women found his hearty humor, robust spirit, and athletic sexuality equally enticing. He had been teased by his chums in the Bern legation in 1918 for the mash notes he received from Mrs. Vera Whitehouse, a New York society lady who had been sent to Zurich to run the American propaganda campaign among the Swiss. Mrs. Whitehouse's naive earnestness earned her bemused tolerance among Murphy, Dolbeare, and the other clerks until her unabashed crush on Allen turned her into a figure of fun.[14]

Clover got an early and thoroughly disturbing introduction to her husband's attraction to and for other women in Constantinople. Another fan, an American missionary named Fanny Billings, confessed her platonic crush on Allen quite often to Clover.

Allen Dulles was a womanizer by any standards. It is inconceivable that he would have been hired by the CIA at all, let alone serve as its director for as long as he did, if today's intense scrutiny and censorious attitudes had existed in the 1950s. His penchant for flirtations and flings drew frequent rages and warnings from Clover, so much so that each dalliance quickly became common gossip within his inner family circle and the wider band of friends in New York and Washington. But there the matter stayed. Back then there were self-correcting devices that kept private peccadilloes from becoming public scandals or the subject of press coverage. Allen also lived under the vastly more *laissez-faire* code of sexual ethics enjoyed by men of the Anglo-American upper classes fifty years ago. The only fact in mitigation that can be drawn from his philandering is that while Allen had numerous affairs outside his marriage during most of his later life, he most definitely did not chase his secretaries around the desk; his lovers were women of his own social standing, and nearly all remained firm friends long after the fire had gone out.

It is also remarkable that many of the women who became involved with Allen did so because he offered them something more than romance. In several cases, Betty Carp being one, Allen drew women to him for help in his work; he could quickly spot women whose ambitions ranged beyond the boundaries that society used to hem them in. In Betty's case, Allen prized her gift with languages and her razor-sharp skill at analyzing personalities and how they might react in different situations. In 1925 he even recommended she be brought to Washington to work on Fred Dolbeare's political analysis staff; "as a judge of human nature, she takes the cake."[15] In 1940 he would bring her to New York to draft the first profiles of major political figures for the OSS. Allen Dulles offered a heady mix of romance and the excitement of being involved in important clandestine business.

Incredibly, many of these women remained friends with Clover, too. His dalliances were no secret from her, nor from his children or the rest of the family. By all accounts, Clover was not at all pleased by his straying; there is a family legend that each time she found out about an affair it cost Allen an expensive piece of jewelry. But Clover recognized that many of these women had been extraordinarily helpful to Allen in times of crisis. She also came to realize that her husband's sexual appetites had little to do with true "infidelity." Allen would love Clover all his life, but he also needed and demanded a constant companion, a soothing haven to resort to when his hectic career exhausted him. Later in their lives Clover would watch her sister-in-law Janet Dulles fill that same function for Foster by being a constant companion who traveled where he went, never left his side, and remained his private consort at all times, even to the neglect of her own children. Clover, on the other hand, was determined to care for her children herself even if that meant letting Allen off the leash from time to time. She was wise enough to realize that her choice was to leave Allen or put up with it, for he would never change. So there were private fights and rages but no ultimatums. Neither of their two daughters, Toddy and Joan, remembers his straying being a big issue. As Joan Dulles remembers, "Father had his girlfriends and we knew it. But that was about it."[16]

In Constantinople, Clover may have gotten her first warnings, but Allen remained relatively chaste with other women. After all, the two were still in the honeymoon phase of their marriage. Later, in 1922, Clover became pregnant in Constantinople, prompting the couple's return to America.

Allen's return to Washington was in professional triumph. During his stay, Allen had spent considerable time in Ankara, where Kemal Ataturk had established his nationalist government and was poised to assume power over all of Turkey. Plans were in the works for a new treaty (signed in Lausanne in 1923) that would remove the sultan and lead to the international recognition of the Ataturk regime. Britain and France persisted in demanding their prewar concessions from the new regime. Ataturk instead wanted longer-term development of his country's vast mineral resources in order to pay for an even larger program of construction of railroads, ports, hydroelectric projects, and irrigation systems. America had the technology and the capital, but it did not have colonial territorial ambitions in the region, and Dulles convinced Ataturk the United States could be trusted. Allen revealed in one cable home that the nationalist government "declares that the oil resources which are considered by them as the greatest undeveloped wealth are open to American companies now and not pledged to other companies.... It is my opinion that the best results would be obtained through a conference which would necessitate my return to the United States."[17]

President Warren Harding's secretary of state, Charles Evans Hughes, also agreed it was time for Allen to come home. American interests were now spread throughout the region, and someone with firsthand experience was needed in the department. It must be remembered that in those days the senior staff of the State Department in Washington amounted to no more than fifty officials of the second secretary level or higher. Regions that had been unknown territories before the war suddenly assumed a vital importance to the government; men with successful firsthand experience in operations in those regions were highly prized. In March 1922 Allen was notified he had been appointed head of the Middle Eastern Affairs division of State. He and Clover bade farewell to their remaining friends (the Belins had already been posted to Paris) on March 20, and traveled again on the Orient Express. They spent a brief holiday in Paris before arriving home on April 7 with the exciting news that Clover was five months pregnant. A week after he reported for duty in Washington, Betty Carp wrote an affectionate letter to Clover and closed with an aside to Allen, "You are becoming immortal at the Embassy, Mr. Dulles, because your successor is rather brainless."

CONSTANTINOPLE HAD BEEN exciting, but Washington was even more so. Harding was in the White House, and America was embarking on a period of unprecedented economic expansion, which included an expansion of the nation as a world power. The quest for peace was hardly forgotten; indeed, the new optimism that had swept into the capital city the year before was in part based on the conviction that the Republican way of achieving peace through traditional alliances and specific treaties was infinitely superior to Wilson's notion of handing some international body a blank check drawn on America's sovereignty. The Washington Naval Disarmament Treaty of 1922 was viewed as the triumphant cornerstone of Harding's diplomacy. But the formula for the number of battleships the great powers could maintain further aroused the resentments of would-be powers such as Japan, Italy, and Germany, and the treaty today is judged a failure. Still, the 1922 naval arms pact served to accomplish one thing the Paris Conference had not. America was now formally drawn into a continuing series of multinational discussions on how to solve the disputes of other nations and preserve peace.

As the prostrating Washington summer heat closed in, Clover took refuge with her family in Newport, Rhode Island, and in August gave birth to their first child, a daughter named after herself, Clover Todd Dulles, but who would always be known as Toddy. Except for hurried long weekends, Allen languished in Washington, and their letters show how much they missed each other; their misery was compounded by the fact that neither was well. Clover's pregnancy was difficult, and Allen came down with a chronic throat infection that left him feverish and weak. He could not join her on vacation because he was too newly arrived at his job; in any event, they had agreed that he must start night law school classes that September at George Washington University, Foster's old school. He did manage to "hide out" a couple of long weekends at Longwood, the spectacular Du Pont estate in Delaware, with his old friends Mott Belin and his wife. There he could golf and play tennis and rest in the lap of luxury. Although Allen shared the Dulles taste of living modestly himself, all his life he enjoyed the hospitality of friends who could offer a more lavish lifestyle.

Back in Washington, the work mounted. The Middle East division had just five clerks to help Allen process the stream of correspondence and telegrams that streamed in from legations, touring businessmen, and American churchmen whose missionary and relief efforts were regularly ensnared in the tangled politics of the region. By the end of 1922, Turkey was at war with Greece and had expelled all Christians from its borders, whereupon the Greeks retaliated and sent its Muslim minority packing. Millions of displaced persons between Macedonia and the Afghan border were, moreover, in dire straits as the ravaging of the Caucasus by the Soviets grew more violent. Huge relief efforts were mounted, financed largely by generous private contributions, but the whole network of catastrophe had to be monitored on a daily basis.[18]

Allen was also thrown together with another major figure in the future of American intelligence, Robert F. Kelley, who had been in military intelligence in Denmark, Finland, and the Baltic states until he joined the department in 1922. In 1925 Kelley became head of the Eastern European division and, in the process, created an intelligence information capacity about the Soviet Union that the Russians themselves envied. During the secretaryships of Hughes, Frank Kellogg, and Henry Stimson—which spanned the Harding-Coolidge-Hoover era—many of the foreign resources of the old U-1 spy office were farmed out to either Kelley or Dulles. Their specific mandates read like a list of the European trouble-spots during that decade. Kelley and Eastern Europe (or the Russian desk, as it was known) were responsible for State's intelligence flow from the Soviet Union, the Baltic states, Austria, and Poland. Allen's Middle Eastern "camel pashas" kept watch over Afghanistan, Albania,

Armenia, Azerbaijan, Bulgaria, Egypt, Georgia, Greece, Mesopo-
tamia, Palestine, Persia, Romania, Yugoslavia, Syria, and, of course,
Turkey and the other nearby mandates of the European powers.
Kelley employed such promising Russian experts as George
Kennan, Robert Murphy, and Charles E. Bohlen. Murphy became
adept at building files on Soviet subversion and propaganda efforts
inside the United States; Dulles was aided by George Wadsworth
and a support staff of four others. Both men answered directly to
Leland Harrison, the old spy chief, who was now assistant secretary
of state.

   It was a bare-bones way of keeping watch by today's standards. Yet as intelligence historian Rhodri Jeffreys-Jones has
argued,[19] it is not right to look at America's hastily gathered and
often duplicative intelligence operations during World War I and
then to conclude on the basis of the reorganizations of the 1920s
that Washington recklessly "dismantled" its spy capacity entirely. It
must be recalled that, prior to 1916, there was no systematic effort
at all to gather, let alone analyze, foreign intelligence in many of
these regions. After the panicky buildup of the war and subsequent
Peace Conference, some budget cuts and shifts in responsibility
were desperately needed. U.S. military intelligence personnel in
Washington alone numbered 1,441 and drew a budget of $2.5 mil-
lion in 1918; some cuts were inevitable.

   Jeffreys-Jones cites the case of the closing of the Black Chamber cryptographic enterprise shared by the State and War
Departments by Secretary Henry Stimson in 1929 (occasioning the
infamous and possibly apocryphal quote, "Gentlemen do not read
other gentlemen's mail") not as a false economy but perhaps as a
clever way of smoking out Stimson's suspicion that the department's own codes had been broken by foreign intelligence agencies.
Closing the Black Chamber was painful, he concludes, but not fatal.
Later the army's Signal Intelligence Service under the legendary

William Friedman built a cipher, a code-breaking type of computer, that translated messages in Japan's *Purple* diplomatic code faster than the Japanese Embassy staff in Washington. The navy's code-breakers built their expertise to the point that they could monitor Japanese fleet maneuvers during the 1930s with perfect accuracy. Thus the disaster of Pearl Harbor was not the failure of America to intercept and decode the Pearl Harbor attack notice of December 1941; rather it was the age-old failure of leaders to read and understand the intelligence they were provided.

Looking at the condition of American intelligence during the 1920s reveals that the government's capability to gather and assess confidential information was hardly nonexistent. As Jeffreys-Jones concludes, "Beginning with World War I, a highly select band of brothers came into existence who maintained a continuing interest and personal involvement with intelligence, both directly and indirectly, in subsequent years. These persons became intelligence professionals... they were among the first to recognize that intelligence and control of the process which produced it was the *sine qua non* of America's future dominance of the international environment."[20]

Allen Dulles was one of those "brothers." And if the revised way of doing business suited policymakers such as Hughes and others, it was in part because of their conviction that foreign affairs were best settled among like-minded individuals and not by committees of bureaucrats. The 1922 Washington Naval Conference had proved that point to them. Such a view still had some validity because the number of active participants in foreign policy formulation—whether in the United States or other leading nations—was still very tiny indeed, and men like Dulles occupied a prominence that enabled them to get things done that it would take a far larger bureaucracy to achieve just twenty years later.

For example, Allen's return to Washington in mid-1922 prompted a flood of cables to London from Robert Craigie, who was now the first secretary in the British Embassy in the American capital. Craigie volunteered and was quickly deputized to negotiate directly with Dulles over a dispute that was threatening to tie up the Lausanne Treaty with the Ataturk government. Craigie argued the official line that any oil concessions from the new government had to be allocated through the old informal understanding with Turkish National Oil; Dulles countered that the United States did not care how the deal was constructed as long as Standard Oil got the share it wanted. Over the summer, the two friends worked out a compromise that left everyone happy.[21]

The following two years absorbed all of Allen's considerable energies. He enrolled at the law school at George Washington University, where the course took three years and not all of the classes were available in the evening, so he had to juggle his daily duties at the State Department with his academic schedule. Clover became pregnant again in 1923, and their second child, Joan, was born in December. Their social life calmed down somewhat. That suited Clover, for she increasingly found Washington's rigid social rituals boring. She was more drawn to her children and to a solitary introspection that she applied to studies of various philosophies and psychological theories.

As 1924 turned into 1925, Allen began to prepare the department's negotiating position for the next big international peace conference—the 1925 Conference on the Traffic in Arms, to be held in Geneva. America would send an official delegation, and Allen was to be one of the delegates. An appraisal of the American delegation sent by the British Embassy to London noted, "I am told Mr. Dulles is likely to be the most active member of the delegation."[22]

Although the United States had sent observers to League of Nations conferences as early as 1921, and even official delegates to minor conferences on narrow issues, the decision by President Coolidge to participate formally in the 1925 Arms Traffic Convention was an important first considering the fact that America still refused to join the League of Nations itself. The decision was an enormous boost for the prestige of the league and raised the prospect that substantive progress toward one of the problems of ensuring peace would be made. The British press reflected its government's pleasure at the "strong" American delegation.

The treaty conference in Geneva was concluded in a remarkably brief three weeks. Before returning home Allen stayed on for a week of law study mixed with a holiday trip to a lakeside inn with Hugh Gibson and his family. He wrote to Clover, "Two exams are over. Trusts I took Sunday night and Corporations last night. I have just one left to take and that is only a half subject and I think I shall take it on the way home. I don't know how well I did but I have a chance of passing I think. I put in four hard days of work but with it all I had some exercise, tennis, golf and plenty of bathing." On his way home, he stopped through London to brief Frank Kellogg, then the ambassador but soon to succeed Hughes as secretary of state. The agreement to limit international trafficking in weapons drew a lot of public praise, and Allen came in for his share on both sides of the Atlantic for his skills at negotiating around the various obstacles to a final agreement. Sadly, lobbyists for American armaments producers were not caught napping as they had been in 1922–1923, so enough pressure was put on the U.S. Senate that American ratification was voted down yet again.

The failure of the 1925 Arms Traffic Convention was a short-term defeat that had longer-term consequences. Public opinion inside the United States turned from determined hands-off isolationism to a demand that Washington take the lead toward a more ambitious world peace pact. Kellogg, as the newly arrived secretary of state, brought new energy and an ardent personal desire to work for some broader international agreement to outlaw war. Scarcely had Allen returned home for Christmas and the end of 1925 than

Kellogg appointed him to go to London in the new year for the preliminary meetings for a much more ambitious naval disarmament negotiation, this time to consider not only warships but also submarines, aircraft carriers, and cannon size. Those talks stalled and spilled over through 1926 and were to be revived in Geneva in 1927, again with Allen slated to play a leading role.

Abruptly, the State Department changed its mind. He was notified in the summer of 1926 that he would be sent as counselor to the U.S. Legation in Peking later that year. It is hard at this distance to read what such an appointment meant. China was in turmoil and certainly needed the best diplomats America had in its service; with Japan threatening all over the Pacific, Allen's strong intelligence background would have been useful. It also was a major promotion in Foreign Service rank. Another factor was that Charles MacMurray, the ambassador to China, and his wife were friends of long-standing. Allen's first impulse was thus to accept the posting and take Clover and the two girls off for a minimum three-year tour in a dangerous although fascinating job.[23]

At this point, Foster Dulles intervened. William Cromwell had not been an active manager of the law firm for more than twenty years; the sudden death of three of the most senior partners forced the firm in the summer of 1926 to reorganize around a four-man executive committee headed by Foster. He was thirty-eight. Within a year, the firm reshuffled again, and Foster emerged as the managing partner of the firm and held that post until 1949. One of Foster's acts that summer of 1926 was to offer Allen a job in New York at a sum considerably greater than the $8,000 per year he would have to live on, school his children, and formally entertain in Peking. The sum was well above what a recent law school graduate could expect on the open market. After a month's leave spent at Henderson Harbor discussing the matter with Clover and the rest of the family, Allen returned to Washington on September 22 and submitted a formal resignation that noted, "For some time I have feared that I could not continue indefinitely in this service. As you know, the financial burden involved in the acceptance of the higher positions in the Diplomatic Service is such that outside resources are increasingly necessary...." Kellogg's response commended Allen's "ability, energy and efficiency" and specifically mentioned his work on the two disarmament conferences. He added a prophetic personal note: "I very much hope that some day you will feel that you may return, either in the State Department or abroad, to the Service in which men of your character and ability are much needed."[24] He departed the State Department on October 15.

Shortly afterward he sent a plaintive note to his good friends, Mott and Frances Belin, who had gone back to Istanbul:

> I am writing now to tell you of a rash decision we have made. I put in my resignation. Am not going to China and in a couple of weeks, starting work in New York with my brother. It was a tremendously hard decision to make particularly with the lure of China ahead. But I reached the conclusion that after China I would in any event, be forced to resign and the New York law firm made me a rather attractive offer which I knew would not be open to me in four or five years. Both Clover and I are very much broken up over the decision but I am sure it is a wise one for a person in my situation. Goodness knows I don't look forward to exchanging Peking for New York but I shall be better able to stand the New York life now than later....[25]

What might have been the most exciting ten years of another man's professional life were coming to an end. For Allen Dulles, however, it was just the beginning of an even more exciting phase.

CHAPTER FIVE

1926–1933

*"Expressions of pious wishes inserted in legal
documents, whether treaties or business contracts,
generally come back to plague their authors."*
—*Allen Dulles,*
Foreign Affairs, *July 1931*

ALLEN DULLES'S RESIGNATION from the State Department in the
fall of 1926 caused an uproar. Allen was pictured in leading newspapers as "one of America's most promising young diplomats," and
his resignation for financial reasons stirred a front-page furor all
over the country, fanning anew the controversy about the U.S.
Foreign Service and the low salaries its diplomats were paid. The
New York Times noted, "A Franklin could live in modest chambers
and wear the plainest of clothes while representing the infant
republic. But the world—like the American people—demands
today that the United States be less niggardly toward its officials
abroad." The *Wall Street Journal* mourned, "Thus, young, able Mr.
Dulles is lost to the Department of State after serving with distinction for ten years in Europe and the Near East." Photographs that
accompanied the article showed that Allen's face had filled out,
softening his jutting jawline, with a fuller mustache and hair parted
in the middle. He continued to wear a stiff collar and appeared the
prototype of the serious, practical young American professional.
The image was bolstered by the press furor, including this com-
plaint from his old friend Walter Lippmann in *The New Republic*:

"Ten years of training in the practical conduct of foreign affairs are lost to the nation... through the resignation of Allen W. Dulles from our Foreign Service, following a recent promotion that entailed added expenses but no higher salary."[1]

Allen's arrival at Sullivan & Cromwell was hardly smooth sailing—he failed his bar exam. He would not go through the formalities to become a member of the New York State Bar until 1931, although he qualified in 1928 on his third try. The bar examination in those days was in two parts, one focusing on the candidate's knowledge of national precedents, federal laws, and tax matters, the second half devoted to the details of New York State laws. Allen passed the first section on his first try and failed the New York section a second time in 1927 before succeeding a year later. Considering how little time he had to prepare, the result may have been embarrassing but was certainly understandable.

While failing the bar is not the first thing a law associate wants to do upon arriving at a firm, Allen at thirty-four was no ordinary fresh graduate. Nor, for that matter, was Sullivan & Cromwell an ordinary Wall Street law firm. It was, upon Foster Dulles's accession to the post of managing partner, the biggest, most powerful, most respected law firm in the world. Its clients were national governments, major corporations, even entire industries. Yet it continued to bear the personal imprint of the flamboyant William Cromwell until his death in 1948, and that was due partly to the fact that Foster Dulles kept the firm doing what it did best.

Cromwell affected a flowing white mane and Edwardian dress, for it suited his personality. But he was in the forefront of the development of American legal practice from the final decades of the nineteenth century through the first decades of the twentieth. If it was an innovative tactic in business law, William Cromwell probably had a hand in it. While he lived a storybook life, much of it in

Paris and away from Wall Street, nearly everything Cromwell did
had a direct tie to his beloved firm. His love of France and things
French kept him out of the daily affairs of the firm but not out of
its principal mission: securing a legal advisory role in every possible significant business deal that was going on in the world at that
moment. Although Sullivan & Cromwell lawyers knew their way
around a courtroom, the firm was not known as a litigation specialist; it was a deal-maker. Cromwell had shown an early genius for
helping industrial giants such as Morgan, Harriman, and Rockefeller construct their mammoth trusts in the last decades of the
nineteenth century. Then, as the century turned and trust-busting
was in flower, the old man had shown his clients how to restructure, divest, and reorganize. He was a major force in both the political and the financial support for the Panama Canal, and, through
his personal ties to the J. Henry Schroder banking house of
London, the firm had a ready source of foreign capital before the
First World War to finance the mammoth investments in railroads,
mining, and factories that turned America into the arsenal of the
Allied cause. William Cromwell did not just represent clients; he
was Wall Street's lawyer to the world.

In the aftermath of the war, the flow of capital from Europe
to the United States began to go the other way as the victors paid
renewed attention to the bleeding continent and the newly developing group of nations. Cromwell once again was on top of every
deal he could get his hands on. Much of the financing of the 1920s
and 1930s in Europe had ties—either direct or by implication—to
the reparations or voluntary debts that resulted from the war. The
old man gloried in the identification of the firm with his chosen
protégé, Foster Dulles, the acknowledged expert on such matters.
For his part, Foster as the new managing partner was determined
to maintain that advantage. The firm's strength was a potent
combination: Its legal abilities were acknowledged, its sources of

outside financing were well established, and its political connec-tions—in Washington, Paris, London, and elsewhere—were the best on Wall Street. It was in that last area of power brokering that Allen Dulles found his legal niche. Allen's arena was not the court-room, but the familiar halls of the State, Navy, and War building at 17th and Pennsylvania Avenue in Washington.

Almost as soon as he moved to New York, Allen began to commute back to the State Department to secure legal permits nec-essary for the firm to complete its big financing deals. Early in World War I, the government had placed the Treasury in an over-sight role for all bank and private loans overseas; the situation was further complicated after the Dawes plan for Germany's repara-tions loans installed a formal U.S. reparations commissioner who could recommend Treasury limits on future loans. Dulles showed how easy it was to cut through the government's feeble safeguards. He was credited with (or blamed for, depending on the source) winning State Department pressure on the government of Colom-bia to provide oil concessions claimed by a partnership of the Morgan and Mellon interests, even though it was formally opposed by the Commerce Department. He also assisted in winning the Treasury's approval of a $30 million loan to the Prussian govern-ment even though the reparations commissioner had firmly opposed it. It was the largest Wall Street loan to a foreign govern-ment up to that time. Between December 1926 and June 1927, Allen was Sullivan & Cromwell's point man at the State Depart-ment on loans to Bolivia ($13 million), Colombia ($10 million), Denmark ($5 million), Sicily ($5 million), and Germany ($20 mil-lion)—all the loans representing enormous sums at the time.[2]

Only a few months of this kind of private practice elapsed before Secretary Frank Kellogg called him back into service in early 1927, "as an adviser to the American Representation at the Naval Limitations Conference which is to meet at Geneva on June 20."

What overtook the naval parley was a much more dramatic proposal—that war itself be declared an international outlaw.

On April 7, 1927, the tenth anniversary of America's entry
into the First World War, French Foreign Minister Aristide Briand
proposed to the American people that the two powers sign a bilateral agreement to make war illegal. Briand had been put up to it by
American internationalists such as James T. Shotwell of Columbia
University and Nicholas Murray Butler, the university's president,
who feared that the endless bickering of international disarmament
conferences was leading nowhere, as in the case of the Geneva naval
talks. Briand's proposal was one of those casual gestures that produce public reaction beyond the dreams of their makers. Popular
opinion in the United States leaped at the idea, and even the most
isolationist members of the U.S. Senate were swept along in the
wake. Briand suddenly found himself an international hero, and
other nations took up the idea. Secretary Kellogg, who doubted that
any such promise would work absent an enforcement provision,
nevertheless knew a good idea when he saw one. He went Briand
one better and turned the idea into a multinational pledge. So on
August 27, 1928, a full fifteen nations agreed to outlaw war "as an
instrument of national policy"—with the usual fudging. Britain
specifically retained the right to defend its empire, and the United
States reserved enforcement of the Monroe Doctrine—this, in the
context of the invasion of Nicaragua that year by a task force of five
thousand U.S. Marines sent in to preserve the power of a regime
supported by the American banks that had lent heavily to that
Central American nation.

Although often derided as an idealistic charade, the Kellogg-
Briand Pact in fact was another step along the road Woodrow
Wilson began to build in Paris. First of all, there was its universality;
in time, sixty-four nations, including five of the Dominions of the
British Empire and even the Soviet Union (which, like the United

States, had not yet joined the league), threw over the historic barri-
cade that strict neutrality had afforded some nations when other
nations went to war. From that time on, all nations promised to
exert a common moral force against any nation embarked on
aggression against another. "It may be that a moral commitment is
necessary before more active sanctions against war are possible,"
mused historians Dumas Malone and Basil Rauch. In their *War and
Troubled Peace*,[3] they argue that when one views this era of successive international conferences and treaties as a historical progression, it becomes clear that by the time the United States signed the
Kellogg-Briand agreement in 1928, it had moved a long way from
the provincial pacifist convictions of William Jennings Bryan and
toward a "system of international law required by the policy of collective security against aggression. As such the Pact committed the
United States to apply 'moral sanctions' against aggressors in the
future."

Allen Dulles's life straddled this world of nonstop talks about
peace and full-throttle preparations for war. His years became
neatly divided. From 1928 through 1934, each spring and early
summer usually found him shuttling between Geneva, Paris, and
London on one international conference or another, rising steadily
in rank and international reputation. The summer holiday would
be crammed into a few hasty weeks in Henderson Harbor, and
then he would return to Sullivan & Cromwell for the autumn and
winter months. Understandably, his career could not be that easily compartmentalized. There was considerable overlap in serving
U.S. foreign policy and private client interests to a degree that
today would be strictly illegal.

But part of this conflict of interest came from the way government did business sixty years ago. The State Department was
still a short-staffed agency. Allen Dulles had a level of expertise that
did not exist in-house and an international reputation that could
not be duplicated. So the secretary of state retained Sullivan &

Cromwell and paid it, not Allen, for his services; the law firm was paid the nominal salary of a Foreign Service officer, and Allen was paid his higher law associate's salary by the firm. Today's suspicion in Washington of business and law did not then exist. The official delegate whom Dulles served most frequently as legal adviser at these Geneva and London parleys was Norman Davis, a Morgan banker whose own commuting between Wall Street and posts at the U.S. Treasury had also begun at the 1919 Paris Conference. The goal of all these international conferences was to halt the use of military aggression, yet the negotiators realized there were profound economic issues at stake that, if not resolved, could derail the basic quest. Agreements to limit the use and disposition of increasingly sophisticated systems of war could scarcely be reached without having a dramatic impact on major industries—oil development and metals manufacturing, to name two—and the complexities of the reparations dilemma overhung the entire peace process.

Talks on limiting naval warship tonnage and firepower resumed again in 1929, and Allen was once more in London. That golden summer of 1929, Allen and Clover joined Foster and Janet for a long idling cruise by open sailboat around the eastern shores of Lake Ontario. It was pure Dulles-style sailing, with the foursome taking shelter at night in tents they had packed along or occasionally in the abandoned hunting shacks that dotted the various small islands. There were two meals a day, a hearty breakfast and a sumptuous dinner of fresh-caught fish at night; the rest of the time was spent sailing from one point to another, a forced march by water. By family reports, Janet enjoyed it because it gave Foster pure relaxation and joy; Clover reveled in the unbroken plunge into nature. She also kept secret during the trip that she was pregnant again.[4]

The crash of the stock market a few weeks after Foster and Allen returned to New York that autumn must have shocked the Dulles brothers with its ferocity, but they had been aware for some time that financial trouble was brewing. As early as 1928, Foster had been arguing in those forums that would hear him that the rising walls of protectionist tariffs and quotas that Congress had been building since 1922 were hurting American prosperity. In the nine years since the Paris Conference, U.S. businesses had sold more than $47 billion in foodstuffs and manufactured goods abroad, most of it to Europe. This is a sizable sum today, but it was unprecedented back then. The foreign buyers of American goods had, in turn, sold billions of dollars worth of products back to the United States, and in so doing had helped pay installments of the debts left over from the war. But the foreigners had a trade deficit with the United States of some $11 billion built up since 1919, and that sum equaled the same amount of new foreign loans made by the New York banks. Foster argued that to shut off trade was to shut off the system that allowed the foreign debts to be paid and American goods to be sold abroad. But the collapse of Wall Street's prosperity machine angered Americans as much as it frightened them. Quick solutions were demanded, and reason went out the window.

The Germans did not help matters. History treats the Weimar Republic as a well-intentioned regime of socialist persuasions and inept performance. This is only partly true. Weimar statesmen had shown a positively Prussian determination to rebuild its military might with clandestine aircraft and shipbuilding projects hidden away in Sweden and Japan for the better part of the decade. German officers, especially combat flyers, were being trained at secret bases inside the Soviet Union. In Italy, Mussolini's bellicosity echoed the length of the Mediterranean, and Japan was just a year away from its rapacious invasion of Manchuria. The Germans kept arms inspectors baffled by subterfuge and poised the country for a rapid vault into arms supremacy at some more auspicious moment.

Brave statements and treaties to the contrary, the painful truth was that the United States lagged behind in building its own navy while the rest of the world had moved on to construct the next generation of war vessels; it would not be until 1934 that Congress approved a sizable navy shipbuilding program, and even then its goal was merely to build back up to the levels of the 1922 pact on battleships and the 1930 limits on other craft. On the intelligence front, Germany and Japan were installing clandestine networks around the world. The Soviet Union, which had acquired diplomatic recognition by most nations except the United States, had poured intelligence agents, *agents provocateurs*, and polemicists abroad. This only fueled domestic uncertainties and suspicions.

Washington, however, continued to put its faith in conferences. After finally achieving a naval agreement in 1930, the major nation members of the league began to dream of a more ambitious goal, to take Kellogg-Briand to its next step—a general disarmament agreement that all nations would sign and abide by. By maintaining only enough troops for self-defense, all nations could live without the fear of stronger neighbors on their borders. The proposal was not new; the Soviets had put forth a version earlier. But one mammoth final effort seemed called for, if only because of the frightening sounds of arsenals being stocked and troops drilling that echoed out of Germany, Italy, Japan, and Russia. Something had to be done to head off such an armaments race before all nations were drawn in.

IN THESE EARLY PREWAR YEARS, Allen Dulles began to make the transformation from being an extremely competent technician to developing his own theoretical base. He argued privately, and then publicly, that nations must reach past specific and narrow conferences and commit to a joint mechanism to ensure the safety of the whole globe. Sooner than Foster, Allen began to search for solutions in a world where he saw the peacemakers being outpaced by the war planners. He was doubly worried because he watched the tide in Washington running backward from the way history was headed; if the 1920s was the time of brave new treaties publicly agreed to, then the 1930s in America was to become the era of "strict neutrality." As wars threatened, seemingly all over the world, there was an increasing danger that the U.S. government would bend to pressure from the isolationists and withdraw into a shell. That might be fine for a tiny nation such as Switzerland, but it was dangerous folly for a nation as powerful and as vulnerable as the United States. There was a real threat that America might push the clock back past the neutrality efforts of Woodrow Wilson in search of an idyllic evocation of Thomas Jefferson and his futile attempts to seal America off from a discordant Europe.

But what was the right antidote to "strict neutrality"? And were Germany, Italy, the Soviet Union, and Japan mounting threats to world peace or, as some argued, merely victim societies looking for a just and equal place at the table of the great powers? Could these increasingly warlike governments be soothed into peace? By what methods could this be done? At what price?

For Allen Dulles the linkage between intelligence and foreign policy remained inseparable. If America could no longer hide from the world, then it followed that the nation had to play a leadership role in the quest for peace; that in turn demanded far better flows of intelligence than the current leaders of the United States government felt was needed. Not only would Congress not appropriate the funds for such services, even internationalists such as Herbert Hoover (before and after he became president) were reluctant to counter, let alone match, the intrusions of the secret services of Russia, Japan, and Germany with an official spy service at home.

It is now a matter of historical fact that during the late 1920s and early 1930s all three powers followed aggressive intelligence activities around the world, and the sluggish reaction of the United States is part of this dismal history. This reluctance had its roots in Wilson's damning of Robert Lansing and the accusation that the dissident secretary had used his spy service against the chief executive. Hoover and Secretary of State Henry Stimson, especially, were reluctant to share with other men the political power that intelligence brings. Spies, they believed, owed no political loyalty, let alone gratitude, to their superiors.

Many of the men with whom Dulles had served in intelligence at the State Department had bailed out for better career opportunities abroad in formal diplomacy. Joseph Grew had gone to Turkey, Leland Harrison had become ambassador to Sweden, while Hugh Wilson and Hugh Gibson spent several years shuttling between the embassies in Brussels and Bern. Many others of the young State Department diplomats from the Paris Conference era drifted into the private sector, and, not surprisingly, a great deal of active intelligence-gathering drifted by default into private hands. This was done with the full knowledge and consent of men like Kellogg and Stimson and Presidents Coolidge and Hoover.

It is fruitless to argue whether the cadre of leaders in the pause between the world wars was hopelessly naive or politically pragmatic. The formal bureaucracy of intelligence drifted, but some intelligence work *was* being done. Indeed, while much of the State Department's facilities were dismantled and many of its key officers dispersed, the FBI under J. Edgar Hoover developed a considerable intelligence capacity, including its own network of informants throughout radical leftist circles in Latin America. Then too, still more of the work of fact-gathering, collating, indexing, and reporting fell into private hands. Colonel Ralph Van Deman, the army's Military Intelligence director in World War I and head of intelligence at Paris, was on reserve status during the peace but went ahead compiling a list of suspects who might, in wartime, be subversive. At least one account of his list says it was based on a secret list of 105,000 World War I suspects compiled by the navy and ordered destroyed by President Wilson when he learned that some of his academic friends were among them. Van Deman merely took the lists into private practice.

This was an era when private citizens of some stature, along with journalists and business travelers, could and did gather information, conduct interviews, and report back to Washington on their foreign journeys. Therefore, it was not long before a group of influential businessmen, bankers, and diplomats with intelligence backgrounds began to pool its information and share its insights systematically with both Washington and London.

Not much has been written about The ROOM, but to set down its membership and actions calls up images of the well-bred hero-spy novels that were so popular in those days. The ROOM was founded in 1927 by Vincent Astor, scion of the wealthy family, and a sailing adventurer. Astor, with his good friend Franklin Roosevelt, had helped organize the U.S. Naval Reserve during World War I. He later became FDR's personal intelligence adviser during World War II. Roosevelt was an enthusiastic booster of official spying dating back to a 1917 trip to London, where the young navy official was entranced by being allowed to observe some deliberately faked intelligence operations organized in his behalf by Admiral "Blinker" Hall's clandestine teams, who penetrated German coastal defenses.[5]

Along with Kermit and Theodore Roosevelt, Jr., Astor secured an apartment in an obscure building on East 62nd Street in New York, and there a secret band of top business and banking leaders met regularly to share information gathered from all over the world. Among the regular visitors to The ROOM's quarters were Winthrop W. Aldrich, the chairman of Chase National Bank; Marshall Field III, the publisher; and David K. E. Bruce, then a businessman and later Allen Dulles's colleague from the London

OSS station. In all, about three dozen prominent men, most with intelligence backgrounds and all with the means to gather information abroad, were brought into this group.[6]

An important member of the group was that old British spymaster Sir William Wiseman, who had been sent by Admiral Hall at the outbreak of the First World War to coordinate Anglo-American intelligence. Wiseman had ostensibly retired at war's end and taken a job at the Wall Street firm of Kuhn, Loeb & Co. Another figure who joined at once was William Donovan, who had won a Congressional Medal of Honor and a host of other decorations for bravery during the war and now was a prospering Wall Street lawyer. Soon after the founding, Allen Dulles was invited to join the gatherings of The ROOM.[7]

Without doubt, The ROOM was a precursor of the World War II OSS operation. In the period between the start of the conflict in 1939 and America's entry in 1941, it even provided clandestine money laundering and covert operations; during the years of active wartime combat, Astor and others became rivals with Donovan for President Roosevelt's ear. It also established the precedent for leaders of corporate America to provide the government with cover and subsidized operations—through transportation, finance, and propaganda—which Washington could not undertake alone.

While his membership in The ROOM was exciting to Allen, his early membership in the Council on Foreign Relations would prove much more important to his development. The beginnings of this influential foreign policy forum go back to the spring of 1919, when a growing number of British and American diplomats at the Paris Peace Conference acknowledged to themselves a sense of despair over the final product. They had been appalled at the level of misunderstanding that existed between governments. And they were ashamed at how much of the treaty's final terms had been dictated by ill-informed and narrowly manipulated public opinion from the delegates' home countries. But they had been heartened at the way the British and American staffs had been able to cooperate during the various treaty-drafting conferences, and they had hope that by continuing contact and sharing views in a formal setting, the more attainable quest of the conference might be kept alive.

These founding members were avowedly internationalist by conviction. On March 30, 1919, Lord Cecil, head of the British delegation, held a luncheon at the Hotel Majestic to organize what was called an Institute for International Studies for both countries. Among the Americans who came were General Tasker Bliss and Colonel House, who were commissioners, and inquiry aides Archibald Coolidge, Whitney Shepardson, and James Shotwell of later Kellogg-Briand fame. The British would go ahead and form their institute rather quickly after the conference in Paris ended. After some fits and starts, the Council on Foreign Relations was born in 1922. Membership was by invitation only, and the council set itself three objectives: to promote study and discussion within the membership toward a more thoughtful and internationalist foreign policy, to provide a forum for public speeches and debates by leading foreign affairs statesmen of all political persuasions, and to reach out to an audience beyond the council by publishing a quarterly devoted to learned articles that would educate, inform, and promote a greater participation in the debate on American foreign policy.

From the beginning, the Council on Foreign Relations carried heavy weight, politically. John W. Davis was its first president, and former Secretary of State Elihu Root was an active sponsor. Others who lent their prestige to the group were Newton Baker, Isaiah Bowman, and Archibald Coolidge, Dulles's old boss on the Austrian and Czech issues in Paris. For many years, Professor

Coolidge was a driving force in the council's activities, and his greatest contribution was in the selection of a young *New York Evening Post* journalist and former military intelligence officer named Hamilton Fish Armstrong to take over the operation of the council's showcase publication, *Foreign Affairs*. Starting in the summer of 1922, *Foreign Affairs* got off to a roaring start. Root, an icon of Republican respectability, contributed the lead article, which argued that the United States stood at the threshold of a new era of internationalism. This new era placed the United States in a special position and imposed a new responsibility on the nation and on its people. Considering who the author was and what he was believed to stand for, it was just the kind of bombshell article a new opinion magazine needed. There were other notable articles in that first issue: Edvard Benes, then the foreign minister and later president of Czechoslovakia, wrote about politics along the Danube; John Foster Dulles provided an essay on future economic problems in Europe resulting from the reparations agreement. Within five years *Foreign Affairs* would have a paid subscription list of 27,000 of the most influential figures in American politics, business, and academia.

Allen Dulles accepted a Council on Foreign Relations invitation in 1923 after his return from Turkey, and he remained a member for the rest of his life. He served as its president from 1946 until 1950, and as we shall see, throughout his life he drew as much from the council as he contributed. Through its various study groups and special projects, Dulles continued a high intensity course of postgraduate study on the evolution of American foreign policy. In countless articles he wrote for *Foreign Affairs* (his first was published in 1924), Dulles established a worldwide reputation as a constructive and thoughtful force in world political matters. Perhaps most important, his long friendship with Hamilton Fish Armstrong would be an enormous source of comfort and support. Armstrong, among his other talents, was one of those editors who drew the best from those who wrote for him. While Allen Dulles possessed the clarity of expression that was part of his family heritage, he lacked the instinct that can illuminate writing beyond its words. In two books they coauthored (*Can We Be Neutral?* in 1936, and *Can We Stay Neutral?* in 1939) Armstrong helped Dulles move into the front ranks of American foreign policy debate and bolstered his reputation for progressive vision, which, at that time, exceeded his brother's.

During this period of reputation-building and debate, Dulles became embroiled in controversies of another nature. Not everyone applauded the disarmament talks that convened in Geneva and London at this time. While many bankers and manufacturers took a broad view of world politics, others reacted noisily when their own industries were called upon to sacrifice. The reductions in the U.S. Navy that came out of the 1922 agreement caught the so-called Big Navy lobby of steel, chemical, and petroleum producers by surprise. To their horror, subsequent peace agreements raised the prospect that future shipbuilding and weapons development could be postponed, perhaps even canceled permanently. The public outcry against "the merchants of death" alarmed still other arms manufacturers, and, not surprisingly, they struck back. While the preparatory agenda sessions that Dulles attended in 1926, and others like them, could be kept private, the actual treaty conferences could not. Lobbyists began to appear, sometimes as official observers, more often as accredited journalists for newspapers known to have specific political agendas of their own. Americans were scarcely alone in this. There was soon a regular community of special interest peddlers who used statistical information, emotional argument, and, occasionally, outright bribery to affect the outcome of the conferences.

William Shearer was a big, blustering glad-hander who arrived in Geneva with accreditation as a reporter for the *New*

York World. He was also on a secret retainer from Bethlehem Steel and other producers of navy ship hulls. Shearer was an impressive, if irritating, source of opposition to efforts to limit the various classes of warships because he had an undeniable knowledge of ship tonnage and the various designs and specifications of the weaponry each vessel could carry. Later he would be accused of using physical intimidation and bribes to block various parts of the agreement and, ultimately, the treaty. In turn, Shearer wrote articles and, on his return to America, made a number of public accusations that Allen Dulles used his privileged position as a negotiator to work out oil concessions for Sullivan & Cromwell clients; worse, Dulles was charged with agreeing to reduce the strength of the U.S. Navy in order to secure those concessions.

Had Shearer stopped there, he might have done some real damage. But the spotlight of sudden celebrity unhinged the man; he extended his charges to include Norman Davis and Hugh Gibson and alleged a broader plot to sell out America's first line of defense that reached into the State Department and perhaps even to the White House. When a Senate committee investigated the Geneva talks in hearings in early 1928, Shearer ran amok and at one point physically threatened one of the witnesses during a committee session. Dulles's reputation was saved by testimony from Drew Pearson, another journalist who had covered the conference. Pearson, a liberal muckraker who would be a major figure in the McCarthy dispute twenty-five years later, refuted the accusation that Dulles had traded national security for oil leases because he knew it was false; Pearson, however, intensely disliked Dulles because of his privileged background, and suspected that Shearer had been at least partly right, that work for Sullivan & Cromwell clients had gone on in Geneva. In that, of course, he was right. From 1927 on, Dulles had used the Sullivan & Cromwell office at 39 Rue Cambon in Paris as a home away from home during his diplomatic missions to Geneva and London.

The uproar might have been greater had the full extent of Dulles's conflicts of interest been understood at the time. As one illustration of how interwoven his ties and activities became, the Dulles papers at Princeton have an *aide memoir* dictated by him in 1963 concerning the Shearer accusations.[8] In it, Dulles recalled that after he returned from Geneva in 1927 to Sullivan & Cromwell, he received a telephone call from Paul D. Cravath, a prominent New York attorney and the senior partner of the rival firm in those days called Cravath, deGersdorff, Swaine, and Wood. Cravath was a founding member of the Council on Foreign Relations, and he and Dulles held memberships in the same Long Island golf club. Allen Dulles, as befit his somewhat reduced status at the law firm, was laboring in The Pit, a common office space shared by half a dozen younger lawyers. Cravath insisted on coming over to Sullivan & Cromwell's offices for a private talk; Dulles hurriedly appropriated the vacant office of a senior partner away on vacation and waited. Cravath said he wanted to retain Dulles on a matter of extreme delicacy.

> Mr. Cravath said, "You know our firm is counsel for the Bethlehem Steel Corporation." I said that I knew that. He said, "We have found a most unfortunate development.... Did you run across a man called Big Bill Shearer at the conference?" I said, "Oh, yes. I knew Bill Shearer very well and saw a good deal of him. He is very well up on naval strength. He can tell all the guns on all the vessels of all the navies in the world. He is a freelance newspaperman, I believe."
>
> Mr. Cravath said, "Here's the situation. We have just discovered that, without consulting counsel or the president or the chairman of the board... or any of the other senior executive officers, the vice president of

the Bethlehem Steel Corporation at the Fall River
branch where we do a great deal of shipbuilding, got in
touch with Mr. Shearer and gave him a retainer to go to
the Geneva conference and follow it for us. Of course
he wasn't to interfere or to do anything other than to
keep us advised...."

I said that I knew what Shearer had done over in
Geneva and I thought that he had been about as effective a man as there was in blowing up the conference.
"Well," he said, "I'm afraid that's the case and I would
like very much to retain you to go down to see [Secretary
of State] Kellogg and explain to him the very unfortunate situation in which we are placed.... He is causing
us trouble. Our friend in Fall River had only given him
a retainer for one particular job. However, Mr. Shearer
is now suing the Bethlehem Steel Corporation on the
grounds that he had a $10,000 a year retainer for an
indefinite period of years. The papers in this case are
likely to be filed and I think Mr. Kellogg ought to know
about this beforehand."

According to the memo, Dulles refused the retainer but
agreed to break the news to the secretary.

Mr. Kellogg was a man of rather short temper and he
was a lawyer. When he heard this report, he almost went
through the roof of the State Department. I never saw a
man so mad in my life. He would see the international
implications of this—American delegation arranges,
through Bethlehem Steel, to wreck conference and all
sorts of headlines of that kind. Kellogg had been very
stout in his attitude about the conference and had taken

a pretty strong stand against the proposals that the
British had presented, and I think quite rightly, but he
could see that this was all going to go up in the air and
that the Bethlehem Steel Corporation would be the big
bad wolf that had wrecked the conference....

What would have happened had the Dulles mission for Paul
Cravath been uncovered at the time can only be imagined.
Perhaps more remarkable is the clear tone that, even thirty years
later, Dulles did not concede that he had acted inappropriately. It
just never entered his mind.

In 1930 Allen, Clover, and their three children (Allen Macy
Dulles had been born that January) moved to Paris for a year of
duty. He was now a full-fledged partner in the firm, and, despite
the fright caused by the Wall Street crash of the previous autumn,
the full depth of the Depression could not even be imagined. Nor,
for that matter, could most people focus on the clear portents of
war, what with the attainment of peace so tantalizingly close. That
same year, the German military intelligence group, the *Abwehr*,
began secret photoreconnaissance flights over Poland. Production
of German artillery shells began at secret plants in Russia, and the
Nazis gathered enough votes in the election that summer to
become the second largest party in the Reichstag.

In October 1930 Dulles wrote to his friend Ham Armstrong:

Clover and I have taken a part of an old French house
which is just what we have been looking for, and we are
very comfortably installed. As a result I am rather
expecting to stay here until after the first of the year,
particularly as work has been cropping up in sufficient
volume to keep me very busy.

Earlier this month I spent a couple of weeks in

Berlin working on the legal end of the large credit recently extended to the German government. The situation there... is extraordinarily interesting and I was glad to have this opportunity of getting in touch with the official governmental and banking circles and learn their reaction. *Personally, I feel that the Hitler menace is greatly exaggerated in the American and European Press and that for sometime at least they will not play a decisive part in determining the course of events, as, while numerically strong, they lack leadership...* [emphasis added].9

Dulles and many others can be forgiven if peace seemed closer at hand than it actually was. In January 1931 the League of Nations hurried to keep the momentum of the 1930 London navy pact by calling for a world conference on disarmament to meet in Geneva in February 1932. Dulles viewed the prospect of yet another Geneva round with some trepidation. In a lead article for *Foreign Affairs* in the summer of 1931, he warned:

International conferences are not an unmixed blessing. Often they are inevitable, as at the close of wars; but unless inevitable they should be called only when the groundwork has been so carefully prepared that there is reasonable expectation of successful results.... Expressions of pious wishes inserted in legal documents, whether treaties or business contracts, generally come back to plague their authors.... When the Allies at Versailles were endeavoring to induce the Germans to accept highly unpalatable provisions respecting their military and naval establishments, they prefaced this section [the disarmament demands as]... "the first steps towards that general reduction and limitation of armaments which... will be one of the first duties of the League of Nations to promote."[10]

Yet when the call came for Dulles to be part of the 1931 U.S. delegation to yet another Geneva parley, he accepted quickly. He moved the family back to New York over objections by Clover, who by this time was tired of the separations, especially now that there were three children to raise alone when he was away. He won her agreement, in part, by promising she could return to Europe on a visit in the summer of 1932, leaving the children in the care of his mother. Minding the three children was seen as a welcome distraction for Edith Dulles; Reverend Allen Macy Dulles had died in 1930 while Allen was away, and his mother needed some occupation. Clover was scarcely mollified and began to worry; her husband's eye had started roving, and he had advanced beyond the simple flirtation stage.

Keep in mind that the United States still was not a member of the League of Nations. Thus the decision of President Hoover to send Secretary of State Stimson as an observer-delegate to Geneva was a clear signal that Washington intended a major breakthrough in weapons reduction. Norman Davis would be the functioning head of the delegation, which included Dulles as the official legal adviser. Also included in the group was an old friend from Bern and Berlin, Fred Dolbeare, who now was a banker with Schroder & Co., the New York branch of the J. Henry Schroder Bank of London. Davis, Dulles, and Dolbeare would also be doing diplomatic work on the league's economic commission, which was involved in the Young Plan, again to restructure Germany's foreign debt burdens. It was in support of that refinancing that Dulles had been involved in a second series of huge loans arranged for the American banks to the German government during his Paris tour for Sullivan & Cromwell a year and a half earlier.

In later years, these visits, and the Dulles brothers' position on the Schroder U.S. branch's board of directors, would be used by Soviet disinformation agents to allege that both men had maintained ties with the German bankers who financed Adolf Hitler's rise to power. This canard gained credence by repetition, to the point that it is now stated as fact in most Dulles family biographies that Foster and Allen maintained discreditable ties to the Nazis before, during, and after World War II. The proof offered was that a Schroeder Bank in Germany was run by a Hitler loyalist, General Baron Kurt von Schroeder, and that the brothers were therefore indicted by implication. In addition to the different spelling of the surname, the lie ignores the fact that the Schroder firm was an all-British institution founded in 1804 in London and that there was no German subsidiary of it called Schroeders. Moreover, the bank General von Schroeder applied his name to was the Cologne banking house of J. H. Stein, which he commandeered when he retired from military service.[11] This was easy enough after 1933, when a spate of Nazi laws made Jewish ownership of key industries and financial institutions illegal. There never was any proof that Sullivan & Cromwell, or the Dulles brothers, or the London Schroder Bank, ever had any ties to or dealings with von Schroeder, but the lie lives on.

But a genuine division of attitude developed between Allen and Foster Dulles on the extent to which Hitler and the Nazis were moral menaces and how much of a threat to world peace Germany would become under their rule. History has established that few people inside Germany, let alone in America, foresaw where the Nazi Party plurality in the Reichstag elections of 1932 would lead, or what Adolf Hitler would dare do when he was offered the prime minister post in January 1933. But Allen Dulles was quicker than most to recognize the danger, especially after his first meeting with the dictator in April 1933. Foster Dulles continued to place his trust in the permanent institutions of German society to control

the excesses of the Nazis. As brutal and repugnant as Hitler's elec-
toral rise was, more deadly violence around the world distracted
observers. In the early 1930s the world had apparently gone mad
with atrocities in Ethiopia, rape in Manchuria, the genocidal policies of Stalin in Russia, and, from 1935 onward, the Spanish Civil
War. Foster's error came from the lawyer's trust in the resilient
strength of the law, of treaties and institutions; his moral flaw was
one shared by millions of Americans who simply turned away
from the fearful realities of what was happening in Europe and hid
behind an American neutrality in word and deed.

If Foster Dulles continued to cling to the comfort that neutrality offered, Allen Dulles had no such illusions from the 1930s
onward. But even he recognized that Sullivan & Cromwell had a
vested interest in preserving the stability of the German economy
no matter who was in power; fully one-third of all the foreign
bonds that defaulted to their American investors during the
Depression were on loans made to German government units and
businesses, bonds which the firm, and he and Foster personally,
had a large hand in facilitating.

WHEN THE AMERICAN DELEGATES set out on the *S.S. Ile de
France* on April 9, 1932, all that was ahead of them. Until Secretary
Stimson and the other foreign ministers had finished their get
acquainted meetings, there was not much the technicians could
do, so Dulles initiated Davis into the pleasures of the various golf
courses in the area and, coincidentally, learned that the older man
shared another of Allen's tastes—attractive women.

One of the unpleasant aspects of Allen Dulles's personality
was not that he persistently had flings with other women, but that
he insisted on letting Clover know about them. It is hard to know
when he first strayed after they were married; Clover destroyed
much of their personal correspondence after his death in 1969.
But there are indications that as they began a more active social

life in New York in 1926, Allen began light flirtations that pro-
gressed into occasional affairs; by the time their son Allen Macy
Dulles was born in 1930, they had become a serious annoyance to
Clover.

Sex, it appears, was to Allen Dulles a form of physical therapy,
something one did to keep fit for more important things. Clover's
insistence on staying home with the children and her increasing
preoccupation with prisoner rights were treated by him as a kind of
betrayal of her obligation to be his good and faithful companion.
After all, Janet Dulles went everywhere Foster traveled, and there
was hired help to care for their home; they usually employed a
cook, a maid, and sometimes a butler-driver during these years. If
Clover would not travel when Allen asked, then he could not really
be blamed if he diverted himself with other women, always of his
own class and station. Yet Dulles realized how much his infidelities
hurt the wife he truly cared for, and so he wrote letters to her well
into the final years of his life in which he would intersperse protests
of loyalty and love with promises to "be good" in the future.
Usually, the same letters included confessions of dates, dinners, and
weekend trips with other women with such frequency that they can
only be considered taunts. On May 1, 1932, he sent Clover a letter
on stationery from a hotel at a lake resort outside Geneva:

> Dearest, We are off for a weekend.... The "we" in this
> case consists of Mrs. August Belmont, Mrs. Eliot
> Wadsworth (now Nancy), Norman Davis and I. I think
> I wrote you that we saw a great deal of Mrs. B & W on
> the boat and they turned up in Geneva last week. B. is
> one of the leaders in the New York unemployment
> relief and will undoubtedly put us both to work on
> that when I get back. She is a very delightful person
> and as you probably know (but I didn't) was the Miss
> Rokon of the stage many years ago....[12]

The letter goes on to report some of the events of the conference and closes with his acknowledging a letter from her after
a period of silence: "I thought you had given me up as a bad job—
I wouldn't blame you very much. So far however my conduct over
here has been quite exemplary." This last was probably meant to
assure Clover that he had not quite made it into bed with the
showgirl wife of the society millionaire and horse fancier, but it is
doubtful that this was much solace to her sitting at home in New
York. Clover sought the advice of Mrs. Norman Davis, who said
that one way to limit Allen's flirtations was to spend as much time
with him as she could. For once, she took the advice to heart.
Stashing the children with relatives, she sailed for Europe at the
end of May. For the rest of that summer, Dulles would be under
close supervision. It was probably just as well for both Dulles and
Davis that Clover came over when she did. With so much at stake
at the conference, the peccadilloes of two such prominent
Americans could scarcely have remained at the gossip stage. Back
home in America, Davis was considered the odds-on choice to be
secretary of state if the Democrats should choose his friend
Franklin Roosevelt to run for president that autumn. Indeed,
Davis was under some pressure to return to the United States and
campaign among his fellow Wall Streeters, who distrusted FDR.

As the summer of 1932 wore on, it became plain that the
issues in Geneva were too complicated to be resolved in a few short
weeks. Davis had resisted pressure to return to campaign for
Roosevelt until too late into October to do his own career any good;
Cordell Hull drew the appointment to State. Had Davis become
secretary of state, Dulles would probably have joined him there in
a senior position; from there his career could well have taken a different path that could have ended in his beating Foster to the top
chair.

In the meantime, Foster was gently nudging his brother to
return home with Clover at the end of summer. Allen responded

in one letter by reporting that he had attended an intimate dinner with Davis, Sir John Simon, and Heinrich Bruning, the German chancellor who had recently outlawed Hitler's political storm troops, the brown-shirted *Sturmabteilung*. It was an invaluable dinner meeting, for through Bruning, Dulles was widening his contacts among the anti-Hitler circles in Germany. All this in the cause of Sullivan & Cromwell, he assured his brother. Later during World War II, those contacts would be pressed into the service of Dulles's OSS operations.

"Most of the diplomatic representatives of the various Powers in Paris," Dulles wrote, "are included on their Geneva delegations, and it may at some future time be useful to have known them. I of course try to let it be known quietly that I am a lawyer and not a diplomat, that I am in Geneva for legal work, and that my connection with the government is only in connection with legal work for the delegation at the Conference," Allen added to clinch his argument for remaining. Foster agreed. In October, Allen was asked to stay on through the autumn to be the U.S. representative at the committee meetings that continued to hammer away at the air power and naval limitation agreements. He accompanied Davis home as far as London. Here, Dulles was able to put his close ties with old British friends at Whitehall to some use. While Davis made farewell calls to Number 10 Downing Street, Dulles and his old friend Robert Craigie met with the British and American naval officers who were the chief technical negotiators on the war vessel reduction clauses to the treaty.

During that holiday, despite his awareness of just how unhappy Clover was, he wrote a series of letters that were incredibly insensitive, bordering on the cruel, given what was at issue between them. The series begins with a letter written on Sunday, October 16, 1932. He had moved to the Astor family estate at Cliveden, a palatial country mansion that later would lend its name to "the Cliveden set"—those members of the British upper class who flirted much too long with Hitler before the war. He and Davis were part of a huge weekend house party that included editors, members of Parliament, bankers, and business leaders. It is a gay, witty letter about a glittering occasion, but he rounds it off with, "Now I must go down and talk Russia with a young English damsel, one of the weekend guests who seems hipped on the subject as a result of several months spent there recently. Love, AWD."

The next night, back in London, he closes another chatty letter, "Now dearest I have almost caught up to date at the risk of losing much sleep. I love you more than you or I realized and I have a sort of apprehension as to what may be happening to you but this may be due to the lateness of the hour."

Several days later, on October 24, he writes from London: "Dearest, It may well be a surprise to have three letters from me all written within 24 hours. There's nothing in my past history of letter writing to explain any such phenomenon. In fact, I cannot fully explain it myself. For some strange reason I have suddenly acquired the desire of letter writing to you and exactly at the moment when you have abandoned it. This has not resulted from any spirituous intoxication or from being enamored of any other female or even from being inspired by any ideas that I felt should be put on paper for future generations, however, I shall write on...."

Yet in the next paragraphs he goes to some length to tell Clover that he had met and formed an instant friendship with Rebecca West, the noted British author and political essayist. He describes West as "clearly a beauty in her youth with extraordinary eyes." He also describes her husband Henry Andrews, a Schroders banker, as a "charming person as well as an extraordinarily able businessman." In fact, this may well have been one of the purely innocent friendships that Dulles developed with other women aside from his romances. In later years, as West gained in reputation for her writings on tyranny and democracy, she became a regular and valued correspondent with Dulles, and she and Andrews became friends of Clover as well. Allen then closes the letter, "I would add that I am quite sane and sober and realize that I can't keep your love by letter writing but am moved by some strange desire to indulge in it. Meanwhile are you running off with strange Gods? How are the children? I came off without any picture of Sonny [Allen] but yours and the other children are with me now. Allen. P.S. Please don't let my letters lie around indiscreetly but don't destroy them until I return."[13]

By now the strain was telling on Clover. She had enough to do running a house and keeping an active entertaining and social schedule when Allen was around. But his frequent trips away and his profligacy drove her into periods of despair and depression; in reaction she sought solace and understanding in books on mysticism, psychology, and the occult.

She made a gallant effort to resist these immobilizing periods of sadness. Using her experience in the Russian concentration camps in Turkey, she had become active in reforming the conditions of New York's prison system, especially the institutions for women. And she maintained a platonic friendship with an older man involving intellectual intimacy and nothing more. In the end, it was enough that Allen and Clover continued to love one another, no matter how often he hurt her. As with so many women of her time, she chose to endure because the alternatives were few and unacceptable.

Finally, in November, Dulles returned home. The Geneva conference had been recessed for six months, and the defeat of President Hoover by Franklin Roosevelt left Dulles and Davis on the beach. From Europe, Dulles had written in *Foreign Affairs* that the 1933 session of the talks would have to merge the three issues of arms reductions, the overhang of World War I reparations claims, and the increasingly burdensome load of international debts that all the major nations carried. In March 1933 the newly installed Roosevelt administration reappointed the Hoover delegates to go to the second round of general disarmament talks in Geneva. Cordell Hull wrote to Allen, "I know that it is asking an appreciable personal sacrifice of you but the importance of the work to be done, the special qualifications you have shown and your familiarity with the situation justify telling you how much I hope you will see your way to accepting...." The same letter appointed him, along with Davis, to attend as a delegate the conference on economic problems that the league was running at the same time.[14]

Ambassador Davis and Dulles, along with a small group of aides, arrived in London at the end of March and quickly learned how much the now worldwide economic Depression was threatening any final agreement on weapons. The Americans made what was to be an informal call on Ramsay MacDonald at Number 10 Downing Street on the morning of March 30 and found Foreign Secretary Sir John Simon waiting there. Instead of a few minutes of courtesies exchanged, two days of heated talks between the two Americans and the British showed how far apart even the two democracies were on how best to achieve peace. MacDonald went straight to the point. Would the new Roosevelt administration demand that all the participants to a disarmament treaty be up-to-date in their reparations payments (none was, except Finland) before such a treaty would be approved? Davis replied that Roosevelt and Hull had instructed him that the United States wanted the league's economic conference to focus on a plan for all the nations to work their way out of the Depression together. But, he added, most of the new United States Congress had been elected on platforms that promised "they would not agree to any cancellation, reduction or postponement of the debts."

Dulles spent his fortieth birthday on the boat-train to Paris, where the Anglo-American disagreements were mirrored among the French. Because no real progress was likely in Paris, Dulles was able to slip off to the Rue Cambon offices of Sullivan & Cromwell, where he learned from associates that Hjalmar Schacht, first met in Berlin in 1920, had become the key financial adviser to Hitler and that informal soundings has been made as to whether Foster Dulles would come to Germany to discuss foreign debt issues with the new German government. In part because of his brother's advice, Foster decided against the commission, especially after hearing what Allen and Davis had to say of their trip to Berlin to interview Hitler.

On April 8, at 4 PM, the two U.S. diplomats joined the American ambassador to Germany, George Gordon, and Baron von Neurath, a German foreign affairs adviser, for their first meeting with Adolf Hitler in his office in the old Chancellery, which was across the Wilhelmstrasse from the U.S. Embassy of Allen's time. Acting as interpreter was Hans "Putzi" Hafstaengl, the charming Harvard-educated Hitler crony whose job it was to put a human face on the Third Reich for American visitors. What followed, according to Dulles's minutes from the meeting, was one of those out-of-sync conversations in which one party has a hidden agenda and the other is talking, unaware of what is really going on.

Hitler was committed to accelerating the long-standing rearmament policies of the German establishment and securing that power to his own control; for the moment, however, it suited him to continue the pretense that Germany still wanted universal disarmament and that he, personally, insisted on merely restoring his nation to the first rank of national powers. Davis and Dulles were both under the impression that the Geneva deliberations could soon progress to a final agreement on getting rid of specific weapons systems and that Germany could be coaxed into staying disarmed if it was assured that other nations would soon join it.

American bewilderment at the conversation can be sensed. A memorandum sent to Washington under Davis's name and based on Dulles's notes stated:

In my conversation with Hitler it was difficult to get him off the topic of the necessity for an immediate revision of the Versailles Treaty. At times he spoke in an excited and oratorical manner. He stressed again and again the intolerable conditions for Germany, exposed as she was to attack on the Polish frontier. In fact, he came back to this so often that it made me wonder whether he did not have a purpose in doing so in order to help prepare public opinion in case later an incident should occur or be manufactured on that frontier. I made it clear to Hitler that while there was considerable sentiment outside of Germany favorable to reasonable modifications of the Treaty any attempt to effect a forceful revision would destroy confidence internationally, that by making a public issue of revision he would defeat his own ends and that the only solution I saw was to work quietly toward the rectification of specific points where hardship for Germany might be involved. Hitler stated categorically that Germany did not intend to attempt treaty revision... by use of force. In one excited moment he did say that irrespective of all opposition Germany will insist upon and obtain the armaments necessary for defense of her eastern frontier.[15]

The conversation with Hitler bordered on the surreal. At one point he asked Davis and Dulles what would have happened in the United States, after the Civil War, if the northern states had tried to force the South to sign a treaty that held them in subjection for an indefinite period of years. Davis, a southerner, proceeded to lecture the German leader on the history of the Reconstruction period in such detail that Hitler, for the moment, was stunned into silence. Abruptly he changed the subject. He had perhaps chosen a bad example, he said; civil wars are always bitter affairs. But, take the Franco-Prussian War of 1871, and he was off again on how Germany had generously forgiven the perfidious French. He continued with a litany of complaints and fears—of the French, of the Polish, of the world in general. At the end, Davis could only weakly suggest that revisions of the treaty might be worked out in Geneva if only Hitler would not talk about his demands so loudly in public. There was a second meeting with Hitler the next day, but the Americans came away worried more about the public anger that boosted the Nazis than about Hitler's ability to make anything of that anger.

On the train back from Berlin, the Americans held an impromptu conference with Francois Poncet, the French ambassador to Berlin, who had undergone a similar harangue from Hitler just hours before Davis and Dulles. Clearly, the French and Americans came away from Berlin with the same faulty analysis of the situation: Hitler was not a man to fear; he was merely an orator, a crowd agitator who used forensic ability to overcome a shockingly poor grasp of history or political reality. Indeed, there was a consensus that Reich President Hindenburg could dismiss the Nazis easily. They believed that Hitler risked being replaced as Nazi Party leader by more able men such as Hermann Goering and Joseph Goebbels, should they choose to take over the movement.

Still, on April 20, Dulles flew to London to brief the British Foreign Office on what had happened in Berlin. Lord Cadogan, who heard him out, recorded his own bewilderment at what worried the Americans so much: "I confess the real object of the visit still remains rather obscure to me." The British diplomat calmly dismissed Dulles's warning that Hitler appeared set on provoking some sort of trouble with Poland; he merely reported without comment that Dulles had taken time to visit German banking and lawyer friends and "was shocked to find the state of intimidation to which these people were reduced."[16] In all, the British were not impressed by Hitler either; he was just one of a host of problems that had to be dealt with.

During that long summer in Geneva Dulles joined with Anthony Eden (a prime minister in the 1950s) and his colleague, Sir William Malkin, to form a technical trio to hammer away at the French, Italians, and Germans on the tedious specifics of which weapons to give up, how many each nation might retain, and what existing arms must be destroyed. Bit by bit, however, there was steady progress, and a sense of tense anticipation began to infuse the conferees in Geneva. At the same time, however, Hitler began to consolidate his hold over his nation's war machine, and the pace of Nazi rearming accelerated. That summer, German airmen went to Italy for secret fighter training, and the clandestine tank school and air bases inside Russia were closed and the officers brought home to begin operational drills. In early October, the school to train U-boat officers and sailors was secretly opened at Kiel.

The first week of October saw Dulles, Eden, and Malkin editing and overseeing the printing of a final draft of the general disarmament proposal, which would be submitted to the league for formal action by the more than fifty nations in attendance. The French, the Italians, and even the German representatives had expressed their belief that this document could be the basis for serious negotiation. The draft was just that close, but it got no closer. It would prove to be the high-water mark of the effort that began in 1919 in Paris to bring peace to the world. More than a dozen years would pass and another world war would be fought before the nations of the world sat down again and planned for peace.

On October 14 Hitler ordered his representatives to withdraw from the conference, and on October 23 Germany formally withdrew from the League of Nations. Secret talks with Poland led to a nonaggression pact that freed the German dictator to devote the full resources of his government to all-out rearmament; within the next year he seized the office of Reich president and proclaimed himself führer. Dulles and others were shocked and realized that Hitler had never intended to cooperate.

In a memo sent to Washington on October 27, Dulles provided the following analysis:

> Germany has left the Disarmament Conference not primarily because of her dissatisfaction with the work of the Conference, but to indicate her revolt against the entire regime of the Treaty of Versailles, as shown by her simultaneous withdrawal from the League, disassociation from the World Court, etc. There is no reason whatever to believe that Germany would shortly return to the Conference if certain technical changes were made in the Disarmament program which was presented to her two weeks ago. The circumstances of her withdrawal show, first, that she does not wish to discuss Disarmament as an isolated subject and, second, that she does not wish to discuss Disarmament within the League framework, that is, with fifty different nations....
>
> In the absence of Germany it is questionable whether it is wise at this juncture to attempt to work out the technical details of a Disarmament Convention.... The Conference machinery should be kept in being but it should not to be allowed to do such active work as to give Germany the satisfaction of seeing a division among the other Powers....[17]

Basically, that is exactly what happened. In 1934 and again in 1935 President Roosevelt made proposals which revived hopes that the continuing peace effort at Geneva could be renewed. But the efforts for peace lagged further behind as outbreaks of war in Asia and the Middle East moved toward that final dress rehearsal for the war in Europe, the civil war in Spain. The reaction among the broad masses of American people was to shrink from the carnage they saw in terrifying newsreels from all over the world. A renewed cry went up for neutrality, a deliberately vague euphemism for pulling back from the kind of multinational debate that had gone on in Geneva for more than a decade. As Allen Dulles sailed for New York in that autumn of 1933, he did not know it but his role as an international arms negotiator had ended, and he was about to move on to a new phase in his career and life.

CHAPTER SIX

1934–1941

*"It is obviously useless for the United States to fight in Europe
every twenty-five years; let us say in 1914, 1939, 1964, and
thereafter if, during the intervening years we follow the policy
of nonintervention in European affairs to which both our
traditions and our sentiments have committed us."*
—*Allen Dulles,* Foreign Affairs, *1934*

ALLEN DULLES WAS FINALLY pulled down from his role as
America's leading arms control technician. The proximate cause
was trivial enough considering the time, yet the enemies who
struck at him were in dead earnest, and their real target was
internationalism itself. He and Norman Davis were asked by
President Roosevelt to return to London in the autumn of 1934
and try to organize a new round of heavy ship naval limitation
talks; most of the provisions of the 1922 Washington Treaty were
on the verge of expiration, and FDR particularly wanted to head
off a new round of capital ship construction that could only
worsen the already grim world scene. While both accepted the
posting, Dulles was beginning to doubt that another round of
talks would do any good.

"If the problems which confront the European countries are
to be worked out by agreement it is not merely a Disarmament
Conference which Europe needs, but a second Peace Conference
in which the disarmament question would be only one of the
major problems to be solved," Dulles wrote in *Foreign Affairs,*
adding, however, that until Germany and the Allies had worked

out their differences, there was no choice for the United States but to stay out of the negotiations.[1]

Yet neutrality had no lure for him either. He remained Robert Lansing's nephew and John Watson Foster's grandson; the world had become too small a place to hide. A war that threatened the rest of the world, by the nature of modern warfare, threatened America as well.

Late in the summer, forces promoting isolationism sought to embarrass the president by focusing on both Norman Davis and Allen Dulles as targets of controversy. It was a replay of the attack launched in Congress fifteen years earlier against Robert Lansing when Woodrow Wilson was the real target. This time the isolationists sought to discredit President Roosevelt's internationalist leanings by hitting at his emissaries.

For the moment Davis proved too big to bite, but Dulles was another matter. On October 4 Davis telephoned from Washington to Dulles in New York with a warning. State Department informants said that newspaper columnist Drew Pearson was about to attack Dulles for the work he did for Sullivan & Cromwell while he was representing the government in Geneva and London. Although Pearson was at heart pro–New Deal, much of his popularity as a syndicated news columnist was due to his willingness to attack establishment figures when they appeared to claim undue advantage. Dulles had previously been criticized in the "Washington Daily Merry Go Round" syndicated column that Pearson wrote along with Robert S. Allen. Previously, the columnists accused Dulles of rigging the 1932 Colombian elections in order to influence that government to grant oil concessions to Sullivan & Cromwell clients. What worried Davis was that this time there were hints that Pearson was being fed more embarrassing information that could involve Dulles and him in congressional hearings. Pearson's style was to begin an attack with a fairly low-key accusation and to save his most dangerous accusations for other columns, to give the impression that a scandal was developing in dramatic fashion.

Taking the advice of the older man, Dulles promptly telegraphed Secretary of State Cordell Hull that he wished to resign his appointment to go to the London talks. Hull just as promptly accepted on October 9, and Roosevelt wrote an official soothing letter on the same day, praising Dulles for his long service and regretting that events conspired against his further service. All of this tended to weaken the first salvo of Pearson's column, which had been written and sent to subscribing newspapers days before, when it actually appeared on October 10.

> Washington, October 9—A strenuous inter-government battle has been raging behind-the-scenes over the question of whether or not Allen W. Dulles shall go to London as disarmament adviser to Ambassador Norman Davis.
>
> The State Department is for him, and the Navy Department is against.
>
> Dulles has been under heavy fire for some time. He was criticized for advising on war debts while he was—and still is—partner in Sullivan & Cromwell, [a] prominent Wall Street law firm. And he was also attacked for his lobbying on oil concessions with his former colleagues at the State Department.
>
> However, Dulles' grandfather, John W. Foster, and his uncle, the late Robert Lansing, both were Secretaries of State. So the State Department has stuck with him.
>
> But the Navy Department has not. It has voiced vigorous opposition to his advising on naval affairs at London.[2]

By resigning, Dulles robbed Pearson of the excuse to continue the attack. It stung, but it was probably for the best that Dulles did not go on with his involvement in the peace talks abroad. The time had come for him to address both obligations and opportunities at home in New York. Early in 1934, the Council on Foreign Relations was spurred into action by the threat of a "strict neutrality" law being enacted by Congress in the next session. The group began to hold conferences aimed at solidifying the internationalist position on two important and conflicting questions: (1) Should the United States go back to the pre-Wilsonian days of neutrality in case war broke out in Europe? (2) How far should American neutral rights and privileges be sacrificed in order to help the other major nations of the world collectively preserve the peace? For many of the American internationalist establishment, it marked the first confrontation of a new idea in U.S. foreign policy—collective security.

As the year progressed, Dulles became more directly involved as an active public speaker on foreign policy issues. He had a pleasant baritone voice and a clear, unaccented way of speaking that lent itself particularly well to the early radio broadcasts of public debate. His first broadcast was a 1929 network national broadcast debate on general disarmament issues.[3] By the mid-1930s he had become something of a radio personality; his output of writing on foreign policy issues also grew as the controversy over neutrality heated up. He wrote, again for *Foreign Affairs*: "The fact is… that no nation can reach the position of a World Power as we have done without becoming… entangled in almost every quarter of the globe in one way or another. We are inextricably and inevitably tied into world affairs. We should not delude ourselves that like Perseus of mythology we can put on neutrality as a helmet and render ourselves invisible and immune to a world in conflict around us."[4]

ALLEN'S FAMILY OBLIGATIONS had become a problem that could no longer be avoided. He finally had to come to grips with the stress his absences and romantic flings were causing his family. Toddy, the eldest daughter, was starting to have problems in school and at home, no doubt partly reflecting her mother's own unhappiness. She also began to suffer from a lifelong battle with manic-depression. Son Allen had an easier time in school but had all the growing pains that come with being a boy with a largely absent father.

Clover and Allen decided to break up the pattern whereby she and the children would decamp for Henderson Harbor for lengthy summer stays while he stayed on in the city. The family would spend more time together closer to home. Foster and Janet Dulles had built a house in Cold Spring Harbor on Long Island in a community that was rapidly becoming fashionable for Wall Streeters who could commute into the city on a convenient train. Allen and Clover found property in Lloyd Neck, a few miles from Foster and Janet and other friends, and began to make plans for a summer and weekend retreat. They would occupy the house in the summer of 1935, and it became their real home base, especially on weekends and long holidays.

At about that time Clover took Toddy and Joan out of their private schools in New York. Archibald Roosevelt, the son of the late president, had created a school in his Long Island home for his own brood of children, and the two girls were boarded there. Clover and Sonny, as young Allen was called, spent weekdays in New York so she could pursue her prison reform work and keep the increasing social schedule that her husband's life required. It was, the children would recall, a very good time in their lives. There were pets, horses to ride, and sailboats nearby. For the adults there were long days of golf and tennis at the nearby Piping Rock Club. In the evenings frequent dinners brought the Dulles families and their friends together; invariably Allen and Foster would fall to arguing over politics, and while the debate could get heated over their widening differences on how to secure peace, the brothers remained personally close.

Allen began a more active role in the legal business of Sullivan & Cromwell, handling a number of Latin American financing deals. His ability to get things done was moving him up the ladder of responsibility at the law firm and in his older brother's estimation. Increasingly, Foster began to rely on Allen's judgment.

In the spring of 1935, Allen sailed on the *S.S. Europa* for a series of business-legal conferences that took him back to Berlin and as far as Budapest. As usual, Dulles was traveling under two flags. On June 3 he appeared as the chief American delegate, representing the Council on Foreign Relations at a League of Nations conference on collective security. Dulles compared his years spent as a disarmament negotiator to a naval battle "stern chase" in which the quarry is always just out of range of the pursuers. "Concrete proposals that might well have proved acceptable a few months before they were proposed," Dulles said in a speech, "have been presented when public opinion and national aspirations have moved forward to more advanced positions.... We are faced with the same difficulty in dealing with the problem of Collective Security. It is not only vital to build up our substitute for war but we must build it up in time."[5]

Dulles had earned considerable recognition for the speech, and he proudly sent back one of the official copies to Clover. This time, on the trip over, his letters had been most conciliatory. "On the whole I have kept rather free from any entanglements and in particular there have been no ladies on board with whom I have particularly consorted." As in other letters, he reported on his energetic athletic activities and his recurring episodes of gout, which confined him to bed for days or hobbled him with crutches.

This time the trip was free of serious health problems, and Dulles was in a good mood. He closed the letter, "I'm glad we have the house for the summer. Let's have a fine time together there for the first time in years."[6]

Once the conference was over, Dulles pushed on to the Continent on law firm business, indeed the main purpose of the trip. The task was to check the prospects of ever recovering full payment on the $1.5 billion in loans, bonds, and share issues that American investors had poured into European debts. These were now being heavily discounted, to the point at which some were worth next to nothing. What he saw alarmed him so much that he returned hurriedly to report to Foster.

Allen argued to Foster that Sullivan & Cromwell must close its Berlin office at once. Throughout Germany he had been pressured by old friends and even strangers to help them sequester financial assets outside the grasping reach of the Nazi Reich. Foster recoiled from dropping out of Germany. It ran contrary to his basic trust in institutions and procedures; one did not just pack up and leave a country because of an odious government that could come tumbling down any day. But Allen forced Foster's hand. He brought the matter up at the next partners' meeting. Jewish members of the law firm had long been uncomfortable with the firm's business dealings inside Germany; others realized those ties could come back to haunt the firm later on. "You couldn't practice law there," Allen later recounted. "People came to you asking how to evade the law, not how to respect the law. When that happens, you can't be much of a lawyer."[7] Foster relented in tears.[8] So the office was closed, and the firm's business activities inside Hitler's Germany ceased. Most biographers of Foster Dulles repudiate any notion that he had any sympathies for Hitler. But most take him to task, and rightly so, for being too aloof to what was going on in Germany during the 1930s. In this Allen and Foster Dulles saw their difference of opinion widen into a gulf as the decade moved closer to war.

Allen sought closer contact with the Council on Foreign Relations and his friend Hamilton Fish Armstrong. Through much of 1935, he and Armstrong worked on a book to explore a more pragmatic viewpoint. *Can We Be Neutral?*, which the two wrote in 1935 and published in 1936, was a 120-page distillation of the opinion representing the more activist wing of the internationalist movement at the time.[9] The answer to the title's question was a conditional yes. America could remain neutral if two other major powers went to war but not if American travelers and merchants insisted on the same kind of freedoms that Wilson had demanded during the early days of World War I. Ironclad neutrality pledges were no good either; they were too inflexible and ignored the fact that while America might not be directly concerned in the outcome of a war—for example, in a war between Japan and China—it could never be unaffected or uninterested. More, there were bound to be cases where to stay out of a fight was to affect the outcome of that fight in ways that might prove harmful later on.

Flexibility of response was the first Armstrong-Dulles recommendation. In preceding years, Congress had been voting a series of increasingly stringent neutrality laws much in the same way that it had built progressively higher protectionist tariff laws during the 1920s. It would continue to do so and, in the minds of the authors, increasingly tie the hands of the president to maneuver quickly and decisively enough in times of crisis to take steps to protect American interests short of war itself. Armstrong and Dulles also dismissed complicated laws that imposed trade embargoes on combatants. Reliance on the League of Nations, they added, had merely demonstrated the built-in flaw in the kind of mechanisms that Robert Lansing had warned of; such organizations would always depend on agreement of the most powerful members, and if the most powerful nations disagreed, what then? The book had the effect of propelling both the Council on Foreign Relations and Dulles into the forefront of the debate over what America should be doing if neutrality offered no security.

While the council itself remained concerned mainly with preserving peace through peaceful means, a growing number of its members evolved a more hawkish faith in preparedness for war as the surest way of avoiding it. One found a wide array of opinion leaders coming together to urge a stronger stand against aggression. There were Paris and Geneva hands such as Frank Polk, the State Department's first intelligence chief; Whitney Shepardson, a Polk aide; and Allen Dulles. But the preparedness committees also drew from outside: publisher Henry Luce, lawyer Dean Acheson, ministers and academics such as James Conant and Henry Sloane Coffin, and even a young and rising political writer named Joseph Alsop.

As prominent as these men were, they were in a distinct minority at the start. The horrors of World War I, a still-strong anti-British feeling, and a public admiration for the visible efficiencies of Italian and German fascism fueled a fear among Depression-era Americans that a future foreign conflict must be avoided lest it spill over into our own country this time. Prominent men, including Joseph Kennedy, FDR's ambassador to Britain, and aviation pioneer Charles Lindbergh, warned that European democracies were too corrupt to stand alone and could only drag us down. Most newspapers boosted the neutrality line; H. L. Mencken, the leading columnist of his day, specifically accused Roosevelt of fomenting a foreign war in order to strengthen his own dreams of dictatorship. It was a time of strong opinions advocated with high emotion.

Things also heated up on the intelligence front. Vincent Astor's ROOM organization began to meet more frequently, and

Allen Dulles became a more prominent attendee, as did William Donovan. Donovan by this time had become a national figure. He had returned to New York after World War I as one of the nation's legitimate combat heroes. As colonel of the 69th New York Regiment (the famed "Fighting Irish'") Donovan had with his brash bravery won a chestful of medals, including the Congressional Medal of Honor.

He resumed his law practice with John Lord O'Brian, his old mentor. O'Brian had spent the war as head of the War Emergency Division of the Justice Department and as such had controlled that agency's domestic intelligence operations. In 1925 O'Brian and Attorney General Harlan Fiske Stone gave Donovan a leg up; he was named assistant attorney general and, later, put in charge of the antitrust division of the department. It is reported in a number of histories that, during this time of reform at Justice in the wake of the Teapot Dome and anti-Red scandals, Donovan had tried to block the accession of J. Edgar Hoover to run the FBI. True or not, Hoover and Donovan shared a mutual antipathy that was demonstrated on countless occasions over the next forty years.

Donovan eventually moved back to New York in 1929 and opened an international law firm that competed with Sullivan & Cromwell, representing many of the same clients overseas. He also nurtured an ambition for high political office that included the presidency. Donovan had the misfortune to run as the Republican candidate for governor of New York in 1932—the same year that the national juggernaut that was Franklin D. Roosevelt used his lengthy coattails to carry Democrats into office; Donovan lost by a wide margin. He then devoted his time between the law firm and an increasing volume of speeches and articles that sought to redress what he saw as a shameful neglect of America's defense needs. By that time the U.S. Army with its 120,000 regulars was ranked thirteenth in the world's military tables, and not one new capital ship had been added to the navy since the end of the war. Donovan saw a conflict with fascism as inevitable, and America in great peril to defend itself. Worse, he increasingly began to fear that the American people's will to defend themselves was being eroded by outside forces.

By the mid-1930s, he and Allen Dulles were friendly acquaintances, different though they were in age, religion, and class. They shared a fierce enthusiasm for intelligence strategy and a growing alarm at America's peril. Donovan did not particularly like Dulles as a friend and never would. Donovan, despite his "Wild Bill" wartime nickname, was anything but an exuberant extrovert. One devotee describes him as "a roly-poly man, soft of voice and manner… he had soft blue eyes and a gourmet's demeanor."[10] Dulles, by contrast, was boisterously athletic, and even though he now affected rimless spectacles and his ever-smoldering pipe, his manner could suddenly shift from jolly to brusque. Dulles made Donovan irritable. Yet Donovan had reason to be grateful and to respect him. Dulles in 1927 had been one of the few lawyers who had publicly refuted accusations that during Donovan's tour as the antitrust chief he had been too soft on monopolies. The two also possessed the kind of boundless energy that enabled them to work on well past the point of exhaustion for other men. Through their meetings at The ROOM and with other groups of the growing preparedness movement, the two men built a common cause on the need for a renewed government intelligence capability. As yet they had not formed a firm idea of what that capability should look like; they just knew more organized intelligence gathering around the world was needed.

Through 1936 and 1937 Dulles continued to travel widely. He went abroad for Sullivan & Cromwell, and to cities and universities across America, including Princeton, to speak on the neutrality and preparedness issues. In the latter year, Dulles took a Pan Am Clipper inaugural flight to Latin America. What he found as he toured the region was not reassuring; much of the more than $250 million in debt issues that Sullivan & Cromwell had helped promote for official and corporate borrowers in South America was in very perilous shape. The Depression had sharply curtailed raw materials exports from the region, and resentful governments regretted the tough payment terms the Yankee lawyers had imposed upon them. At the firm's partners' annual dinner in November, Foster sat silently while Allen read a gloomy list of recision and damage suits that stretched the length and width of the southern continent; it was not the firm's fault, of course. "Lawyers cannot set up bond issues [that are] proof against economic disasters or political revolutions," he told them. But in the future, he told the partners, Sullivan & Cromwell had to be more careful about the loans it promoted for its clients.[11]

On that same trip he gathered information on an even more disturbing development that could turn into a strategic threat to the United States. Almost from the beginnings of the Third Reich, thousands of Germans had emigrated to various Latin American countries. Many of these transplants were tied to their homeland through various pressures, some patriotic, some compulsory. The Hitler regime's Condor Airlines helped many new airlines spring up in South America and served an increasingly important role in the still-primitive transportation systems of these countries. German trading and export offices did business at concessionary rates, and their executives doubled as both intelligence officers and clandestine agents. Germany's support of Franco in Spain and later of Argentina's military dictatorships had won it enormous popularity among the conservative elements in South America, where neither Britain nor the United States was considered to be a friendly power. The surge of German influence in so much of South America was an unforeseen development that shocked Washington and led President Roosevelt to launch a number of diplomatic initiatives to win friends for the United States. Assuredly, the rest of the hemisphere could no longer be ignored.

In 1938 Clover and Allen traveled to Europe once more and spent considerable time in Berlin and Paris sampling the vastly different views of Hitler's forcible merger of Germany and Austria into the Greater German Reich. Allen was so alarmed by what he saw that when he returned to New York, he decided to run for Congress as a preparedness candidate. The campaign was a disaster from the start.

In that summer of 1938, Franklin Roosevelt set out to purge his party's congressional wing of those who opposed the New Deal. One of the rebels was a popular veteran Tammany Hall pol who had long held sway in the Sixteenth Congressional District of New York, which took in the East Sixties, where Allen and Clover had their town house. The district was overwhelmingly Democratic by registration, but Dulles was persuaded to run for the Republican nomination in the hope that without the incumbent as the Democratic nominee, he might be able to squeeze through on the preparedness issue. The trouble was that under New York's election laws, a candidate could file for any or all party nominations and voters could cross over in primary contests as they pleased. So the pro-Roosevelt loyalist Democrats nominated another man, but the banished incumbent blithely picked up the nomination of the leftist American Labor Party of New York and filed for reelection both as a Democrat and as a Republican. This meant the issue in the voters' minds was whether Franklin Roosevelt could dictate who their local congressman would be, not whether America's defense needs were being attended to. It was also something of a referendum on the New Deal itself.

All this left Dulles in a hopeless situation. He ran a dull, dignified campaign that won the endorsement of respectable newspapers such as the *New York Herald Tribune*. The campaign was confined to formal speeches to various political groups in the district, and there the Dulles precision of speech reassured rather than sparked the crowds. There is, in the printed campaign literature and newspaper articles about the race, a placidness about the Dulles campaign that contrasted with the rowdy effort to oust the incumbent that the Tammany forces were fighting out in the streets. Daughter Joan Dulles Buresch, who was fifteen at the time, remembers, "Mostly it was fun for us kids. We could lick envelopes after school and put up posters around the neighborhood. I do remember a lot of crowded rooms full of smoke and people, and I do remember that while he was disappointed at losing, it was not a big deal for my father or for us."[12]

It was a good thing, for the incumbent lost the Democratic nomination but beat Dulles by a three-to-two margin for the GOP nomination. There is an intriguing piece of correspondence kept in the Dulles campaign papers for 1938, a consoling note he sent in 1966 to another Republican friend and ex-OSS veteran who had suffered a political reverse. He wrote, "Dear Bill, I grieved at the results of the primary but hope that you are not discouraged. In my first efforts in politics a good many years ago, I got licked by a Democrat in the Republican primary." The note was to William J. Casey, who would become CIA director during the Reagan presidency.

The defeat drove Dulles more deeply into active GOP party politics. The loss had hardly disgraced him; if anything it had made him better known among New York Republicans, and he had at least fought in a good cause. He was, after all, just forty-five and was in his prime as a high-income Wall Street lawyer with an equally high profile in foreign affairs. Although partners' salaries remained closely guarded secrets at Sullivan & Cromwell, it has been estimated that in those years Foster, as senior partner, was pulling down in excess of $300,000 annually from the firm, not counting what he received for the various corporate directorships he held. It is not unreasonable to guess that Allen probably commanded a six-figure income as well from both the firm and his own corporate directorships.

Clover and Allen entertained a great deal. "They went to parties, they gave parties, a lot of dinners, as I recall," says Joan. "My father was a real extrovert, he loved parties and he loved to entertain. I think my mother did not enjoy the parties themselves, but she took pleasure in running the house side of things well. She took enormous satisfaction in arranging things, flowers, decor and functions; I just don't think she enjoyed the actual dinners and cocktail parties that much."

Eleanor Elliot, a cousin who later became Janet and Foster's social secretary during his time at the State Department, remembers as a young girl the lavish Christmas Eve dinner that Clover and Allen held during the late 1930s.

"Clover was very proud of her Maryland background, and they would have wonderful buffets of oysters and clams on ice brought up from the Chesapeake; they regularly had a terrapin brought up on the train to cook just before the party, and Clover used to stash it alive in Allen's bathtub, which always caused an uproar," she recalls.

"They were a very attractive couple. She wasn't beautiful in the traditional sense but she was statuesque all of her life and had a beautiful figure that she kept in good shape. Even when they had a lot of money, she never dressed expensively, but she dressed well. She went to Valentina, one of the top fashion designers of the day who did designs for Garbo and Gertrude Lawrence, and she would buy one or two dresses there and wear them rather than buy a lot of less expensive stuff," Elliot adds.[13]

Although Allen had not forsworn his romances, he at least settled down to a more sedate pace. For one thing, much of his travel at the time was by airplane, which was hardly as conducive to flirtations as the five-day trans-Atlantic crossing. At home, he was pretty much limited to a long-running and fairly public affair with a neighbor's wife who frequently partnered with him in tennis club doubles tournaments.

Joan Dulles Buresch recalls, "Oh, Mrs. Hawkins. Yes, we knew about her. She was a blonde tennis partner of Father's. She was lovely and a great tennis player and had an unfortunate husband, who was a friend of my mother's and who was in and out of state mental hospitals at the time. But Mrs. Hawkins was there with her family, and we saw them a lot. I remember we all felt sorry for her because her husband was often being confined in some institution or other for his problems. In fact I think my father and Mrs. Hawkins won some of those tennis tournaments, too."

One of Foster Dulles's sons also recalls that as a curious teenager he sometimes skulked beneath the stands of the tennis club hoping to catch a glimpse of "Uncle Allen and his lady friend up to something." Father Avery Dulles, now a much respected Jesuit theologian at Fordham, chuckles at the reminiscence. "Who told me about Mrs. Hawkins? My sister, probably. Who told her? Mother. I'm sure it was not my father; he never would have spoken to anyone about Uncle Allen. I doubt if he ever spoke to Uncle Allen about it."[14]

Says Eleanor Elliot, "My memory of those days was that Allen and Clover were very active and very social. There was always tennis on Long Island in the summer, and there was a lot of nightclubbing when they were in Manhattan. They not only went to the better clubs with law firm clients, but they went on their own for fun and to dance; they were always on the go, it seems."

She adds, "Yes, Allen had his romances and was not that discreet about it. But as far as I know, they were with women of a certain kind; not just of his class, but women who were in command of themselves, and I think many wanted something more out of life. I also know that however much they fought, and Clover and Allen had fierce rows sometimes, there was never any question of them separating, not that I can recall, and our families were very close at that time."

Often the rows centered on the increasing troubles their children faced. As Toddy approached young womanhood, her bouts of manic-depression became more acute and troubling. Young Allen now began to show some of the cost of not having his father actively involved in his life. Clover decided to hire a young man to be the boy's companion and sports tutor; the young man soon ran off to California with Toddy in an abortive elopement. One gets the impression of this time that like other branches of the Dulles clan, Clover, Allen, and the children were bound together by their love for each other, but as individuals it was increasingly hard to find happiness.

Even their social life began to change as the 1930s came to an end. Clover and Allen were more drawn toward the Republican smart set of young bankers and lawyers who looked to the end of Franklin Roosevelt's second term as an opportunity to vault ahead of their elders. A year before his congressional bid, Dulles had met Thomas Dewey, then thirty-five and a rising young district attorney for New York. Dewey was a hot political prospect with a national reputation as a tough lawman who fought organized crime in the huge metropolis. Despite the age difference, the two men quickly became friends and found they shared many of the same views. They made common cause with a growing number of Republicans who saw that their only hopes to wrest control of the White House in 1940 lay in repudiating the dour, do-nothing isolationism of the middle western wing of the GOP. They wanted a party that advanced a less grandiose version of the New Deal, along with a strong pro-preparedness position on defense. Such a party, they reasoned, stood a good chance at the polls even if the unthinkable occurred and Roosevelt stood for a third term. A third term was unthinkable, to be sure, but Roosevelt obliged the Republicans by running.

IT IS GENERALLY REPORTED that William Donovan did not get around to drafting plans for a spy service until well into 1940, and that he did not try to recruit Allen Dulles until the middle of that year. The most common story is that Donovan approached Dulles at the Republican National Convention in Philadelphia in the summer of 1940, took him into a hotel bar, and recruited him for a job in what would be the office of the Coordinator of Information, the precursor of the OSS.

But it looks more likely that Donovan was well into detailed discussions about the organizational structure of a new American spy service as early as 1937. It is certain that he was regularly gathering foreign intelligence for the U.S. government as a private citizen as early as 1935, so the topic of a future spy agency had to have been very much on his mind. Dulles and many others were also involved in such musings, especially Vincent Astor and the other ROOM members. President Roosevelt surely was aware of what was going on.

First confirmation of this comes from Allen Dulles himself. In his book on the German army's surrender in northern Italy in advance of V-E Day, Dulles pays tribute to Donovan's early concern with America's lack of a coordinated intelligence service: "In the years before the outbreak of World War II [Donovan] was already at work studying military affairs and *planning the type of intelligence organization America would need as soon as we became a belligerent*—which he felt was inevitable [emphasis added]."[15]

This fits other known facts about that period. As early as 1937, British military and naval intelligence officers hosted a secret conference in London with their U.S. counterparts in Army G-2 (general staff intelligence) and ONI (Office of Naval Intelligence) to discuss sharing information. Donovan and other private citizens took an early lead and assumed growing importance in fashioning a formal government secret service. The White House did not want to embroil itself in the controversy of setting up another intelligence service while the neutrality fevers ran so high on Capitol Hill. But something had to be done in the meantime.

Among the surviving firsthand witnesses to these early planning meetings is Edmund "Ned" Putzell, a close aide to Donovan at the time and, later, a senior OSS and CIA officer until he retired to go into private business. Putzell recalls coming down from Harvard Law School, where he was in his second year and being hired as a law clerk by Donovan in the spring of 1937. One of his early tasks was to help write Donovan's speeches and to accompany him, as a secretary, to the various confidential meetings he had on intelligence planning.

About that time, Putzell recalls, Donovan "began to beat on Roosevelt about the importance of a central intelligence, a strategic intelligence function. He had made a life's study of the impact of intelligence on world events. He had collected enough for four or five volumes on the subject...."

Putzell is firm that both Foster and Allen Dulles were active participants in these early discussions about the form and function of a spy service even though they may have given little thought of going to work in such an agency. "Both Dulleses had been friends with Donovan, and through him, I met them. I lived in New York for a while before I went to Washington [in 1939], and Donovan was talking to both of them even then. He needed people both with experience and ability, and they had it. You could not afford early missteps, so we looked to those he knew. He was very concerned about ability. Donovan had a house in Washington as well as the one in Beekman Place [in New York].

Allen Dulles was there one night, well before the election of 1940. My recollection is that it took Dulles some time to make up his mind [about playing an active role]. And understandably so, it was all a lot of pie in the sky at the moment."[16]

It might be advisable at this point to review just what was going on regarding a spy service in those days prior to the war in light of the common perception that America had no intelligence capacity and that Donovan "invented" one. First, there were no less than eight government agencies gathering intelligence over a wide area of coverage. In addition to the army's G-2 and navy's ONI, the FBI was having marked public success in rounding up German spies and saboteurs. There were also active programs within the Treasury's secret service, the Labor Department (immigration), as well as State, Commerce, and the Federal Communications Commission, which monitored international radio traffic.

Neither Donovan, Dulles, nor any of the others who partici-pated in these early talks intended to replace or even to preempt this existing intelligence system with a superimposed creation of their own. Rather, they focused on the two areas where America was particularly vulnerable. One was the arena of psychological warfare and propaganda, which the Nazis, Soviets, and other totalitarian aggressors had turned into a potent weapon that undermined the will of a target people to resist aggression. The other was an inability to take the already large flow of informa-tion that came into the existing intelligence establishment and examine it all as a first step in formulating policy choices. This lack was generally conceded by President Roosevelt and others in government and was referred to in the days before the attack on Pearl Harbor as "the twilight time."

After December 7, 1941, this failure to coordinate and inter-pret was called "the Pearl Harbor syndrome." The information was there, but policymakers could not manage it adequately.

Donovan had no particular desire to become the chief of just another spy agency. He had larger ambitions. If he could not be inside the cabinet, he would prefer an active military combat command, and he suggested, even as he was putting the final touches to his spy agency proposals, that he be put in charge of training a commando regiment to his specifications. Dulles also had no desire for a dreary desk job. He had long ago been weaned from the lure of government service. He was playing a larger role at the law firm and having all the satisfactions of the intelligence life as he traveled around the world for Sullivan & Cromwell without any of the constraints of working for a formal spy agency. He was also playing a more active political role that promised to make him a major force within the Republican Party, even if elected office was probably beyond his grasp.

Dulles was among a group of younger Wall Street lawyers who had begun to work within the Republican Party organization in New York to win the 1940 presidential nomination for Tom Dewey. Much of history wrongly demeans Dewey as a dullard and ignores what a revolutionary wind he blew through the dispirited ranks of the GOP. The humiliation of the Alf Landon debacle in 1936 had brought discredit on the traditional midwestern arch-conservative wing of the party. The younger, more urban Republicans wanted to fashion a new party look. By 1939, with the war in Europe an imminent threat, Dulles and others had difficult choices. They repudiated the strict neutrality stance of the establishment wing of the party. Yet they all opposed Roosevelt's attempts to collect more powers to the presidency under the guise of preparedness.

Ever immune to the risk of a conflict of interest, Allen became part of the intelligence planning debate in behalf of FDR even as he became a key adviser on foreign policy for Dewey. Not that Dulles was the only anti-Roosevelt participant whose advice on intelligence structure was being funneled back to the president.

Certainly Vincent Astor and the other well-born clubhouse spies were avowed Republicans; Donovan himself was an outspoken critic of the New Deal domestic programs but enjoyed FDR's special confidence on foreign matters. This perhaps had as much to do with Roosevelt's own attitudes toward men and issues. It helps to remember Roosevelt's Wilsonian ties; he had been a particularly energetic undersecretary of the navy during World War I and certainly was no stranger to the operations of the ONI or America's debt to British intelligence. FDR also had a capacity to put his trust in men regardless of whether he liked them personally. He never particularly warmed to Donovan, despite their having been law school classmates, yet FDR trusted him on intelligence. Later, in a similar vein, he would pick two senior Republicans for his War cabinet, when he named newspaper publisher Frank Knox as secretary of the navy and cabinet veteran Henry Stimson as secretary of war.

Donovan also had an advantage that virtually no one else had—a thorough grasp of intelligence theory. He had actually been out in the real world of global conflict and knew what trends were developing firsthand. In Thomas Troy's authoritative biography of Donovan,[17] the chronicle of his journeys to far-flung battlefields was unique to any military observer of the day because of his ability to gain access where others could not. The trail began in 1935 when, with the War Department's approval, Donovan paid his own way to Rome, where he secured from Mussolini personally all the passes he needed to get full briefings from General Badoglio on Italy's invasion of Ethiopia.[18]

Just what Donovan was up to that early in the day has recently become the focus of renewed speculation. Intelligence historian Brian R. Sullivan, who teaches at the Naval War College, asserts that he was on a secret mission from FDR to sound out Mussolini. According to Sullivan, "Roosevelt believed that Hitler was preparing for a war of conquest, probably by 1938 or 1939. Unable to take active measures against Germany himself, Roosevelt sought an international partner who could act for both of them. Roosevelt soon realized that the British and French governments did not possess the necessary determination. Instead, the president increasingly placed his hopes in the Fascist Italy of Benito Mussolini."[19] The Italian dictator apparently won credibility with FDR when, in July 1934, he rushed four infantry divisions to the Brenner Pass and forestalled a German occupation of Austria in the wake of the Nazi murder of the Austrian Chancellor Dollfuss.

But in 1935 Mussolini's true objectives were made plain when Italy invaded Ethiopia; the aggression provoked an economic embargo of Italy by the League of Nations. The attack also threatened to draw Britain into the war in order to protect its vital interests in the Suez Canal. Donovan's mission clearly was to find out where the Italians stood in their campaign and what impact there might be on FDR's worries about the other fascist state—Germany.

With passes signed personally by *Il Duce*, Donovan went everywhere and inspected Italian military innovations from huge bombers to hospital ships and transport motor pools. He went to the front lines of that barbaric conflict. His interviews with commanders at the brigade level covered army camp layout, combat tactics, diet, troop morale, and even the condition of the mules and horses. On his way back to Washington he shared his findings and picked up other intelligence from American diplomats throughout Europe, and all of it was digested and given to Roosevelt personally in the early weeks of 1936. For the next two years Donovan roamed seemingly at will through Europe as it prepared for war. He attended German army maneuvers on a regular basis, inspected Czechoslovakia's defenses, toured the Balkans, and was General Franco's personal guest in Spain during the attack along the Ebro River. Each time he returned, his detailed reports were gratefully absorbed throughout the prewar intelligence establishment.

History teaches there is no inevitability to events. The development of a central intelligence capability might have rested there, and Donovan could have gone on into a combat command during the war. But Donovan fell heir to an ally, and that new alliance probably tipped the historical balance between the creation of the OSS as we know it or some other variant under some divided command. The new arrival was Donovan's old dining partner from his intelligence visit to London in 1916, William Stephenson.

Stephenson is memorialized forever as the "Man Called Intrepid."[20] He had ended World War I as one of the Royal Air Force's most decorated flying aces; despite his war wounds he had toughened himself up to win a world championship belt as an amateur lightweight boxer. Returning to Canada, he had become a millionaire many times over with inventions in mining machinery, but his ties to British intelligence, and especially to his old colleague William Wiseman, remained strong. Wiseman, too, had remained in America after the war. Nominally he had become an investment banker with the New York firm of Kuhn, Loeb and Co., but actually he remained an agent in place for the MI6 service.

The story of Britain's involvement in the establishment of the OSS—and indeed, of its campaign to drag the United States into its second European war—has been well told in any number of other histories, and we need only recount a summary from the standpoint of the involvement of Allen Dulles.[21]

On September 15, 1939, FDR initiated the first of the long series of confidential communications between himself (code-named POTUS) and "Naval Person," as Winston Churchill was known, for he had become first lord of the admiralty to the luckless Neville Chamberlain. That autumn and winter, Stephenson used his cover as an internationally recognized metals expert to learn that the Germans had specific plans of using a hydroelectric plant in Norway to produce the heavy water their scientists needed to construct an atomic bomb. In March 1940 Stephenson brought back firm evidence that an atomic bomb program was going on inside Hitler's Reich. By April he was in Washington bearing that news as well as Churchill's proposal for a cooperative effort on intelligence for North America and Britain. Stephenson was to link British security services with the Royal Canadian Mounted Police and the FBI.

Once inside the United States, Stephenson set himself up on the 35th and 36th floors of Rockefeller Center in Manhattan as the representative of the British Passport Control Office and proceeded to go his own way, despite J. Edgar Hoover's protests and interference. In time, he eased out of his ties with Hoover and made common cause with Donovan. While the MI6 and FBI operations against sabotage and subversion in South America were working well enough, Stephenson needed help with the other part of the mission Churchill had assigned—"to assure sufficient aid for Britain... and eventually to bring the United States into the war."[22] Neither prospect looked good. FDR faced a reelection campaign for an unheard of third term. The temper of Congress already was fiercely isolationist, and the lawmakers had specifically barred Roosevelt from handing over any material aid to Britain even though London was desperate for warships to keep its vital sea lanes open for supplies. U.S. Ambassador Joseph Kennedy spoke for many State Department firsthand observers who witnessed France's collapse that spring when he urged Roosevelt in a July 4 message that America must not be "left holding the bag in a war in which the Allies expect to be beaten."

American public opinion was solidly against joining in the war. The top-secret *Weekly Political Intelligence Summary*, which

MI6 circulated only to senior British cabinet officials and select heads of Commonwealth governments, glumly noted in the spring of 1940 that a series of Gallup Poll surveys commissioned by the agency in September 1939 had asked, "If it appears that Germany is defeating England and France should the United States declare war on Germany, and send our army and navy to Europe to fight? In that poll, 56 percent of the respondents had said 'No'; last October 71 percent; and now 77 percent."[23]

Stephenson turned to a sympathetic new face in the Roosevelt war cabinet, Navy Secretary Frank Knox, and together they advanced the notion to the president that Donovan would be the ideal man to go to Britain and see firsthand if the British could hang on. On July 14, after a hurried briefing by Roosevelt at the White House, Donovan flew to London, where he was given the kind of head-turning treatment and access that Britons are noted for when they want something. Not that Donovan minded much; he was being sent there by FDR to be seduced.

Donovan had detailed conferences with Churchill (by then prime minister) and the entire cabinet. There were emotional conversations with King George VI, and riveting briefings that argued, correctly, that the Royal Air Force was winning the Battle of Britain. America's help was a vital part of what must be a final triumph over the fascist reign of terror in Europe. Donovan returned on August 8 and threw his law firm headlong into the detailed research and legal brief that gave FDR the justification he needed to bypass the congressional strictures and to authorize the transfer of fifty-four U.S. warships of the destroyer class to Britain at once. The deal was a swap for the American right to set up advance warning naval and air bases on British islands in the North Atlantic.

He also returned with another important item, a firm proposal from Churchill for British assistance if the United States would go ahead and set up its own intelligence service above and beyond that which currently existed. After Roosevelt's reelection in November, he turned with understandable reluctance to face the hardest prospect of all, that America must, somehow, get ready to enter a European war on Britain's side. Since that was so, and Churchill never doubted it, America would need a full-dress spy service that could cover both European and Pacific theaters. It also must secure the Western Hemisphere since, in the worst of scenarios, the British authorities had planned to move their royal family and government to Canada should their home islands be overrun.

On December 17, 1940, Donovan left New York again for a three-month British tour of the Mediterranean theater of war organized by Churchill. Once again, Donovan roamed the front lines from North Africa to the Balkans, often frightening his hosts with the risks he took to get firsthand information. Donovan was impressed by Churchill's emphasis on a strong effort to foster resistance and sabotage behind the enemy lines directed by an Allied espionage offensive. One of the souvenirs carried away by Donovan from a briefing was a small canvas-covered pamphlet that was an astonishingly accurate primer on the German intelligence services; the booklet carries a red stripe across its cover and the stern warning: "Under no circumstances is this to be removed from the Imperial War Room." It is one of the treasures of Donovan's papers at the U.S. Army War College in Carlisle, Pennsylvania.[24]

In addition to the invaluable personal witness to the war that Donovan brought home, he arrived with a firm outline of a plan for a new American spy service and for British assistance to the United States in building it. He was almost too late with his proposal. Hoover and General Sherman Miles of G-2 continued their squabbling over turf and manpower. The FBI's friction with Stephenson's now full-blown operations in New York City moved President Roosevelt out of frustration to name Vincent Astor to be "coordinator" of intelligence operations in New York, and, later, it was proposed that Astor act as "referee" between the warring services. Donovan, however, was able to put a broad-brush organization plan into the hands of Frank Knox by April 26, and on the strength of that, Roosevelt asked Donovan on May 31 to draw up a detailed table of organization. This was what Donovan had been waiting for. Ned Putzell reports that he and other Donovan aides had moved to Washington late in 1939. The Donovan team began to work in basement quarters at the White House during most of 1940 and the early months of 1941, operating under cover, all with Roosevelt's personal approval. The British Royal Navy had added formal weight of its own to press the case for Donovan's plan. Admiral John Godfrey, head of British ONI, and his aide, Lieutenant Commander Ian Fleming (later the creator of spy hero James Bond), arrived to urge the president to move. On June 11, 1941, Donovan submitted to President Roosevelt a detailed proposal for a "Service of Strategic Information."

On June 18, 1941, Roosevelt met with Donovan and then penned a note to officials in the Bureau of the Budget to set up the office of Coordinator of Information (COI) and to fund it initially out of the $100 million in secret, unvouchered funds that Congress had appropriated for that and other preparedness actions. Donovan was to be paid no salary and reimbursed only for billable expenses; he even had to pay the government for the cost of the secret scrambler phones that were installed in his homes in Georgetown and Beekman Place. The formal marching orders were intentionally vague. The COI was "to collect and analyze all information and data, which may bear upon the national security... correlate such information and data... [and make] such information and data available to the president and to such departments and officials of the Government as the president may determine." The official creation of the COI was set for July 11. Buried in the

Federal Register notice published on July 15, there also was what the British called the "special means" clause, which empowered the new agency to conduct "such supplementary activities as may facilitate the securing of information important for national security not now available to the Government...." Thus the power to gather covert intelligence and conduct clandestine war by all means possible was established at last. Once more, the spy service was authorized by executive order, albeit without reference to Congress.

Although the COI was now authorized it hardly was encouraged. The Budget Bureau planners who followed FDR's directive assumed that a budget of slightly less than $1.5 million would be ample funds for the first year for the ninety-two officers and staff the COI was originally organized around; after all, Army G-2 had only eighty personnel in Washington and another thirty military attachés around the world. How much bigger did Donovan think he needed to be? The answer came with disconcerting speed. Before the year was out, COI had more than six hundred people on board, and Donovan was demanding, and getting, another $10 million from the shocked budget keepers. By the end of the war, the OSS (which COI was renamed in 1942) would have grown to more than thirteen hundred. The ultimate downfall of the OSS could be attributed in part to the constant unease that gripped the accountants of the Bureau of the Budget over the huge outlays of unvouchered money.

The OSS would be for the post–World War II generation of young leaders what the Paris Peace Conference had been to the Dulles brothers' generation. When we look ahead twenty years to the end of Allen Dulles's career, it is astonishing how many of the "fresh faces" of the Kennedy and even later administrations— men like Walt Rostow, Arthur Schlesinger, Jr., Dean Rusk, Arthur Goldberg, Ralph Bunche, William Colby, Richard Helms, and William Casey, to name a few—had earned their spurs in Bill

Donovan's band of brothers. The OSS was assembled with astonishing speed because young men and women were passed onto
the agency through the established network of college professors,
bankers, industrialists, newspaper publishers, and the like who
were friends of Donovan.

During these hectic and formative months, Allen Dulles was
of service to Donovan on the outside. From 1939 onward, Dulles
had become one of the leading public proponents of the view that
America's own defense security was inextricably entwined with
that of Western Europe, and particularly with that of Britain. That
year, he and Hamilton Fish Armstrong published a sequel to their
1936 argument against isolationism. In *Can We Stay Neutral?*[25]
the two advanced the argument that the very notion of neutrality
was something of a threat to American security because laws that
mandated an insularity from world events limited the ability of a
president to maneuver in times of crisis. Further, if the United
States really were to remain aloof from the war crisis around the
world, then the safety of other, smaller neutrals would be equally
in jeopardy.

Dulles also became an active campaigner for Thomas
Dewey's 1940 run for the Republican presidential nomination. He
took the job of heading the small team of activists who drafted
foreign policy papers for the candidate. In February, Clover and
Allen joined their friends the Lamott Belins for a motor holiday
along the Florida Gulf Coast to New Orleans. Then Clover
returned to New York while Allen pushed on through a series of
Dewey campaign speeches to Republican clubs as far west as
Houston. He and Belin also actively tapped into Du Pont family
resources for campaign contributions for Dewey. But the prosecu-
tor was viewed by party regulars as being too liberal, too Eastern,
and too internationalist; they were more reassured by Wendell
Willkie, who, though a successful Wall Streeter, played up his mid-

western roots and used a shrewd last-minute campaign blitz to battle through the convention in Philadelphia in late June. It did not help that the final days of the campaign saw the evacuation of more than 300,000 British troops from Dunkirk and the German conquest of most of northern France in the weeks that followed.

In several versions of his reminiscences, Allen Dulles would assert that he was not offered a job in the COI organization until after the Pearl Harbor disaster. However, it appears from the OSS's own history that Donovan was waiting for Dulles when he returned from his holiday and formally asked him to open the agency's important New York office in October 1941; Dulles apparently agreed at once.

Dulles commandeered part of Room 3603 in Rockefeller Center, a suite occupied by Stephenson's British security coordinator's office. Stephenson himself was busy shifting the first American recruits to the combat, cipher, and operations training center the British had set up in Ontario, and Donovan and his Washington staff were busy interviewing and leasing farmland in Maryland and Virginia for expanded training camps. They also had to compile the first archives of maps, tidal reports, crop data, political profiles, and other vital information on regions of the world where America had not bothered even to have diplomatic relations. COI, as it turned out, was too busy getting started to be blamed, later, in the bitter recriminations that followed Pearl Harbor.

As discovered in the aftermath investigation, the famed navy *Magic* decryptions of the Japanese diplomatic and naval traffic in the days before the attack were denied to Donovan or to any of his aides during the weeks leading up to the disaster of December 7. It was probably just as well for COI's future that Donovan was cut out of the *Magic* loop. There is no evidence that the new agency would have been any more alert to the impending attack; in fact, an argument can be made that it would not. In September 1941

Donovan hired Edgar Ansel Mowrer, a friend and talented political journalist, to go on a three-month tour of the Far East to assess the situation. Mowrer wrote for the *Chicago Daily News*, owned by Navy Secretary Knox, and he carried Donovan's personal letter of introduction plus credentials from Knox that gave him access to American and British officials from Pearl Harbor to Australia to Burma. His job was "to set down any conclusion reached as to Japanese intentions and possibilities in the near future."

Mowrer was a seasoned China hand as a journalist and an indefatigable traveler. He ranged through Manila, Singapore, Batavia, Bandung, Bangkok, Chunking, and Hong Kong. He judged the British defenses of Singapore "sufficient" and "invulnerable" and toured an Australian air base where, he noted approvingly, all the aircraft were American. He met with young Joseph Alsop at the air base in China where Alsop served as the secretary to the legendary Colonel Claire Chennault and his "Flying Tigers" air volunteers. In Manila, he heard General Douglas MacArthur argue dismissively that the Japanese had "a first class fleet... but a shoddy one- to two-billion–dollar Army which has completely broken down and shown its worthlessness in China." The consensus was that, having failed to move in the summer of 1940, Japan now faced the dilemma of either attacking somewhere new against prohibitive odds or giving up some of its gains. The consensus bet was that the Japanese might well attack further north through Manchuria and China to carve off easternmost ports of the Soviet Union. "Japan is in a fix," Mowrer concluded.[26]

His report on Japan's war capabilities was sent to Donovan dated December 3, 1941.

CHAPTER SEVEN

January–November 1942

"From my experience I would say that one-third of the mistakes come from disregarding the intelligence available, one-third come from a false analysis of the intelligence available and about one-third from not having the intelligence available."
—*Allen Dulles*

ALLEN DULLES LIKED TO reminisce that he was relaxing at the Lloyd Neck house on Long Island listening to a radio broadcast of a football game between the old Brooklyn Dodgers and the New York Giants when the announcer broke in with the news that the Japanese had attacked Pearl Harbor. Part of the yarn was that William Donovan was at the Polo Grounds watching the same football game when he was called to a telephone; James Roosevelt, the president's son and White House aide, told him the news of the attack and ordered him back to Washington. "A few days after that I joined up with Bill Donovan and from then on I was quite busy," Dulles recalled.[1]

It is unlikely that Donovan had waited that long. His top priority was to get the COI fully operational in New York City. If the analysts Donovan recruited by the dozen for service in Washington were to have anything to analyze, much of it would first have to be gathered in New York. Wanted urgently were the mundane raw ingredients of intelligence: maps, directories of names, geographical surveys, tidal charts, memberships of labor unions, dues rolls of political groups and émigré organizations, shipping schedules, and radio broadcast frequencies. Liaison had to be started in earnest with William Stephenson and the MI6 operation in Rockefeller Center. Allen Dulles was the obvious choice to get such an operation rolling.

"In those days we were starting from scratch. No one was beating on our doors to get in. Few people knew about us to begin with, and the concern about the war was not as great in those days before Pearl Harbor because we were not close enough to hostilities," recalls Ned Putzell, Donovan's aide. "New York was the logical first place, and Dulles was the logical guy because of his contacts. He started bringing people in right away."[2]

Early in February 1942 Dulles had fully staffed his offices at 3603 Rockefeller Center. Among the tenants that had been ousted had been one of Stephenson's own sections, although Dulles whimsically kept the same sign on the door, "Rough Diamonds, Ltd." Among the first people recruited was Betty Carp, who, significantly, left Istanbul before the Pearl Harbor attack on a perilous airplane journey of five weeks across Africa and the North Atlantic. She was at once put to work compiling biographies of the major political players of the Balkans, many of whom she knew personally. She also resumed a friendship in Washington with a Russian woman who was the private secretary to Maxim Litvinov, the Soviet ambassador to the United States. She began a regular schedule of visits to the lonely woman, who liked to pour out her troubles, and an astonishing amount of inside information, to the sympathetic Carp. Betty proved to be one of the most versatile intelligence providers within the COI organization. Unescorted and relying only on her language ability and nerve, she crashed a private club for Greek merchant sailors in the New York dock district. Even though the club was being run by communists for their own recruitment purposes, Betty began to round up likely prospects for the agency among the sailors who would be sailing back to Mediterranean ports.

Another priceless provider of intelligence biography was Sigrid Schultz, who had spent most of the between-the-war years as a journalist in Berlin for major newspapers such as the *Chicago Tribune*. She had known most of the Nazi hierarchy from their beginnings as vulgar street brawlers, and her chronicles of the murderous power struggles among Hitler's henchmen were spiced with delicious gossip about the sexual predations and larcenous corruption of most of them. Of more use and interest to Dulles and Donovan were Schultz's updated reports on the whereabouts and positions of those prominent Germans who were known to be firmly anti-Hitler.

This was crucial information. America was late to the wartime intelligence game. Unlike the previous war, plausible visits by observers behind enemy lines would not be possible; dropping trained agents into the Third Reich was going to be a high-risk, low-yield process that was valuable only when it was used to gain immediate military intelligence needed for combat operations. While the British and French had years to insert "stay behind" agents who remained in place after the German frontiers had closed, the COI would have to reach out to sympathetic Germans who could be trusted on both sides of the barbed wire. The list of prominent anti-Nazi Germans compiled in New York in 1941 contained most of the final group of desperate plotters who tried and failed to kill Hitler in the disastrous 20th of July plot in 1944. Those on Dulles's list were prominent Germans he had dealt with as a peace negotiator and lawyer for twenty years, including such men as Count Helmuth von Moltke and Adam von Trott zu Solz, aristocrats with important positions in the Foreign Ministry. There were Arthur Nebe, a police official close to SS leader Heinrich Himmler; such generals as von Hammerstein, Beck, and Falkhausen; and Colonel Count Klaus von Stauffenberg, who would actually put the bomb in Hitler's headquarters in East Prussia three years later.

Dulles needed more than well-intentioned assassins, however; he needed labor leaders, church leaders, editors, academicians, and moderate government officials who not only could assist the war effort but also could form the basis for a new democratic Germany after the war was over. To that end, Donovan set up a separate operation in New York and recruited Arthur Goldberg to come from Chicago in February 1942 to begin systematic contact with refugees from the European trade unions who still had contacts in the occupied countries of Europe and inside the Third Reich itself. Goldberg, the future Supreme Court justice, had wide experience as a labor lawyer, and he was assisted for a while by Gerhard ("Gary") Van Arkel, who had been general counsel for the National Labor Relations Board before he was recruited into the COI. Men of science and scholarship as well as anti-Nazi government officials such as Konrad Adenauer, the mayor of Cologne, all had to be listed, studied, and ranked according to their suitability both for clandestine contacts during the war and for postwar positions of power in a Germany that would have to be built anew. A valuable source of insight into these personalities was Emmy Rado, a Swiss-American psychiatrist and wife of Sandor Rado, the Hungarian analyst and colleague of Sigmund Freud.

"Things developed so quickly and so many people began to show up that we got a little concerned," Ned Putzell recalled. "I remember being scared to death when Bill Stephenson brought down from Canada a woman who claimed to have been educated at Moscow University and to have spied on the Germans for the Russians. We were afraid that she might even be a triple-agent and wouldn't let her near the Rockefeller offices."

Dulles's New York offices certainly were outgrowing their space and spreading around town as new functions were added. Foreign broadcast monitoring became a major job. David Bruce was put in charge of the Special Activities Branch within the COI, which in part meant he had to create a counterintelligence capability to protect the new agency even though it was explicitly forbidden in its charter from carrying on spying activities inside the United States. That task should have been reserved to Hoover's FBI, but Dulles and Bruce quickly had reason to suspect that the Justice Department agents had placed observers within the New York office and were tapping the COI telephones. When almost verbatim reports of COI conversations began to appear in the syndicated newspaper columns of Drew Pearson and other Hoover journalistic favorites, the fledgling agency began to protect itself from its own government as well as from enemy penetration.[3]

The product of basic intelligence information in graphic and narrative form began to flow out of the COI to the White House and then on through the highest levels of the policy-making structure. There could be no doubt that the intelligence service was up and running by the time FDR signed the formal charter turning the COI into the OSS on June 13, putting it under the supervision of the Joint Chiefs of Staff. Donovan did not get all the independence he wanted, and some commanders, most notably General MacArthur, barred OSS operations from their theaters altogether. But Donovan also was assured that his child would not now be taken over by the rival intelligence services and that, by the time the first American soldiers went into combat, agents of the OSS would be established in enemy territories waiting to help them come ashore.

Donovan proposed to President Roosevelt a plan to make Switzerland a key outpost for the OSS penetration of Hitler's Germany and for the support of the resistance groups in Italy and France, key elements in any successful invasion of Occupied Europe. He argued:

Switzerland is now, as it was in the last war, the one most advantageous place for the obtaining of information concerning the European Axis powers. Analysis of the telegrams reaching the State Department from various posts in Europe in which we still have representatives shows that the information from Switzerland is far more important than from any other post. Nevertheless, the activities of our Legation must remain official and circumscribed, and the Minister and his associates may not be in a position to take the necessary steps to greatly extend the scope of their information....

We have finally worked out with the State Department the appointment of a representative of this organization to proceed to Bern as "Financial Attaché." The representative is a man of almost a life-time experience in an analogous type of work. He will head up our service there... carry on the clandestine work; handle the machinery of contact, transmission of messages, etc.... However, we need badly a man of a different type; some person of a quality who can mingle freely with intellectual and business circles in Switzerland in order to tap the constant and enormous flow of information that comes from Germany and Italy to these people. Such a man as I envisage would have no relation to the clandestine work other than making his reports through the Financial Attaché, although he would, of course, consult with the Attaché whenever advisable. The pretext of the presence of such as man in Switzerland under present conditions is extremely difficult to find. The pretext would have to be highly adequate; otherwise, a man moving around the country would be immediately suspected. We may be driven to adopting some official cover for such a representation. As soon as we find the man we need and check him with the Department of State I shall advise you.[4]

Donovan had already begun serious talks with Allen Dulles in New York about an overseas assignment. London station chief was one prospect, but neither man was enthusiastic about putting Dulles there. David Bruce turned out to be an inspired choice. Besides, Dulles abhorred the amount of administrative work the London operation would necessarily involve. London was too close to Washington but not close enough to where the action really was—inside Europe itself.

Ned Putzell remembered, "Bern and Allen Dulles were a natural. He wanted it, Donovan wanted it. Donovan believed all along that we had to have some means of reading the Germans from Switzerland, it was such a hotbed of intelligence. He set three places as main stations, London, Bern, and Madrid. They talked about it for years. The big question was, what would happen if Allen were locked in? The question was, would the Germans invade Switzerland? Even though he wanted to go, Allen debated it for quite a while; I remember one night down at the Beekman Place house, doing the pros and cons with him and Donovan."

After all, Dulles was forty-nine and had a family to consider. His health, while still robust, was a question because of the increasing severity of gout attacks, which sometimes immobilized him for days if he were under stress. And Bern would be stressful enough; in fact it would be downright dangerous. With only a narrow exit window to the rest of the world through Vichy France, Switzerland was virtually surrounded by the Axis menace, and an actual invasion by the Germans was feared at any minute.

But Switzerland was the only place in Europe where all of the major participants in the global war could have a common meeting place. Even the Japanese delegations to the various capitals within Hitler's Fortress Europe liked to gather in Bern to have a private conversation. The Chinese and Russians were there as well, and so were representatives of exile groups from other nations, along with the remnants of the various League of

Nations international agencies and the relief and refugee groups of a score of religious and charitable organizations. Switzerland was also a major business and banking center for Europe, and across its borders passed a steady stream of travelers, refugees, and espionage agents. In short, Switzerland was one big clandestine conversation, and Swiss intelligence knew it. But the Swiss were serious about maintaining their posture of neutrality, and the last thing they wanted was to give either Hitler or Mussolini any provocation that might move them to send troops in. So the staffs of foreign embassies, especially those of the Axis and the Allies, were under strict watch.

As one OSS report noted: "In Bern and other cities transparent plain clothes men were planted in all important hotels and restaurants. For reasons of economy the Swiss did not go to the expense of employing many of these men, so that it was impossible not to spot them all after a time. For over two years one of these men was assigned to the Schweizerhoff Grill to watch Americans and British. Searches of hotel rooms were by no means uncommon. The mails were never safe. Even letters dropped by messenger in mailboxes inside private houses were intercepted and photographed. For this reason OSS correspondence was usually sent by courier to consulates to be called for. The telephone was under constant surveillance, practically all conversations were recorded on disks... there were patrols on railroad trains and in stations. Provocative agents were occasionally planted...."[5]

A related reason Donovan had for not being fully candid with the State Department about his choice of Bern station chief lay in the fact that State already had a very good intelligence operation inside the American Legation, and the diplomats were most alarmed that Donovan's spies might rampage around the country and invite sanctions from the Swiss government. The ambassador was none other than Leland Harrison, who had started State's intelligence program for Robert Lansing nearly twenty-five years earlier. He was supported by the legation's military attaché, General Barnwell ("Barney") Legge, a highly effective military intelligence veteran of the previous war. Unlike in 1917, the legation was fully staffed with trained personnel who had been in place since 1940. Harrison's operation had already set up close operating partnerships with the exile group intelligence services of those countries overrun by either Germany, Italy, or the Soviet Union.[6]

So Donovan began to build his Bern base with some circumspection. In early March he had sent Gerald Mayer to Bern as a legation "technical adviser" to set up the propaganda services needed by the Office of War Information. In May, even before Donovan's letter to Roosevelt, the "financial attaché" had been picked out of a group of three men who had undergone training in codes and intelligence procedures at the COI's training center. Charles B. Dyar was a Treasury finance officer whose language skills were listed as "excellent German, French and Dutch, good Italian and Spanish." He did have an important job to do as the American liaison with the Swiss banks, the Swiss National Bank central institution, and the multination clearinghouse Bank for International Settlements.

Germany was desperate for gold and for the hard currencies of nations outside the war zone. This money was needed to finance purchases of vital war materials such as tungsten from Spain and metals and other products from Latin America and Africa. Moreover, Switzerland was the base for Berlin's shipments of money to the Ausland Organization and other clandestine groups around the world that were to continue the fifth column struggle. The British, for example, had already reported to Washington that huge sums of Nazi money were being funneled to several of the independence movements in India; other sums were going to support a radio-relay link set up in South Africa by the sympathetic Boer government there; still other amounts were supporting German efforts in

Ireland. And there was reason to believe that even larger sums were going to South America, not only to preserve the flow of raw materials but also to stir up enough pro-German sentiment in the Western Hemisphere to frighten Washington. The British were as anxious as Donovan to find out how much gold and money was coming out of Switzerland and to shut the flow off tight.[7]

While Donovan and Dulles continued to plot, Clover Dulles was unhappy at the prospect of being left in New York for an indefinite time. While Clover was pleased that her husband was reunited with his beloved intelligence craft, she understood that the post would be too dangerous for him if she were there as a potential target. This left Clover facing a bleak future. Toddy was now out of school for good and ultimately would move to Washington where she would get a job as a research analyst and assistant inside the OSS. Joan was finishing her college term, and young Allen was getting to the age where he would be sent off to a prep school.

Allen's departure for a foreign adventure also spelled the end of their active social life and meant that even with Sullivan & Cromwell paying her his partner's stipend there would be financial constraints that Clover would have to face alone.

"My mother definitely was not a committee woman type of the kind they had in those days; you know, rolling bandages, tea, and so on. She had her prison work, and that was important, but it clearly would not be enough. So she got a job as a supervisor at a factory over in Brooklyn, I think, that made radium dials for fighter planes and bombers. She worked very hard at it and was quite proud," daughter Joan remembers. "I think she would have liked to have gone with Father but knew she could not; but she certainly went to Europe the first opportunity she got."

Dulles had a rush of meetings in both Washington and New York before he was ready to go.[8] He was given more than one hundred letters of introduction from American residents to Swiss relatives and friends who might be helpful information sources. There were also liaison meetings with the intelligence services of the exile groups, including an important cooperative agreement that Dulles and Arthur Goldberg worked out with David Ben-Gurion and Chaim Weitzman, who were in the New York offices of the Jewish Agency; both men would later be founders of the nation of Israel. Through their New York director, Emanuel Neumann, both Weitzman and Ben-Gurion agreed to share the intelligence flows that they received from their outposts in Sweden, Turkey, and, most important for Dulles, from Switzerland, as well as to undertake joint operations with the OSS in the Middle East.[9]

The OSS-Zionist cooperation is an important incident in the history of World War II intelligence. For Allen Dulles, it meant he was able to plug into one of the most skilled intelligence operations of the war; the Zionists kept contacts throughout Europe, even deep inside the Third Reich itself. But the deal meant more in a broader policy sense. During the previous war, matters involving Zionist affairs, indeed Jewish matters generally, were treated as the exclusive province of Britain's Foreign Office and MI6. But by the outbreak of war in 1939, the Zionists were no longer passively lobbying for a homeland in Palestine, and U.S. diplomats were no longer resigned to viewing the Middle East as an exclusively British sphere of influence.

More immediate tasks faced Dulles once he got to Bern. The military planners getting ready for the Operation Torch invasion of North Africa desperately needed order-of-battle information about the location of German divisions inside Occupied Europe, and especially in southern France. The amount of basic organizational information the Army G-2 needed from Dulles was staggering; the American planners even lacked simple organizational tables for different *Wehrmacht* combat unit formations on the Mediterranean coast. Nor could the British provide locations for specific *Panzer* tank divisions or even whether any *Wehrmacht* troop concentrations were inside Italy at all. Beyond that, the Research and Analysis (R&A) wing had an insatiable appetite for information of almost any consequence from inside Fortress Europe. Not only did R&A want to know the target locations and coordinates of every chemical, fertilizer, metal, tool, and transport manufacturing plant in Europe, it wanted the latest information about products such as aircraft engines, armaments, synthetic fuels and rubber, plastics, clothing, and food items. It wanted up-to-date maps, train schedules, work passes, identity cards of all nations and occupations, military uniforms of all services, samples of any and all weapons, and copies of daily newspapers. R&A needed everything Allen Dulles could lay his hands on.

Needless to say, he was not going to undertake the task by himself. Frederick J. Stadler, who had Swiss citizenship, was sent to Bern in August to head up a counterintelligence program to protect the U.S. operation from penetration by friend and foe alike. Later, he would be succeeded by Paul Blum. Another helper was a former Standard Oil scientific expert, Fred R. Loofbourow, who went in October as petroleum attaché in Zurich, under the guise of being vice consul there, so he could keep contact with Swiss chemical and petroleum companies that did business throughout Occupied Europe. Dulles had drafted Max Shoop, an old Sullivan & Cromwell colleague from the firm's Paris office, to open offices in Geneva under the cover that he was an international lawyer who was trying to clear up wartime confusion involving business deals and financial claims for American clients. His job was to handle the financing and support of most of the resistance chains in Italy and the French *maquis* (resistance) groups. Royall Tyler, an American who worked for the Bank for International Settlements, provided links to financiers who traveled across the border to all the occupied countries. Others would be recruited later. Donald Jones surfaced in Locarno and was put to work organizing Italian resistance groups across the border under the cover of a vice consul's office there. Walter Sholes, who was a legitimate diplomatic consul at Basle, was recruited for intelligence tasks involving that important banking and railroad center.

But Dulles had to get to Bern first; he almost did not make it. The paperwork for the station chief dragged on and on through the bureaucratic maze as his long-standing foes took their revenge. There were disputes over compensation and expenses and who would bear the cost for his various operations. Even though there had been formal discussions about the appointment since spring, it would take three months after Donovan formally notified the State Department in July that Dulles was to go before the final papers came through. At one point, in late October, Dulles was reduced to formally forswearing any government pay for his service.

> I do not propose to take any salary, but I should expect to draw, for my necessary living expenses, entertainment, etc., subject to any accounting which you may wish me to make. I shall probably make a cable remittance, either personally or through my firm, of some five thousand dollars, or so, which I can use initially for living expenses, and which would be reimbursed by OSS. I might also ask for a small allowance of a few hundred dollars to cover incidental expenses in connection with my departure and the purchase of equipment which I would not otherwise require. We might also discuss the question of drawing funds for any operational expenses and how that would be worked out between Drum [at the legation] and myself.[10]

Even though, in the strictest sense, such an arrangement was not orthodox even for those times, it was not unprecedented. Donovan himself drew no government salary during his OSS years until he received his elevation to general. He even refused to bill for expenses when he found out he had to itemize each claim. Other veterans of the rush to build up either the OSS or other wartime agency staffs have told the author that they were supported at least for a time by their old corporations, banks, or law firms while their families were adjusting to the expensive move to Washington.

For Allen Dulles, the final days before his departure grew crowded as the minutiae of spycraft competed with negotiations with Foster to wind up his legal affairs and to make sure his family would continue to be supported by Sullivan & Cromwell. He was given the OSS code designation "110," with Donovan being "109," and David Bruce "105." Dulles in his capacity as Bern station chief was to send cables to "Victor" in Washington from his station, which was given the transparent designation "Burns."[11] Fred Dolbeare, his old friend from the early days in Vienna, took over as head of the New York office.

The agency he left behind had already changed beyond all recognition from what it had been fifteen months earlier. Training camps in the Maryland hills and Virginia hunt country were processing the first classes of OSS officers who would test themselves against the Axis war machine. Many would go on to distinguished careers in Cold War intelligence work; any list of them has to include such men as Stewart Alsop, Tom Braden, Tracy Barnes, Andrew Berding, Frank Canfield, Richard Helms, William Colby, Arthur Schlesinger, Jr., and Walt Rostow. The OSS had outgrown Donovan's original headquarters at the Apex Building and managed to appropriate a relatively new compound of buildings at 2430 E Street N.W. "The Kremlin," as it remains known, was home to both the OSS and the succeeding spy agencies through Dulles's own directorship of the CIA. The complex is a collection of federal period mansions arranged like a campus on the tree-shaded hill that overlooks the Lincoln Memorial as one approaches it from the 23rd Street side of the State Department. The navy had built the complex during the 1930s to house its medical research facilities. Its built-in system of underground tunnels and huge metal storage safes for medical supplies was made to order for a spy service home. Moreover, it was one of the more salubrious locations in the summertime pesthole that Washington often was. Its North, East, and South buildings formed a U-shaped crescent that faced Theodore Roosevelt Island across the Potomac River, and the cool breeze off the river was most welcome in those pre–air conditioned days. That Allen Dulles dreamed that someday he would take command in the same first-floor office in the East Building that Donovan claimed for his own is pure conjecture; but there can be no doubt that "The Kremlin" was his kind of headquarters environment.

Finally, on November 2, he was off, flying to Lisbon. The plan then was to go by train across Spain and Vichy France to Geneva. But as Dulles tells the story:

> Unfortunately, because of bad weather, my plane for Lisbon was held up a couple of days in the Azores. I had lost valuable time. The [Operation Torch] landing, I knew, was imminent. From Lisbon I flew to Barcelona. The rest of the journey across Spain and Vichy France was to be by train. It was already November 8th when I took the train from Barcelona. On the way from Barcelona to the French frontier I had met some Swiss friends and we were lunching together at Port Bou, the last stop in Spain before crossing over into Vichy France, when the Swiss diplomatic courier, who was well known to my friends, came up to our table. "Have

you heard the news?" he exclaimed in great excitement. "The Americans and British are landing in North Africa."

I was still in neutral Spain and able to turn back if necessary, or I could go ahead and gamble on the possibility that the Nazis would take a few days to make up their minds about what to do. I had to assume, however, that at least they would occupy the lines of communication across France and would stop and search trains. I knew that my trip would be through an area close to where plenty of German troops were stationed. If I was picked up by the Nazis in Vichy France, the best I could hope for would be internment for the duration of the war. My diplomatic passport would be of little use to me. It was a tough decision, but I decided to go ahead. Across the frontier, in Vichy France, I received a reception in the town of Verrieres as though I were a part of an American liberation army come to free them from the Nazis. The French were delirious.

They had some sort of misconception that the American forces would be coming across the Mediterranean within a few days. As it turned out, they had to wait almost two years.

While my train made its way through France that night, I decided that if there were evidence of German controls I would try to slip away at one of the stops and disappear into the countryside in hopes of making contact with the French resistance, eventually perhaps to get over the border into Switzerland unofficially— or "black," as we used to call it.

At Annemasse, the last stop in France where all passengers for Switzerland had to alight to have their passports examined, I found that a person in civilian dress, obviously a German, was supervising the work of the French border officials. I had been told in Washington that there would probably be a Gestapo agent at this frontier. I was the only one among the passengers to fail to pass muster. The Gestapo man carefully put down in his notebook the particulars of my passport, and a few minutes later a French gendarme explained to me that an order had just been received from Vichy to detain all Americans and British presenting themselves at the frontier and to report all such cases to Marshal Petain directly. I took the gendarme aside and made to him the most impassioned and, I believe, most eloquent speech that I had ever made in French. Evoking the shades of Lafayette and Pershing, I impressed upon him the importance of letting me pass. I had a valid passport and visa and there was no justification for holding me up. I assured him Marshal Petain had many other things to worry about on that particular day besides my case. I also let him glimpse the content of my wallet. Neither patriotic speeches nor the implied offer of a small fortune seemed to move him. He went off to make his telephone call, leaving me to pace the platform. I began to case the areas in the hope of carrying out my plan of slipping away on foot to avoid being trapped there. It wouldn't have been easy.

Finally around noon, when it was about time for the train to leave for Geneva, the gendarme came up to me, hurriedly motioned for me to get on the train and whispered to me, "Allez passez. Vous voyez que notre collaboration n'est que symbolique [Go ahead. You see our cooperation (with the Germans) is only symbolic]."

The Gestapo man was nowhere to be seen. Later I learned that every day, promptly at noon, he went down the street to the nearest pub and had his drink of beer and his lunch. Nothing, including landings in Africa, could interfere with his fixed Germanic habits. The French authorities had gone through the motions of phoning Vichy, as they had been ordered to do. But once the Gestapo man had left his post for his noon siesta, they were free to act on their own, and they did. Within a matter of minutes I had crossed the French border into Switzerland legally. I was one of the last Americans to do so until after the liberation of France. I was ready to go to work.[12]

It had been a close call. Hitler was in a rage at the successful Allied landings. Operation Torch had been the first triumph of the fledgling OSS. The American aid "observers" had organized potent sabotage and guerrilla bands among disaffected Moroccan tribes; clandestine radio stations had reported the state of readiness of Vichy French forces and even the details of tidal changes along the coast. A disinformation campaign had foxed the Germans completely into believing the invasion would come on the Atlantic coast further south near Dakar and not on the Mediterranean side at all. Sensing betrayal by some of the Vichy leaders in Algiers who had ordered their troops not to oppose the U.S.-British force, Hitler ordered his *Wehrmacht* divisions in southern France to push past the lines established during the previous year's armistice and to assume *de facto* control over all the territory ruled by Petain's regime. The border to Switzerland, the last pathway through to the outside world, was to be shut tight, and any suspect foreigners were to be interned at once, regardless of what kind of passport they carried. The Gestapo would sort them out later.

Still, Dulles had made it and was in a triumphant mood when he arrived at the U.S. Legation in Bern late on the tenth. The iron-clad procedures of the security system required Ambassador Leland Harrison to go through the dumb show of a sign-countersign exchange with Dulles, whom he had known for all of his adult life. By the prescribed formula, Dulles presented himself in the Bern legation that afternoon and Harrison greeted him by asking, "Where did you have dinner your last night in Washington, D.C.?"

Dulles replied, "At the Metropolitan Club." His booming laughter echoed down the halls of the legation, and the startled staff realized that the new "special assistant to the minister for legal affairs" had arrived. Unlike the roles of Dyar and some of the other "vice consuls," everyone in the legation knew what role Allen Dulles had come to play. Everyone in Switzerland who cared knew the same news within hours after that. The OSS master spy had arrived. The game was afoot. Soon after his arrival a Swiss newspaper recorded his arrival in the capital and described him as "the personal representative of President Roosevelt" with a "special duty" assignment. It was as good as hanging a brass plaque on his office door to advertise that he was setting up a spy shop. "It had the result of bringing to my door purveyors of information, volunteers and adventurers of every sort, professional and amateur spies, good and bad," he recalled, happily.[13] After all, that was why he was there.

FIRST, DULLES HAD TO FIND a place to live and to get settled. He had traveled light so he needed new clothing. He also had to straighten out his financial affairs, for, while he did carry with him a large sum of money (perhaps as much as $10,000), it was probably not the $1 million amount that legend credits. Moreover, much of what he did carry was in traveler's checks, which the Swiss National Bank had embargoed as part of its currency struggles with the U.S. Treasury. Fortunately, Dulles had friends in Bern. One of the first men he looked up was an Austrian lawyer named Kurt Grimm.

Grimm had left his home country in 1938 and set up a law practice in Switzerland through which he ran an aid-relief organization for Austrians who were caught there by the war. In his late thirties, Grimm had been part of a Viennese law firm that was a correspondent in business deals with Sullivan & Cromwell clients, and he had taken a large sum of money with him when his family emigrated. Grimm was set up in a luxurious apartment at a lakeside hotel, from which he ran an extensive intelligence service through former law colleagues in Germany and other top-level business contacts throughout Occupied Europe. He was happy to take his old friend Allen Dulles to his tailor. He was even happier to become what one senior British intelligence official would tell this author was "one of the three major sources of Allen Dulles's rather remarkable operation in Bern."

Dulles was delighted with Grimm's arrangements. Grimm's choice of living accommodations also proved to be inspired. Dulles described finding "an apartment in the Herrengasse, in the delightfully picturesque and ancient section of the Swiss capital near its cathedral. This arcaded and cobblestoned street ran along the ridge high above the River Aare. It was near where I had lived and worked twenty-four years before in the last months of World War I."[14]

The house at 23 Herrengasse was the last house of a row of adjoining five-story townhouses built in the fourteenth century by the Bernese city government to house dignitaries. The street itself ended there in a cul-de-sac, and the land fell sharply away beyond a low wall down to the vineyard terraces that stepped down to the Aare, which made a horseshoe bend around the ancient city walls.

Cordelia Dodson Hood, who later joined the OSS operation in Bern, and who lived in one of the top floor apartments at 23 Herrengasse after the war, describes it as "fairly conspicuous."

"His apartment was on the ground floor," she remembers. "It was a beautiful apartment with a big terrace in the back that overlooked the Aare, then you looked up and saw the whole Bern Oberland mountain range, the Eiger, and the rest of the mountains. It was almost kitschy it was so postcard perfect. The land the building was on sloped down into the vineyards and to the Aare and was part of the original fortifications. There were all kinds of wine cellars back there and, most importantly for Allen, a back entrance that people could walk to along the terraces when they came to see him at night."[15]

As an added precaution, Dulles pulled some strings and had the streetlight opposite his front door turned off for the duration of the war, but most clandestine guests came and went by the back door, whatever the hour. The apartment was ideal for his needs. "There was an enormous reception room at the front, then the first door to the right was a study, this was along the river side of the house," Mrs. Hood recalls. "Behind it to the back was a big salon. The first door to the left was into the kitchen and then back to the dining room with a pass-through window between them. There also was a pantry and servants' quarters with a bathroom. Across the back of the apartment were the bedrooms with a bath in between them. It was very airy and light with those huge windows, and there were fireplaces. He would have most of his meetings in the big salon, but he would have his most confidential conversations in the little room in front."

Gerald Mayer and his War Information propaganda operation had taken office space in 24 Duforstrasse, across the street from Number 21, home of the U.S. Military Mission run by Barney Legge. Although there was now no real secret about what Dulles was up to, a circumspect concern for Swiss sensibilities dictated that he at least seek a headquarters that could claim diplomatic immunity, so he moved into 24 Duforstrasse with Mayer, who shortly was forced to seek other quarters once the Dulles operation got moving in earnest. Later in the war, when counterintelligence and preliminary postwar tasks provided new assignments for the Bern OSS station, Dulles expanded his operation even more and took over the office building next door at Number 26.

"I guess people thought he had a lot of people running around helping him, but Allen never had more than a dozen people in his office even at the end of the war, and for most of the war he had eight or fewer. At the beginning, he had even fewer than that," Cordelia Hood notes. "He had two secretaries—Mildred Gasser, she was Swiss-American and had worked in the consulate. And Betty Parsons, who had come from Italy, where she had been living; she later worked on some of his books after the war. And there was Baldwin, the fixer."

Henry Baldwin, who was British, had been a butler at the U.S. Legation and earlier had served a British intelligence officer's home in Cairo. He and his wife moved into the top floor of the three-story building at 26 Duforstrasse and oversaw the maintenance of the growing OSS establishment. A true fixer, Baldwin could organize numbers of cars for hasty trips out of Bern; he could arrange to have trains met or watched; he could get telephones tapped and other people's mail opened. Allen and his American colleagues assumed that Baldwin was a planted agent of the British as well. When questioned by the author about Baldwin's possible double role, British intelligence officers who were in Bern at the time invariably denied that they would do such a thing to their close allies; but then they also invariably laughed, so the reader is left to judge. Certainly Cordelia Hood and others who worked for Dulles maintained he believed it of Baldwin and did not mind:

So we had Baldwin and his wife on the top floor of Number 26, and Allen and his two secretaries were on the second. The Baldwins took care of repairs and things, and they also took care of the pouch of communications that had to be taken to the legation, although we always thought he showed the contents to the British first. And he had a stable of drivers, most of whom had been drivers for wealthy families in the nearby mountain regions of France, the Savoyard, and so on. They were crucial because the borders weren't neatly barbed wired like East Germany later became. You had to know the woods and where you could safely cross over to France or to Germany and where you had to avoid.

On the first floor at the start they had the administration and finance people; later in 1944, Paul Blum and I moved into the first floor of Number 26 and set up X-2, the counterintelligence operation. Allen did not like X-2 all that much, and he particularly did not like the rule that you had to send the names of all your potential new contacts to London to be checked before you could get involved with them. He always said he should be able to talk to the devil if he needed to.

First off though, Dulles had to talk to the British. The British spy outpost in Switzerland was one of the senior posts of the MI6 service. The head of the operation was a genial aristocratic Englishman who had inherited a Belgian title, Count Frederich "Fanny" Vanden Heuvel. His number two was Andrew King, who had been in Vienna until the war broke out with the cover of the representative of director Alexander Korda's London Films Company. British guerrilla warfare and sabotage operations in France and Germany were the province of the Special Operations Executive representative, John "Jock" McCaffery, who had been teaching at a university in Italy when the war broke out and who considered the Italian partisan guerrillas to be his private property. There were two military celebrities on staff at the Bern embassy as well. Freddy West had won a Victoria Cross during the First World War as one of Britain's Royal Flying Corps combat aces. The other attaché, Colonel Henry Cartwright, was another legend, having led a number of successful prisoner escape missions out of German prisoner of war camps in the previous war. Vanden Heuvel's operation was intentionally far away in Geneva so as not to ruffle the feathers of Swiss intelligence. So it was to Geneva that Dulles went in late November to introduce himself.

The officer Vanden Heuvel assigned as liaison with Dulles later recalled that first meeting:

Allen knew who he had to go to and he called on my chief, and I was asked to come in too. And Dulles said, "Well, I've got bags of money, and I've got a fairly authoritative position in Washington; I can get the ear of the president anytime I want it if it's important enough. I have a few memories of what this war work was like in the 1914–1918 war and memories of Switzerland but otherwise I must rely on you boys entirely to tell me what to do and how to do it."

And my chief, who was very charming, not at all a traditional spymaster, he absolutely agreed. He was tremendously pro-American himself and had many happy business visits there before the war. Well, in theory, we collaborated 100 percent from the word go. In practice, of course, it didn't quite work like that, but that was the basis of our agreement. As time went on he built up a staff, and very often I think his staff distrusted his close collaborating with the Brits.

For one thing, we didn't have the money the Americans did. Allen practically put a notice on the door that said, "American Intelligence, good prices paid, agents wanted." And even though we were the favorite chicks of the MI6 brood, we not only didn't have the resources, we also were under strict orders to keep ourselves undercover, to do everything we could not to be ousted by the Swiss. Also, we saw our missions differently. We went after a lot of military intelligence, order-of-battle things, and we weren't too preoccupied with what would happen after the war, just what we had to do to win the war at the moment, whereas Allen saw his mission as much more encompassing.

At the beginning Allen was most conciliatory and was a most charming man, very friendly. I did have a strip torn off me by Dulles once, so I also know he had a terrible temper when it suited him. We had agreed early on that we would not poach each other's agents; we wanted to avoid paying twice for the same information. We had this farmer in the Shothausen Salient who had been our agent for two-and-a-half years before Allen arrived and very soon afterwards his material started coming up in the material that Allen shared with me. I said to the agent, whom I used to run myself, we've seen this material come through the Americans and you can't get away with it, so don't try it again. Then I went to Dulles and said I'd done this and said further that it just was not on, he was our agent and so on. And he got most angry. I can still see him glowering at me from behind his desk there in the Herrengasse, his pipe smoking away. He said, very angrily, that he represented the president of the United States and that I had no right to tell anybody

who could or could not work for the United States government; such a question was entirely for him to decide.
And I guess I said, Oh, well, I am sorry, but we do have
this agreement and he happens to be our agent. But he
was unmoved; that isn't for you to say and don't every do
it again. I came out with my tail between my legs.[16]

One area where the British did allow Dulles to buy his way
into a valuable source was in the case of Madame Halina
Szymanska, the widow of a slain Polish officer who had become
the mistress of Admiral Wilhelm Canaris, head of the German
military intelligence service, the *Abwehr*. When the war broke out,
Canaris, whose political loyalties appear to have taken a backseat
to his own personal advancement, managed to spirit the lady and
her daughters to Switzerland, where she was supported, and
quickly suborned, by both the Polish and British spy services.

Nicholas Elliot, who succeeded Vanden Heuvel as head of the
Secret Intelligence Service in Switzerland toward the end of the war,
explained, "Madame Szymanska was a formidable lady. Canaris
used to come to various neutral countries to lay her. And in the
course of the pillow talk he used to talk to her freely and once told
her about the secret meeting between Franco and Hitler [in
Hendaye, France, in October 1940]. It is clear to me that Canaris
knew exactly what he was doing and that she would pass this on."

This much is certain, that early in 1941, when the whole
world was braced for Hitler's expected invasion of England,
Canaris, through his mistress, sent word to the British that a new
strategy called for German troops to swing east and invade Russia
instead. It appears now that for Canaris and a growing number of
high-ranking German military officers, the decision to provoke a
war with Russia was the final evidence that Hitler had to be
removed before Germany was totally destroyed. From that point

onward, Canaris and many of his aides inside the *Abwehr* were plotting actively with Allied intelligence representatives in Bern to bring down their leader one way or another.[17]

Dulles also turned to his old World War I mentors, the Swiss intelligence service, which had a separate section known as *Buro H* to share sensitive secrets on a highly confidential basis with foreign spy services. Thus Dulles was introduced to Brigadier General Roger Masson, who headed the bureau. Masson, among other tasks, kept covert communications going with the top leaders of Germany's diverse, and usually warring, intelligence services—a delicate task indeed. Dulles also met two men who were assigned by Masson to keep contact with U.S. intelligence, Captain Hans Haussamann and Major Max Waibel. Throughout the war Dulles had regular meetings with Haussamann at the Zurich home of Emil Oprecht, a wealthy Swiss publisher and patron of the arts. Waibel, whose intelligence duties focused mainly on German activities in the Lucerne area and over the border into Italy, would play a critical role in Dulles's most dramatic intelligence coup toward the end of the war. In the meantime, the Swiss and Dulles settled into an easy, if guarded, relationship. They told him about Soviet intelligence operations in Occupied Europe, the famed *Rote Kappelle* (Red Orchestra), and he gave them advance knowledge of selected Allied bombing raids in Germany and Italy that might be close to their borders. The Swiss also abetted his intentions to make contact with the *Schwarze Kapelle* (Black Orchestra), which was the name the Gestapo had fixed to those Germans who were committed to overthrowing Hitler and the Nazi regime. German émigrés in America and Dulles's own widespread contacts throughout Occupied Europe had identified the principal leaders of the German underground, which OSS code-named "Breakers"; the hard part was to establish a working contact with the group that would be safe for both sides.

The Germans did have their successes, particularly in Switzerland, where sympathetic Swiss citizens could be used to gather information rather than Germans, who would be immediately spotted. Nazi agents also redoubled their efforts against the Americans once Dulles had arrived so publicly; agents watched the front door of 23 Herrengasse twenty-four hours a day from across the street. And for all that, the Allies were perhaps not as security conscious as they should have been about counterespionage defense in the early days of the war. Even before he left New York for Bern, Dulles cabled David Bruce and Hugh Wilson in Washington:

> Colonel Sadowski writes me that his London headquarters have received unconfirmed reports from German occupied France that the Gestapo, in conjunction with French police, had succeeded in getting hold of our embassy cipher code. He adds that correctness of this report is being investigated and that he will communicate any further details.[18]

When he got to Bern, Dulles discovered that at least one of the leaks was across the street from his own office. A Swiss janitor in Barney Legge's military affairs shop had become disgruntled over pay and had decided to supplement his income by taking the carbon paper discards out of the wastebaskets to the German Embassy. But was the code that Harrison and his staff used actually broken as well? It would take another month of probing before it could be confirmed that the State codes had been compromised, too.

In the meantime, Dulles moved quickly in December to scoop up an extraordinary asset that the Germans and Vichy French had carelessly left in Switzerland. On November 22 the

German army finished its occupation of the rest of Vichy France and moved to take control of the port of Toulon. This provoked the French navy officers whose ships were berthed in the harbor to go over to the Gaullist Free French side and to scuttle three battleships, seven cruisers, and more than two dozen destroyers and submarines. In retaliation, the Germans dissolved Petain's armed forces altogether. One result was that the Vichy diplomats in Bern were told to send their military attachés home and to cease all intelligence operations of any kind. As with the doughty passport control officer at Annemasse, French cooperation with their Nazi masters was more symbolic than actual. The French military security service officers who had been operating in Switzerland were quietly told to make themselves scarce, and no attempt was ever made to send them home. Instead, they went looking for a new sponsor.

Credit for confirming that Allen Dulles ran not one but two separate intelligence operations within the French resistance movement must go to Fabrizio Calvi, the authority on the French maquis, who identified Major Gaston Pourchot as the French intelligence officer who brought his entire Deuxieme Bureau operation into the American fold. Pourchot's group was estimated at 250 agents operating in both France and Germany. At the fiftieth anniversary conference that marked the OSS founding, held by the National Archives in Washington in 1991, Calvi said that in December 1942, Barney Legge was authorized to provide the sum of 45,000 francs a month to support Pourchot's operation.

Pourchot, or "Gaston P.," as he was known, was a real find. His most important triumph was a precise order of battle location of all the German forces in France shortly before the D-Day invasion of Normandy.

As Calvi said, "Gaston P.'s position was delicate and difficult indeed. Passing information to the Americans was treason according to Vichy law. But after December 1942, he was in a more difficult situation—no work, no money, and no legal existence. The money was very little at the time but it helped to keep his chains of fine operators going; it is important to note that most of them were unpaid people."[19]

Dulles was sensitive to the need to treat "Gaston P." carefully and to keep him separate from the other contacts that Max Shoop was building over the border with his own fractious *maquis* forces. Shoop was having remarkable success in part because a French colleague who had been in the Paris office of Sullivan & Cromwell had gone underground with one of the maquis groups and was in contact with Geneva already. Still, the partisans were one thing, but Dulles knew that an already established military intelligence net might well be jeopardized if it was folded in with a still-uncertain civilian operation. He also sensed that the French soldier felt more at home with a wartime comrade such as Legge, so the military attaché was "Gaston's" control officer, although Dulles continued to debrief him regularly. The "Gaston" operation also included two clandestine radio stations, one in the embassy and another elsewhere in Bern. Copies of the intelligence reports were to be provided both for the French headquarters in Algiers and for American listeners in Washington.

As the old year ended and 1943 approached, Dulles had reason to be pleased with what he had accomplished in just the half dozen weeks since his arrival in Bern. He was established with a good base of operations, he had set good relations with allies such as the British and Poles, and he had begun the delicate task of winning active support from the Swiss. "Gaston P." and his chain were a triumph in themselves. Moreover, Bern station had produced some minor information scores already. The orders to scuttle the French fleet at Toulon had been intercepted and sent to Washington ahead of the event. And Dulles was energetically trying to make contact with the "Breakers" plotters inside Germany, not an easy task. Now all he had to do was start producing some important intelligence product from inside Hitler's high command.

CHAPTER EIGHT

December 1942–August 1943

"Peace can come to the world only by the total elimination of German and Japanese war power... [which] means the unconditional surrender by Germany, Italy or [sic] Japan."
—*Franklin D. Roosevelt,*
Casablanca, January 24, 1943

FDR'S DEMAND THAT the Axis Powers surrender their war machinery without reservation turned out to be the defining moment of World War II. It pleased Winston Churchill, the other main conferee at the Casablanca Conference, to pretend that he had been caught by surprise by Roosevelt's demand and that he had loyally followed the lead. Later, in his own history of the war, he was honest enough to concede that the "unconditional surrender" pledge had been jointly bargained between them. Whether the pledge was to be strictly adhered to, come final victory, was another matter.

Neither the German Military High Command nor senior diplomatic strategists in the Wilhelmstrasse (nor even Hitler loyalists such as Heinrich Himmler of the SS) took "unconditional surrender" as an unequivocal demand for total surrender. Such a proposal was unthinkable, according to that relentless Teutonic logic that can defy reality. England and America surely would let Germany survive as an active partner in the struggle against Bolshevism. Adolf Hitler's henchmen were happy to blame him solely for the war. With Hitler out of the way, by coup, by assassination, or whatever, the Allies would quickly come to terms. Others, mostly military officers who had had their early training in the covert bases of the Soviet Union fifteen years earlier, believed that, even if the West sought to impose a Carthaginian peace, they could cut a better deal with Stalin, who wisely continued to insist in private signals sent through neutral capitals that his own ambitions were merely for a buffer zone that might extend into part of Poland and certainly did not encompass the destruction of the German state.

Allen Dulles recognized what "unconditional surrender" meant to his own espionage and intelligence program. Even before the conference, he warned in a December 6, 1942, cable to Donovan: "Whatever may be our finally invoked policy toward a defeated Germany, our line of attack today should be to try to convince the German people that there is hope for them even in defeat, and that while there will be punishment of the guilty through legal process there will remain assurance of protection for the innocent.... [I]t is important to recognize that the chief reason for any hesitation on the part of anti-Nazi and anti-Fascist elements in both occupied and unoccupied Europe to give us their undivided support is due to their fear of Communism. There is a widespread apprehension that we in America may be too distant and the English too weak to prevent Soviet Russia from taking advantage of the temporary social chaos which is likely to follow our victory over Germany and imposing its own type of domination on Europe. There is, of course, no particular enthusiasm at the prospect that Nazi domination will be exchanged for any Communist Russia."[1]

The Casablanca pledge came at a bad time, as Dulles still faced the daunting task of trying to reach into the heavily sealed confines of the Greater German Reich that surrounded him, to penetrate its secrets, and to generate as much internal opposition as possible. Of equal seriousness, he had to establish credibility back in Washington with the ultimate consumers of whatever intelligence he did produce.

Within a few days of the German takeover of Vichy France, Switzerland in that winter of 1942 was sealed off from much of the rest of the world. Commercial airline flights, except those of the Swiss that flew directly into Germany, were banned. Train service was continued into France after grueling searches at the French border; passengers bound for Germany had to disembark, walk through two sets of passport controls, and board *Reichban* trains for journeys into the Reich itself. Even diplomatic courier service was denied the Americans and British. Harrison's legation staff worked out a deal with the Peruvian diplomats in Bern and managed to put its own sealed pouches inside the bags of those deliveries bound for Lisbon, but there were often lengthy delays between such trips, and the security of the documents was a constant worry.

There remained only the telegraph or radiotelephone. Dulles began a series of ten-minute telephone calls at around midnight (so as to reach Washington by the close of the business day) on a scrambler device attached to his apartment telephone, using the fiction that Bertram L. Johnston was calling Charles Baker Jennings. The calls were directed to a specific extension at "The Kremlin" on E Street that turned the calls into recordings that could be replayed the next day at briefings held by Donovan or Whitney Shepardson, the new head of the OSS intelligence section (he had just returned from the London station). The scrambler prevented taps from outside the system from hearing anything useful, but the Swiss authorities who monitored from inside the telephone system itself could hear his conversations clearly and presumably could and did leak whatever might be useful to whomever they were dealing with at the moment. Therefore, whatever Dulles said had to be of the most general and nonsensitive nature. It also meant that an increasing volume of traffic, both from Harrison's own intelligence providers and from Dulles and his fledgling crew, had to be converted into coded messages that could be telegraphed with safety to Washington, London, or Algiers. That meant the use of the cumbersome "one-time" pads that had a cipher of randomly selected letters and characters printed on each sheet. The sender had to translate each page's message according to the cipher for that specific page; only a recipient who had an identical message pad and who could refer to the cipher for each page could unscramble the message. The randomness of the cipher text made breaking the coded messages an impossible task, but it also meant that every message had to be hand-transcribed before it could be transmitted.

Dulles sought permission from the Swiss to recruit ciphering volunteers from the American airmen whose planes had crashed after missions in Germany and Austria and who were interned in camps near Bern after their escape from enemy territory. He was able to secure twenty-four–hour passes for teams of six airmen who would work in a secure apartment on the top floor of 26 Duforstrasse, laboring to put his cables into a one-time format for transmission on the commercial Swiss telegraph lines. Later, in 1944, Dulles was able to get his own clandestine radiotelephone operating, but even then he was cautious about any traffic home that was not formed on the one-time pads because he assumed that everything sent or said was being taken in by the Germans and probably the Soviets as well.

From the start, the volume of information generated by Dulles and his office team caused comment in Washington. On an average in those early months of 1943, cable traffic from Burns to Victor quickly moved more than 150 separate transmissions, each of which might contain half a dozen or more separate news items. Then there were the telephone calls (dubbed "flashes"), which averaged five nights a week and might contain dozens of more general sets of information.

The early flow of news Dulles provided was by necessity somewhat general and occasionally uncertain. But steadily the percentage of traffic devoted to battle order reports of the locations of

Nazi armed forces in southern France and later in Italy began to attract enthusiastic consumers among the military planners in both London and Washington. As one government analysis of Station Burns's performance noted, "Order of Battle reports have become ever more lengthy, detailed and of increasingly better quality. Reports on bombing targets in Italy have received a high rating. Efforts in gathering intelligence material are ever more coordinated...."

It was also noted that cable bills for agent "110" through the Swiss telegraph service were running more than $100,000 a month even in the early days.[2] Despite the widely accepted rumor (which Dulles never bothered to deny) that he had arrived in Switzerland with a million dollars, evidence indicates that, as noted, he actually arrived with no more than $10,000 in traveler's checks, which could not be readily cashed because of the squabble over blocked funds. Money would remain a problem for the OSS operation throughout the war. The U.S. dollar was worth 2.5 Swiss francs in 1942 and would improve through the war to a black market price of just 1.9 per dollar. From the time they were encircled until the late summer of 1944, the OSS secret bank accounts at the Banque Populaire branches in Freiburg (code named "85 Duc") and Bern ("51 Schwan"), did stockpile up to $1 million at a time, but largely because of a deal whereby Dulles was able to borrow Swiss francs from friendly bankers with the understanding they would be repaid at an interest rate of roughly double the prevailing currency loan rates on world markets in other neutralist countries.[3] But of course Switzerland was not just any other neutral marketplace.

In the meantime, Station Burns had to branch out and start penetrating into enemy territory. This was tricky business on a number of fronts. The British considered the various French *maquis* groups to be their private preserves. In London, MI6's operations chief, Claude Dansey, would throw table-pounding tantrums at joint service meetings when the matter of OSS forays into the area was broached. From his standpoint it was a dangerous and wasteful duplication of effort for the Americans to go lumbering around with their cash boxes open, ready to be duped and possibly even to jeopardize nets already functioning for MI6 and the Special Operations Executive.

Although the British did not know it at the time, Dulles operated more than two French networks. In addition to "Gaston P.'s" military spotters and the bands of *maquis* being subsidized, a third French operation was run cooperatively with Gerry Mayer's Office of War Information propaganda program. Dulles had located the Deuxieme Bureau's chief propaganda artist from World War I, whose cover name was "Salembier." He was quickly set up in a printing business in Geneva and produced a flood of pamphlets, leaflets, bogus postcards, and even counterfeit and often insulting postage stamps (FDR insisted on getting some for his extensive stamp collection) for propaganda purposes for use in France, Germany, and Italy. When Goebbels suppressed the respected newspaper *Frankfurter Zeitung,* an edition was run up by "Salembier" and dropped into Germany. The latest speeches of de Gaulle and other Free French leaders were sent in vast quantities into Occupied France. And the latest passes, ration cards, and other identity documents were made to order for cross-border penetrations.

Getting a look inside Hitler's Germany was difficult for Dulles, but he accomplished it by means that offended the intelligence orthodoxy of the day. The traditional doctrine of intelligence services on both sides of the conflict dictated that information from one's own agents inserted into enemy territory was the first order of business. Dulles simply reversed the polarities and went looking for Germans who would help—that is, Germans already in place and often in high places indeed. Among the many letters of introduction Dulles had brought into Switzerland was one from a Standard Oil official to a young German-born American citizen named Gero von Schulze Gaevernitz.

Gaevernitz, then in his early forties, had the polished Euro-aristocratic air that came from his family and its political promi-nence throughout Europe. His father was a well-known pacifist scholar and had served in one of the early Weimar cabinets in the 1920s; now he lived in quiet obscurity and apparent safety inside Germany, teaching economics at the University of Freiburg. Dulles had known the father and also knew that Gero's family, through marriage, had important ties to a major manufacturing group in Germany. Until it had become too dangerous, Gero had shuttled in and out of the Reich, keeping up his contacts until his anti-Nazi sympathies became widely known. Stuck in Switzerland, he had been frustrated at the little use that the British intelligence officials had for him.

In fairness, the British came by their suspicion the hard way. MI6 had been burned badly early in the war in 1939 when two of its senior officers in Europe had been kidnapped and imprisoned by the Nazis in a ruse that used just such apparently sympathetic anti-Nazis. This preoccupation with being undone by counterespionage intruders would keep the British on a cautious track throughout the war. Gero had thus largely been kept as a "cut-out," or go-between.

One of his British contacts was an MI6 Psychological Warfare specialist, Elizabeth Wiskemann,[4] a talented liberal journalist of the 1930s who had been expelled from Germany for her highly critical articles about Hitler and his henchmen. She was now in Zurich compiling lists of friendly and hostile persons and drafting propa-ganda articles to be placed in the Swiss press. Wiskemann also used Gaevernitz as one of the confidential emissaries to visitors to Switzerland from highly placed members of the Kreisau Circle of intellectuals, nobility, and diplomats who were committed to killing Adolf Hitler and toppling his regime before Germany was destroyed. Allen Dulles also knew many of these people from long business and personal relationships that dated from the former war; this was the same group that OSS in Washington had given the code designation "Breakers." Both Wiskemann and Gaevernitz were based in Zurich, and Dulles traveled there often in December 1942, usually meeting them at the apartment of Emil Oprecht, the publisher. First he had to win the confidence of the opinionated Wiskemann (mutual friendship with Rebecca West helped), and then he had to recruit Gaevernitz to full-time work for the OSS.

The Dulles-Gaevernitz friendship was to be a partnership that lasted into the beginnings of the Cold War itself. The young German-American was a double treasure; he was intensely loyal to Dulles, as so many later protégés would be. And he had a keen eye for the kind of anti-Nazi whom Dulles wanted to contact, first for wartime intelligence purposes and, ultimately, for postwar recruitment.

As Dulles later explained in his book *Germany's Underground*, he was searching for

men who felt that a victory of Nazism and the extinction of liberty in Europe and possibly in the world was a far greater disaster than the defeat of Germany. In fact, they felt that Germany's rebirth could be achieved only through the defeat of Hitler, and they wanted to accomplish that defeat as rapidly as possible and before the kernel of civilization in Germany was destroyed by total war. They wanted the Allies to win before Germany was ground to bits and all values, material as well as moral, disappeared. They believed that there was something remaining on which to build a new Germany. They looked primarily to the West for this, but often with a veiled threat that if we refused to hold out any hope to them they would have no choice but to throw themselves into the arms of... Russia.[5]

The search was at one level a more difficult task than it might seem. Switzerland had become the waiting room of Europe. The tiny country was indeed the "happy hunting ground" for spies of all nations, but in some respects it was too much of a good thing for the new arrival. From the start of Hitler's seizure of power a decade earlier, Switzerland had been jammed with true victims seeking refuge. But there also came the morally ambivalent, frauds, swindlers, extortionists, and assassins. Complicating matters were the crowds of what might charitably be called sincere loonies. Switzerland during most of the 1930s had become what one British agent described to the author as "the sort of La-La land that the Big Sur and that part of California became after the war. It was filled with enthusiasts of all kinds who formed colonies of sorts, most of them around various Swiss health spas. There were artists and writers, and psychiatry was very popular for these devotees. Some of these followed a variety of diets, others were spiritualists and faddists, and, not surprisingly, many of them also were fascinated by various Wagnerian myths—of Wotan and Tristan—the nonsense that gripped Hitler, that well-known vegetarian."[6]

Dulles felt that Gaevernitz was experienced; he might be a time-waster, but he could be of genuine use to the OSS. As 1943 arrived, Gero proposed that his new boss meet someone else with whom the British had contacts but, because of their institutional caution, had refused to allow too near.

HANS BERND GISEVIUS was one of the most complex characters in spy lore, which is saying something. While the stereotypical German character is highly conformist, there is also a renegade Germanic personality that seems to be tolerated by the more disciplined majority, perhaps for the same reason rational people put up with outspoken eccentrics. Born to a family tradition of bureaucratic service, Gisevius had early on joined the Gestapo when it was still the state police agency of the Prussian government and headed by Hermann Goering. There he had become friends with Arthur Nebe, head of the agency's criminal investigation division. Nebe was judged a devious plotter even by masters of the art like Reinhard Heydrich and Himmler. Yet Nebe was a mentor for Gisevius and protected him from Heydrich's increasing suspicions, which could have led to a quick death for the younger man. Indeed, Nebe advanced his protégé's interest to the point that Gisevius was considered for promotion to the task of directing the security for the 1936 Olympic Games in Berlin. But both men had been marked for their increasing criticism of the corruption and outright murder that pervaded the Gestapo under its new Nazi masters. Once the Gestapo was merged within the SS organization (Nebe became an SS major), the younger man found it more prudent to work a transfer to the *Abwehr* military intelligence service of Nebe's other ally, Admiral Canaris. It was at this point that Gisevius was inducted into that loose, conflicted, ambivalent, and slightly dotty movement that has come to be known as the German Underground.

Simply to tally the names and positions of many of the key participants in the various schemes to topple Adolf Hitler is to wonder how he lasted as long as he did. Intelligence coordination must have been a nightmare. First off, to have Canaris, head of military intelligence, running an in-house opposition service, using his top aides and even his mistress to communicate with the enemy, has to be judged a major security disaster for Hitler. The German Army High Command (OKW) structure was riddled with other plotter cells, too—ultimately Field Marshal Gunther von Kluge, in charge of the campaign in Russia, and Field Marshal Erwin Rommel, whose tank divisions would have to contest the

Normandy invasion in the West, would be recruited into the final attempt on Hitler's life. The upshot was that many of the most senior commanders on both the Atlantic Wall and Eastern Front were in a constant fever of schemes to shoot, blow up, or poison Hitler during the final three years of the war.

By far the most ill-starred, feckless, and tragic group of plotters was the Kreisau Circle of young well-born intellectuals and foreign service elitists who dithered until they became victims of the most grisly and awful executions that a revenge-maddened führer could devise. Kreisau was the Prussian family estate of Helmuth Graf von Moltke and the base to which scores of plotters and recruits (including the occasional Nazi plant) came to argue endlessly over policy objectives and who would get what job in the new government after Hitler's fall. Absorbed by lofty ideals and paralyzed by details, the Kreisau plotters built lists of assigned duties and areas of responsibility, lists that would later be used to tragic effect.

After the war, in 1946, Dulles tried an unsuccessful first draft of a book about what would become known as the 20th of July plot to kill Hitler. A final ghostwritten version, much more cautious about Germany's prospects as a reformed member of the world society, became *Germany's Underground*, published in 1947. But in the unpublished version Dulles can be excused for lamenting that the plotters' failure cost Germany too much—"the best perished in the struggle."[7] After all, men like Moltke and Adam von Trott zu Solz were very much in the mold of men that Woodrow Wilson had tried to produce at Princeton.

Gisevius became an eager messenger between Admiral Canaris and the Kreisau plotters, just as he had been willing to become a vice consul in the German Embassy in Zurich and serve the admiral as his contact with mistress Halina Szymanska and with the British. He found himself at the center of a fragile web of conspirators whose moods swung from steely determination to sweaty panic at the slightest reverse. Canaris and his *Abwehr* were what Dulles was talking about later when he wrote, "An intelligence service is the ideal vehicle for a conspiracy. Its members can travel about at home and abroad under secret orders, and no questions are asked. Every scrap of paper in the files, its membership, its expenditure of funds, its contacts, even enemy contacts, are state secrets. Even the Gestapo could not pry into the activities of the *Abwehr* until Himmler absorbed it. He only succeeded in doing so late in 1943."[8]

Yet for all his love of plotting and his all too obvious self-absorption, Gisevius was basically an insecure and nervous individual whose adventures during this time put him under a strain that nearly broke him. He was now forty and had been at risk from plots and counterplots in the center of the Nazi nightmare for more than eleven years.[9] Gisevius could not trust even other Germans on his own side. Could he trust Dulles?

On January 8 Field Marshal Beck, Moltke, Trott, and other leaders of the various civilian and military factions met near Berlin; the objective of the young Kreisau Circle members was to prove to the cautious officers that it was time to unite around a fixed plan to assassinate Hitler and topple the rest of his regime by force. The plan that eventually emerged culminated in an abortive attempt to bomb Hitler's plane in March. But before that happened, the Kreisau plotters wanted some firm indication from the Allies of their response. Switzerland was an obvious place to make contact. As the new year began, Admiral Canaris himself was expected in Switzerland for one of his impromptu visits to Madame Szysmanska. On January 10 Dulles noted in a "Breakers Watch" file:

No confirmation presence Admiral C. in Bern. For second time saw yesterday man thought to be one of his

lieutenants. Am trying to keep closely informed concerning this organization [the *Abwehr*] especially as
growing antagonism between it and Gestapo reported.[10]

By January 13 Dulles had assigned "512" to Gisevius and
noted for his records that

he is believed to be working closely with Dr. Schacht
and is one of [Pastor Martin] Niemoller's friends. He
stressed the importance of receiving encouragement
that if the Nazi leaders eliminated Hitler there could be
negotiations for a durable peace with the United
Nations. As he pictured it, the alternative was chaos
and revolution, as Hitler, rather than surrender to the
Western powers, would turn to bolshevism. He said,
also, that his friends did not see any reason to risk their
lives unless there were some hope if the movement
succeeded. I, myself, doubt very much whether this
movement is, as yet, organized seriously.

On January 15 Dulles confirmed that he had been meeting
with "Gesvius [*sic*]" by name and that on the day before he had
met with "von Trott zu Solz." Trott was a high-ranking diplomat
in his own right and thus could move abroad to neutral capitals
to push the group's campaign for a separate peace with the Soviets.
The timing of his visit was keyed to the Berlin gathering of the
broader "Breakers" group, and it came just a few days before FDR
and Churchill opened the Casablanca meeting. The young diplomat complained that the Western Allies had been turning aside
frantic efforts by the circle members to win some sort of encouragement that their vision of Germany would be supported once
Hitler was gone and the war ended. The Kreisau intellectuals

assumed they were making a huge concession by agreeing in advance to give up all of the territories the *Wehrmacht* had conquered in the East, just as long as the dreaded virus of Bolshevism was kept from their doors. To Dulles's surprise, Trott in the next breath warned that if the West did not reward their ousting of Hitler and the Nazis, "there is a strong temptation to turn East." And here his notes to Dulles wandered into vague talk about the racial heritage shared by Slavic and Teutonic peoples, and how the *Wehrmacht*, especially those German officers who were alumni of Russian tactical training schools, respected the Red Army.

It is evident from the record that Dulles did want to preserve a reformed German nation after the war; if pressed, he might well have wished for a more hopeful version of the Weimar Republic. Nor did he hesitate to dangle before the "Breakers" and other German contacts that anything was possible once Hitler was out of the way. But there could be no question of a cease-fire that would allow Germany to keep its gains by conquest, nor could the removal of a few Nazi leaders make the nation acceptable again. The Casablanca declaration of "unconditional surrender" was dismaying to the Kreisau plotters. But Dulles knew, and told both Trott and Gisevius, "to stop short of total military victory, to allow Germany any doubt of its total defeat, would [be] unthinkable on our part."

Those early meetings between Dulles and Gisevius began the pattern that would be repeated hundreds of times over the next three years with scores of other covert contacts. Gaevernitz accompanied the scared new recruit from Zurich to Bern on a January night and guided him along the unfamiliar paths away from the old quarter's streets along the dark riverside terraces and finally to the darkened basement doorway at the rear of 23 Herrengasse. Despite warnings from Vanden Heuvel that the British suspected a Nazi plant, Dulles decided Gisevius, even if he was untrustworthy, was worth talking to for his insights into the opposition groups forming against Hitler.

Instead of following the stiff German custom of address by surname, Dulles relaxed the nervous younger man by insisting on being called Allen from the start. With easy informality and personal warmth, Dulles drew Gisevius to him as a personal friend who understood what a terrible burden he had been carrying. Dulles joked with him and called him "Tiny" because of his huge size. This pattern of personal involvement Dulles would use all his life to bind people to him. Fritz Molden, a young Austrian resistance agent who made many dangerous border crossings during the war to 23 Herrengasse, once told the author, "At the end of every formal debriefing in his big room in the back, it was always the same. Whoever else might be there, Allen would then take me into the little salon in front and close the door. And he would ask me how I was feeling, how my father was holding up. 'Fritz,' he would say, 'do you need anything personally?' For us Germanic types that kind of intimacy is overwhelming, and sometimes I would cry a little just out of relief."[11]

Feeling he could confide in his new friend Dulles, Gisevius let him in on a personal secret. He had been writing a secret testament of faith for some time now. It was a huge manuscript that described in intimate detail some of the dirtiest secrets of the power struggles within Hitler's Nazi madhouse. It could have been written only by a policeman with access to all the files; it would have been written only by a man struggling desperately with his conscience. This testament detailed the various plots and ruination of key figures in German politics and in the army as well as the inside story of the infamous 1934 "Night of the Long Knives"—the murder of scores of SA brownshirt leaders suspected of being rivals to Adolf Hitler's supremacy. Gisevius complained to Dulles that the British had been unwilling to help him translate it into English or to aid in publishing it as soon as the war was over. Surely Dulles must agree that such a clear statement of intentions by a "good" German would do much to help heal the wounds after the conflict ended.

Whatever Dulles thought, he agreed to find a translator, and, in fact, the book was published.[12]

As proof of his good faith, Gisevius produced some fragmentary notes of cable traffic that had passed over his desk which indicated that the Gestapo was actively deciphering the majority of State Department code traffic out of Switzerland. The truly bad news was that German intelligence had intercepted messages which indicated that a plot was in motion among high-ranking Italian government officials to replace Mussolini and seek a peace with the Allies. The American cable traffic apparently identified one of the coup leaders as Count Ciano, *Il Duce*'s foreign minister and son-in-law. The Gestapo counterintelligence coup was presented to Hitler and was at once sent to Mussolini. Ciano's arrest and subsequent execution were presumed to have come directly from this leak.

Through the spring months of 1943, the Station Burns networks began to produce solid intelligence of the highest grade. The steady disintegration of Mussolini's fascist regime was chronicled in detail. Kurt Grimm (now "490"), mining his network of sources in the Reich's technology industries, reported early in February that German scientists were working on a secret weapon described as "a flying contraption perhaps in the form of an aerial torpedo." Another Dulles contact, a German mining and metals company executive who came often to Zurich, Eduard Schulte, added other pieces of information that confirmed that scientists were working on not one but two V-rocket bombs—the slower winged V-1 "buzzbomb" and the larger, higher flying V-2. Gisevius was able to confirm that Hitler had ordered the scientists to have the rocket program ready for use against London by the winter of 1943. Grimm and other Austrian business friends along with Schulte all contributed to the mosaic by identifying factories where parts for the new experimental rockets were being made and, most impor-

tantly of all, pinpointing the barren North Sea peninsula called
Peenemünde as the secret test and development site. The discovery
had political side benefits as well. British aerial photo-intelligence
had spotted new activity along that same coastal area, and the subsequent air raids over Peenemünde on August 17, 1943, put the
dreaded V-1 rocket project nearly a year behind schedule. The OSS
information also showed to doubters how American intelligence
could be used as an equal partner with London's. Instead of being
able to destroy the Allied invasion armada as it lay helplessly at
anchor in British coastal waters, the first V-1 unguided missiles did
not strike England until June 13, 1944, too late to thwart the D-Day
landings a week earlier.

Indeed, Anglo-American cooperation inside Switzerland
became institutionalized on a number of important levels. Each
Thursday, Vanden Heuvel, the British MI6 chief, would send his
top aide up by train from Zurich early in the morning to the
Herrengasse house. The aide recounted those visits for the author:

It was something of a treat. I managed to catch an early
enough train in order to get there in time for breakfast.
And he [Dulles] would give me a very good breakfast
indeed. Even though his cook was supposed to be spying for the Germans, she was a very good cook. Then
we would leave the dining room and go back into his
big study and sit down by the fireplace. He would have
a big briefcase full of papers, and I would have mine.
We would swap reports and discuss what we had
learned in some detail. Then we would talk. About the
war in general and what was going on in our patch. Or
rather, he would ask me questions, and I would talk.

I came to simply adore the man. He made me feel
he genuinely was interested in who I was and what I

thought about things. I don't remember him expressing
many opinions of his own, except in the most general
terms. I can't claim to have known him very well despite
those regular meetings. I don't know that you can. But I
did like him very much and respected him enormously.[13]

Spring also produced hard intelligence of the most grisly,
heart-rending kind. On March 19 Dutch churchman W. A. Visser't
Hooft, general secretary of the World Council of Churches organization in Geneva, had formally notified officials in Washington and
London that evidence of the Holocaust was now undeniable.

"The Secretariats of the World Council of Churches and of
the World Jewish Congress have in their possession most reliable
reports indicating that the campaign of deliberate extermination
of the Jews organized by the Nazi officials in nearly all countries
of Europe under their control, is now at its climax. They therefore
beg to call the attention of the Allied Governments to the absolute
necessity of organizing without delay a rescue action for the per-
secuted Jewish communities...."[14]

A covering letter to Dulles indicates that he and the church
leader had been in regular contact about the mounting evidence of
the murder program since his arrival. Dulles also appears to have
advised the Dutch cleric on the wording of a formal proposal that
an active rescue plan by the Allies be coordinated with as much
diplomatic pressure on Berlin as could be exerted by the neutral
nations such as Sweden and Switzerland. ("We have tried to keep
specially in mind the points which you made and have emphasized
as much as possible the first question of encouraging the neutral
countries rather than the second question of exchange. The kind of
assurance which would seem to be required need not necessarily be
that the refugees would finally be allowed to emigrate to the United
States.")

Moreover, much of the hard information in the "reliable reports" Hooft referred to—details of the mass extermination operations, locations of the death camps, volume of murders involved—had come from reports written by Dulles's own agent "643," Eduard Schulte. In addition to being the managing director of his mining and metals firm, Schulte was on the boards of half a dozen other major manufacturing combines, and many of those widespread business contacts were benefitting from the slave labor the condemned were forced to perform before they were put to death. Holocaust historians Walter Laquer and Richard Breitman identify Schulte as the source of the information used in the famous "Reigner Report" cabled to Washington from Switzerland by a young World Jewish Congress worker.[15] The report is often cited as hard evidence that the American government knew about the extermination terror almost from its inception. Laquer and Breitman make a point of documenting Schulte's work for Dulles and the spymaster's energetic efforts to hasten Schulte's denazification and to help his return as a business leader of the new Germany after the war.

Interestingly, German historian Klemens von Klemperer takes up another link in the relationship, Visser't Hooft's long personal ties with most of the Kreisau plotters.[16] It was to the churchman's home in Geneva that Adam von Trott fled after his disillusioning meeting with Dulles in January; subsequently Trott and others in the Foreign Office began to increase their contacts with Soviet diplomats in neutral capitals to explore whether Stalin might agree to some kind of standstill agreement on the eastern borders of the Reich. Alarmed at what his young friend was doing, Visser't Hooft posed a rhetorical question to Dulles that was meant to be considered in both Washington and London:

Are the United Nations willing to say to the [Hitler] opposition: "If you succeed in overthrowing Hitler and if you then prove by your acts (punishment of Nazi leaders and Nazi criminals, liberation of occupied territory, restoration of stolen goods, installation of a regime which respects the rights of men, participation in economic and social reconstruction) that you have wholly broken with National Socialism and militarism, we would be ready to discuss peace terms with you?" As long as that is not clearly and definitely said, the process of development of an anti-Western, anti-liberal complex is likely to go on. And, as long as that is not said, large groups in Germany, who are psychologically prepared to join the opposition, will remain hesitant and wonder whether, after all, Hitler is not a lesser evil than total military defeat.[17]

By this time, too, Visser't Hooft had become a good enough intelligence source to have his own code pseudonym ("474"), and numerous, similar reports by him contain continuing bits of information and opinion from Trott and other young "Breakers." For all his sympathy, however, Dulles did not buy into the Kreisau Circle as quickly as he might have. After passing on one lengthy essay by "474," Dulles appended a note to State Department analysts: "I am transmitting the foregoing report solely because it may be of interest in connection with the program of psychological warfare and not because I am of the opinion that there is any serious organization of the opposition group in Germany or that, short of a complete military victory for the United Nations, they should expect or be lead [sic] to expect any encouragement from us or any dealing with us."[18]

Meanwhile, the Nazi intelligence hierarchy was hastening to learn more about Dulles. Heinrich Himmler was the second most powerful man in the Reich next to Hitler himself, but he was far from secure; even the corrupt and inept types such as Hermann Goering kept an irreducible amount of power, while far lesser figures such as Martin Bormann had more of the führer's confidence and affection. Like the Kreisau plotters, Himmler's secret ambition to place himself in Hitler's throne backed by his *Schutzstaffel* divisions was conditioned by a single question: Would the Allies come to terms with him *when* Hitler was toppled and let him, as the new leader of Nazi Germany, turn his forces against the Soviets? Allen Dulles was known by now to be President Roosevelt's personal observer across the border. Who better to ask?

The documented record of the famous "Bull-Pauls" conversations in 1943 rests on sources that are among the most curious in that mare's nest of boxes and microfilm files known as the OSS History Record Group in the National Archives in Washington.[19] There in the midst of the carefully sanitized, picked-over, and randomly shuffled collection of cable traffic and memos between Dulles ("110" and "Burns") and Washington ("Victor") is what purports to be a series of reports (in German) to Himmler (and ultimately to Hitler himself) on a number of conversations held in Bern between Dulles and his old World War I friend Prince Max-Egon von Hohenlohe. The topic was about what the American attitude might be toward Germany and its position in a postwar Europe.

The report gives pseudonyms to the participants in the talks, but they are easily decipherable. Prince Max is "Herr Pauls," Dulles is "Mr. Bull," and an American go-between from Geneva with German business contacts named Royall Tyler (the international banker) was "Mr. Roberts." Over a period of three months the talks continued, sometimes with Prince Max talking only to Tyler. There were also talks between Tyler and an Austrian SS officer named Reinhard Spitzy, code-named "Herr Bauer," who chaperoned the prince. Von Klemperer, the German historian, identifies Spitzy as the author of the reports, which he asserts were "repeatedly doctored" in order to have the desired effect on their final audience, Himmler and Hitler.

According to the story in the reports, Prince Max arrived in Geneva in mid-February 1943 and was immediately contacted by Tyler with an invitation from Dulles to renew their acquaintance. Spitzy reports that Dulles urged Prince Max to make the contact through officials of the German Embassy, including Hans von Bibra, who directed fifth column activities inside Switzerland.

One of the interesting facets of the reports is Spitzy's obvious attempt to convince his intended audience of how important a source Dulles was and how much he liked Prince Max. At their first meeting in Bern, Spitzy describes Mr. Bull:

> He is strongly built, an athletic type, tall, about 45 [Dulles was soon to be fifty], with an athletic look about him, good teeth, his manner fresh, simple and broadminded, generous and handsome. He certainly is a man with the courage of his convictions. At his side is the well-known Mr. Roberts, who is a specialist in European industry. Mr. Bull is very energetic and constantly entertains and contacts men of connections from all of the various European organizations. We can easily accept him as a special envoy of Roosevelt in Europe. It was possible for him, even though he came late, to pass through Vichy France into Switzerland even as the German troops were marching into Vichy.

What Dulles is reported to have said to his longtime acquaintance must have made for riveting reading by Himmler and his advisers. The first report states that Dulles greeted Prince Max cordially and they reminisced for a while about their days together in Vienna in 1916 and their later meetings in New York in 1923 and 1931. Then:

> Mr. Bull stated he was glad to see Herr Pauls after so many years to talk with him because he had a good grasp of European problems; that he [Dulles] was fed up with hearing from all the outdated politicians, emigrants and prejudiced Jews. In his view, a peace had to be made in Europe in which all of the parties would be interested, we cannot allow it to be a peace based on a policy of winners and losers; never again must nations like Germany be driven through need and unfairness to experiment with crazy heroics. The German State must remain in any peace settlement as an intact institution, a division of Germany or a separation of Austria cannot be an issue. On the other hand the power of Prussia over the German State must be reduced and other regions must have equal influence in a Greater Germany.

Dulles also reportedly expressed his lack of interest in whether Czechoslovakia would have its lost territories restored after the war, and he advocated using countries like Czechoslovakia, Poland, and Hungary as a *cordon sanitaire* to protect western Europe from both Bolshevism and Panslavism. The document concludes that Dulles was uninterested in helping the Soviet Union dominate Europe after the war, that, indeed, he viewed Germany as the economic leader of the Continent. This led Prince Max to repeat what had become an article of faith with the Nazi strategists: England would probably agree to divide Europe with Russia, while the Americans could be relied upon to help Germany regain its dominance as the bulwark against communism.

Then Prince Max came to the part of his remarks that would cause the most furor after the war. The prince stated flatly that it was "unthinkable" that Jews would ever be allowed to return to their homes in Central Europe or that they would ever be able to recover their lost position in European affairs. He added, as a dig to Dulles, that he felt sometimes that America continued the war in order only to send the Jews who had fled there back to Europe and to get them out of the United States.

> To this, Mr. Bull, who in the course of the conversation had clearly evinced anti-Semitic tendencies, said that in America things had not quite gotten to that point yet and it was in general a question whether the Jews wanted to go back. Herr Pauls got the impression that Americans intended rather to send off the Jews to Africa.

There were subsequent meetings, one the next day between Prince Max and Tyler alone, and later, in March, a series of conversations in which Prince Max, Dulles, and their companions participated. Tyler, it appears from the record, was especially anti-Semitic in his statements out of Dulles's earshot, but both Americans are portrayed as believing that Hitler's big mistake was arousing world opinion against his persecution of the Jews, and that, had Hitler simply attacked the Soviet Union first, England and the United States would have stood by and let him do it. Dulles reportedly called the Casablanca declaration "a piece of paper" that would be scrapped if the Germans really wanted to negotiate a peace. Dulles also reportedly emphasized over and over again that the Allies would never deal with Hitler and that "America did not want wars every twenty years and would rather either destroy Germany or help it be the centerpiece of a new Europe. It was Germany's choice; get rid of Hitler or lose."

Spitzy's narrative includes some hints from Dulles about American military plans. No plan to invade southern Europe through landings in Spain had been laid, but a quick landing operation might be possible, perhaps even somewhere in the Balkans. First, though, Dulles is reported to have said, the Allies would probably make a quick push from Africa to Ploesti, the oil fields in Romania.

The provenance of these documents is as interesting as the information contained therein. Articles about the "Bull-Pauls" meetings first began to circulate in Soviet-backed disinformation publications in the 1950s to support claims that the United States had actively negotiated with leading Nazis in order to prevent the Russians from gaining even greater territorial victories—the pre-emptive rush by American troops into Austria near the war's end still rankled the Soviets. The documents themselves were reportedly recovered by Russian troops, and, as one account argues, the record "exposes Dulles's hypocrisy and double-dealing and shows that one of America's chief present-day policymakers was a kindred spirit and in fact abettor of the Nazis. In his political thinking he is not far removed from the Hitler cannibals."

The documents are probably not a total fabrication, or at least not 100 percent forged by Russian agents. But nor are they an accurate rendering of Dulles's true attitudes at the time, as seen from the earlier documents about the church campaign against the Holocaust. A likely interpretation comes from von Klemperer: "In view of the obvious unauthenticity of the documentary evidence it would be a mistake to hold Allen Dulles responsible for the opinions attributed to him. He was clearly engaged, as he himself later put it, in a 'fishing expedition,' and he did manage to extract some intelligence from his princely friend. The news of dissension within the Nazi hierarchy alone was worth the whole venture."

While OSS records do not confirm the "Bull-Pauls" talks themselves, other files point to frequent enough meetings between Dulles and Prince Max in early 1943 to assign the nobleman the cover designation "515." Early on, Dulles was well aware that Prince Max was primarily interested in preventing either side from confiscating his own Carpathian estates and the properties in Mexico belonging to his wife, a Portuguese marquesa. And aside from Dulles's own suspicions, there was plenty enough doubt about Prince Max's dependability among the OSS analysts back home. Later in 1943, Dulles cabled a response to one such warning from Washington: "Agree that he is a tough customer and extreme caution required. Highly possible he might be used by Himmler for major feelers. On other hand if certain types of information discounted he can be useful. He realizes his property interests which are his chief concern will be better protected if he plays with us than if too closely identified with Nazis. I have obtained several useful clues from him but only pass on selections from total bulk information furnished."[20]

Dulles used Prince Max as a direct pipeline to Himmler, particularly in the latter days of the war when there was a scramble among members of the SS hierarchy to protect themselves from reprisals and to explore possibilities for a separate surrender to the Allies without giving up to the Soviets. Prince Max and Spitzy were clearly being used to convey disinformation to Himmler—warning the Germans off any notion of a U.S. landing along the western Mediterranean coast (where they did land in 1944) and pointing toward a far corner of the Balkans as the most likely site.

More than twenty years later, Dulles remained unaware that a report on the "Bull-Pauls" talks had been written or what offensive remarks Tyler had reportedly made. Gero von Gaevernitz was doing research for his memoirs at the National Archives in Washington in February 1964 when he came across the microfilm record of the infamous exchanges. He quickly penned a note to Dulles, telling him: "You may wish to look at these reports because they contain a rather amazing detailed description of yourself referred to as Mr. Bull, but also because of certain remarks on the Jewish problem made by Roy Tyler to the German agent [Prince Max] which might cause an unpleasant situation if they were published."[21]

Was Allen Dulles capable of putting on a duplicitous face when meeting with an emissary of the enemy? One would hope so; otherwise he would have been a poor spy indeed. And as we have seen repeatedly in the past, one of the hallmarks of the intelligence game is how frequently the major players are better acquainted with their opposite numbers than are the statesmen for whom they work. So it is, for example, that a growing number of intelligence scholars now believe that British intelligence in Switzerland actually fed *Ultra* secret communiqués from the German Eastern Front to Soviet military intelligence by using its famous "Lucy Ring" branch of the *Rote Kapelle* in Switzerland. Rather than just hand over the information formally in an official exchange in London, it now appears that much of Lucy's incredibly rapid transmission of German battle orders inside Russia back to Moscow came through this rather ornate scheme, which enabled MI6 to left-foot its ostensible Kremlin allies whenever it wanted to. It also appears that Dulles was well aware of the *Ultra* leaks to the Russians and that he did not object even though he himself was barred from access to the supersecret code-breaking results.[22] The real importance of the "Bull-Pauls" talks, again assuming their legitimacy, is that they underscore how deeply Dulles had penetrated into the heart of the Nazi fortress so early in the war.

In the meantime, Dulles continued his expanding volume of important raw intelligence and increasingly knowledgeable analysis of events in Europe. From an early date he continued to warn of reports from Soviet sources of Stalin's hardening plans for USSR ascendancy in Europe after the war. He also warned Washington not to count too heavily on the rolling tide of Allied bombing raids into Germany serving to break the spirit of the German people; only by breaking their faith in Adolf Hitler could the Germans be demoralized into surrendering without a clear military collapse. Increasingly he was able to provide rather detailed reports on the damage caused by the bombing raids themselves, and, too often, his reports showed less damage and a quicker recovery of activity than did the intelligence photos of the Allied air command. The unexpected volume and breadth of the flow coming out of Station Burns was not universally praised in Washington; many of Dulles's conclusions about U.S. strategy offended the diplomatic analysts, and his reports on the effectiveness of various military operations (often based on reactions and eyewitness reports) angered many at the War Department.

On April 28 Whitney Shepardson, by now back from the London station and head of Special Intelligence, cabled both a warning and a cheering endorsement:

> It has been requested of us to inform you that: "All news from Bern these days is being discounted 100% by the War Department." It is suggested that Switzerland is an ideal location for plants, tendencious [*sic*] intelligence and peace feelers but no details are given.
>
> As our duty requires we have passed on the above information. However, we restate our satisfaction that you are the one through whom our Swiss reports come and we believe in your ability to distinguish good intelligence from bad with utmost confidence.[23]

Shepardson sent the cable not on the OSS's own wires but through the State Department, with copies to the War Department and to London Station—a sort of bureaucratic raspberry.

THE SUMMER MONTHS of 1943 saw Dulles building other relationships as well. Mary Bancroft was thirty-nine when she met Dulles through Gerry Mayer. Contemporary photos show a dark-haired, short, and somewhat plump woman, but they do not convey the sharp mind or intense enthusiasm that characterized Bancroft's personality. It was her energy and willingness to plunge ahead that transformed her from being the heiress granddaughter of C. W. Barrons, one of the founders of the *Wall Street Journal,* into the romantic whose adventures touched many lives. Her second marriage had brought her to Zurich; her Swiss husband was a moody, distant man who often was away for long periods of time on business trips within Occupied Europe, where her nationality barred her from traveling.

Mary had become one of the most prominent Americans in Switzerland. She used her personal wealth and her husband's contacts to build something of a salon in Geneva; it was an eclectic set of European writers, scholars, journalists, and government officials. Mary was not above keeping lines open to the more eccentric faddists who were devotees of various health and spiritual cults, but she was too tough-minded to fall under their spell.

Bancroft was using her experience as a newspaper features writer to produce propaganda articles for Mayer's press service when he asked her for a drink at the Baur au Lac Hotel to meet the recently arrived Dulles, then being publicly introduced around as Leland Harrison's newest assistant.

I found Gerry sitting beside a man with a ruddy complexion, a small graying mustache, and keen blue eyes behind rimless spectacles; he was wearing a tweed jacket and gray flannel trousers. As the two men rose to greet me, it flashed through my mind that if anyone imagined this new arrival was anyone's "assistant," they were in for a big surprise. My instantaneous impression of Allen Dulles was that he would never be anybody's assistant—at least not for long.

Within a few weeks, Bancroft had been recruited away from Mayer and was writing profiles and political analyses for Dulles; very soon after they became lovers. "I realized not only that he was in love with me, but that I was very much in love with him," she recalled. One of the Dulles traits she found most attractive, she recounted in her memoirs, was his direct, rather blunt approach to their romance. There was no question that he would ever leave Clover, he told her. "I can't marry you," he had said. "And I probably wouldn't even if I could. But I want you and need you now." Said Bancroft, "I suppose some women would have been put off by such bluntness, but I found it admirable. Allen had put the ball squarely in my court, thus forcing me to take full responsibility for my own actions."[24]

Mary Bancroft not only knew a great deal about herself, she also learned in time a great deal about Allen Dulles and about the inner workings of his important family relationships—particularly with Clover and his brother Foster. She contended that the first twenty months of his spy work in sealed-off Switzerland were the happiest time of his life.

Yet once the Swiss frontiers opened and people came flooding in from Washington, his personality underwent what was for me a most disturbing transformation. I never again saw the Allen Dulles I had watched operating with such consummate skill when he was cut off from all outside influence and just acting on his own. It is rather difficult to describe this personality change except to say that much of the sparkle and charm went out of Allen's personality as I had known it. It was rather like the way an exuberant young person behaves when his parents suddenly show up.... I also felt that his attitude toward his older brother, John Foster, played an important role in his soft-pedaling his own personality.[25]

Their relationship lasted beyond the war and in time became a friendship that expanded to include Clover; indeed, daughter Joan Buresch maintains, "Mary actually became a closer friend of Mother's later on." Her role became something of a go-between because she could broach subjects with Allen that caused angry arguments with Clover; fearless Mary could break through the closed curtain Allen would ring down whenever he wanted to avoid a topic. Clover's own introverted spirit could rarely push through that barrier.

Not that Dulles restricted his intense relationships to just one woman even in the hermetically sealed environment of wartime Switzerland. A frequent visitor to the Herrengasse apartment was Wanda Toscanini, daughter of conductor Arturo Toscanini. As the Countess Castlebarco, she kept a villa on the Swiss-Italian border and was an active and heroic link between the OSS and the Italian partisans in northern Italy. She used funds her father raised on concert tours across the United States to keep numerous partisan groups equipped and functioning. Wanda considered herself both of the titled nobility and the more important aristocracy of the arts; Mary Bancroft was derided as a pushy American. Yet she too was intrigued by that bit of Allen Dulles that he always held back. After the war, when Allen and Clover were reunited, Wanda, like so many others, kept a friendship with her old lover and was not above playing up to the children to advance her position.

Mary, not surprisingly, was jealous and referred disdainfully to her ostensible rival as "the Circus." In reality, rivalry for Dulles's affections was a useless enterprise. Throughout his adult life, he appears to have kept an essential part of his inner self closely under guard. Bancroft, like many of his other close friends, quickly learned to distinguish between the "hollow laugh" that he used to turn away questions he did not want to answer and the explosive, booming laugh when he was genuinely amused. Perhaps this mastery over his own emotions was what made Dulles the successful spy that he was, but it made him a difficult man to love.

When Dulles first mentioned his attraction to Bancroft, he made the lighthearted quip, "We can let the work cover the romance and the romance cover the work." She was never to forget, during those wartime months, that Dulles wanted her for more than love. Each morning thereafter at 9:20, he called from Bern with reports he wanted, people to be met and judged, contacts to be made, and research to be performed. Finally he assigned her the numbing task of translating and editing the huge manuscript of Gisevius, the ambivalent German policeman. In early June, after a series of cautious meetings to determine whether Gisevius could trust Bancroft, he handed over to her a first installment of 1,400 manuscript pages. Her job was more than a daunting literary task; in the process of making the testament publishable, she had to win enough of his confidence to pry other information out of him that might be of more current use to Dulles. In his journals Gisevius had chronicled the early meetings that had led to the fragile alliance among the different groups of "Breakers" plotters. Of more immediate use, Bancroft was to get the latest news on how the plot was developing since the German could not easily travel to Bern to see Dulles personally. Ultimately, Bancroft sought help in both the translation and the interrogations from Elizabeth Scott-Montagu, a titled English lady who had been stranded in France as a volunteer ambulance driver, but who had made it safely to Switzerland ahead of the Germans. Gisevius was flattered to have someone from the English nobility working on his memoir, and the two women proved an effective team in flirting and teasing valuable gossip and information out of their skittish subject during their secret afternoon meetings. The range of the information he provided was so widespread in scope that Dulles ended up adding two other code designations to "512"—"Culber" and "Luber"—to distinguish between the various kinds of information for Washington consumption.

In her turn, Bancroft introduced Dulles to another equally valuable source of insight and information. Like many of the American expatriate illuminati in Switzerland, the still-forming mysteries of psychiatry fascinated Bancroft, and she became a devotee and close friend of Carl Gustav Jung, who had established his research facility in a nearby hamlet and gave public lectures in Zurich. Through sessions with Jung, Bancroft was able to cure herself of chronic attacks of sneezing; she in turn had helped popularize Jung with American audiences through a number of magazine profiles that played up his rivalry with Sigmund Freud. Jung, for his part, was pleased by the attention and amused at the adulation of his American subjects; he once observed that Americans took to psychiatry "as a shortcut to culture."

A steadfast anti-Nazi, Jung was nonetheless fascinated with the psychological makeup of Adolf Hitler and other Third Reich personalities. It was that shared interest that drew him and Allen Dulles together after an introduction by Bancroft. Many of Jung's theories are based on the tribal-myth view of societies, and he argued that, unlike other national leaders such as Mussolini and

Stalin, the tremendous psychological hold Hitler had over the German popular mind was due to his instinctive power of speaking, preaching even, to the innermost fears and yearnings of those people. Thus began a strange partnership in which Jung became a frequently consulted adviser ("488") on the propaganda campaign the Allies were beaming into Germany. He agreed with Dulles that it was ineffective to threaten or heap guilt on the German people; rather, they must be made to understand that they must break with Hitler if they were to preserve themselves. One early cable of Jung's insights was eerily prophetic: "It is Jung's belief that Hitler will take recourse in any desperate measures up to the end, but he does not exclude the possibility of suicide in a desperate moment."[26]

Jung's advice proved so valuable that at the end of the war he received a much prized letter of commendation and thanks from General Eisenhower. Later, the analyst and his teachings became a major fixture in the lives and futures of Dulles and his family.

That summer of 1943 was perhaps the busiest time of Dulles's life thus far, including the hectic months in Paris in 1919. Short-staffed and surrounded by enemies, even Dulles's enormous fund of physical and mental energy must at times have been exhausted. The few letters he was able to smuggle out to Clover speak of frequent gout attacks that left him bedridden and fuming. Mostly, however, the portrait is of a man with high enthusiasm for the chase, in constant motion, meeting, judging, and translating the confusing events of a battle in progress. If there was frustration, it was of not being able to be in more than one place at a single time, and of trying to move the huge volume of information and insights he was gathering to Washington more efficiently and in more timely fashion. Intelligence, after all, has a short shelf life; then it becomes history.

What he could not know was that in August 1943 he would win his greatest intelligence coup of the war, and add immeasurably to the enormous flow of information out of Hitler's Germany and onto the desks of the OSS analysis staff. Just as Jung was able to give Dulles valuable insight into the workings of Hitler's mind, he was about to fall heir to another confidential source who could put the spymaster virtually inside Hitler's command center in the Nazi Foreign Ministry in the Wilhelmstrasse in Berlin. Dulles was about to meet the man known forever in intelligence history as "George Wood."

CHAPTER NINE

August 1943–September 1944

*"...arrival of more than 200 highly valuable Easter eggs, which
will be whipped into shape and quickly forwarded..."*
—*110 to Victor, April 11, 1944*

"What a bunny..."
—*Victor to 110, April 12, 1944*

A RETIRED BRITISH INTELLIGENCE officer recently recalled that
on the afternoon of Tuesday, August 17, 1943, a short, stocky
German was ushered into the office of Colonel Henry Cartwright,
military attaché at the British Embassy in Bern. The poor German
was sweating with fear. The blond fringe of hair that ringed the
sides of his bald head was soaked, making him seem to have less
hair than he really had. Yet, as frightened as he was, the man was
determined to say his piece.

To cut a long story short, he said he was an employee of
the German Foreign Office, that he was wildly anti-Nazi,
had been even before the war. He had a whole family of
relations in southwest Africa. He gave their names and
said we could check them out and what they said about
him. And he repeated that he was in the foreign office
and he got access to copies of decoded telegrams, and
here, dear colonel, are twenty copies which I managed to
slip in my pocket and take out of Germany at some risk.
I think that we ought to be able to devise methods of

delivering to you a written supply of information. That
was the proposition.[1]

Fritz Kolbe had good reason to perspire. He was the special
assistant to a top Nazi Foreign Office official, Ambassador Karl
Ritter, who was entrusted with the most important diplomatic
missions involving the *Wehrmacht's* high command, the OKW.
Ritter was both rough and ruthless; he had been the organizer of
Nazi fifth column movements in Latin America before the war.
Now he was the right-hand man to Foreign Minister Joachim von
Ribbentrop. Kolbe's job was to screen and reroute all the top-
secret cables and memoranda that were directed into and out of
the ambassador's office. In short, through the hands of this forty-
three-year-old functionary flowed all of the important secrets and
policy decisions of Hitler's generals and diplomats; only the
führer himself had a better vantage point for German intelligence.

Kolbe, moreover, was the genuine article. He, like Hans
Gisevius, was one of those eccentrics who spoke his mind with such
blunt honesty that other more conformist Germans gave him a
wide berth even in the midst of the frenzy of Hitler adulation that
gripped the nation. Kolbe's life is proof that no tyrant is safe as long
as one honest man is left alive. The son of a saddlemaker, Kolbe had
worked his way up to the position of stationmaster in the state railway system while he studied at night to qualify for the foreign service. In various foreign posts he earned an enviable reputation for
precision as a bureaucrat and was willing to work long hours. So his
superiors overlooked his outspoken political views. He was viewed
as a drudge by his masters, a brusque, prickly character, but one
who could handle important, difficult administrative tasks fault-
lessly. He was five-feet, seven-inches tall, but his stocky build made
him appear shorter; his prominent ears and high-cheeked features
spoke of Slavic forebears that conflicted with the Teutonic ideal in

higher Nazi circles. He had well-known marital troubles and had left a son behind in southern Africa while he tried to divorce his second wife. When the war started, his political views were suspect enough to have him called back inside the Third Reich, but his reputation for skilled work landed him a job at the hub of the Foreign Office's communications network in the Wilhelmstrasse.

As Kolbe later explained, once the Nazi war machine seemed inevitably directed toward conquest, he reasoned that "it was not enough to clench one's fist and hide it in one's pocket, one must strike with it." But how? During the early days of the war he had tried to make contact with various cliques within the "Breakers" group, but he judged many of them to be dilettantes (and many were) and their discretion to be so poor that he doubted they would ever be able to bring off a coup that would save Germany. He concluded that the only way to save Germany was to bring about its defeat by the Allies as quickly as possible. Getting out of Germany with his secrets was the trick.

One of Kolbe's friends was a woman who made travel assignments in the courier section of the ministry. He arranged through her to get one of the assignments to deliver some sensitive documents to the German Embassy in Bern; his excuse was that he wanted to institute divorce proceedings against his wife, a Swiss national, who had refused to return to Germany with him in 1939. Once he reached Bern, Kolbe contacted Dr. Ernst Kocherthaler, a German Jew who had secured Spanish citizenship and had set up practice in the Swiss capital. The two had become friends when Kolbe was stationed in Madrid. It was Kocherthaler who secured the appointment with Colonel Cartwright.

The interview story continues:

Cartwright was a very nice man, but he was awfully dumb. The reason he had been appointed to the military attaché's job was that in the 1914–1918 war he had escaped twelve times from prisoner of war camps. He was very good at escaping, you see, so they sent him to Switzerland to be our military attaché.

Cartwright was as aware as any other British intelligence officer that MI6 by that time was under formal orders from the Foreign Office to dismiss anti-Nazi volunteers, especially those bringing peace feelers. Foreign Secretary Anthony Eden worried lest a suspicious Stalin (who was, after all, bearing the brunt of the war at that moment) sense betrayal; British officials also worried about bolstering the public will to endure the war to its conclusion. Already there had been too many neutral emissaries trying to reach church leaders and other influential friends in Britain.

So this poor man pulls out these thin pieces of paper that he had smuggled out and spreads them before Cartwright, [who] just glanced at the papers and drew himself up. He said, "Sir, you take me for an utter fool. I am not an utter fool. I know that you are sent as a plant to get me into trouble but in the remote possibility that you are not a plant, then, sir, you are a cad. And I do not deal with cads." And he showed him the door and didn't even keep the bits of paper.

That might well have been the end of the Kolbe saga, perhaps even of Kolbe himself. But his friend Kocherthaler had the presence of mind to suggest to his shattered friend that he try the Americans. The next day, Gerald Mayer of the Office of War Information was called by a friend of Kocherthaler from Basle who suggested a meeting with an interesting friend. The doctor went to the meeting at 24 Duforstrasse while Kolbe attended to his official chores at the German offices. After explaining what he was doing, Kocherthaler left with Mayer sixteen of the cable copies that had been brought out in a package strapped to Kolbe's leg. Mayer excused himself, ran up the two flights of stairs to Dulles's office, and showed him the documents, each one stamped with *Geheime Reichsache*—Secret State Document—the highest grade of the Nazi classification system. If the documents were legitimate, they were dynamite. All had to do with intelligence operations. One was about sending German agents into North Africa, another about the resistance in Czechoslovakia, a third reported on British agents being inserted into the Balkans. Even the normally enthusiastic Dulles drew back from bait like this; it smelled just too good to be true.

Dulles and Mayer at this point in the war were not aware of the extent of progress the code-breakers at Bletchley Park had made in penetrating the various German ciphers by spinning their handmade computer off the *Enigma* machine variations at their command. But they were all too painfully aware that the Germans had penetrated at least some of the American codes. If Dulles tried to transmit these Kolbe documents, even in paraphrase, back to Washington in OSS code, it could give the eavesdropping Germans enough points of reference to penetrate even that secure system. And the information itself might be bogus. Another variation might be that the information itself was valid but just "chicken feed" to lull U.S. intelligence into a state of belief that might make a more important lie credible later. At the least, Kocherthaler himself might be an *agent provocateur* who would tip the Swiss authorities off to what Dulles was up to and force them to intervene and perhaps even expel the Americans.

Still, as Dulles would later explain many times, the memory of his missed meeting with Lenin in 1917 pushed him forward. A four-hour meeting was set for Thursday morning with both

Kolbe and Kocherthaler at Mayer's apartment; Dulles was to attend as Mayer's assistant, "Mr. Douglas." This time Kolbe handed over to Mayer "flimsies with 186 other separate bits of intelligence which ranged from verbatim cables to summaries of longer memoranda." The tissue-thin papers were mimeographed copies of the telegraph traffic coming into the communications room of the Wilhelmstrasse from dozens of important embassies and from a host of military command units. The reports covered troop morale on the Eastern Front, an assessment of *maquis* sabotage in France, the Berlin visit of a Japanese ambassador, and various conferences between Foreign Secretary von Ribbentrop and other Nazi officials. Among the other treasures Kolbe brought were a hand-drawn map of Hitler's secret Eastern Front headquarters at Rastenburg, the location of the railway siding nearby for the special trains that the top Nazis used to get there, and one of the German one-time cipher pads.

At this point, Dulles entered the apartment and was introduced to the two Germans. Dulles made no attempt to ingratiate himself with this strange little man, Kolbe. Without waiting to be asked, Kolbe launched into a recitation of who he was, what his job entailed, and what had motivated him to commit the highest form of treason against his government. Under close questioning by Dulles, he gave specifics about his own twenty-year career in the diplomatic service, said that his wife and son were in South Africa, and told where other friends and acquaintances could be found to vouch for him. He wanted no payment for himself, he said, only help in reestablishing his government career; he assumed that those who were known to have resisted Hitler would be given preference over Nazi loyalists. Before he was questioned further, Kolbe told the Americans that he had gone to the British first and they had not believed him. Dulles had known that already, for Colonel Cartwright had run into him the night before and warned lightly that "some cove with a funny name, has a 'tal' in it," had been peddling suspect information.

Dulles decided at least for the time being to keep Kolbe on the string. The German might possibly be able to wangle a second trip soon, but this time it might be to Sweden. Dulles came up with the code name "George Winter," but somehow the last name became "Wood." He was told to bring more information of the same quality as soon as possible. Beyond that, the Americans would not commit themselves. Kolbe said he did not mind; the material would convince them of his *bona fides* soon enough.

Kolbe's second chance came on September 16. By then he had stockpiled a considerably larger cache of flimsies, far more than could be strapped to his leg. He struck on an ingenious solution. As a courier, he would carry an officially sealed envelope of material for the embassy in Bern which was so secured that it could not easily be tampered with, nor could it be inspected either by German police or Swiss customs authorities. The solution was to secure a larger envelope, put the embassy's envelope plus his own inside, and then have it officially stamped and sealed. Once across the border, he merely destroyed the outer envelope, delivered his official consignment to the embassy, and called Kocherthaler to arrange a rendezvous to hand over his own precious cargo.

At nightfall, Mayer picked Kolbe up in his car and dropped him off at the footpath the led along the river to the back door of 23 Herrengasse, where Dulles waited. This time the batch of documents contained disclosures that required both confirmation and action. There was a professional map of the Rastenburg command complex and the latest schedule for the trains running there from Berlin. Among the cable items was a note that the German Legation in Dublin was about to resume broadcasts from the clandestine radio station that it operated there intermittently. Irish officials knew of the station's existence in the German

Legation and earlier had shut it down after strong protests from London that it was used as an important link to the wolf packs of submarines that prowled the North Atlantic. There were also descriptions of a campaign by the Vichy government of Pierre Laval to shoot relatives of soldiers known to be fighting with Charles de Gaulle's forces; of a plot to smuggle vital tungsten supplies from Spain disguised in orange crates; and, most alarming, of a report from the German Embassy in Buenos Aires about the impending departure of a large supply convoy for Britain from an American Atlantic port. Kolbe even had a list of suggested industrial and transport targets for Allied bombers. By now, Dulles was excited. He worked out procedures by which the German could safely send his tissue-paper thin copies of the Foreign Ministry traffic via third parties, and communications codes were agreed upon. Kocherthaler agreed to send Kolbe food parcels that, if they contained coffee, meant the previous shipment of papers had been safely received. Postcards sent from fictitious friends in Switzerland inquiring about the availability of Japanese toys in Berlin stores, for example, might signal a desire by Dulles for more military information about Japan.

There is no exact record of the number of times Kolbe made the perilous journey to Bern himself. The official OSS history puts it:

> For several months, "Wood" managed to go to Switzerland every few weeks. Soon he was bringing cables by the pound, officially packaged and sealed by him in the Foreign Office. The problem of handling this periodic flood of material was a staggering one. The security angle alone was perplexing enough, and the task of translating and encoding took the time of the entire staff at Bern for weeks after each batch of telegrams was

received until the frontier opened in September 1944, and the material could be sent out in bulk.[2]

Between then and the end of the war, more than 1,600 items of pure gold intelligence flowed into Dulles's hands from "George Wood" alone. In terms of timeliness, few of the reports were more than ten days old when they reached Dulles. In range they covered the Nazis' own assessment of German popular morale from the bombings, the actual damage assessments of the raids, and, of vital interest, the breakdown of the *Wehrmacht*'s fighting power on the Russian front. The pattern of distribution, study, and ultimate use of Kolbe's extraordinary cable copies later became an item of study and reflection among Cold War intelligence professionals; it provided a cautionary tale for both gatherers and "receivers."[3]

The flimsies of German Foreign Office cables being smuggled out of Berlin by "George Wood" through the autumn and winter of 1943 assumed an importance far greater than their immediately enormous intelligence potential; the traffic in effect could put OSS into cryptanalysis via the back door since the cables were the answers the code-breakers were seeking in the first place. That is, if they were genuine.

In the midst of this, Dulles sent the first sixteen "Wood" cables over to Count "Fanny" Vanden Heuvel and asked him to transmit them to London. Dulles wanted MI6 to check Kolbe's references and to analyze the content of the cables; a similar cautiously worded file went to Washington. For security and manpower reasons, the entire series of Kolbe documents (now designated "Kappa" between Burns and Victor) was not moved out of Bern until September 14, two days before Kolbe returned with his second batch. He was back again on October 9, this time with two hundred pages, which included ninety-six verbatim telegrams and a ten-page debriefing report. Dulles and Mayer closely questioned him during this three-

day stay and got even more information in the form of gossip—
who had been transferred, where certain offices in Berlin had
moved because of the bombing, and so on. In his covering cable to
Washington, Dulles said he was finally convinced of "the particular
value and authoritative quality of this material."

According to the available "Kappa" traffic files, Washington
did not respond with any "Out" messages about this swelling tide
of information until October 20, and even then the questions
were anodyne and reflected no particular enthusiasm. At the
London OSS station, David Bruce's analysts mulled over the flow
and pronounced a cautious "no evidence against" opinion. By
now, fully half the traffic Kolbe was bringing to Bern was being
sent via the transcribers at the British Embassy to MI6 London,
where the crusty vice-chief Claude Dansey went into a sputtering
rage at the notion that Dulles was paying attention to such a spurious and obvious plant. Even if the cables reflected true events,
they were just "chicken feed" aimed to lure the Allies into swal-
lowing some major intelligence fraud later. At that point, coincidence and a large dose of irony took a hand.

HAROLD ADRIAN RUSSELL (KIM) PHILBY had been recruited
into the Soviet intelligence service as early as 1933. He had been
recommended by spotters at Cambridge University, where he was
the most promising of a glittering set of young intellectuals of that
day, a set that included those other two rogues and traitors, Guy
Burgess and Donald Maclean. During the 1930s Philby did spy
chores for the Soviets as he supported himself in a number of occupations, including a stint as a war correspondent in Spain and in
Austria before World War II. After wangling his way into MI6,
Philby, by his own account, was plotting for advancement within
the agency (the better to serve his Soviet compatriots) when the
"Wood" traffic began to arrive in London and was noisily derided

by Dansey. In his self-serving and occasionally vindictive autobiography, *My Secret War*,[4] Philby tells how he saw the Kolbe-Dulles cables as a vehicle for his own advancement. On his own, he took the messages to the agency's cryptanalysts to see whether their *Ultra* decoding had already spotted the same messages among traffic that had been intercepted independently by the British. Among the items submitted for comparison was an important German report on the Japanese order of battle and assessment of future Japanese intentions sent via the diplomatic channels by the German military attaché in Tokyo. The report came back quickly. Three of the intercepts exactly matched what the Bletchley Park cryptographers had deciphered, and the remainder were of invaluable help in decoding the German diplomatic system.

While the geniuses of Bletchley Park had their own copy of the German *Enigma* enciphering machine, that still left them the chore of working out the permutations of code possibilities each time one military or diplomatic user moved to a different calibration on the machine. In doing this, the British in effect invented the modern computer to help them. But it was an enormous boost to have clear messages to work backward from. Besides, the German technology was giving the British a race for their lives; by that time they were well aware that the *Wehrmacht* was testing a radiotelegraph machine that could be typed in clear, sent in code over the airwaves at high speed, and typed in clear by a machine at the receiving end. That meant more traffic and more codes to break.

At Bletchley Park, Philby was a hero. As more and more of the "Wood" traffic was swallowed whole by the cryptographers, Philby began to circulate selected bits to the various military and diplomatic consumers of such information—careful not to mention that it was originally OSS traffic or its provenance. "The reaction was immediate," Philby wrote. "Army, Navy and Air Force—all three howled for more. The Foreign Office was more sedate, but also very polite."[5] Ever the consummate bureaucrat, Philby made sure he had written endorsements of the "Wood" traffic and demands for more before he bearded Dansey in his den. The old spy was predictably furious when he recognized that the material was genuine, but he was considerably mollified to find out that, thanks to Philby's selective marketing, the general perception was that "Wood" was a British product. It took a while before the misunderstanding was sorted out, but by then, Philby's career was advanced by "our German friend... with his useful suitcase." By the end of the war, Philby was where he wanted to be: head of the British service's anti-Soviet counterintelligence division. In 1949, as the British intelligence representative in Washington, he took part in the ill-fated Anglo-U.S. attempt to topple the leftist regime in Albania and, later, was linked in the 1951 defection to Russia of fellow spies Burgess and Maclean. Philby himself defected to Moscow in 1963, just as the British net was finally closing in. He died in Russia in 1988, with the rank of major general in the KGB.

Philby did at least get the information from Dulles's coup circulated and put to immediate use against the Germans. "George Wood" was not so lucky at the start in Washington. Donovan had turned over the first batch of the "Kappa" traffic at once to counterintelligence and waited, resisting what must have been an awful temptation to rush copies over to the White House for the president's pleasure. Roosevelt was an enthusiastic consumer of "110's" output; sometimes he even arranged to be patched through by telephone to "The Kremlin" so he could listen in to the nightly "Flash" radio monologues. But Donovan realized that "Kappa" was different.

Indeed, it would be the end of December before General Strong's military intelligence personnel even got their hands on the Dulles paraphrases, and it would be January 1944 before the information was generally circulating to top intelligence officials at other agencies, including the State Department. Again, the fear of being lured by "chicken feed" was used by Donovan's enemies to cool enthusiasm. Some—Mott Belin, now at State, was one—were early advocates of the "Kappa" traffic, but that had more to do with their own faith in Dulles than any insight into the material's legitimacy. But Donovan had enough trouble keeping his critics at bay, and with understandable prudence he organized a committee to review the "Boston Series," as its interagency designation identified the cables. General Strong of G-2, James Murphy, head of OSS counterintelligence, and the British service's representative in Washington were handed the early batches.

In the meantime, Donovan urged Dulles to review the "Kappa" traffic at hand and examine the original documents from which the translated paraphrases had been made for signs of holes in the stories. Fortunately for Dulles, just at that time the Allies had liberated the island of Corsica off the coast of France. Through his French *maquis* contacts, Dulles arranged with the engineer of the Geneva-to-Lyons train to install a secret compartment over the firebox in the locomotive cab. Rolls of microfilms of the original "Wood" documents, plus a whole host of other intelligence raw data, could now be secreted in the locomotive; if it was searched on occasion, the engineer merely flipped a lever that dumped the compartment's contents into the flames, where they were instantly consumed. At Lyons, the microfilms were transported by bicycle all the way to Marseilles, where the legendary Corsican smugglers promptly delivered them to waiting planes on the island. Now the critics could not complain that Dulles might be misreading the material. But "Wood" and Dulles won their credibility before the study committee could actually render its decision; the break came during Christmas week 1943.

Kolbe made it out to Bern yet another time on December 27. On the 28th Dulles cabled that more than two hundred documents were in the batch and "I now firmly believe in the good faith of Wood, and I am ready to stake my reputation on the fact that these documents are genuine. I base my conclusion on internal evidence and on the nature of the documents themselves. We are keeping close watch on cipher security in re-wording." In the batch were cramped handwritten copies of longer telegrams along with thirty items of oral information. There was also news about the new German supersonic fighter plane, more information that construction sites were being chosen for the V-1 rockets in Belgium and France. Among the whole telegrams was a blockbuster, dated November 4, from Franz von Papen, the old World War I spy, now in Turkey. Von Papen wired to Foreign Minister Ribbentrop in the Wilhelmstrasse:

> ...a number of [official British] documents have come to us from a new walk-in with whose further exploitation... I have charged SD officer Moyzisch. Because of the compass of the material and in order to provide a better evaluation I have sent him to you with the Saturday courier to make a personal report. For the sake of security very few even here are witting [*sic*] of the matter; in future communications I shall designate this source "Cicero"; request that questions about him be sent eyes-only to the ambassador....

There was much more. Dulles began sending "Kappa" cables on the 29th, and they were still rattling into "The Kremlin" communications center on New Year's Day. Among the "Cicero" citations was his report on the Teheran Conference of Allied leaders that had been filed within a week of the event itself. Moreover, source "Cicero" produced documents showing that the Allies had dropped plans to force troops through Turkey into the Balkans. He also reported that vital Turkish airfields would be made available by the neutralist Ankara government, that the Allies believed Rome would be taken by the middle of January, that combined air operations from Italian islands and Turkey would be used in a campaign for air superiority in the Aegean, and that an invasion plan somewhere in the Mediterranean was code-named "Anvil." Later documents would affix the code word "Overlord" to the expected invasion of Europe by the "Anglo-Saxons" and would even point to the landings taking place in June without pinpointing exactly where.

Source "Cicero" clearly was a coup for von Papen, the slippery old spy and Hitler booster. His mission was to manipulate Germany's old World War I ally, Turkey, into joining the Axis, or, failing that, to prevent Turkey from allowing the Allies to build up a force there for a Balkan invasion. He had considerable cards to play, not least that German air bases in Greece made Istanbul itself a potential target if the Turks chose the wrong side. Istanbul and the capital Ankara, as during Dulles's own tour there, were another "happy hunting ground" for spies, and von Papen had bagged a good one, the valet in the British ambassador's residence. It seems the ambassador, Sir Hughe Knatchbull-Hugessen, was particularly sloppy about leaving secret documents around his dressing room in the official residence instead of putting them in the safe.

The valet—now "Cicero" to the Nazis and OSS alike—began photographing important documents a month after he was hired in September 1943, and Kolbe was gathering copies of von Papen's indiscreet telegrams bragging about his coup and the stolen secrets almost at once. This was a critical time to have a leak from Istanbul directly to Berlin. From November 22 to 26,

Roosevelt, Churchill, and Chiang Kai-shek met in Cairo to set Allied policy in the Pacific theater of the war. Three days later, FDR, Churchill, and Stalin met at Teheran, where the Soviet leader's claims for Poland after the war were conceded and where the commitment was made for an invasion of France by the Anglo-American armies in the year to come.

The "Cicero" case went on to become something of a *cause célèbre* in postwar Britain when it became public knowledge. A number of British historians attempted to assert that British counterintelligence had picked up on "Cicero" almost at once (after all, the British did have the *Ultra* computers working night and day) and that he was "turned" into a double-agent to send disinformation via von Papen until the spy's sense of danger caused him to drop from sight and abandon work for the Germans. Something of a growth industry sprang up surrounding what was undeniably one of the more colorful espionage tales of the war; scores of magazine articles were written, and so were two books—one by "Cicero" himself and another by his German security service control[6]—and a movie.

In a postwar newspaper book review for the German control agent's book, Dulles voiced a theme that is essential to understanding what happened in both the "Cicero" and "George Wood" cases during the war.

> The story well serves to illustrate several interesting points about secret intelligence which my own experience in this field amply bears out. It is often harder to use the product than to get it. The receivers of intelligence generally start out by discounting a particular report as false or a plant. Then when they get over that hurdle they discard what they don't like and refuse to believe it. Finally, when they do get a report they both

believe and like, they don't know what to do about it. And so it was with Operation Cicero.[7]

And so it was with "George Wood," too.

"Wood's" Christmas delivery had brought other material of immense value as well. He had seen the German High Command's own order-of-battle report on Allied divisions stationed in England in preparation for the expected invasion of Europe. The German Army High Command generals were convinced that sixty divisions were already set in place, about a third again more had just arrived, and most were only beginning to train for the assault. There also were alarming reports of a debate going on within the Nazi hierarchy about whether the eight thousand Jews living in Rome were to be deported to the north and then liquidated or, as the German commandant of the Eternal City wanted, put to work on fortifications.

Perhaps braced by Dulles's personal commitment to the "Wood" information, Donovan was finally emboldened enough on January 10, 1944, to send the first fourteen "Kappa" cables to President Roosevelt with this cautious endorsement: "We have secured through secret intelligence channels a series of what purport to be authentic reports, transmitted by various German diplomatic, consular, military and intelligence sources to their headquarters. The source and material are being checked as to probable authenticity both here and in London. We shall submit later a considered opinion on this point. It is possible that contact with this source furnishes the first important penetration into a responsible German agency. We have labeled these reports the 'Boston Series'...." Just one day later, Donovan sent another memo to FDR, this time based on a bombshell contained in the New Year's "Kappa" traffic about Henry Wallace, Roosevelt's vice president. Wallace was increasingly becoming a political worry and embarrassment to the White House because his outspoken political opinions moved steadily leftward as the war progressed. The item accused Wallace of leaking top-secret intelligence from the Moscow Conference (between Churchill and Stalin) to the Swiss ambassador to Washington, a man who happened to be Wallace's brother-in-law.

The following paraphrase comes from German sources, the ultimate source allegedly being the German Foreign Office. It purports to be a report to Berlin by the German minister to Switzerland embodying the substance of a report from the Swiss minister in Washington to the Swiss Foreign Office:

1. K.O. Schweiz [the *Abwehr* station in Switzerland] has seen reports of the Swiss Minister, which were based upon talks with the Vice President. According to these reports, at the start of the Moscow Conference the Americans and British tried to vindicate both the past and future actions of the Allied GHQ's; however, their Russian partner exhibited practically no sympathy or appreciation of their position. On the other hand, it seems that the foundations were laid for coming military cooperation. Not until a second front has been opened, i.e., not until the Allies have carried out a successful invasion of France, will this plan for cooperation go into effect. Until then Russia retains the right to unrestricted action in military and political matters. The Vice President stated, however, that Russian conditions for more complete military cooperation will soon be met.[8]

And so it went. "Cicero" stopped his spying in Ambassador Knatchbull-Hugessen's bedroom sometime in March 1944, because of his own fears and because the Germans had given him enough money in English sterling notes to make a run for it. British security officers sent to Turkey to investigate the "Wood" tip-off wasted weeks sleuthing around the British Legation in Istanbul and the embassy in Ankara, never thinking that the ambassador's residence servant might be suspect. Later, London rather grumpily demanded that Dulles put Kolbe to work trying to track down "Cicero," something the Germans themselves were unable to do at the moment; their revenge was that much of the money given to the spy was counterfeit. Withal, "Kappa" traffic remained much prized at Bletchley Park.

There was progress of sorts in Washington. General Strong of G-2 and James Murphy of X-2 left much of the daily task of reading and checking the "Boston Series" files to Colonel Alfred McCormack, who fought a slow rear-guard action with each cable. Faced with real gold dust, he would issue a qualified "probably authentic" ruling or "sounds like what their originators might send home." But on the whole, McCormack clung to the Dansey "chicken feed" line—that the Germans were giving out stale, harmless secrets easily confirmed by other sources (like subsequent events) in order to build a false sense of confidence for some other forthcoming bit of catastrophic disinformation.

But "Kappa" did win its spurs, and it was Murphy's X-2 analysts who rode to the rescue. The information that finally convinced them, ironically, came out of the Pacific theater of operations, not Europe. During Easter week, Dulles had taken delivery of two hundred more "Wood" cables that he judged "highly valuable Easter eggs" (to which Washington cabled back, "What a bunny"). This time the information was so widespread, so eminently confirmable, and so much more damaging to German interests that the notion of a plant dwindled away. What finally convinced the doubters at the War and State Departments were the disclosures in the Easter "Kappa" lengthy report of telegrams from the German military and air attachés in Tokyo who had been given an inspection tour all around the southern periphery of the Japanese Pacific battle perimeter. It was pure gold. The reports not only confirmed some of the scanty tactical information gathered by MacArthur's own command intelligence service, they also filled in scores of information gaps and corrected a number of big mistakes in the American view of Japan's strategic intentions and capabilities of holding its far-flung island redoubts. The British MI5 analysts in London coincidentally came to the same conclusion about the remainder of the "Kappa" cables that they had analyzed; only 4 percent of them contained identifiable errors, and henceforward they would be received "with enthusiasm," David Bruce ("105") messaged "110."

> According to Broadway [MI6], the [Wood Japanese] report… is amazingly correct and there is small doubt as to its authenticity. They request that special congratulations be offered the source; these we hereby heartily send.[9]

As of May 6, almost ten months from Kolbe's first fearful visit to Bern, Murphy's X-2 began to distribute "Boston Series" information to an eleven-man senior list in Washington, including Marshall, Stimson, Knox, and the intelligence chiefs of the armed services and State Department. FDR would be briefed by the director himself, or from Donovan's personal copy of the material.

In the meantime, Kolbe was operating under increasing strain. He had found an ally in an Alsatian doctor working in Berlin who had links to the French resistance. Together they set up a clandestine photo studio in the doctor's clinic where Kolbe could bring briefcases full of documents to be photographed with Gerry Mayer's microfilm camera. To do so, Kolbe had to brave the dangers of the nightly bombing attacks that turned Berlin's streets into a storm of explosions and shell fragments. Perhaps even more disturbing to him, his own career advanced as his Nazi masters increased their reliance on his bureaucratic skills. At one point shortly before the July 20 plot, he actually found himself working in the Eastern Front secretariat at Hitler's secret Rastenburg headquarters. He began to feel his spying was useless and finally told Dulles he wanted to shift over to a more active relationship with the "Breakers" organization and actually take a hand in the assassination. Horrified, Dulles turned on his considerable personal powers to persuade the shaky man that he was doing far more good as "George Wood" than he ever could inside the Kreisau Circle. For the moment, Kolbe was mollified, but he continued throughout the war to take risks that seemed to dare the Nazis to discover him.

It was fortuitous that Kolbe did as Dulles asked. The "Breakers" conspirators seemed determined to destroy themselves before they even got close to Hitler. Helmuth von Moltke had been seized by the Gestapo in January and was languishing in the Plotzensee Prison in Berlin. He had been caught quite by accident trying to warn a fellow conspirator who was suspected in one of the earlier assassination attempts. But von Moltke in any case had been calling too much attention to himself to have lasted much longer. While Adam von Trott was darting about Switzerland, von Moltke was waging an all-too-open series of visits to Istanbul, where he tried to reach American intelligence and diplomatic contacts about negotiating a separate peace. He was led on for a while, but ultimately the Anglo-American officials in Cairo were less interested in installing the Kreisau plotters in Hitler's place than were the authorities in Washington and London. Now he was in the hands of the Gestapo; what few secrets there were about the Hitler plotters were being tortured out of him. As it turned out, Himmler already had a list naming most of the major conspirators in the Kreisau Circle and in ex-mayor Carl Goerdeler's government group. He was lacking only the third piece of the conspiracy, the identity of the military officers who would attempt Hitler's murder.

German intelligence and Dulles's network of contacts there were hit by more turmoil. The von Moltke arrest had led to the seizure of others, including a number of top aides to Canaris. Then a number of *Abwehr* agents defected to the Allies, most notably in Sweden and Turkey. Hitler went into a rage against the *Abwehr* and against Canaris personally. In February he ordered the *Abwehr* folded into the *Sicherheitsdienst.* The resulting creation was the *Reichssicherheitshauptamt* (RSHA), and it was put under the direction of Heinrich Himmler, the leader of the Reich SS and chief of the German police. Thus, the German *Wehrmacht* became the only combatant army of World War II not to have its own intelligence service on the eve of the Allied attack. Direction of the RSHA was given to a man named Walter Schellenberg, a protégé of the assassinated monster Reinhard Heydrich. Canaris, for his part, was treated leniently, considering Hitler's anger. Schellenberg, as much a plotter as Canaris, was not about to have the Gestapo rampaging through his newly created agency, even if it meant protecting suspects like Canaris. The admiral was put under protective house arrest for the time being and in charge of a division of the RSHA for economic warfare back in Berlin. It was not until the roundup of the July 20 conspirators that Canaris was scooped up by the Gestapo and finally executed.

In those spring months of 1944, Dulles was working at a fearsome pace. The Normandy invasion had been definitely set for the end of May or the first week of June. Operation Anvil, the landings in southern France, were to follow closely behind, but logistical troubles began to intrude in the final planning stages. If the Allied Expeditionary Force was to put ashore the number of troops that General Eisenhower's strategists insisted upon for Operation Neptune, it would take nearly all the landing craft and supporting battleships and cruisers in the Allies' possession. To then shift many of those same craft, after netting out expected casualties, all the way around to the North African coast in just a few weeks was foolhardy planning. Moreover, while there were troops in North Africa, the bulk of the combat units would have to be siphoned off from the Anglo-American forces battling their way up the peninsula of Italy. Worse, the Allied command in Alexandria expected the Germans to contest the southern landings almost as fiercely as they would those on the Normandy coast. There were important *Panzer* and elite *Waffen SS* units in the Vichy sector of France; if they were not lured north by the Normandy offensive, they could decimate the Allied forces attempting to come ashore in the south.

William Quinn, a colonel in charge of G-2 for General Alexander Patch's Seventh Army, had to make the tough decisions, for those units would have to get ashore and fight their way north through the Rhone valley to link up with General George Patton and his Third Army. As he explained, "We had to land where the Germans *weren't*. So that meant we had to find out where the Germans *were*, and then convince them that we were going to try right in front of them."[10]

"The way we were set up," Quinn explained, "the Allied Forces Headquarters [AFHQ] was in Algiers. General Patch was to be in charge of the invasion, but all of us were under the command of Field Marshal Sir Harold Alexander, the theater commander. So we were obliged to rely on their British intelligence services and what they could tell us about conditions inside France, and it wasn't encouraging."

This was understandable since Alexander and his staff were disquieted by the prospect of having to divert troops from the Italian front for a speculative landing in another area; one does not divide one's command needlessly. Moreover, British intelligence operations among the French *maquis* were more keyed to build up and support forceful resistance action once the main Neptune offensive in Normandy began; they were to concentrate on identifying bridges and key railheads for sabotage once the signal was given, not to be prowling around *Wehrmacht* units trying to identify them and their strength. The British, particularly the covert Special Operations Executive, had their hands full in France locating and establishing communications with hundreds of active *maquis* contacts who were airdropped with an increasing volume of light arms and explosives for the uprising, which would be timed for D-Day, whenever that was to be. It was bloody, heartbreaking work. In May the Germans launched a "Blood and Ashes" campaign of reprisals and executions; in one area alone, nearly one hundred captured *maquis* were publicly hanged. There was little time or inclination to use scarce resources to check every landing beach, Nazi fortification, or gun emplacement from Genoa to Gibraltar. But Quinn had his own D-Day to prepare.

"No one had heard much about OSS, not where we were, anyway," Quinn reported. "Then one day Donovan called on me and said, 'Look up a guy named Henry Hyde.' So I went to this little place outside of Algiers and got briefed by Hyde, and by God, he's got these agents reporting to him from southern France, right in our target area. So I said, 'Henry, listen, God, this is beautiful stuff. What are you doing with it?' He was just sending it all back to AFHQ. But I said I wasn't getting any of it back. I am not saying there was duplicity there. I'm just saying that what he told me that he was giving the British was stuff I did not know.

"So what I did," Quinn continued, "was take this stuff raw from Henry, and I set up a little group of one major and a sergeant and a clerk in a special area in my office in Patch's headquarters. It was almost clandestine within ourselves. So for a month I tested

Hyde's stuff, I asked questions that I had the answers to already. And it not only proved out, it also revealed there were some double agents in the British networks, agents actually working for the Germans. So we used them to inform the 19th German Army that we were going one place when we really were going someplace else."

British G-2 at Alexander's headquarters got wind of Quinn's new intelligence assets and moved quickly to close off that source. "They were pretty angry that I had bypassed them," Quinn explained. "They said those agents in France are just being run by that Dulles fellow up in Switzerland and he'll believe anybody. Those are suspect sources; we forbid you to use them, and that's an order from headquarters. Well, I threw them out of the office. Then I went to Sandy Patch and said, 'General, I've just come to say good-bye. I'm about to be fired.' He said, 'Have you raped a native?' I said no, and told him the story. He said for me to do what I thought would produce the best intelligence for Dragoon [the invasion code name]. And I did."

Dulles's preparation for the invasions had begun in October 1943 when he convened a series of conferences in Geneva for the various resistance groups. The French representatives brought with them detailed information on what reasonably could be done to support the invasions and what material would be needed. By November a complete plan of railroad and communications sabotage was sent to London. Once the invasion started, key routes and junctions would be paralyzed.

LOOKING OVER THE INCREDIBLE list of accomplishments of the Bern station, one could easily bypass just what Dulles was able to accomplish in France when compared with other, flashier coups such as the recruitment of Gisevius or "George Wood." But an argument can be made that, in terms of its direct impact on winning the war itself, defeating German arms, and saving American lives, Dulles's success in building an American-run resistance movement in southern France may have been the most important thing he did. As the OSS official history retells:

> Before the Allied invasion of France in June 1944, OSS/Bern had means of ascertaining the day-by-day developments in the Vichy Government through a channel which went to the immediate entourage of Marshal Petain. Through other sources it received copies of the important messages sent by the German diplomatic representatives in both Vichy and Paris. It had eight separate networks, with hundreds of agents, working in France and was able to identify and locate all of the important German military units there.[11]

Dulles's penetration of Paris was so thorough that he was able to provide pre-invasion planners with maps of German anti-aircraft gun emplacements and the exact location of key Nazi administrative offices inside the city limits. Working with Gaston Pourchot's network of military observers and Max Shoop's liaison with the *maquis* groups drawing support from the United States, Dulles was able to skillfully plant disinformation, which when combined with the faulty analysis of the *Abwehr*, convinced German Army High Command planners that any southern landing would have to focus on the key port of Marseilles and the landing areas to the west. Instead, on August 15, the Franco-American task force of eight divisions struck farther east between Cannes and Toulon. Only one landing beach was hotly contested; overall casualties were extraordinarily light, and the Germans were clearly caught by the surprise. The French divisions quickly captured both Toulon and Marseilles while troops of the U.S. Seventh pursued the doggedly retreating Germans up the Rhone. They linked up with Patton's Third Army at Dijon on September 11 and rolled up 57,000 prisoners in a three hundred–mile race to the German West Wall. There, however, the Americans became bogged down as early autumn arrived.

In addition to their sabotage and guerrilla operations, the French *maquis* had provided the advancing Allied troops with intelligence that every corps commander knows is absolutely priceless—knowledge of what is just around the next bend or over the next foothill. But pushing on into the Third Reich itself was another matter. There was no waiting band of brave resisters; local populations were too cowed or too hostile to offer assistance of any kind, and the *Wehrmacht* was on its home ground, soil it had fought over for more than three centuries.

Quinn turned to the OSS and Dulles again. The OSS representative assigned to the Seventh Army was the remarkable Henry Hyde, whose own exploits running various resistance operations inside France deserve a book of their own. It was Hyde who maneuvered the Special Operations Executive into dropping radio operators code-named "Penny Farthing" into France. After meeting with Dulles in Lyons (the border was now effectively open), Hyde reported to Quinn that the Bern chief had said, "You know there is an awful lot of dissidence among the Germans. You fellows ought to be taking advantage of it."[12]

Recruiting spies from among prisoners of war was specifically forbidden under the Geneva War Conventions, and a strict ban had been imposed by the rules of engagement set by Eisenhower's Supreme Headquarters Allied Expeditionary Forces (SHAEF). Yet having pushed across France since June, most of the Allied armies were stuck in front of the German West Wall; Patch's own Seventh Army was on the eastern banks of the Moselle, just fifty miles from the German border. It was what lay around the next bend that had them stalled. With a wink from Patch and

Quinn, the pragmatic Hyde got an unofficial go-ahead from Donovan, who by now was installed in London on one of his numerous "fact-finding" missions.

Dulles was not being merely intuitive with his advice to Hyde. He knew from experience that plenty of Germans, both captured prisoners and exiled dissidents, could be recruited for various dangerous missions inside the Third Reich. Again, such tactics ran in the face of orthodox intelligence-gathering. There was an undeniable risk that, once safely across the border, such recruited agents would merely betray the Allies; the related risk was that even if they remained faithful, they might be captured and forced to disclose the secrets of other missions. The trick then was to draw one's agents from those whose loyalty could be counted upon and who had the necessary tough skills to survive in a clandestine environment and accomplish their objectives.

Such a pool of talent lay over the Swiss border in the numerous internment camps run by the Vichy government for communists and other suspect European refugees who were caught on the run from the war. In the case of the communists and socialists, whose nationalities were spread across Europe, many had been forced over the border out of Spain at the end of that nation's bloody civil war in 1939. Much of the relief and aid that these internees received came from humanitarian refugee organizations based in Switzerland. As it turned out, the man leading the Unitarian Church project was Noel Field, the young State Department colleague of Allen Dulles at the London Naval Conference of 1935.

Field was the son of Dr. Herbert Field, the well-meaning refugee aid official who threw into confusion the American Legation's fledgling spy apparatus in Bern in World War I. Noel Field, however, was quite another matter. A man of extremely fey intellectual brilliance, the Harvard-educated Field was marked for early star status in the State Department. But he also became an enthusiastic convert to communism early in his career. According to the later testimony of Soviet agents who claimed to have recruited Field and his German-born wife Herta, he was purposely forbidden to join the American Communist Party or any of the other noisy and all-too-visible organizations that sympathized with Stalin. Instead, Field was to provide the Soviets with intelligence from inside the State Department, and he became, by his own lights, a kind of Fritz Kolbe, fighting for a greater good inside his own corrupt nation's government. But even a true believer like Field would go only so far, it seems. In 1936, the year after he and Dulles worked in London, Field turned down a promotion and appointment by State to Germany; his Soviet controllers say they were dismayed when, despite their explicit orders to accept the job, he resigned from the government and took a position with the League of Nations in Geneva. He later explained to friends that he reasoned that by working for the league he could not be accused of working for or against any nation, not even his own. Thus he continued to provide intelligence, lower grade to be sure, from the increasingly moribund league secretariat to Soviet operatives in Geneva.

At the end of the Spanish carnage Field was sent on behalf of the league's Disarmament Commission to take the weapons away from all the combatants and make sure that the troops sent there were returned to their home countries. The onset of World War II later in 1939 ended Field's job at the league, but he quickly found work in France parceling out financial and material aid from the Unitarian Church to refugees who had begun to rush into France, first from Spain and then from all parts of Europe. The Fields were based in Marseilles and formed firm links with the communist organizations in the south of France; indeed there were such widespread complaints that the communists were getting most of the

Unitarian relief resources that other aid agencies routinely sent displaced persons suspected of being communists around to Field's
offices. In November 1942, with the Germans swarming into the
Vichy sector, Noel and Herta made a dash for Switzerland and ran
a highway checkpoint at Annemasse on the same day Allen Dulles
was talking his way past at the train station. The Fields also made
arrangements to rescue from a grim imprisonment in a French
concentration camp a seventeen-year-old German girl, the daughter of some communist friends.

Erica Glaser's father had been a doctor who ran a hospital for
the leftist Loyalist International Brigade in Barcelona during the
civil war. During the expulsion of communists and other Republican partisans from Spain in 1940, Erica was hospitalized with a
severe case of typhoid fever. Her parents ultimately made it safely
to Britain, where a son was flying with the Royal Air Force, but the
Fields rescued the girl and brought her to Switzerland to conva-
lesce. As Erica Glaser Wallach, she would play a dramatic role in
the Fields' 1949 defection to Hungary, but at that time in 1942, she
was just a malnourished teenager, still shaky from her illness. She
soon became involved in the dangerous covert operations that
Field was engaged in with his former disarmament colleague,
Allen Dulles. She recounted to the author her impressions of the
Fields:

> You want to know what they were like? I had nothing
> when I came to them. It was on my seventeenth birth-
> day. I had cloth shoes, a skirt that came down to my
> ankles, a man's shirt, and a leather coat. Nothing else at
> all, not a comb or even a toothbrush. And Mrs. Field
> was waiting for me with a light blue, silk bed jacket. It
> still makes me mad. Noel was out of touch in a different
> way. He had to work everything out in his mind; he read
> everything and set it out in order. He was very method-

ical, and he had very strong opinions once he had made his mind up. He also was a big list maker, and that was important too. Because he had vast lists of people among the Spanish refugees who were communists; he knew where everyone was and what they could do. It was natural that he could give those lists to Allen Dulles and help him recruit those people interned in France so they could either join the resistance there or be recruited by OSS.

So there was this exchange going on. Allen Dulles provided money and arms across the border to those who would fight in France, and he would get those out of France who could be put into Germany or Austria. Even I was dragged into it occasionally and took guns to the border crossings. Crossing the border was not like the Berlin Wall came to be. There were no barbed wire fences around Germany or between France and Switzerland. You would cross over the mountains if you knew the paths and rendezvous with people at prearranged places and times. And if you were careful you would be all right. I would go with a bicycle and no papers and just be a girl who had gotten lost, but I was never stopped. The Swiss helped us.

It was certainly true that Noel Field gave information to Allen Dulles, and so he was a spy. And he took money from Allen Dulles to give to the communists, so he was a communist spy and an American spy. But he did not consider himself a communist, in that he always insisted to me that he had not joined the party. But he was a great sympathizer, he said, and he was especially willing to work in that direction when Russia and the United States were on the same side of the war to fight the Germans.

Noel was not a pawn, he was an active participant. He was a naif in many ways, trying to justify
everything. He always looked at things from a right or
wrong standpoint.

He thought it would all come right because he
was doing the right thing. Dulles had his own agenda
too, of course. One time I was given orders by the
German communists in Switzerland to pick up two
men who were to be transferred out of France into
Germany with weapons and money. And I drove them
and hid them and got them to Basle, where they
crossed over. Several months later when I was with the
OSS in Wiesbaden, here one of these guys shows up in
an American uniform. And I say, "How did you get
here?" And he said, "Didn't you know? This was an
Allen Dulles operation all the way."[13]

By the time Allen Dulles suggested that Henry Hyde scour
the prisoner of war camps for willing German agents, the OSS
station in Bern had built a lengthy list of Europeans of all nationalities and political allegiances who might be used for various
purposes both in the war and afterward. Long before D-Day had
confirmed the beginning of the end for Nazi Germany's tyranny
over the Continent, Dulles had been gathering lists of names and
contacts with persons who might play important roles in establishing democracy and, equally important, stability in Europe
once the hostilities had ended. To that end, Dulles was committed
to rooting out Nazis from Germany's power base, but he was
equally concerned that the power vacuum not be filled by the
Soviets; if that meant dealing with socialists or communists with
a strong nationalist bent in the various countries of Occupied
Europe, so be it.

Perhaps the most important misjudgment Dulles made during his period of isolation in Switzerland was in his assumptions
of the role he himself would play in the postwar political and
intelligence aspect of reconstructing Europe. Again, he can be
excused for believing he would have a bigger role than he actually
received. For one thing, he was the man that a growing number of
resistance groups were approaching to establish their claims for
power after the war by undertaking acts of opposition against the
Germans and their collaborators. In March, the head of an
Austrian resistance group made it out to Bern for formal talks
with Dulles. After his arrest that summer, a second group made
contact in September through the remarkable Fritz Molden, who
undertook numerous trips across the dangerous border between
Austria and Switzerland. In May, various factions of Italian partisan groups came to a conference Dulles chaired in Lugano, and
out of that meeting formed a central resistance group and an
agreed-upon strategy for combating the German forces in the
north by sabotage and guerrilla attacks. Not surprisingly, the
group leaders fully expected a major role in Italian politics once
the war was over, and Dulles had no qualms assuring them they
would.

But Germany remained the focal point of Dulles's intelligence and political objectives and his personal ambitions. As soon
as Allied forces were able to secure air bases in France in the late
summer of 1944, Dulles began to get some extra help from outside. Cordelia Hood and Paul Blum flew in and set up the first real
counterintelligence operations of the war for Station Burns.
Significantly, their main target was Soviet espionage efforts inside
Switzerland; the Swiss had suddenly awakened to the fact that
Germany was no longer the immediate threat to their sovereignty
and that there soon would be nothing to stop Soviet troops, once
they reached Austria, from continuing to march west into their

country as well. But Dulles was able to ask for and get sent to him Emmy Rado, the psychiatrist whose profiles of leading Axis personalities for the New York COI office had been so accurate. Her job was to compile the "Crown Jewels" list—names of churchmen, academics, civil servants, and other political figures who were as clean of Nazi involvement as possible. Official policy had determined that there would be war crimes trials of those accused of barbarity, and to replace as many Nazi and collaborationist public officials as possible with Germans, Austrians, and Italians who had clear antifascist records. Gerry Van Arkle, the labor attaché, was compiling his own list of labor leaders in conjunction with "Crown Jewels" and recruited young Erica Glaser to winnow through the lists of German communists provided by Noel Field. It was exciting work—it was nothing less than an inventory of leaders for a new Germany and a Europe where democracy was being planted anew.

If Allen Dulles aspired to be the architect and spy boss of a new Germany, he had other reasons besides his own ambitions. The job had virtually been promised to him months before. In December 1943 Frederick Mayer, who would later distinguish himself as an OSS agent inside Germany, was on the German desk in "The Kremlin" when he wrote a memo to Whitney Shepardson, head of Special Intelligence:

> Our 110 is the man, in my opinion, to head our German Occupation Intelligence activities—at least to set them up and get them started.... It would seem to me unwise "to freeze" any idea in London at this time that it would head up our German Occupational Intelligence activities. Furthermore, I doubt the wisdom of establishing on British territory the base for operating such an important and comprehensive American intelligence

system in Germany. Switzerland would be much better, I should think, and the overall supervision should be clearly understood as Washington.[14]

So it was with some sense of expectation that Dulles received orders on September 6 to fly to London to meet with Donovan and David Bruce to coordinate strategy for the final months of the war. Dulles slipped over the border to a secret hide-out of the French resistance in the Rhone valley near a disused airfield, there to await a clandestine flight to London. To his astonishment, Donovan was waiting for him; he had come along for the ride when Operation Dragoon invaded Nice and to pick up Dulles and Henry Hyde on his way back to London. He had another surprise for Dulles; they both were going back to Washington. But Dulles was to stay only a week at home before returning to Bern to soldier on. There was no question of Dulles's moving on to become head of European operations at the end of the war; he would have quite enough to do in Germany. Donovan wanted no petty princes setting up in the business of continental intelligence; if there was to be a postwar intelligence agency—and Donovan never doubted it—he wanted to remain in firm command of such an organization. Allen Dulles must never become a rival.

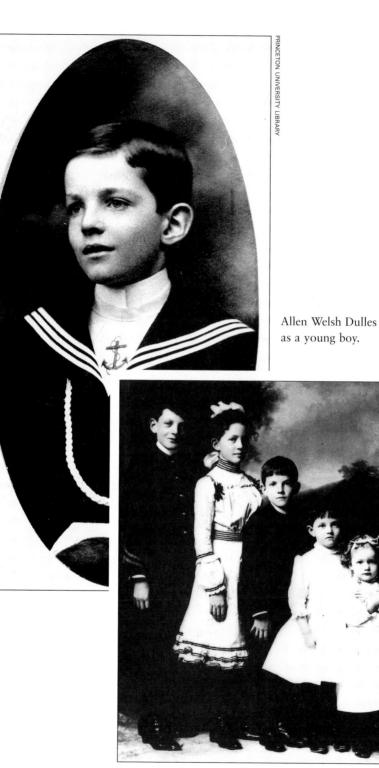

Allen Welsh Dulles
as a young boy.

Allen and his siblings. From left to right: John Foster,
Margaret, Allen, Eleanor, Nataline.

General John Watson Foster, Allen's maternal grandfather, was a formative influence in Dulles's life. General Foster himself had a long diplomatic career, culminating in a short stint as President Benjamin Harrison's secretary of state.

The Dulles family, circa 1912. Allen, sporting the clipped mustache he would wear the rest of his life, sits in the back right-hand corner of the room.

Secretary of State Robert Lansing, Allen's uncle, is flanked by members of the White House press corps. By mishandling President Woodrow Wilson, Lansing fell from power and was subsequently disgraced—a lesson Allen took to heart in advising later presidents.

Dulles and his fellow staffers at the Paris Peace Conference in 1919. From left to right, sitting: Frederic Dolbeare, Colonel Ralph Van Deman, Ellis Dresel, E. T. Williams, . H. Stabler. Standing: Dulles, J. G. D. Paul, Major Roy Tyler, Major DeLancey Kometze.

A young Clover Todd, who wo
become Mrs. Allen Dulles.

Allen and Clover's wedding day, October 16, 1920. From
left to right: best man John Foster Dulles, maid of honor
Lisa Whittal, Clover, Allen.

A happy moment for the young couple.

Clover as a young woman. Depression would shadow Clover throughout her life.

The growing Dulles clan.

Allen and Clover enjoy a sail. Allen and his brother Foster had enjoyed sailing since boyhood.

Clover Dulles and their son, Allen Macy Dulles, circa 1937. "He was a beautiful, winning child, big blue eyes, curly hair; people would stop on the street and stare at him," his older sister Joan said. "Father never appreciated how unique he was. He loved us all, but he never really understood us."

Allen Dulles, with his ubiquitous pipe, talks on one of the three phones necessary to maintain his vast intelligence network.

Dulles and colleagues in Prague, 1945. From left to right: Hans Gisevius, a member of the German Underground who helped Dulles infiltrate Nazi Germany; Mary Bancroft, one of Allen Dulles's many mistresses—and later one of Clover Dulles's closest friends; Erica Glaser, a young German woman who became involved in Dulles's covert operations; Dulles.

Dulles stands outside the Zurich home of Swiss publisher Emil Oprecht, where he held regular intelligence meetings throughout World War II.

General William Donovan was head of the Office of Strategic Services, the precursor to the Central Intelligence Agency.

Allen Dulles and William Donovan in Wiesbaden in late summer 1945.

Second Lieutenant Allen Macy Dulles (second from left) at a pre-battle briefing in November 1952, the night before he suffered the massive head wounds that would force this young man of great promise into a life of hospitalization and psychiatric care.

Director of Central Intelligence Allen Dulles (left) and Secretary of State John Foster Dulles work side-by-side. Under President Eisenhower, the two brothers were key architects of American foreign policy.

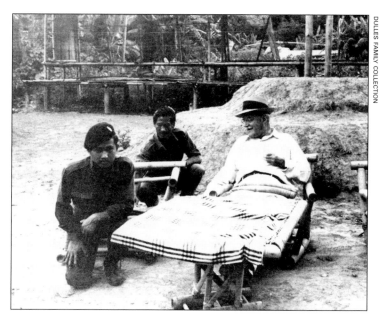

On a fact-finding mission in Thailand in 1956, Dulles suffers from an immobilizing gout attack.

As Dulles looks on, President Dwight D. Eisenhower lays the cornerstone of the CIA headquarters in Langley, Virginia. The creation and completion of the complex had been a near-obsession for Dulles.

President John F. Kennedy presents the National Security Medal to Dulles. Kennedy fired Dulles after the Bay of Pigs fiasco, although history has too harshly judged Dulles's role in that failed operation.

CHAPTER TEN

September 1944–May 1945

"I can see how much you and Allen care for each other—
and I approve."

—*Clover Dulles to*
Mary Bancroft, 1945

AS DONOVAN LED Allen Dulles and David Bruce into the American Bar of London's Savoy Hotel in that first week of September 1944, the OSS agency was seriously vulnerable, and at least part of the problem lay with the growing controversy over the agency chief himself. The OSS was being publicly derided as "Oh So Social," a bunch of playboys and dilettantes who were not man enough to join the active combat services. Much of the slander was fed to tame political columnists by a wide and growing list of enemies, such as J. Edgar Hoover and the military brass, to name just two sources.

But there were legitimate grounds to criticize as well. The agency had an undeniable reputation for free-spending, and the largesse that OSS personnel had at their command sometimes slopped over into inexcusable waste. There were also intelligence gaffes. In Spain and Portugal, the rivalry with the FBI (whose Secret Intelligence Service had placed outposts there because of its Latin American mandate) caused George Kennan and other diplomats in those countries constant headaches; at one point OSS ties to Basque separatist groups came close to provoking an open break with Franco's government. And there were the inevitable failures of mission—"Sparrow" in Hungary, half a dozen in Italy—and scandals that discredited the agency's station chief in Istanbul.

William Donovan was many things, among them a war aficionado who loved the smell of burning cordite in the morning. He had turned up as a frontline tourist for most of the major invasions in the European theater: Sicily in 1943, Normandy and Nice in 1944. He had flown into OSS outposts behind Japanese lines in the jungles of Burma, and between 1942 and 1945 his travel logs show him out of the United States for more than eighteen months, more days than at his desk in "The Kremlin." A recurring memory of aide Ned Putzell is of Donovan, wrapped in an enormous sheepskin greatcoat against the cold of an army air corps transport, working into the night on papers on some secret mission throughout Europe as they narrowly skirted *Luftwaffe* interception perimeters. He spent much time in Cairo and Algiers, ostensibly helping to plan the intelligence operations that would precede the invasions of Italy and southern France. And he did advance work for the various Churchill-Roosevelt summits. He undertook missions into the Balkans and successfully negotiated a liaison agreement in Moscow with the NKVD (the Soviet security service) that would have put an OSS presence in the Soviet Union and a Russian intelligence officer in Washington for the better exchange of information (J. Edgar Hoover quickly blocked that notion). While his personal courage was undeniable and his level of energy positively awesome, some part of Donovan seemed to consider World War II a personal entertainment and the OSS his personal war chariot.

None of this would have mattered if Donovan had won the personal confidence of Franklin Roosevelt, but he had not. FDR had a hearty appetite for OSS intelligence exclusives, and he appreciated the personal insights that Donovan brought back from various missions. But neither Donovan nor the OSS shaped or provided the main intelligence product upon which Roosevelt plotted his strategic decisions. And the two men did not click personally. Roosevelt suspected Donovan of using his wartime service for future political advantage (in that, FDR was pretty close to the truth), and he worried that the OSS might be turned into something more than a wartime spy agency.

Roosevelt also had plenty of other strong, incisive intellects to advise him—Marshall, Stimson, Hull. Each had his own institution with its own facts and information to contribute, and each was never very far from the president in Washington. Donovan, on the other hand, might be anywhere, and who knew what he was up to? Nor, in his lengthy and frequent ventures abroad, did Donovan allow the OSS to develop its own voice and its own constituency as an agency. The OSS remained Bill Donovan's fiefdom. There were numerous "palace revolts" in which frustrated but still loyal department heads would plead for greater coordination, for a chief of staff who would improve internal communications so the disparate forces at work could be more efficient. But that meant sharing power. As a result, another of Donovan's loyal friends, Ned Buxton, worked himself to a frazzle trying to keep operations functioning and putting out brushfires when he could. The result was that, despite its triumphs, coups, and recognized accomplishments, it was clear to all who cared to look that the OSS probably would not survive the war. That is, unless Donovan could find a postwar mission for the agency and its spy network.

On that September 1944 afternoon, the three men had the Savoy cocktail bar pretty much to themselves; the first V-2 rockets had landed on London earlier in the day, and more were expected. Donovan needed all of his considerable persuasiveness with his two star intelligence properties. David Bruce wanted to go home as soon as he could and resume a more public career in diplomatic service. Dulles, who wanted to stay and advance, also had the blandishment of a lucrative law career waiting for him at home. The few letters from Foster that had made it through the obstacle course of war to Switzerland were full of praise and admiration for his brother's accomplishments, but the tone of the letters was unmistakable; the needs of Sullivan & Cromwell should be attended to as soon as the country's needs were served. Allen, however, was willing to stay on as long as whatever Donovan was planning meant an enlarged mission.

On the air trip from Lyons to London, Dulles had made his first pitch for promotion. OSS would need a European coordinator for a vastly expanded intelligence network that would have to be built throughout the Continent after the shooting stopped. Wherever that coordinator was based (Bruce was on his way to set up offices in Paris near Eisenhower's SHAEF headquarters), the man for the postwar job was Allen Dulles.

Donovan said no. There in the bar he explained to both men that he had originally intended to bring Bruce back to America but that he had never intended for Dulles to take over in London or to take on an expanded role in a postwar European OSS. The fact was, Donovan did not think Dulles was a good administrator, which is strange considering how slapdash Donovan himself was. But he was politic enough to argue from another point.

Donovan is quoted as telling Dulles, "I didn't want anyone to be unhappy over David's replacement. There are lots of guys shooting for the job, good guys with marvelous records—the best men we've got. But they can't see that it isn't the sort of job they're suited for. Just because they're brilliant station chiefs doesn't mean they can handle London—all that administration. Nearly all of them are lousy administrators. They could foul things up at a vital stage in the war. So I'm ordering David to stay on, just as I'm asking you to do the same. God knows what would happen if we had a change in Bern at this juncture. We just can't afford to lose you."[1]

Then Donovan made Dulles an offer that he could not easily refuse. Dulles could not be European station chief after the war, but he could be the OSS chief for the occupation of Germany. Both men shared the belief that the hope of a stable, democratic (read non-Soviet) European continent depended on transforming Germany into a stable, prosperous, and truly democratic Germany. If the Allies (read the United States) could successfully revive the national governments created at Paris in 1919 and manage this time to bring Germany back to full membership at that table of nations, then a war-shattered USSR posed no threat. But no one doubted that the task of rebuilding Europe in an American image lay squarely with the United States, and the essential foundation of that task lay in the successful establishment of an intelligence network that saw everything, knew everything, and could do anything in every corner of bombed-out Europe. The focal point for this network and the success or failure of the mission lay squarely in Germany. Allen Dulles was clearly the man for *that* job; he did not need a fancy desk in London or Paris and a lot of administrative bother.

And so the two of them left David Bruce in London and flew the long night-flight back to Washington. Donovan was going home to produce the final draft of the plan for the future of OSS that he had been mulling over for several months now. Dulles would stay for just a week to deliver the suitcases full of secret documents that he had been unable to smuggle out before and to report on the dramatic events of that summer that had led to the historic invasions of Normandy and Nice. There was much to report and more in the way of policy guidance to receive.

One crucial assessment that had to be made was about the failed attempt by the "Breakers" plotters to kill Adolf Hitler on the

20th of July. Those who were miraculously still alive were on the run. Scores had already been arrested and shot; thousands more of their relatives and friends would die in the next six months. This last attempt had been a total catastrophe. Hitler survived the attack because the bomb-laden briefcase placed near him by Colonel Count Claus von Stauffenberg, a "Breakers" leader, had been moved to a spot behind a thick table leg that partly shielded the führer when the blast went off. He was only superficially injured, although several other staff officers in the map hut were killed. Stauffenberg had compounded the disaster by leaving Rastenburg early and not confirming that Hitler was really dead. The result was that this time the plotters in Berlin had so over-played their hand that they were readily identifiable for the Nazis' uncontrollably savage revenge. Once again, the perverse angel who protected Hitler against dozens of attempts to shoot, bomb, kidnap, or poison him had kept the tyrant alive a while longer.

At least part of the vulnerability of the "Breakers" lay in their insistence on detailed lists, agreements, compacts, and tables of organization. The young noblemen of the Kreisau Circle spent years drafting manifestoes and romantic justifications for why their higher duty to Germany was more important than their per-sonal oaths of allegiance to Adolf Hitler. There were detailed lists of who would be given what jobs in the new government, assum-ing the Nazis were overthrown. The generals, for their part, debated at scarcely clandestine meetings over their own duty to their führer. Himmler once boasted to Canaris in 1943 that he already knew who the major plotters were (although he did not suspect Canaris himself at the time).

Most astonishing of all, the various plotting groups resolutely clung to the conviction that, once their *putsch* had succeeded, the British and U.S. governments would allow them to about-face and insulate Europe from the plague of Slavic Bolshevism. By January

1944 most of the plotters realized that the Red Army was not going to be stopped at the far edges of the eastern Reich unless some hurried accommodation was reached with the West.

Hans Gisevius, the regular link Dulles had to the "Breakers" groups, had stopped going into Germany because of Gestapo hints that he would be more closely questioned about his alibi—that he frequently met with Dulles because he was spying on the American spies. Gisevius had been scrupulous about slipping in and out of 23 Herrengasse by the terrace approach at night, but his visits had not escaped the notice of the Dulles apartment's cook and housekeeper, a Swiss woman named Selma. As with other clandestine visitors, Dulles would tell Selma to stay out of the library–living room in the rear of the apartment whenever he had guests. Each arrival would be announced by some cover name—in Gisevius's case, it was "Dr. Bernard"—and Dulles would take the further precaution of playing gramophone records to cover the conversations. But Selma noticed that "Dr. Bernard" did not speak German with the customary Swiss accent. Curious, she had checked the lining of the large man's topcoat and the inner lining of his hat, which he had hung in the entrance hall. She noticed the Berlin tailor's label on the coat and the initials "H.B.G." on the hatband. Since she picked up extra pocket money by reporting to the German Embassy, she brought this curious information there, and Gisevius underwent a Gestapo grilling the next day. Fortunately, he had the presence of mind to go on the offensive. Of course, he was meeting with the American representative of President Roosevelt; it was a matter of vital Reich security importance. He was under direct *Abwehr* orders, and his actions were none of the Gestapo's business. There the matter rested. But when the churchman Dietrich Bonhoeffer and some friends inside the Canaris service were arrested, Gisevius was reluctant to trust his luck in Berlin. Too late, Selma was arrested by the Swiss and jailed.

This left Eddie Waetjen, the lawyer and *Abwehr* source whose cover was as German consul general in Zurich. Gisevius turned over to him the task of shuttling in and out of Berlin itself while another *Abwehr* agent, Theodore Strunck, was given the job of courier between the "Breakers" and Bern. In April 1944 Waetjen and Gisevius brought to Dulles an announcement from General Ludwig Beck and Carl Goerdeler, a high civil servant, that their groups were ready to lead a coup d'état against Hitler. Beck had retired as OKW chief of staff in 1938 after two other *Wehrmacht* leaders had been railroaded out of their jobs by Nazi plots. He kept close contact with his former brothers in the high command, just as Goerdeler had done within the network of municipal and provincial civil servants and politicians. Details of a consensus offer came again in May. Once the führer was removed from power (bloodlessly if possible) and his loyalists rounded up, a new government would be formed, and the OKW would be ordered (with the cooperation of leading generals) to allow the Allies to make a quick, unopposed landing in France.

Gisevius, in his memoirs, conceded that the "Breakers" still believed a separate peace was obtainable, despite Dulles's unmistakable assurances to the contrary. Bitterly, he recounts:

> Goerdeler retained his hope that some political arrangement would be attainable after we had succeeded in overthrowing the Nazis. Beck held a more skeptical view; but he, too, thought he recognized the necessity of asking for an armistice as soon as possible, never planned his first act as chief of state of the new German regiment would be the sending of an emissary to Eisenhower's headquarters in order to negotiate immediate surrender. It is quite possible that some persons in the group of younger military leaders—

though… not Stauffenberg, who looked toward a reconciliation with Russia—might have harbored their
own plans behind the backs of the political leaders of
the fronde. This is quite likely in view of the general
political confusion which was the chief characteristic
of the preparations for the July Putsch.[2]

As Dulles cabled to Washington:

The group was reported ready to help Allied units get
into Germany if the Allies agreed that the *Wehrmacht*
should continue to hold the Eastern Front. They proposed in detail: (1) three Allied airborne divisions
should land in the Berlin region with the assistance of
the local army commanders, (2) major amphibious landings should be undertaken at or near Bremen and
Hamburg, (3) landings in France should follow, although
Rommel cannot be counted on for cooperation, (4) reliable German units in the area of Munich would isolate
Hitler and other high Nazis in Ober Salzburg.

Dulles noted, "To these overtures, the OSS representative
said little beyond expressing his strong conviction that the United
States would never act without previous consultation with the
USSR."[3]

The Normandy invasion on June 6 brought more converts
to the "Breakers" ranks from among the generals in France. The
collapse of the Army Group Center in Russia added to the
urgency of the plotters. On July 8 Strunck arrived in Bern with
final details of the coup, which by now had escalated into an
assassination attempt against Hitler as well as Goering and
Himmler. On July 11 Gisevius could no longer stand his self-

imposed exile. Mary Bancroft had completed the translation and editing of four thousand manuscript pages of his testament; Canaris and other friends had been either arrested or removed from power. It was time for him to join the "Breakers" in the front ranks of those who risked everything to save their nation. He and Strunck traveled to Berlin to take part in Operation Valkyrie, now known forever as that sad debacle, the 20th of July plot that failed. Waetjen's cover had been completely blown, and he was forced to stay behind lest he jeopardize the other two.

In the summer weeks that followed, Dulles knew nothing of Gisevius's fate and assumed that, as had happened to Strunck, he had been caught almost at once and summarily executed. The death lists rolled out of Berlin with grim precision, and although there was no mention of Gisevius, Dulles feared the worst, for the Nazis seemed to be murdering innocents almost randomly while they kept the truly active members of the plot alive for more exquisite reprisals. Colonel Count von Stauffenberg, the officer who actually placed the bomb, and some fellow principal plotters in Berlin were taken out and shot at once; General Beck and others committed suicide; still others such as Helmuth von Moltke, Carl Goerdeler, Adam von Trott, and socialist leader Julius Leber were forced to endure torture and humiliating sham trials before being executed in the most grisly fashion months later. Finally, during the last weeks of the war in April 1945, Admiral Canaris, Pastor Bonhoeffer, and others tangentially linked to the "Breakers" were simply murdered to silence their witness to the desperate plot.

DURING HIS WEEK of briefings at "The Kremlin" in Washington, September 14–21, Dulles did not have much time to go into high policy with Donovan and his senior planners. Donovan himself was engrossed in working out a new organizational plan that would save the OSS and perhaps convert it into a fully established intelligence service after the war. He had seen a previous suggestion shot down earlier in the year. That early proposal had been for the OSS to be turned into one of four major armed services after the war. There were already debates over a possible merger of the military services into a single cabinet agency; that plan included creating a separate air force out of the army air corps. So, why not a fourth military force—the "Strategic Service"—fully equal with the army, navy, and air services, with its own chief of staff under the defense agency? The plan had been dismissed out of hand.

Now Donovan was returning to the idea that he had proposed in 1939—a civilian intelligence agency that would answer first and only to the president. This central agency would draw intelligence material from every government agency and service that produced it and "coordinate" it into a single intelligence product for the chief executive's own use and that of his key policy advisers. In September 1944 the notion that had failed to appeal five years earlier had several new factors that helped its credibility with other Roosevelt advisers who were advancing their own strategies.

For one thing, there was a sense of urgency that the war might be over by Christmas; the dramatic penetration of France by the combined Allied armies was moving at a thrilling pace and would for some weeks more. This had brought forward the question of just what the Allies (mainly the United States) planned to do with Germany once it had capitulated. It was essential that the Soviet Union be persuaded to enter the war with Japan (which Stalin had thus far avoided doing), because there was no reason to believe that the one-and-a-half million Japanese troops ravaging China would meekly surrender. Stalin's price for that was for FDR and Churchill to concede his territorial demands in Eastern Europe. Roosevelt (and especially Churchill) had no intention of merely turning all of Western Europe over to the Russians as a sphere of total influence. Germany must continue as some kind of border between East and West; the question was, what kind of country was Germany to be?

There were hard-liners around the president who wanted a full and open-ended Allied occupation of Germany, a repeat of the onerous Reconstruction period that the Union had visited upon the prostrate states of the Confederacy after the Civil War. Hawks such as Henry Morgenthau, Jr., and even Bernard Baruch, had argued that the main mistake of the 1919 Paris Conference was letting Germany reconstitute itself after the First World War; it must not be allowed such a luxury again. Indeed, Morgenthau hotly pushed a plan that would parcel out whole sections of the traditional Reich to nations that had been victimized by the Nazis, while the central provinces were to be reduced to a flat landscape where only peasant agriculture could prosper. Others, such as Adolph Berle and a group within the State Department, argued the position of the 1919 planners who occupied Maxim's restaurant in Paris; any hope for permanent peace in Europe lay in bringing a (justifiably) suspicious Soviet Union into full partnership with the Western Allies.

For a while, Morgenthau and his supporters held the upper hand. Even as Dulles and Donovan arrived in Washington, FDR and Churchill were in Quebec for the Octagon Conference. There, the two leaders approved Eisenhower's tactical plan for his troops, who were just then crossing the Rhine into Germany. And they also gave preliminary approval to Morgenthau's scheme to "pastoralize" Germany after the war. It took considerable convincing before the two weary leaders could look to the harder necessities that lay ahead; a quick, cleansing punishment seemed so much more satisfying.

One center of policy opposition to both of these extremes lay within the Research and Analysis (R&A) division of the OSS as well as among top-level leaders, including both Donovan and Dulles. The R&A division's story underlines one of the secret truths about intelligence, which is how politicized the final product can be when it is sent to policymakers. Despite the pious orthodoxy that good intelligence analysis must be politically neutral, and that policy decisions must be reserved for those charged with broad strategy, the truth is that the analytical conclusions of intelligence advisers are inevitably freighted with political bias, opinion, and agendas. In the case of the questions about postwar Free World strategy, it scarcely could have been otherwise.

That the American foreign policy of post–World War II was rooted in German restoration and resistance to Soviet ambitions is well-documented historical fact. How that came to be, however, is still the subject of hot and constantly revised debate. Some recent analysts argue that American officials became so wedded to their Eurocentric view of Cold War strategy that they tried with indifferent success to impose the same vision of reconstruction, democratization, and economic homogenization on the nations of both Asia and Latin America. Conspiracy theorists of both the Right and Left have flourished into the third generation, arguing the roots of this American policy.

The historical organization of the R&A branch of OSS has been portrayed, but not beyond a certain point. When Donovan went looking for scholars and researchers to flesh out and interpret the intelligence data his spies would bring in, he sought out Librarian of Congress Archibald MacLeish to help organize what the director knew would be the heart of his proposed agency. MacLeish in July 1941 went recruiting among such scholastic gatherings as the American Council of Learned Societies and the Social Science Research Council, as well as to specific university leaders of his acquaintance. It was from that milieu that James Phinney Baxter III was called from his post as president of

Williams College to be director of R&A, and William Langer of Harvard was asked to supervise the scholars and ultimately, in September 1942, to succeed Baxter. This so-called College of Cardinals that the three scholars recruited was indisputably the cream of academic authority on everything from diplomatic history to geology and economics. While the cardinals ranged in discipline and region from Joseph Hayden, who taught government at the University of Michigan, to Calvin Hoover, the Duke economist, nearly all were creatures of the Ivy League, and, more importantly, nearly all were confirmed internationalists who viewed the current war as an opportunity to put right the errors of the previous failed efforts at peace.

The cardinals brought with them to R&A what might be called the curates—younger scholars of promise and accomplishment who were given reach and responsibilities far advanced over anything their academic careers could have brought in peacetime. Sherman Kent was put in charge of the enormous Europe-Africa desk. Conyers Read covered the British Empire, sharing jurisdiction with Ralph Bunche of Howard University, who focused on postcolonial policies and race questions. There were historians of the caliber of John Fairbank and Crane Brinton, as well as five future presidents of the American Economics Association and a future Nobel laureate. Intellects of the caliber of Walt and Elspeth Rostow, Arthur Schlesinger, Jr., Gordon Craig, and Charles Kindelberger found themselves in policy apprenticeships that groomed them for larger contributions later.

If Langer had stopped there, R&A would have been a formidable resource for the government there and then. But in the spring of 1943, a third tier of less-publicized recruits was brought into OSS service—the "Germans." These were a collection of European, mainly German, refugees from Hitler who had first found refuge at the International Institute for Social Research at Columbia. These scholars and intellects, many of them Jews, mostly far left in their political beliefs, constituted within the Central European section of the OSS a truly unique collection of cutting-edge intelligence.

The group's leaders were Franz Neumann, Herbert Marcuse, and Otto Kirchheimer, all leading social and economic theoreticians of the neo-Marxist Institute for Social Research in Frankfurt. The Frankfurt School, as it was known, was one of the first academic facilities in the Reich to be banned when Hitler came to power. All three had been prominent in forming the doctrines of the Social Democratic Party during the Weimar days, but the R&A "Germans" were more diverse in their opinions and skills than that. To cover culture and propaganda, Neumann recruited Bertold Brecht and Siegfried Kracauer. To analyze the Nazi oppression of religious institutions and future implications, the group added Paul Tillich and Heinrich Bruning (the ex-chancellor), both prominent in the now-banned Catholic Center Party. Walter Gropius, the founder of the Bauhaus school of design, surveyed European housing and urban intelligence; Eugene Fodor, the guidebook author and polylinguist, was brought in, as was Finnish architect Eero Saarinen, who was put to work in the Visual Presentations unit. It was said, truthfully, that not even Admiral Canaris had as many German intelligence experts working for him as there were within R&A.

That such a group would fall to arguing on nearly every issue of intelligence interpretation was inevitable; there were Gaullists and Giraudists, those who were pro-Mikhailovich or pro-Tito, those who feared the Soviet Union and those who despised Poland. But surprisingly, the quality of the analysis gradually, albeit painfully, moved beyond purely partisan advocacy, and the analysts began to focus a finely honed consensus on the task of winning the war in front of them and then, later, arguing over the peace that would follow. They were assisted, often over

their objections, by a projects review committee headed by
Richard Hartshorne, a University of Wisconsin geographer who
laid down the dictum, "Intelligence reports find their literary
merit in terseness and clarity rather than in expressive description.... Proust, Joyce, or Gertrude Stein would all be equally out
of place in R&A."[4]

Two reasons help explain both the positive and the harmful
impact on the stature of the OSS made by the "Germans." First,
for the good, a quite large volume of analysis began to pour
almost at once out of R&A. This created an almost instant market
for still more product from other government policy agencies that
were charting future strategies in their own jurisdictions. An
obvious and enthusiastic customer was the State Department's
own specialists committee on the economic reform plans that the
United States should insist upon for Germany after the war. This
committee included Eleanor Dulles and many of her colleagues
from the Bureau of Labor Statistics, and intellects from other
agencies such as Harry Dexter White from Treasury and Donald
Hiss, brother of Alger.

"I remember a sense of great excitement," Eleanor Dulles
recalled. "We were, after all, going to be rebuilding a brand new
society—at least we thought we were. Even after work, we would
gather in somebody's apartment or house and argue late into the
night; the people from OSS were in the middle of it, too. We all
considered ourselves very progressive, even those of us who did
not particularly consider ourselves liberal or left-wing. So we were
eager for anything that sounded progressive, especially if it confirmed our own attitudes about what should be done."[5]

Thus, in addition to the quantity and acceptability of the
analysis by the Central European desk analysts, many of the planning and theory specialists in other agencies focused on Germany
rather than any other aspect of the wartime political dilemma.

There was not, it was obvious, any remotely comparable group of Soviet scholars or Asian (let alone Japanese) experts who would tilt the policy debate about America's global responsibilities and objectives after the shooting ceased. The British might have their Foreign Office Arabists and plenty of experts on the Indian subcontinent in London's Colonial Office. But there was no force like that inside the OSS, and what came out of the OSS often had a great weight among the client agencies; the OSS had its "Germans," and they had considerable clout.

But they were also controversial, even suspect. Many of the R&A scholars were undoubted communists; none of them could escape the cultural biases that came with coming of age between the world wars in Europe, which had endured much more instability and uncertainty than had America. But they showed a remarkable objectivity in the analysis they prepared for others, especially when it came to the emotive question of what would happen after the war. Barry Katz, the Stanford professor whose book on the OSS intellectuals is the authority on the group, concludes that early in 1944 "the Central Europeanists turned their attention to anticipated problems of the postwar era and launched an extensive research program designed to assist American officers in the military occupation and governance of a defeated Germany. If one can speak of an R&A 'line,' it was to steer a middle course between the extremes of a punitive Morgenthauism and the call to rebuild Germany as rapidly as possible as a bulwark against the Soviet Union. Whereas the OSS in general exercised little influence on the actual conduct of the war, the Europeanists of R&A did play a demonstrably significant role in preparing for the peace that followed."[6]

These "Central Europeanists" had another impact. Early on, they made it respectable for Allen Dulles to openly recruit socialists and communists out of the internment camps of Spain and France and put them to use in his intelligence and resistance network without any outcry from Washington. Dulles had leaped at an offer by Noel Field to put him in contact with Julius Leber, the German socialist labor leader, and other exiled union officials who kept open lines to potential saboteurs and spies in factories and on railroad lines. By the final year of the war, few trains moved within the German Reich that were not reported to Dulles within hours; the Rhine River bargemen had been organized into a network, and even the water levels of the Rhine itself were radioed to Eisenhower's Paris headquarters, lest the Germans open the floodgates during an Allied crossing.

Dulles headed back to Bern with a new target in sight. At this point in late September 1944, he had achieved miracles in setting up functioning intelligence and resistance groups in France, northern Italy, and Germany itself. His web of contacts and two-way flow of information reached inside the top levels of many other Eastern European governments, and he was deeply involved even in the tangled and contradictory Allied dealings in that mare's nest known as Yugoslavia. But until now, not much attention had been given to Austria. The Austrians had been blamed by Allied strategists for welcoming Hitler's annexation of their land too warmly to qualify them to be considered a conquered people. The Austrian military had become a trusted cohort of the *Wehrmacht,* and Austrian Nazis became energetic auxiliaries in the administration of the Greater Reich. There was an opposition, to be sure, but the arrest of many key underground leaders midway through the war led strategists to lump Austria in with Germany as an enemy to be subdued first and reformed later. If Stalin had limited his demands at Yalta merely to the occupation of Berlin, it might have remained that way. But the Soviet insistence on hegemony over Austria as well as Yugoslavia suddenly confirmed for Western leaders that Soviet intentions were as threatening as many of their advisers had been warning.

Other factors emerged that autumn to focus Washington's attention on the Alpine region of Europe. American and British troops were having a tougher time than expected slugging their way up the northern part of the Italian peninsula. The Allied drive had stalled at what was called the Gothic Line and no further advance was possible until April 1945. Allied leaders dreaded a campaign to pry the Germans out of dug-in positions in the Austrian Alps and Tyrol regions. And a whispered threat became a worrisome fear: the Final Redoubt. Goebbels had begun promising the German people that come what may, loyal SS troops would retire to an Alpine fortress stronghold that would be more impregnable and fearsome than anything the Swiss might have achieved. Cadres of fanatically faithful Hitler Youth were to form into commando death battalions known as the Werewolves. From their mountain lair, these young avengers would sortie out into the lands held by the Anglo-Americans and the Russian Slavs and wreak a terrible vengeance. The enemies of the Reich would know no peace.

The Final Redoubt turned out to be something of a fantasy, and Dulles came in for a share of criticism for his guarded communiqués warning about reports of a huge-scale construction effort of fortifications, arsenals, and connecting mountain tunnels. But the point often overlooked is that quite a formidable opposition in southern Germany, Austria, and the Italian Tyrol could have been organized, one as bloody and difficult to defeat as the German defense of France itself. Field Marshal Albert Kesselring, who commanded the Army Group South-West, had more than a million troops at his disposal in northern Italy and the Alpine regions, many of them hardened SS and *Panzer* units transferred from the Eastern Front. As the German tide rolled back upon itself under pressure from the Russians, the southern flank of the Reich took on a new strategic importance. Redoubt or no redoubt, some way had to be found to prevent the Germans from digging into those mountain regions. Otherwise the war in Europe could sputter on for another year, or even longer.

Dulles had much to consider during his briefings at "The Kremlin," and not much time for a reunion with Clover. There was just a day together, but it was enough. Despite Dulles's ability to put various parts of his lives in strict compartments, Clover was too much a part of his life to be put on a shelf and taken down when needed. He had missed her and the children. Despite the romance with Mary Bancroft and flirtations with other women, only Clover provided the faithful affection and support he needed most. One measure of how much he missed her during the twenty months of separation was that he never teased her about his flirtations while he was truly cut off from her. Her letters, often much delayed, had been an unsatisfactory link between them, as this brief letter from him from late January 1944 shows:

Dear Clover: After a long period of no letters whatever, I received three in a row. Your microfilm letter of September 17 and a letter from November 16 and 22nd. The latter came over [from] London and was liberally censored and tested for all sorts of secret writing. However, it got through in legible style. It was good to hear some news of your daily doings, of the house in the country and the children's schooling and Toddy's troubles. I know how worrying the latter must be but I suppose we have to go through with them. I imagine you must be deciding Allen's schooling very shortly. I certainly do not want him to go to a school that he does not himself wish. I have no objection to St. Marks. It is a little more of a social school than I would have liked in this day and generation but I suppose we can wait and toughen him up later.

I often wonder how your money problems are getting on. I assume that Foster will take care of it out of my balance with the firm. If you get short, don't hesitate to call on him as the money is there and belongs to me. You can hardly imagine how busy I am. Sundays are just like any other day except that I often use them for trips that I have to take. One evening a week I am in Zurich and about as frequently in Geneva. I see a great deal of Royall Tyler and he is a great comfort. Tell all the children that I am very proud of them. Joan's record at college and Sunny's at school have certainly been magnificent and I am delighted to know that Toddy is working away and I suppose I will find her an expert stenographer and typist when I get back and I hope this won't be so very long now although I am afraid it will not be as soon as I had once hoped. Affectionately—7

When he got back to Bern, Dulles wrote a lighthearted letter to let her know he had arrived safely. It was full of bright chat about how he had run into Whitney Shepardson in London and traveled with him to Paris, where they had quite a gala reunion with David Bruce "and other old friends from earlier times." Then, a few weeks later, a more plaintive letter:

The opening up of Switzerland has greatly changed my work and put considerable strain on our small organization. Everybody wants everything at once. I have to travel from Bern to Port Ayer and to Annemasse. Every minute is taken. Unfortunately, a bit of gout has hit me. Not really a bad attack but enough to keep me a little more quiet than I need to be. I am being careful with it so don't worry…. Now that the border is opening up, I

wonder if you could come over for a visit? Let me know
what you think.[8]

Clover did not have to think. She began the tedious campaign for necessary permits and visas at once.

Dulles, in the meantime, had to effect the rescue of Hans
Gisevius. While others of the "Breakers" group had been rounded
up, Gisevius had found a hiding place in Berlin and gotten word
out to Bern of his whereabouts. Getting him out would not be
easy. A full description of him was at every border post in the
Reich. Travel, even on authorized purposes, was getting increasingly difficult throughout Germany. New permits, documents,
and limitations on where civilians could go presented problems to
the Allied forgers, this assuming that the daily bombings of Berlin
and key railroad lines did not kill Gisevius first. But Dulles was
determined. Gero von Gaevernitz was able to steal the latest passports and travel documents out of the German Embassy in Bern,
and he flew with them to London, where MI6 forgers were waiting to create a new identity. They had settled on a plausible dis-
guise for the easily recognizable giant German—he would escape
from Germany as an official of the Gestapo. It would be easy
enough for Gisevius to pretend to be what he once had been. The
only real difficulty was the fabrication of the Gestapo's own identity disc, which each member of the policy agency carried on his
person like a talisman. It was an oval, rather large belt-buckle–
sized disc made of an unknown silver alloy, but somehow the
British had managed a credible counterfeit. Dulles was able to
take delivery of the package of documents in late October, but
even then it was two months more before a trusted courier could
be found who would travel into war-shelled Berlin and make his
way to Gisevius's hideout.

While Dulles was waiting for Gisevius to escape, he was fully
occupied with a stream of new emissaries out of Europe.

Himmler and his spy chief, Schellenberg, had begun a series of cautious feelers to Dulles about yet another possible *putsch* of Hitler. More importantly, Dulles found out that the German security chief was having even more detailed and ambitious talks with British officials in Sweden, talks that the Americans were unaware of, talks that the British steadfastly denied were going on. Dulles, for his part, was suspicious that Himmler was playing a double game, which might include a genuine peace offer, but which might also be used to smoke out whether the Allies were negotiating with any other group of Reich officials. It was a natural enough suspicion because Dulles was also involved in a series of uneventful talks with a group of *Wehrmacht* battlefield commanders about a general surrender along the Rhine battle line.

In the midst of all this, Dulles was visited by another extraordinary walk-in. Fritz Molden was a young Austrian who had been conscripted into the army during the war as penalty for having belonged to one of the antifascist student groups in Vienna. He was the son of a prominent anti-Nazi publisher in the center of an underground group of about five thousand Austrians who planned armed resistance against the Germans once Allied troops crossed the border. Most of the opposition in this Provisional Austrian National Committee had served in previous prefascist governments, and most were socialists or communists who had gone to ground in 1938 during Hitler's *Anschluss* of Austria. They had begun to form in earnest after the Moscow Declaration at the end of 1943, in which the Allies guaranteed Austria that it would recover its independence from Germany. Their objective, once the Allies had been victorious, was to seek status as one of the political groups that would form a new democratic government after liberation. After serving on the Eastern Front in a punishment battalion, Molden managed a transfer to Italy and deserted after convincing the German military police that he was dead. With a new, stolen identity, he managed to cross over the border into Switzerland, where Swiss intelligence quickly brought him to Dulles. Still in his early twenties, Molden had a feisty quality that Dulles liked at once. Would the young man agree to go back over the border into Austria and make contact with the resistance group his father belonged to? The answer was an enthusiastic yes. He became "K-28."

First Molden was sent to SHAEF headquarters to be debriefed about conditions in Austria and then provided with the list of questions Allied planners wanted to ask the underground group. His appearance in Paris sparked a stormy argument with British intelligence. This time, Dulles had gone too far. Dansey and others in MI6 had made no secret of their feelings that while Dulles had done some undeniably good work—the "Wood" cables by now were acknowledged gold dust—Dulles's willingness to deal personally with the most obvious frauds and double agents was dangerous, if only from a security standpoint. It was bad enough that they had to go to the trouble of rescuing his pet Gestapo agent; now they were being asked to provide an Austrian army deserter with information that could jeopardize MI6 personnel who had been parachuted into the Tyrol and other parts of Austria, and just on Dulles's say-so. It was not discussed, but it was an open secret between OSS and MI6 officials in London that Vanden Heuvel's heavy squad had already "liquidated" one highly dangerous agent who had continued to be received at 23 Herrengasse, this after Dulles had been repeatedly warned that the man was from Schellenberg's RSHA and an assassin to boot. Lest the British appear too brutal by comparison, it should be noted that the OSS official history notes that whenever Dulles suspected a walk-in of being a German plant, he routinely gave him a mission into France, where the resistance could execute him summarily.

Much later, Molden said he believed the British wanted to kill him, too, rather than take the risk. "I know, because Allen told me much later, that the British wanted to let me go back into

Austria on a mission and then they would tip off the SS. If the Germans let me go back across the border into Switzerland then that would be proof that I was a Nazi agent. And the British would shoot me. If the Germans shot me immediately, it would be proof that the British had been wrong about me but—poof—that was not such a big loss. Dulles stopped them though. I was his man, and I must be protected. He saw to it that the Swiss knew it too and that I was not to be accidentally shot coming across the border; you know the kind of accident I mean."9

Molden made repeated trips to such dangerous spots as Milan and Vienna and built up a contact network around Salzburg and other Alpine checkpoints that would be invaluable to the American troops that later in 1945 raced the Soviets to gain the Austrian capital. He also added to a markedly increased flow of battle order information that began to stream out of Bern in that final winter of the war. Dulles had finally secured Swiss approval to locate a clandestine radiotelephone transmitter in the American Legation; this vastly improved security and enabled the Americans to transmit fuller texts of information more quickly both to Washington and to Allied military headquarters in Paris and Caserta, Italy. Partisan watchers were able to bring to Lugano for transmittal almost daily reports on *Wehrmacht* traffic through key railheads such as Verona; key German divisions such as the *Panzer* Hermann Goering, Rizer Gustav, and Trident could not move easily without being spotted and bombed in transit. From Lugano, Dulles established regular courier service to Milan, Venice, and Turin.

Earlier, in 1943, Dulles had helped a tiny Italian enclave inside Switzerland to rebel against the Mussolini regime and declare its allegiance to the pro-Allied government in the south. Using this non-Swiss territory as a "neutral" base, Dulles was able to set up direct radio links with the Allied command in Caserta and to stage partisan raids into the northern provinces. At the same time, Dulles built a closer liaison with the U.S. Army G-2 staffs of the Twelfth and Sixth Army Groups and Patch's Seventh Army as they at last pushed into Germany. Through his network of resisters in Munich, the OSS was able to touch off a *putsch* of local Nazi leaders and surrender the city to Patch with little struggle.

Meanwhile, Clover had pulled every wire at her disposal and produced the necessary visas and travel permits for a civilian to enter what was still an active war zone. A shipment of automobiles was being sent to Lisbon and then driven across the Iberian peninsula and France to Paris for use by the State Department. Clover got a "job" as a relief driver for the trek and set out shortly after New Year's Day 1945. During the ship crossing, Dulles got a telegram from Washington that Clover's mother had died after a long illness; it was too late to tell her or for her to turn back. He did not have the heart to tell her until she reached Bern, but that would take some time.

Clover's trip to Paris took the better part of two weeks, and after a brief stay there she headed off to Switzerland and an unforeseen adventure of her own. Although no mention of it can be found in the Dulles family papers, British intelligence sources insist that Clover had a near brush with a pocket of German troops still hanging on to a border outpost in France. According to the British account, Clover had accepted an invitation from a French army officer who had commandeered a Rolls Royce in Paris for a trip to Lyons, a convenient crossing point for Switzerland. The officer decided they would detour so he could show her the terrible devastation of the Vercors massacre of French civilians and *maquis* forces, and they became lost and wandered perilously close to the German battle line; there may even have been some gunfire, but no harm was done. Finally, in late January 1945, Clover and Allen were reunited and in residence at 23 Herrengasse. One of the first people Dulles introduced her to was Mary Bancroft.

The Bancroft-Dulles love affair had gone its way by then, as was the case with so many of Allen's affairs. During that almost idyllic time of isolation and high adventure in Switzerland the passion had been real enough. Dulles had been charmed by her quick and irreverent wit; Mary rather famously had once attacked Henry Luce at a Zurich dinner party, criticizing the tortured "Time-style" of his magazine and the right-wing nature of his politics and contradicting him about his analysis of his recent tour through Europe. Luce was captivated by such feistiness in a woman; so was Allen Dulles. Mary brought Allen up short on numerous occasions, including one tale she retold often of their being in bed one night in the Herrengasse apartment when suddenly his front doorbell rang. Dulles ignored the caller, who began to pound on the door and ring the bell in alternate bursts of noise.

> Allen put his left hand over my mouth and, reaching for a pad and pencil on the night table at the head of the bed, he scrawled, Don't move. Don't make a sound.... After the fourth ring, I looked at Allen and raised my eyebrows inquiringly. He shook his head and scrawled on the pad again, smiling delightedly: Persistent bastard, isn't he?... Eventually, after what seemed to me an unconscionable amount of time but which was probably not more than another ten minutes, he jumped up. "I guess he's gone," he said. To which I countered, "How do you know it was a 'he?'"[10]

Dulles's laughter, the hearty true booming guffaw, echoed throughout the apartment. There would be much other laughter and companionship. And there was the tremendous excitement of the work they shared. But the astute Bancroft began to realize that the ten years that separated them in age were a considerable barrier in their relationship. In time Mary began to rein in Dulles's impromptu visits to her apartment for the quick assignations he claimed he needed "to clear his head." The romance cooled into a genuine friendship. Both understood it could never lead anywhere.

Yet Mary was loyal enough as a friend to come up from Zurich when Clover arrived. Dulles simply could not face being alone when telling his wife that her mother had died. Mary was happy enough to befriend the "shy, almost otherworldly" Clover. She quickly pierced the rather vague outer shell that Clover used to keep strangers at a distance and spotted the underlying sharp wit and keen observer that lay beneath. They would be close friends until Clover's death in 1974. During those later years, Mary would often referee some of the hot shouting matches between the couple. "She and Allen had terrible fights, which Allen invariably won by the simple device of clamping an iron curtain down between them," Mary recalled. Clover quickly spotted that something beyond friendship had gone on between her husband and her new friend. Mary quotes Clover during one of their early meetings in Bern as saying, "I want you to know I can see how much you and Allen care for each other—and I approve."[11]

It was a constant source of pain to Clover that, although she was the closest person in the world to her husband, their intimacy and sharing could go just so far and no further. She also puzzled at the constant drive of both Allen and Foster Dulles, the drive to be doing, always on the move. She told Mary she christened the brothers in her own mind "The Sharks," because sharks must constantly move and feed to stay alive. Allen was soon referred to in their private letters as "The Shark," and the two women formed an alliance, becoming "The Killer Whales," the only creatures strong enough to deal with the constantly predatory sharks.

Mary did Clover another significant service; she introduced her to Carl Jung. Clover was fascinated by the personal warmth and insights of the legendary psychologist. He in turn was attracted by her enthusiasm for greater self-knowledge, and he felt sympathy for the obvious pain she endured. He arranged for her to work with an associate analyst who lived in Bern and thus began a Dulles family relationship with Jung and his institute in Zurich that is now in its second generation with daughter Joan Dulles Buresch, a Jungian analyst in Santa Fe.

Dulles welcomed his wife's deep interest and determination to study Jung's teachings. He was now working flat out on a number of chancy but important projects. In the first week of January, Dulles met secretly with Edda Ciano, the daughter of Mussolini and widow of his former foreign minister, Count Ciano. She had escaped to Switzerland to a sanitarium but not before she had hidden the explosive personal diary her late husband had kept during his years as *Il Duce*'s first minister and emissary to Hitler. She was desperate for money and some way to save herself and her children from postwar revenge by the partisans. Dulles tracked her down and persuaded the terrified woman to turn the diaries over to an OSS team that, using a hand-held camera, photographed every page of the intimate autobiography over a five-day period. Dulles, for his part of the bargain, provided her with a modest amount of cash and put her under his personal protection for the rest of the war.[12]

All the while, Dulles was receiving periodic communications from November onward that could only be coming from Heinrich Himmler. The emissary was the German consul in Lugano, Alexander von Neurath, who was the son of a former German foreign minister. Neurath had also made overtures to the British consul in Zurich, and Dulles was not sure whether the peace feelers were genuine or an attempt to drive a wedge into the Anglo-American alliance. By December another contact surfaced. General Wilhelm Harster was commander of the RSHA police and security forces for Italy. He began to ask the same cautiously worded

questions about a separate surrender through various Italian contacts of Dulles. It had also become clear that Himmler's chief
deputy, Schellenberg, had been in personal contact with Count
Bernedotte, the Swedish diplomat, about similar proposals.

To confuse matters further, in January 1945 Max Waibel, the
Swiss intelligence officer in charge of counterespionage against
the Germans, told Dulles that a there were messages from an
emissary of SS General Karl Wolff. The general was head of the
divisions of both the SS troops as well as the RSHA security police
in Italy. In that theater of operations, Wolff was General Harster's
superior officer and answered only to Field Marshal Kesselring.
What tantalized Dulles was seemingly that Wolff made this
approach on his own, without Harster's participation but with
Himmler's knowledge. Dulles was about to embark on Operation
Sunrise-Crossword, one of the most dramatic and controversial
intelligence triumphs of his career and his last major coup of
World War II.[13]

THE FIRST CONTACTS from the Wolff group began in late
February 1945. By March 3 Dulles was able to dispatch Paul Blum,
the OSS counterespionage chief for the Bern station, to Lugano
for a direct parlay with Nazi officers who claimed to represent
Kesselring, Wolff, and Harster. Dulles had instructed Blum to
demand the Germans prove their good faith by releasing two
prominent Italian resistance leaders who were being held by the
Gestapo in Milan—one was Ferruccio Parri, later a postwar premier of Italy. Parri, who thought he was being taken out of his cell
to be shot, was astonished to find himself safely hidden in a Swiss
hospital a few days later. In the meantime, Allied commander
Field Marshal Alexander had signaled from the Caserta headquarters near Naples that Dulles was to proceed cautiously with
talks, but on the understanding that there could be only an

unconditional surrender of the German divisions in Italy and that the Russians would have to be involved in the final negotiations.

On the night of March 8 General Wolff and some aides arrived in Zurich dressed as civilians, having used the good offices of the Swiss authorities to sneak over the border. Dulles said that, while the others in the German delegation cooled their heels in a Swiss safe house, he and Gaevernitz would meet Wolff by himself at a secret apartment the American spy chief kept in that city. Wolff agreed and sent ahead a set of credentials to identify him. The two OSS men could scarcely keep a straight face; among the documents was a full-page photograph of the general cut from a German photo magazine along with a list of his official titles. Attached was a memorandum of references that Dulles could check to be sure of Wolff's *bona fides*: the top of the list was Rudolf Hess, the Hitler aide whose peace flight to England had landed him in a British jail. The second name on the list was that of Pope Pius XII. But other documents were not so loony. Wolff also appended a list of art treasures from the Uffizi Gallery in Florence, including the king of Italy's coin collection, which were under his care and which he would see were returned to the Allies.

In his personal notes, Dulles later recalled the meeting:

> Wolff was a good looking fellow. There was a question of whether I should shake hands with him. Since I was not a military man, it seemed to me that it would be in order to shake hands with him if he offered, since I felt if I refused our talk would start with an insult to him. He offered his hand and I shook it. He was a strange, "Goethesque" [*sic*] guy, likable and talked well—said the war was over and he wanted to end it as soon as possible to save lives. (I was supposed to be a special representative of President Roosevelt in Switzerland.) This

idea had been spread by word-of-mouth by the Swiss and was so referred to in Gestapo records. The more we denied it the surer the Gestapo was that I was Roosevelt's special representative... it made good cover.

Wolff did not have Kesselring convinced about the surrender.... [He] went back to headquarters and found that at that moment, by coincidence, [Kesselring] had been ordered by Hitler to take over command of the western front. The props were out from under the plan and we were on a spot. I immediately sent a report to Donovan, OSS-Italy (for General Alexander) asking for advice. Alexander said go ahead.

The situation was even worse than Dulles knew at the time. Kesselring, after giving Wolff vaguely worded assurances that he approved of a surrender, had moved to his new headquarters and was refusing telephone calls from the increasingly frantic SS general. Still worse, Wolff was called by Himmler's top SS commander, Ernst Kaltenbruner, and directly ordered to cease his contacts with Dulles since they might jeopardize talks that were going on elsewhere; so Himmler *did* know about the talks, and Wolff's very life could be forfeited at any moment.

After starting so promisingly, the situation on the German side deteriorated badly over the next weeks. Kesselring's replacement as army commander in Italy was an old-school soldier who refused to countenance surrender because he was still bound by his personal oath to Hitler. In the meantime, Wolff narrowly missed being killed by an Allied bombing raid near his headquarters in Bolzano. The Allied staff at the Caserta headquarters had sent two high-ranking officers, General Lyman Lemnitzer and British General Terrance Airey, up to Switzerland to negotiate directly in behalf of the Allied commanders. In deference to Swiss sensitivity, the two Allied generals came disguised as U.S. Army sergeants; they regularly forgot the cover names on their dog tags.

On March 19 Wolff made another perilous secret trip, again in civilian clothes, this time to two resort cottages that Gaevernitz had leased in Ascona near the border. When he returned to Bolzano again, Wolff permitted Dulles to send a radio operator (a Czech OSS agent who had escaped from Dachau) to slip over in a German uniform and be secreted with a wireless sender in a room in the general's headquarters. Two of the general's top aides were then taken to Caserta and presented with the official terms of surrender; they had Wolff's permission to sign on his behalf even though he had not secured Kesselring's assent or even that of his subordinate battlefield corps commanders.

In the midst of this, Donovan telegraphed to Dulles in Ascona that the U.S. Joint Chiefs had expressly forbidden the talks to go further. The Soviets had become suspicious, and an exchange of increasingly insulting telegrams from Stalin to Roosevelt threatened to rupture their alliance in the final weeks of the war. From Stalin's standpoint, the British and Americans were clearly betraying the Soviet Union by agreeing to truce talks that allowed the Germans to shift divisions to the Eastern Front. In one of the increasingly angry exchanges, Stalin charged to Roosevelt: "The Germans have on the Eastern front 147 divisions. They could without harm to their cause take from the Eastern front 15–20 divisions and shift them to the aid of their troops on the Western front. However, the Germans did not do it and are not doing it. They continue to fight savagely with the Soviets for some unknown junction Zemlianitsa in Czechoslovakia which they need as much as a dead man needs poultices, but surrender without any resistance such important towns in Central Germany as Osnabruck, Mannheim, Kassel. Don't you agree that such a behavior of the Germans is more than strange and incomprehensible?" Roosevelt, who was now days away from dying, roused himself in anger. He was joined by the doughty Churchill in rebuking Stalin. At that point, the Soviet leader cooled off just as quickly and, after a fashion, apologized. But the schism was visible, and the threat was growing. Liberated countries such as Rumania and Yugoslavia had suddenly been taken over in internal power grabs by groups of declared Communist parties. Moreover, while the Russians had only informally guaranteed Austrian independence, Moscow had not yet officially signed the agreed separation pact, and the question was rapidly being rendered moot by the onrushing tide of the Red Army.

A sense of unbearable urgency began to build at Allied headquarters in Caserta. The spring offensive against the Gothic Line had not yet started; if the Germans dug into Alpine fortifications, hundreds of thousands of lives would be lost, and the campaign could last twelve to eighteen months. In the midst of all this uncertainty, Dulles was suddenly summoned to Paris, where, to his surprise, he found Donovan ensconced in the Ritz Hotel and in a frightful mood. President Roosevelt had died two days earlier, and Donovan knew he should be back in Washington protecting his agency and befriending the new president. But he was stuck in Paris until he could find out what Dulles was up to and build a case to take back to an angry Joint Chiefs of Staff who felt (correctly) that they were being misled by both the OSS and Caserta. Dulles reassured him, partially, by revealing that Wolff had been called back to Berlin by Hitler and Himmler and might not be able to return to Italy, might even be shot for his efforts. There was nothing yet so concrete about the talks that should worry anyone; as far as the Soviets were concerned, Operation Sunrise could still be plausibly denied. Donovan repeated, and Caserta confirmed, that for the time being Sunrise was shut down as an ongoing surrender negotiation.

But by April 23 Dulles was wiring Caserta and Washington that Wolff and the senior aide to his *Wehrmacht* superior (Kesselring's replacement) would arrive in Lucerne with full powers to effect a surrender. Hiding out at the house of Major Waibel in Lucerne, the German envoy was reduced by the strict orders from Washington not to see him in person but to talk to Dulles and Gaevernitz on the telephone in Ascona. Wolff assured Dulles he now had full powers to effect a surrender, and he gave a full report of his April 18–19 meetings in Berlin.

What Dulles had to report to Caserta and Washington was an astonishing view into the unreality that gripped the Nazi leadership in their final hours. Himmler and Kaltenbruner had upbraided Wolff for seeking Dulles out, but then told him to go ahead with a surrender if he could effect the quick release of the German troops and evacuate them safely back to Germany. Then the general had gone to Hitler's bunker under the Reich's Chancellery, where Hitler, he said, "seemed in low spirits but had not given up hope. He stated, 'We must fight on to gain time; in two more months, the break between the Anglo-Saxons and the Russians will come about and then I shall join the party which first approaches me. It makes no difference which.'"

Finally, on April 29 in Caserta, two representatives of General Wolff signed the formal surrender of more than a million German troops in northern Italy. Now the problem was how to convey that news over a battle line that ran hundreds of miles through forbidding terrain; unknown to the Allies at the time, Wolff had not by any means secured the support of the other top German commanders, and at one point he had to imprison several of them in a salt mine and ring his headquarters with tanks to keep from being arrested by his own field commanders. It took time for the full text of the surrender to be sent to Switzerland, translated, and then radioed to Bolzano; the deadline for the cease-fire and formal surrender was noon on May 2, and time was running out.

By this time Dulles had been running between Paris, Bern, Ascona, and Annemasse, the French-Swiss border crossing where a nearby airfield allowed him to commute to and from Caserta. Coming back from his confrontation with Donovan in Paris, he had one of his more serious gout attacks. At one point, he brought Clover along for company to Ascona and put her in a hotel on the small lake nearby. Suddenly a delegation from Wolff's staff showed up, and Dulles told Clover to make herself scarce; dressed in a pair of light shorts and a shirt, she took one of the hotel skiffs out for a row on the lake and waited for a signal that it would be safe to come back. The day passed slowly, and toward dusk, a sunburned Clover rowed ashore and found to her amazement that the clandestine conference had ended hours earlier. The Germans had gone back to Italy, and Dulles had forgetfully driven off without her to the cottage kept by Gaevernitz. In time, the incident became a family joke.

Finally, it was over. Hitler's suicide on April 30 was officially confirmed on May 1, and many German officers felt they were released from their loyalty oaths to their führer. Those who had threatened to fight on or to try to thwart Wolff gave in and issued orders to their troops. Even Kesselring had surfaced and, after an emotional confrontation, had agreed to endorse Wolff's and the other generals' declaration of surrender. Two days later he sent his own message to Eisenhower in Paris offering to surrender the rest of the divisions under his command in the entire Alpine region of Austria. Allied troops beat Russians into the key Mediterranean port of Trieste and swept through the Tyrol into Vienna, thereby confirming in Stalin's mind that Operation Sunrise had all along been a terrible plot on the part of Washington and London.

History tells us that V-E Day was May 8, 1945, when the Germans formally surrendered to Eisenhower and the other Four Power commanders. Without Dulles's secret surrender, the fighting could have lasted far longer.

CHAPTER ELEVEN

1945–1950

"Peace will need to be worked out as diligently as war has been."
—Council on Foreign Relations Report
for 1944–1945

MOST SENIOR PLANNERS in Washington assumed World War II would continue through 1946 and possibly into 1947. Had that been so, the odds are strong that the OSS would have been dismantled and parts of it absorbed into other departments well before the shooting stopped. So the trap was already closing on the spy service and its creator; it merely accelerated when the war rushed to an abrupt conclusion in the summer of 1945.

As early as 1943 powerful forces within the military services and the State Department agreed that the flamboyant William Donovan (now a major general) had no place in a postwar intelligence service. Those parts of the OSS that were acknowledged successes—such as the top two tiers of R&A scholars or the paramilitary units—were expected to be salvaged and sent into some other jurisdiction. But even though President Roosevelt had grave doubts about the OSS, he was also concerned about the capacity of the military and diplomatic intelligence branches to provide what he needed on their own.

The ghost of Pearl Harbor loomed everywhere. Thus Donovan was included among those FDR turned to in October

1944 to contribute a general outline for a peacetime intelligence service. The OSS chief had been drafting such a plan since his return from Europe with Allen Dulles. In November he sent to the White House his blueprint for a "Permanent World-Wide Intelligence Service."

That first Donovan plan called for a central authority that reported directly to the president and not through the Joint Chiefs of Staff or any other agency. Its job was to set objectives and coordinate the material a president and his senior advisers would need to plan and execute "national policy and strategy." Donovan's new agency would retain the power to conduct secret intelligence collection abroad and to wage covert operations, but it would be forbidden to have any police powers or to spy at home. More immediately, Donovan argued to FDR that the changes should come at once and that the OSS should be transformed into this proposed intelligence service; there should not be, he argued, a demobilization of the tremendous assets and talents already acquired. The OSS, he concluded, should not be torn down and rebuilt; it should be expanded on its present base.

But Thomas F. Troy, the respected Donovan biographer, reports that Roosevelt was being urged at the same time by his close friend Harry Hopkins to dismiss Donovan; to that end FDR assigned one of his bright young men in the subterranean Map Room of the White House, army Colonel Richard Park, Jr.,[1] to analyze the record of OSS shortcomings. Hopkins, in the meantime, circulated to Roosevelt and others a report from that old nemesis, G-2's General George Strong, that called the OSS "possibly dangerous" and argued that it ought to be "liquidated in a perfectly natural, logical manner."[2] All during the early spring of 1945 the battle raged. It even slopped over into the newspapers with a series of leaked stories in the *Chicago Tribune* written by Walter Trohan that Donovan was advocating the creation of an American

"Gestapo" to spy on foreigners and citizens alike. Most historians have believed that J. Edgar Hoover was the source of that particular malice, but Troy quotes Trohan himself as confessing years later that Steve Early, FDR's press secretary, had given him a copy of Donovan's blueprint at the president's urging in order to test public reaction.[3] Public reaction to an expanded spy service was not good; congressional reaction was even more hostile.

The issue being struggled over had moved well beyond the traditional question of *whether* America would have a central intelligence service. The question was who would control such a central service once the war ended, and just what tasks would be assigned to it. Less obvious was a second issue that was often debated as a separate matter. This was the still unsettled question of what America's role was to be in the new, unstable world of peace that lay in the future. If the foreign policy of the United States was to rest on a narrow and military solution—the open-ended armed occupation of both Germany and Japan—then intelligence could very well be left to the armed services with the kind of Joint Intelligence Board that the British used for oversight and coordination.

Allen Dulles was one of the early voices that argued the other side of the debate. In March 1944 Dulles had sent a lengthy memorandum to Donovan that was circulated to FDR and other cabinet officials and then sent via the British Security Coordination office in New York over to the Foreign Office for comment. Dulles began his analysis by concluding that the war had progressed to the point that "under no circumstances can Germany win now even a partial victory."

> The only real question today is whether constructive regenerating forces will control and direct the fate of Europe, or whether forces of disintegration and anarchy

will prevail. The answer to this question depends firstly upon the policy adopted by Russia, and secondly upon the vigor, strength and direction of the policy adopted by America and Great Britain.

Our policy seems to have been predicated upon the idea that a military victory plus unconditional surrender was all that was needed. This, I think, is mistaken. We in the West have yet failed to understand the social and spiritual factors which are playing a vital part in determining the trend of events in Europe today. As a result it is Russia rather than the Western powers which is tending to dominate the scene, not only because of its military victories but on account of the growing belief in many parts of Europe, particularly where Russia is little known, that the common man will fare better in a Europe under Russia than under Western influence.... We have not yet dictated and given to the people of Europe any clear indication as to what economic and social regime we propose to favor, or to give life and figure to a program which appeals to the common man.

The people of Europe have moved far to the Left. By and large, they do not want communism. But they do want a new social order which will constitute a very definite break with the past. They feel that in our Italian and French policies the Western powers have shown a disinclination to break with the past, or to seek the aid of those forces which, I believe, will be the coming elements in the Europe of tomorrow. As regards Germany, we are certainly reaching a point where daily more and more people are becoming reconciled to a Russian solution....[4]

But, as so often happens in the pace of historical events, the debate was resolved in an abrupt and unanticipated fashion. Franklin Roosevelt died on April 12, 1945. Harry Truman succeeded as president, and V-E Day followed quickly on May 8. One of the first items handed to the new president was Colonel Park's report that had been commissioned by FDR six months earlier. Park's indictment of the OSS listed 120 instances of, as Troy describes, "poor security, incompetence, waste, nepotism, inadequate training, extravagance, corruption, alcoholism, orgies, foreign penetration—you name it." Park recommended that Donovan be fired at once and that the OSS be scattered to the winds. Truman heard much the same line of argument in the weeks that followed. Dean Acheson, who was assistant secretary of state under Henry Stimson and who would be elevated to undersecretary when James Byrnes succeeded Stimson that summer, campaigned to have R&A sent to the State Department. The Pentagon services had their wish lists; J. Edgar Hoover had his hit lists. If Roosevelt had been ambivalent about Donovan, Truman actively disliked him—for ignoring him when he was vice president, and because he resented the spy chief's patronizing manner. It needs remembering that Donovan still saw himself as a possible presidential candidate at this time and that Truman knew it.

In the midst of this, Dulles was sweating out the final weeks of the Operation Sunrise negotiations with the Germans. He began to be approached by Japanese diplomats in Switzerland who claimed to represent high officials of the peace party inside the Japanese government. There were cautious inquiries about surrender terms. Dulles's first cable to Washington was dated May 12, but there is evidence that he had been seeking guidance about the approaches as early as mid-April. "One of the few provisions that the Japanese would insist upon would be the retention of the Emperor as the only safeguard against Japan's conversion to

Communism." In a memo to President Truman, Donovan had handwritten the question, "Should we pursue this?"[5]

Dulles at this point was of the opinion that the feelers were merely from "local boys," Japanese diplomats isolated in Switzerland, far from home, and out of the political power circles in Tokyo. But a few weeks later, Dulles was approached by the well-known Swedish economist Per Jacobsson, one of the founders of the Bank for International Settlements in nearby Basle. Jacobsson, a trusted friend, said that two of the Japanese senior officials at the bank had brought a serious peace offer authorized by ranking officers in both the Japanese navy and army in Tokyo. The Japanese had approached Jacobsson because he had just done service as the chief negotiator of the peace agreement between Finland and the Soviet Union. Dulles by this time was packing to move on to his new assignment as OSS director for Germany in Wiesbaden. He reminded Jacobsson that the Japanese had to face a total surrender, but then hinted that preservation of the imperial family's status might be possible. His cables sparked action by a friend, Joseph Grew, at that time undersecretary of state to Stimson and the last U.S. ambassador in Tokyo when war broke out. For six weeks Grew lobbied President Truman to acknowledge publicly that the emperor might be saved and finally got such a statement issued from the White House on June 10. This was just eight days before the final strategy session to fix American plans for the last stage of the war in the Pacific, the perilous invasion of the Japanese mainland known as Operation Downfall.[6]

At that point, the prospect of winning the war with Japan was likely, but victory would come at a ghastly cost. War Department strategists drew up the landing operations called Olympic and Coronet, a detailed strategy for an island-hopping campaign to invade Japan that would begin four to five months after American troops could safely be withdrawn from Europe and sent

to Pacific staging areas. Operation Olympic was the name for the
first landings on the island of Kyushu, the southernmost of the
island nation chain, in November 1945 at the earliest. An invasion
force of 766,700 American troops was contemplated. The planners
told President Truman that the Japanese military and civilian population could be expected to defend its homeland with fierce
determination. Based on the cost of liberating other Pacific islands
in the war, he could expect more than 260,000 killed or wounded.

Operation Coronet was to be the attack on the remainder of
Japan's heavily fortified homeland, beginning in March 1946. The
planners called for a force of more than two million troops and at
least six months to a year of hard fighting. Americans killed and
wounded could be expected to be between 600,000 to 750,000; victory would probably entail the devastation of all of Japan's major
cities and a Japanese civilian death and injury toll in the millions.[7]
These predictions horrified everyone from Truman on down. More
horrifying, even after conquering the Japanese home islands, the
Americans would still face a Japanese army of one-and-a-half million in the field in mainland China. The prospect of continued warfare in Asia for another five years could not be ruled out.

Even before that date in mid-June, when the war plans for a
conventional attack were being set, Truman and his top advisers
agreed that if the atomic bomb could be perfected and manufactured, he would use it to short-cut the catastrophe of an invasion.
The question, in those final weeks of June, was whether the bomb
would be ready in time. And, even if it worked, would it prod the
Japanese to surrender?

Japanese officials in Tokyo chose that moment to blunder.
Despite cables from Bern stressing the importance of Dulles as a
peace negotiator (had he not just arranged the capitulation of a
million German troops?), the faction of senior ministers seeking
peace decided to approach the Soviet ambassador in Tokyo, Jacob

Malik. Since the Soviets were not yet in the war with Japan, could they not use their good offices to broker a peace that saved their honor? Malik stalled. The Japanese cabled their embassy in Moscow to hurry things along; the cables were immediately intercepted and sent back to Washington. There was no response from either the White House or the Kremlin.

President Truman in the meantime prepared to journey to Potsdam for a meeting, his first summit with Churchill and Stalin. The Potsdam Conference, which began in July and lasted into August, finally divided Germany into four zones of occupation and confirmed the Soviet hegemony over Eastern Europe that Stalin had claimed at Yalta. On July 14 Dulles relaxed in the garden of his new quarters in the village of Biebrich (near Wiesbaden), just a short distance from the new regional OSS headquarters that had been set up in a commandeered champagne factory. It was a Saturday, and the weather was extremely hot for Germany at that time of year. Per Jacobsson had called the day before with an urgent message that the Japanese were now prepared to enter into direct negotiations with the Allies. Dulles arranged for a car to bring the economist the 350 miles from Switzerland. This time Jacobsson brought a list of specific questions that the diplomats had assured him were key to overcoming the objections of those in the Japanese cabinet who still favored a struggle to the death. He also brought with him Dulles's old assistant, Gero Gaevernitz, who had been one of the intermediaries in the early talks with the Japanese.

The Japanese wanted to know the following: In Dulles's personal opinion, would America agree to preserve the imperial dynasty? Would the Allies agree to a new Japanese constitution along the lines of a quite liberal one that had been adopted in 1889? Could President Truman halt the war at once?

Throughout the hot evening the two men argued over the true meaning of the overtures. Dulles suspected a ploy designed to disrupt the Potsdam meetings, which were to begin on Tuesday.

Jacobsson argued that some accommodation had to be made to the personal fears of the Japanese ruling class if it was to overcome its reluctance to face defeat. The next morning, on Sunday, the talks continued at the champagne factory. Dulles agreed to send a memo to Truman via diplomat John McCloy, who was passing through the area on his way to Potsdam. Jacobsson was sent back through the ninety-degree heat and told to sit tight. He was to tell the Japanese who wanted peace, "The safest way is to take the risk" and surrender. Yet, as the economist was climbing into the OSS car for the journey back to Switzerland, Dulles reassured him that the matter would not drop. "This is the biggest thing on our map right now. I'll see that it gets through." He decided to take the news directly to Potsdam himself.

Dulles later remembered:

> Our flight to Potsdam took place on the 20th of July 1945. It was just one year to the day after the abortive attempt of the German resistance to kill Hitler…. At Potsdam, Secretary Stimson received me as an old friend. As I recall, his close associate, Harvey Bundy [father of McGeorge and William Bundy], was the only other person present. He heard my story and all its details to the end. He thanked me for the information, which he said fitted in with other intelligence he had received. He gave no clue as to his own decision, nor did I expect it…. There was one other item of news I did not know then, namely, that four days earlier, on July 16th, the atom bomb had been successfully detonated. Today one wonders whether if the Japanese negotiators had come a little sooner and with clear credentials of authority, the Hiroshima explosion would have taken place.[8]

That question will probably provoke debate forever.

AFTER THE ATOMIC BOMBS were dropped and claimed an estimated 250,000 lives, Japan surrendered on August 14. President Truman set out almost at once to dismantle significant parts of the American war machine, including the OSS. The Lend-Lease program of aid, which had propped up the economies of both Britain and the USSR, was shut down five days after V-J Day. Other programs and operations quickly followed. But while Washington rushed to peacetime, the country was moving rather seamlessly out of the shooting war and into a more ominous Cold War. Allen Dulles spent those late summer months directing the gathering of evidence for the Nuremberg trials as well as drafting lists of Germans who were qualified and anti-Nazi enough to work in the reconstituted government bureaucracies of the defeated Reich's towns and provincial ministries. Gerry Van Arkle had brought young Erica Glaser with him from Bern to help with the lists of labor union communists who could be recruited for responsible positions. "It was a game really, as far as I was concerned," she recalled. "I saw my job [as] to make sure that the government jobs were not all taken by socialists and democrats, that as many communists as possible could be brought in. One problem was that the German communists were not at all sure that they wanted to be brought in."

To reassure the communists that the West could be trusted, Dulles turned to Noel Field and sent him to Paris to convince top OSS officials at headquarters to make a formal liaison with a group of German exiles who wanted to return home and take up positions in the new occupation government. One of the OSS officers involved in the case was Arthur Schlesinger, Jr., the distinguished historian, then a young intelligence specialist on Western Europe. Schlesinger recalled later:

> Field wanted us to support an organization of exiles
> that was the western edition of the Free German

Committee, which the Soviet Union had set up among the prisoners it had captured on the Eastern Front and among exiled German communists. I interviewed Field with another officer, and it was evident to us that Noel Field was a communist and that this was a Stalinist racket organized among their prisoners for the future benefit only of the Soviet Union. So we recommended against OSS getting involved, and Dulles did not complain about it. There was always a certain concern among some of us about what the communist resistance groups were up to; we certainly had no illusions about it, I don't think. But the big change in mood from worries about the Nazis to worries about the Russians did not come until after I returned to the United States in October 1945. Then there was a big change in mood, particularly when some of the people came home from Eastern Europe. After Allen left Wiesbaden he was replaced by Frank Wisner, who had been in Rumania, and he really moved in on the Cold War. That was also a time when OSS and others began to make deals with former Nazi intelligence groups.[9]

Dulles had quite a staff of intelligence talent working for him at the champagne factory. There was Richard Helms, a young naval officer and former United Press correspondent who had covered Germany before the war. He was a deputy for special intelligence for Germany. Frank Wisner, also a navy officer, joined them from operations in the Balkans to become head of special operations; after succeeding Dulles for a time in Wiesbaden, he became head of the State Department's intelligence operations branch until it was folded into the CIA. Gero Gaevernitz soon came from Bern to join Dulles's staff. Branch offices were quickly established in Berlin, Munich, and Frankfurt. The OSS became

more military in appearance than it had been during the hostilities; those who were detailed from military branches wore their
regulation uniforms. Civilians like Dulles, and even Gaevernitz,
wore rather baggy army-issue officers' uniforms without insignia.

But by early September, the OSS was finished, and even
Donovan knew it. Even as he was waging his last-minute campaign
for a reprieve, Donovan was forced to go ahead with the unavoid-
able directives to begin liquidating the OSS as a functioning entity
of wartime government. Truman was in a hurry to get started on
constructing a new intelligence service even if he had no idea what
its shape would be. The Soviets had taken the place of Hitler's Nazis
as a serious security threat to the United States, perhaps even more
serious. The new secretary of state, James Byrnes, was in London
for the Council of Foreign Ministers meeting to draft the peace
treaties for the defeated Axis nations. He sent a stream of complaints to Truman about Soviet obstructionism. In the midst of all
this, Truman was deluged with plans for the new intelligence service. Dean Acheson, as acting secretary of state (during Byrnes's
absence), formally asked that the OSS be sent intact to his department. The Joint Chiefs wanted it at the Pentagon. Truman had
commissioned a study group under Ferdinand Eberstadt, which
recommended that a central authority report directly to the president's top national intelligence advisers, the National Security
Council. The postmaster general argued that, since his agency
opened mail already, it was the logical repository for a spy service.
Even as this argument went on throughout early September, the
dismantling of the OSS was well under way.

On September 18 Donovan cabled "110, AMZON," which
was Dulles's new designation in Wiesbaden:

(1.) We submitted to Budget Bureau a liquidating budget of $10,500,000 which is to cover our expenses from

1 July to end of liquidation.... (2.) Active consideration is being given in official circles to proposal for a central intelligence agency. JDC [Joint Defense Committee] have revived their earlier study of my proposal.... Meanwhile, JCS [Joint Chiefs of Staff] has directed us to return all military personnel to army and navy as quickly as can be done without disrupting essential work.... (3.) We should begin immediately to turn over to the military or to stop altogether any tactical intelligence work we now are undertaking. At the same time we shall strengthen our Strategic Intelligence organization during next three months so as to assure that our government will not suffer through neglect on our part in the event a new intelligence agency is established. By tactical intelligence I mean in general that which is primarily of use for specific activities of... the military agencies..., whereas strategic intelligence has significance of a policy nature and is primarily of use to those determining policy. (4.) Our withdrawal from tactical intelligence will involve the disbanding of our German and Austrian missions as they are now constituted.[10]

Truman officially disbanded the OSS on September 20. But just seven days after that, Donovan cabled Dulles again that he and his team were to stay where they were. There would be immediate reductions in force of the sixteen thousand personnel on the OSS rosters, but many of them were merely to be returned to the military services from which they had come. Key elements of Secret Intelligence comprising more than nine thousand intelligence specialists and officers had been shifted to the War Department into a new branch called the Strategic Services Unit. The R&A functions, which were to be pared down to 1,300 analysts, were to go to State and be put under the charge of Colonel Alfred McCormack, the man who had upheld the "chicken feed" view of the "Wood" traffic. Luckily for Dulles and others still in place, the Strategic Services Unit was put under General John Magruder, who had run OSS operations in China and then became deputy director of Secret Intelligence in 1943. Magruder picked Colonel William Quinn as the man who would actually preserve the Strategic Services Unit's human assets during this interim period. Quinn and General Patch, because of their triumph with the landings in southern France, found themselves stranded without a mission after V-J Day. It had been planned that they would direct the actual Olympic landings in Japan if the war had proceeded by conventional means. At least for the time being, a friend of the OSS—and of Dulles—was in a position to salvage and protect.

But for Dulles himself there was the question of a mission. Harry L. Rositzke, an OSS officer who came from London to Wiesbaden, recalls the confused slide from one kind of war to another. Rositzke joked:

> We lived in a place called the Horn Rabbit House. The owner had been a big hunter of those rabbits with horns, and these stuffed heads of rabbits were all over the walls there. Living there were Dulles, Dick Helms, Frank Wisner, and a couple of my boys. I had the great responsibility of having the hot cinnamon red wine ready every evening. When we got there in May there was no focus at all. You see, after V-E Day there were no intelligence targets for us in Germany. The main thing was running counterintelligence against the leftover Nazis and trying to get hold of their records. But the army's CIC [Counter Intelligence Corps] took over

a lot of that. There was no focus on the Russians either, at least from what I knew of, before the winter of 1945. There was stuff in Berlin going on, and Allen went up there a lot. We had a colonel from the NKVD [Soviet intelligence] come over to our side, and that was exciting. Still, you could see something was coming. The Russians had moved a thousand miles to the west. As soon as they got to Berlin they started putting up wire and guardposts around their sector.[11]

One common thread of the recollections of men like Rositzke, Helms, and others who were working in Wiesbaden in the autumn of 1945 was an overwhelming desire to get home to the United States and get on with their civilian lives. There was also a pervasive feeling that for all its triumphs, the OSS needed a shakeup. More exactly, the men who had actually served in European operations believed Washington needed to define more clearly what was wanted from an intelligence service and how that service should be organized.

This is not to say that the OSS had not been a successful attempt, especially considering that it was created out of very little in the way of a formal intelligence structure four years earlier. As Harry Rositzke notes, "When the whole thing was over, I had a chat with the British General [Kenneth] Strong, who was Ike's chief of G-2, and he said he thought our tracking of just two of those SS divisions in the south of France, the *Das Reich* and the *Lehr,* and the way they were slowed down getting to the Normandy beachhead saved at least 10,000 lives. That, alone, to my mind, paid for the entire OSS operation around the world."

Richard Helms, a lieutenant commander in the navy when he worked for Dulles in Biebrich, remembers being not much concerned about the breakup of the OSS at the time. "I remember wanting to get home and get out of that uniform. Then I would decide what to do with my life." Shortly after his discharge that winter, Helms was back working in the Strategic Services Unit, as head of the special intelligence section for Central Europe. During his career in the CIA, Helms rose through the ranks to become one of Dulles's most relied-upon deputies and became director of Central Intelligence himself in both the Johnson and Nixon administrations. More recently, he looked back from the vantage point of his long career and provided this assessment of OSS and Allen Dulles:

> I have looked back on it as a great training ground for what came later, but when it comes to whether we would have won the war with or without the OSS, I don't think it made any difference, or much difference. Remember, this was an infant, the OSS. We didn't know anything about running agents or writing intelligence analysis or anything else.
>
> It hadn't existed in the United States government before. This was the first shot at it. Everybody had to learn their business. Most of the operators learned it at the feet of the British because they were the only people we could communicate with who would like to help. So it was learned pretty much as a British trade craft. But suppose you had organized it differently. You still had to figure out where to go and all the rest of it. I don't think organizational structure was a terribly important thing in those days.
>
> OSS was a great venture. It got together a lot of surprisingly able and dedicated people. They worked their asses off to try to affect the outcome of the war one way or another. There were some successes, but it

was not a howling success as an organization. That fact that it was kept out of the Far East mostly—you have to wonder about its ultimate impact. You asked when we started considering the Russians an intelligence target, well, hell, we only started on Russia well after V-E Day and after everybody suddenly realized that the Russians were going to be pretty tough to deal with. There wasn't anybody working against Russia before that time. That's all poppycock.

We were so goddamned busy winning the war with Germany, there was no time to spend on anybody else. I don't think people realize how close the Allies came to losing that war. Where everybody gets the idea that the war was such a fan dance, I can't figure out. Just suppose Hitler had invaded Britain before he went into Russia. What do you think would have happened? He would have taken Britain without question. They were in no position to resist him. So then, how would we have gotten him out of Europe?

Would we even have tried? Probably not.

Our job was to get any useful military information out of Germany. And it was very tough. Everybody was involved in that full time. Scandinavia, Iberia, Italy, any place you served, that's what you were supposed to be trying to do. When you look back on the amount of Europe that Germany held up until the time of D-Day, you see that this was a hell of a problem. We used Poles and the Dutch, Belgians, and Norwegians, anything we could lay our hands on. And most of them got wrapped up [captured]. It was very hard to survive in that environment. So this idea of derring-do and so forth just wasn't there. A lot has been exaggerated in the writing about [William] Casey's dropping agents into Germany. It was nothing as fancy as it is made out to be, or as successful. Some of those fellows survived, but they didn't produce much intelligence that made any difference one way or the other.

The most useful material was the "Wood" material. Code-breaking was an aspect of life that we knew nothing about at the time. OSS was not allowed to share in *Ultra*, except perhaps with respect to counterintelligence and then only with respect to suspected double agents. I'm quite sure I'm right about that. We never saw any *Ultra*.

That is why the "Wood" material was so important. All that stuff about Allen Dulles and his pipe and his genial nature and so on, that was just staging. Sure he contributed to it. But if you look at his work in Switzerland, keeping that "Wood" thing going, trying to use the "Breakers" group, the "Crown Jewels" project, the negotiations with Wolff and Sunrise—that's enough for anybody. Dulles was a very serious worker, and he worked very hard, and there was no bullshit about it. That is why, pretty early on, Dulles left Wiesbaden and took himself up to Berlin to be in charge of the branch operation up there.

That is when we first started to focus on what the Russians were up to. We had not focused on it up to the summer of 1945. But then we began to realize that this was going to be pretty tough sledding; that these were not four allies working together. It was three allies and one enemy. That became manifest before very long. What were the Russians doing with their troops in their zone? It didn't take long to figure out they weren't going to tell you a damn thing. In fact, they were going to keep you out of there, and they were going to be very hostile. Gradually we began to get into the business of trying to find out what they were doing. And G-2 was doing the same thing. We were all working together on this for a while.[12]

Helms's recollection of Dulles's operating in Berlin is borne out by fragmentary OSS records that show him away from Wiesbaden and working there with an undesignated group of army officers and OSS personnel from July 4, 1945, through the early autumn months. Recall that at that time the Soviets had exclusive control of the German capital by right of capture and it would not be until later that a Four Power Allied division of the city would be established. Just what operations the Dulles-army group undertook is unclear. At first, it appears the Americans contented themselves with the old mission of tracking down sought-after Nazis. But as the Soviets tightened their grip on Berlin and its people, that mission changed; reports grew that they were also unbolting as much of the German industrial machine as they could reach and were shipping it back home. Against their own personal preferences, American policymakers back in Washington began to demand much more information about Soviet-controlled target subjects. For a brief moment, it appeared that the remnants of the OSS might be revived.

But not for long. It soon became apparent that, even with the Strategic Services Unit inside the War Department as a division of the army, the Military High Command in Germany did not want civilians involved in intelligence operations. If there was rising concern about the Soviet allies, the military intelligence officers had a card of their own up their sleeves. Shortly after V-E Day, the army had taken prisoner German General Reinhard

Gehlen, who had been in charge of a senior intelligence group called *Fremde Heere Ost* (Foreign Armies East), the main intelligence analyst of Soviet order of battle intentions and capabilities for the German Army High Command, the OKW. Gehlen and his organization had provided increasingly gloomy analysis for Hitler and his command staff, so gloomy that, in April, an angry führer dismissed both him and OKW Chief of Staff General Heinz Guderian. Gehlen thereupon put away in a safe place a treasure-trove of detailed records about the Russian military capacity, only shortly to be taken prisoner by the Americans. With others from his staff rounded up from Allied POW camps, the Gehlen Organization became one of the star assets of G-2.

By early October it was clear to Dulles that his European adventures were at an end. President Truman had directed his three senior advisers—the secretaries of state, war, and navy—to come up with the final plan for an intelligence service that all three could agree upon and live with. At the first meeting of the three cabinet members, the only name put forward to head such an organization was that of Allen Dulles. Word filtered out to Dulles, and it was clear he would be in a better position back in the United States, where he might have some say in the shaping of this new agency. He would not learn for some time that Donovan had discouraged such an idea whenever he could; Dulles simply was not a good enough administrator. Or at least, that is what he said.

Dulles put in his papers to be relieved of duty from the Strategic Services Unit and was formally discharged into civilian life on December 2. He and Clover had returned to New York by then. They left behind their daughter Joan and his sister Eleanor Dulles, who had surprised everyone by deciding, early in 1945, that she wanted to put the economic reconstruction theories she had been working on for twenty years to practical work. By sheer force of personality she got herself appointed to the military government organization that was to take over the American zone in Vienna. Despite objections by the State Department visa office, she also managed to round up travel documents and passports for her son and adopted daughter, and for Joan, who had been recruited for the trip to serve as a nanny.

This strange collection arrived on Clover's doorstep in Zurich in April 1945. When Allen had left Bern for Wiesbaden, Clover had stayed behind to continue her studies and psychoanalysis. She had moved to Zurich to be closer to Dr. Jung and his institute. Eleanor had paused in Zurich long enough to get the three young people settled in, and then rushed off to Milan. There she commandeered a seat on General Mark Clark's personal airplane for the flight to Vienna. She would go on to play a vital role in the economic reorganization and revival of the Austrian economy. In 1947 she would be put in charge of a similarly successful program to rebuild and revive the totally shattered infrastructure of West Berlin. Of all the Dulleses, Eleanor is the one the Germans, especially the Berliners, hold in fondest regard and respect to this day.

With Clover due to leave Switzerland with him, Dulles secured the necessary permits and transportation authority for Joan to move herself and Eleanor's two children to Vienna. Even with all the documents that Dulles could provide for the three, the journey was uncertain because of the scarcity of transport and the high priority for military travelers over mere civilians. He turned to Fritz Molden, his brave border-crossing courier to the Austrian underground, to get the three Dulleses safely through their journey. Molden carried off his mission and, in the process, fell in love with twenty-two-year-old Joan, who stayed on in Vienna to study art. Two years later they married, and Molden later went on to a prominent career in the Austrian foreign ministry and as a publisher.

The return to New York and civilian life was all Dulles could have hoped for. Not only was he warmly welcomed back at

Sullivan & Cromwell by Foster and the other partners, but he also found himself being accorded an unexpected recognition in the other arena of his life that he valued, among the scholars and statesmen of the Council on Foreign Relations. Members of the Council on Foreign Relations had played a significant role in forming America's wartime policies; more than two hundred of the group had held senior positions in a wide variety of government service, from the State Department and the OSS to the military services and refugee relief agencies. Its War and Peace Studies program had been a private and much-valued resource for State Department policy strategists. Indeed, with Norman Davis and *Foreign Affairs* editor Hamilton Fish Armstrong as chief lobbyists, the Council on Foreign Relations had been a major party to the drafting of the United Nations charter.

With the Cold War so rapidly threatening the newly won peace, the council turned again to Dulles to direct an active campaign for a more bipartisan and progressive foreign policy on Europe. In a reorganization of its study and policy groups, the Council on Foreign Relations in the winter of 1945 created nine separate policy areas where its members felt they could make positive contributions; many of these were focused on specific global regions such as Britain and its empire, and Latin America. The regional group on "Western European Affairs" quickly became absorbed with issues involving Germany and its reconstruction. Dulles was unanimously selected to direct that panel's studies.

The selection of Dulles to head the Council on Foreign Relations policy group on Europe during this time of transition was not due solely to his returning from the war with an aura of espionage glamour. He had been a director of the council since 1927 and was listed as its secretary from 1933 through 1944 (notwithstanding his exile abroad). More to the point, Dulles brought back from Europe impressive credentials of firsthand experience with what was going on in the war-torn continent and with the menace that Soviet ambitions posed to world stability. Michael Wala is a German historian who edited a recently discovered book written by Dulles in 1947 (but not printed at the time) to promote the Marshall Plan. Wala sounds a familiar theme in his analysis of the returning spymaster's post-Occupation attitude:

> Earlier than many of his peers in the United States, Dulles had concluded that Germany was at the focal point of a number of important decisions determining the future political, strategic, and economic situation of Europe and consequently of the postwar world. Germany was vitally important for European economic restoration, and it was the site where the future predominance of the Soviet or of the American economic and political systems in Europe would be determined.
>
> Dulles was certain that clashes between the USSR and the U.S. were almost inevitable and only "insulating the two systems" promised a chance for a lasting peace. The European infrastructure of roads, railroads and waterways had been nearly totally destroyed by the war. "Europe as a whole," Dulles reminded the [Council on Foreign Relations] members, "cannot get back to anything like normal conditions, not to speak of prosperity, with a completely disorganized Germany."[13]

Specifically, Dulles and others began to campaign against the Joint Chiefs of Staff directive known as JCS 1067, which was imposed on General Eisenhower as the plan to rule a conquered Germany with a firm hand for an indefinite period. The plan was dubbed "the Four D's," because of its objectives—demilitarization, denazification, decartelization, and democratization. The

Morgenthau plan for an agrarian Germany under permanent
Allied supervision had been put aside by Roosevelt as an official
policy, but it survived in the stark rules of JCS 1067 and in the
sense that there was no alternative strategy then being considered
in Washington.

Dulles argued at the December 3, 1945, meeting of Council
on Foreign Relations leaders that "Germany ought to be put to
work for the benefit of Europe and particularly for the benefit of
those countries plundered by the Nazis." The rigidly enforced
denazification policies of the Allied military rulers of Germany
would result in barring many of the very people who could get the
infrastructure of the shattered country to function again. "We
have already found that you can't run railroads without taking in
some [Nazi] party members."[14]

Wala, among others, dismisses the accusation that Dulles had
become soft on fascism in his zeal to thwart the rising tide of communism. "Dulles, by no means a 'friend of Germany,' detested
Nazism fervently and was, like most of his peers at the Council, an
Anglophile. He simply wanted to put Germany back to work," he
says. He was not alone in this view by any means. Dean Acheson
and James Riddleberger, a State Department specialist on European
affairs, had been campaigning for some time for a more constructive policy. But what should it be?

In January 1946 Dulles outlined in some detail a reconstruction plan that is one of the earliest notions of what would, a
year later, be known as the Marshall Plan. Dulles's views were later
greatly shaped by other Council on Foreign Relations study
groups, but this was his own first response to what he had seen
over the past four years. One month later, in a speech to the
Foreign Policy Association in New York, Dulles warned that the
U.S. military occupation forces in Germany could not continue to
indefinitely imprison without trial those persons suspected of

war crimes simply by virtue of their past Nazi associations. General Eisenhower had said in a press interview that more than 100,000 Germans were being held at the time in the American zone, and that under the arbitrary rules of what constituted a war crimes suspect, the total could run to half a million.

"We find ourselves in the concentration camp business on a large scale," Dulles argued. "I believe in exemplary punishment for the Nazis. I do not believe in keeping vast numbers of people in concentration camps, housed, fed, and guarded at our expense for an indefinite period without trial.... When the Nuremberg trials have fixed the principles of justice, let us apply those principles to the Nazis whom we have arrested according to the evidence in each case.... We should decree punishment quickly...."

The focus of his speech, however, was on the need for prompt action to restore the German economy as a necessary prerequisite to the reconstruction of Europe. "Continued unemployment is one of the greatest dangers we face in Germany," he went on. "A man out of work is a danger in any society. Without some imports of raw materials it is difficult to see how German industry can continue to provide work for the unemployed, and this is an issue we and our allies will now have to face. The circle is a vicious one. Some industry is essential to export. Export alone can provide the foreign exchange for the necessary imports of food and additional raw material.... Without some imports of food and raw materials over these next five years there seems no alternative to widespread starvation and unemployment, political unrest, and possibly the seeds of a philosophy as dangerous as Nazism."[15]

Everyone in the audience knew which philosophy he was warning about. In later speeches he refined the notion of a federalized political system for Germany as an antidote to the Prussian type of centralized authority. And he warned audiences that year not to expect democracy German-style to be a reassuring copy of the American republic. "We should not be disturbed at, in fact we should welcome, a liberal and leftist oriented Germany. Here and in the labor unions we are likely to find the sturdiest anti-Nazi Germans."[16]

Shortly thereafter, Dulles was elected president of the Council on Foreign Relations, a position he would occupy until 1950, when he joined the CIA.

At that time, of course, the CIA had not quite come into being, although the process was under way.

ON JANUARY 22, 1946, President Truman created a four-man National Intelligence Authority (the secretaries of state, war, and navy and a presidential representative) and a Central Intelligence Group. The three cabinet agencies represented in the National Intelligence Authority were further directed to provide "persons and facilities from your respective departments..." to the new Central Intelligence Group, which would be "under the direction of a Director of Central Intelligence [who would] assist the National Intelligence Authority."[17] What Truman had set into being was a better-organized collection and distribution method for intelligence, which would be gathered and processed by the existing, and competing, intelligence services of the military services and the State Department. The director of Central Intelligence, commonly known as the DCI, was allowed to sit in on National Intelligence Authority sessions with the president but was not allowed a vote in the final intelligence interpretations that would be provided.

It was clearly a stopgap measure, one in which Truman himself apparently did not put too much faith. The compromise pleased neither the State Department, which wanted direction over the DCI's actions, nor the military services, which wanted control by the Joint Chiefs of Staff. Two days later, Truman summoned to a White House luncheon Admiral Sidney Souers, his designated DCI.[18]

Souers is often dismissed as being ill-suited to the task of being the first DCI. He was a naval reservist who was anxious to get back to his civilian life as a grocery chain executive in the Midwest. Yet Souers was one of the few men available who understood that creating a functioning secret intelligence service that would withstand the realities of Washington's political conflicts took time. And Souers understood, even though Truman's directive was muddy on the issue, that the Central Intelligence Group was not to collect intelligence of its own (much less to engage in covert operations) but was, in the words of the directive, to correlate, evaluate, coordinate, and distribute the intelligence product—not directly to the president, but to the National Intelligence Authority in recommended form. In short, the DCI worked for the National Intelligence Authority.

Soon the Central Intelligence Group was swamped with reports to draft. Truman, like Roosevelt before him, had been used to receiving a highly informative foreign affairs digest of sensitive intelligence material that was provided by the British Foreign Office to a limited list of "heads of Allied Governments only." The weekly reports were gossipy but informed, and the two American presidents had especially enjoyed the rather dry judgments that the British made about leading U.S. political figures and their doings. But with the war over, Whitehall abruptly canceled the distribution to the White House, and Truman promptly ordered Souers to begin a *daily* digest for him to read at breakfast that took precedence over anything else the reports staff might have been planning. Since Souers had no budget of his own and had to draw personnel from other services, the Central Intelligence Group quickly approached gridlock.

Truman began to move to deal with some of the crises facing the United States. In February the State Department had handed him the famous "long telegram" from George Kennan, the chargé d'affairs at the U.S. Embassy in Moscow, which warned that Stalin's animosity aside, the USSR could never compromise or cooperate with the democracies of the West and that this presented a clear danger to the United States. Reports coming in from Central Intelligence Group stations in Europe reported a steady subversion of the wartime agreements the Soviets had signed at Yalta and Potsdam and the brutal imposition of communist-dominated regimes in a pattern that began in Eastern Europe but that marched steadily west. A few days after Kennan's warning from Moscow, Winston Churchill made his famous "Iron Curtain" speech in Fulton, Missouri. The potent image was a confirmation that the Cold War had begun in earnest.

By June, Souers was ready to go home, and at that time Truman appointed Lieutenant General Hoyt S. Vandenberg as his successor to the DCI post. Vandenberg, age forty-seven, had compiled a splendid record as an army air corps commander in the war and had open ambitions to become the first chief of staff of the U.S. Air Force, which was about to be created as a separate service. Along with his own credentials and drive, the general benefitted from being the nephew of Senator Arthur Vandenberg, who was both chairman of the Senate Foreign Relations Committee and Senate president pro tempore. A tour of duty that could demonstrate his administrative and political skills was just what Vandenberg wanted, and he moved with energy to transform the Central Intelligence Group into something beyond its original mandate. Even before taking over from Souers, Vandenberg embarked on a whistle-stop trip to the major intelligence service posts still operating in Europe, some of them caught in a bureaucratic limbo from the old Strategic Services Unit to the new Central Intelligence Group. To the intelligence officers on the ground who were understandably worried about pay, careers, and, most of all, their mission, Vandenberg brought words of cheer and encouragement: Just hang on for a bit and the agency will be up and running even better than it had during OSS days.

In the first three months of his eleven-month tour as DCI, Vandenberg radically changed the role of the Central Intelligence Group and his own function as director. He pushed the reports staff into what became the Office of Reports and Estimates, which continued the daily briefings but began a flow of timely analytical papers with a longer-term focus. The first, ORE 1, was "Soviet Foreign and Military Policy," and updated Kennan's earlier warnings about Russian objectives. Vandenberg also insisted that these intelligence estimates had to be under the sole control of the DCI and that the final documents had to be considered the opinion of the director alone. The other members of the National Intelligence Authority were free to append dissents and disagreements, but the estimates themselves became firmly the province of the Central Intelligence Group.

Vandenberg then moved quickly in July to absorb the remaining agent assets and facilities still held under the Strategic Services Unit. Between then and September, he won approval from the National Intelligence Authority and the president for three other demands: the right of the Central Intelligence Group to collect intelligence on its own apart from the other agencies; the right to conduct intelligence research into communications, atomic weapons developments, and other areas; and separate financing authority. In one final test of strength, Vandenberg also wrenched away from J. Edgar Hoover the FBI's mandate to conduct intelligence operations in Latin America. Once again, the intelligence service had been lucky to have the right man in charge at the right time. While Vandenberg had little interest in intelligence operations or in fashioning the estimates sent to the president, he did use his authority to move the Central Intelligence Group from its subservient role under the other cabinet-rank intelligence services to close parity with them. If the Central Intelligence Group was not the first among equals, it was at least on its way. By the end of his tour as DCI, the organization no longer was merely a "group" but had become an "agency" in fact.

One of the steps Vandenberg took in August to strengthen his hand was to write to Allen Dulles and recruit him for a "small select Board of Consultants to advise me personally in the discharge of my responsibilities."[19] Others who agreed to serve included Kingman Douglas, William H. Jackson, Robert Lovett, Paul Nitze, and Admiral Souers. It was difficult for the group to meet frequently enough to suit Vandenberg, and finally Dulles was being called upon separately, often by telephone to his New York law offices. Thus, after an exile of only six months, Dulles was back in the intelligence game in earnest. What Vandenberg wanted most of all was Dulles's advice on how best to structure the new agency and how to sell the idea to a doubting Congress.

This was a busy time for Dulles. Sullivan & Cromwell was back in the swing of major bond financing and legal representation all over the world; the war had interrupted uncounted business agreements and loan deals, and nearly all appeared headed for one court or another. The Council on Foreign Relations committee on Germany also began to meet more frequently and to attract a far larger interest among council members than anyone had anticipated. While most of the Council on Foreign Relations policy study groups had at best fewer than two dozen active participants, the Dulles group on German reconstruction had drawn one hundred active members, including many from outside New York. At the same time, Dulles was trying to write a book about his experiences with the "Breakers" plotters. He had a simple but important point to make. Not all Germans had been mindless, enthusiastic Nazis. In fact, there had been a considerable underground opposition to Hitler and his evils. That the story of the "Breakers" ended in unspeakable tragedy made it all the more important that Americans understand what had happened, if only to realize that no society is immune to despotism.

The trouble was that Dulles was a pedestrian writer. The unpublished raw manuscript of "The 20th of July Plot" in his private papers at Princeton lumbers and digresses. The raw manuscripts for his scores of articles in *Foreign Affairs* and the two books on neutrality he coauthored are not available, but it is apparent that he relied heavily on Hamilton Fish Armstrong, the editor for the Council on Foreign Relations, as something more than a copy fixer. Whether Armstrong actually ghostwrote all of Dulles's articles, or sharply reworked them, remains unknown. But Dulles clearly needed a ghostwriter for his book on the "Breakers," and fortunately the right one volunteered for the job. Wolf von Eckardt was a German-born U.S. soldier in military intelligence during the war. As part of his duties he had ransacked the Nazi offices in the Berlin suburb of Waansee and brought back to the American zone boxes of records, among which were the details of the "Breakers" plotters and the terrible fate they met. The full details of the attempt to kill Hitler in 1944 were just becoming known in early 1946, and along with the fascination of the war crimes trials that were going on, public interest was very high. Von Eckardt shared Dulles's views on the need to recognize the churchmen, labor leaders, and others who had paid the price for their opposition to Hitler, but he recognized that because he was German himself, he could never get such a book published under his own name.

Von Eckardt's wife Nina recalls: "Early in 1946, Dulles met Wolf and agreed with him that the book was a good idea. Wolf was to go to back to Germany to work on the war crimes trials later that year, but in the meantime he went over most days to Dulles's house in New York; it was very quiet there, and he worked on the manuscript. It was a gentlemen's agreement, and it was a wonderful thing for him; he would have been about twenty-five at the time."[20] *Germany's Underground*[21] was published the next spring with an acknowledgment to von Eckhardt and Betty Parsons, his Bern secretary, "for helping me piece together and reduce to manageable proportions the mass of data on the German underground...." The book was a best-seller. Wolf von Eckardt later became a well-respected writer on architecture and design for the *Washington Post*.

Truman's response to the Cold War was to push for passage of the National Security Act of 1947, which sought to modernize America's defense capabilities. Dulles journeyed to Washington in April to present to the Senate Armed Services Committee recommendations to build a Central Intelligence Agency within whatever new defense setup Congress wanted to create. Dulles proposed:

> To create an effective Central Intelligence Agency we must have in the key positions men who are prepared to make this a life work, not a mere casual occupation. Service in the Agency should not be viewed merely as a stepping stone to promotion in one of the armed services or other branches of the Government. The Agency should be directed by *a relatively small but elite corps of men with a passion for anonymity and a willingness to stick at that particular job* [emphasis added]. They must find their reward primarily in the work itself, and in the service they render their Government, rather than in public acclaim....
>
> Because of its glamour and mystery, overemphasis is generally placed on what is called secret intelligence, namely the intelligence that is obtained by secret means and by secret agents. During war this form of

intelligence takes on added importance but in time of peace the bulk of intelligence can be obtained through overt channels.... I believe the agency which is to be entrusted with assembling and analyzing intelligence should be predominantly civilian rather than military, and under civilian leadership....

Much of our thinking relating to an intelligence agency is colored by our recent dramatic war experiences. Intelligence work in time of peace will require other techniques, other personnel, and will have rather different objectives. The prime objectives today are not solely strategic or military, important as these may be. They are scientific—in the field of atomic energy, guided missiles, supersonic aircraft, and the like. They are political and social. We must deal with the problem of conflicting ideologies as democracy faces communism, not only in the relations between Soviet Russia and the countries of the West, but in the internal political conflicts within the countries of Europe, Asia, and South America. For example, it may well be more important to know the trend of Russian communism and the views of individual members of the Politburo than it would be to have information as to the location of particular Russian divisions.[22]

The plan Dulles presented to Congress was not a reflexive repeat of his OSS experiences. He was describing a job he wanted, to be sure, but it was a new job with new, broader responsibilities. The Dulles plan differed from a number of previous versions sponsored by others in that it recognized a sharp difference between America's intelligence needs during a full-scale war (à la the OSS) and those of peacetime. That he advocated strong civilian

and nonpolitical control of the agency is a natural enough out-
growth of his background and experience. But Dulles also showed
he had been looking ahead to the Cold War problems the new
agency would face—a mission that must include collecting intelligence on political, economic, social, and technical questions as
well as defense strategy. Dulles urged that the agency report
directly to the president but that it be supervised by a small group
of senior cabinet officials (ideally only the secretaries of defense
and state and a presidential representative).

The agency Dulles wanted would differ sharply on another
key issue: its role as a shaper of foreign policy. Dulles wanted an
activist agency except in that one area. His proposed CIA should
have total free access to all sources of intelligence gathered by
other services, including the jealously guarded *Magic* and *Purple*
intercepts of the military. It also ought to have sole responsibility
for carrying out secret intelligence operations, and it would have
its own personnel and independent budget. But it must not,
Dulles repeatedly argued, be involved in recommending policy
actions. That must be the job of the president's National Security
Council or other advisory group, and ultimately the decision of
the president alone.[23]

In light of his later reputation for being preoccupied with
running secret operations (hence the nickname "The Great White
Case Officer"), it is interesting that Dulles argued to the senators
that "80 percent of CIA's information would come from open
sources and only 20 percent from secret sources," a term that he
used to cover communications intelligence as well as espionage.[24]

He also drew sharp lines of distinction between clandestine
intelligence and covert operations for reasons far beyond the
Dulles habit of precise descriptions. Clandestine operations are
meant to be secret and stay secret; breaking an enemy's code or
running an agent like Fritz Kolbe must never be suspected. A
covert operation is an act that by its nature will be noticed—a

bridge blown up, an assassination, a guerrilla raid—but whose hand struck what remains a secret. Dulles even recognized a marked philosophical difference in the intelligence methods of war and peace. To Hanson Baldwin, a *New York Times* editor and fellow Council on Foreign Relations expert on defense and intelligence strategy, Dulles wrote:

> Intelligence in wartime requires rather different techniques than intelligence in peacetime. In time of war, in dealing with an enemy or those friendly to your enemy, there is a justification for the use of ruthless methods which I would hardly favor in time of peace. If one's activities are uncovered in wartime that is too bad but there are no serious political repercussions. In time of peace, however, *one must be far more careful and subtle* [emphasis added]. One should not take the long risks or act on impulse as one has to do in time of war. Secret intelligence in peacetime should be a long-range affair, methodically and carefully built up with every emphasis on security and with an avoidance of the slap-dash, cloak-and-dagger methods which may be justified in time of war.[25]

In the midst of the congressional debate, the intelligence service had another change of command. Vandenberg, as expected, moved out in the spring of 1947, on his way to be the first air force chief in October. In his place, Secretary of Defense James Forrestal succeeding in promoting a recently elevated rear admiral, Roscoe Hillenkoetter. An affable man of good intentions, Hillenkoetter had considerable experience as the naval attaché at the U.S. Embassy to the Vichy French government. Unfortunately, in the eyes of many intelligence historians, Hillenkoetter saw his job in part as trying to reduce the tensions that existed between the

Central Intelligence Group and the other services. Even after the National Security Act was adopted in July 1947, he declined to push the agency's frontiers into new territory, and even abandoned Vandenberg's claim to be the "executive agent" of the other national intelligence advisers (now called the National Security Council) to the president. In fairness to Hillenkoetter, he lacked a clear mandate to do otherwise.

The National Security Act did create a Central Intelligence Agency and a director of Central Intelligence. But it did not clearly define just what the CIA was to do, nor did it specifically put the DCI in full control of the agency, let alone give him any authority over the other near dozen government agencies that collected sensitive information of a security nature. To the contrary, the act provided that "the departments and other agencies of the Government shall continue to collect, evaluate, correlate, and disseminate departmental intelligence," but there was no direction as to how the CIA was to coordinate it all. Authority to conduct covert operations was nowhere mentioned. The uncertainty left Hillenkoetter and his aides immobilized over what to do next; all too soon, the CIA leaders became distracted by the ceaseless maneuverings and challenges of the rival intelligence services and by a steadily deteriorating world situation. Not surprisingly, morale sagged badly during the next two years. An unsigned internal memo based on a survey of "top operational staff" reflected the sense of drift:

> The Admiral and staff are the cause of most of the lack of progress and failures on the operational levels. Neither the Admiral nor staff have had any experience in the field nor have they operated the work from a "desk" in Washington. No idea or programs can reach the Admiral except through staff.
>
>   Most operational staff are still loyal to the agency. Most want a clean sweep of "The Kremlin."

The unanimous choice of successor is Allen Dulles. Why Dulles? Because he knows all the tricky problems of the business from personal field and desk experience in addition to *being an able administrator* [emphasis added]. If Dulles is not available, any good administrator who would cooperate with the operational level would do.

Closer cooperation is needed between "The Kremlin" and Operations. The Chief or member of his staff should be available to any desk man who has a legitimate problem to discuss which can only be decided on a higher level.[26]

For the time being, that was out of the question. President Truman was happy enough to give Dulles the Medal of Merit that summer for his OSS exploits. But both Allen and Foster were increasingly involved in the policy planning for Thomas Dewey's third attempt at the Republican presidential nomination, and Truman despised Dewey of all Republicans. The same disdain did not apply to the Dulles brothers by any means, but Truman was reluctant to bring them too quickly and too closely into his inner circle just a year away from his own planned election bid.

One of the problems the president faced, however, was that the advisers he did have were clearly overworked. Thus, in January 1948 Truman acquiesced when Forrestal recruited Allen Dulles to head a special study group to reorganize the CIA. The two other men on the panel were also Wall Street lawyers with intelligence experience, Matthias Correa, a former New York district attorney, and William H. Jackson, who had been General Omar Bradley's chief of intelligence and, later in the war, an aide to General Donovan. It had become clear that the National Security Act of 1947 had not really addressed the intelligence issue, and that the stream of directives coming out of the White

House merely patched over some old problems without dealing with new problems or basic structural flaws. A fresh look at both intelligence theory and practice was required.

The "Dulles-Jackson-Correa Committee," as it came to be known, soon developed into a two-horse race between Dulles and Jackson. Jackson was an imperious southern aristocrat who had left wartime service and taken over the investment banking firm of J. H. Whitney and Co. with the avowed intention of augmenting his family's already considerable wealth. He had won wide respect during the war for his combat intelligence skills, so much so that Bradley had used him as a foil in dealings with Eisenhower's SHAEF headquarters staff. His feuds with General Walter Bedell Smith, Eisenhower's chief of staff at SHAEF, were legendary and bitter. As the war ended, General Donovan posted Jackson to London, where he underwent a lengthy tutorial on British intelligence methods at the hands of none other than Anthony Eden. Jackson became known in American intelligence circles as an expert on British methods and an advocate of the British system, which gave control over the clearly divided intelligence operations to a Joint Intelligence Committee made up of top policymakers. Both Dulles and Jackson had been recruited by General Vandenberg for his advisory circle, and, to the extent that Admiral Hillenkoetter bothered to seek outside advice, they had remained as consultants to the DCI.

Throughout 1948 Dulles became the far more dominant force in shaping the report. He had prepared his earlier proposal to Congress, but he did not actually do the writing of the Dulles-Jackson-Correa report. As we have seen, he had his hands full working on the questions of broad foreign policy and intelligence strategy, if not for the president, then for the Council on Foreign Relations committee on Germany and, lest we forget, for Thomas Dewey. He was, however, determined that the reforms of the agency follow the course he had outlined in April. Correa was not

sure any agency should have the double responsibility of coordinating intelligence estimates and engaging in intelligence operations, open or covert. Jackson wanted the fragile balance of the
British Joint Intelligence Committee system, in which separate
streams of intelligence came together only at a narrow opening at
the top of the analysis funnel. A Forrestal aide, Robert Blum, did
the actual writing of the report, and Jackson wrote the summary,
ever afterwards referring to the paper as the "so-called Dulles
Report." But crediting Dulles for the report was accurate enough,
for its recommendations more accurately reflected his views than
those of the others.

   When the three hundred–page (still classified) report was
presented to the president in January 1949, it caused an immediate uproar. The survey placed blame on the CIA for numerous
failures (there were fifty-seven specific complaints) and bluntly
attributed those failures to "a lack of understanding on the part of
the Director of Central Intelligence."[27] The report was quite an
accurate summation of the problems faced by the government.
Even Hillenkoetter, ever fair and patient, conceded more than
two-thirds of the accusations. The momentum increased when
the National Security Council reacted to the Dulles Report by
asking Secretary of State Dean Acheson and Secretary of Defense
Louis Johnson (Forrestal had committed suicide in March 1949)
to recommend what action the National Security Council should
take; they handed over the responsibility for creating the policy
directive that became known as NSC 50 to General Joseph
McNarney. The general, an army intelligence expert, turned to
none other than Robert Blum. Blum drafted NSC 50 off the recommendations of the Dulles Report, and on July 7, 1949, the
National Security Council accepted the reforms.

   Hillenkoetter, who had borne the criticism with some grace
in the early part of the year, was personally wounded by the
National Security Council action and became immobilized in his

office in "The Kremlin"; it had been clear from the Dulles Report that he had to go, and it was Hillenkoetter's fervent wish all along that he be returned to active sea command.

In the meantime, Thomas Dewey had failed in his third bid for the presidency. The Dulles brothers had staked a lot on the Dewey candidacy and had been active campaigners as well as chief foreign policy advisers for the campaign. The authority and accuracy of Dewey's charges against Truman's foreign policy in the previous three years enraged the president all the more because he suspected (correctly as it turns out) that much of the information was being slipped to the Dulles brothers by insiders in his own administration.

Dewey's upset loss, then, was a tremendous shock to them both. Fritz Molden, who had returned to New York with Joan on a visit, remembers the scene on Election Night in November 1948. "It's the only time I ever saw Papa (that's what I came to call Allen) drunk. We were in a special family box at the Hotel Roosevelt, up in the balcony. And someone said that if Dewey carried Philadelphia he would win, because Philadelphia, for some reason, had always voted for the winning president. And Dewey carried Philadelphia early in the evening, so we all began to celebrate. But around midnight, someone came into the box and said something was going wrong; we were still ahead, but the reports from the Middle West were bad. So we stayed up nearly all night drinking and watching, and it got worse and worse. By dawn we went out into the street with Dewey still ahead by the slimmest of margins. Allen was staggering but trying to cheer up everyone else. But by then they knew it was over and they had lost. It was awful for them. Allen wasn't angry or anything, just down."[28]

Despite Dewey's defeat and the confusion after the submission of the Dulles Report two months later, Dulles may have continued to entertain thoughts that he could become DCI himself.

There was plenty of debate about who should succeed Hillenkoetter, and Dulles's name came up often. Defense Secretary Louis Johnson proposed General McNarney, but Truman's antipathy to Johnson blocked that. Dean Acheson was now secretary of state, but Truman pointedly never asked him for his recommendation. William Donovan threw his hat into the ring from his New York law offices; it was tossed back. Robert Lovett and David Bruce were asked by Truman to consider the job of DCI, but Bruce wanted to keep his job as ambassador to France, and Lovett had joined a Wall Street banking firm. Even J. Edgar Hoover and Dean Rusk (who had combat intelligence experience in Burma and was a rising State Department star) were considered and rejected.

America's secret war against the Soviet Union struggled along separate and often conflicting paths. After its inception in 1947, the CIA installed an Office of Special Operations that was limited to clandestine information gathering. After 1948 Frank Wisner (the OSS operations chief in the Balkans) became head of the Office of Policy Coordination, which was set up at the State Department to undertake covert operations—sabotage, guerrilla action, economic warfare, and other paramilitary actions. The Office of Policy Coordination's covert operations quickly began to chafe the clandestine intelligence teams of the CIA's Office of Special Operations. Wisner did not want to share control of his operation with the CIA, and Hillenkoetter did not try to extend his mandate to the more senior department's activities. As a result, operations were rarely coordinated, and there were recriminations about duplicate agents, botched jobs, and errors from field offices all over the world.

WHATEVER IMPACT THE 1948 Dewey defeat had on Foster Dulles's prospects, for Allen the deep disappointment may also have been something of a physical relief. In the final months of the campaign Allen had been on the road almost as much as the

ALLEN DULLES

candidate himself. He logged more than 26,000 miles in trips around America, either in Dewey's staff entourage of speech writers and policy advisers or off making foreign policy addresses on his own.

In addition to the final work on the report on CIA reforms, Allen had been involved from the start in 1947 in the effort by General George Marshall to put a comprehensive plan of economic reconstruction to work in Western Europe. Marshall had come home from a two-month Foreign Ministers Conference in Moscow, alarmed at Soviet intentions to control Germany and appalled at the conditions he had seen in Western Europe on the return journey. This was just a month after the White House had formulated the Truman Doctrine (March 1947), which committed the United States to economic aid and the military protection of Greece and Turkey. Public reaction to Truman's pledge of involvement in such a remote region of the world had ranged from indifferent to openly hostile. Marshall and his undersecretary, Dean Acheson, knew that a careful campaign of publicity and argument was needed if Congress was to be persuaded to appropriate the $20 billion in aid money most experts believed would have to be invested to do any good. Among the sources of support Marshall and his advisers sought was the Council on Foreign Relations, particularly the Dulles committee on German resuscitation.

Dulles, too, had gone on a tour of Western Europe in the spring of 1947. He returned to New York just five days before Marshall used an invitation to speak to the Harvard University commencement exercises on June 5, 1947, to unveil what would be known as the Marshall Plan. It was central to Marshall's needs that the plan of reconstruction and aid be open to all European nations, whatever their political coloration. There was still an outside chance that some if not all of the governments that had come under Moscow's domination might be coaxed into participating in this free-enterprise experience; Stalin, however, must under no circumstances become alarmed by an apparent American confrontation at this point. So while, as secretary of state, Marshall knew he must sell his plan as an open, peaceful gesture to all of Europe, someone else had to sell the notion in the United States for what it really was: America's economic and political response to the Soviets' effort to take over Europe by stealth and force.

No direct evidence has been found that Dulles took his fact-finding tour of Europe at Marshall's request. But it can scarcely be coincidence that on June 16 both men appeared at the graduation ceremonies at Brown University to accept honorary degrees. Nor is it coincidence that Marshall accepted his award and then excused himself to the audience because he had to return to Washington at once for "an important conference with President Truman." This left the podium and the audience's attention free for the keynote speaker, who was Dulles, and the topic, which was the Marshall Plan.

"Personally, I do not feel that there was ever a time, even in the dark days of 1917 and 1940, when more depended upon what the United States was prepared to do," Dulles warned the audience. He then proceeded with a ringing endorsement of the Marshall Plan, but clearly keyed to its importance as America's chief weapon in the Cold War in Europe. Casting the proposal's net beyond Germany, Dulles reported on his findings in Great Britain, France, Italy, the Netherlands, and other Western European countries. "It is by restoring the economic life of a country, and by this alone, that we can meet the threat of dictatorship from a fascist Right or a communist Left." He spoke of a "common cause of democracy and peace." And he argued that, with the plan, "We should thus confront communism, not with arms or atomic bombs, but with a restored economic life for the men and women of Western Europe.... There is little use in feeding people indefinitely just to keep them barely alive. The improvement of the conditions of the laboring man and the farmer will, in the long run, be far more effective as a block to the advance of militant communism than arms and munitions. Conversely, communism will not need military forces to advance into Western Europe if economic chaos and starvation should rule the day there."[29]

Michael Wala, the German historian who has studied the origins of the Marshall Plan probably more closely than anyone else, believes, "This was no coincidence. Marshall could not confront Russia at that time. But Dulles could say the things that needed saying and as a private citizen; Marshall could not be held responsible."[30]

A few weeks later, Dulles accepted the job of consultant on the plan to the House select committee that had been formed to study the proposal; Christian Herter, his old Versailles chum, was now a Massachusetts congressman and vice chairman of the panel. In October, Dulles worked with Henry Stimson, the former war secretary, and with other Council on Foreign Relations members, including Alger Hiss, to organize a citizens' lobby, the Committee for the Marshall Plan. It was under the committee's auspices that Dulles set to work on his lengthy pamphlet in behalf of the proposal. "The Marshall Plan is not merely a philanthropic program. It is an attempt, in one vitally important area of the world, to protect free institutions, because we feel that in the world today we cannot live safely if these institutions disappear elsewhere.... We do not propose, if we can help it, to permit a great power, with a system incompatible with ours, to overrun Europe or Asia." The pamphlet lay in dusty manuscript form among his papers in Princeton and in the Marshall Library in Lexington, Virginia, until Wala brought it to light in the early 1990s.[31]

Even though Dulles was in the midst of the public campaign to elect Dewey, he circulated the manuscript, and, in the ensuing six months until the plan was enacted by Congress, he made more than eight major addresses to generate support for the controversial program among the very business and political groups that were opposed to the Truman administration on general principles. The quick adoption of the plan in April 1948 was an unalloyed triumph for both Dulles and the Council on Foreign Relations. It was also a challenge.

As has been noted countless times elsewhere, the Marshall Plan was not a "plan but an idea." Now the task was to implement the congressional mandate, and for that considerable organization lay ahead. While Congress had approved an administrative body (the Economic Cooperative Administration), the men put in charge of the operation quickly turned to the Council on Foreign Relations to play a major role in providing guidance on what kind of aid should be sent and where it should go. In his role as Council on Foreign Relations president, Dulles quickly ordered the creation of a new study group on "Aid to Europe" to advise the new Economic Cooperative Administration. That panel had to be led by someone of impressive credentials and scrupulous apolitical reputation. Which certainly ruled out either of the Dulleses; indeed, no one closely associated with the council leadership could really take on the task. At this point, the Dulles luck once again asserted itself.

Dwight Eisenhower had left the army to become president of Columbia University and was a bored and unhappy man. A recruiting committee made up of Dulles; John W. Davis, the former Council on Foreign Relations president and Democratic presidential nominee; and Henry Wriston, president of Brown University, went to Eisenhower's offices at Columbia on November 3. After a cautious appraisal, Eisenhower agreed to serve as chairman of the group and start work in January 1949. Although he had no academic training in the issues central to the plan, Eisenhower had a good mind and was willing to work hard. He saw the chance for a first-class education in the interdependence of military, economic, and political matters in foreign affairs, and he took it. Until he moved to Paris in January 1951 to become the first commander of NATO forces in Europe, he missed only two of the aid committee's meetings.

Even as the education of Eisenhower was proceeding, and as world crises were springing up on almost a daily basis, the question of who would lead the CIA suddenly came to a head. One morning in May 1950, Sidney Souers asked President Truman with studied casualness whether he had thought any more about a possible successor for Admiral Hillenkoetter. Truman replied, "How would Bedell Smith do?"

General Walter Bedell Smith had been Eisenhower's chief of staff during the war and was believed by some to have been the organizational genius behind the Overlord invasion plan for Europe. He was just ending a tour as U.S. ambassador to Moscow, where Truman had been impressed by his quick grasp of Russian intentions and thinking. Like Truman, he was a largely self-educated man who possessed a steel-trap mind and legendary toughness; one had to be tough to start out as a drill sergeant in the Indiana National Guard and achieve the rank of general ahead of many West Pointers of his age. The drawback was that Smith was in ill health and facing serious surgery from a stomach ulcer. He begged off until he saw how his recovery progressed; he frankly wanted to retire and make some money in private industry.

THE KOREAN WAR intervened. On June 25, 1950, North Korea invaded South Korea, and Truman committed U.S. air, ground, and naval forces five days later. Hillenkoetter, fearing he would be left out of the war, asked immediately to be reassigned to sea duty. By August it was clear that General Smith would recover, and Truman baldly ordered him to take over as DCI. This was not just a case of the commander in chief being peremptory; Truman, Smith, and everyone else firmly believed that World War III had just begun.

While he was preparing to take over at "The Kremlin" in October, Smith began to cast about for the important key staff aides. He told Souers after his appointment, "I know nothing about this business. I shall need a deputy who does." It was not quite the truth. As a combat planner, Smith had used Donovan's OSS material during the war and had continued a running conversation with the old spymaster and other intelligence experts, including Dulles, on the need for better collection and handling of intelligence. But he was not a spy and had no intention of becoming one.

Smith went to New York to recruit William Jackson, who was as surprised as anyone when the man he had feuded with five years earlier urged on him the job of deputy director. Smith, who feigned not to know much about the Dulles Report, nevertheless dangled the task before Jackson of sole responsibility for putting those reorganization recommendations into effect. Smith would be the outside man, he said, and Jackson would be the inside man with the mandate to structure the agency as he saw fit. Jackson was charmed and accepted.

Then Smith called on Dulles. "You wrote the damned thing," he said, referring to the Dulles Report. "You've got to come to Washington to help me put it to work." Dulles demurred; he did not fancy working for Jackson. But that was not the job Smith had in mind for him. The divisions inside the CIA over the conflict between operational covert actions and intelligence collection threatened the agency. For his own reasons, Smith did not want simply to merge the two main clandestine offices into one, but he proposed that Dulles come for six weeks as a consultant to advise the new director on how best to make the ill-fitting clandestine espionage pieces work more efficiently.

Dulles arrived in Washington on November 16, 1950, as an unpaid consultant. By December 1 he had become deputy director for operations (later changed to deputy director for plans). On

December 22 he presented to Smith a contract that stated he would work full-time as deputy director without pay (except for a per diem and travel expenses back to New York) from January 1, 1951, until July 1. At that time he and Smith would review the bidding.

Allen Dulles was back in the intelligence business running operations.

CHAPTER TWELVE

1950–1953

"Dulles! Dammit, Dulles, get in here!"
—General Walter Bedell Smith

GENERAL WALTER BEDELL SMITH understood that Allen Dulles knew how to run covert operations, and not just because of the triumphs of the Bern and Wiesbaden operations of the OSS.[1] Plenty of evidence has since surfaced that Allen Dulles did not stop his involvement in clandestine intelligence collection when he left the OSS. In fact, he was engaged in a series of secret efforts to advance American intelligence capabilities throughout Europe and the Middle East right up to the time he joined the CIA as a consultant to Smith in October 1950. Thus, the real reason General Smith brought Dulles in from the cold was so Dulles could help to create order out of what had become from 1945 to 1950 a freelance and uncoordinated jumble of forces to keep America in the Cold War spy game.

It was at least partly because of the confused melee going on in Washington that Dulles kept active in propping up old networks and helping establish new ones all over the Cold War battle line in Europe and the Mediterranean. In the five years between his retirement from the OSS until he came on board as an unpaid consultant at the CIA, Dulles crossed the boundary between overt and covert activities abroad a bewildering number of times. How much of this activity was officially sanctioned may not be known for some time. It is a matter of official record that he frequently visited Washington for senior staff level consultations "on foreign affairs" with everyone from Dean Acheson (then undersecretary of state), to George Kennan at the National War College, to Christian Herter (who had been elected to Congress) and other hawks on Capitol Hill. Documentation from that period is scarce; some sadly has been lost or disappeared out of neglect. Some historians of the CIA maintain that many files of the army's Strategic Services Unit postwar stewardship of intelligence assets remain inaccessible because they have been misplaced inside the Pentagon's archives.

Yet clearly, the United States did not stop spying or undertaking covert operations just because the war against Germany was over. There was no intelligence hiatus between World War II and the Cold War. What went on was clumsy and unfocused. Nevertheless, intelligence collection and covert operations were part of America's first tentative counterstrokes against the Soviet testing of Western resolve. Most of the techniques were simply shifted over from the war just ended. At the same time the fight within the U.S. government over intelligence control revived and grew in fury. Lawrence Houston, the senior legal counsel from the days of the Strategic Services Unit until the third decade of the CIA's existence, recalls the period between October 1945 and January 1946 "as some of the toughest infighting and maneuvering that I have ever seen before or since."[2]

The most open and sanctioned of the intelligence collection and operational work was performed by the army's Military Intelligence Division and its Counter Intelligence Corps. The army continued "ops"—operations—throughout Western Europe well past 1949, the year it turned over to the CIA the running of its Gehlen Organization, the cadre of former *Wehrmacht* spies in

Germany and Eastern Europe. As late as 1951, the Military Intelligence Division was running "ops" in Germany and was rewarded with intense criticism twenty years later when it was learned that it used unrepentant Nazis such as Klaus Barbie in some of its campaigns. As a generalization, the army's efforts were moderately successful, but the price of its disasters was judged too high, and there were too many controversial liaisons with operators who had been on the enemy side during the war.

Then there was the growing intramural conflict between intelligence gatherers and covert operators that went on even after Frank Wisner's Office of Policy Coordination was formally put under the command of the DCI in 1948. It probably will never be known for sure just how many spies and analysts Colonel William Quinn was able to keep functioning and to hand over to General Vandenberg and his Central Intelligence Group in 1946. But it was certainly more than a staff of 150, which is the number cited most often. A closer look at the records shows that the R&A part of the OSS, which was sent over to the State Department between 1945 and 1947, never had fewer than five hundred people on its roster. The basic spy and counterintelligence assets kept by the Strategic Services Unit under the War Department budgets had funds for nearly three thousand slots, although many of those were not filled until after the CIA was established in 1947.[3]

Another friction point between the intelligence gatherers of the Office of Special Operations at the CIA and the new "ops" people who came aboard Frank Wisner's Office of Policy Coordination in 1948 was that many of the collectors had never left government service when the war ended. The Office of Special Operations considered itself the senior service and had a cool view of the action service; thus, the schism between "eggheads" and "cowboys" began. The rivalry over competing jurisdictions reached its most ludicrous point in 1950–1951, when the Office of

Policy Coordination undertook to send a specially trained task force of Chinese Nationalist troops into the mainland through Burma. The objective was to create a "second front" that would distract Peking's commitment to the Korean War. Office of Special Operations intelligence officers in Burma could not convince their rivals that the Chinese force was riddled with Red Army spies who were betraying the guerrilla band's operations; their attempts to remove some of the suspects by force provoked such a violent confrontation between the two American teams that they were near to pistol point before Washington intervened.

Such active espionage did not immediately improve the quality of understanding among the intelligence analysts who had to educate the president and other policymakers. Within the government there were constraints amid the confusion. Harry Rositzke, last seen with Allen Dulles in Wiesbaden and Berlin, was given the unenviable task of starting the first intelligence desk devoted to the Soviet Union at the Strategic Services Unit. "There was nothing there, just me," Rositzke recalls. "No card indexes, no files, nothing. I went out to Sidney Kramer's bookstore and bought what I could find, a copy of *Das Kapital,* and other books on Russia and Soviet politics, and on communism. And I tried to create a syllabus on what communism and the Soviets were all about for our case officers. That was the first manual of theory we had on Russia, but when I went to circulate it among our desk officers, the security office made me stamp it 'Classified,' and restrict its use. Their excuse was that the document might leak out and we would be accused of conducting communist indoctrination inside the Strategic Services Unit. That's the level we were working on in those early days."[4] Undaunted, Rositzke went on to create for the CIA a greater repository of fact and insight into Soviet matters than existed even inside Russia.

But the Strategic Services Unit did keep much of its field operations going, and many of its early station chiefs were the foundation stones of the CIA that followed. Richard Helms returned from a brief civilian respite to plant networks throughout all four German zones occupied by the Allies; Alfred Ulmer in Vienna successfully blocked trainloads of machinery and raw materials being pirated by the Soviets out of Austria on to Russia; James Angleton was in Rome checkmating a communist takeover; Frank Wisner and Albert Seitz roamed through Eastern Europe and the Balkans in an effort to keep the old spy and counterinsurgency chains going; and James Kellis covered the turmoil in China. Other operations in the Middle East and Asia never stopped in this inter-regnum period; a Vietnamese rebel leader named Ho Chi Minh provided American intelligence with news of what was going on within Mao Tse-tung's revolution in China as well as his own strug-gle against French colonial rule.

Just on the other side of the official-private boundary line was William Donovan, who alternated between a public cam-paign in the press to create a unified government spy service and secret efforts to build a clandestine operational service that would be privately funded and run by civilian veterans of the old OSS. Donovan, in effect, tried to create his own private intelligence ser-vice. Almost as soon as the OSS was officially closed in October 1945, Donovan moved to create the Veterans of Strategic Service, nominally an alumni group to lobby in behalf of a strong intelli-gence service for the government. By 1948 the Veterans of Strategic Service had 1,300 active members. Publicly, there was an all-out media campaign, including magazine articles by members (Dulles wrote in such diverse outlets as *Foreign Affairs*, the *New York Times Magazine*, and *Collier's*) that raised the specter of the subversive Soviet menace. Newspapers confirmed the fear with headlines about stolen atomic bomb secrets and Russian spy rings deep inside American institutions. Hollywood put out a series of spy thriller films based on OSS exploits; even comic books about secret agent heroes were commissioned.

More significantly, Donovan and the Veterans of Strategic Services worked tirelessly behind the scenes as well to keep old overseas networks alive and functioning during a time of increasing peril. The organization was considered a "ready reserve" that could use its members' covers as business executives and academics to go anywhere and do almost anything. Donovan, even out of power, was successful in enlisting the help of corporate America for funds and logistical support for the various campaigns he undertook, and plenty of doors were still open to him in Washington, despite President Truman's dislike of the man. William Stephenson, the representative of Britain's MI6 in New York who had helped build the original Coordinator of Information (COI) organization for Donovan, quietly took his own network of agents and some OSS operatives into private retirement and kept them busy posing as a trading company in South America.

With a combination of hard-dollar contributions and soft-dollar services, major American corporations were enthusiastic supporters of both government and private cloak-and-dagger campaigns. Correspondents for major newspapers, magazines, and broadcast networks (most notably Time-Life, NBC, and CBS) doubled as collectors while the media outlets themselves shaped programming to propaganda needs. International communications firms such as ITT, RCA, and Western Union regularly monitored private telephone calls and telegraph messages abroad. Banks such as Citibank and Chase Manhattan aided in shifting huge sums of clandestine funds about the globe, while the Grace shipping lines and airlines such as Pan American and TWA provided transport on demand to faraway places. Hollywood moguls such as Spyros Skouras were especially important sponsors of both government and Donovan projects. The movie industry united to fight communism through its screenplays and by smothering the effort for control by leftist unions.

Early on, the Cold War had started to get dirty. In June 1946 Donovan wrote to Dulles to express concern that many of the agents left in place by the OSS in Berlin were beginning to disappear. A week later, Dulles replied that he, too, was aware that something was happening. "Certainly the possibility you suggest always existed and I understand that steps are being taken to extract 'Wood' of Boston fame and bring him over here for a cooling-off period. I understand he is still about the most useful man we have in Berlin but certain events have caused our people over there to feel he is no longer safe."[5] Dulles did succeed in getting Fritz Kolbe and Hans Gisevius placed in safety in the United States, despite State Department visa office objections that the two had been in the German government. Unfortunately, neither man prospered in the United States (Kolbe's business partner swindled him), and both finally returned to Germany to live out rather dismal lives, reviled as traitors to the nation they had tried to save.

Despite all the strife in and out of the agency, the CIA had managed a number of spectacular clandestine coups and covert triumphs from its earliest inception. The best known was the help provided in 1948 to the centrist Christian Democrats in Italy to win an election campaign that April, the first general election since the war and part of a series of tests of the parliamentary democracies in other Western European countries. It bears remembering that the CIA in those days was not supposed to go near covert operations. General counsel Lawrence Houston, who drafted the actual charter language, recalled that he personally believed the CIA should stick to intelligence collection and analysis and leave "ops" to the military. But as he recalled later, "I had a notion that something more might be required of [the agency]." So he drafted the now famous Paragraph Five of the National Security Act, which required the CIA "to perform such *other functions and duties related to intelligence* affecting the national security as the National Security Council may from time to time direct [emphasis added]."[6] Through that narrow window covert action slipped into the CIA.

The success of the American effort to defeat the Italian Communist Party in the April 1948 election campaign gave those who wanted the CIA to have a more aggressive covert capability the dramatic victory they needed. At a cost of only about $10 million in subsidies to the Christian Democrats and other anti-left parties (and helped by a massive letter-writing campaign organized within the Italian-American community to relatives in Italy), the victory was a narrow but convincing one. And the break between Tito and Stalin at about the same time handed Moscow its first clear setbacks of the Cold War struggle. Significantly, the CIA still did not have a staff or administrative mechanism for repeating even such a modest venture. The Italian operation had basically been transferring funds to James Angleton, who had parceled it out judiciously among various politicians who had to bribe a few newspapers and get the voters motivated enough to go to the polls. The task was handled within the agency's Office of Special Operations; these intelligence collectors did not at all like being involved in "dirty tricks." They were even more unhappy when the "cowboys" of the Office of Policy Coordination showed up on the horizon.

It is clear from the outset that few of the top policy strategists of the Truman administration had any idea of the dimensions of involvement in covert meddling and violence that the CIA would be directed to undertake in subsequent decades. One of the strongest advocates of covert operations at the beginning was the distinguished diplomat George Kennan, whose advocacy of a "containment" strategy against Soviet aggression would form the intellectual underpinning of American actions for the next forty years. But even Kennan has conceded that what followed was not what

was intended. Kennan gave this description of the prevailing atti-
tude at the State Department in 1948–1949 to the Senate Select
Committee to Study Governmental Operations with Respect to
Intelligence Activities, chaired by Senator Frank Church, in 1975:

> We were alarmed at the inroads of the Russian influ-
> ence in Western Europe beyond the point where the
> Russian troops had reached. And we were alarmed
> particularly over the situation in France and Italy. We
> felt that the Communists were using the very extensive
> funds that they then had in hand to gain control of key
> elements of life in France and Italy, particularly the
> publishing companies, the press, the labor unions, stu-
> dent organizations, women's organizations, and all
> sorts of organizations of that sort, to gain control of
> them and use them as front organizations....
>
> That is just one example that I recall of why we
> thought that we ought to have some facility for covert
> operations....
>
> It ended up with the establishment within CIA of
> a branch, an office for activities of this nature, and one
> which employed a great many people. It did not work
> out at all the way I had conceived it or others of my
> associates in the Department of State. We had thought
> that this would be a facility which could be used when
> and if an occasion arose when it might be needed.
> There might be years when we wouldn't have to do
> anything like this. But if the occasion arose we wanted
> somebody in the Government who would have the
> funds, the experience, the expertise to do these things
> and to do them in a proper way.[7]

Whatever the early intentions of Kennan and his State
Department planners were, others had a vastly different view of
how often, how aggressive, and how confrontational covert operations were to be. Allen Dulles, for one, knew that it would be the
rare president who, once handed the weapon of covert operations,
would put it down again easily. Nor could Kennan have been
unaware that in September 1948 there were secret talks among the
U.S. and Western European military planners who were to set up
the North Atlantic Treaty Organization (NATO). At one such
meeting of the "NATO Treaty Military Committee," a British
Foreign Office internal summary lists the agreed-upon "War
Objectives of the Allies":

To counter the threat to Allied security and well being
posed by the USSR, our general objectives with respect
to Russia, in time of *peace or war* [emphasis added]
should be:
(a) to reduce the power and influence of the USSR
to limits which no longer constitute a threat to peace....
(b) to bring about a basic change in the conduct of
international relations by the government in power in
Russia to conform with the... United Nations Charter.
(c) ...to destroy Russia's capacity to make war....
(d) ...destroy the rule of the Communist Party...
[and] rid Russia of the Bolshevik Regime....[8]

THE ARRIVAL OF ALLEN DULLES at "The Kremlin" in the
autumn of 1950 coincided with a dramatic episode of a long-
running scandal that was an intense personal embarrassment to
the Dulles brothers, involving Alger Hiss and the eccentric Noel
Field. Hiss had been a prominent and well-respected State Department attorney. During the war, Hiss had been mentioned as a

possible general counsel for the OSS. He had been a trusted aide of President Franklin Roosevelt at the Yalta Conference with Churchill and Stalin that plotted postwar boundaries. He had become something of a protégé of Foster Dulles after he had assisted Foster at the 1945 San Francisco Conference that established the United Nations. Hiss was now forty-two years old and as much a part of the State Department establishment as anyone; he was reported to be in line to be the first secretary general of the new UN, a tremendously sensitive position. There were recurrent rumors that he had dabbled with communism when he was young, but the whispers were dismissed by his superiors as probably untrue, or, at most, a youthful indiscretion.

In 1946 Foster Dulles was asked to fill in as temporary chairman for the prestigious Carnegie Endowment for Peace, a foundation devoted to furthering the old steel magnate's commitment to the Hague peace process earlier in the century. The Washington institution needed a new president, and men such as Adlai Stevenson and William Fulbright were mentioned. After several candidates turned down the job, Foster Dulles put forth Hiss as "the next most available person." In December 1946 Alger Hiss left the State Department with high praise and became president of the Endowment. Hiss had close ties to Allen Dulles and the Council on Foreign Relations as well. He had been a longtime member of the Council on Foreign Relations and in 1947 was asked by Allen to join a group that included Dean Acheson, Herbert Lehman (the former New York governor and the head of the UN's Relief and Rehabilitation Administration), and others to help coordinate the council's public relations campaign in behalf of the Marshall Plan. For the next two years, both brothers fended off a series of unproved accusations that Hiss had maintained his communist contacts while in government and had even been a Soviet agent.

In February 1948 Hiss was called before a federal grand jury in New York City that was probing Soviet subversion in government. Foster Dulles became aware that the FBI had begun an active probe of Hiss. In August, Whittaker Chambers made his now famous accusations to the House Un-American Activities Committee (HUAC) that Hiss had been an active intelligence operative of the Soviets; a few days later, Hiss appeared before the same HUAC panel and, before a riveted public gaze, began to disintegrate in confusion and contradiction. On August 11 Richard Nixon, the young California congressman who had been an active pursuer of the Hiss accusations, asked Foster and Allen Dulles if he could come to New York to seek their advice. The brothers told him to come to the Dewey campaign headquarters in the Roosevelt Hotel, and Nixon and another congressman, Charles Kersten, caught a late afternoon train that same day. Nixon was anxious to turn the heat up under Hiss, but he recognized the risk to the Dewey campaign if any of the political fallout landed on Foster, the candidate's chief foreign policy architect. Nixon had never met Foster and confessed later to being nervously deferential. He was relieved to see Allen there as well; they had become acquainted the year before when both men went on the inspection of European conditions set up by Christian Herter's congressional panel on the Marshall Plan.

Hiss had based his defense against the Chambers accusations on the impossibility of the two men ever having met at the times stated, let alone that they ever knew each other and plotted together. Nixon brought for the brothers' inspection some still-secret transcripts in which Chambers convincingly showed that Hiss was lying, that they had met and did know each other. Nixon later recalled:

I remember he [Foster] paced the floor after reading [the testimony] and was convinced—and the issue at

that point was whether or not Hiss knew Chambers—
he said there was no question about Hiss knowing
Chambers. It was very difficult for Foster Dulles to
believe that Hiss had misled him, because he had been
one of those who had recommended him for the
Carnegie foundation job.

But at the end of the conversation, what impressed
me about it was that when I came to the key point, as to
whether the investigation should be pressed, he had no
hesitancy at all. He said, "There's no question but that, in
view of this testimony, you must press the investigation."
And he said this, knowing that it would be embarrassing
to him. This was quite impressive to me, because I knew
Foster was probably going to be Secretary of State, and I
knew that this would mean that some of the critics of
Dewey, particularly on Foster's internationalism, in the
Republican Party would bang him hard when it became
known that he had been misled by Hiss.[9]

One does not betray a Dulles with impunity. Moving quickly,
Foster summoned Hiss to New York and flatly told him he wanted
his immediate resignation from the Carnegie Endowment. Hiss
refused, so Foster moved to isolate him from any command
responsibilities, at least until the HUAC hearings were concluded.
Later, Dulles would provide damaging testimony of his own on
how Hiss had misled him; Hiss was later convicted of perjury and
sent to prison.

Whatever embarrassment Foster Dulles might have experienced from the Hiss affair was dwarfed by Dewey's shocking
defeat at the hands of Harry Truman three months later. As far as
Foster was concerned, the Hiss matter became part of that greater
disaster. Nor was the Hiss case an isolated affair for Allen Dulles
either. As the HUAC probe into communist subversion bored

onward into 1949, other names were brought into focus, including that of Noel Field. Much of the case against Hiss had been from witnesses such as Chambers who themselves were confessed former Soviet agents. In other testimony, they alleged that there had in fact been two separate cells of Moscow operatives inside the State Department in the 1930s, the one that Hiss had belonged to and another one that controlled Noel Field.

By the late spring of 1949, Field had lost his refugee relief job in Europe and was broke. One day he took an Air France plane from Paris to Prague and disappeared. His wife Herta followed him to Czechoslovakia, and she, too, dropped from sight. Shortly afterward, his brother Hermann Field vanished in Poland. By this time Erica Glaser had dropped out of active Communist Party membership. She had been suspect because of her OSS ties and because of her disquiet over the Russian domination of what was supposed to be a German political reformation. She also had married an American, Robert Wallach, who had been in the Counter Intelligence Corps, and they lived in Paris. She had just given birth to their second child when concern about the Fields' disappearance began. Out of loyalty, Erica went to Berlin and forced herself into a Communist Party office in the Russian zone. She confronted old comrades and demanded to know what had happened to her friends and saviors. She was promptly arrested. After extensive torture and interrogation she was tried in an East German court for espionage for the CIA. She was sentenced to death and ultimately endured seven years of imprisonment, including four years at hard labor in a Siberian gulag, before she was freed in the political thaw that greeted Stalin's death.

What had happened was that Field and his wife and brother had been rounded up by Stalinist security services in Poland and Czechoslovakia and accused of having recruited anticommunist networks there, first for the OSS and later for the new CIA. Instead of being feted as heroes of the revolution, Field and his wife underwent weeks of the most rigorous torture, which inevitably ended in their both becoming pliant witnesses for a series of sweeping purges and show trials that replaced Eastern Europe's old-line nationalist communists of the war years with a new cadre of faceless, Moscow-trained thugs. Month after month, Noel Field was taken from country to country where he openly confessed that he had been "head of the U.S. Secret Service" under his controller, Allen Dulles, the famous OSS pro-Nazi spymaster. His confessions led to the imprisonment or execution of some of the most prominent names in the wartime communist pantheon: Lazlo Rajk and Tibor Szoenyi in Hungary; Wladislav Gomulka in Poland; Trailscho Kostoff in Bulgaria; and Leo Bauer (who *had* helped the OSS in Bern) in East Germany—all were brought down in the turmoil. But it was in the notorious Slansky Trials in Czechoslovakia that Field did his greatest damage. His carefully orchestrated denunciations in 1950, and for several years thereafter, led to the ouster of nearly 170,000 members of the Czech Communist Party (one-tenth of its membership). Ironically, Rudolf Slansky, who led the purge, was himself arrested a year later in one of the other waves of accusations.

Erica Glaser Wallach, who died in 1994, was among a small but adamant group of survivors of that period who remained convinced that Noel Field had been deliberately set up by Allen Dulles, who spooked him into making a break for Prague and then had him denounced through CIA channels to his communist captors. Dulles, she believed, counted on Field's ability to cling to his bizarre vision of a higher Marxist duty and willingly do what his tormentors wanted him to do, to denounce his old colleagues in the movement for imagined sins. Field was arrested and accused, she said, by a Polish security official named Jozef Swiatlo, whom the Americans had co-opted a year before. Swiatlo defected to the United States in

1954 and lived in obscurity for another fifteen years without ever speaking publicly about the Field case. But Wallach asserted:

I believe it is so because I was told it was so after I got to the United States. Also, it makes sense. You in America only remember your McCarthy Era and the political purges over here in the 1950s. You aren't aware that the communist governments in the east of Europe went through the exact same thing at the same time, only more so; people were shot, not just denounced. In that sense it was an enormous victory for Allen Dulles. The Slansky Trials and the other show trials of that time in the Eastern Bloc devastated those governments for years afterward. Nobody was able to do anything over there; they were paralyzed by fear and by the arrests and disappearances. So there was no economic reform, no progress, and they never recovered from those purges, not ever.

Would Allen Dulles do such a thing? Of course. It was his job. And it was easy enough to do. They [the CIA] had contacts everywhere in those governments. They recruited this man Swiatlo [the Polish security officer] in 1948, and it was he who had Field arrested and directed the interrogation. Evidence is easy to come by. And remember, many of those early party leaders had connections with the OSS during the war, it was a natural thing. But what made it all work was having Noel Field there, still loyal to communism and willing to denounce anybody for anything.

Allen Dulles's motives are easy to imagine. When they could get their hands on a high official of the Polish secret service, this Swiatlo, of course you grabbed him.

Anything that destabilized the situation in Eastern
Europe was good for U.S. interests. Stalin was paranoid
enough. The crackdown there was real enough. By
fanning the flames, you could turn people against communism. It makes sense. If you can topple the real communists then you are making progress. And then we have
this fool Noel Field, a romantic, he had been everywhere,
he was full of these enthusiasms, he went back and forth
into these countries freely. I don't think Allen Dulles
hated Noel Field, not at all. But the opportunity was too
good to miss. And I blundered into the middle of it.

So Field was a romantic, and Allen Dulles was a
romantic too. Allen Dulles had a certain arrogance in
which he believed that he could work with the Devil,
anybody's Devil, and still be Allen Dulles. He could
work with Noel Field and betray him. He could work
with the Nazi Canaris or with the communists. He really
did think himself untouchable by these experiences,
and, of course, you cannot help but be touched, be
affected no matter how noble your cause is.[10]

The Dulles-Field story does not end there. Erica Glaser
Wallach was freed under an amnesty declared by Soviet Premier
Nikita S. Khrushchev in 1955, but she was unable to join her husband and two daughters in the United States because of State
Department visa office alarm over her previous Communist Party
membership. It took intervention by Dulles to get her reunited with
her family in America in 1957. The Field family had already been
released from captivity in 1954. Brother Hermann returned to
America, but Noel and Herta settled in Budapest, where they
remained unrepentant apologists for the regime that had tortured
them. Field had written while in a Czech prison, "My accusers

essentially have the same convictions that I do, they hate the same things and the same people I hate—the conscious enemies of socialism, the fascists, the renegades, the traitors. Given their belief in my guilt, I cannot blame them. I cannot but approve their detestation. That is the real horror of it all."[11] Historian Arthur Schlesinger, Jr., who had checkmated Field's bid to win OSS funds for a German communist-front group during the war, later had the best observation: "Field's simple-mindedness was indestructible."[12]

But was Allen Dulles actually responsible for Noel Field's betrayal? There have been recent attempts to turn Dulles into a super-superspy, the *real* director of the CIA during this period, who used Admiral Hillenkoetter as a "cutout" and kept his cover of the mild-mannered international lawyer. But lacking any firm proof, one is forced to look both at what is possible and what is probable in the Field case. It is more probable that Noel Field went to Prague to explore the possibility of a later defection, and also that his wife, brother, and friend followed after him in all innocence to try to find him and were rolled up in turn. And it is possible that once they found out about the arrests, CIA officials saw an opportunity to sow discord, and, with Allen Dulles's active consent and advice, helped, as Erica Wallach said, to fan a blaze fueled by uncontrolled paranoia and cold-blooded Stalinist terror. It is certain enough that Allen Dulles was delighted at the chaos that resulted and shed not a tear for the harsh treatment meted out to the Fields. He coldly turned away all efforts by Elsie Field, a sister, and other family members to help rescue Noel and Herta.[13]

In a network radio interview done during the time of the Rajk and Szoenyi trials in Hungary in the autumn of 1950, Dulles rejoiced in what he described as "a conflict between Moscow and the local communists." Asked about the fiery denunciations of him personally and about the allegations that he headed up active operations to destabilize Eastern Europe, Dulles mildly replied that he assumed it all stemmed from his recent work to establish another private sector anticommunist organization, the Committee for a Free Europe. He explained to the audience, "Communism has driven out of the Iron Curtain countries many democratic leaders… eminent and tried liberals, who have sought here the kind of asylum for which this country has always been famous. They are trying to keep alive the ideals of freedom and we [the committee] are trying to help them." Asked if the work might "cause something to happen over there," Dulles was quite emphatic. "Yes, with Tito and now Rajk, there is a spirit of revolt in every one of these countries and we hope that this spirit may bring about a liberation from Moscow control by means of internal uprising."[14]

The Committee for a Free Europe had been organized by DeWitt C. Poole and set up under the auspices of Dulles and the Council on Foreign Relations in 1949 at the request of George Kennan. It drew no less a personage to be its president than Joseph Grew, the former U.S. ambassador to Japan before the war and an old colleague in Dulles's at the State Department and the council. The makeup of the group's board provides an interesting insight into the unanimity of purpose among a fairly diverse group of high-level American opinion-makers and into Dulles's influence. Fred Dolbeare, the old spy comrade from World War I, was brought out of retirement to be the group's secretary; Frank Altschul, a prominent Council on Foreign Relations member, was its treasurer; and DeWitt Poole was its executive director. Board members were Adolph Berle of the State Department; James Farley, a Democratic Party leader; Dwight Eisenhower; DeWitt Wallace, the *Reader's Digest* founder; and film studio executives Spyros Skouras and Darryl F. Zanuck. The nominal objective of the Committee for a Free Europe was to generate public support for the Truman administration's policy of aggressive containment (as defined by Kennan) of Soviet attempts to subvert democratic nations around the globe.

Its real purpose was to help organize the floods of Russian and Eastern European refugees who had fled from the Soviets into a resource for both open and covert opposition. Poole had been head of the OSS branch on foreign nationalities and had pursued the refugee problem within the study groups of the Council on Foreign Relations. In a few months, General Lucius D. Clay came home from his tour as American commander of the occupation zone in Germany and became president of the related action group, the Crusade for Freedom.

Both groups served the purposes of Frank Wisner, the head of the Office of Policy Coordination, the covert action service of the CIA. Wisner was desperate to organize the various exile groups into a cohesive force, but he had no official place to put them for "quarters and rations," nor to give them a specific task to undertake at once. The Committee for a Free Europe in 1950 started Radio Free Europe, which was based just outside of Munich and began to collect information and broadcast in local languages to all the captive nations of Eastern Europe; much of the financial support and staff came from Wisner and the Office of Policy Coordination. Well into the late 1950s personnel of Radio Free Europe and its related network, Radio Liberty, could buy fuel and get maintenance for their automobiles from U.S. Army facilities throughout Europe, and they had free access to the Post Exchange and army postal facilities as well.[15]

An often overlooked part of Dulles's intelligence record occurred in the spring of 1949, when he went to Iran for six weeks as the legal adviser to a consortium of leading U.S. corporations that had agreed to help the shah organize the first attempt at economic development since the war, a private sector Marshall Plan. He took considerable time to do his own firsthand reporting on intelligence matters in the area. That part of the world had long been the intelligence province of the British government, but both London and Washington had reluctantly come to the conclusion that the United States was a major player with interests in every arena. The slow transfer of the power and tasks of the British Empire into American hands had already begun.

BY THE TIME "BEEDLE" SMITH came on board at the CIA in October 1950, the task facing him was not to create an intelligence service but to get control of a mishmash of disorganized efforts that were ill-suited either to guide tactics in time of war or to design longer-term strategy to cope with the confusing world that lay ahead. Smith faced four immediate crises when, on the morning of Saturday, October 7, 1950, he formally relieved Admiral Hillenkoetter and sat down at the same desk in "The Kremlin" that had been occupied by his predecessors going back to William Donovan. First and foremost, the general had to make it absolutely clear in the minds of everyone else in the far-flung intelligence establishment that he, and no one else, was the *director* of Central Intelligence. Smith had to establish tight control over the wide number of military and civilian shops that provided the raw material.

His chance came at the close of business the next Tuesday, October 12. Admiral Leahy, the White House military adviser, telephoned General Smith to say the president wanted six detailed intelligence estimates to take with him to his historic confrontation with General Douglas MacArthur on Wake Island. Truman was to leave in less than twenty hours. He wanted to put a damper on MacArthur's increasingly vocal disagreements with the administration, but he wanted to argue from the latest intelligence on the points he demanded from General Smith. Over the previous three years the National Security Council had handed over day-to-day relations between the CIA and the other intelligence arms to the Intelligence Advisory Committee, which was made up of five of the intelligence chiefs at State, army, navy, air

force, and Joint Chiefs of Staff. The Intelligence Advisory Committee had evolved into a board of directors of the CIA and had
gotten into the habit of overruling requests from Admiral
Hillenkoetter and generally going its own separate way. None of
the Intelligence Advisory Committee members considered that the
committee was under any obligation to the DCI. But when Smith
telephoned each of the five representatives that evening there was
no doubt who was in command. They all were ordered to report to
"The Kremlin" by seven o'clock. When one unfortunate objected
to being called away from his dinner table, Smith loosed the full
repertoire of drill-field curses and made it quite clear that since he
was the senior lieutenant general on duty in Washington, he would
brook no interference.

    The task that faced them when they arrived in Smith's office
was as daunting as the general himself. Truman had asked for
explicit estimates on the six toughest questions of the Korean War.
The president needed to know: (1) What was the threat of a
Communist Chinese intervention on the side of the North Koreans;
(2) what was the threat of a direct Soviet intervention; (3) would
the Chinese invade Formosa; (4) would they invade Indochina; (5)
were the Communist Chinese capable of being a threat in the
Philippines; and (6) what were Soviet and Communist Chinese
general intentions and capabilities in the Far East over the foresee-
able future?[16] The six separate reports were to be on Smith's desk
for review by eight o'clock the next morning; the Intelligence
Advisory Committee chiefs had less than twelve hours to drag
their staffs back to the Pentagon and produce the estimates. There
were some initial expressions of concern, which Smith silenced at
once. Not only were the six reports provided in time, but the
assembled staffs were able to answer a seventh question that had
occurred to Truman overnight—would the Soviets use the Korean
conflict to precipitate a global war? Even given the haste of the
exercise and that the estimates really were nothing more than the

consensus wisdom of the moment, six of the seven reports were, remarkably, on target. And the seventh, erroneous estimate had beneficial side effects insofar as the development of a strong CIA was concerned. The Intelligence Advisory Committee opinion had been that the Chinese army would not intervene with troops in North Korea for fear of American retaliation on the mainland. This had been the steadfast opinion of General Charles A. Willoughby, the crusty intelligence chief of General MacArthur's staff, and the error helped put an end to barring the CIA from the Pacific.[17]

The way General Smith handled the hurried assignment from the president is instructive. While there was no doubt in anyone's mind about who was in charge, Smith saw to it that the preparers of the estimates did their work in the Pentagon, on their home ground, with maximum and efficient access to information. And he let the specialists get on with their work; he sent over Ludwell Lee Montague, then chief of global surveys for the Office of Reports and Estimates, as a single agency overseer of the joint operation. A week later, when Smith convened the first formal meeting of the Intelligence Advisory Committee, he went out of his way to avoid confrontation with the panel, and during his two years as DCI he made sure the group members were secure in the knowledge that, while they were now members of *his* team, they remained in charge of their own bailiwicks and were solely responsible to their own internal constituencies. Nor did Smith heed the advice of his two staff lawyers, Lawrence Houston and Walter Pforzheimer, that he seek specific authority from the National Security Council. Instead, he personally visited George Marshall at the Pentagon and Dean Acheson at the State Department to assure them that, while he was taking command at the CIA, the cooperation and full participation of their intelligence divisions would be eagerly accepted as part of the process of assisting the DCI to present the best information to the president.

In that approach, Smith set a pattern that Dulles later followed, to the dismay of many of his own advisers. Both men knew that some things are better left understood and did not need to be set out on paper. Both had learned from bitter experience how to coax, placate, and coordinate fractious allies into putting forth their best efforts. Neither man would ever try to assert his or the CIA's supremacy over the other intelligence arms (it is doubtful either could have done it anyway) as long as the work got done and he was the one directing the work. In that sense, both engaged in skillful bureaucratic politics. But they also left standing very real walls of jurisdiction through which CIA oversight never passed. Some tasks (such as logistical support for covert operations) became the province of the military. Another sacrifice was that total control of the American intelligence effort would never be fully coordinated or directed from a central authority. It was enough for Smith and, later, for Dulles that the poisonous plotting and obstructions that hamstrung Donovan and the OSS were smothered and that coordination on specific projects could be achieved. There would be no private intelligence services.

The Truman assignment allowed Smith to move quickly on to his next objective, the capability to produce better intelligence estimates with a longer focus and a broader scope than the current intelligence bulletins that were produced daily and weekly by the Office of Reports and Estimates being run by R. Jack Smith and Ray Cline. Smith and William Jackson persuaded William Langer, who had run the old R&A branch of the OSS, to take a year's leave of absence from Harvard to create an Office of National Estimates; Langer brought with him Yale scholar Sherman Kent, who would succeed him at the end of his tour. Langer and Kent set up a system that was to survive well into the 1970s and profoundly influence the way the final intelligence product was prepared for the president. Most immediately, Langer effectively put up a wall between his Office of National Estimates and the current intelligence staffs of Smith and Cline. He and Kent saw the role of their staff as the final editors and drafters of the reports that the DCI took to the White House. The actual research and analysis were assigned as separate projects to the relevant outside agencies— political reports came from the State Department, and tactical and other military data were compiled by branches of the Military Intelligence Division. It all would be assembled, analyzed, and put into final form at the Office of National Estimates. Current intelligence from the Office of Reports and Estimates was accepted, but Langer and Kent kept a tight grip on the final product despite the expected resentment.

Langer and Kent also created a panel of outside senior advisers, the Board of National Estimates. This group was made up of retired military and diplomatic officers, distinguished academics, and other informed specialists on foreign affairs, economics, intelligence, and strategy. Men like Hamilton Fish Armstrong, George Kennan (who had retired from the State Department), and atomic scientist Vannevar Bush met periodically to critique formally the language and content of the estimates that were about to go forward from the Office of National Estimates to the DCI's desk. The group became known as the Princeton Consultants, because it met most often near the campus; later its meetings moved to the enhanced privacy and more salubrious facilities of the Gun Club outside of Princeton, and the name stuck. After the Gun Club had passed on a paper, it would be sent to the five Intelligence Advisory Committee members for review and comment, and, unless there was some major problem, the estimate was then run through the cabinet-rank National Security Council and on to President Truman. With someone of Smith's stature actually delivering the estimates at the National Security Council meetings with President Truman, the final products became the dominant ingredient in the administration's policy discussions on the conduct of the war in Korea and on the government's responses to ploys by the USSR.

General Smith also turned to the Dulles Report when he created a new division to do research in the fields of science, technology, and economics. This became the Office of Research and Reports, and, among other tasks, it was to have exclusive jurisdiction over studies about the economic stresses and patterns within the Soviet bloc. The Office of Research and Reports also housed the old OSS mapping division with its expert cartographers. But the office quickly became submerged in the economic research task that was directed by a Jackson recruit, Max Millikan, the well-known economist at the Massachusetts Institute of Technology. In his one-year tour, Millikan succeeded in nearly doubling the manpower of the Office of Research and Reports to eight hundred researchers (most freshly recruited from the best graduate schools). The agency was quickly developing intelligence expertise in topics from raw materials to manufacturing technology to theoretical science.

Another of the permanent foundation stones of the CIA was being set in place. For the first time, both finished intelligence product from the Office of National Estimates and basic intelligence research from the Office of Research and Reports reached outside the government. Until that time, the Office of Reports and Estimates and other collectors and analyzers had stayed close within the confines of the other intelligence agencies, with occasional requests for data from the nongovernment data collectors.

When General Smith signed the contract for Allen Dulles to become the CIA's deputy director for plans on January 2, 1951, the task of putting a single harness on the clandestine collection of intelligence (done by the Office of Special Operations) and the more aggressive efforts to combat and confound the enemy were complicated by the fact that Smith and Dulles disagreed on both ways and means. Using the delicate touch that often was overshadowed by his more spectacular rages, Smith wanted intelligence and operations to be kept separate for administrative purposes but under the active oversight of a single director. Dulles insisted on the more difficult approach of mutually shared efforts. In the 1949 Dulles Report chapter on "Secret Intelligence and Secret Operations," he argued:

> The collection of Secret Intelligence is closely related to the conduct of Secret Operations in support of national policy. These operations including covert psychological warfare, clandestine political activity, sabotage, and guerrilla activity, have always been the companions of Secret Intelligence. The two activities support each other and can be disassociated only to the detriment of both.[18]

In the preliminary draft of that report sent in May 1948 to the National Security Council, Dulles had been more specific. Secret Intelligence and Secret Operations must be "under the same roof." While collection and covert operations should be separate channels of work run on parallel tracks so as not to endanger the security of either effort, nevertheless, "Operations must have full access to SI [Secret Intelligence] resources." To Jackson's annoyance, Dulles was able to point to the British experience of separating its Special Operations Executive paramilitary wing from MI6 during the war, only to merge the two services immediately afterward. When Smith and Dulles arrived in the autumn of 1950, the conflict between the Office of Special Operations and the Office of Policy Coordination as it stood was, Dulles said, "a situation unsound."[19]

No one considered tearing down the clandestine services and starting over by reexamining the functions of each. The task was to make the existing machinery work more smoothly. Also worth noting, at each step in the construction of the CIA since 1947, the National Security Council and the president had *increased* the for ever more aggressive covert action. NSC 68 in April 1950 had called for nonmilitary, economic, political, and psychological counteraction specifically directed at the USSR. Another intensification (NSC 10/5) was ordered in October 1951, partly in response to heightened war needs in Asia. In response to the Korean War, the Office of Policy Coordination undertook to become operational in every possible theater, including the previously taboo ground in the Far East. The covert operations also became aggressively paramilitary. Wisner's budget the year before the Korean War had been $4.7 million for a staff of 302. By 1952 the Office of Policy Coordination had 2,812 personnel working away in elderly World War I "temporary" buildings down the hill from "The Kremlin," toward the Lincoln Memorial, and another 3,142 staff and operatives were classed "overseas contract" personnel in forty-seven stations abroad; the total budget cost was $82 million.

The Office of Special Operations was far from being left totally in the cold. General Willard Wyman and his successor, Lyman Kirkpatrick, had been aggressive enough in building their own overseas collection service out of the OSS networks that survived the war. They had scored a major coup in 1949 when the Gehlen Organization was able to secure for them the plans and test records of the MiG-15, the Soviet's first jet fighter plane. But because the Office of Special Operations had been carried as a budget item for the CIA while the Office of Policy Coordination had had access to separate State Department funding, a widening disparity had opened up in the "quarters and rations" provided for the two services. Office of Special Operations personnel considered themselves the purists and the more senior professionals, and they had the lower salaries to prove it. They considered the Office of Policy Coordination to be "cowboys" who overspent and over-reached. Each side blamed the other for fouling up carefully contrived operations, for suborning agents already on one payroll, and for being gullible to "paper mills" being churned by spurious exile groups.

Most tellingly, the Office of Special Operations blamed the covert action service for tilting the whole culture of the CIA away from systematic collection and analysis, and there is some truth to that charge. The agency did indeed move away from its original conception as Harry Truman's "quiet intelligence" provider and became the chief executive's action service. In fairness, Harry Truman wanted it that way. Others in the administration concurred that while better understanding was wanted, it was to be "intelligence by objective," intelligence to answer specific questions and to provide the ways and means to solve problems.

Allen Dulles's summons of Wisner and Kirkpatrick to their first meeting on closer coordination in February 1951 was part of the long evolution of the American intelligence services. As intelligence historian Rhodri Jeffreys-Jones observed, "The formation of the CIA in 1947 did not represent a sudden break in the history of American espionage. The CIA grew from the practices of the preceding half-century."[20] The tension between providing better understanding of situations that frustrate political leaders and giving the far more satisfying prompt action to solve those frustrations dated back to when Leland Harrison sent State Department clerks around to the German Embassy to try to steal the kaiser's codebooks. By 1951 the attention of the president was more sharply focused than ever on the pervasive fear that the United States was sliding inexorably into a final all-out war with the Soviet Union. The Russians had demonstrated (in 1949) that they had created their own atomic weapons capacity with the help of secrets stolen from the United States. Their advances in jet aviation lengthened the reach of their air force. Implicit in the American strategy was the alarming conviction that the Soviets had both the capability and the intention to resort to an aggressive global war to achieve their ambitions. The task was to thwart, block, and defeat the enemy, just as it had been against Japan and Germany.

In fairness to General Smith and Allen Dulles, the agency had more customers than just the president. The Pentagon and State Department got into the habit of turning to both clandestine services for help in specific theaters of operation. It was obvious from the start that as successful as it was, the Office of Special Operations could not be expected to repeat its triumphant "op" in the Italian elections on demand. Nor could the Office of Policy Coordination function on an ad hoc basis. If the clandestine services were to function, there had to be training of staff, compiling of data, and maintenance of facilities. That meant budgets. As Senator Frank Church's committee concluded in its history of the agency's development, "With budgeting came the need for ongoing activities to justify future allocations—rather than leaving the flexibility of responding to specific requirements." So, the Office of Special Operations and the Office of Policy Coordination under Dulles adopted projects and a budget system that supported projects rather than a financial system that was organized around broad policy objectives. The Church staff analysis concluded, "The project system had important internal effects. An individual... judged his own performance, and was judged by others, on the importance and number of projects he initiated and managed. The result was competition among individuals and among the... divisions to generate the maximum number of projects. Projects remained the fundamental units around which clandestine activities were organized...."[21]

Both Dulles and General Smith grasped at once that in the CIA whoever controlled the clandestine services was a long way to controlling the agency itself. Whatever his judgment on the abilities of Allen Dulles to organize and run "ops," Smith had no intention at all of elevating his deputy for "plans" to that level of power.

Dulles, on the other hand, had no doubt in his mind that the Office of Special Operations and the Office of Policy Coordination must be merged and that he would control that integrated force; even if it meant he would never be DCI, he would run the people who did the "ops."

The issue of control over how the clandestine branches would be coordinated slipped out of Smith's grasp without any single chance for him to force a showdown so he could reverse the drift toward merger or, if he had to, fire Dulles for bucking him. Dulles moved in small, manageable steps that the DCI grudgingly approved. In June 1951 the two services stopped feuding over South America and began to coordinate collection and operations throughout the Western Hemisphere. By August 1952 Smith had agreed to the formal wedding of the Office of Special Operations and the Office of Policy Coordination under a Directorate of Plans, with Wisner named deputy director of plans and Helms from the Office of Special Operations in the number two role as chief of operations. William Jackson, who was having increasing alcohol problems, wanted to go back to the private sector, and that is how Allen Dulles moved up to become Smith's deputy director. Whatever the elevation in title, Dulles remained directly responsible for the operational side, just as Sherman Kent was determinedly digging in to protect his turf on the research and reports side of the agency.

General Smith did not surrender control by any means. Dulles became the most frequent target of the DCI's provoking rages. The general was not particularly interested in the details of operations, either collecting or covert. His fascination and satisfaction came from winning the bureaucratic battle to make the agency grow and the administrative struggle to make it more efficient. The already high-strung Wisner became terrified of Smith's rages and was increasingly unsettled by the DCI's "don't bother me with details" retort whenever he was asked for detailed guidance on an upcoming project. Dulles cheerfully occupied the deputy director's office which adjoined Smith's at "The Kremlin" and kept his door open (which Jackson had refused to do) so that he could quickly respond when the general shouted "Dulles! Dammit, Dulles, get in here!" for yet another peremptory order or bawling out.

Colonel L. K. "Red" White was brought into the agency at about that time to become the assistant to Deputy Director for Administration Walter Wolfe. White had been a combat infantry officer during the war and had gone on to be the deputy chief of the Foreign Broadcast Information Service of the Central Intelligence Group, where he undertook a complicated reorganization of the radio monitoring force. He recalled the tense morning meetings where all the department chiefs under Smith's command reported:

> "Beedle" was as gruff as everyone says, but if you didn't let him scare you, you were all right. At one morning meeting, he was laying down the law about the new administrative structure and somebody said he didn't know that he could agree with the new line. And "Beedle" said, "You don't ever disagree with me, do you understand that?" And he asked everyone that question around the table, and they were all so scared they just nodded. So Allen was the last one around the table, and he laughed that chuckle of his and said, "Oh, sure 'Beedle,' we all understand." Smith could make Frank Wisner break out in sweat when he chewed him out, but he never ruffled Allen, and that sometimes made him angrier. I've seen Allen, and Wisner walk away from one of those sessions, and Wisner would be shaking his head. Allen would be laughing and saying, "Wasn't that something?" He wasn't about to be stampeded out of that job.[22]

CHAPTER THIRTEEN

1953–1958

*"I was probably a fool to take the job instead of retiring to the
quiet practice of law for the rest of my days. However, the die is
now cast and I am here until I am thrown out or wear out."*
—*Director of Central Intelligence Allen Dulles,*
February 10, 1953[1]

EARLY ON THE MORNING of Monday, February 26, 1953, messengers bustled about the shabby corridors of the "temporaries" (since World War I), as the cluster of CIA staff offices adjoining "The Kremlin" was known. A single piece of paper was placed on each desk; its message was simultaneously clattering over the teletype machines in scores of agency stations all over the world. The message was from the new DCI. In it, Dulles gave special thanks to General Smith, crediting him with winning for the agency "a respected place in government." But Dulles also made it explicit to all hands, "The reorganization period, except for minor changes, is over."[2]

Dulles's taking command at the East Building corner office at "The Kremlin" complex marked another cycle in American intelligence evolution. What Allen Dulles was about to do was take the foundation stones that had been put in place by himself and others and erect a service that transcended procedures and physical facilities. Under Dulles, the CIA became a culture of its own. His agency pseudonym for cable purposes, "Ascham," delighted him when he learned (from CIA official biographer Wayne Jackson) that

Herodotus in his *Histories* had written about a warrior class that served the Egyptian pharaoh Psammetichus; "Ascham" in Greek meant "those who stand on the left hand of the king." That fit in with Dulles's own image of the elite status he wanted for his agency. The spy had come a long way from the back alleys. Under Dulles, espionage moved up the ladder another rung to the honorable government service that Donovan had decreed; the American intelligence officer was destined to become a praetorian guard that served the left hand of the president—the hand that did the sinister deeds that statecraft requires.

President Eisenhower's appointment of Dulles as DCI had a certain inevitability about it even though there were competitors for the job. "Beedle" Smith personally disdained Dulles, but he acquiesced because Ike had persuaded him to accept the post of deputy secretary of state, where he believed he could keep a watch on his old agency. Men like William Donovan and Gordon Gray, a wealthy diplomat, never really had a chance. Ike gave Dulles full credit for helping make him a major political figure before he joined the NATO command, and afterward.

Back then, in 1950, Dulles had taken charge of a lengthy policy letter drafted by the general that urged a massive defense buildup. President Truman had a visceral dislike of Eisenhower (and for all West Pointers) and would have rejected such unsolicited advice. But Dulles skillfully conveyed the suggestions to Averell Harriman, a trusted adviser to Truman, who, with equal delicacy, slid the recommendations into a stack of proposals already on the president's desk. When Truman approved the military rearmament program contained in NSC 68 (which called for covert operations aimed at the Soviet Union) and then declared a state of national emergency on December 16, 1950, Ike's recommendations were pointed to as proof of the bipartisan nature of the president's policies. Everyone won on that exchange, and Eisenhower never forgot the role Dulles played.[3]

Allen's appointment was publicly popular as well. His promotion was cheered inside the agency, and he found he was far more welcome on Capitol Hill than General Smith had been. Congressional leaders had feared Smith's abrupt rages; he had not helped matters when he stated at a hearing just before the 1952 elections that he assumed communists had penetrated both the State Department and the CIA. When Dulles went before the Senate Armed Services Committee for his confirmation hearing on February 19, 1953, the session took exactly ten minutes, time enough for each of the nine senators to praise the appointment and then to vote unanimous consent.[4]

One of Dulles's first jobs was to bolster the security of his own agency. General Smith had spoken from direct knowledge that the Soviets had penetrated deep into the U.S. government, although not into the CIA itself. There had been too many cases of servicemen stationed at sensitive communications and defense installations being approached for (and sometimes agreeing to provide) secret documents; one army sergeant handed over all the Russian codes the communications interception listeners used to monitor Soviet military radio signals. This was a time of national dismay over the Red menace. The unscrupulous fanned those fears, but the menace had a dangerous reality to it.

Admiral Arleigh A. Burke, a World War II naval hero of the Pacific sea battles, in early 1951 was among the American and South Korean officers who were trying to negotiate with the North Koreans a cease-fire line across the Korean peninsula. At the time, the North Koreans had pushed the battle line below the thirty-eighth parallel, which had been the previous boundary between the two countries. The United Nations forces managed to regain lost ground by launching attacks on the section of the armistice line that would be discussed at the next meeting. In the midst of this forceful but successful way of negotiating, the order came from the White House that the Allies were to hurry through the talks about the cease-fire line. The dividing point had to be established where it was, well into South Korean territory. Angry protests from the negotiators, backed up by General Matthew Ridgeway, the UN commander, were to no avail; the word from Washington was explicit: Hurry it up. Burke resigned his job and made the arduous flight across the Pacific to Washington in a last attempt to convince President Truman to hang on a little longer and to allow the negotiating team to win strategic and politically important gains. But despite warnings from his navy superiors that a protest could cost his career (Truman had taken him off the promotion list once already for his outspokenness), Burke called the White House, and the president agreed to hear him for fifteen minutes that afternoon. Years later, Burke recalled:

> I told him who I was and that I'd come back from Korea, and I said, "Mr. President, I am very distraught at the decisions that have been made. I think we ought not to accept the present battle line as the final line of demarcation." And I gave him my reasons and we talked. He asked me a lot of questions, and I stayed there about two hours. He canceled the rest of his appointments.
>
> Finally he said, "Admiral, this is not a decision that the United States is making by itself. We represent the United Nations. I agree with you, but I don't see how we can avoid it. If the United Nations votes against us on this when it comes to an open vote we will lose our negotiating position. This is a helluva thing we're in."
>
> And he said, "Even the British are against us on this. Several times a week we meet down in the cellar here [the old Roosevelt War Situation Room] with

representatives of all the allies that have troops over there. And they pound on me all the time to hurry up and get a cease-fire at any cost. They have a guy who comes down here from the British Embassy named Guy Burgess who really pushes for this."

It wasn't until five or six years later that I learned that Burgess had access to all of our dispatches [from Truman to the UN command] and that he was the one who persuaded the British government on the cease-fire. He had sent the dispatches to us to accept the present battle line as the final line of demarcation to the communists. I had no idea that all our communications were cleared with Russia before we ever got them. So the communists were getting our orders before we were. It was a horrible damned thing. Of course, President Truman had no idea it was going on. I don't know that he ever knew.[5]

The penetration of Anglo-American security by two of that famous trio of British traitors, Guy Burgess, Donald Maclean, and H. A. R. "Kim" Philby, has come to dwarf every other tale in the history of espionage. Considering how long these men ran their string of deceptions, how deeply they penetrated their own security service (Philby at one point was being groomed to become head of MI6) and that of the United States, and the actual secrets they passed on to their Soviet controllers, the three were uniquely damaging. Philby, that sardonic, charming monster of mannered cynicism, by himself changed the shape and direction of the Cold War. Looking over the list of World War II secrets he passed from the OSS (the "Wood" traffic being just one set) and MI6 to the NKVD, one wonders about the direction the Cold War might have taken without him.

The survival of Philby, Maclean, and Burgess is all the more remarkable because the intelligence services of three nations had been on their trail since 1945. That was the year that Igor Gouzenko, a Soviet intelligence officer, defected to the Canadians with proof of Soviet espionage activities there, in the United States, and in Britain. J. Edgar Hoover had begun a probe and assigned one of his most dogged agents, William Harvey, to interrogate Elizabeth Bentley, one of the early suspects quizzed in the probe. Bentley confessed to being a courier for Soviet operations in Canada and the United States, and she named more than one hundred others as members of the spy group. Two dozen of those named were officials placed throughout the U.S. government, including the State Department (she named Alger Hiss), the Justice Department, and even the Board of Economic Warfare, where Eleanor Dulles, Donald Hiss, and other intellectuals labored on postwar reconstruction.

As the war ended, the hunt for the Soviet spies stalled for lack of hard evidence to convict. This is not the same as saying that the FBI lacked hard suspicions backed by evidence. A detailed publication of the so-called Venona decryptions—thousands of enciphered telegrams sent by Soviet spies in the United States to Moscow—has recently appeared. Prodded by the revelations of Gouzenko, Bentley, and Whittaker Chambers, the U.S. Army Signals code-breakers and a team directed by FBI agent Robert Lamphere were able to peel away the stubborn code covers and identify hundreds of American informants who worked for the Soviet cause. The code-breaking singled out scores of senior leaders of the supposedly naive Communist Party of the United States. White House aide Laughlin Phillips, Treasury adviser Harry Dexter White, atom bomb spies Julius and Ethel Rosenberg, and Alger Hiss were all identified by Venona and confirmed by subsequent probes. But since the confirmation often came via illegal telephone wiretaps and other legally excluded tactics, convictions were few and the national frustration level grew.

Part of that frustration stemmed from the fact that President Truman was kept informed about the progress of the decryptions and the growing list of Soviet agents in high places within the government. But even after he won the 1948 election in an upset, he seemed unwilling to mount a public campaign against the spies lest it give comfort to the Red-baiting Republicans in Congress. He mused in a memo to Attorney General Tom Clark, "I wonder if we could not get a statement of facts from the FBI about the meddling of the House Un-American Activities Committee and how they dried up sources of information which would have been accessible in the prosecution of spies and communists. Their meddling efforts were in fact a 'red herring' to distract attention not only from the shortcomings of the 80th Congress but also contributed to the escape of certain communists who should have been indicted...."[6]

In 1947 a frustrated Harvey quit the FBI and was quickly recruited into the fledgling CIA's counterintelligence branch, which had just inherited the European counterintelligence assets of the Strategic Services Unit. Among the files that were transferred were the boxes of even newer Soviet codes that Wisner and others had grabbed in 1944 and that, despite Roosevelt's order to return them to Stalin, had been copied by Donovan. A year and a half later, in early 1949, the cryptanalysts deciphered for the first time a 1945 message sent by a Soviet agent in New York that contained the complete text of a telegram sent by Churchill to President Truman through the secure lines of the British Embassy in Washington. The message included the embassy's own reference numbers. The conclusion was inescapable, and more translations of other messages brought even more ominous discoveries. Not only was there a Soviet spy high up in the British Embassy in Washington, but he had been passing to the Russians advance tips on the FBI probe of the atomic spy ring. The decoded Soviet traffic also helped provide the clues that led British investigators to Klaus Fuchs, a British physicist who had provided the Russians with key elements of the Manhattan Project's details. Arrested and under questioning, Fuchs led the investigators to Harry Gold (who had been named by Elizabeth Bentley five years earlier), and Gold, in turn, produced the key evidence that led to the 1950 trial and conviction of Julius and Ethel Rosenberg for conspiracy to commit espionage. The Rosenbergs were executed in 1953 despite misguided worldwide protests of their innocence.

As Harvey's team pushed on with the deciphering, it went back over old records of previous hints provided by Russians who had defected even before World War II. A profile of the Soviet plants in the British Embassy began to emerge. There were two men, it seemed; one was known to be of Scots background, the other had been a war correspondent during the Spanish Civil War. Harvey by this time had been joined by James J. Angleton, who had returned from his OSS and early CIA successes in Italy. The irony is that the closer the American and British probers got to Maclean and Philby, the higher these traitors climbed in trust at MI6 and the more their capacity for damage increased. Throughout 1949 and 1950, Philby was the embassy's liaison for a number of joint Anglo-American covert operations. One was the support of the Ukrainian insurgents. Another was a program to insert bands of trained operators and guerrillas into Albania to organize the overthrow of despot Enver Hoxha. Hundreds of insurgents were rolled up by the waiting Soviets and killed; whole villages of sympathizers were relocated by force. Burgess, deep in the White House War Room, was able to assure Moscow that President Truman was determined not to use atomic weapons if the Chinese were to intervene in the Korean War. Russian historians have since confirmed that with those assurances, Stalin was able to convince a reluctant Mao Tse-tung to commit his troops over the border.

While the ties between MI6 and the CIA functioned during this time, Dulles never allowed the "Special Relationship" to be as open and free as it had been during the war. The spectacle of Philby's survival in the British secret service for more than a decade after Burgess and Maclean had decamped to Moscow had a broad impact on Allen Dulles and on the CIA's development. Unlike William Jackson and others within the agency, Dulles had no intention of ever letting MI6 have access to all the agency's secrets or be a full partner in all of its undertakings. This is not to say that Dulles did not believe in that loosely informal but nonetheless binding understanding that the Americans had many more vital interests in common with the British than with other nations of the world. In that sense, the legendary "Special Relationship" is still alive and well even today. But during the Dulles directorate, it was established that the CIA had to go its own way in the world. America would never again be the junior partner in intelligence ventures with the British. A series of secret negotiations between MI6 and the new CIA in 1947 tried to cod- ify just how tight that common interest was and who would do what in which areas of the world. With the exception of dividing the world into sectors for purposes of monitoring broadcasts and other signals intelligence (SIGINT), the British and Americans could not agree on the kind of theaters of primary influence for intelligence collection and covert operations that had been set up during the war.

Dulles had already decided the CIA must reach into every corner of the world. Among the first orders of business when James Angleton was made head of the agency's counterintelli- gence force was an ambitious program of outreach to the spy ser- vices of Turkey, Taiwan, South Africa, and even Tito's Yugoslavia, in addition to the more obvious relationships set up with the Israelis, the French, and, of course, Dulles's old friends, the Swiss. One of the most common sets of ties saw the CIA giving these "friendlies" useful information gathered from its increasingly pervasive monitoring of Soviet radio traffic, in exchange for fair sharing of the local service's coverage of its internal intelligence collection.

The Liaison Section Angleton established is one of the least understood, but perhaps the most successful, of the counterintelligence tasks he supervised. His division also established its own research section, which provided custom-designed information and guidance for the "ops" he directed from his office. One of the problems in evaluating Angleton's performance and contribution is that so much of what he did remains unknown even to trusted veterans of other branches of the agency. Counterintelligence was sealed off from the other clandestine services. Part of this was due to the administrative culture that Smith set in place and that Dulles later refined and expanded. But it is also generally agreed that during the Dulles years, Angleton's eccentric and driven style of counterintelligence kept the CIA far safer from Soviet penetration than any other U.S. security agency did. When Angleton's reputation later came to grief, some of the blame must be aimed at Dulles and how he dealt with his most senior aides.

Colonel L. K. "Red" White, who was the chief of administration for the agency, describes Dulles's management style: "You can organize horizontally, in which case everyone doing similar functions such as operations is aware of what everyone in that area is doing. Or you can do what Dulles did and organize vertically so that functions were sealed off from each other; the excuse was the need for security, for a "need to know" rule. The argument was that as you broaden the number of people who know about something, you weaken the security of that operation. So no one knew what Angleton was doing except Angleton, and then the director, when he was told by Angleton. The problem is obvious; it's hell to administer. And people who might have something to say about an operation don't get the chance to comment. It opens you up to very serious mistakes." As we shall see, that is exactly what happened a number of times.

In Angleton's case, the counterintelligence chief himself was "hell to administer" and drove the men charged with oversight of his operations to raw frustration. One officer who was involved with a number of counterintelligence projects recalls, "Jim came in late and left early. He took long lunch hours and was well known to drink a lot, even though he handled it. If a paper was routed to his office, you played hell getting it back. He also was fixated on certain properties of his which no one else in the agency could touch; he really was jealous of his contacts with the Israelis, for example. Nobody but Jim knew as much about Israel. And he was suspicious of defectors, and he wrecked the careers of several dozen agency officers during his time. But he did protect the agency from penetration, and Allen Dulles let him have free rein even though he perhaps should have paid closer attention."7

One of the first areas of liaison that Dulles and Angleton targeted after Israel was West Germany. The Bonn government was in the process of regaining national sovereignty and assuming control over its own security. When Dulles assumed command at "The Kremlin," the West German legislature approved the treaty for the European Defense Community, which preceded its joining the NATO military force in 1955. Even at this early date, the CIA's sponsorship of General Reinhard Gehlen's band of spies was entering a new phase. The Gehlen Organization had come a long way from that day in the spring of 1945 when the general ordered the burial of fifty sealed cases of his most sensitive secrets about the Red Army and told thirty of his most senior aides to go into hiding until they could surrender safely to the

Americans. By the early 1950s, the Gehlen Organization had more than four thousand staffers and perhaps an equal number of occasional agents who were passing freely to and from Eastern Europe. Their successes were impressive, but it was painfully clear that the Soviets and East Germans had been just as successful in penetrating the fledgling West German government of Konrad Adenauer and the Gehlen Organization. The German group's former masters, particularly General Arthur Trudeau, the newly appointed head of Army G-2, began to campaign to have Dulles cut all links with Gehlen for security purposes; the distaste over using former Hitler advisers also surfaced.

In the early summer of 1953, Dulles took an extended tour of Europe, his first as DCI. After London and Paris, Dulles went on an inspection trip to Munich, where Harry Rositzke was busy setting up the CIA's main operational base for the Cold War in Europe. While there, the director went out to the village of Pullach, five miles down the Isar River, to visit Gehlen, whose headquarters was behind a secured set of buildings that resembled a housing complex on the riverbank. The questions before both men were how soon the Gehlen Organization could be taken off the books of the CIA and what the prospects were that the Adenauer government would officially take Gehlen on board as chief of intelligence with his ready-made service. Those two questions caused serious doubts, and from them a third question naturally followed. Assuming the Gehlen Organization did become Germany's official intelligence service, what would its relationship with the CIA become? The hard fact was that, even though Dulles was paying all the bills, the Gehlen Organization was very much under Gehlen's autocratic control and following his intelligence agenda.

This was a prickly problem for Dulles. He was already under pressure from the Pentagon to cut the Gehlen Organization loose and deal at arm's length with whatever intelligence service the

Germans put in place. But he knew he could not do that; American efforts to put agents in place in the Soviet Union and in other communist-dominated governments had been disastrously unsuccessful. The group, vulnerable as it might be, had agents in place already. But the Germans already considered themselves an independent force despite the lump-sum budget allocation from Washington; Gehlen's staffers considered themselves the general's men, not employees of the CIA.

The relationship Dulles was able to achieve with Gehlen and his successors was unique. The British referred to the agency as "the cousins"; by that standard the CIA and its German counterparts were second cousins—related but at a distance. The Germans, for their part, recognized the debt they owed the agency and Dulles for keeping the Gehlen apparatus alive and intact at a crucial time, but they jealously prized their independence. General Eberhard Blum was a postwar recruit to the Gehlen Organization service and later was one of Gehlen's successors when the organization was taken into the West German government as the *Bundesnachrichtendienst* (BND, or Federal Intelligence Service) in 1956. General Blum describes the delicate balancing act that Dulles and Gehlen worked out with each other's service:

> Allen Dulles was a tremendous father figure to us and a very impressive man. He had a capacity to make people trust him and follow him. He certainly showed confidence in Gehlen's project, and he stuck with us even when there was political opposition before we became official. I think the Gehlen Organization at the beginning of the Cold War had a monopoly on intelligence on the military threat from the east. But then the American technology began to have greater influence and effect. Our contribution to the CIA always remained strong in

certain areas, but Dulles's philosophy always was to be independent as a national service and to get their own intelligence for their own needs. We were counted upon to help, but they never depended on us as the sole source of information. Dulles never was dependent on any of the allies, the French, the Israelis, or the British. He knew, although many thought otherwise at the time, that there never would be a NATO intelligence force to confront the Soviets. He knew, and he was right, that it would always remain a group of national services.

You know, a book that will never be written is the relation of the BND and its contacts with the third world countries. It is interesting that we were never considered a colonial power in the third world. Many of the new governments in Africa, Asia, and the Middle East had no direct memories of us, or Hitler, or even of the First World War. So while they did not welcome their old colonial masters, or especially the United States, we found we were welcome. This was the time of the Cold War, and the nonaligned movement was very popular. We offered them friendship, and aid, and were not perceived as colonialists, so we had a very good entrée.

And I must say that worked too, even in countries in Europe that we had conquered under Hitler; even before we could admit to having political or military ties, there were good relations with the intelligence services. And despite the fact that we had been their enemies, Gehlen was very successful there. He had a political mind, like Dulles, that went beyond just swapping information for information. He went beyond that and felt it was good for Germany if the BND gave intelligence to those countries even though they might not have things of equal value for us at that time.

So we were welcome in places in the world where Allen Dulles was not, and he became a beneficiary of that. And there were cases where he made our entrée to a given country much smoother. You have to understand his standing throughout the world of intelligence in those days. He was such a godfather figure everywhere that it made his sponsorship of us extremely helpful in certain countries. And in those places where we could go freely, we could help him with them. Our dealings were always bilateral, mind you. But the impact went many times beyond that.[8]

Dulles's first trip to Germany as DCI in 1953 also took him to Berlin. He arrived just in time for the first serious riots in East Germany. A labor union dispute had gotten out of hand and turned into an old-fashioned Berlin insurrection. Soviet troops and tanks were called in by the regime of Walter Ulbricht, and the suppression that followed was brutally unmistakable proof to the world of the real terror of the workers' paradise. By coincidence, Eleanor Dulles had arrived at the same time on one of her periodic inspections of the economic and physical reconstruction of the free sections of Berlin. This was too much for the communist propaganda machine, and a loud outcry went up that the infamous brother and sister had masterminded the riots in order the destabilize the East German government.

This was one of the few times in 1953 that Allen and Eleanor had occasion to share a good laugh. What should have been a good year indeed for the Dulles family had been blighted badly. Foster had not behaved well when he arrived at the State Department in January. One of his first acts was to try to fire Eleanor from her job in the German affairs department at State for the spurious reason that it caused embarrassing comment among the newspaper columnists. Having gained the position his grandfather and uncle had achieved, he perhaps did not want the distraction of a sister as he prepared to devote his full energies to the task ahead; having a brother as DCI seemed to be another matter entirely. Part of the estrangement lay in Eleanor's habit of lecturing Foster on matters in which she assumed her considerable expertise in economic strategy was superior to his. This annoyed Foster so much that the ever-protective Janet refused to let her sister-in-law visit their home on all but the most social occasions.

Eleanor, characteristically, did not go quietly. She sought help from a friend in the department, James Riddleberger, who had worked with her in Vienna and had been the highest-ranking civilian in the Occupation government of West Germany while she was there. Eleanor explains:

Jimmy Riddleberger went to see Foster and said he couldn't fire me because I was in the department first; it was unfair. And Foster told him he just couldn't have me around, it didn't look right, or something. And Riddleberger said, Look, give her a chance.

Give her a year and if she doesn't get into trouble, it will probably be all right. And Foster agreed. And after a hard year, it all blew over. But I never did understand why he did what he did.[9]

Eleanor's unhappiness was overshadowed by the tragedy that struck Allen and Clover. Their son, Allen Macy Dulles, had been the one most likely to take the family to new glories. "I don't think people realize just how brilliant he was," his sister Joan believes. Along with his mother's fair features and his father's rugged build, young Allen had been a top student and one of those natural leaders that other boys instinctively rally around. Robert Abboud, who later became a prominent international banker, remembers a debating contest in which he represented Boston's Roxbury Latin School against Allen Dulles and a team from the Exeter Academy prep school he attended. "It's funny how you remember some people from your youth and not others. Allen was one of those who stood out; he was just that good at what he did."

After graduating at the top of his class of 250 at Exeter, Allen followed family tradition and went to Princeton, winning a Naval Reserve Officer Training Corps scholarship. But he chafed at Princeton's lack of challenge. His sister Joan recalls, "At the end of this third year, he wrote them a letter telling them off. And then he got into Bailiol College at Oxford and got his degree from there in history; I remember his dissertation was on the history of the permanent undersecretary system of the British Foreign Office, and it was judged good enough to get his degree from Oxford and, on the strength of it, his degree from Princeton too." This left the twenty-two-year-old Allen faced with his college obligations to the Naval ROTC; the Korean War was under way, and the draft was calling up a new intake of young Americans. He joined the Marine Corps and was commissioned a second lieutenant. By the summer of 1952, he was in South Korea with the First Marine Division and was put in charge of the light machine gun squad that supported Company "B," a frontline rifle company. On the night of November 14, Lieutenant Dulles took command of a rifle platoon dug in at an observation outpost in front of the fortified lines. Almost at once he was wounded when a North Korean shell fragment nicked him in the leg. Robert Abboud, who by coinci-dence was "B" Company's executive officer, later recalled what happened:

There was heavy sniper fire out there, and Allen went out toward it. He went out with a corporal who got hit, and Allen organized the evacuation. Then he charged the three snipers by himself; they shot his weapon out of his hand and wounded him in the wrist. He didn't have to do any of that, but I guess he felt he had something to live up to. He never wanted to be treated differently from the rest of us.[10]

The next morning, after Dulles had his wounds attended to, he was back at the outpost as a Marine air strike strafed the area. The young lieutenant sent the enlisted men of his platoon back to the fortified bunkers while he stayed at the post. While the jets were pounding the area around him, Dulles noticed that a communist mortar and machine gun nest had been set up within range and was firing on the company's left flank. He called for a nearby mortar platoon to zero in on the position, and, taking some rifle grenades, he crawled to within thirty yards of the enemy and began to direct the Marine mortar fire ahead of him. Just before the enemy withdrew from the position, he was hit by an 81-mm mortar shell and suffered severe head wounds. His commanders later put him in for a Navy Cross. Abboud remembers, "I was there when they brought him in. He kept trying to get off the stretcher and go back. Some of his men were crying. I've never really known anyone quite like him."

Allen was evacuated to a navy hospital in Japan. Clover, who had been staying with Mary Bancroft in Zurich on one of their Jung study courses, flew at once to be with him. Considering how deeply the mortar fragments penetrated his skull and the extent of the injuries to his brain, young Dulles made a remarkable physical recovery. By February 1953, Allen and Clover were able to get him home and into the Bethesda Naval Hospital. That summer he was allowed to come home, and Allen was able to prevail on friends within the State Department to find him a light research job in the archives; Uncle Foster could scarcely object to that. His sister, Dr. Joan Dulles Buresch, recalls, "We did not know anything about how injuries to the temporal lobe of the brain can sometimes lead to troubles with paranoia. They didn't know how to deal with it until much, much later. It was all very upsetting to us. He was so good and bright and had such promise."

But it was a promise that was not to be fulfilled. A steady job proved beyond his capacity, and although he was well enough physically, young Allen often was immobilized by waves of despair and fear. After a series of disturbing incidents proved beyond Clover's ability to cope, a young Marine veteran friend was invited to be a companion. Over the next few years, there were longer stays in various hospitals and clinics in New York; each time hopes would rise and then be dashed. Finally, in 1962, the family sent Allen to the Sanitarium Bellevue in Kreuzlingen, Switzerland, for extended psychiatric care.

The emotional strain on Clover and Allen's marriage was compounded by chronic money problems to which the son's expensive hospital bills added. The Allen Dulleses had never been rich and had long since exhausted whatever partner's equity Allen might have built up at Sullivan & Cromwell. When he became General Smith's deputy at the CIA, his salary was the standard $14,000 a year for a senior government official of that day; becoming director meant the salary increased by only $800. For the 1950s this was hardly meager wages, and the couple could afford the upkeep on their home at Lloyd Neck on Long Island, but they were never able to own a home in Washington. After renting a series of houses near upper Wisconsin Avenue in the Cleveland Park section of Washington, Clover and Allen in 1954 were offered the use of a three-bedroom house at 2723 Que Street N.W. in the Georgetown section of the city, where most of their friends lived. The Que Street house was on a property that included the larger house, tennis court, and gardens of the family of Peter Belin, a relative of Dulles's old colleague Mott Belin. The rent was a token and provided access to the tennis court, of which Allen made full use. The couple made their home there, and Allen turned the basement into a cluttered library and file room after his retirement from the agency while he worked on his various speeches and books.

By the time Allen became DCI, he and Clover had come to a marriage relationship that provided comfort and support if not total satisfaction. Clover had come into an inheritance when her parents died that enabled her to establish a trust fund for each of the three children and to travel and study. In 1947 she had returned to her Jungian studies in Switzerland and would continue them all of her life. Her trips to Zurich usually lasted about six weeks, but she was often absent from the Que Street house for extended trips to visit young Allen at one clinic or another. At least part of her decision to separate from her husband had to do with his resuming his affair with Wally Toscanini, who showed up in New York early in 1947 in part to escape the privation of war-torn Europe. Allen had helped secure her visa to the United States and sponsored her application for citizenship on the grounds of her war work with the partisans and her conductor father's energetic fund-raising for the Allied cause.

Joan Dulles Buresch recalls, "Wally flattered all of us in the family. I think Toddy was the friendliest with her; she was a bit too much for my taste with all this countess thing she threw about. Besides, I knew Mary Bancroft first, and I knew Mary was Mother's friend too. In any event, Wally did not stay around for very long before she began to fight with her father and she went back to Europe."[11]

While Clover and Joan may have favored Mary Bancroft in

the romance sweepstakes, other family members detested her. On learning that Mary had come back to New York and applied for membership to the chic Cosmopolitan Club for fashionable women, Janet Dulles had her blackballed at once. Whatever was happening with Allen's career at the time, the family scene was in a constant state of uproar. Joan and Fritz Molden had divorced, and she had married another Austrian, Eugen Buresch, a diplomat. They were stationed in Teheran at the Austrian Embassy during some of this period. Toddy in turn married Jens Jebsen, a Norwegian-born banker who became a senior executive of the Manufacturers Hanover Bank, and they lived in London for many years. But her bouts with depression deepened, and there were periods during which she had to be hospitalized. Small wonder then that Clover began to look elsewhere for her happiness.

Clover also resumed sketching and painting, which she had studied in her youth. For a while in the middle 1950s, she and Mary Bancroft discussed various drafts of a book that would combine Clover's drawings of Jungian dream-myths with their insights on the psychologist's teachings. Her friendship with her husband's former mistress grew very close, and a steady stream of "Dear Shark" letters of confidences flowed between them wherever their travels took them. Clover and Allen did not really separate; rather, they developed separate lives that came together frequently but remained on distinctly different paths.

Daughter Joan explains:

My father was very, very extroverted. He loved to be on the go constantly. He would work hard and then he wanted to go to a party, or to give a party. He wanted people around him, movement, action. My mother was an introvert and liked to have time to think about things, to read and to be alone. For an introvert, it often is painful to be around an extrovert who crowds himself and others in around you. Marriage is tough enough. It is now, it was then. Basically, my mother loved my father but had to have time away. My father always wanted her around him, to go places with him, to travel with him, far more than she could. I remember one time when we were living at Lloyd Neck they had left us at home and gone to some tennis party all day at the club, and Father wanted the two of them to go on to dinner someplace and then to go to a party; but she wanted to come home so she could spend some time with us before we were put to bed. That was how she thought; that was how he thought.[12]

Despite her dislike of Georgetown's crowded social scene, Clover soldiered on as Allen's official hostess and companion. The Que Street house became one of the prestige addresses on the Sunday afternoon "tea" circuit of cocktail parties and tennis matches. Her own sojourns to Switzerland and to visit her son aside, it was Allen who was most often away at work when callers came. Often visitors were of the clandestine variety who preferred to seek out the head of the CIA at his home rather than risk being seen at the gates of 2430 E Street. Throughout his term as America's spymaster, Dulles kept his telephone and address listed in the public directory, and the front door to the house was often left unlocked in the evening, just as the back gate at 23 Herrengasse had been. More than once, Clover presided at a formal dinner party at which she was introduced to none of the guests present, or they would have obvious cover identities.

"I had a lot of regard for Clover considering what she had to put up with," a family friend from CIA days notes. "Whenever it would get too crowded in the living room, or if the gathering got just too overwhelming for her, she would just go sit down for a while off by herself. I remember at one party that lasted too long, I found her sitting reading a book and so deep into it she had tuned us all out. When she got up, I went and looked—it was *Pilgrim's Progress.*"

One comfort to Clover was that Allen's romances dwindled as he got older and stopped altogether when he became DCI. Only one of his many women colleagues at the agency who were interviewed for this book acknowledged an affair with Allen, and she asserts that at the time he had not yet come on duty officially; it was just a brief fling before Clover moved to Washington in 1953. As she remembered years later, "I was alone and had some personal problems. Allen was so kind and was genuinely interested in my troubles. He was affectionate and understanding, and I needed that a lot at the time. We remained good friends after that. Sexual harassment? Probably by today's standards, who knows? But I enjoyed it, and he enjoyed it. And then, we went on with our lives."[13] Even Dulles's sharpest critics agree that whatever his past, Dulles stopped his womanizing when he became DCI and never took advantage of the women who worked in his secretarial pool or personal office. Barbara Pindar Smith, one of the long-serving secretaries in Dulles's office, is emphatic: "It never occurred to us that such a thing might happen. We knew him as 'The Director' and called him 'Mr. Dulles,' and, while he was cordial and friendly all the time, there never was any doubt that we all were there to work."[14]

The hearty Dulles cordiality worked its wonders throughout the young officer class of the agency. He routinely sought out officers who had just returned from abroad from some post or mission and demanded that they brief him on the journey even before they reported to their own section chiefs. He treated them with the same deep attention and personal concern as he had Fritz Kolbe and Hans Gisevius in Bern. He also had a child's enjoyment of the adventures of his officers.

One current officer recalls a youthful escapade that brought him to Dulles's attention. "I had been in Paris and went to meet a French communist official in what we thought was one of their safe addresses, a top floor apartment. All of a sudden, we heard the door downstairs crash open and footsteps running up toward us; I absolutely could not be caught in that apartment with that man, so out the window I climbed. I can still hear Dulles's laugh and the way he slapped the desk top as I told him how I had to shinny up a drain pipe and escape over the rooftops of Paris to get away. Then he called General [Charles Pearre] Cabell into the office and made me tell the story all over again."[15]

The director was not above a bit of subterfuge to instill *esprit de corps* in his young charges. The author heard numerous versions of this same event that happened to a number of young case officers who were summoned to his office on a matter of some importance. As one veteran agency official recalled:

> I had never met the director until that minute, and my division chief had not been called in to the meeting. It was just the two of us. And Mr. Dulles said, "Now, young man, what do you think about the situation here?" And when I started to mumble something about the information still being too soft, he cut me off. "I know all that, but what do you think is going on?" And so I took a deep breath and told him. He said, "Well, I disagree with you. Why do you think you're right?" So I defended myself as best I could. At that point the telephone rang and he answered it. To my horror, I heard him say, "Well, sir, I was just discussing that very matter with some of my staff. And here is what we think is going on." He repeated my conclusions and arguments and then hung up. "Well, young man, I hope you're right. That was the president of the United States that I was just

talking to." It scared me half to death. I never forgot the lesson that my judgments were ultimately going to turn up at the White House.[16]

Barbara Pindar Smith confirms that Dulles had a button under his desk that signaled her when he wanted her to ring his telephone, either to cut off a tiresome discussion or for some other bit of theater he wanted to perform. Yet there was never any doubt among the agency staffers that served on the front lines of the secret war that Allen Dulles was a sincere personal friend who cared deeply about their welfare and success.

DULLES'S HEALTH BEGAN to deteriorate slowly but markedly at about this time. He had been fifty-eight when he came to Washington as a consultant to "Beedle" Smith. During his eleven years at the agency, the bouts of brutally painful gout would hit without warning and often force him home to bed. During his first year as Smith's deputy director, Dulles had to take nearly a month's worth of sick leave from "The Kremlin." He began to rely on heavier doses of the drugs of the time, colchicine and Benamid, even though both medicines had strong side effects. Later he would become mildly diabetic, and, when his gout doctors switched him to the more powerful Butazoladin, he developed painful problems with edema and with his digestion.

It is all the more amazing then that Dulles continued to outwork everyone else in the agency. Unless he was confined to bed with one of his attacks, he routinely worked a twelve-hour day and often put in full days on the weekend. It was so well known in the government that Dulles was usually at his desk by nine on Sunday mornings that President Eisenhower would occasionally drop by "The Kremlin" unannounced before he went off to one of his golf outings. Barbara Pindar Smith recalls:

He was just so exuberant and so enthusiastic that even now I can't quite get used to the idea that he was more than sixty when I worked for him or that he had the gout; I knew he had gout, but I can't say I was ever aware of it, although he must have been in pain now and then. What does come to mind is that he would always get up and come to the door to greet whatever visitor came to see him. Whoever came into that room must have thought they were the most important person on earth at that moment because he was so sincerely glad to see them.

He came in at eight in the morning and never left before seven at night, and often then it was to go someplace else. We had to use a system of what we called "long notes" which we would give him. They would say so-and-so wants to see you about such-and-such and the tentative time for the appointment, and he could write in, yes-no, another time or whatever questions he wanted to know before the meeting. And he would take them home with him sometimes and get them all done. There was usually the staff meeting first thing in the morning, and then from that point on, it was one appointment after another. He would be over to the White House for a National Security Council meeting, or up on Capitol Hill, and there was a steady stream of people in and out of the office all day long. All the time, though, he kept reading memos and handing things back to us.

We were on duty until he left each night. He would come out from his office through my office to the front door of the DCI offices, and he would always stop at my desk and speak. But there was never any chitchat; it was very formal, and he was clearly an old-school gentleman around the secretaries. We all were thrilled to have those jobs.[17]

Undeniably, the years Dulles spent as head of covert operations and later as director were the golden years of the CIA's clandestine war against the Soviets. He was helped along by the weakening of British determination to be an equal voice of power in the Anglo-American partnership and by the arrival of Dwight Eisenhower and John Foster Dulles to take command of the conduct of the Cold War in Washington. The policy of containment was set aside. The world, after all, was a vastly different place from what it had been in the darkest postwar hours. World War III was not imminent, not in the conventional sense that had alarmed Truman, Marshall, and Acheson. Winston Churchill had returned to Number 10 Downing Street in 1951, but the implacable foe of Hitler's despotism had no desire to roll back the Iron Curtain he had decried, not at the cost of more British lives and treasure. Churchill's government argued a more conciliatory line toward Moscow; he also acknowledged the force of reality.

The president and his advisers believed they had no other choice but to go it alone and adopt an even more confrontational and aggressive line with the USSR. Stalin was dead, and the leadership that coalesced around Nikita Khrushchev was in a bellicose and dangerous mood. There was a bloody, inconclusive shooting war going on in Korea, and Americans were heartily sick of it. Years of temporizing (as it appeared) by Washington had resulted in millions of Europeans being dragged behind the Iron Curtain. From being the supreme atomic power in the world in 1945, America in 1953 had to face that it lagged behind Soviet progress with the hydrogen bomb. And the Soviet menace of long-range bombers brought a new threat many times more alarming than the fears of a conventional World War III clash of armies; the destruction of entire civilizations was now possible. The time had come for America to go on an offensive of its own. Covert operations should be increased in intensity and number. The Soviets should operate unopposed in no area, and maximum pressure must be applied to force the Russians into mistakes or, ideally, into retreat.

The covert operations started under the Smith directorate were expanded. Efforts to quell the Huk insurrection in the remote part of the Philippines became a laboratory experiment in winning the "hearts and minds" of the rural poor by setting up schools and clinics, and by pressuring corrupt local officials to reform. Ultimately the CIA, under the gifted Edward Lansdale, succeeded in placing the reformist Ramon Magsaysay in power there, and the rebellion faded. Other, more confrontational "ops" continued in the Balkans, Greece, and Turkey.

In the summer of 1953, as Dulles returned from his European inspection tour, he recommended that the agency take on a new target for operations—Iran. The old shah, who had been interned during much of World War II for his Nazi sympathies, had been replaced by his son, Reza Pahlevi. But the young shah proved to be weak and had let power be seized from him by the premier, a dramatically eccentric politician named Muhammad Mussadegh. Backed by a coalition that included the radical Communist Party (the Tudeh Party) that was feared to have alliances with the Soviets, Mussadegh had won widespread public support when he nationalized the lucrative Iranian oil industry, broke royalty agreements with British petroleum producers, and, finally, expelled Britain's diplomats. An important source of supply to the British petroleum industry had been cut abruptly; it must be restored.

C. M. Woodhouse, the British intelligence officer for the region, had been campaigning for some time to have Washington take a more active role in the deteriorating situation. "I was convinced from the first that any effort to forestall a Soviet coup in Iran would require a joint Anglo-American effort. The Americans would be more likely to work with us if they saw the problem as one of containing Communism rather than restoring the position of the [Anglo-Iranian Oil Company]," Woodhouse recalls.[18] One of the early converts to the plan was Kermit Roosevelt, the scholarly grandson of President Theodore Roosevelt and the Middle East desk chief in Washington for Frank Wisner, who had recently been renamed deputy director for plans. In July, Roosevelt secretly arrived in Teheran and convinced the frightened shah that both London and Washington would back him if he seized back control of the police and armed forces and then ousted Mussadegh. Operation Ajax was under way.

In the end, it all looked absurdly easy. Woodhouse had close ties with key members of the officer corps, and the rank and file soldiers were pro-shah as well. The Iranian Gendarmerie had been largely trained and directed during the war by H. Norman Schwarzkopf, the former head of the New Jersey State Police and the father of the future U.S. commander of the 1991 Desert Storm war with Iraq. At a cost of about $200,000 Roosevelt was able to organize massive public demonstrations in support of the shah, and the police suppressed the counterdemonstrations in support of Mussadegh. Emboldened by the show of public support, the shah issued the required decrees and ordered the arrest of Mussadegh, then fled to Rome to await results. Dulles flew there immediately, and with the help of the shah's more resolute sister, steadied his nerve during the ensuing turmoil. In the end, Operation Ajax was judged a complete victory for all concerned. American oil companies, along with the British, turned on the oil pumps again, and Iran got a more generous royalty agreement. The shah restored some measure of stability, and Foster Dulles pushed a $45 million aid program through Congress at once. The

Soviets (who may or may not have been planning a coup) got a visible black eye, and America established itself as a major force in the region until the shah was deposed in 1979.

Roosevelt's reward was to be offered a job to direct a similar "op" in Guatemala. He turned it down. In his report on Ajax, which he delivered personally to Eisenhower and the Dulleses, Roosevelt explicitly warned that the agency should not get into the habit of relying on covert intrusions into the affairs of other nations unless it was absolutely necessary for U.S. security. Covert "ops" were not a cheap and easy substitute for direct military intervention.

"I tried to tell them that these operations never work," Roosevelt said, "if you are going against the grain of events. You have to have so much going your way before you dare undertake them. First and foremost, you have to have the vast majority of the people behind you. We did in Iran. And you have to have a leadership that is better than the one in power and one that can take control. We had that in Iran in the army and the power structure; and the shah himself was a very gentle and reasonable person, although later he turned into a tough customer. In Guatemala it was a case of going against the grain, it was going against the situation and the way the country was developing." Roosevelt would resign from the CIA after rejecting another offer of an "op," this time to forcibly remove Colonel Gamal Abdel Nasser, one of the Egyptian officers who had ousted King Farouk in 1954. The American had befriended Nasser in the early days of the revolution and maintained that he could be kept friendly to the United States despite his clear anti-British, pro-Soviet stance. "Foster [Dulles] became too demanding. He had the idea that I could solve almost anything, anywhere. That just wasn't true. Allen was upset about it and recognized eventually that I couldn't take it any longer. Allen tried to protect me and he would try to reason with Foster as long as he thought he could, and then he would give up and go to ground."[19]

The Guatemala operation, led by rising case officer Tracy Barnes, with Dulles protégé Richard Bissell as overseer, was an even more spectacular success because it involved such little expenditure of money and manpower. Washington had become alarmed when Jacobo Arbenz was blamed for the assassination of a more moderate political opponent when he took power in the small Central American country. Arbenz and his wife were believed to be ardent communists, and they confirmed Washington's worst fears when the regime moved to nationalize the extensive properties that the United Fruit Company had developed there. More persuasive was the president's brother, Milton Eisenhower, who returned from a fact-finding mission in Latin America and convinced Ike and Foster that Guatemala was on the verge of becoming the first communist outpost in the Western Hemisphere. Guatemala by the autumn of 1953 had built the largest military force in that part of the world, and when in May 1954 the CIA spotted a boat unloading a shipment of arms and equipment from Czechoslovakia, the White House decided to move. Direct military intervention was impossible because the custom of sending U.S. Marines into Latin Caribbean countries had long been politically offensive at home and abroad. So Operation PB Success, as the venture was optimistically called, was put into effect.

Frank Wisner was assigned to put a covert team into neighboring Honduras to support a rebel faction headed by Colonel Carlos Castillo Armas, an army officer in exile with a few followers. The team included David Attlee Phillips, E. Howard Hunt, and other young CIA operatives who would learn much about the craft of insurgency on this job. The CIA provided a clandestine radio station that broadcast from Honduras a series of warnings that vastly overinflated the forces (about 150 in all) and popularity of the Armas rebellion and issued dire warnings about the impending collapse of the Arbenz regime. Three elderly B-26

bombers were flown by CIA contract aviators, and the agency provided the trucks that carried the rebel forces unopposed over the
border into their homeland on June 1, 1954; Castillo Armas rode in
the lead of this ragtag caravan in a battered station wagon. The procession stalled six miles inside the border, and for three weeks there
was stalemate, with Armas unwilling to move forward and Arbenz
unable to leave Guatemala City to attack. Finally, one of the B-26
planes flew over the capital and dropped a single bomb, while the
CIA radio station broadcast signals that portrayed Armas's soldiers
as moving into position on the outskirts of the city. That was
enough. Arbenz resigned and sought sanctuary at the Mexican
Embassy, which was quickly jammed with hundreds of his supporters. Castillo Armas and his band were flown to the airfield outside of town and marched in triumph to take over the government.

His triumph was more than matched ten days later when the
principal CIA officers involved in Operation PB Success were
brought to the White House to conduct a full briefing before the
envious eyes of the Joint Chiefs of Staff and the cabinet. At the
end of the briefing, an obviously pleased and impressed President
Eisenhower shook their hands and then turned to Dulles.
"Thanks, Allen," he said. "And thanks to all of you. You've averted
a Soviet beachhead in our hemisphere."[20] Whatever doubts Allen
Dulles may have shared with Kermit Roosevelt about the wisdom
of toppling unfriendly governments were put to rest.

Strictly speaking, the CIA did not undertake to repeat its
Iranian and Guatemalan triumphs until 1958, when it backed an
abortive effort to overthrow the Sukarno government of
Indonesia. But neither of the Dulles brothers nor Frank Wisner
was in the mood for such fine distinctions. The CIA undertook a
stepped-up campaign of covert intrusions into the political and
economic lives of a whole host of other nations—friendly,
unfriendly, and close ally, alike.

There is a temptation to look at this period of the Dulles-CIA history as the golden time for elitist schoolboys who went on a Cold War rampage of their own devising and became, in time, a secret government within the government of the United States. It is noted that men like Wisner and his deputies, Tracy Barnes and Desmond FitzGerald, were all from the prep school, Harvard, Wall Street background; these men are thereby turned into schoolboys on an adventure in which other, less privileged people pay the cost of their mistakes. Indeed there are those who today argue that the Cold War itself was an American miscalculation spurred by these selfish aristos.

But to sustain that argument is to ignore other truths of the time. While there was a high Ivy League content to the agency at the time, it was neither exclusive nor overwhelmingly dominant. For every Wisner, Barnes, and FitzGerald, there were men like Richard Helms, William Colby, Raymond Rocca, Harry Rositzke, and Sam Halpern, whose backgrounds were far from elitist and whose energies were just as fiercely dedicated to the CIA's mandate. The other point is that the CIA under Allen Dulles was far from the "invisible government" it is accused of being—not with Foster Dulles at State, not with Dwight Eisenhower in the White House. If the agency undertook reckless missions, it was because the president of the United States so ordered for motives far beyond the reach of its action service team leaders. Vietnam, which was far away from the European theater beloved by most CIA veterans, is a case worth recalling.

In 1954 the Eisenhower administration agreed to play a more active role in Indochina. France was about to withdraw from Vietnam after an eight-year war with the Viet Minh had ended with the disastrous defeat at Dien Bien Phu. As in Korea, a demarcation line was drawn, this time at the seventeenth parallel, which had established a cease-fire that allowed the communists to take hold in the north. Edward Lansdale was sent to Saigon to repeat his win in the Philippines. When it became obvious that Viet Minh leader Ho Chi Minh would not abandon his Marxist intentions, Lansdale in 1955 engineered a popular election that picked Ngo Dinh Diem as the first president of the Republic of Vietnam. But just as Diem had resisted both the French and the Viet Minh, now he went his own way as soon as Lansdale had trained his presidential bodyguard. There would be no noisy Filipino-style democracy for Vietnam. All too quickly the rule invoked by Kermit Roosevelt began to prove true in a hundred small, worrying ways. Corruption flourished and quickly immobilized both government and the economy; groups once loyal to Diem out of fear of the communists drifted away. Lansdale returned to Washington to lobby Foster Dulles for some direct American pressure on the Saigon regime, but to no avail. Despairing, he requested a transfer home, and within a year, the first North Vietnamese terror campaigns erupted in the south.

One of the problems in confronting the mistakes in Vietnam was that the country was so far away. Europe was still the major theater of confrontation between Washington's "Kremlin" and Moscow's Kremlin, and Dulles had thrown himself totally into that struggle. By 1954 he had organized the agency the way he wanted it. As his deputy, he had chosen Lieutenant General Charles Pearre Cabell, a fifty-year-old former chief of the air force's intelligence arm and a skilled administrator. Dulles entrusted to Cabell the broad oversight of the CIA's rapidly building staff (personnel would peak in the late 1950s at around fifteen thousand) and global activities; in Colonel "Red" White, both Dulles and Cabell had an able administrative chief who held the administrative controls over the operations side of the agency and so worked more closely with Dulles himself. Sherman Kent continued to refine and improve the National Intelligence Estimates and, like

James Angleton in counterintelligence, jealously prevented any jurisdictional intrusions except by Dulles himself. Operations, both collection and covert action, remained the province of Wisner and Richard Helms. As one wit observed, Dulles had organized the agency so that every important job was the responsibility of somebody other than himself. The genius of that arrangement was that it left him free to be involved in the covert operations side of the agency—the side that most interested the president and Foster, the side where the quickest results could be enjoyed, and the side where the biggest risks of disaster lurked.

The result was that Dulles, with his surplus of energy, was all over the agency, popping into conferences, calling case officers directly, and looking over everyone's shoulder. He showed no compunction about bypassing the very men he had made responsible for departments and dragging low-level case officers up the hill from the "temporaries" for a long chat about some far-off place or some obscure political figure. Richard Bissell, who later succeeded Wisner as deputy director for plans, once objected to being bypassed when Dulles had called in some young officer without telling him. Bissell recalled, "I told him, you can't operate that way. You have to go through me to my people, otherwise how am I to know what's going on in my own department? And Allen really jerked me up. He was quite angry. He said he would talk to anyone in this agency about anything, anytime. 'If I tell somebody to do something or to send an order, it will come across your desk and you can object then. If I want to talk to somebody I will, and it is your job to find out about it, not mine to tell you or ask you.' And he was right, of course."[21]

Dulles's first priority in those early days was penetrating Eastern Europe and especially the Soviet Union itself. Since 1949 there had been an uninterrupted flow of agents dropped by parachute or sent by other clandestine means into the Iron Curtain region, either to set up reporting stations by radio or to undertake specific tasks. Most of these were refugees displaced by the war, who could be trained and dropped with credible cover stories back in their homelands; it was a matter of pride to Richard Helms that the complex set of identity documents that the agency provided its operatives were virtually discovery-proof. Nevertheless, the return on the investment in training, the risk to manpower, and the cost of failure was unsatisfactory in the extreme. Agents almost always were arrested eventually. Sometimes the Soviets would turn the operators around and use them to send fabrications back.

Defectors to the CIA came from various communist intelligence services, and Dulles relied on his experience with Fritz Kolbe and Hans Gisevius to get around James Angleton's visceral distrust of "walk-ins." But the Soviets had defectors from the West as well. One of the most publicized CIA-MI6 joint ventures was to dig a tunnel into East Berlin and to tap into Soviet military telephone cables. Operation Gold cost $30 million but produced such a flood of precise military and political information that both services could scarcely manage the traffic. The trouble was that a British traitor named George Blake had tipped Moscow off about the tunnel almost at once. With remarkable restraint, the Soviets let the telephone taps stay in place for more than eleven months before they "accidentally discovered" the operation and shut it down.

Getting intelligence was only one part of the CIA's job. What is made out of the raw information is the final test of any spy agency. Quite early, the analysts of Sherman Kent's National Intelligence Estimates staff had concluded that the military risk to the United States did not lie in Soviet conventional air power. Against alarmist predictions put together by air force intelligence (in part to justify its own demands for bomber development appropriations) the Russians had not pushed all-out to build the kind of substratospheric jets that the United States was building. Instead, the National Intelligence Estimates began to warn with steady precision that Moscow was putting considerable resources into the development of guided missiles based on the old blueprints (and using many of the captive German scientists) from Hitler's V-rocket program. When the Pentagon adjusted its view of the Soviet danger to take in the missile threat, it tended to overestimate the range and payload of the rockets under construction. Alarm was widespread throughout Washington that the Russians were about to put all their effort into intercontinental ballistic missiles that could hurl megatons of nuclear warheads at the United States. Kent and his analysts waged a steady campaign against this alarmist view, coming up with proof after proof that the Soviets were trying to develop a tactical mix that included medium- and intermediate-range rockets that would be usable in Europe or any other conventional theater of war.

Another consideration was that times had changed. As Harry Rositzke, the Munich station chief at the time, describes it:

Air dispatch of radio-equipped agents virtually ceased in 1954. Not only were the losses too high and the expenditure of effort too great for the results achieved, but the Soviet orbit was beginning to open up after Stalin's death and the war scare in Washington had toned down somewhat. Finally, too, illegal overflights violating Soviet terrain were being assessed for what they had always been: a direct provocation of the new Soviet leadership…. [T]he solution would ultimately lie in the air. A high-flying airplane with a precise camera could produce in a few hours more visual data than a hundred agents could in a year of observing and reporting.[22]

With the development of the U-2 spy plane, Allen Dulles and the CIA were about to push the craft of intelligence from back alleys and listening posts into the space age.

CHAPTER FOURTEEN

1958–1960

*"...it should not be forgotten that the Director of the CIA and
the Secretary of State happen to be brothers."*
—*British Foreign Office memo*

BOTH FOSTER DULLES and the president were haunted by their
inability to see behind the Iron Curtain. There was no way to
know what was going on in vast tracts of the East Bloc or within
the Soviet Union itself. Soviet diplomats in the United States
openly bought maps and rented airplanes for photomapping
jaunts around major American ports and industrial centers; by
comparison, the CIA was not actually sure where the major railroad lines went in parts of the USSR. The fear of Pearl Harbor
raised its head again. Even though no one really believed the
alarmists at the Pentagon, no one—not even Allen Dulles—could
be sure what was going on.

In the spring of 1954, Eisenhower recruited James Killian,
president of the Massachusetts Institute of Technology, to organize
a crash program to examine ways to put science to work for
America's security. Killian responded by assembling a task force of
forty-six top scientists who were assigned specific areas of technology and science to examine for possible development into defense
and intelligence use. One of those panels was chaired by Dr. Edwin
Land, the reclusive inventor of the Polaroid-Land camera and a host

of other photography and lens patents. Land was sure he could develop a camera that held a huge canister of film and used the biggest, most accurate lens he could devise.

By coincidence, Kelly Johnson, a legend in aircraft design, had been asked to submit a plan for an air force study for a high-altitude jet surveillance craft. Johnson ran the history-making "Skunk Works" for the Lockheed Aircraft Corporation, which had turned out so many World War II and postwar military aircraft. Operating mostly on speculation, Johnson had come up with a wide-winged airplane that could fly at more than seventy thousand feet for as much as four thousand miles. The Pentagon could not decide whether to proceed with it. Johnson sought out Allen Dulles, whom he had met through Charles Wrightsman, a Texas oilman and director of Lockheed who was an old friend of Dulles's. Clover and Allen Dulles frequently took winter holidays at the Wrightsmans' villa in Palm Beach, Florida, and helped Wrightsman publicize Lockheed's early *Constellation* and *Superconstellation* jet passenger planes by taking numerous inaugural flights abroad in them.

Here again, Dulles's willingness to reach out to the private sector for unofficial assistance underscores his wide range of personal contacts and his unique willingness to look past bureaucratic procedures and focus on end results. That the private sector responded without hesitation—be they Hollywood moguls, Wall Street financiers, labor union leaders, or industrial chief executives—shows how less cynical those times were and how real the threat of war was to most people.

Land and Killian agreed with Dulles that putting together a high-altitude plane with the inventor's giant camera was too hot a project to be held up until the full Killian Committee report could be presented to the White House. The three went directly to President Eisenhower and, to their surprise, received an immediate go-ahead. One restriction was imposed by Ike—no American military personnel could be used to fly missions over Soviet airspace. The flights were provocative and could cause serious trouble with Moscow. But the old lure of plausible deniability persuaded Ike that the final insult of U.S. military involvement could be avoided. In subsequent meetings the president quickly agreed to a $35 million budget for the project, and the project was handed over to the CIA to run because it, alone of the federal agencies, had permission to issue contracts to single source providers without having to go through the cumbersome and insecure open bidding process. Despite the logic of the move, air force officials began to suspect they had been outmaneuvered by Dulles.

If the U-2 spy plane project was an informal way of doing business, it was typical of the way top policy decisions were made by President Eisenhower and his closest advisers. "The Boss," as his aides called him, firmly believed in a highly organized staff structure to keep watch on the details. But like Allen Dulles, Eisenhower wanted to be free to cut across jurisdictional lines and take prompt action on his own. What quickly evolved was a sort of lopsided triangle of foreign policy decision-making with the president at the top, then Foster Dulles and, slightly below, Allen Dulles and the CIA. Below them was a series of advisory groups and their staffs including the cabinet, the National Security Council, and an Operations Coordination Board (which consisted of undersecretaries of the various departments). The rise of the CIA as a major foreign policy force stunned other intelligence services, particularly British intelligence. Anthony Eden was so puzzled by the way the Eisenhower administration made up its mind that he ordered a secret study by Sir Roger Makins, which stated that the old way of doing business through diplomats was over:

> I draw two main conclusions. First that the State
> Department does not alone determine, nor even

always accurately reflects, the administration's attitude in respect of particular issues; and secondly that for this reason it is essential for my staff to continue to keep in close touch with agencies other than the State Department in the field of foreign relations.... The absorption of the United States with Communism and means of combating it enhances the neglect of the diplomatic aspect in favour of other aspects of foreign policy. The United States Government is not really interested in the maintenance of relations as such with the governments of the Satellites, and perhaps not always with that of the Soviet Union; it has declined to recognize the Peking regime. American policy towards the Communists is rather a mixture of research, propaganda and intelligence operations in which non-governmental assistance is widely sought and used.... It is erroneous to regard the CIA as concerned with covert operations only. It is in fact the most important research organ of the United States Government in the connected fields of national security and foreign affairs, in which it operates on *a larger scale* than does the Department of State [emphasis added].... Both the research and the operational sides of the agency have a share in the making of recommendations on policy which are submitted to the National Security Council. Independent experts such as Mr. George Kennan and Mr. Richard Bissell, are now working with or for the CIA.... A clear distinction should be drawn between the influence and role of the State Department and such and the influence and role of Mr. [Foster] Dulles personally.... As far as we can tell, Mr. Dulles has access to a considerable amount of information not

available to, let alone submitted by, the relevant bureau
of the State Department. In this connection it should
not be forgotten that the Director of the CIA and the
Secretary of State happen to be brothers.[1]

Selecting Richard Bissell to direct the U-2 development program was another of the ad hoc decisions that marked the
Eisenhower-Dulles triumvirate. Richard Mervin Bissell, Jr., was an
economist by training, not an aerospace project manager. He had
impressed a generation of Yale undergraduates (including the
Bundy brothers) by teaching a course on Keynesian economics
from his own notes taken at lectures by Keynes at the London
School of Economics. After World War II, he had earned even
greater regard for his administrative skills when he worked on the
Marshall Plan program in Europe. His first job upon joining the
CIA was as an aide to Frank Wisner on the Guatemala operation.
Bissell was an undeniable favorite of Dulles. He combined a bril-
liant academic mind with a gritty toughness, and he was willing
to undertake anything the director ordered.

On a rainy November 24, 1954, the Wednesday before
Thanksgiving Day, Bissell was planning, like most CIA staff, to get
away early to join his family. "Allen came back from the White
House and called me in," Bissell recalled. "He said there was going
to be a staff meeting over at the Pentagon at four o'clock and he
wanted me to sit in. When I went, it was obvious that very little
thought had been given to just how the project was to be brought
off, how it was to be organized."[2] Bissell's organizational techniques
fit neatly with the informal preferences of Allen Dulles. Rather than
build a formal bureaucracy to oversee the U-2 project, he turned
much of the actual design, construction, and testing over to
Lockheed and Polaroid and let them get on with the job. The results
were astonishing. Just eight months after Eisenhower's decision, the

first U-2 spy plane was rolled out of its top-secret hangar in
California for a test flight in July 1955; the cost of the first fleet of
twenty-two U-2s delivered in the next twelve months was $3 mil-
lion below the original $35 million estimate.

The results were just as impressive. The plane's ability to
climb to 85,000 feet put it beyond the range of the most advanced
Soviet jet fighters. The three thousand–mile range (it would be
lengthened later) meant it could soar over the Russian heartland
from Pakistan to bases in Scandinavia without refueling. At its film-
ing altitude of 55,000 feet, the special seven-lens camera Land had
designed could record a 125-mile strip of land in a single frame and
resolve details so fine that it could determine the height of a man.
The U-2 also carried equipment that monitored and recorded the
new generation of "Elint," electronic intelligence about radar and
radio beacons that pointed to Soviet missile bases. The payoff was
that the CIA was able to validate Eisenhower's position that the
Soviets had not gained a dangerous advantage in guided missile
production, and the plane's photographs began to gain wide use
and importance as a strategic tool in other theaters of the Cold War
conflict. In the late summer of 1956, the British, French, and Israelis
had caught the White House off-guard with a military attack to
regain control of the Suez Canal and to force Colonel Nasser from
power in Egypt. London and Paris were, in turn, surprised when
both Foster Dulles and President Eisenhower resolutely refused to
back the raid on the Suez or join in the bloody Egyptian-Israeli war
that followed. At least part of the U.S. resolve came from U-2 photographs (including a dramatic set showing the British bombing
the Cairo airport) which convinced the White House that American
forces should not be fed into the dangerous—and ultimately
failed—venture.

At least part of the reason Dulles and the CIA could operate
on such a freewheeling basis was that he and the agency had become

a magnet for a host of able young academics in the Bissell tradition. It also became popular among young labor union leaders and peace activists of the 1950s to work for the agency. Dating back to his days with Arthur Goldberg and Gerry Van Arkle in the OSS, Dulles had kept close personal ties to key union leaders such as George Meany of the AFL-CIO and Walter Reuther of the United Auto Workers union. He recognized that the American labor leaders, like the European socialists, had goals that were in direct competition with Soviet communism; many of the American leaders also had close personal ties with various ethnic groups at home and abroad.

While the ghost of Alger Hiss forever haunted Foster and kept him from adequately defending State Department liberals from the accusations of Senator Joseph McCarthy and his staff, Allen Dulles felt no such fear. Thus he was able to recruit liberal journalist Tom Braden for an Office of Policy Coordination project to support cooperative labor unions, both American and foreign, as a bulwark against the Moscow brand of union propaganda. Dealing with union officials who had tasted from the Marxist well in previous years did not bother Dulles in the least as long as they would do what was needed to support the CIA-sponsored International Confederation of Free Trade Unions and other national union groups in Italy, France, and West Germany. When Braden left the agency in 1954, he was replaced by Cord Meyer, who had first met Dulles when they argued against each other in a radio debate in the 1930s about whether the League of Nations could ever be the foundation for a world federal government. Meyer remained active in the World Federalist movement and in those days probably could not have gotten a job anywhere else in Washington except the CIA. Dulles, however, personally recruited him to expand Braden's program to embrace pro-Western groups of students, intellectuals, and promising young anticommunist politicians throughout the world.

One of the Braden-Meyer triumphs was getting philosopher
Sidney Hook to help establish the magazine *Encounter* under the
aegis of the agency-supported Congress of Cultural Freedom.
Published in London and boasting editors like Melvin Lasky and
Stephen Spender, *Encounter* provided welcomed income and a
prestige showcase for the political writings of a generation of
young leftist political figures who would come of age in the
Labour governments of Harold Wilson and James Callaghan
twenty years later. It was said, in jest, that in the mid-1950s there
were enough CIA operatives among high officials of French
unions and political parties to constitute a majority in the
General Assembly. William Bundy, who later was a top security
adviser to both Presidents Kennedy and Johnson, recalled his days
as an analyst for the CIA:

> I represented the liberal Democratic Party attitude of
> the day, and he [Dulles] understood that. Dulles was
> not an opportunist nor a zealot in any way. That gave
> him the capacity to run an agency that was incredibly
> ecumenical. In that he was vastly different from Foster.
> Right through the CIA there were people decidedly
> more liberal than many of the Republicans who were in
> charge. That explains people like Cord Meyer and Tom
> Braden. Sherman Kent's brother was chairman of the
> Democratic Party in California during those days. They
> were very liberal people who never would have been
> able to work there if there was in inflexible mind at the
> top. Allen saw the possibilities and knew the kinds of
> Europeans to whom the agency could reach out. He
> knew the difference between a socialist and a commu-
> nist, and he knew in Europe that the socialists were the
> very kind of people the communists hated most.

I never saw Allen indicate the slightest degree of prejudice toward any person or minority group. He did not have hang-ups like that. Everyone felt they had a special relationship with him. That is a very unusual quality. But he listened to you. You felt he knew what you were talking about and that he had his own thoughts about it. I spent most of my agency career with Robert Amory in the business of getting estimates to the [National Security Council], and our people were pretty liberal on the whole. On more than one occasion we had NIEs [National Intelligence Estimates] that were very critical of Foster Dulles's leadership. But this sort of thing Allen could take without getting uptight about it.[3]

The old guard conservatives in the GOP railed at the Dulles brothers for being "New Deal Republicans" and particularly at Allen for filling the intelligence agency with such an obvious mix of liberals and exotic refugees. Far from being a fraternity house of "old boys" from privileged and aristocratic backgrounds, the Dulles CIA was the "elite," liberal, and university-select band that he had urged on the Congress in 1947. It was true that nearly one-quarter of the agency's top officials had at least one degree from Harvard, but an equal percentage had advanced or postgraduate degrees from other universities; 40 percent of the staff were women (very high for any government agency in those days), and three-quarters of all personnel in the mid-1950s had some foreign language skills. The agency would remain virtually all-white and mostly male at the top ranks for twenty years past the Dulles directorate, but at the time, the CIA without doubt was a liberal haven for the young, the gifted, and the ambitious of both sexes.

Part of the agency's high morale in those days was based on an intense loyalty by the younger staff to Dulles himself. This loyalty was best shown in the incident when Senator McCarthy suddenly turned his Red Scare guns on the CIA. In the summer of 1953, McCarthy was scrambling to obscure a minor scandal within his own staff; one of his lawyers had made a speech that accused the Protestant clergy of the United States of being procommunist. To deflect the outcry, McCarthy announced that there were more than one hundred communists inside the CIA and that he was going to unmask them.

The first target was William Bundy, the son of wartime State Department official Harvey Bundy and the brother of Dulles's Dewey campaign colleague McGeorge Bundy. Bill Bundy was just the kind of liberal intellectual that set the right wing's teeth on edge. He had joined the agency in 1951 and had become an assistant to Robert Amory, the deputy director for intelligence. In the time between leaving the army at the end of the war and joining the agency, Bundy had practiced law with Dean Acheson's law firm and had married one of Acheson's daughters, thus becoming a brother-in-law to Alger Hiss. When Hiss was indicted for perjury in the case, Bundy contributed $400 to his defense fund. Later, he recalled:

I had been [Amory's] staff assistant to the [National Security Council] for two years or so when it was given oversight of the Atomic Energy Commission. That meant I had to get a top-secret "Q" clearance. I had told Allen long before that I had made the contributions, and Allen had said he understood, and the agency investigation put together a file that said I was okay. I did not look mole-ish. But then this "Q" clearance thing had to be sent over to the FBI, which checked on the AEC. I am sure of this next, but I can't prove it. But within forty-eight hours of my file going

to the FBI, Roy Cohn had his hands on it. The next
thing I knew, Bob Amory told me to get out of town
and stay lost for a while. So I went up to Massachusetts
and played golf with my father.[4]

Cohn, who was chief counsel to McCarthy's investigating
subcommittee, had telephoned Walter Pforzheimer, the agency's
legal counsel for congressional relations, at nine o'clock in the
morning to say that Bundy must come before the panel in less
than two hours. Allen Dulles was locked up in a National Security
Council meeting at the White House, and Eisenhower never permitted interruptions. Acting quickly, Pforzheimer made sure
Bundy got lost and then confronted an enraged Cohn with the
bland statement that his quarry had already left on a holiday trip
and could not be reached. It was a tough day for Pforzheimer;
Cohn immediately threatened to subpoena him to take Bundy's
place at the witness table and explain his absence. It would have
been folly to lie to a congressional committee, both for the agency
and for the lawyer's career.

Meanwhile, Dulles had returned to "The Kremlin," and
while Cohn raged in repeated telephone calls to Pforzheimer, the
decision was made. Cohn could subpoena whom he liked, but
only the DCI answered to congressional committees "where
appropriate." If a subpoena came, Dulles planned to take it to the
White House. But a telephone call to the president made it clear
that he did not relish a challenge to Congress's right to investigate.
Dulles, at Amory's suggestion, turned to Vice President Richard
Nixon, who supported him in his determination to protect CIA
employees; when the summons did come, Dulles merely passed it
on to the vice president, who had it quashed.

Rather than let matters rest there, Dulles met behind closed
doors with McCarthy and stressed that the security of the agency

would be seriously harmed if its staff were dragged in the public limelight. As a sop to the senator's prickly pride, Dulles agreed to set up procedures with the subcommittee so that it could obtain information about CIA personnel without actually calling them up in public. But he demanded that McCarthy turn over specific evidence of any subversion, and the senator grudgingly promised to provide damaging information about Bundy; he never did. The two men posed for news photographers, and Dulles made conciliatory statements to help matters along. The press treated the affair as a serious defeat for McCarthy, who, as the *New York Times* asserted, "retreated in effect from the most direct challenge he has made so far—that the top secret CIA is not 'immune to investigation'...."[5] This was by no means the end of McCarthy's attempts to bring the agency to heel. Pforzheimer spent much of the next two years deflecting aides Cohn and Robert Kennedy until, finally, McCarthy was removed from the subcommittee's chairmanship. Although Dulles was careful not to sneer publicly at the senator, he did recognize the significance of having McCarthy give way on Bundy. A mass meeting of CIA staff was called, and Dulles reviewed details of the confrontation and what it meant for the agency's own sense of security.

The Bundy case was an important element but not the only one in the development of a tremendous *esprit de corps* that characterized the agency in those days. The CIA felt it could go anywhere and undertake any task set by the president. By the late 1950s the battle orders were changed; it was not enough merely to fight the communists wherever they attempted to gain power. America had a duty to promote democracy and freedom everywhere; that was the best defense against Moscow. The lesson of Guatemala had been taken to heart; the seeds of Marxist revolt against vulnerable right-wing tyrants must be headed off. The corrupt and brutal dictatorships of Rafael Trujillo in the

Dominican Republic, Anastasio Somoza in Nicaragua, and Fulgencio Batista in Cuba were examined.

TROUBLE CAME, insofar as Allen Dulles and the CIA were concerned, when Eisenhower and Foster Dulles in their final years began to alter their foreign policy goals. The president and his secretary of state began to muse about the prospects of attempting a peaceful dialogue with the less threatening Nikita Khrushchev. At the same time they tried to micromanage the smaller annoyances of a fretful world scene. America began to interfere in insoluble conflicts in Africa and the Middle East, to topple a distasteful dictator here and there, and to try to pick winners among competing insurgent groups. The prospect of replacing tyrants with acceptable moderates, even socialists, began to be studied in earnest. A promising young lawyer named Fidel Castro, Eisenhower was told, was organizing a coup against Batista in Cuba; there were others elsewhere.

Eisenhower most wanted system and order from his intelligence director. He wanted an Army G-2 operation that guarded against his being caught by surprise, the cardinal sin of a good general. Also, he wanted a routine of systematic reviews of world problems, a statement of probabilities, and a menu of suggested responses from which he would then choose—with Foster Dulles's advice. When he gave orders, he wanted prompt and literal implementation. Sometimes he got the feeling that Allen Dulles would receive his marching orders and then go slightly off in a direction of his own choosing. The president also lamented that while Dulles had a pretty good grip in the CIA, he had not exerted his full range of power over the other intelligence services. Better coordination was what Ike wanted—more order, more control.

An almost nonstop series of studies, watch committees, and operations control boards were put in place to exert more power over the entire intelligence process. But Ike also knew that Dulles was dead set against a turf war of that kind. This annoyed Eisenhower, but, as he confessed, there was not much he could do about it. "I am not going to be able to change Allen. I have two alternatives, either to get rid of him and appoint someone who will assert more authority or keep him with his limitations. I'd rather have Allen as my chief intelligence officer with his limitations than anyone else I know."[6]

Part of Allen Dulles's acknowledged contribution to Eisenhower's policy decision process lay in his unique relationship with Foster Dulles. One of the reasons historians have not devoted more than obvious comment on the ties between Foster and Allen lies in the maddening fact that, while there are exhaustive telephone logs of their conversations, those exchanges through the years had condensed into monosyllables to the point that they verged on mental telepathy.[7] But whenever they both were in Washington (the two were exhaustive travelers) it was rare that two hours passed without one calling the other. Even after official business hours, the dialogue continued. Since the CIA complex of buildings at 2430 E Street was near the State Department, one brother could easily swing his car by the other's office, and they would ride home together; most often, if it was Foster's limousine, they would remain idling outside 2723 Que Street deep in conversation. Sometimes, if events were developing in dramatic fashion somewhere in the world, the telephone calls would go on into the night, or Allen would drive in the evening to the apartment that Foster and Janet kept in the Shoreham Hotel.

Two impressions stand out from the reams of summaries of these telephone calls, which long-suffering secretaries listening in on extensions had to take down. One is the extraordinarily large range of topics that the two discussed. A single call could deal with half a dozen developments in as many countries. By the end of the

day the Dulles brothers would have surveyed the globe. They criticized each other's speech drafts and counseled each other on press
relations and congressional testimony. It was as if thirty years had
been rolled back and the Dulles brothers were back in the Crillon
Hotel fighting the rearguard battles for Woodrow Wilson's vision of
world peace. Through it all, the second impression runs of how
hermetically sealed they were from the more traditional pressures
of government foreign policy; the only outside opinion they really
valued was that of "the Boss"—Eisenhower.

Then, too, no government bureaucrat ever had such a blank
check as that handed Allen Dulles by a succession of House and
Senate leaders of both parties. Part of this *laissez-faire* attitude
stemmed from the general American ambivalence toward espionage; most members of Congress in those days agreed that spying was a necessary government undertaking, but few wanted to
confront what was involved. But it also is true that Dulles, perhaps more than any other department chief of that time, worked
hard at and was successful in winning friends for himself and the
agency that was so closely identified with him. Wayne G. Jackson,
Dulles's official biographer for the CIA internal study, describes a
now-familiar pattern of the DCI's ability to win converts:

> [Dulles] had a vast number of friends and acquain-
> tances; he corresponded with many and made a great
> many people feel that they were making valuable con-
> tributions to the national welfare by passing on their
> thoughts, observations, or impressions. This was true
> even when the material in their letters or reports—and
> his files contain many of them—was of a most banal
> sort. All the people who worked near him felt that he
> saw too many visitors and made too many speeches. If
> taxed on this score, his answer invariably was that the

public relations of the agency required it. And there were few who did not recognize his expertise and "feel" in this area. It should be noted again that he was a past master in the art of appearing to talk frankly about sensitive information. He would seem to be skating on the thin edge of indiscretion. But when what he had actually said or written was recalled, it was evident that he had cloaked generally known information with an appearance of sensitivity.

His relations with the press were, with a few exceptions, excellent. He had his favorites, but with them he exercised his highly developed ability to give the impression of candor and freedom of information while revealing nothing.... His attention to the Congress, and to individual members, was constant and successful. This was by no means limited to those Congressmen who served on committees which had a direct responsibility for CIA.... [H]e often offered to brief Congressmen who were going on foreign travels and asked them to report their observations and impressions when they returned. This obviously made the travelers feel more important.... His active social life included circles in which he saw and established cordial relations with important members of the Congress, particularly Senators.[8]

The funding for the CIA in those days was buried in the appropriations for the Pentagon, State Department, and other agencies, but Dulles, like every other bureaucrat, had to trek up to Capitol Hill each year to make his pitch. The jurisdiction over the agency was in the House and Senate Appropriations Committees, each of which had a subcommittee on the armed services that considered CIA funding in secret session, often without any staff present. Dulles, in fact, paid little attention to the staffs of the congressional committees, to the profound annoyance of his chief of liaison to the lawmakers, Walter Pforzheimer. To be sure, he did not need to. During most of this time, the armed services panels were chaired by the full committee chairmen—Representative Clarence Cannon of Missouri and Senator Richard Russell of Georgia. What they said, went. Colonel "Red" White, the head of administration, often accompanied Dulles to these hearings, lugging along a black loose-leaf book prepared in anticipation of questions on specific situations around the world. He remembers:

The director always began with a summary of the world situation in the most general terms. But the way he said it, it sounded very inside and confidential. Usually, that would be it. Clarence Cannon more often than not would say, "Now there is one question I want to ask. Do you have enough money to do your business properly?" And Dulles would say, "I think, Mr. Chairman, I have asked for as much as I can spend wisely. If I get into trouble, I will come back to your committee." And Cannon would bang his gavel, "Meeting adjourned." That was that.

Sometimes, a congressman or senator would actually ask a question, usually something they had read in the newspaper. Just as often as not, Senator Russell or Cannon would interrupt, "Now don't tell us about that if we don't need to know." If he actually had to refer to the black book, Dulles would usually make a big deal about the confidential nature of what he was about to reveal. He would ask for a delay while I was sent out of the room. Me! I'd brought the damned

thing into the room in the first place. I knew everything in that book. But out I'd go, and they ate it up.[9]

On one occasion Walter Pforzheimer, the legislative counsel,
had to track down Chairman Cannon to find out why appropriations hearings for the CIA had not been scheduled. Waylaying the
congressman in the Capitol's Statuary Hall, Pforzheimer pressed
his case but was disturbed by the response. Some members of the
committee had said they would like to attend a session and ask
questions. That would not do. But there had to be a hearing,
Pforzheimer insisted; Dulles intended to ask for a 10 percent budget increase for the next year. Cannon stepped back into one of the
alcoves of the hall, beckoned Pforzheimer to follow, and said, "All
right, Walter, you tell Mr. Dulles that he had his hearing and that he
got his 10 percent."[10]

Though the CIA's covert aggressiveness increased through-
out the Dulles directorate, that period was generally considered
by those who worked at the agency to have been, as historian
James Billington says, "the golden age of the National Intelligence
Estimates. The NIEs themselves were quite good and, under
Dulles, they were an important component of the National
Security Council process during the Eisenhower years to a degree
that was not true later under John Kennedy."[11]

The raw ingredients of the estimates themselves came from
Sherman Kent and his National Intelligence Estimates staff as well
as from all the involved cabinet-level agencies and armed services.
The task then was to meet President Eisenhower's demand for forecasts that were crisply written, authoritative, and with realistic
options. William Bundy, who was involved in shaping the drafts of
National Intelligence Estimates that came out of Kent's office,
recalls:

I'm biased, but I think that the estimates were as good as bureaucratic prose is ever likely to get. An estimate often had quite a lot of lift to it. You could see what they were trying to say, and you could get a pretty accurate picture of what they felt the odds were on this or that event taking place. They were pretty frank, certainly never consciously the other way. When you had people like Sherman Kent around he would say, "When we say a thing is likely to happen, what are we saying? Is it a 50 percent chance? Or 65 percent?" And he would try to get it so it would be understood by those who had to understand where to place the bets. There was a lot less gobbledygook if you compare our estimates with those of the British Joint Intelligence Committee output. Theirs would be suggestive but never as really down-right on the gut question of do you, or do you not, think "X" is going to happen. I thought ours were a very creditable performance and, for a government bureau-cracy, a remarkable performance.

Now, as for Allen Dulles, I was in the briefings we did the night before he went before a National Security Council meeting. He did not intervene in the process of shaping the NIE documents to the degree that later DCIs have done. He did not rewrite them when they came to him. But he had done his homework and knew what would go in the digest form in the first part of the paper. Like Walter Bedell Smith, he continued the stance that the NIEs were the director's estimates, and he presented them to the National Security Council as such. He also stayed pretty far away from expressing policy recommendations; that was Foster Dulles's job. He never disassociated himself from the estimates, but he could and did say, this is what the intelligence community thinks, but I have these reservations. You have to remember he had all these other outside contacts who were talking to him all the time from everywhere. I remember one instance, and there were others, but this one was in the fall of 1956, just about the time that Hungary looked as if it would blow up. And we had done an estimate on Poland with the conclusion that Soviet control there was as strong as ever. When the papers were sent to Allen, he signed off on it, but at the National Security Council meeting he said, they may be right, but the marker buoys—the people I have talked to recently—they tell me it is decidedly more volatile there than this estimate suggests. Poland could blow before Hungary, he said. And it did. I've seen him do that time and again.[12]

The nickname "The Great White Case Officer" tended to obscure his involvement in the final intelligence analysis product presented to the National Security Council and the president, but was certainly deserved. Covert operations gave Dulles's intuition its full play and provided his greatest satisfaction when successful. The business of estimating was a collegial exercise; "ops" were individual, high-risk, and dangerous. And Dulles knew full well what many intelligence professionals do not like to admit: Presidents love "ops" more than analysis. As much as Eisenhower grumbled about coordination and needing more precise forecasts, both he and Foster were enchanted by the darker side of the clandestine struggle; the frustrations of politics could be laid aside, the enemy could be struck and could strike back. There was a sense of accomplishment in a successful operation—even one as banal as bribing a third-world politician—that did not come from the most trenchant National Intelligence Estimates.

The operational side of the agency's work also gave Dulles free rein for his need to be in constant motion. He traveled more than perhaps any public figure of his day; if he had a rival it was Foster Dulles. On a battered passport in his CIA personnel file the visa stamps for the late summer of 1955 show Dulles spending five days in August in Switzerland, flying to Rome on August 31, to Munich the following day, and then returning to Rome for five days. After he left Rome he traveled through Turkey and Greece before flying by military transport to England on September 15. On September 22, the passport shows an arrival stamp at the airport in Saigon.

In the summer of 1956, with the presidential campaign in full cry, Dulles left Washington and went on an epic tour around the world with Clover. The public reason was a fact-finding mission. One of the other purposes was to take side trips to examine the secret installations in Pakistan and elsewhere that were to serve as the bases for the U-2 spy plane missions. James Billington, now the librarian of Congress, had joined the army after his graduate work in history at Yale and was assigned to Kent's estimates staff at the Office of National Estimates. He and Ray Cline, a senior analyst, accompanied the Dulleses but were largely outnumbered by the other CIA officers who represented the operations side of the agency's global contacts. Billington remembers:

It was astonishing, that 1956 trip. The first thing was how many people he knew. The second was how he inspired tremendous affection among people who were in this business. There was much hugging and reminiscing wherever he went. In that sense his life was all of one piece, it was a steady parade of people who had known him at different times. When we were in Paris there were people who had known him when he was there with Woodrow Wilson in 1919. When we got

to Istanbul, there were all these Turkish officials lined
up to greet him—some thought he was the secretary of
state—and there was this aura of real consequence. Allen
walked by them all and said, "I want to see Betty Carp."
And this rotund, elderly lady came forward and they had
a bear hug and went off talking and left us all standing
there. That was not on the schedule, I can tell you.

But there also were high heads of state who knew
him and loved him. I remember when we arrived in
India, Nehru was giving everyone trouble, but he
stopped everything and had a long talk and kept calling Dulles "Mr. Allen," and there were these reminiscences about Allahabad so many years before. What
this trip turned out to be was a continuing conversation all around the world. It was an elegant discourse
by an old-world gentleman with a lot of laughter and
good fellowship with old friends, and it was very civilized and affectionate. I don't read many of these espionage novels, but it was nowhere as grim or dry as they
make such meetings out to be. It was just Dulles picking up the conversation with friends where they had
left off years before. It was amazing to me. It was so
laid back.

Then there would be the technical conversations,
and I did not sit in on many of those; I was a mole from
the intelligence side, and Ray and I were trying to see
just how many of these longer estimates we could get
him to read on the trip. But from what I did see, I drew
an impression of an inordinate number of people who
sought him out along the way who tried to get him and
the agency involved in various plots and schemes.
There were official visits, there were visits from dissi-

dents, exile groups, the strangest collection of people. The feedback I got from the covert types was that he had this marvelous ability to say no to these schemes. He listened to them all patiently and politely so no one went away angry. But he would turn to me or someone and say, "Another one of those. Keep an eye on that one, will you?" He had this ability to make quite cold-blooded assessments while remaining warm and gracious that was quite remarkable. People talk about the Cold War frenzy, but I admit I slept better after that trip knowing that some of these plans never got off the ground. I know the CIA has another reputation these days—the rogue agency and all that—but I never saw it nor believed it of Dulles. He was terrific at warding off these crazy schemes; he had this inner compass that kept him from being distracted. And he had this ability to assess people that kept him from being seduced or taken in.

The other things that stand out from that trip— one was the endless hours. He never really stopped working, stopped thinking about intelligence and what was happening in the world. The other thing was this deep understated sense of obligation to the world. He was a real Wilsonian, and the substructure of Wilsonian moralism—in the best sense of the word—was very deep. Allen Dulles was not in the world to make money, nor to make trouble, but to make the world a better place for freedom. The only time I saw him lose his temper was when we got to Thailand, there was this thug of a general running the place and he really lavished a lot of entertainment on us. During one of the tours Clover had admired a particularly ornate riverboat on one of

the klongs, the canals. It was quite a work of art. The
next day when we got to the air force plane, there was
the boat. A gift to Clover from the general. That whole
affair offended Allen's Presbyterian sense of propriety
and he got quite angry, but not so angry that he did not
say politely to the Thais that he thanked the general for
his generosity, but would they please give the boat back
to its owner; the poor fellow had probably been murdered. But Allen was having none of it.[13]

Eisenhower still trusted both Foster and Allen Dulles. But the
president searched constantly for more control over events and for
men who would jump when he gave orders. This led to the formation of what first was called the "5412 Committee" and later
became the Special Group. Its makeup was fairly fluid over the
years, but basically it consisted of representatives of the secretaries
of state and defense, the Joint Chiefs, the CIA, and other agencies
as specific projects dictated. The first chairman of the Special
Group was Gordon Gray, a wealthy North Carolinian who had
served as Truman's secretary of the army. Gray had a background
in intelligence and had been a possible rival for Allen Dulles as DCI.
He and another major figure, Nelson Rockefeller (who was chairman of the Operations Coordinating Board), sold an already pre-
disposed Eisenhower on the notion that the problem with covert
operations in the past was that they were either not aggressive
enough or, if they were, they risked America's (and the president's)
reputation as a world peacemaker. The concept of "plausible deniability" had become hard policy by then. It argued that covert operations should be more selective, narrowly focused, result-oriented,
and, most of all, covert enough that the rest of the world should
never be able to lay blame on the United States government. Gray
was particularly concerned that CIA activities not embarrass the
president. Thus the Special Group was to serve as a "circuit breaker"

between the president and "ops" that might blow up in his face. Intelligence historian Rhodri Jeffreys-Jones writes:

> The fallacy here was that the Special Group could at the same time be a secret committee and a publicly displayed "circuit breaker" in times of trouble. Over the years, the group was to be disinterred and reburied in a series of farcical attempts to deceive public opinion.... Experience was to show that the Special Group's existence protected neither president nor nation, and certainly not the CIA.... As to the reputation of the United States, foreign opinion made no distinction between the president and an executive committee because the distinction was irrelevant to the citizens of the nations affected by what the CIA did. As it turned out, a more satisfying method of vindicating president and nation was to blame the CIA when things went wrong. As one agency veteran put it, "It is part of the CIA director's job to be the fall guy for the president."[14]

And Soviet expert Harry Rositzke notes, "The CIA became an all-purpose instrument of action like the Office of Strategic Services" throughout Southeast Asia. From the middle 1950s onward, the agency was successful in Laos in checkmating the communist Pathet Lao, which were backed by the North Vietnamese, training and supplying them with an army of Meo tribesmen. That war went from guerrilla to conventional and had fifteen thousand troops in the field by the end of the Dulles era. Without the CIA presence in South Vietnam, the Diem regime would not have lasted as long as it did.

But sometimes the Kim Roosevelt rule against covert operations that lack popular support or able leadership would take hold with dismaying results. In 1958 the agency backed an uprising of Indonesian army officers who wanted to overthrow the Sukarno regime; the reason given was that Sukarno had been seeking development aid and closer military ties with Moscow. The decision to train, support, and assist an armed uprising in Indonesia came out of a pervasive sense of frustration rather than any deep concerns that Sukarno was a direct threat to the United States. Part of that frustration was that previous agency efforts to oust him had ended embarrassingly. There had been an attempt some years earlier to counterfeit what were to appear to be filmstrips from a pornographic movie that the Soviets had concocted to show Sukarno participating in various sexual acts. The idea was not to capitalize on the Indonesian leader's well-known appetites but to make the Soviets appear to be the villain in a sex-blackmail scheme. Even though the movie strips were produced for the agency through the good offices of film star Bing Crosby, the prints that were circulated through East Asia caused more laughter than disgrace, and some internal embarrassment within the agency.

So it was that the agency expended much money and material in the 1958 insurgency, including sending three military advisers and a group of B-26 bombers flown by pilots of the agency's clandestine Civil Air Transport airline. The Djakarta government ultimately crushed the revolt and in the process exposed the CIA's involvement to the world. The lesson lost on the Special Group was that the CIA's own chief of paramilitary warfare at the time, Desmond FitzGerald, and the head of the clandestine service's Far East desk, Al Ulmer, had raised doubts about the project but had been overridden by the Special Group itself. Nor was the truth acknowledged a year later when the Chinese Red Army wiped out a guerrilla army of Tibetans set up and trained for five years by the agency.

Harry Rositzke describes the hardening of the White House's resolve: "For the first dozen years of the Cold War there

was no talk of assassination in Washington. Even in those sometimes hysterical times I knew of no one at any level who seriously
proposed that X or Y be wiped out to advance the national interest. Then, between 1959 and 1962, the White House, the National
Security Council and its Special Group, and members of the cabinet talked seriously about killing foreign leaders and, in two
cases, authorized the CIA to arrange their murder...."[15]

The Special Group debated several assassination plans
(Egypt's Colonel Nasser and Red China's Premier Cho En-lai were
two) before dropping them as too risky. In 1960 Dulles got orders
for an ambitious program of air support and paramilitary aid to
Colonel Joseph Mobutu's bid for control of the Republic of the
Congo (later Zaire). Mobutu had led a coup against Patrice
Lumumba, the charismatic, emotional (and some believed mad)
prime minister in the first postcolonial Congo government of
Joseph Kasavubu. An army revolt led Lumumba to seize control of
the regime, and he alarmed Washington by seeking aid and support
from Moscow. The Special Group saw this as a clear danger that the
Soviets might gain a vital stronghold in Africa, and President
Eisenhower was particularly alarmed at Lumumba's hot denunciations of the West for its oppressive heritage in Africa. Although an
investigation a decade later by CIA Inspector General Scott
Breckenridge turned up no explicit orders for an assassination by
either the president or the Special Group, Lawrence Devlin, the
CIA's station chief in Kinshasa, had no doubt that he was to do
more than just provide guns and money to the Mobutu insurgents.[16] Vials of poison were produced and sent to Devlin for the
attempt. That Mobutu's henchmen went ahead and captured and
executed Lumumba and others on their own without any help
from the CIA is really beside the point. America was blamed for the
death by Africa and the world, and the CIA was the fall guy. Some
of the drugs and mechanisms of death were products of the

agency's own laboratories, or of projects funded at leading universities which explored mind-altering concoctions that might be
added to the nation's arsenal.

On the main front of the Cold War battlefield, the stakes
rose higher all the time. The Soviets had successfully tested the
first version of their intercontinental ballistic missile in 1956. On
October 4, 1957, the world was shocked into the space age when
the Soviet's "Sputnik I," the first artificial earth satellite, was
launched into orbit. Three days later the USSR announced the
successful test of "a mighty hydrogen warhead of a new design."
Suddenly the frustrations of Korea, Red China, Southeast Asia,
and Eastern Europe receded, replaced by a general alarm across
America. The fact that the U.S. was able to launch its Vanguard I
and Explorer III satellites within five months of Sputnik demonstrated how close the missile race was in technical skill. But the
panic merely spread. American schools were no good; the dicta-
torial Soviet method produced better scientists. America's moral
fiber was weak; the communists were dedicated. The Kremlin had
succeeded; the White House had failed. America was in the greatest peril since the days before Pearl Harbor.

President Eisenhower and his chief advisers knew better, of
course. The testing of the Atlas intercontinental missile with its
8,800-pound payload and its dependable ability to get into orbit
and stay there actually put the United States at a considerable
advantage if the race was merely to see who could drop the biggest
nuclear warhead the furthest distance with the greatest accuracy.
And there was ample intelligence evidence that the U.S. aerospace
industry could produce bigger and more accurate missiles at a far
greater rate than Russian industry. Moreover, while Khrushchev
was pushing the missile program in the Soviet Union, there were
clear signals coming out of Moscow that he did not seek to attack
the United States or, for that matter, Western Europe. Tentative

feelers were put out by both superpowers to try to exploit areas of common understanding that would reduce world tension. Khrushchev reduced the Red Army by one million troops and began a round of nuclear disarmament talks with U.S. diplomats that opened in Geneva in early 1959. Britain's new prime minister, Harold Macmillan, began a series of shuttle diplomacy visits between Moscow and Washington.

But Eisenhower sided more with his in-house advisers who counseled that, while they should sincerely hold out the olive branch to Khrushchev, there was also the need for tougher direct action against communist subversion in crucial areas of the world such as the Middle East and Latin America. The United States landed fifteen thousand marines in Beirut in 1958 to prevent the Lebanese government from being toppled by communist-backed insurgents. And despite private, but nonetheless angry, protests from Moscow, the president continued to authorize U-2 overflights through Soviet airspace. Each one was tracked in helpless frustration by Russian radar-directed antiaircraft missile batteries that did not have the range of the thirty thousand–foot arcs the U-2s made.

AT THIS TIME ALLEN DULLES was dismayed to find himself and the CIA gradually moving to the margins in the Eisenhower councils. One heavy blow was the death of Foster Dulles on May 24, 1959, at the age of seventy-one. He had been on medical leave since February, battling the cancer that had hit him three years earlier. His successor, mild-mannered Christian Herter, himself a partial invalid from polio, proved to be neither a protector of the CIA nor a collaborator with Allen. The pace picked up as the CIA was transformed from its first role of intelligence analyst and interpreter of events for the president and became more a tool for direct action.

One of the focal points of Eisenhower's attention became the U-2 program. With Khrushchev appearing to soften, the White

House began to order a diminishing number of the offensive over-flights. From 1958 through April 1960, only a few dozen flights took place, and most of those were surveys along the Soviet Union's vast borders. The president had always feared the world outcry if one of the U-2s should crash inside Soviet borders; those fears increased as information came in detailing the rapid advances the Russians were making in radar-guided antiaircraft missile technology.

The hopes of administration officials that there might actually be a thaw in the Cold War began to build in the summer of 1959 when the Soviet leader and entourage made a hugely popular tour of the United States—the first ever for a Russian leader. In a dramatic private conversation at Camp David, Khrushchev agreed to remove the Soviet presence in Berlin. An important summit meeting of East and West leaders was to be planned for a year hence, and there were hopes born that a genuine disarmament pact and new era of peace might serve as the capstone of Eisenhower's eight years of crusading for freedom.

But the public fears of the Cold War threat could not be turned off so easily. The 1958 congressional elections had expanded the Democratic Party majorities in both House and Senate. As 1960 approached, the Democrats began to believe they had a chance to capture the White House after an eight-year absence. The "missile gap" became a frightening public image and a valuable political weapon for leading Democratic hopefuls. These charges were seized upon by a particularly potent Senate leader with declared presidential ambitions. Senator Stuart Symington of Missouri had been secretary of the air force in the Truman administration. Symington was lobbied by the air force, and by a collection of aerospace industry executives, some of whom held grudges against the CIA for grabbing the U-2 program. White House critics began to coalesce around the Senate Armed Services Committee and to feed its members alarming data about the various "gaps" in America's defense system. These charges invariably found their way into the press. Repeatedly, Symington charged that America had been "in retreat" since World War II. In numerous secret sessions on the missile gap, Dulles emphatically stated that the USSR enjoyed no such strategic superiority; the reverse was actually true. Of course, he could in no way refer to the secret evidence obtained by the U-2. The spy planes had spotted several ICBM bases under construction in Russia, but all of them were far from operational. And when he challenged Symington to identify his sources in one hearing, the senator refused and accused the CIA of meddling in politics.

By April 1960 it appeared that the White House could replace the risky and offending U-2 spy plane with a Discoverer spy satellite launched by an Agena rocket. The Operation Corona project had been jointly run by the CIA and air force and offered even better photo-intelligence production without the political risk. The capsule containing the exposed film could be brought out of orbit and parachuted to safe recovery outside Russian territory. Another project was also in development; the SAMOS satellite used even newer technology to scan targets with a television camera and transmit the pictures back to earth.

On April 9, 1960, a U-2 was authorized to take off from the secret CIA base in Peshawar, Pakistan, and to fly over the Soviet heartland to Bodo, Norway. Bissell and Dulles asked for one more flight to pinpoint that Russian ICBMs were being brought to operational status at Plesetsk, six hundred miles north of Moscow. Allen Dulles sent Bissell off on a deserved weekend break and returned to "The Kremlin" to send the orders for what was to be the final flight of the U-2 over Russian airspace, at least until the Paris summit was over, and possibly forever. It was Saturday, April 30, in Washington; in Peshawar it was already Sunday morning, the absolute final day that the president had said the mission could be undertaken before the crucial Paris meeting.

There remains an unresolved dispute over exactly what happened, but Dulles personally believed (based on National Security Agency tracking reports) that the U-2 being flown by civilian pilot Francis Gary Powers had a flameout and that the spy plane drifted below forty thousand feet as he attempted to restart the jet engines.[17] At that altitude, he was well within range of Soviet surface-to-air rocket batteries that had been tracking his progress from the moment he crossed the Russian border. Powers was hit and bailed out over Sverdlovsk in the Ural Mountains. It had been assumed at the CIA that in the event of a U-2 crash inside the Soviet Union, the plane would be destroyed beyond the ability of the Russians to reconstruct any secrets, and that the pilot would not survive the fall from seventy thousand feet. On the basis of these suppositions, the White House issued its bland first confirmation that an American civilian pilot had strayed by accident into Russian territory and nothing more. The capture of pilot Powers, who was very much alive and most cooperative, and the recovery of the nearly intact U-2 (which was promptly put on display in Red Square) was a public relations disaster for the president.

The White House's first version of the story had to be recalled, doubling the embarrassment and fueling the public uproar that followed. The president had to go before the press and confess that the United States had been involved in aggressive espionage, and had been caught. Then there was the collapse of the Paris summit when Khrushchev walked out. Eisenhower manfully took full responsibility for the overflight program and its spectacular failure, but his unhappiness with Dulles deepened, and his frustration with the CIA and its free-spending command of budget resources became part of the litany of complaints that dominated the president's final days in the White House. Nevertheless, Eisenhower withstood advice by many of his advisers that Allen Dulles should resign (he offered) and that more of the blame should be placed on the CIA for its recklessness.

Despite the U-2 disaster, Eisenhower continued to press his DCI for a larger number of covert operations over a wider arena. There was the affair with Patrice Lumumba going on in the Congo; the secret war in Laos needed shoring up; Vietnam's Diem regime was tottering. Closer to home in the Caribbean, the president had decided in March 1960 to do something about two vexatious problems in the region: the corrupt regime of Rafael Trujillo in the Dominican Republic, and the subversion of the Cuban revolution of 1959 by Fidel Castro and his group of Marxist guerrillas. In the case of Trujillo, it was supporting a coup being organized by enemies of the dictator.

Castro's case was a different matter. He had been part of a broader revolt that had driven Fulgencio Batista into exile; then Castro had seized the revolution, and many of his former comrades were forced to follow Batista to the United States to escape imprisonment or death. Castro sealed off Cuba so tightly that any operation to topple him would have to be based on sparking an uprising among the general populace. The flood of Cuban exiles to the United States from 1959 on presented a problem for the planners of any uprising. Among the vast majority of Cubans, most of them desperately poor, Castro's campaign to expropriate the land of the rich and to take over major businesses met with enormous support. The strictures of Kim Roosevelt's rule applied in Cuba; there was no cadre of leaders to take power, and there was little visible public support for toppling Castro, at least not on the island itself.

Informal discussions about how to generate popular support for such a rebellion had been going on for the winter months of 1959–1960. Dulles and Bissell had even presented to the Special Group and the president a scheme for sabotaging the biggest sugar refining complex in Cuba and thereby striking a blow at the already shaky economy. It was not enough for the president. He wanted action against Castro personally, and if it could not be done during his term in office, then planning could commence

for a covert operation that could be handed over to his successor—
probably Vice President Richard Nixon. On January 18, 1960, a
special group called WH/4 Branch (for the Caribbean region of
the Western Hemisphere) within Bissell's covert action office at
CIA was created "to begin an examination of the possibility of
overthrowing Castro."[18] On March 17, 1960, Eisenhower ordered
the CIA "to begin the training of Cuban exiles... against a possible
future day when they might return to their homeland."[19] The specific purpose for the exile group was as yet undefined, and only a
few hundred were recruited. Requests for arms and support had
come from disparate anti-Castro groups inside the country; perhaps the guerrillas could help unify those forces, perhaps they
could take off for the Sierra Maestra Mountains—as Castro had
done—and sow the seeds of revolt. In the meantime, the agency
and State Department would try to sort out the most plausible
coalition of Cuban émigrés and former officials who could be supported to form a legitimate government-in-exile, and then to sue
for legitimacy at the United Nations and the Organization of
American States. This organizational task would be as difficult as
the paramilitary operation. Cuban politics was rooted in a history
of coups and counterrevolutions by loose confederations of rebels
who rarely hung together for long. The actual expedition in which
Castro and his 26th of July guerrillas made their first landing in
Cuba three years before had been financed by the former Cuban
president, who had been thrown out of the country by Batista in
the 1940s. Rival groups plotted to return to their homeland, and
against each other, in the public coffeehouses and through
Spanish-language newspapers from New York City to Miami.

General Andrew Goodpaster, the White House military
affairs adviser, is emphatic that "President Eisenhower left no
doubt in anyone's mind that any paramilitary operation sent into
Cuba had to be pegged to efforts by Cuban leaders themselves to

take back their government. We could help them, but they had to do the work themselves. The president was emphatic about this."[20] The general also remembers that while recruiting and training was organized and conversations were started with the various exile groups, little further discussions considered in a specific plan for the operation. But it also is clear from the subsequent interviews gathered by various investigative groups that the staff officers of the agency, the Pentagon, and the State Department were sure that Castro was to be removed from power at all costs. Scott Breckenridge, the agency's inspector general during the 1960s, and others have failed to find a paper trail with an explicit statement, but everyone understood that if Castro had to be killed while he was being ousted, so be it. As Breckenridge's investigation in 1967 showed:

> In that same month [as the exile training order] the National Security Council... discussed the "removal" of Castro. This was in the context of the invasion plan, and the word "assassination" was not used, but the personalized connotation was there.
>
> In the late spring/early summer of 1960 CIA's Deputy Director for Plans [Bissell] asked the head of the Technical Services Division to review capabilities in the general area of "incapacitation and elimination," assassination being one of the capabilities to consider.
>
> In the fall of 1960 the Special Group... discussed "direct positive action" against Castro. That language may be subject to various interpretations but it has an ominous ring. In early 1961 [Bissell] instructed Bill H. [William Harvey has more recently been identified] to establish what was referred to as an "executive action capability," which was understood to mean the ability to

kill selected individuals. In giving this instruction the
Deputy Director for Plans stated that he had been urged
twice by the White House to do this. While the instruction was stated in general terms, without specifying a
particular target, it was very much in the time period of
the mounting program against Castro and his regime.[21]

Some of the schemes the CIA discussed with President
Eisenhower (and later with President Kennedy) bordered on the
lunatic. There were suggestions that Castro could be sprayed with
hallucinogens, or his cigars laced with botulism, or his shoes dusted
with thallium powder in the hope that his beard would fall out. But
it also appears from the record that these discussions remained
nothing more than that and were put on hold in August until the
results of the presidential election were known.

Bissell began to assemble the men he wanted for what became
known as the Cuba Project but ran into trouble from the start. It
was viewed by some of the other top operational people within the
agency as another chance for the director's anointed favorite to
show off while the rest of them had to do the hard work of the Cold
War. Even though William Harvey, the old counterspy and Berlin
Tunnel boss, was organizing a general assassination capability that
had Castro as its main target, he refused to have anything to do
with the invasion plan and made his doubts known to anyone who
would listen. Others, like Richard Helms, who had to take over the
rest of Bissell's job as deputy director for plans, had enough to do
already without getting involved in the Cuban venture. But other
division directors were a bit malicious when Bissell sent out a call
for operational personnel to be sent from various offices to help
out. Some of the men who were involved were able veterans of the
Guatemala coup and countless "ops" since then. The overall staff
director was Colonel J. C. King, head of the agency's Western

Hemisphere division and a covert war veteran. E. Howard Hunt
became the liaison with the recently formed *Frente Revolucionario
Democratico* (FRD), which brought together a fractious group of
Cuban exile politicians who ranged from moderate Christian
Democrats to radicals on the run from Castro's own 26th of July
movement. But as one agency official later judged, "A lot of the
division chiefs sent their castoffs over to Dick Bissell. They didn't
like him much, by then, and they didn't want to waste good people.
But they didn't help matters with some of those people who were
sent over for Cuba."22

Still, at the beginning, hopes were high within Bissell's group.
No one doubted that if Richard Nixon won the 1960 election, the
plan would go ahead that autumn even before his inauguration. On
August 18, at a cabinet meeting, Eisenhower approved a $13 mil-
lion budget for the project; it was specified clearly that no United
States military personnel were to be used in any combat portion of
the operation. This was largely a moot point to the Eisenhower
planners, for the doctrine of "plausible deniability" had become
firmly understood. Also, there was no lack of Cuban volunteers
among the young émigrés of the exile community. But a new sense
of urgency drove events. There were reports that selected Cuban air
force officers had been sent for advanced combat jet training in the
Soviet Union, and there were indications that among the tangible
rewards Moscow was willing to give Castro was a squadron of new
MiG-21 jet fighters to replace his aging fleet of American surplus
trainers and light bombers. With only ninety miles separating the
two countries, the threat of attack became very real to most
Americans and a source of enormous alarm to the residents of
Florida and their congressional delegation.

Something would have to be done as soon after the
November elections as possible.

CHAPTER FIFTEEN

1960–1961

*"The general expectation within the Kennedy administration
has been that Mr. Dulles... would step down in 1961...."*
—New York Herald Tribune

NO ONE WAS IN A more truculent mood in those final days
before the 1960 election than Richard Nixon. He counted himself
among the people injured in the U-2 spy plane affair. The vice
president had begun the race as a clear front-runner pursued by a
pack of Democratic rivals. During that long summer he had
watched his lead erode and now was in the unenviable position of
having to campaign as the heir to a tired administration that had
stumbled badly. Worse, he had heard that John Kennedy, the
Democratic nominee, had received secret briefings from Allen
Dulles that had laid out in detail the Cuba Project, among other
covert operations in the works. Nixon did not think it was coincidence that in his debates with Kennedy, the senator had homed in
on Eisenhower's apparent inaction on the threat posed by Fidel
Castro. But with just as much vigor he criticized the growing
speculation in the press that the Eisenhower White House *was*
planning some sort of paramilitary interference in Cuba—this
violated a long-standing American policy against intervention in
the affairs of its Latin American neighbors, he argued. It was obvious to the vice president that Kennedy was having it both ways; he

knew full well that there were secret plans in the works and that
he, Nixon, could not refer to them in defense. Since Nixon was
always capable of letting his native suspicion run unchecked, he
concluded that Dulles had decided to help the Kennedy campaign—and said as much in his subsequent memoir.[1]

Allen Dulles had indeed briefed John Kennedy in the summer
of 1960 on at least three occasions, and the deputy DCI, General
Cabell, had conducted at least one other briefing. Candidate briefings during presidential races go back to George Marshall's confidential briefings of Thomas Dewey, and Dulles had personally
attended to the briefings given Adlai Stevenson in both of the
Eisenhower-era campaigns. But Dulles was emphatic at the time
and later that he had never given Kennedy any information about
any planned covert operations.

It is also true that Allen Dulles liked Jack Kennedy. In later
years, he would hint that he had voted for Richard Nixon since he
"generally voted Republican." And it is likely that under a Nixon
administration, Dulles could have stayed on as DCI for three more
years, until he was seventy. By that time, most of his senior aides
believed, he would have resolved in his mind whether his successor
should be Richard Helms or Richard Bissell, the favorite of the
moment. Indeed, by handing over full control of the Cuba Project
in the summer of 1960 to Bissell, Dulles was seen as giving him his
chance for a star-turn success if he could pull it off. It would prove
whether the lanky, professorial Bissell could handle a complicated
covert "op" that involved intricate interagency coordination and
extreme political sensitivity. Dulles never appears aware that numbers of his top aides were betting that Bissell would get into trouble.

When John Kennedy won his narrow victory over Nixon on
November 7, Dulles was not disturbed. As it turns out, John
Kennedy was another of those important future leaders that Allen
Dulles had taken time to cultivate years before. Dulles had known
Joseph P. Kennedy, the family patriarch, from Kennedy's days as a

Wall Street securities dealer. Later, with his credentials as a securities regulator and former ambassador to Britain, Kennedy had been on one of the civilian commissions that had studied and criticized the CIA. While the two men had their differences, it was no bar to Dulles being invited to visit the Kennedy family during his frequent holidays with Clover at the Palm Beach mansion of Charles Wrightsman, the wealthy oil and aerospace executive and close friend. The Wrightsman estate was within walking distance of the Kennedy family compound on Palm Beach. In a 1964 oral history interview Dulles gave to journalist and former CIA colleague Thomas Braden, Dulles recalls meeting the youthful politician as early as 1956 and engaging in an informal series of tutorials in Florida that grew into a warm friendship as time went on.[2] Dulles remembers:

> [Kennedy] was always trying to get information, I don't mean secrets... particularly, but to get himself informed. He wanted to get my views, and when my brother was there [at the Wrightsmans'] his views on what we thought about things, and we had many, many talks together.... The contact was fairly continuous because my trips to Palm Beach were quite frequent... and whenever he was there we always got together. I respected his views. I thought he had a very keen appreciation of foreign problems, and being in the intelligence business, I pumped him as much as I could to get his views on things and his reaction to things, and that continued on during these days until the days when I served under him for a short time as director.[3]

Dulles had hoped he might stay on at "The Kremlin" for a while longer under Kennedy, but he was surprised at how quickly the president-elect moved to reappoint him and J. Edgar Hoover.

On the morning of November 10, just three days after the election, Kennedy called Dulles at his office and, without preliminaries, told him he wanted to announce his reappointment as quickly as possible. Pleased and flattered, Dulles made what he considered the appropriate qualifiers that he was near retirement age, that Kennedy might not want to keep him on indefinitely, and that he would be willing to stay on to help with an orderly transition. Kennedy briskly put those considerations aside; he wanted to announce the CIA and FBI appointments right away and to talk about longer-range plans later. Although he was not to be sworn into office until January 20, 1961, Kennedy wanted to get moving. The oft-repeated anecdote that Kennedy hesitated to keep Dulles is untrue. Retired *Washington Post* editor Ben Bradlee, a close friend and neighbor of the president-elect, is a frequently cited source of the tale. But he recently told the author, "[David] Halberstam and others have misunderstood what I said. The night after the election my wife and I were at the Kennedys' for an informal drink and a light meal. Jack jokingly asked us to name our top cabinet recommendations, and I and another guy said, fire Dulles and Hoover. He laughed at us and that was that."

On November 18 Dulles and Bissell flew to Palm Beach to inform the president-elect on some of the confidential intelligence that had been denied him as a candidate. The Cuba Project was discussed at length. So, too, was the situation in Laos, the crisis in the Congo, and the latest disagreements among the NATO commanders. Kennedy, for his part, had some news for Dulles about changes he wanted to make in the way he as president would formulate foreign policy and receive his intelligence guidance. During the Eisenhower years, Dulles had grown accustomed to opening the Thursday morning meeting of the National Security Council with one of his famous tours of the horizon of world problems. Kennedy, it turned out, had little patience for such deliberate consideration. He wanted two major changes. One was that he receive each morning a tightly written briefing memo on the major events of the previous twenty-four hours and whether specific action was needed. The weekly systematic reviews by the National Security Council and the Special Group were to be downgraded. The style of the men around the new president fit his own taste for a more informal, more action-oriented response to foreign affairs. This preference was out of the textbook of management techniques of Robert S. McNamara, who would be Kennedy's secretary of defense and the most important of the New Frontiersmen coming to Washington—more important even than Dean Rusk, the careerist, who would be the secretary of state. This shift in the power structure was noted immediately throughout the bureaucracies that served the president. McNamara was unknown to Washington, but his reputation as a high-efficiency Ford Motor Company executive come to apply modern methods to government's old ways was part of the excitement of the Kennedy advent. Task forces known as "working groups" were to be organized to deal with specific problems. The theory was that one could better select quick responses with just the right advisers to deal with the problem, and then disband the group and form another, custom-tailored team to deal with the next crisis.

There were three important results of this change in the way the White House related to Allen Dulles and the CIA. At one level, the DCI was excited by the way Kennedy involved himself, to a far greater extent than Eisenhower, in the daily details of foreign affairs. The new president was determined not to get caught on the blind side by some unforeseen development, and so the morning memos usually led to a series of telephone calls to Dulles by the president or his military aides with questions.

But the new system had some doubtful effects as well. With this less hierarchical and supposedly more responsive approach,

Kennedy effectively severed the lines of responsibility that had enabled the State Department and other security agencies to keep watch over the broader National Intelligence Estimate briefings that the agency provided. There was no one to take a long view when the momentum behind the various covert "ops" began to build. The third unintended impact was that during the months leading up to the inauguration, Dulles found himself being pulled more to serving the instant needs of the new president, and spending less time overseeing the details of the operations the agency was bringing over from the old administration. The result was a loss of control over the very area of CIA work that had been his primary focus.

That loss was still some months away. Meanwhile, the Cuba Project was not on hold. It changed radically before the November 7 election and continued to evolve steadily right up to January 20. On November 4, three days before the election, the Special Group had agreed with Bissell to keep a small group of guerrilla raiders on hand and to train the bulk of the 1,200-plus volunteers formed in Brigade 2506 for a full-blown amphibious *and airborne* attack.[4] The decision was sparked by intelligence (which the State Department made public a few weeks later) of a massive buildup in the Cuban military supplied by Moscow; the actual number of troops under arms was ten times what Batista had maintained two years earlier, and 28,000 tons of military supplies had been seen entering Cuban ports from Eastern Europe. Worse, the few bands of insurgents inside Cuba were virtually useless as a base upon which to build a revolution. If Castro were to be toppled, it would take a full-scale invasion by a trained amphibious force backed by heavy firepower and air support. A few days later, after Dulles's return from briefing Kennedy in Palm Beach, the enlarged Brigade 2506 was sent to special training for the larger operation. It would be Guatemala's PB Success operation, only bigger.

THE VERY WORDS "BAY OF PIGS" have become a synonym for ill-planned disaster. In the raw human terms it was a terrible debacle. Of the 1,200 brigade members who waded ashore on the beach of the Bay of Pigs on April 16, 1961, more than a thousand would languish for twenty months in Castro's prisons before Washington could swap loads of medicine and medical equipment for their freedom. The actual operation was a nightmare. Even before the invaders had embarked on their transports from Nicaragua on April 12, details of the invasion appeared in leading U.S. newspapers. On the night of April 14–15, a diversionary landing in Oriente province had to be aborted because of bad sea conditions. When the first air strike against Castro's airfields did take place on April 15, one of the brigade's bombers was shot down and two others developed mechanical troubles that forced them to land at Key West and Grand Cayman Island, respectively. Cover stories that the planes were flown by defectors from Castro's air force were quickly unmasked by reporters, and criticism began to build in the United Nations. This provoked Adlai Stevenson, the American ambassador to the UN, to protest to Rusk that his personal integrity had been jeopardized. Stevenson's emotional tirade further unsettled the secretary. The decision was taken to cancel plans for a second air strike, and permission was withdrawn for the remaining brigade planes to fly in support of the men, who by midnight of April 16–17 were wading ashore in the darkness. On the landing beaches of the Bay of Pigs the next day, mistakes turned into disasters. Transport ships did not get the men ashore soon enough and were caught in the bay by Castro's planes. One vessel, which had all the ammunition, was sunk; another was run aground. Castro's militia men had been alerted to a possible invasion and rushed to the area. Tanks and artillery were moved up against the invaders. Trapped on the beaches, the brigade endured three days of artillery fire and strafing runs from

Castro's planes, which fired .50-caliber machine guns on the troops' exposed positions. That the brigade had fought bravely and well was documented by the Castro government.[5]

Those whose emotions and professional careers link them forever to the memory of John Kennedy damn the CIA and its director for leading the young president and his inexperienced team of advisers into a swamp more impenetrable and dangerous than the Zapata marshes that ringed the Bay of Pigs. Those who cherish both Dulles and the agency sneer at the "touch football" brand of intelligence handling and foreign policy formulation that Kennedy and his chief advisers brought to Washington. The indictments and the anger are specific on two questions. First, could the Cuba Project in any of its configurations ever have succeeded in toppling Castro, or was the whole scheme such a violation of Kim Roosevelt's rule that it was insane to try? If the answer to the first question is yes, then, second, how fatal was President Kennedy's decision to deny the brigade forces adequate air cover for the landing?

A third view is not often discussed but may be the most plausible conclusion about the Bay of Pigs disaster. The chief villain in the tragedy may be that tempting seducer, the concept of "plausible deniability." The notion that American presidents who function in our system of democracy can never have the benefits of military action without paying a political price was never seriously considered at the time or in the immediate aftermath. Previous setbacks such as Indonesia and the U-2 crash had been explained away as anomalies and accidents.

After the Bay of Pigs disaster in April, President Kennedy asked four men to form an investigation into just what had happened. General Maxwell Taylor, who later became the president's chief military aide, was the group's chairman. Admiral Arleigh Burke, Allen Dulles, and Attorney General Robert Kennedy were the other members. The Taylor Committee report compiled a narrative of events that makes it clear that those responsible for the actual planning of the invasion were in regular and detailed contact with President Eisenhower, Christian Herter, and the Special Group during the waning days of Eisenhower's administration, even as they were informing the president-elect. This was no rogue operation. Between December 10, 1960, and February 8, 1961, CIA officer Tracy Barnes (Bissell's case officer on the project) and former Ambassador Whiting Willauer attended to these detailed informal briefings. The Taylor investigation also notes that the details of the invasion plan had become quite specific well before the Kennedy administration took command. The report reads:

> [Allen Dulles] briefed the President on the new paramilitary concept on 29 November 1960 and received the indication that the President wished the project expedited. The concept was formally presented to the Special Group on December 8, 1960. At this meeting, [name deleted] in charge of the paramilitary section for the Cuba project, described the new concept as one consisting of an amphibious landing on the Cuban coast of 600–750 men equipped with weapons of *extraordinarily heavy firepower* [emphasis added]. The landing would be preceded by preliminary air strikes launched from Nicaragua against military targets. Air strikes as well as supply flights would continue after the landing. The objective would be to seize, hold a limited area in Cuba, maintain a visible presence, and then to draw dissident elements to the landing force, which hopefully would trigger a general uprising. This amphibious landing would not entirely eliminate the previous concept for infiltrating guerrilla teams. It was expected that some

60–80 men would be infiltrated prior to the amphibious landing.

The Special Group was also briefed on the quality
of the Cuban force in training in Guatemala. [identity
deleted], in charge of training, described the superior
characteristics of the individuals, particularly as to motivation, intelligence and leadership qualities. He expressed
the opinion that such a force would have no difficulty
inflicting heavy casualties on a much larger militia
force.[6]

By this time there even was a new name for the operation,
the Trinidad Plan; the Cuban town of Trinidad on the southeast
coast was where the amphibious forces would come ashore. On
January 11, even before the new Congress convened, Allen Dulles
appeared in secret sessions before the Senate Foreign Relations
Committee chaired by William Fulbright and discussed in broad
terms the plans to overthrow Castro using Cuban paramilitary
forces that were completing their training at that moment. He was
accompanied by the agency's intelligence chief, Robert Amory.[7]

On that same day in January, nine days before the inauguration, a "working committee" of staff members from the agency,
State and Defense departments, and the Joint Chiefs was formed to
coordinate the logistical details of the invasion plan. On January 22,
two days after President Kennedy took office, his top advisers had
their first briefing on the Trinidad Plan. Present were Dean Rusk,
the new secretary of state; Robert S. McNamara, the defense secretary; Chester Bowles, the undersecretary of state; and Attorney
General Robert Kennedy. The briefing was conducted by Dulles
and General Lyman Lemnitzer, the chairman of the Joint Chiefs
and Dulles's old colleague from Operation Sunrise. They advanced
the concept of the operation as a joint project and presented a list

of possible actions of ascending degrees of force needed to topple Castro. President Kennedy got a similar briefing six days later at a White House meeting at which Vice President Lyndon Johnson, Secretaries Rusk and McNamara, and such top foreign policy aides as McGeorge and William Bundy and Assistant Secretary of State Paul Nitze were brought up to date by General Lemnitzer and Dulles. At that meeting, Kennedy ordered the CIA to step up its current propaganda and sabotage efforts and to continue its U-2 flights over Cuba to monitor the arrival of the new Soviet jet planes. The Pentagon was ordered to review the Trinidad Plan for military logistics and tactical details and to coordinate changes with the CIA. Rusk and his aides were told to try to win support from the other Latin American governments to isolate the Castro regime and, if possible, to involve the Organization of American States as an arbitrator once a credible rival government could be established.

At around this time, President Kennedy took a fateful step that may have done more than anything else to put the invasion plan out of control. He abolished the Operations Coordinating Board and took oversight of the Trinidad Plan out of the hands of the Special Group and into a more dispersed "working group" of White House aides and close advisers. Kennedy had plausible reasons for doing so. One of the most entrenched groups within the State Department's diplomatic corps was a band of Latin American experts and a smaller group with deep and emotional ties to Cuba. These men were among the most hawkish of the political forces working on the invasion plan, and both Kennedy and Rusk wanted to isolate them. This was a perilous time for Rusk, who was a comparative outsider among the close-knit crew that had come to help the president.

Kennedy and his "working group" were understandably cautious about the Trinidad Plan, but they were by no means appalled by either its objectives or its strategy. Those in the

president's inner circle, after all, were no strangers to covert operations and their risks. Walt Rostow, Arthur Schlesinger, Jr., and
Dean Rusk came out of the OSS tradition; William Bundy had
worked for Dulles at the CIA; and Paul Nitze had been in the
senior intelligence councils of the government since the Roosevelt
administration. While the Kennedy team knew full well the haz-
ards involved in covert operations, it shared a common belief that
paramilitary force was preferable to either doing nothing or risk-
ing all-out war. The president's stirring inaugural call to
Americans to come to their country's service also was a rallying
call for freedom-loving people everywhere. Rise up and an elite
American force would come and help, whether it was a member
of the Peace Corps or the Green Berets.

President Kennedy and his aides knew full well the paradox
they faced with Castro and Cuba. Political scientist Hans J.
Morgenthau best described this recipe for disaster: "The United
States was resolved to intervene on behalf of its interests, but it was
also resolved to intervene in such a way as not to violate the princi-
ple of non-intervention.... The United States failed to assign prior-
ities to these two interests. The United States jeopardized the
success of the intervention... and we lost much prestige as a great
nation able to use its power successfully on behalf of its interests....
[I]t sought the best of both worlds and got the worst."[8]

As the meetings on the Trinidad Plan continued through
February and March, bits and pieces began to fall off, and finally
the plan itself was radically altered into an unhappy compromise
that became known as Operation Zapata, named after the barrier
swamp that lay inland from the new landing site, the *Bahia
Cochinos*—the Bay of Pigs. The decision to change the mission
was made on March 11; the Trinidad Plan was too "spectacular."
The president told Bissell and his assistants to come up with a
"quiet" landing, preferably a night amphibious assault. The new

location came out of Rusk's urging that the site be near an airfield, to preserve the illusion that this was a locally sponsored
uprising that was flying its own planes.

During this time, in March, Dulles and others remember
Kennedy having his most serious doubts, but doubts as much
about preserving "plausible deniability" as about the success of
the mission. During one meeting in the Cabinet Room with the
Joint Chiefs and Vice President Johnson in attendance, Kennedy
called Dulles into an adjoining room known as the Fish Room for
its collection of stuffed game fish caught by President Truman
and other anglers. Alone, he confronted his DCI with his doubts
and asked, "Allen, what do you think of this? Would you do it or
would you not do it?" Dulles advised him at that point to put back
the invasion for another month, that more planning was needed.
A month later, as Dulles recalled:

> There was a general feeling that it was very important
> to do something here…. [S]hortly before the decision
> was made… we sent down… a Marine colonel… who
> had been doing a good deal of supervision of the
> training, and I wanted to get a report from him…. It
> was a very optimistic report…. [T]hat report had a
> great deal of influence on me, I know it had a great
> deal of influence on the President.[9]

And there was the often retold incident of the dramatic White
House meeting during which President Kennedy demanded a show
of hands from his top advisers as to who stood against going ahead
with the invasion. The only hand raised was that of Senator
Fulbright, who voiced moral compunctions about what was about
to be done. At least one ranking adviser was so offended at the sanc-
timonious tone the senator used with Kennedy that he silenced his

own doubts and voted in the affirmative; he regretted it ever after. Others in the room have confessed that they, too, kept silent. Although they worried about Operation Zapata failing, they worried more about how they would appear in the president's eyes. The only area of agreement among those who debate the matter these days is that there was plenty of individual blame to go around for what happened.

At the time though, many blamed Allen Dulles for the entire disaster. It was his agency, it was his handpicked team, it was his operation, and it was his fault. Admiral Arleigh A. Burke was one of the most vocal critics. Admiral Burke was the chief of naval operations who had to organize the navy task force that was ordered to stand by helplessly as observers while the Brigade 2506 members endured three days of murderous heat and shell fire before a handful of them could be pulled off the beaches. Burke freely admits that he never had much regard for Dulles but that he considered that the director's withdrawal from the debate over the daily changes of the plans amounted to negligence.

> I always thought his brother had more substance than he did. But the fact is that he just wasn't involved in that operation. He showed up for the meetings and sat there smoking his pipe. Dick Bissell and Tracy Barnes were the ones who actually sold President Kennedy on the plan. We have our share of the blame, too. Those of us in the navy were kind of fired up that we had a navy man in the White House for the first time since Roosevelt, and I do think many of us didn't say anything about our doubts because we didn't want to appear chicken in front of our new commander in chief. But the idea that you could do this kind of an amphibious landing with that small a force and no air

cover, well it was just a stupid idea. If you want to
know the truth, I think a lot of people in the agency
and the Pentagon thought that, despite the president's
warning that he would never use U.S. military forces,
once the brigade got stuck in there good and proper,
he would be forced to send in the Marines. I believe the
folks at the agency thought they could force the president's hand. But in the end I also have to fault Allen.
He left the organization of that operation largely to his
subordinates. And they organized it within various
elements of the CIA independent of other elements.
They had this separation of secret operations from
intelligence and that sort of thing; one hand did not
know what the other was doing. And finally, I blame
him for not being there. More than once, on similar
occasions—I think of the Indonesian thing, for one—
Allen was out of town.[10]

Of all of President Kennedy's personal advisers, historian
Arthur Schlesinger, Jr., has been the most critical of Dulles's role
in not stopping the operation at the beginning:

The Bay of Pigs seems to be a real case where Dulles
and Dick Bissell were just carried away by advocacy and
by their identification with the project. They misled the
White House. I don't say that Dulles had immersed
himself in the operational details. Dick Bissell, after all,
was an extremely intelligent man and a very lucid and
persuasive advocate. But I believe Allen Dulles was a
frivolous man. He was most intelligent and a man of
great charm, unlike his brother. But he was frivolous in
the sense that he would make these decisions which

involved people's lives and never really would think them through. He always left that to someone else.[11]

Even harsher judgments are aimed at McNamara and Rusk. Unsure of just where the power lines lay at the Pentagon, McNamara let the Joint Chiefs move ahead with their tactical preparations. An early memorandum by the service chiefs explicitly warning that adequate air support was essential to *any* amphibious landing was misplaced on his desk until after the disaster.

Dean Rusk has blamed himself for not speaking up more forcefully against going ahead with the operation at all. "I served President Kennedy badly," he wrote later. His fault, he said, was that he confined himself in the early days of the administration to matters dealing strictly with the State Department when, as a veteran of the guerrilla war in Burma, he could have been more critical of the military preparations. Rusk had never met Kennedy until he was asked to be secretary of state, and he did not know McNamara either. "There was a tendency for each one of us to sit upon our own specific responsibility."[12]

But one of the CIA staff aides to William Harvey who attended many of those planning sessions blames Rusk for urging most of the changes that ensured the operation's failure. According to him:

The original plan was not to go into the Bay of Pigs, it was to go into Trinidad. That was because if you could not hold on at Trinidad, then the force could at least get away and up into the Escambray Mountains, as Castro had done. Trinidad is midway between Santiago de Cuba and the Bay of Pigs. Do to Castro what Castro did to Batista.

So Rusk argued that it was "too professional," that the landing would look too much as if the Americans had picked the landing site. We should pick a place that looked as if the Cubans had chosen it. And as for air support, he says, I was in OSS in Asia during the war and air support was not that important in jungle warfare. The whole thing began to fall apart. And neither Allen Dulles, nor Pearre Cabell, nor Dick Bissell, I believe, ever sat back and looked at the entire final plan for flaws. I don't believe for a minute that Bissell or anyone at the agency knew that they were putting all the brigade's ammunition on one ship [which was bombed and sunk by Castro's air force]. Everyone had a piece of it, but no one had it all.[13]

This view is ratified by Richard Helms, who was left to run the rest of Bissell's covert shop while his boss concentrated on the invasion. Thus, Helms and the other operational people in the agency had no opportunity to know about or comment on the holes that were starting to appear in the fabric of the plan. He points to two major problems with the concept of the operation:

First of all, it was started in one administration and ended in another. Under Eisenhower, they were told, as I understand it, that if there was any trouble, the U.S. Navy would come in and bail the force out. It is my impression that when the new president came in, Allen Dulles and Bissell were so busy selling this whole concept that they did not stop to ask the Kennedy people the same questions they had of the Eisenhower people. "Do you have the same view that Eisenhower did? If such-and-such happens, do we do this or that?" They may have assumed what the president would do. If that is what they did, then it was too bad.

The other thing is that the entire operation was too big to be kept secret. You talk about Iran and Guatemala, they were secret operations. But they had to set up that air force and set up the bases, and you had all these guys down in Guatemala being trained. And there are no secrets in Washington anyway, everything leaks. Then the agency had to turn over to the Pentagon a lot of the project because we did not have that kind of capability. Too many people were involved.[14]

To add to the confusion, there were conflicting views over just what Brigade 2506 was supposed to do, assuming that it could land successfully. It is apparent that at least part of the determination by the president and his top aides to limit the amount of visible air protection for the invaders was the assumption that the landing would spark an immediate and general uprising among the Cuban people. Waves of bombers and jet fighters would be unnecessary if the people supported their liberators, and such an air presence would merely discredit the notion that this was strictly a Cuban insurgency.

But just the opposite view was held by Bissell and Dulles. Bissell recalled:

Neither [Dulles] nor I thought it was going to be an instant revolution. The scenario I had in mind was that we could seize and hold the beachhead. And there would then follow a period when we were doing a lot of strategic air attacks from the beachhead [there was an airstrip nearby], and Castro would find it impossible to dislodge the brigade and suffer considerable losses in the attempt. My notion was that at that stage of the game, you could try for a diplomatic ploy in the form of an [Organization of American States]-supervised cease-fire and then some form of election, or power-sharing. Now in the Bay of Pigs case one of the most damaging limitations imposed on us was that we could not even use genuine U.S. volunteers. If we had been able to recruit a number of B-26 aircrews it would have greatly strengthened the air force we did have. That to me was an example of sacrificing an operational capability in the interest of plausible deniability, a very vain thing. I must confess though, I did not argue the point at the time, so this is nothing more than hindsight.[15]

While Bissell and Dulles are guilty of not asking the right questions, President Kennedy and his aides must share in some of the guilt for not speaking more emphatically about their determination that the brigade essentially had to go into the beach on its own. William Bundy had come from the CIA as a senior security adviser. He recalls:

I remember exactly what Dick Bissell said at the time. It was much more measured than what the military was saying at the time. He said, of course it all depends on whether there is a real rising of the people. I cannot assure you there will be a rising of the people. But we have a great deal of information that there is that kind of opposition once the fire is lit. It was a very measured statement, and it sticks to me like a burr. I remember getting into an argument with Arthur Schlesinger and he was damning the agency root and branch, and I said the agency was more measured than the military were. None of us looked as hard as we might have, but the agency did not sell the project and Dick Bissell did not mislead us.

But having said that, we did inherit from the previous administration. And I do believe Eisenhower was slipping by then and Allen Dulles was less acute than he had been; he was sixty-eight by then. You add to this the strong feeling that Castro is a real enemy. And then Dick Bissell did have this aura of can-do; after all, he had done.

All of us could have done better. I wasn't as articulate about my doubts as I should have been. And I heard the president say in one of those sessions, "We are not sending U.S. forces in. That is categorical." But he never said it in the presence of the military or the agency. I remember being in Paul Nitze's office and asking some of them what they thought the real chances of success would be for the brigade on its own, and they said 35 to 40 percent. And I said, "Christ, is that the impression they have?" Their assumption had to have been that the president would go in to rescue the tethered goat. I do not remember the military ever being in the room whenever the president repeated his opposition to U.S. troops being directly involved. And it is a very sad reflection on the state of communications between the president and the Joint Chiefs, of which McNamara was a big part.[16]

Bundy's "tethered goat" thesis is borne out by the actions of the CIA project staff when Operation Zapata was actually launched with D-Day set for midnight, April 16. The invasion plan was specific when it came to just what air cover the landing force would receive. There was to be an air strike on the day before the landing to wipe out Castro's force of American-made jet trainers and light bombers while it was on the ground. The brigade itself had a tiny force of eight B-26s that were to be flown by Cuban trainees. There was no question of U.S. combat planes coming either from the nearby navy task force or from any U.S. bases. That meant that the Cubans had to fly each run from their base in Nicaragua, thereby severely cutting down the time they had to run sorties over Cuba before their fuel ran out. Then on Monday, on D-Day itself, the brigade's air force would be restricted to bombing and strafing Castro's forces as they approached the landing site; there was to be no air-to-air combat and no operations over the landing site itself. The assumption was that the Cuban air force would be destroyed by then. Another Rusk limitation was that the invasion planes had to occupy the nearby airfield for refueling— again, the preoccupation with the fiction that this was a spontaneous raid. Other preparations were scrapped or went by the board. The efforts to organize the exiled Cuban leadership into a rival government fell into confusion in an attempt to keep secret what the whole world knew about the invasion. And the ambitious diplomatic efforts to win support within the Organization of American States were shelved because they, too, conflicted with the notion that the White House must not be seen to be involved.

The sense of hesitancy communicated itself throughout the staff level and led to one of the remarkable side dramas of the whole sad affair. On Saturday, April 15, President Kennedy went to his hideaway farm in the Virginia hunt country for the weekend. McGeorge Bundy was left as the watch officer at the White House; Dean Rusk was on duty at the State Department. Allen Dulles was in Puerto Rico, fulfilling a long-standing speaking engagement to a young business executives group. His remarkable absence underscores just how unaware the main parties involved appeared to be about the perils of the operation. Richard Bissell was on duty at a special war room and communications center that had been set up in "T-30," one of the "temporaries" on the West Potomac Park along Riverside Drive. From hundreds of miles away, the Cuba Project officers tried to direct the support ships, air strikes, and landing by radio. The first test was the D-minus-2 air raids, planned to hit three of Castro's air bases and immobilize his defenses.

By the early afternoon of Sunday, D-minus-1, it was clear that the raids had not come close to knocking out Castro's planes. The operational staff in the basement at once ordered what it euphemistically called a "follow-up" strike while there was still some daylight and in advance of the provisional plans for D-Day air cover flights. According to eyewitness accounts, General Cabell chose this minute to visit the war room; he had been on a Sunday afternoon golf outing and had dropped by "The Kremlin" to see how things were going. Cabell, it appears, was worried that the White House would think the agency had overstepped its mandate and called McGeorge Bundy, over the strenuous objections of the operational staff, who knew what would happen next. Bundy called Rusk. The secretary of state, who had fretted all along that the air raids were a clear American signature, forbade the "follow-up" raid. Soon thereafter, Bundy called again and said D-Day air support could not be authorized unless it was clear that the brigade's B-26s had secured the nearby airfield or a strip on the beachhead. With the curses of the operational staff in their ears, Cabell and Bissell hurried by car to the State Department at about 10:15 PM to protest to Rusk in person. They were told by the secretary that he was acting on orders received that day in a telephone call from the president. If Cabell wanted to argue the point with Kennedy, he was free to do so, Rusk told him. The general decided (probably correctly) that he would be unable to change Kennedy's mind and so did not make the call—a decision he regretted the rest of his life.[17]

The operational staff, headed by Colonel J. C. King, believed that leaving the skies over the beachhead and the waters between the land and the brigade's support vessels unprotected was a fatal error that doomed a better-than-even-money chance for success. Bissell and General Cabell returned from the State Department after midnight; it was now D-Day, the 17th. The brigade members were disembarking in the darkness and heading toward the beach; there was no way to call them back. Worse was to come when daylight broke. Photoreconnaissance showed that the preemptive raid on Castro's bases had destroyed only five planes and had left more than half his air force undamaged. Colonel King told the Taylor Committee:

> We had a very violent discussion over what had happened and we spelled out as best we could to the General that we expected to lose every ship the next morning and that this had to be understood.... If we had conducted our D-Day strikes as planned, I know we would have knocked out the task force in Managua [the main Castro air base] and we would have destroyed at least a portion of the remaining aircraft.... If we could have accomplished this, we would have piled the enemy tanks up as they came in along those roads, and they wouldn't have been able to use their artillery against us because of the flat country and the fact that they wouldn't have any planes in the air to direct the artillery fire.... It was after midnight when they came back, because at the time they gave us the information, the troops were already in the process of transferring into the [landing craft]. At that point recall would have been impossible....
>
> [Question: Would you have recalled it if you could?]
>
> Yes. I would have recalled the brigade if it was within my power, because this was a delicate operation

and we had calculated it down to such a fine point. I
thought we had better than a fifty per cent chance of
succeeding provided that we got all the support we
were counting on…. [and succeeded in] establishing a
firm beachhead which could sustain itself for a pro-
tracted period of time.[18]

General Cabell and Bissell tried once more to salvage some
protection for the invaders, who were already under fire from
Castro's rural militia. Admiral Burke had ordered the aircraft car-
rier *Boxer* with a brigade of Marines to stand by out of sight of the
Cuban coast in case it was needed to support the invasion. At
4:30 AM, Cabell woke Dean Rusk at home and asked that, at the
least, the U.S. Navy planes be allowed to protect the ships that had
to land more men and critical supplies during the daylight. Rusk
called Kennedy and patched Cabell through on the connection so
he could make the request in person. Then Kennedy and Rusk
discussed the matter, and, as Cabell stated to the Taylor Committee, "The Secretary informed me that the request for air cover was
disapproved."
    It is tempting to ask whether, if Allen Dulles had been on
duty at "The Kremlin" that fateful weekend, he could have talked
President Kennedy into changing his mind. Most of the principals
involved agree that by that point Kennedy's mind was set on the
matter. One of the people who always wondered if he could have
prevented the debacle was Dulles himself. In an oral history interview with journalist Tom Braden, he was asked how important he
thought calling off the second air strike had been. Dulles mused:

The lesson I would draw from [the Bay of Pigs] is that
one ought never to leave the chief of state, the man
who has to reach the final decisions, in any state of
uncertainty as I think the president must have been as

to the points of the plan which are absolutely essential. I don't think he appreciated fully the vital importance, the absolutely essential character of these particular air strikes.... [T]here's one thing that I do feel badly about, because I think I had a responsibility there that I didn't fully carry out. That is before we went into this I should have said, "Mr. President, if you're not willing to permit us to take the steps necessary to immobilize for X period... the Cuban air force... the plan to get this brigade ashore with its equipment and supplies is a faulty one." That seems to me to be... the point that I would stress, that I don't think I made that absolutely crystal clear to the president.[19]

Dulles had returned with Clover from Puerto Rico late on that D-Day Monday and was briefed at home that the landing had not succeeded in putting all the men and equipment on shore, that opposition from Castro's forces was not overwhelming but was stronger than anticipated, and that the air cover had been pulled off the operation. Yet much of the brigade had gotten ashore, and there had been some success. The operation was in trouble, but time would tell. Several years before, Dulles had shifted the DCI offices out of the corner on the first floor of the East Building to a South Building suite that had its own communications center. He arrived there at daybreak on Tuesday morning, and signs unmistakably pointed to a total operational disaster. One of the remedies he tried, oddly enough, was to ask Richard Nixon to call on President Kennedy to order the nearby navy jets to take up active combat support for the brigade. Nixon did not hesitate and went to the White House at once. But it was too late, Kennedy said grimly.

Later in the day, Colonel "Red" White, the administrative aide, went to brief Dulles on another matter and found the director turned away from his desk and staring out the window behind him at the perfectly framed view of the Lincoln Memorial through the trees. After delivering his report, the trusted friend stood by silently. When Dulles spoke it was in a quiet voice that lacked his usual deep heartiness; it was frail and sad.

"Red, this is the blackest day of my life."[20]

THE MEN GATHERED around President Kennedy were seized by moods sharply shifting between rage and emotional paralysis during the three days of April 17, 18, and 19, as the Bay of Pigs raiders were killed or taken prisoner by Fidel Castro. Walt Rostow, who had been a key foreign policy adviser to the Kennedy campaign, was summoned to the White House on Tuesday, April 18, for a 7:00 AM meeting. A Yale historian and former OSS officer, Rostow had witnessed many covert operations failures, but not one that had so thoroughly demoralized the high command. He joined McGeorge Bundy in the Cabinet Room, where he found Allen Dulles, General Charles Pearre Cabell, and Richard Bissell waiting, seated together at one end of the long cabinet table. The president entered the room; none of the other senior aides who had been involved in the Bay of Pigs was present.

"The largest contribution I made in eight years at the White House," Rostow recalled, "was my role in helping to mop up the Bay of Pigs failure during those three weeks. All my friends and colleagues were having nervous breakdowns. They were in terrible shape; literally, they could not function. So my job was to be cheerful and help John Kennedy." Rostow listened to the three intelligence experts brief Kennedy on the weakness of the brigade's perimeter and their estimates of how long the troops could last. "I could never figure out how grown men like Dick Bissell, who I loved, and Pearre Cabell, a good friend, and Allen, a good friend, got carried away into it," Rostow added. "In retrospect I have concluded that there was this belief in the CIA and the Pentagon that once they got the invasion started, Kennedy would have to involve the U.S. armed forces. It was absolute nonsense and Kennedy had made it clear beforehand; the fact that he was strong enough to hold the line and to take the blame on himself later explains the operation."[21]

Rostow set up shop in the "T-30" operational center and began the difficult process of monitoring the steady erosion of the brigade's strength and its plaintive radio messages for support, calls that quickly turned to bitter curses. "The morale of the Washington team engaged in the operations progressively disintegrated," Rostow said. "This was not the first tactical defeat Americans had ever suffered, nor even the worst that I had observed; but it was painful to see their composure break up." That night, at Bissell's request, Rostow asked Kennedy for one more meeting to consider sending U.S. forces to aid the invasion. There was a White House reception going on for new members of the U.S. Congress. Kennedy, Rusk, and McNamara were in white tie; General Lyman Lemnitzer, the Joint Chiefs chairman, and Admiral Arleigh Burke, the head of Naval Operations, were in full uniform and medals. Bissell laid out the options and pressed both for navy jets and for the task force to come within firing range of the beachhead, if only to support an orderly evacuation. Kennedy was troubled by the fate of the troops, but he was firm. He would not start a war in Cuba. A limited number of fighters could fly cover, and the navy could stand by to rescue those brigade members who could get back to their landing boats. But the word had to be passed: It was every man for himself.

The reaction to JFK's decision among the president's personal team on Wednesday, the 19th, was one of dismay. Rostow remembers Robert Kennedy shouting at the advisers gathered in the Cabinet Room that they had to come up with some way to save the operation. Rostow notes:

Of course, Robert Kennedy did not have the substance his brother had. He was really angry; we would be called "paper tigers" by Moscow. We just could not sit by and let this happen. We had to do something. I asked him to come with me out of the room into the Rose Garden, and we walked along that portico outside the president's office. I told him, if you are in a fight and get knocked on your ass, the worst thing to do is get back up and start swinging. That's the way to really get hurt. This is the time to dance around until your head clears. We will have all the chance in the world to prove we are not "paper tigers"—we have all these problems in Berlin, in Southeast Asia. This is the time to think. This is the time to regain our momentum. And he looked at me for a long time with that cold stare of his. Finally he said, "That's constructive."

I think that's the best day's work I did during that time.[22]

In the immediate aftermath, President Kennedy gave no sign that he held Allen Dulles particularly responsible for the Bay of Pigs failure. For one thing, the full horror of the affair did not become public immediately. World attention that week was distracted by the crisis between President Charles de Gaulle and the rebellion in Algeria that threatened to plunge France into civil war. At home, Kennedy's standing in the public opinion polls rose rather than fell after he forthrightly took responsibility for the operation's failure; shortly afterward he made a well-received speech in which he reaffirmed America's determination to thwart communist subversion in the hemisphere. Dulles later recalled:

The president, without any hesitation, assumed personally full responsibility for the action that had been taken. And without issuing orders he made it clear that... he did not expect his subordinates, others that had been working on this matter, to go out and do some after-game quarterbacking on the thing, and do a lot of talking about it.... I think the country owed him a great deal for that very courageous decision.... I admired him for that stand.... I talked to him a great deal about it afterwards, and while I did have a feeling that he thought I had let him down, there never was one harsh or unkind word said to me by him at anytime thereafter. He never blamed me. He never said you ought to have warned me more about this. You ought to have made it more clear to me—and I think there maybe we did make a mistake—you ought to have made it more clear to me that this air cover was absolutely a *sine qua non*, that this was absolutely essential. We kind of thought we had made that clear, but I guess we hadn't made it clear. You can't land naked vessels with ammunition and supplies on board in the face of any kind of hostile aviation that controls the air.... We had many talks about it and I could hardly tell—I'm sure it had some effect on his views as to my judgment, maybe he felt that I had persuaded him too much. I tried not to.... I may have appeared in that light to him. It was a very difficult decision because if you didn't do it, you had the problem of trying to reverse a line of policy in connection with the training of these men which had set in motion a great many hopes.... [P]olicies were affected, and it wasn't just a thing you could easily turn off the spigot and go off and forget it. You left behind you quite a trail that would have affected our relations with Cuba, and affected, if we ever wanted to do anything like it, affected our ability to do that again.[23]

Kennedy, like Eisenhower, would scarcely have been human if he had not been able to acknowledge his own responsibility in the affair, but still feel he had been let down by his chief central intelligence adviser. Arthur Schlesinger, Jr., reports that the president told him soon after the disaster:

> I probably made a mistake in keeping Allen Dulles on.... It's not that Dulles is not a man of great ability. He is. But I have never worked with him and therefore I can't estimate his meaning when he tells me things.... Dulles is a legendary figure and it's hard to operate with legendary figures.... [As for the CIA] we will have to do something.... I must have someone there with whom I can be in complete and intimate contact— someone from whom I know I will be getting the exact pitch.... Bobby should have been in CIA.[24]

While Kennedy himself never rebuked his intelligence chief, the ground was quickly falling away from beneath Dulles's feet. Blind quotes from unnamed sources began to appear in the leading newspapers. On April 28 David Wise wrote in the *New York Herald Tribune*:

> President Kennedy had planned an overhaul of the Central Intelligence Agency after its Director, Allen W. Dulles, retired at the end of this year or early next year, it was learned today.
> The timetable for the review of the CIA was moved up as a result of last week's ill-fated invasion of Cuba by rebel forces. The President last Saturday named General Maxwell D. Taylor (Ret.) to investigate U.S. intelligence capacities, including the CIA.

The general expectation within the Kennedy administration has been that Mr. Dulles, Director of the CIA since 1953, would step down in 1961 or 1962, it was understood. At that time the administration planned to take a hard look at the controversial agency. The timing of the plan to overhaul has been advanced because the CIA is the agency that organized and executed the unsuccessful rebel invasion, according to informed sources here. When Mr. Kennedy reappointed Mr. Dulles CIA Director as one of his first acts after the election, he did so with the understanding that Mr. Dulles would not be expected to remain on for four years.[25]

Illustrating the article was a photograph of Dulles holding his head in both hands taken at a congressional hearing some months earlier. The message was clear: Dulles was in trouble. The clamor rose. One syndicated columnist reported from "lower echelons of the Kennedy administration" that Dulles had to go because Nikita Khrushchev had complained about him to the new president. Other speculation was that he was about to be replaced by General Taylor, or by General Cabell. In exasperation, Dulles ordered Stanley Grogan, the CIA's press liaison, to track down who was spreading the rumors; Grogan reported back that many of the stories were coming from Richard N. Goodwin, the assistant special counsel to the president. But apparently the leaks were authorized by someone higher up. The suspicion was that Robert Kennedy was the motivating force.

On the same day the blind-source piece by Wise appeared, the Senate Foreign Relations Committee began closed-door hearings into the Bay of Pigs affair. For much of the month of May, Dulles shuttled between sessions on Capitol Hill and the Executive Office Building that adjoins the White House; there, the

Taylor Committee began to take testimony from all the principals who had been involved in planning and running the operation. Political agendas dominated both investigations to an extent that neither Dulles nor Bissell had had to confront in similar covert operations failures, including the U-2 crash. It became clear that the issue of whether Cuba's citizens could have been expected to rally to the brigade's cause was going to be used as a rebuttal to any implied criticism of the president for denying the rebels adequate air protection. It became like the dog that did not bark in the night in the famous Sherlock Holmes story; its significance lay in that the uprising did not happen. Kim Roosevelt's rule that popular support was a key ingredient in any attempt to topple a despot had come home to roost once more.

Senate Foreign Relations Committee Chairman William Fulbright, who was determined to have his original objections underscored at someone's expense, seized on the popular revolt issue and targeted the CIA as the main culprit in his opening address: "The basic mistake, I think, of CIA was the assumption that if you sparked a revolution, sparked this movement, by only a few people, that there would be an uprising, and this just was not so. Their political judgment of the conditions in Cuba was quite wrong. I also think they made technical mistakes as to judgment with respect to the terrain and other matters." On May 1 Secretary Rusk took up the theme and cited for the senators "three misjudgments," each of them the fault of the CIA. The first was "an overestimation of the capacity... of the Cubans inside Cuba to take matters into their own hands. The second was an underestimation of a buildup of the control apparatus in Cuba by mid-April, and the buildup of the weight and quantity of arms which might be brought to bear speedily against this particular enterprise." The third flaw, Rusk asserted, was the mistake the field commander of Brigade 2506 made when, faced with stronger opposition than expected, he did not at once order his 1,500 men to fade into the impenetrable Zapata swamp and slip unnoticed through enemy-held territory to the sanctuary of the Escambray Mountains far away. In short, it was all the CIA's fault.[26] The State Department's neglect in building a popular and political base of credibility for the Cuban government in exile was never mentioned. The failure of the individual Joint Chiefs who rushed the tactical orders for Zapata through in a few days was ignored.

Dulles and Bissell faced the realization that others were trying to pin full responsibility on them and the agency in order to deflect criticism of their own failures. General Lucian K. Truscott, the liaison between military intelligence and the CIA during the Eisenhower years, tried to get Walter Bedell Smith to attack Dulles publicly and to lobby his friend General Taylor to put more blame on the intelligence estimates than on the military operations plan put together by the Joint Chiefs.[27] Admiral Burke, who had represented the navy in the drafting of the Zapata order of battle, protected the navy's reputation during the Taylor testimony sessions. When the time came for both Bissell and Dulles to undergo questioning before the senators or the Taylor group, they could answer only what they felt to be true: There was enough blame for everyone involved, but the agency was not solely at fault. The fatal flaw was the last minute denial of air support. The issue of an instant rally of support by the Cuban people was a non sequitur; the mission had long ceased to be to infiltrate a small band of guerrillas into the populace—it had become an attempt to create an independent force for rebellion in a zone that could be held and expanded. If Castro was as popular as many Kennedy apologists later argued, why was America trying to overthrow him? As history has since demonstrated, a considerable part of the Cuban population might have rallied to the brigade's cause, provided it had lasted long enough to be credible. It was that failure that was fatal.

Whatever the effect of the testimony before Fulbright's committee, the evidence that the Taylor Committee gathered put a reasonable portion of blame on everyone's plate. Bissell and Cabell were explicitly singled out for blame for not adequately informing the president about the essential nature of air cover and, on the fateful Saturday night, for not lobbying hard enough with Rusk and Kennedy.

General William Y. Smith, then an air force major and aide to General Taylor during the probe, agrees that the decision to cancel both the Sunday "follow-up" and the D-Day strike killed any chances of success. But he also points to three fatal flaws in the basic conception of the invasion, flaws that both Dulles and the president should have realized:

> If one looks at it objectively, there is no way there could have been plausible deniability. It was already in the press that we were training those people. You can criticize JFK's advisers the most for thinking they could get by with a plausible denial after all that had been done at that point.
>
> Another thing, and I looked into this. The final plan for the Bay of Pigs operation was developed within a period of ten days to two weeks. The main weakness in those documents is that the chiefs did much of the work themselves without staff assistance. It was not a clearly concise battle plan, not properly staffed. You can't do something of that magnitude in that little time. That is where you get these notions that they could escape into the mountains. No one really did the planning. They misloaded the ships with all the ammunition on one ship and the weapons on another. All that was because of the pressure of time.

Third, I believe there was hope within the CIA that there would be some response from within the nation of Cuba, from among the Cuban people. One of the things that was disappointing was there was no uprising. There were some CIA reports that did say there was no likelihood, but the assumption was they could start it and get away with it. Part of that belief I also believe is that both the chiefs and the CIA thought that if the brigade got into trouble, the United States would have to bail those people out as a matter of course. At that point, you would be so far along that the Cuban people would join in and you could manage whatever backlash you got from Latin America.

As for Allen Dulles, I think it is correct that he wanted this to be Bissell's operation. In fact, if you look at the planning records after January you don't see much of Dulles at all. The only place Dulles could have said something was after the first air raid on Saturday.... He might have made a contribution to what to do next. He might have said on Sunday night, if the president will not go ahead on air strikes then we must call the whole thing off. He could have done that at that moment. But think about that for a moment. It is unlikely he would have interfered. If he had been called in Puerto Rico on Sunday night, he would have said, what does Bissell want to do? And then he would have said, do what Bissell wants done. I would have been surprised if General Cabell had made such a call, or even called the president directly. The only advantage in actually calling the president at that point is to make him tell them directly for their own political advantage later. Military people generally don't think that way, they believe in the chain of command.

I was there with General Taylor after the committee finished [Taylor became Kennedy's chief military aide], and Allen Dulles was very much around. Kennedy was much less irritated with the CIA than he was with the military, that's how I remember it. People remember that Kennedy fired Bissell and Dulles, but Bissell was given a good job as head of the Institute for Defense Analysis. And most people forget that within a year, all of the Joint Chiefs had been replaced— Burke, Lemnitzer, White of the air force, they all were retired, all very quietly.[28]

CHAPTER SIXTEEN

1961–1969

"If this were England and I were Prime Minister,
I would have to resign. But it isn't England and I can't resign.
It's you who have [sic] to go."
—*John F. Kennedy to Allen Dulles,*
August 1961

FAR FROM BEING cautioned by the Bay of Pigs debacle, John Kennedy and his aides were more captivated than ever by covert operations. Within weeks of that failure, the agency had an unexpected success. Plans to help pro-U.S. rivals assassinate Rafael Trujillo in the Dominican Republic were outstripped by the rivals themselves; they ambushed the dictator and shot him dead without the active assistance of the CIA station chief. As with Patrice Lumumba, the agency had helped along the inevitable but had not actually pulled the trigger.

Instead of heeding the rules promulgated by Kermit Roosevelt and other covert veterans, Kennedy and his aides (and those who continued on to advise President Johnson) were prompted by the death of Trujillo to increase their bets in the Dominican Republican intrusion every time the situation deteriorated. The result was a strategic lesson that should have affected the early involvement in Vietnam, but did not. By May 1965 the United States had 23,500 Marines and army troops committed to the Dominican Republic even as President Johnson was planning the Vietnam troop buildup that destroyed his presidency three years later.

Moreover, instead of chastening them, the Bay of Pigs set-back whetted the appetite of the Kennedy's men to get rid of Fidel Castro at any cost. Attorney General Robert Kennedy was the most active advocate of a renewed and personal attack. In October, while Dulles was clearing his desk to leave the CIA in the next month, he and Bissell were ordered by President Kennedy to put Operation Mongoose—the assassination of Castro and as many of his top aides as possible—into readiness. William Harvey was put in charge of Mongoose, which he ran on a separate track from the broader special assassination group with the cover name ZR/Rifle, which had been set up in 1960.[1]

As with the Bay of Pigs affair, considerable confusion sur-rounded who was aware of the Mongoose project, and when per-mission was given to renew existing CIA contacts with Chicago Mafia boss Sam Giancana and Johnny Roselli, a Las Vegas gang-ster. The plan was to use a former Howard Hughes aide named Robert A. Maheu as a "cut-out"—a go-between—to arrange for a Mafia assassin to kill Castro. The killer presumably was to be a mob member left behind in Havana from the days when American gangsters controlled most of the resort hotels and gam-bling casinos there. A payment of $150,000 for the hit was sup-posed to be made to Roselli, and funds were authorized in May 1962, after Dulles had left the agency. As it turns out, no attempt was made, and a tiny sum of the money was spent on expenses.

In 1990 the CIA declassified a 1975 memorandum from Charles N. Kane, the agency's director of security at the time, that was part of the preparation for the Church Committee investiga-tion into covert operations. The report questions previous reports that Operation Mongoose was a "rogue operation"—one con-ducted without the knowledge or approval of senior agency offi-cials such as Dulles and Bissell, and without authorization from anyone within the Kennedy White House. Yet the 1975 report states, "A review of the Office of Security files relating to Robert A. Maheu, Johnny Roselli, and Salvatore (Sam) Giancana disclosed that the operation against Fidel Castro was approved by Allen Dulles, who was DCI at the time.... Further, our files reflect that *six* [emphasis in original] agency people were aware of the operation—Allen Dulles, William Harvey, Richard Bissell, Sheffield Edwards [head of CIA's security division], Colonel J. C. King [head of the agency's Western Hemisphere division under Bissell], and [still classified]."[2]

One of Harvey's chief aides was CIA veteran case officer Sam Halpern, who was called to testify before the Church Committee examination of Operation Mongoose. He recalled later:

> Everyone involved in Mongoose knew it was a Kennedy operation. We had one officer whose sole job was to go to all the people on the criminal side that Bobby Kennedy sent him to. This operation was not just dictated by the president, it became the sole responsibility of his brother, the attorney general. From the beginning, I did not like it.
>
> This did not have anything to do with the United States of America; it had to do with the Kennedy name, the Kennedy escutcheon. That reputation was blemished in the Bay of Pigs, and, goddamnit, they were going to get even.
>
> Bobby Kennedy believed the Mafia had lots of interests in and people in Cuba; he was absolutely convinced that they had left stay-behinds in Cuba and all they had to do was tap into those stay-behinds. Now remember, the CIA had no assets in Cuba, not a pot to piss in. We did have lots of resources, but Castro had rolled them up. So Bobby had this guy of ours, and he

had a telephone to that guy from the attorney general's office that could not be traced through the CIA. Whenever the telephone rang it was from Bobby. And this officer of ours, we gave him a nice sounding Italian name; he went to Chicago and to Canada and New York to have meetings with the mob, and whenever he came back, he met first with Bobby. It was a waste, of course, since the mob had no assets on the island at all.

This was separate, by the way, from Bill Harvey's own operation which he was running in Miami with his Mafia connections. I was his executive officer, and even I did not know what was going on with that one, because he kept it all to himself. He would go to Miami, where he had stashed weapons and cash. All I was supposed to do was call Miami and tell the station chief there to have a car at the airport. That one didn't go anywhere either. But Allen Dulles could not have stopped that operation; we had signalled everyone by then that Cuba was our first priority.³

As the full extent of the Bay of Pigs tragedy began to be grasped by the public, pressure built on the president to replace his top security advisers. Since Dulles still had plenty of friends in high places, Kennedy was reluctant to appear too vindictive. Congressman Clarence Cannon, the chairman of the House Appropriations subcommittee which had jurisdiction over the agency's funding, sent a letter to President Kennedy hoping to offset the increasing rumors that Dulles was about to be fired. The letter said, "Of course, no member of the Legislative Branch of the Government would presume to make any suggestion to you with relation to the appointment of strategic members of your Administration. But the Subcommittee on CIA which, naturally, has been in touch with Mr. Dulles for many years, have found him exceptionally reliable, efficient and competent." The letter was signed by Democrats George Mahon and Harry Shepard and Republicans John Tabor and Gerald R. Ford.[4]

Where and how Allen Dulles got the word that he, General Cabell, and Richard Bissell would have to go remains unclear. The best evidence is that Robert Kennedy was the first to speak to Dulles in the last week of August about leaving. One clue is a note on White House stationery, dated August 29, from Walt Rostow: "Dear Allen: This is merely to record my sadness at your impending resignation. As I told Mrs. Dulles, I have had few heroes and you are one. I learned many things from you, among them how a man behaves when things go wrong...."[5] At about that time, Dulles came back from the White House and reportedly told John Earman, one of his executive staff officers, "I've been fired." On September 27 President Kennedy announced that John A. McCone, a wealthy shipbuilder and former chairman of the Atomic Energy Commission, had been named DCI. Former President Truman, on his first visit to President Kennedy at the White House, made an impassioned plea that Dulles be kept on as DCI; to fire him "is a goddamned shame." It was not too late, Truman argued, for McCone to be given another job in the administration.[6] But it was too late as far as JFK was concerned. Dulles's publicly announced retirement was allowed to stand.

In the six weeks after the formal announcement of the change of command, Dulles briefed McCone on the vast enterprise he would be directing. The two went on a lengthy trip to Europe on which they visited all the major CIA stations and had important conferences with British, French, and German intelligence chiefs on what the change in command would mean to what had been personal relationships with "The Kremlin."

Although McCone would win general approval for his performance as DCI (mainly for his cool head during the Cuban Missile Crisis the next year), the foreign chiefs could not help but contrast Dulles's comfortable bonhomie with his successor's rather dour and formal manner.

The last weeks on the job were also taken up with the completion of a project that had been one of the focal points of Dulles's personal involvement in the agency—the creation and construction of the CIA's new headquarters complex on a fifty-acre campus in Langley, Virginia, outside of Washington, D.C. It had been obvious from the days of Walter Bedell Smith that the agency needed better quarters than "The Kremlin" and its ramshackle warren of "temporaries" along the Reflecting Pool. Dulles had won the $50 million appropriation from Congress (an enormous sum for the time), had selected the site, and worried over every stage of the design and construction. He made no secret that this headquarters was to be his permanent monument. Dulles fretted over the decor of rooms down to the light switches, and designed the DCI's office so that it had an open doorway into the office of the deputy director. Ever the clandestine craftsman, he ordered that there be separate waiting rooms with separate entrances to his office, so, as he chuckled, "The Arabs can come in one door as the Jews go out the other." At the start of the construction project in 1958, he fretted until President Eisenhower agreed to attend a formal ceremony to lay the cornerstone, with Dulles's name firmly engraved on it. Colonel L. K. "Red" White recalled:

> He and I had gone out to see the new Atomic Energy Commission building, which was the first major federal building to be built out of the center of Washington. After he saw that, he said he wanted a cornerstone-laying

ceremony. And I said, "But boss, we don't even have a road out there. Why not wait until the building is up and looks great?" And he said, "Red, there will be a new election soon and we may get a new president who won't keep me around. And I want my name on that building, but not on some copper plate that somebody else can take down later." He was not vain, but he had his pride.[7]

On November 28, the day before Dulles's formal departure, President Kennedy flew by helicopter to Langley for a ceremony to honor him in the building he had created but would never occupy. The occasion showed the Kennedy grace and wit in what must have been a bitter occasion for all concerned. The event was held in the lobby of the main CIA building, and seven hundred officials and employees were assembled as the president arrived with his party, which included Robert McNamara, General Taylor, and Robert Kennedy. Kennedy presented Dulles with the National Security Medal, which joined his Medal for Merit and the Medal of Freedom, the other two top civilian honors. The president said:

I know of no man who brings a greater sense of personal commitment to his work, who has less pride in office than he has. Your successes are unheralded—your failures trumpeted. I sometimes have that feeling myself. But I am sure you realize how important your work is, how essential it is, and how in the long sweep of history, how significant your efforts will be judged.

Dulles was unable to leave that abruptly. He relinquished his director's office with its view of the Lincoln Memorial and moved into quarters nearby. During the weeks that the agency staff was packing up to move from "The Kremlin" to Langley, Dulles annoyed McCone to distraction by popping in unannounced and intruding on meetings to which he had not been invited. When McCone finally moved to the new headquarters, no provision for Dulles was made. Dulles kept a provisional office in "The Kremlin," which remained an agency annex until 1994, but after the center of action moved away, he remained at home an increasing amount of time.

After returning from a Christmas and New Year's holiday in Santa Fe and Phoenix, Clover and Allen began to make the adjustment of living together more closely than they had for thirty years. She still had an active life of her own, and a decision soon had to be made to move their son Allen to an expensive sanitarium in Switzerland. There were plenty of calls for Allen's advice and counsel by old friends in government, but it was obvious that he was no longer wanted at either the White House or the CIA. During the crisis in Berlin, where the East Germans began to build the first of the barricades that would become the Berlin Wall, and later during the showdown with Khrushchev and Castro over the Soviet missile bases in Cuba, Dulles was purposely ignored, although the president was actively seeking advice from old guardsmen such as Dean Acheson and Clark Clifford.

Dulles in the meantime tried to refute a particularly poisonous and error-filled report on the Bay of Pigs debacle prepared by the agency's inspector general, Lyman Kirkpatrick. The report was submitted to McCone in October, six weeks before he became DCI, but kept from Dulles, Cabell, and Bissell until just before their departures; they had not been interviewed or asked for notes on the operation. The purpose was clear: to condemn both the DCI and the monopoly his deputy director and the deputy director for plans had over covert operations. Wayne Jackson, the agency's official biographer of the Dulles years at the agency, bluntly accuses Kirkpatrick of using the report to argue to McCone and the White House that the CIA needed a chief of staff "so as to further his own ambitions."[8]

Dulles now had to face up to the fact that he needed money. Clover's own inheritance had been parceled out to the children, much of it for son Allen's care. Dulles's final years as DCI had seen his government pay climb to the lower rung of a senior executive, $21,000 (a four-star general at the time received $27,000), but the retirement system of the time credited his "twenty-four years, eleven months" of government service as qualifying for an annual pension that netted just $8,732. He was taken back at Sullivan & Cromwell on an "of counsel" basis at $50,000 per year, but at the end of 1962 he had to ask Arthur Dean, the senior partner, to end the stipend because of the claims on his time by the Council on Foreign Relations and other pro bono organizations that interfered with his law work. He would go back on the payroll intermittently after that, but never received a full year's compensation. As a result he and Clover began to scale back on those expenses they could control. Son-in-law Jens Jebsen took over the mortgage payment on the Lloyd Neck house when he and Toddy moved into it on their return from London; Allen and Clover began to take their August holidays back at Henderson Harbor; and they relied heavily on their seven-year-old Pontiac now that he had no CIA car and driver.

Like many men forced from public life, Dulles turned to public speaking and writing to fill up his hours and his bank account. During 1962 he spoke at nearly forty public functions and nearly three dozen the year after. Many were standard off-the-cuff luncheon addresses that are a staple of Washington life. But others were more remunerative convention addresses that required considerable preparation and arduous travel. In 1963 he was asked to prepare the article on intelligence for the *Encyclopedia Britannica Yearbook*. The 41,000-word article was reprinted in *Harper's* magazine and, later that year, was the core of his book, *The Craft of Intelligence*.[9] The book became a Book of the Month Club selection and a best-seller. It led an old friend and contact, *Harper's* editor Cass Canfield, to suggest that Dulles take some of the amusing tales he liked to tell around dinner tables about Operation Sunrise and make a book out of the story. This led to another profitable book two years later, *The Secret Surrender*.[10]

Although both books were immensely popular, Dulles did not receive the full royalties from either. He had inherited the precise but ponderous Dulles writing habits. Without DCI McCone's knowledge or approval, friends at the agency had been detailing talented writers from the staff to help Dulles with his speech- and article-writing since his departure from "The Kremlin." E. Howard Hunt had labored mightily to rewrite an early Dulles book on the Cold War and intelligence, but it could not be salvaged. Then an enduring partnership was formed between Dulles and a CIA officer named Howard Roman, who had retired from the agency to become a novelist—like Howard Hunt and numerous other intelligence experts who knew they could do better than Ian Fleming, and often did. Roman effectively rewrote the bulk of *The Craft of Intelligence*. He went with Dulles to Switzerland in the summer of 1965, where they joined old colleagues such as Generals Terrance Airey and Lyman Lemnitzer and Swiss spymaster Max Waibel for a reunion during which they recorded reminiscences about Operation Sunrise. *The Secret Surrender* was a collaboration with Gero Gaevernitz, who included his own memoirs and who was active in a related scheme to produce a movie script for a Hollywood producer. It still fell to Howard Roman to pull the manuscript together, and, to Dulles's credit, he was generous with the royalties both books earned. Later, Roman selected much of the material for two anthologies of spy stories that appeared and gave credit to Dulles as the editor.[11] Both books sold well, but the income to Dulles was much reduced.

Dulles also lectured at dozens of universities, most frequently at Princeton. He continued to attend regular meetings of the Gun Club, which argued over National Intelligence Estimates that the Kennedy team no longer relied upon. The lecturing did not pay well but afforded him the opportunity to speak his mind about the craft he loved so much and about the state of intelligence. Increasingly, Dulles found himself called upon to defend the agency. He was able to say publicly things that the succeeding DCIs could or would not say in its defense. Increasingly in his retirement years, Dulles was pulled back into public view and into public controversies and crises.

The investigation of the shocking murder of President Kennedy in November 1963 was part of a sad and ultimately unsuccessful attempt to rehabilitate Allen Dulles. President Johnson appointed him to be a member of the Warren Commission to probe the assassination, along with Chief Justice Earl Warren, Senators Richard Russell and John Sherman Cooper, Congressmen Hale Boggs and Gerald Ford, and diplomat John McCloy. The Warren Commission was a source of dissatisfaction even to its members; it became in reality a board of editors who faced a mountain of documentary, and sometimes conflicting, evidence about the killing of the president. The correspondence in Dulles's personal papers shows that a major preoccupation of all the commission members was to satisfy the American public that Lee Harvey Oswald had acted alone and, above all, had not had any ties to the CIA, the FBI, or any other arm of the government. That matter of intense personal concern to Lyndon Johnson lent weight to the determination to calm public doubts about what exactly had happened in Dallas on that tragic day.

The record also shows that Dulles was not that much involved in the commission's work. He attended most of the formal meetings, which were held twice or three times a week that spring and early summer of 1964. But in June, he was deputized by President Johnson as his special representative to rush to Mississippi to demonstrate the White House's outrage and concern at the murder of three civil rights workers. The president had a reason for picking Dulles for the job, although, as Allen confessed, he had not involved himself in the civil rights struggle and was not even sure who the governor of Mississippi was. The kidnapping and murder of the three young activists had come at a time when tempers on both sides had reached the flash point. Johnson was working hard to win passage by Congress of the 1964 Civil Rights Act; he had shed many of the common white southern prejudices and was trying mightily to coax many of his old Senate and House colleagues into line. What Dulles had to do was convince all sides that the federal government would aggressively pursue the murders and that they must remain calm while the political process worked its way in Washington. It is a tribute to his personal charm that on his return after an arduous but successful two days of meetings he left a calmer Mississippi.

Some were offended at Dulles's return to public life. Johnson, who seemed determined to rehabilitate Dulles almost to spite JFK loyalists, appointed him to a special study commission headed by Roswell Gilpatric on future policies for nuclear weapons development. And Dulles would be a member of an informal panel of foreign policy advisers who could be summoned to the White House on short notice for the kind of impromptu sessions that President Johnson liked to have when he was confronted with a problem.

Dulles was called upon increasingly to appear on television debates on the host of conspiracy theories that challenged the Warren Commission hearings. He joked in private that the conspiracy buffs would have had a field day if they had known of a number of strange coincidences—that he had actually been in Dallas three weeks before the murder (on a book tour to promote *The Craft of Intelligence*); that one of Mary Bancroft's childhood friends had turned out to be a landlady for Marina Oswald, the assassin's Russian-born wife; and that the landlady was a well-known leftist with distant ties to the family of Alger Hiss.

More frequently, Dulles was called on to take on the public defense of his beloved CIA. A growing frustration over increased American involvement in Laos and Vietnam had become a favorite topic in the press, and the agency was a favorite target. Books began to be published describing the CIA as a cabal within the federal government that concocted violence all over the world without authority or supervision. And revisionists within the Kennedy clan blamed the agency and Dulles personally for leading an unwitting President Kennedy into the Bay of Pigs disaster. Kennedy White House aides Theodore C. Sorensen and Arthur M. Schlesinger, Jr., published articles in *Life* and *Look* magazines in mid-1965 that portrayed a young, trusting president being inveigled into the Zapata morass by a wily DCI and his cold warriors at the agency. Dulles was accused of promising Kennedy that the operation would be more successful than the Guatemala "op" and that a spontaneous uprising of the Cuban people was assured. Books, expanded from the articles, were published later in the year.[12]

Part of the motivation for the pieces lay in the conviction held by Kennedy loyalists that Dulles had betrayed JFK first. In September 1961, shortly after Dulles had been told he was fired, the business magazine *Fortune* carried a long story about the Bay of Pigs and other administration foreign policy crises during the first nine months of the Kennedy presidency. The article was written by Charles J. V. Murphy, a senior Time-Life correspondent and a friend of Dulles. Murphy wrote: "Nevertheless, in any full review of John Kennedy's first months in office, there must be reported a failure in administration that will continue to inhibit and trouble American foreign policy until it is corrected. This failure raises a fair question: whether Kennedy has yet mastered the governmental machinery, whether he is well and effectively served by some of his close advisers, and whether they understand the use of power...." The Murphy story so angered the White House that General Maxwell Taylor was twice sent to New York to demand corrections and retractions from Henry Luce; he was turned down both times.

The specific nature of Murphy's disclosures, particularly of the decisions on air cover, convinced the White House that Dulles was responsible for a leak to his friend. He was not. The CIA's own history of the event, which calls Murphy's version "essentially correct," also notes that Murphy offered to show Dulles a copy of the manuscript before publication, but Dulles wanted nothing to do with it. Indeed, while many sources Murphy relied upon came from within the agency, others were from men within the Kennedy circle who thought the president had been ill-served by other rivals.

As for Dulles, what angered him most about the Sorensen and Schlesinger pieces was what he saw as a violation of Kennedy's own decision that he personally would take the responsibility for the Bay of Pigs and that there would be no second-guessing.

Encouraged by Cass Canfield, Dulles set out to correct the record. During the autumn of 1965 he labored on a rebuttal for *Harper's* magazine; at one point, writer Willie Morris was detailed to help Dulles lighten up and condense his prose until finally a seven thousand–word article was set in galley proofs. The recounting shows that Dulles was badly hurt by Schlesinger's quoting Kennedy's lament at having reappointed him as DCI. He was further distressed that Sorensen and Schlesinger, especially the latter, had written the offending pieces. He wrote:

> Were these offhand comments given in moments of great tension and stress, or were they President Kennedy's carefully considered opinions? Were they given after calm deliberation, or in moments of strain? Was

President Kennedy speaking for the record, or merely finding relief from the emotions of the moment?

As he himself points out, Sorensen knew nothing about the Cuban operation until it was over. He only knew how I might have felt and the nature of my advice at second hand. Schlesinger was deeply involved in the arduous task of dealing with the Cuban refugee leaders and was not directly concerned with operational planning. Neither was in a position to see the planning at close quarters. Neither was in on many confidential sessions others and I had with President Kennedy. Neither knows more than a small part of the story.[13]

In his own defense, Dulles recalled his early and affectionate ties to John Kennedy and his close friendship with Jacqueline Kennedy. She had given him his first copy of an Ian Fleming novel from the "James Bond" series, and he had importuned his friend Fleming to keep the first lady supplied with first editions of the series as they appeared. "If I appeared to President Kennedy as a legendary figure, I think the feeling of affection and respect remained," he wrote. He was, after all, appointed to the Taylor group to investigate the operation; that must stand for something.

Finally, the Dulles article came as close as he ever would to criticizing Kennedy himself: "Great actions require great determination. In these difficult types of operations, so many of which I have been associated with over the years, one never succeeds unless there is a determination to succeed, a willingness to risk some unpleasant political repercussions, and a willingness to provide the basic military necessities. At the decisive moment of the Bay of Pigs operation, all three of these essentials were lacking."[14] Then, having vented his anger, Dulles handed the galley proofs to Clover to read. She advised him that those who knew the true story did not need the article to bolster their opinion of him; those who chose to believe otherwise would never be convinced. He agreed, and to the magazine's dismay, he withheld it from publication. Life was too short.

The last three years of Allen Dulles's life saw his health deteriorate more markedly. He had his good days—trips to the Bahamas with Clover, long visits to Europe where old friends could be counted upon to fete them at every stop along the way. Honorary degrees (from Columbia and Princeton) and medals (the French Legion d'Honneur) also arrived, and Dulles frankly relished the role of elder statesman. His children had weathered their various storms. Toddy and Jens Jebsen were in Lloyd Neck. Joan had divorced again, taken up the study of Jungian psychology in Switzerland, and become an analyst herself. In 1966 she moved to Santa Fe, New Mexico, and brought her brother Allen there so she could keep watch on his care; they live there still. Grandchildren were a large and happy part of those final years. Clover and Mary Bancroft kept up their close friendship, and Allen did the honors in giving away Mary's daughter when she married.

Old friends from forgotten wars arrived in Washington and came to the house on Que Street for one last candlelit night of laughter and for tales that were just a little taller than they had been at the last retelling. As always, Dulles kept to his reputation for elusive discretion; "chatty as a clam," one wit described him.

But Dulles began to pay the inevitable price for the hectic life he had led. In his final years as DCI, his gout, despite steady dosages of colchicine, had often confined him to a large easy chair with a high footstool in his office at "The Kremlin." He would bound out of his car in the morning and limp back to it late in the evening on crutches. Eugene Olsen, the official stenographer who often worked the long weekend shifts in the DCI's office, remembers: "When I think of Allen Dulles, I see him with his glasses up on his forehead, hunched over some paper as he read through it. And he would be massaging those huge knuckles of his, rubbing away the pain, but you would never guess that he was in pain. When he was thinking, he would fuss with that pipe of his, clean it and put tobacco in it, and then he would call somebody and tell them what he had decided. Then he would turn to me and say, 'Welllll, Gene, what's next?' And on we would go for hours. Only when he got up to leave would you realize that he had another attack of gout, he would be all bent over."

Not surprisingly, Dulles developed hypertension and began to put on weight. His last CIA physical listed him at 190 pounds, at least thirty pounds heavier than when he had joined the agency eleven years earlier. In 1962 he was hospitalized with a painful kidney stone. He began to be mildly diabetic and in 1964 suffered a burst blood vessel in his eye that restricted his reading for a time. A year later, another clot, this time a mild cerebral accident, also affected his sight for a while. By 1966 visitors to Que Street began to notice that Dulles had trouble keeping his balance. Arthur Schlesinger, Jr., recalls one visit when Dulles had to hold onto the backs of the chairs as he moved about the room. Dulles began to consult specialists at Wayne State University's neurology department. At that time he was taking daily doses of Orinase for his diabetes; Anturane and colchicine for his gout; Dipaxin, an anticoagulant, for his clots; and Arlidine for hypertension. In addition, he reported frequent use of Seconal to get to sleep at night.

The public speaking trips were drastically cut back but still numbered more than two dozen in 1966 and fifteen or so the next year. He also devoted an increasing amount to time to advising his successors at the agency on how best to counter the flood of books that had begun to criticize the CIA, some of them by journalists who had benefitted in the past by agency confidential briefings. He and a secretary devoted their mornings to corre-spondence and to collecting material for the anthologies he and Howard Roman were producing. Often he would go to lunch at the Metropolitan Club or his other favorite hideaway, the Alibi Club, a nearby luncheon and social club for the most powerful of Washington's power elite. Then there would be visitors in the afternoon. If Clover was there, they had at least one dinner a week with guests. If she was in Switzerland or visiting elsewhere, he often accepted invitations out at night and cadged a ride home with one of the other guests. Allen Dulles in black tie, with black cloth slippers to cover his gnarled feet, was a common sight in those final years.

During the last two years or so left to him, Allen began to suffer recurring bouts of short-term memory loss. Cousin Eleanor Elliot, who had moved back to New York after her job as Foster's social secretary, kept close contact with Clover during those years.

"Uncle Allen," she said, "would go off to lunch at the Metropolitan Club or the Alibi Club and forget how to get home. Sometimes he would just get lost in the neighborhood, and peo-ple who recognized him would bring him back. Clover was so worried. I remember one night a doctor, a specialist, came to the house. I could not hear what he said, but it was clear that he was telling Uncle Allen that his condition could only get worse—per-haps it was what we call Alzheimer's disease today. But I could hear Uncle Allen in that deep voice of his asking the doctor whether he was sure, absolutely sure that nothing could be done. And finally, I heard him say, 'Well, thank you, Doctor. Say, could I make contribution to your research department? Maybe you can help someone else later.' That was so like him."

Yet when death did come, it was unexpected. He and Roman had nearly finished editing *Great Spy Stories from Fiction* in

December 1968 when he was put to bed with a severe case of influenza. He and Clover tried to treat it at home for a week or so, but the infection settled in his lungs and made breathing difficult. There is a malicious and fabricated legend that he was found, gasping and alone in his bedroom, by guests attending a Christmas Eve cocktail party hosted by an oblivious Clover. But he was admitted to Georgetown University Hospital just before the holiday, where his condition improved, then worsened, over the next month, finally turning into pneumonia. During the moments when he felt better, Dulles wrote cheerful, forward-looking notes to friends, including congratulations to Richard Nixon, whose inauguration was a few days away. Toward the end of January, Clover herself was put to bed with a severe sinus infection; she postponed plans to go visit their son Allen in Santa Fe. At 11:00 PM on January 29, Allen Dulles died of the complications from his illness. He had been napping all day when he had difficulty breathing, lapsed into unconsciousness, and never revived.

"The next morning, Dick Helms called and said Allen had died and to get over there [to the Que Street house] fast," Colonel "Red" White remembered. "We got some phone lines put in there to handle the condolence calls, and some people started looking through his files. Eleanor, Jim Angleton, and Charles Murphy worked on the eulogy in his office. I don't think the minister was too happy about having someone else write his stuff, but Eleanor made short work of that. Clover was upstairs, as I remember."[15] Late in the day, the news media was notified that Dulles had died.

It is tempting to compare the funeral services that were held two days later on February 1 for Allen Dulles at the Georgetown Presbyterian Church with the enormous spectacle of Foster Dulles's farewell at the National Cathedral in 1959. Foster's had been the formal national ceremony of a government official who had died in office. Network television cameras were there to record the parade of world greats, including General de Gaulle, and the representatives of every free nation in the world. Foster went to his rest after lying in state, accompanied by an honor guard of troops. Flags were lowered to half-staff on all government buildings for a month of official mourning. Tributes from prime ministers and presidents of other countries flowed into Washington, and President Eisenhower was publicly stricken by the loss of his close adviser.

Ten years later, Allen Dulles had his final remembrance in far more modest surroundings. Few of the great men he had served came to say goodbye. President Richard Nixon sent Vice President Spiro Agnew in his place, though the president did send flowers. An assistant secretary of state, his successor John McCone, and the ambassadors from Britain, New Zealand, and Australia were the only other dignitaries who showed up to honor a man who had left official power eight years before. But it is fitting that both of Allen Dulles's families—his own and the CIA—filled the church to overflowing. The Dulles clan rallied around the still ailing Clover, who was escorted down the aisle by Richard Helms, loyal to the end. Then came the honorary pallbearers: Arthur Dean, his old law partner; Hamilton Fish Armstrong, his comrade from the Council on Foreign Relations; General Alfred Gruenther, an ally of both hot and cold wars; Peter Belin and Charles Murphy, his neighbors and friends; diplomat Livingston Merchant; and agency stalwarts James Angleton, James Hunt, and "Red" White.

Hundreds of the other family, the officers and staff of the CIA, filled the remaining seats, and hundreds more stood outside the church in silent tribute to a man who had touched each of their lives. At the end of the service, they listened as the minister, Russell Stroup, read the eulogy to Allen Dulles, a remembrance to "a splendid watchman… a familiar and trusted figure in clear outline on the American ramparts, seeing that the nation could not be surprised in its sleep or overcome in the night....

"Allen Dulles began his public life as a Wilsonian Liberal. To the end he believed with Wilson that Americans were 'destined to set a responsible example to all the world of what free government is and can do.' He lived by this belief and he, himself, never bent to compromise. Allen Dulles's faith, public philosophy, and life itself, were all of a piece.... Men everywhere knew where Allen Dulles stood. This is what has made his many colleagues a band of brothers."

Dulles was buried that afternoon in the Baltimore cemetery plot of Clover's relatives, the Gilman family. She joined him there seven years later.

WHAT, THEN, DOES ONE make of Allen Welsh Dulles?

As one of a series of directors of Central Intelligence, his flaws and failures are, as President Kennedy noted, easy to trumpet. He kept too many things to himself. He did play favorites among his staff and often worked those favorites to collapse or past their levels of competence and endurance. Men like Richard Bissell, Frank Wisner, William Harvey, and, arguably, James Angleton were as much victims as they were beneficiaries of Dulles's favor. But Dulles also had the capacity to keep the loyalties of men whom he sometimes misused: Walter Pforzheimer, who was sent to confront Roy Cohn; or Lawrence Houston, who was handed a hundred cans of legal worms to deal with; or Richard Helms, who endured his share of slights.

But no one ever doubted that Dulles matched their dedication and shared their cause. He also gave even the lowest-ranking case officers a most precious gift, the encouragement to do the best job they could. If the Dulles style defied bureaucratic doctrines, it inspired the men and women of the CIA to a level of

involvement and energy that did not exist elsewhere in government service then and does not now. The agency under Dulles
became the elite service he had urged in 1947, a happy band that
shared with Dulles his belief in their common cause—to provide
the presidents they served with the best insight available on the
"capabilities and intentions" of America's friends and enemies
around the world. The personality of the CIA became Allen
Dulles's, and it remained so for a long time after his passing.

Allen Dulles did not, as many within the intelligence community argued, push the CIA into the single dominant intelligence authority over the Pentagon and State Department—turn it
into another KGB—because he knew from the past that war with
the other services was folly. But he did enhance the quality of the
National Intelligence Estimates prepared for the president and the
National Security Council. Although aware that those who govern
often ignore the estimates and make decisions based on emotions
such as fear, prejudice, and anger, by the same token he moved
with enthusiasm as one president after another developed a taste
for the quick fixes of covert operations. He had learned that lesson in Bern in two world wars: You can listen endlessly to theorists,
but it is the secret surrenders and the covert victories that shape
history, if only on a short-term basis. If that is an unpleasant
truth, Allen Dulles did not invent it; it came with the world he
moved in. He often recalled to aides during the dark hours of
some watch that he had become the only man in America during
peacetime who could order a man to face death for his country.
He did that hundreds of times to thousands of men and women
who went where brutal things are done in good causes.

To make those kinds of decisions, any person would have to
build a kind of mask, a public persona behind which to hide one's
true feelings and emotions. Otherwise, he or she could not survive for long, and Allen Dulles was a survivor. Some took the

mask as the real Dulles, seeing only the jovial, professorial hearty in a tweed suit and bow tie. Some were offended by his private life, ignoring that his family bore his frailties with love and no apologies. Some only saw the man who loved to go to parties and to play tennis; they heard yarns about how he would summon young aides to his office on a Saturday afternoon to drink beer and listen to a baseball game on the radio and miss that a tutorial was also being conducted, and young minds were being tested. It was easy to dismiss Allen Dulles as "frivolous."

But ask the question another way: If Allen Dulles were alive today, how would he judge what his agency has become in the decades since his departure? How would he advise those who even now are trying to erect a new intelligence edifice for the new century?

First, he would be alarmed. The agency he handed to his successors was truly the central collecting agency for American presidents and their most senior advisers. The CIA had both control over the mechanisms of intelligence and access to the ultimate consumers. It was the central marketplace through which other competing intelligence gatherers brought their wares to the attention of the policymakers. Today numerous agencies of government are larger, better funded, and on independent missions beyond the CIA mandate, such as the Photographic Reconnaissance Office, which interprets the images bounced back to earth from the dozens of spy satellites the United States keeps aloft these days. Even the Joint Chiefs of Staff, which once had no in-house intelligence capacity of its own, now has a private war room in the Pentagon where the latest satellite and signals intelligence data can be ordered and analyzed—this over and above the intelligence capacities of the separate military services and the Defense Intelligence Agency.

Not only has the agency lost its preeminence in the technology of intelligence, but its final product of analysis—the ultimate reason for its being—is no longer the raw material of policy; often agency insights are spurned by chief executives. The situation deteriorated so badly during the Reagan administration that the president's top security advisers set up their own intelligence service—complete with covert operations capacity—inside the White House until the Iran-Contra scandal engulfed them. George Bush, to name another president, considered himself his own best counsel on such matters. Bill Clinton, for another, has a personal distaste for intelligence matters and relies on summaries prepared by senior aides.

But Dulles would not have been too surprised by the discovery of Aldrich Ames, the Soviet mole, inside his CIA. The shift from vertical organization, the disarray of supervisory personnel, the loss of a sense of mission that characterized the 1980s made an Ames inevitable. It is the apparent loss of a mission that would worry Dulles most. Today, the intelligence architects have begun their debate on the future of American intelligence by conceding at the start that no single agency of government can be the central director of guidance to the White House; nor is there much public concern about the spread of intelligence gathering and of covert operations among other government services, even into the private sector of high technology government contractors.

The competing sources of intelligence among various agencies today would disturb Dulles, but he would be appalled at how much of America's clandestine flow of information and analysis is coming from private sources. In another area, the happy days of the congressional blank check are gone, but even Dulles would have applauded that change, for he recognized that the studied indifference of congressmen and senators was really a sham attempt at building their own plausible deniability. But the competition for funds, the expensive nature of satellite and electronics technology, and the global mandate of America's watch-services have meant that increasing numbers of private contractors now operate spy systems and direct the flow of information that official decision-makers have no choice but to use. When the United States began to take an active role in forcing a disengagement of the warring factions in Bosnia, the NATO satellite interpretation was done from the secret Molesworth base in England by a staff of private contractors on loan from the U.S. Joint Chiefs. During the 1991 Desert Storm war, radar intelligence personnel provided by low-bid private firms threatened to leave Kuwait when the first Scud missiles landed nearby. That would most certainly make the old case officer shudder.

Yet Allen Dulles was a great believer in open-source intelligence. As seen, he credited it with as much as 80 percent of the final product. Presumably, then, he would rejoice in the information revolution that computer technology has brought in recent years. He would also presumably urge that congressional leaders be brought even closer into the intelligence loop—to deny them plausible deniability, and to tighten the controls on the confidentiality lacking among committee staffs.

Most important, Allen Dulles would call for a new elite to be drawn into the ranks of the CIA and insist that it resume its role as the central and civilian-run informant of presidents. This new elite would not need to come so predominantly from one class or university community. The excellence and variety of the American university system has spread and prospered to an astonishing degree since his day, and he would rejoice in it. He would urge a focusing of the agency's access to its greatest asset outside the government, the best minds of those universities and corporations. He would not balk at private contracting per se, but he would demand that private sources of information understand their obligations as being to more than personal profit.

Finally, Allen Dulles would sound the alarm that America's internal security is only marginally better today than it was in the final days of the Cold War. True, one need no longer fear Soviet tanks rumbling through the Fulda Gap toward France. The menace has metastasized however into a thousand smaller virulent tumors of terror. Organized crime, drug cartels, religious and ethnic radicals, and rogue nuclear warlords have demonstrated with chilling clarity that America's borders are easily penetrated with horrible effect. At a time when America's future increasingly lies in foreign arenas, the nation's domestic vulnerability has rarely been so threatened. This is not the time for the false economy of budget cutting or of parceling out the final responsibility for providing hard information about the intentions and capabilities of our enemies.

Dulles would surely argue that the role of the United States as world citizen, as major economic force among other nations, and as occasional referee is a logical progression from the Wilsonian idea of mutual security. America is not the lone policeman of the world, but it has relations and obligations that involve other nations and regions that bring us tremendous benefit and prosperity even as they confront us with problems. We cannot shrink from those problems today any more than we could have remained strictly neutral in 1939. To stay in the world under these conditions, our intelligence resources must be rebuilt and nurtured by men and women of the same dedication that Allen Dulles and his band of brothers and sisters had for more than forty years.

Dulles was, throughout his life, much more than a fixture of the Wilsonian ideal that has dominated American lives for the past eighty years. He brought a rich heritage of commitment to his ambition; he was indebted to both his grandfather and uncle for his conviction that the safety of a free society must be protected by that institutional paradox, a publicly accountable secret service. If that ideal was wrong, then Dulles was wrong, and the concept on which the CIA was founded was also wrong. If the past fifty years were wrongly cast then the Truman Doctrine, the Marshall Plan, and the Cold War were all ghastly mistakes. And indeed, there are those who lately argue just that—that by aggressively fighting and confounding the ambitions of the Soviet Union, the United States exacerbated Moscow's fears and made it more militant than it might have been. But it is necessary to cast a full reckoning of recent history.

Any fair accounting of Allen Dulles and his agency must "trumpet" the failures: Vietnam, Indonesia, and, of course, the Bay of Pigs, which occurred on Dulles's watch. We blanch at the assassination plots, the drug experiments, and some of the other bizarre schemes that he ordered during both his OSS and CIA days. But then consider the map and condition of the world that Allen Dulles and that first "band of brothers" confronted when they arrived at the Hotel Crillon in Paris in the winter of 1918. Consider the community of nations they erected out of the destruction of World War I. Recall the decades of work at conferences to win a lasting peace among those nations. Faced with a more horrifying conflict between despots and democracy, Dulles and those brothers—now no longer boys—rallied yet again, and won that next battle, too. Their response—to try to build more democracies, to labor in yet another forum for the peaceful resolution of world conflicts—was truly remarkable. When that faith was tested yet a third time by those who would subsidize their own cruel power by enslaving others, Allen Dulles could hardly have viewed the Cold War as anything but a struggle from which only one side could survive, a struggle which could never be ended by conciliation or surrender.

Fairness dictates that any accounting of the life of Allen Dulles and his agency must also acknowledge the list of "unheralded" victories and ask whether the Japanese, the Filipinos, the citizens of a dozen European countries and of entire regions of

South America and Asia are the better for the existence of both the CIA and Allen Dulles.

Then look to the future. How much has really changed since Allen Dulles began his quest in Vienna in 1916? This century has had few moments when some war of aggression has not brought fresh carnage and horrors to America's door. We have tried and discarded a variety of responses. We have shrunk inward only to learn again that we cannot hide. We have experimented with every known form of intelligence gathering and counterthrust and have been confronted time and again with basic truths such as those devised by William Donovan, Allen Dulles, and Kermit Roosevelt. Now, it seems, we are about to learn those lessons again, and again at some painful cost.

One of the great pleasures of Dulles's last year of life came in March 1968, when "Red" White and Richard Helms invited him out to the Langley headquarters of the CIA to unveil the bas-relief medallion that carried his portrait. The medallion hangs in the central lobby of the CIA headquarters building, and its inscription is a rough translation of a Latin motto, *Si monumentum requiris circumspice*. White and Helms had written, "His monument is around us."

They meant the agency and its traditions. In truth, Allen Dulles's monument lives on in the world around us. So do the truths that guided him.

NOTES

CHAPTER ONE

1 Chalmers Roberts, Interview with author, 1995.

2 John Watson Foster, *Diplomatic Memoirs* (New York: Houghton Mifflin & Co., 1910); *also,* William Castle, *John Watson Foster,* Volume VIII of the series *American Secretaries of State and Their Diplomacy* edited by Samuel Flagg Bemis (New York: Alfred A. Knopf, 1928); *also,* Townsend Hoopes, *The Devil and John Foster Dulles* (New York: Atlantic-Little Brown, 1973); *also,* Dulles Family Papers, Boxes 290–295, Seeley G. Mudd Library, Princeton University.

3 Edith Foster Dulles, *The Story of My Life* (1934, unpublished). From the private papers of Eleanor Lansing Dulles, by permission.

4 Ibid.

5 Eleanor L. Dulles, *Chances of a Lifetime* (New York: Prentice-Hall, Inc., 1980).

6 Deane and David Heller, *John Foster Dulles: Soldier for Peace* (New York: Holt, Rinehart & Winston, 1960).

7 Daniel M. Smith, *Robert Lansing and American Neutrality* (Berkeley: University of California Press, 1958), 1.

8 "The Boer War, A History," Allen W. Dulles, first privately published in 1902. From a copy reprinted by the Central Intelligence Agency in 1953, Mudd Library, Princeton.

9 Edith Foster Dulles, *The Story of My Life.*

10 Allen W. Dulles, Private Papers, Seeley G. Mudd Library, Princeton University [hereafter "AWD Papers"], Box 2.

11 Class of 1914 Yearbook, Princeton University Press. From a copy in the Mudd Library Alumni Records section at Princeton.

12 AWD Papers, Box 3, Interview with United Press International, July 31, 1964.

13 Walter Lord, *The Good Years* (New York: Harper & Brothers, 1960), 333.

14 AWD Papers, Box 24.

CHAPTER TWO

1 David Smith, *Robert Lansing and the Wilson Interregnum 1919–1920* (Berkeley: University of California Press, 1957).

2 British Foreign Office, Files for the Washington Embassy, 1915. File FO 115/1977, Public Record Office, Kew.

3 Robert Lansing, Private Papers, National Archives microfilm box M743, Washington, DC.

4 Herbert O. Yardley, *The American Black Chamber* (Indianapolis: Bobbs-Merrill, 1931).

5 Robert Lansing, Private Papers.

6 Julius W. Pratt, a profile of Lansing in *The American Secretaries of State and Their Diplomacy* (New York: Alfred A. Knopf, 1928).

7 Pratt.

8 James Kerney, *The Political Education of Woodrow Wilson* (New York: Century, 1929).

9 Pratt.

10 AWD Papers, Box 241.

11 U.S. State Department Personnel File, Allen W. Dulles, File 123D88, National Archives, Washington, DC.

12 James Cabell Bruce, *Memoirs* (Baltimore: Gateway Press, Inc., 1975).

13 Nigel West, *MI5: British Security Service Operations, 1909–1945* (London: Stein and Day, 1981).

14 William R. Stevenson, *A Man Called Intrepid* (New York: Sphere Books, 1977); *also,* H. Montgomery Hyde, *Room 3603* (New York: Farrar, Straus & Co., 1962); *also,* other sources spoke to the author on their experiences in both MI5 and OSS only on an off-the-record basis.

15 Anthony Cave Brown, *The Last Hero: Wild Bill Donovan* (New York: Times Books, 1982).

16 Nigel West, *MI6: British Secret Intelligence Service Operations, 1909–1945* (London: Weidenfeld & Nicolson, 1983).

17 Thomas F. Troy, *Wild Bill and Intrepid* (New Haven: Yale University Press, 1996).

18 Robert Lansing, "The President's Attitude Toward Great Britain and Its Dangers, 1916," a confidential memo in the Lansing Papers, Mudd Library, Princeton.

19 U.S. State Department Personnel Files, Allen Dulles, Files 1910–1929, Files 123D85/72 and 123D8960-Box 1330, National Archives, Washington, DC.

20 Michael Beschloss, *Mayday* (New York: Harper & Row, 1986), 126.

21 Sanche De Gramont, *The Secret War* (New York: G. P. Putnam's Sons, 1962).

22 AWD Papers, Box 4, 1917.

23 Lansing, Cable to Dulles, March 28, 1917; *also,* Robert Lansing, *The War Memoirs of Robert Lansing* (New York: Bobbs-Merrill Co., 1935).

24 Ronald W. Pruessen, *John Foster Dulles: The Road to Power* (New York: The Free Press, 1982).

25 Barbara Tuchman, *The Zimmermann Telegram* (New York: Macmillan Publishing Co., 1958), 7.

26 Dumas Malone, *War and Troubled Peace, 1917–1939* (New York: Appleton-Century-Crofts, 1960).

CHAPTER THREE

1   U.S. State Department Personnel File, Allen W. Dulles, File 123D88, National Archives, Washington, DC.

2   Robert Murphy, *Diplomat Among the Warriors* (New York: Doubleday, 1964).

3   AWD Papers, Boxes 4 and 5, 1917–1918.

4   AWD Papers, Box 4, May 21, 1917.

5   R. L. Craigie, Jr., Interview with author, 1993.

6   AWD Papers, Box 5, 1917–1918.

7   Anthony Read and David Fisher, *Colonel Z* (New York: Viking, 1984), 148; *also*, Author's interviews with British intelligence sources.

8   Robert Lansing, Copies of personal and confidential letters to President Wilson. Documents 364–368, Box M743, April 8, 1917, Microfilm Collection of State Department Documents in the National Archives, Washington, DC.

9   Lansing, *War Memoirs*, 174.

10   AWD Papers, Box 5, December 1917.

11   AWD Papers, Box 8, Paris Peace Conference, January 29, 1919.

12   G. J. A. O'Toole, *The Encyclopedia of American Intelligence and Espionage* (New York: Facts on File, 1988), 192–193.

13   Ibid, 358–359; *also*, Rhodri Jeffreys-Jones, *American Espionage: From Secret Service to CIA* (New York: The Free Press, 1977), 71–85.

14   Ray Stannard Baker, Conversation with Vance McCormick, July 15, 1928. From Series IB of the Baker Papers Collection in the Library of Congress.

15   John Foster Dulles, Personal Papers, Daily Record March 27–August 24, 1919, Reparations Commission File, Mudd Library, Princeton.

16   AWD Papers, Paris Peace Conference Files, February 16, 1919.

17   John Foster Dulles, Personal Papers, Memorandum dated April 1, 1919; *also*, Pruessen, 40–41.

18   AWD Papers, Box 8, August 29, 1919.

19   AWD Papers, Box 7, Letter to Alexander Kirk, dated November 13, 1919.

20   AWD Papers, Box 7, Letter to John C. Hughes, dated November 29, 1919.

21   AWD Papers, Box 7, Letter to Alexander Kirk.

22   AWD Papers, Box 9, Letter to John M. Colt, dated January 14, 1920.

CHAPTER FOUR

1   AWD Papers, Box 9, February 8, 1920.

2   AWD Papers, Box 9, April 5, 1920.

3   Pruessen, 58–65.

4   Lansing, *The Peace Negotiations* (New York: Houghton Mifflin, 1921), 3–4.

5   "Wilson Acted Alone for U.S. in Drafting Treaty, says Lansing," *New York Sun*, August 7, 1919, 1–2.

6   Daniel Smith, "Robert Lansing and the Wilson Interregnum, 1919–1920," *The Historian*, Vol. XXI, no. 2, February 1959, 135–161; *also*, "The Bullitt Mission to Russia; the Testimony before the Committee on Foreign Relations of the United States Senate of William C. Bullitt," *New York Times*, September 13, 1919.

7   Allen W. Dulles, "Woodrow Wilson: Prophecy and Perspective for the Present," Speech for Lamont Lecture, Yale University, November 27, 1956. Copy in AWD Papers, Box 72.

8   U.S. State Department Personnel and Cable Records for Allen W. Dulles, File 123D88, 1919–1920, National Archives.

9   AWD Papers, Box 9; *also*, AWD Papers, Box 9, Letters to Mrs. Allen Macy Dulles File, dated November 5, 1920.

10 British Foreign Office Memoranda, File dated November 19, 1920, FO 371/5291, Public Record Office, Kew.

11 Clover Todd Dulles, Correspondence, Box 9, Dulles Papers, November 18, 1920, Mudd Library, Princeton.

12 Clover Dulles, Personal Correspondence, dated December 13, 1920.

13 AWD Papers.

14 Murphy; *also*, AWD Papers, Correspondence from Mrs. Vera Whitehouse, Box 5.

15 AWD Papers.

16 Joan Dulles Buresch, Interview with author.

17 Allen W. Dulles, Telegram to Secretary of State, February 23, 1922, No. 48605 Commerce Papers-Turkey, Herbert Hoover Presidential Library, Ames, Iowa.

18 U.S. State Department Diplomatic Record Group Box 5240 (old index numbers in the 800 series) for 1924–1927, National Archives.

19 Jeffreys-Jones, *American Espionage*, Chapters 9–10.

20 Ibid, 73.

21 British Foreign Office Records, Memoranda and Minutes, Files dated 1922, FO 115/2785 and FO 115/2866. Public Record Office, Kew.

22 British Foreign Office Records, Memoranda and Minutes, File dated April 1925, FO 371/17356, Public Record Office, Kew.

23 U.S. State Department Personnel Files for Allen Dulles, Document 123D 88/73, dated May 17, 1926, National Archives.

24 Ibid, dated September 22, 1926; *also*, AWD Papers, Correspondence from the Secretary of State, Box 11, dated September 24, 1926.

25 AWD Papers, Box 11, September 24, 1926.

CHAPTER FIVE

1   Articles in the *New York Times*, the *Wall Street Journal*, the *Journal of Commerce*, the *Utica* (NY) *Press*, the *New York World*, the *Louisville* (KY) *Times*, the *Cleveland Plain Dealer*, the *Washington Post* and *The New Republic*, all dated between October 10–20, 1926. Available in AWD Papers, Box 11.

2 State Department Diplomatic Record Group 59 and 165 and 5332, National Archives.

3 Dumas Malone and Basil Rauch, *War and Troubled Peace* (New York: Appleton-Century-Crofts, 1960), 84–90.

4 Allen W. Dulles, Memorandum on Naval Disarmament, June 27, 1929, State Department Record Group Box 5240, National Archives.

5 Christopher Andrews, *For the President's Eyes Only: Secret Intelligence and the American Presidency from Washington to Bush* (New York: HarperCollins, 1995).

6 Jeffrey Dowart, "The Roosevelt-Astor Espionage Ring," *History*, Vol. 62, no. 3, 1981.

7 Author's interviews with Edmund "Ned" Putzell, who at that time was a lawyer for Donovan's firm. He later was a Donovan aide with the OSS and became a senior officer in the CIA.

8 AWD Papers, Box 11, Memo, File 6, dated February 8, 1963.

9 AWD Papers, dated October 27, 1930.

10 Allen W. Dulles, "The Disarmament Puzzle," *Foreign Affairs*, Vol. 9, no. 4, July 1931.

11 J. H. Schroder Bank, plc., Statement to author, 1992.

12 AWD Papers, Box 12, Files 14–15, Geneva Conference correspondence, 1932.

13 AWD Papers, Boxes 12–15, Correspondence, dated October 1932.

14 Norman H. Davis, Memoranda of Conversations (by Allen Dulles), March 30–June 22, 1933. Available in AWD Papers, Box 13; *also*, British Foreign Office, Anglo-American Naval Discussions, October 12–14, minutes by R. L. Craigie, FO 371/16432, Public Record Office, Kew; *also*, Hugh R. Wilson Papers, Files on Allen Dulles, Herbert Hoover Presidential Library, Ames, Iowa.

15 Norman H. Davis, Memoranda of Conversations (by Allen Dulles), April 8, 1933.

16 British Foreign Office, Memorandum of Arthur Lord Cadogan, April 20, 1933, File FO 371/17356, Public Record Office, Kew.

17 AWD Papers, Box 13.

CHAPTER SIX

1 Allen W. Dulles, "Germany and the Crisis in Disarmament," *Foreign Affairs*, Vol. 12, January 2, 1934, 260–270.

2 Drew Pearson, "Washington Daily Merry Go Round" syndicated column, October 10, 1934.

3 Allen W. Dulles, Radio speech on disarmament, sponsored by the National League of Women Voters and broadcast by NBC on June 5, 1929. Speech text in AWD Papers, Box 11.

4 Allen W. Dulles, "The Cost of Peace," *Foreign Affairs*, Vol. 12, no. 4, July 1934, 567–578.

5 Allen W. Dulles, "Collective Security," Speech to League of Nations conference at London School of Economics, June 3, 1935. Copy in AWD Papers, Box 14.

6 AWD Papers, Box 14, Correspondence.

7 Allen W. Dulles, John Foster Dulles Oral History Project, 1962, Mudd Library, Princeton.

8 Hoopes, 47.

9   Hamilton Fish Armstrong and Allen W. Dulles, *Can We Be Neutral?* (New York: Harpers, 1936).

10 William J. Casey, *The Secret War Against Hitler* (Washington, DC: Regnery Gateway, 1988), 13.

11 AWD Papers, Box 15, November 18, 1937.

12 AWD Papers, Box 14, 1938; *also*, Joan Dulles Buresch, Interview with author, 1994.

13 Eleanor Elliot, Interview with author, 1995.

14 Joan Dulles Buresch, Interview with author, 1993; *also*, Father Avery Dulles, Interview with author, 1993.

15 Allen W. Dulles, *The Secret Surrender* (New York: Harper & Row, 1966), 4.

16 Edmund Putzell, Interview with author, 1993.

17 Thomas F. Troy, *Donovan and the CIA* (Frederick, MD: University Publications of America, 1981), 29–70.

18 Brian R. Sullivan, "A Highly Commendable Action," *Intelligence and National Security*, London, Vol. 6, no. 2, 1991, 336–337.

19 Ibid.

20 Stevenson.

21 Kermit Roosevelt, editor, *History of the OSS* (Washington, DC: U.S. Government Printing Office, 1976); *also*, F. H. Hinsley, *British Intelligence in the Second World War* (London: H. M. Stationery Office, Vols. 1 and 2, 1981); *also*, Troy; *also*, Brown; *also*, Rhodri Jeffreys-Jones, *The CIA and American Democracy* (New Haven: Yale University Press, 1989); *also*, Stevenson; *also*, Nathan Miller, *Spying for America* (New York: Doubleday & Co., 1989); *also*, G. J. A. O'Toole, *Honorable Treachery* (New York: Atlantic Monthly Press, 1991); *also*, Stewart Alsop and Thomas Braden, *Sub Rosa: The OSS and American Espionage* (New York: Reynal & Hitchcock, 1946); *also*, West, *MI5, MI6*.

22 Robert Sherwood, *Roosevelt and Hopkins* (New York: Harper Bros., 1950), 270; *also*, Thomas E. Mahl, *Desperate Deception* (Dulles, VA: Brassey's, 1998); *also*, *British Security Coordination* (London: St. Ermin's Press, 1998).

23 H. M. G. Imperial War Ministry, *Weekly Political Intelligence Summary*, February 6, 1940. From the General Jan Smuts Archives, Pretoria, South Africa.

24 Brown.

25 Hamilton Fish Armstrong and Allen W. Dulles, *Can We Stay Neutral?* (New York: Harper Bros., 1939).

26 Edgar Ansel Mowrer, "Final Report to Colonel William J. Donovan Concerning a Mission to the Far East in the Autumn of 1941." Available in AWD Papers, Box 17; *also*, AWD Papers, Box 101, File 1940 Donovan, Conversation notes between Allen W. Dulles and Edgar Ansel Mowrer recorded in 1962 in Washington.

CHAPTER SEVEN

1   AWD Papers, Boxes 15–17, Correspondence File, Letter to Frances Miller, January 19, 1965.

2   Edmund Putzell, Interview with author, 1993.

3   Roosevelt; *also*, Edward Hymoff, *The OSS in World War II* (New York: Richardson & Steirman, 1986), 40–49; *also*, Troy; *also*, Joseph E. Persico, *Piercing the Reich* (New York: Viking Press, 1979), 18–19; R. Harris Smith, *The OSS: The Secret History* (Berkeley: University of California Press, 1972); *also*, Robin Winks, *Cloak and Gown* (New York: Quill, 1987), 122–185; *also*, Kenneth McDonald, "The Secrets War," Lecture on July 11, 1991, at the Fiftieth Anniversary Conference on the Founding of the OSS, National Archives, 10.

4   William J. Donovan, Memorandum for the President No. 537, May 27, 1942, PSF Box 166, OSS Files, Roosevelt Presidential Library, Hyde Park, NY.

5   OSS History Files from the CIA Archives, Box 11, File 478.

6   OSS History Files, Record Group 226, Entry 92, Box 58, Files 7874 and 1645, April–May 1942, National Archives.

7   Memo on German Financial Transactions via Switzerland, from C. Belfrage of British Security Coordination, New York to Murray Gurfein, OSS, New York, November 24, 1942. Available in Allen Dulles, Records, Entry 165, Box 174, File 13075, National Archives.

8   OSS History Files from the CIA Archives, Box 11, File 478, Interoffice Memo to David Bruce, July 27, 1942.

9   OSS History Files, Record Group 226, Entry 92, Box 64, File 8282, Memos to and from Allen Dulles, June 2–23, 1942, National Archives.

10 OSS History Files, Memo to David Bruce, NND 877092, October 21, 1942.

11 OSS Personnel File for Allen Dulles, No. 9330. Available in OSS History Files.

12 Dulles, *The Secret Surrender*, 13–14.

13 Ibid, 15.

14 Ibid, 15.

15 Cordelia Dodson Hood, Interview with author, 1993.

16 Author's interviews, 1991–1994, with a British intelligence officer who requested anonymity.

17 Nicholas Elliot, Interview with author, 1992.

18 OSS History Files, Entry 92, Box 122, File 10,794, September 8, 1942.

19 Fabrizio Calvi, "OSS in France," Lecture to OSS Conference at National Archives, July 12, 1991.

CHAPTER EIGHT

1   OSS History Record Group 59, Box 52, File 103.918/744 Burns to Victor, National Archives.

2   William Donovan, Papers, Box 120, Switzerland Folder 82, Special Funds, U.S. Army Military History Institute, Carlisle Barracks.

3   OSS History Record Group 59, Box 171, File 11939, National Archives.

4   Elizabeth Wiskemann, *Europe of the Dictators* (London: Fontana Press, 1966); *also*, Elizabeth Wiskemann, *The Europe I Saw* (London: Collins, 1968).

5   Allen W. Dulles, *Germany's Underground* (New York: Macmillan Company, 1947), 125–133.

6   British intelligence source, Off-the-record interview with author, 1994.

7   Allen W. Dulles, *Conspiracy Against Hitler* (1946, unpublished). Available in AWD Papers.

8   Dulles, *Germany's Underground.*

9   Heinz Hohne, *The Order of the Death's Head* (London: Secker & Warburg, 1969), 87–88, 248.

10   Central Intelligence Agency, OSS History File, Box 6.

11   Fritz Molden, Interview with author, 1993.

12   Hans Bernd Gisevius, *To the Bitter End* (New York: Houghton Mifflin Co., 1947).

13   Author's interviews, 1991–1994, with British intelligence officer who requested anonymity.

14   OSS History Record Group 59, Entry 125, Box 5, National Archives.

15   Walter Laquer and Richard Breitman, *Breaking the Silence* (New York: Simon & Schuster, 1986) 167–219.

16   Klemens von Klemperer, *German Resistance Against Hitler* (London: Clarendon Press, 1992), 280–281.

17   W. H. Visser't Hooft, *Memoirs,* 157. Available in AWD Papers.

18   OSS History Group, DD 13033, January 14, 1943.

19   OSS Microfilm History Group Box T-175, Roll 458, Frames 2975007-15, "Aufzeichnung uber Aussprachen mit Mr. Bull und Mr. Roberts."

20   OSS History Record Group 59, Entry 125, Box 7, Folder 131, Telegram Burns to Secstate, Washington, November 20, 1943.

21   AWD Papers, Box 124, Dulles Correspondence, Gero von Gaevernitz.

22   Laquer and Breitman, 176.

23   Whitney H. Shepardson, Cable SI to Burns, April 28, 1943, OSS Record Group 59, Box 165.

24   Mary Bancroft, *Autobiography of a Spy* (New York: William Morrow & Co., 1983), 129.

25   Ibid, 138.

26   Ibid, 139.

27   OSS History Record Group 59, Box 171, Burns to Washington, February 3, 1943.

CHAPTER NINE

1   Author's interview with British intelligence officer who requested anonymity, 1991.

2   Roosevelt, Vol. 1, 279–280.

3   "Alias 'George Wood'" by "Anthony Quibble," *Studies in Intelligence,* Spring 1966, Vol. 10, no. 1, Central Intelligence Agency, Record Group 226, Box E193. Copies of this previously classified document, based on still-classified OSS and Dulles papers, were made available to the National Archives in 1976; *also,* Ernst Kocherthaler, "Background of the George Story," a deposition made November 17, 1964. Available in Central Intelligence Agency, Dulles Files, Box 5, File 6-1092; *also,* AWD Papers, Box 36, Deposition in support of Fritz Kolbe, January 15, 1948; *also,* see Box 20 for related documents; *also,* "Boston Series" (OSS code reference for

the cable traffic based on the "Wood" documents), recently put on microfilm, File M-1746, National Archives.

4   H. A. R. Philby, *My Secret War* (New York: Grove Press, 1968), 100–104.

5   Ibid, 103.

6   Elvesa Bazna, *I Was Cicero* (New York: Harper & Row, 1962); *also,* L. C. Moyzisch, *Operation Cicero* (New York: Coward-McCann, 1950).

7   Allen W. Dulles, *New York Herald Tribune Book Review*, October 29, 1950, 5.

8   "Boston Series," National Archives; *also,* "Alias 'George Wood.'"

9   "Boston Series," USTRAVIC (London) to Burns, May 12, 1944, National Archives.

10 General William W. Quinn, Interview with author, 1991; *also,* Henry Hyde, Interviews with author, 1991–1992.

11 OSS Official History, Vol. 2, Part V, 181.

12 Persico, 108–109.

13 Erica Glaser Wallach, Interviews with author, February 1993.

14 F. L. Mayer, Memo to Chief, SI, December 30, 1943, OSS Record Group 125, Box 162.

CHAPTER TEN

1   Richard Dunlop, *Donovan, America's Master Spy* (New York: Rand McNally, 1982); *also,* Corey Ford, *Donovan of OSS* (New York: Little, Brown, 1970).

2   Gisevius, 482–483.

3   OSS Memo to the President, Overtures by German Generals and Civilian Opposition for a Separate Armistice, May 16, 1944, Map Room Box 73, File J-205, Roosevelt Library, Hyde Park; *also,* Peter Hoffman, *History of the German Resistance* (Cambridge: MIT Press, 1977), 1–13.

4   Barry M. Katz, *Foreign Intelligence* (Cambridge: Harvard University Press, 1989), 9–16.

5   Eleanor Lansing Dulles, Interview with author, 1992.

6   Katz, 34–35.

7   AWD Papers, Boxes 21–23, 61, Correspondence.

8   AWD Papers, Boxes 21–23, 61, Correspondence.

9   Fritz Molden, Interview with author, 1993.

10 Bancroft, 150–161.

11 Ibid, 244.

12 OSS/Bern Report, Dulles Papers, Box 11, Central Intelligence Agency, 32–33.

13 OSS History Files, "Sunrise Material," Record Group 226, Entry 190, National Archives; *also,* Allen W. Dulles, Personal Notes on Sunrise, OSS Files Box 6, Central Intelligence Agency; *also,* Allen W. Dulles and Gero von Gaevernitz, "Report on the Sunrise-Crossword Operation to Major General William J. Donovan," May 22, 1945, OSS History Record Group 226, Entry 110, Box 2, Folder 1; *also,* AWD Papers, Motion Picture Treatment for *The Secret Surrender* (edited by von Gaevernitz), 1966; *also,* Dulles, *The Secret Surrender.*

CHAPTER ELEVEN

1 Thomas F. Troy, "Knifing the OSS," *International Journal of Intelligence and Counterintelligence*, 1986, 95–107.

2 Troy, *Donovan and the CIA*, 229.

3 Troy, "Knifing the OSS."

4 British Foreign Office Records, Security Coordination Files, F.O. 371/38633, 162–167, April 26, 1944.

5 OSS History, Dulles Files, Box 5, Central Intelligence Agency; *also*, AWD Papers, Personal notes for 1965 television interview; *also*, OSS Files for June–September 1945, Box 15, Truman Presidential Library, Independence, MO; *also*, Basle Centre for Economic and Financial Research, *The Per Jacobsson Mediation*, Series C, no. 4, 1968.

6 Thomas Allen and Norman Polmar, *Code-Name: Downfall* (New York: Simon & Schuster, 1995).

7 General William Quinn, Interview with author, 1992; *also*, Samuel Halpern, Interview with author, 1994.

8 AWD Papers, Personal notes for 1965 television interview.

9 Arthur Schlesinger, Jr., Interview with author, 1992.

10 OSS History Record Group RG 132/192 ("OUT-AMZON") cable traffic, June–December 1945, National Archives.

11 Harry Rositzke, Interview with author, 1993.

12 Richard Helms, Interview with author, 1992; *also*, David E. Murphy, Sergei A. Konpdrashev, and George Bailey, *Battleground Berlin* (New Haven: Yale University Press, 1997), 3–13.

13 Michael Wala, editor's introduction to *The Marshall Plan* by Allen W. Dulles (Providence: Berg Press, 1993), xix–xx; *also*, AWD Papers, Box 21, Dulles's own manuscript, "Talk at CFR, 12/3/45."

14 Council on Foreign Relations, "Digest of Discussion, 12/3/45."

15 AWD Papers, Box 25, Speech to Foreign Policy Association luncheon, January 19, 1946.

16 AWD Papers, Box 25, Speech to Foreign Policy Association luncheon, January 19, 1946; *also*, AWD Papers, Box 26, Speech to a Princeton Conference on Development of International Society, October 12, 1946.

17 Harry S. Truman, Executive Order of the President, January 22, 1946. Copy from "Leahy Files" of the Joint Chiefs of Staff Record Group 218, National Archives.

18 Truman diaries, quoted in Daniel Yergin, *Shattered Peace: The Origins of the Cold War* (Boston: Houghton-Mifflin, 1977) and Trevor Barnes, "The Secret Cold War," *The Historical Journal*, Vol. 24, no. 2 (1981), 399–415; *also*, Diary of Admiral Leahy, Library of Congress.

19 Wayne G. Jackson, *Allen Welsh Dulles as Director of Central Intelligence* (Washington: Central Intelligence Agency DCI Historical Series, No. 2, 1973 [declassified 1994]), Vol. I, 12.

20 Nina von Eckardt, Interview with author, 1993.

21 Dulles, *Germany's Underground*.

22 Allen W. Dulles, Memorandum Respecting the Bill to Provide for a National Defense

Establishment to Senate Armed Services Committee, April 25, 1947. Available in Dulles Files, Box 1, Central Intelligence Agency.

23 AWD Papers, Box 26, Testimony to Senate Armed Services Committee, April 27, 1947.

24 Ludwell Lee Montague, *DCI Historial Series-One* (Washington, DC: Central Intelligence Agency, 1971), Vol. 1, 25.

25 AWD Papers, Box 30, Letter to Hanson Baldwin, November 13, 1947.

26 Central Intelligence Agency, Dulles File, Box 9, File 001505, undated, unsigned.

27 Montague, 89.

28 Fritz Molden, Interview with author, 1993.

29 AWD Papers, Box 30, Address to the 179th Commencement of Brown University, June 16, 1947.

30 Michael Wala, Interview with author, 1993.

31 Allen W. Dulles, *The Marshall Plan* (written in 1947), edited by Michael Wala (Providence: Berg Press, 1993), 125.

CHAPTER TWELVE

1 Arthur Darling, *The CIA, an Instrument of Government to 1950* (Washington, DC: Central Intelligence Agency DCI Historical Series, 1954 [declassified 1989, published by Penn State University Press]), 410–430.

2 Lawrence Houston, Interview with author, 1989.

3 Central Intelligence Agency, *The CIA Under Harry Truman* (Center for the Study of Intelligence, 1994), 40–44; *also*, Bradley Smith, *Shadow Warriors* (New York: Basic Books, 1983), 390–414; *also*, John Ranelagh, *The Agency* (New York: Simon & Schuster, 1986), 128–129; *also*, William M. Leary, editor, *The Central Intelligence Agency—History and Documents* (Montgomery: University of Alabama Press, 1984), 11–54; also, Jeffreys-Jones, *The CIA and American Democracy*, 19–60.

4 Harry Rositzke, Interview with author, 1993; *also*, Harry Rositzke, *The CIA's Secret Operations* (New York: Reader's Digest Press, 1977), 38.

5 AWD Papers, Box 24, Dulles-Donovan Correspondence, June 29, 1946.

6 Central Intelligence Agency, *The CIA Under Harry Truman*, 134.

7 George F. Kennan, Testimony before the Senate Select Committee to Study Governmental Operations, October 28, 1975, pages 8–10 (also quoted on page 37 of the committee report).

8 British Foreign Office File 115, Folder 443, September 25, 1948, Public Record Office, Kew.

9 Richard M. Nixon, Interview, March 5, 1965, John Foster Dulles Oral History Project, transcript.

10 Erica Glaser Wallach, Interviews with author, 1993; *also*, Erica Glaser Wallach, *Light at Midnight* (New York: Doubleday, 1967).

11 Noel Field, "Hitching Our Wagon to a Star," *Mainstream*, January 1961.

12 Arthur Schlesinger, Jr., "Book Review of *Red Pawn: The Story of Noel Field*," *New York Review of Books*, February 11, 1965.

13 AWD Papers, Box 40, Correspondence Files, November 1949.

14 AWD Papers, Box 222, Speech and Interview Files, Interview with NBC in New York, October 1, 1950.

15 Frank Wisner, "Chronology on How U.S. Embarked on Covert Operations," Memo to Allen W. Dulles, dated August 31, 1962. Available in Central Intelligence Agency, Dulles File, Box 10, File 005610.

16 Ludwell Lee Montague, *General Walter Bedell Smith as Director of Central Intelligence* (Washington, DC: Central Intelligence Agency DCI Historical Series, 1971 [declassified 1990]), Vol. II, 24–30.

17 General William Quinn, Interview with author, 1991.

18 Central Intelligence Agency, excerpt from Chapter 9 of the still-classified "Dulles-Jackson-Correa Report," January 1, 1949. Available in Central Intelligence Agency, Dulles Personnel File, Box 9.

19 Ibid, Preliminary report dated May 13, 1948.

20 Jeffreys-Jones, *American Espionage*, 200.

21 U.S. Senate Select Committee to Study Governmental Operations with Respect to Intelligence Activities (the Church Committee), "Staff Report on Foreign and Military Intelligence" (Washington, DC: Government Printing Office, 1976), 25–40.

22 Colonel L. K. White, Interview with author, 1993.

CHAPTER THIRTEEN

1   AWD Papers, Letter to William Lacy, February 25, 1953.

2   AWD Papers, Box 58, February 26, 1953.

3   Blanche W. Cook, *The Declassified Eisenhower* (New York: Doubleday, Inc., 1981), 89; *also*, Michael Wala, Interview with author, 1994; *also*, Dwight D. Eisenhower, Transcript of interview, John Foster Dulles Oral History Project, July 28, 1964.

4   AWD Papers, Box 56, "Senate Armed Services Committee, Report of Proceedings—Nomination of Allen Welsh Dulles of New York to be Director of the Central Intelligence Agency," February 19, 1953.

5   Rear Admiral Arleigh A. Burke, Interview with author, 1985.

6   Robert Louis Benson and Michael Warner, editors, *Venona: Soviet Espionage and the American Response, 1939–1957* (National Security Agency and Central Intelligence Agency, 1996), 119.

7   Confidential source, Interview with author, 1994.

8   General Eberhard Blum, Interview with author, 1993; *also*, Mary Ellen Reese, *General Reinhard Gehlen* (Arlington, VA: George Mason University Press, 1990); *also*, E. H. Cookridge, *Gehlen* (New York: Random House, 1971); *also*, Heinz Hohne and Hermann Zolling, *The General Was a Spy* (New York: Coward, McCann & Geoghegan, Inc., 1972).

9   Eleanor Lansing Dulles, Interview with author, 1992.

10 A. Robert Abboud, Interview with author, 1992.

11 Joan Dulles Buresch, Interview with author, 1995.

12 Joan Dulles Buresch, Interview with author, 1994.

13 Confidential source, Interview with author, 1994.

14 Barbara Pindar Smith, Interview with author, 1993.

15 Confidential source, Interview with author, 1991.

16 Confidential source, Interview with author, 1993.

17 Barbara Pindar Smith, Interview with author, 1993.

18 C. M. Woodhouse, *Something Ventured* (London: Granada, 1982), 110.

19 Kermit Roosevelt, Interview with author, 1992.

20 David Attlee Phillips, *Secret Wars Diary* (Bethesda, MD: Stone Trail Press, 1989), 135; *also*, Stephen Schlesinger and Stephen Kinzer, *Bitter Fruit* (New York: Doubleday, 1982); *also*, Ray S. Cline, *Secrets, Spies, and Scholars* (New York: Acropolis Books, 1976), 133–135; *also*, Ray S. Cline, Interviews with author, 1990–1991.

21 Richard Bissell, Interview with author, 1992.

22 Rositzke, *The CIA's Secret Operations*, 38.

CHAPTER FOURTEEN

1 Sir Roger Makins, Memo to Sir Anthony Eden, "Reorganization of the Conduct of U.S. Foreign Policy," March 17, 1955, British Foreign Office Records FO 371/114365, Public Record Office, Kew.

2 Richard Bissell, Interview with author, 1991.

3 William Bundy, Interview with author, 1992.

4 William Bundy, Interview with author, 1992.

5 *New York Times*, July 19, 1953.

6 Jackson, Vol. IV, 84, citing letter to Jackson from Gordon Gray.

7 Eisenhower-Dulles-Herter Collection, Telephone logs kept by Ann Whitman, Eisenhower Presidential Library, Abilene, KS.

8 Jackson, Vol. IV, 96–97.

9 Colonel L. K. White, Interview with author, 1993.

10 Colonel Walter Pforzheimer, Interview with author, 1991.

11 James Billington, Interview with author, 1994.

12 William Bundy, Interview with author, 1993.

13 James Billington, Interview with author, 1994.

14 Jeffreys-Jones, *The CIA and American Democracy*, 92; *also*, Rositzke, *The CIA's Secret Operations*, 239.

15 Rositzke, *The CIA's Secret Operations*, 196.

16 Scott D. Breckenridge, *CIA and the Cold War* (New York: Praeger, 1993).

17 Beschloss, 356.

18 Central Intelligence Agency, "Memorandum of Paramilitary Study Group Meeting (The Taylor Committee investigation), May 22, 1961," Nineteenth Meeting. (Author's note: This summary of the testimony of Colonel J. C. King, head of the WH/4 Branch, has only recently

been declassified. It is omitted, therefore, from the previously published version of the hearings edited by Luis Aguilar and referred to in footnote 4 for Chapter Fifteen.)

19 Dwight D. Eisenhower, *Waging Peace* (New York: Doubleday & Co., 1965), 533.

20 General Andrew A. Goodpaster, Interview with author, 1993.

21 Breckenridge, 110; *also*, Interim Report of the Select Committee to Study Government Operations with Respect to Intelligence Activities, U.S. Senate, 94th Congress, "Alleged Assassination Plots Involving Foreign Leaders," Report No. 91-465, November 20, 1975, 110–181, see footnote 17.

22 Confidential source, Interview with author, 1994.

CHAPTER FIFTEEN

1 Richard M. Nixon, *Six Crises* (New York: Doubleday, 1972).

2 Allen W. Dulles, Interview by Thomas Braden, December 5–6, 1964, for the John F. Kennedy Library, quoted by permission of Dr. Joan Buresch, 1991. Copy in AWD Papers, Box 126.

3 Ibid.

4 Luis Aguilar, editor, *Operation Zapata*, the edited record of the Taylor Committee investigation of the Bay of Pigs operation (Frederick, MD: University Publications of America, 1981), 6. (Author's note: The nineteenth meeting of the Taylor Committee on May 22, 1961, which was absent from this edition because it was classified, has recently been made public by the Central Intelligence Agency Historical Office under the title "Memorandum for Record, Paramilitary Study Group Meeting, May 22, 1961.")

5 G. J. A. O'Toole, *The Encyclopedia of American Intelligence and Espionage*, 57–59.

6 Aguilar, 7.

7 *Executive Sessions of the Senate Foreign Relations Committee* (Historical Series), Vol. XIII, Part 1 (1961), published in April 1984, 322–323.

8 Hans J. Morgenthau, "To Intervene or Not To Intervene," *Foreign Affairs*, December 1961.

9 Allen Dulles, Interview by Thomas Braden.

10 Admiral Arleigh A. Burke, Interview with author, 1985.

11 Arthur Schlesinger, Jr., Interview with author, 1992.

12 Dean Rusk, *Washington Post*, August 1, 1988, A-11.

13 Author's interview with still-active CIA officer, 1993.

14 Richard Helms, Interview with author, 1992.

15 Richard Bissell, Interview with author, 1991.

16 William Bundy, Interview with author, 1992.

17 General Charles Pearre Cabell, Interview for John Foster Dulles Oral History Project, 1964.

18 Colonel J. C. King, Taylor Committee report on Nineteenth Meeting.

19 Allen Dulles, Interview by Thomas Braden.

20 Colonel L. K. White, Interview with author, 1993.

21 W. W. Rostow, Interview with author, 1994.

22 W. W. Rostow, Interview with author, 1994; *also*, W. W. Rostow, *Diffusion of Power* (New York: Harper & Bros., 1977), 208–210.

23 Allen Dulles, Interview by Thomas Braden.

24 Arthur Schlesinger, Jr., *A Thousand Days: John F. Kennedy in the White House* (New York: Houghton Mifflin, 1965), 276.

25 David Wise, *New York Herald Tribune*, April 28, 1961, 1.

26 *Executive Sessions of the Senate Foreign Relations Committee*, Vol. XIII, Part 1 (1961), published in April 1984, 313–450.

27 Letter from General L. K. Truscott, Jr., May 18, 1961. Available in Smith Papers, Eisenhower Presidential Library, Abilene, KS.

28 General William Y. Smith, Interview with author, 1994.

CHAPTER SIXTEEN

1 Herbert G. Schoonmaker, *Military Crisis Management, U.S. Intervention in the Domincan Republic* (New York: Greenwood Press, 1990), 34–41; *also*, Ranelagh, 383–389.

2 Central Intelligence Agency, Dulles Personnel File, Box 11, File 14, Memo: Roselli/Maheu Matter, May 23, 1975, declassified September 1990.

3 Sam Halpern, Interview with author, 1993.

4 AWD Papers, Boxes A–C, Selected Correspondence File, Representative Clarence Cannon, Letter to President Kennedy, May 15, 1961.

5 AWD Papers, Boxes U–Z, Selected Correspondence File, W. W. Rostow, Letter to Dulles, August 29, 1961.

6 Stanley J. Grogan, Memo for DCI, October 19, 1961, Central Intelligence Agency, Dulles Personnel File, Box 1.

7 Colonel L. K. White, Interview with author, 1993.

8 Jackson, Vol. III.

9 Allen W. Dulles, *The Craft of Intelligence* (New York: Harper & Row, 1963).

10 Dulles, *The Secret Surrender*.

11 Allen W. Dulles, editor, *Great True Spy Stories* (New York: Castle, 1968); *also*, Allen W. Dulles, editor, *Great Spy Stories from Fiction* (New York: Castle, 1969), posthumously.

12 Theodore C. Sorensen, *Kennedy* (New York: Harper & Row, 1965); *also*, Schlesinger, *A Thousand Days*.

13 Allen W. Dulles, "My Answer on the Bay of Pigs" (1965, unpublished). Copy in AWD Papers, Box 244.

14 Ibid.

15 Colonel L. K. White, Interview with author, 1993.

BIBLIOGRAPHY

RECOMMENDED PRIMARY RESOURCES

There are three desk references that should be at hand for anyone beginning research in the broad topic areas covered in this book. One is *The Encyclopedia of American Intelligence and Espionage*, by G. J. A. O'Toole (New York: Facts on File, 1988). The second is the comprehensive bibliographical guide *American Intelligence, 1775–1990*, edited by intelligence scholar Neal H. Petersen (Claremont, CA: Regina Books, 1992). The third is more specifically focused: *From Hitler's Doorstep: The Wartime Intelligence Reports of Allen Dulles, 1942–45* (University Park, PA: Pennsylvania State University Press, 1996). It is also by Neal Petersen and includes his insightful commentary. This guide assembles the wartime cable traffic between the various posts of the Office of Strategic Services (OSS) and Allen Dulles's spy center in Bern, Switzerland. It is a valuable tool for anyone trying to wade through the thousands of cubic feet of documents about the OSS operations held in the various library collections.

ARCHIVAL SOURCES

OSS Operational Archives; Record Group (RG) 226, National Archives, Washington, D.C.: This collection of more than 3,000 cubic feet of records has recently been moved to the Archives facility in College Park, Maryland. Of special interest are Entry 180, which contains 193 rolls of microfilm copied by OSS director William J. Donovan and which is available both at the Archives and at the Donovan papers collection at the U.S. Army Military History Institute, Carlisle Barracks, Pennsylvania. Also at the Archives, another 132 rolls, designated M1642, contain the files of the OSS Washington Director's Office.

Central Intelligence Agency: The agency's Center for the Studies of Intelligence has undertaken a program of declassification and publication of various documents relating to previously withheld OSS documents and of early agency papers that relate to the Cold War. Specific requests under the Freedom of Information Act are always an option. The agency also has an extensive, but somewhat dated, "Selective Bibliography" that tracks the extensive literature published by Mr. Dulles and press accounts about him.

Seeley G. Mudd Manuscript Library, Princeton University, Princeton, New Jersey: This collection contains 264 boxes of Allen Dulles's private papers plus a broader collection of family papers, correspondence, and photographs. Papers concerning John Foster Dulles are also collected here and at the School of Diplomacy that bears his name at Princeton.

Dwight D. Eisenhower Presidential Library, Abilene, Kansas: The Eisenhower Library holds the private papers of Eleanor Lansing Dulles and other notable figures of American diplomacy and intelligence history.

Franklin D. Roosevelt Presidential Library, Hyde Park, New York: The FDR Library has three major collections worth study. The Map Room Files and the President's Secretary Files hold OSS documents, including Dulles's reports. There are also the Naval Aide Files.

Herbert Clark Hoover Presidential Library, Ames, Iowa: Not to be confused with the Hoover Institution collections at Stanford University in California, this collection holds the private papers of a number of important figures.

Department of State Records, National Archives, Washington, D.C., and College Park, Maryland: Record Group 59 contains OSS and Dulles material throughout the European War files. RG 84 contains post material for Bern, Geneva, Basel, and Zurich.

Archives of the Special Operations Executive, The Admiralty, London, England: By appointment and with written specific requests, this collection has valuable material on the joint operations and frictions between Britain's covert action group and the OSS.

Public Record Office, Kew, England: This main British archive has valuable documents in the War Cabinet series (CAB), Confidential Papers (PREM), and War Office files (WO-series 193 through 219).

Georgetown University Library, Washington, D.C.: Georgetown is home to the Russell Bowen Intelligence Collection, a huge holding of books and manuscripts, many not found elsewhere.

BOOKS

Accose, Pierre, and Pierre Quet. *A Man Called Lucy.* New York: Coward-McCann, 1966.

Aguilar, Luis, ed. *Operation Zapata.* Washington: University Publications of America, 1981.

Allen, Thomas, and Norman Polmar. *Code-Name: Downfall.* New York: Simon & Schuster, 1995.

Alsop, Stewart, and Thomas Braden. *Sub Rosa: The OSS and American Espionage.* New York: Reynal & Hitchcock, 1946.

Andrew, Christopher. *For the President's Eyes Only: Secret Intelligence and the American Presidency from Washington to Bush.* New York: HarperCollins, 1995.

———. *Her Majesty's Secret Service: The Making of the British Intelligence Community.* New York: Viking, 1986.

Armstrong, Hamilton Fish, and Allen W. Dulles. *Can We Be Neutral?* New York: Harper Bros., 1936.

————. *Can We Stay Neutral?* New York: Harper Bros., 1939.

Bancroft, Mary. *Autobiography of a Spy.* New York: Morrow, 1983.

Baudot, Marcel, et al., eds. *The Historical Encyclopedia of World War II.* New York: Facts on File, 1989.

Bazna, Elyesa. *I Was Cicero.* New York: Harper & Row, 1962.

Berle, Adolph A. *Navigating the Rapids.* New York: Harcourt Brace Jovanovich, 1973.

Beschloss, Michael R. *Kennedy and Roosevelt.* New York: W.W. Norton, 1980.

————. *Mayday.* New York: Harper & Row, 1986.

Bissell, Richard M. *Reflections of a Cold Warrior.* New Haven: Yale University Press, 1996.

Borovik, Genrikh. *The Philby Files.* Boston: Little, Brown & Co., 1994.

Breckinridge, Scott D. *The CIA and the U.S. Intelligence System.* Boulder, CO: Westview Press, 1986.

Brown, Anthony Cave. *Bodyguard of Lies.* New York: Harper & Row, 1975.

————. *"C": The Secret Life of Sir Stewart Graham Menzies, Spymaster to Winston Churchill.* New York: Macmillan, 1987.

————. *The Last Hero: Wild Bill Donovan.* New York: Times Books, 1982.

Bruce, James Cabell. *Memoirs.* Baltimore: Gateway Press, 1975,

Calvi, Fabrizio. *OSS: La Guerre Secret en France, 1942–1945.* Paris: Hachette, 1990.

Carlton, David. *Britain and the Suez Crisis.* London: Institute of Contemporary British History, 1988.

Casey, William J. *The Secret War Against Hitler.* Washington, D.C.: Regnery Gateway, 1988.

Chalou, George C., ed. *The Secrets War: The Office of Strategic Services In World War II.* Washington, D.C.: The National Archives and Records Administration, 1992. Collected lectures from a 1991 fiftieth anniversary conference on the OSS.

Cline, Ray S. *The CIA Under Reagan, Bush, and Casey.* Washington, D.C.: Acropolis Books, 1981.

———. *Secrets, Spies, and Scholars.* Washington, D.C.: Acropolis Books, 1976.

Cline, Ray S., and Roger W. Fontaine. *Foreign Policy Failures in China, Cuba, and Nicaragua.* Washington, D.C.: United States Global Strategy Council, 1991.

Colby, William E. *Honorable Men.* New York: Simon & Schuster, 1978.

———. *Lost Victory.* Chicago: Contemporary Books, 1989.

Colby, William E., and Peter Forbath. *My Life in the CIA.* New York: Simon & Schuster, 1978.

Constantinides, George. *Intelligence and Espionage: An Analytical Bibliography.* Boulder, CO: Westview, 1983.

Cook, Blanche W. *The Declassified Eisenhower.* New York: Doubleday, 1981.

Cook, Fred J. *The U-2 Incident.* New York: F. Watts, 1966.

Cookridge, E. H. *Gehlen.* New York: Random House, 1971.

Copeland, Miles. *Without Cloak or Dagger.* New York: Simon & Schuster, 1974.

———. *The Game Player.* London: Arum Press, 1989.

Corson, William R. *The Armies of Ignorance.* New York: Dial/James Wade, 1977.

Corvo, Max. *The OSS in Italy.* New York: Praeger, 1990.

Costello, John. *Ten Days to Destiny.* New York: Morrow, 1991.

Darling, Arthur. *The CIA, an Instrument of Government to 1950.* Washington: Central Intelligence Agency DCI Historical Series, 1954; declassified 1989, published by Penn State University Press.

De Gramont, Sanche. *The Secret War.* New York: G. P. Putnam's Sons, 1962.

Dowart, Jeffrey. *The Roosevelt-Astor Espionage Ring.* New York History, Vol. 62 (1981), no. 3.

Dulles, Allen W. *The Boer War* (written 1902). New York: Gordon Press, 1974.

————. *The Craft of Intelligence.* New York: Harper & Row, 1963.

————. *Germany's Underground.* New York: Macmillan, 1947.

————, ed. *Great Spy Stories from Fiction.* New York: Harper & Row, 1969.

————, ed. *Great True Spy Stories.* New York: Harper & Row, 1968.

————. *The Marshall Plan.* Providence, RI: Berg, 1993. Written but not published in 1947, edited by Michael Wala.

————. *The Secret Surrender.* New York: Harper & Row, 1966.

————. *The United Nations.* New York: The Foreign Policy Association, 1946.

Dulles, Edith Foster. *The Story of My Life.* Printed privately, 1934. In the Dulles family papers at the Seeley G. Mudd Library, Princeton University, Princeton, NJ.

Dulles, Eleanor Lansing. *Chances of a Lifetime: A Memoir.* Englewood Cliffs, NJ: Prentice-Hall, 1980.

————. *John Foster Dulles: The Last Year.* New York: Harcourt Brace & World, 1963.

Dunlop, Richard. *Donovan: America's Master Spy.* New York: Rand McNally, 1982.

Edwards, Bob, and Kenneth Dunne. *Study of a Master Spy.* London: Housmans, 1961.

Eisenhower, Dwight D. *Waging Peace.* New York: Doubleday & Co., 1965.

Foot, M. R. D. *SOE in France: An Account of the Work of the British Special Operations Executive in France, 1940–1944.* Frederick, MD: University Publications of America, 1986; a reprint of a 1966 British official history.

Ford, Corey. *Donovan of OSS.* New York: Little, Brown, 1970.

Gates, Robert M. *From the Shadows.* New York: Simon & Schuster, 1996.

Gisevius, Hans Bernd. *To the Bitter End.* London: Jonathan Cape, 1948.

Godson, Roy, ed. *Intelligence Requirements for the 1980s.* Washington: National Strategy Information Center, 1980.

———. *Intelligence Requirements for the 1990s.* Lexington: Lexington Books, 1989.

———. *Dirty Tricks or Trump Cards.* Washington: National Strategy Information Center, 1995.

Godson, Roy, Ernest May, and Gary Schmitt. *U.S. Intelligence at the Crossroads.* Washington: National Strategy Information Center, 1995.

Heideking, Jurgen, and Christof Mauch. *American Intelligence and the German Resistance to Hitler.* New York: Westview Press, 1996.

Heller, Deane and David. *John Foster Dulles: Soldier for Peace.* New York: Holt, Rinehart & Winston, 1960.

Hinsley, F. H. *British Intelligence in the Second World War.* London: H. M. Stationery Office, 1981 (five volumes).

Hoare, Geoffrey. *The Missing Macleans.* London: Cassell & Co., 1955.

Hoffman, Peter. *History of the German Resistance.* Cambridge: MIT Press, 1977.

Hohne, Heinz. *The Order of the Death's Head.* London: Secker & Warburg, 1969.

Hohne, Heinz, and Hermann Zolling. *The General Was a Spy.* New York: Coward, McCann & Geoghegan, Inc., 1972.

Hood, William. *Mole.* New York: Norton, 1982.

Hoopes, Townsend. *The Devil and John Foster Dulles.* New York: Little, Brown & Co., 1973.

Hunt, E. Howard. *Give Us This Day*. New Rochelle, NY: Arlington House, 1973.

Hyde, Montgomery. *Room 3603*. New York: Farrar, Straus, 1963.

————. *Cynthia*. New York: Farrar, Straus, 1965.

Hymoff, Edward. *The OSS in World War II*. New York: Richardson & Steirman, 1986.

Jackson, Wayne G. *Allen Welsh Dulles as Director of Central Intelligence*. Washington: Central Intelligence Agency DCI Historical Series, No. 2, Vols. I–IV (1973—declassified 1994).

Jeffreys-Jones, Rhodri. *CIA and American Democracy*. New Haven: Yale University Press, 1988.

————. *American Espionage: From Secret Service to CIA*. New York: Free Press, 1977.

Jeffreys-Jones, Rhodri, and Christopher Andrew. *Eternal Vigilance? 50 Years of the CIA*. London: Frank Cass, 1997.

Kahn, David. *The Code Breakers: The Story of Secret Writing*. London: Weidenfeld & Nicolson, 1967.

————. *Hitler's Spies: German Military Intelligence in World War II*. New York: Macmillan, 1978.

Katz, Barry M. *Foreign Intelligence*. Cambridge: Harvard University Press, 1989.

Kent, Sherman. *Strategic Intelligence for American World Policy*. Princeton: Princeton University Press, 1966.

Kirkpatrick, Lyman. *Captains Without Eyes*. London: Macmillan, 1969.

————. *The Real CIA*. New York: Macmillan, 1968.

————. *The U.S. Intelligence Community: Foreign Policy and Domestic Activities*. New York: Hill and Wang, 1973.

Klemperer, Klemens von. *German Resistance Against Hitler*. New York: Clarendon Press, 1992.

Knightley, Philip. *Philby: KGB Masterspy*. London: Andre Deutsch, 1988.

Kornbluh, Peter. *Bay of Pigs Declassified*. New York: The New Press, 1998.

Langer, Walter C. *The Mind of Adolf Hitler*. New York: Basic Books, 1972.

Lankford, Nelson D., ed. *OSS Against the Reich: The World War II Papers of Colonel David K. E. Bruce*. Kent, OH: Kent State University Press, 1991.

Lanning, Lieutenant Colonel Michael Lee. *Senseless Secrets*. New York: Birch Lane Press, 1996.

Laquer, Walter, and Richard Breitman. *Breaking the Silence*. New York: Simon & Schuster, 1986.

Leverhuehn, Paul. *German Military Intelligence*. New York: Praeger, 1954.

Lewis, Flora. *Red Pawn: The Story of Noel Field*. Garden City, NY: Doubleday, 1965.

Lisagor, Nancy, and Frank Lipsius. *A Law Unto Itself: The Untold Story of the Law Firm of Sullivan & Cromwell*. New York: Morrow, 1988.

Lord, Walter. *The Good Years*. New York: Harper & Bros., 1960.

Lowenthal, Mark M. *U.S. Intelligence: Evolution and Anatomy*. Westport, CT: Praeger, 1992.

Lynch, Grayston L. *Decision for Disaster*. Dulles, VA: Brassey's Inc., 1998.

Mahl, Thomas E. *Desperate Deception*. Dulles, VA: Brassey's Inc., 1998.

Malone, Dumas, and Basil Rauch. *War and Troubled Peace*. New York: Appleton-Century-Crofts, 1960.

Manchester, William. *The Arms of Krupp*. New York: Little, Brown, 1968.

Marchetti, Victor. *The CIA and the Cult of Intelligence*. New York: Knopf, 1974.

May, Ernest R., ed. *Knowing One's Enemies: Intelligence Assess-*

ment Before the Two World Wars. Princeton, NJ: Princeton University Press, 1986.

May, Ernest R., and Philip D. Delikow. *The Kennedy Tapes.* Cambridge: Harvard University Press, 1997.

McGarvey, Patrick J. *CIA: Myth and Madness.* New York: Saturday Review Press, 1972.

McIntosh, Elizabeth P. *Sisterhood of Spies: The Women of the OSS.* Annapolis: Naval Institute Press, 1998.

Meyer, Cord. *Facing Reality: From World Federalism to the CIA.* Washington, D.C.: University Press of America, 1982.

Miller, Nathan. *Spying for America.* New York: Doubleday & Co., 1989.

Molden, Fritz. *Exploding Star: A Young Austrian Against Hitler.* London: Weidenfeld & Nicolson, 1978.

Montague, Ludwell Lee. *DCI Historical Series-One.* Washington, D.C.: Central Intelligence Agency, 1971.

———. *General Walter Bedell Smith as Director of Central Intelligence.* Washington, D.C.: Central Intelligence Agency DCI Historical Series, 1971 (declassified 1990).

Moyzisch, L. C. *Operation Cicero.* New York: Coward-McCann, 1950.

Murphy, David, Sergei Kondrashev, and George Bailey. *Battleground Berlin.* New Haven: Yale University Press, 1997.

Murphy, Robert. *Diplomat Among Warriors.* New York: Doubleday, 1964.

Nixon, Richard M. *Six Crises.* New York: 1969.

O'Toole, G. J. A., ed. *The Encyclopedia of American Intelligence and Espionage.* New York: Facts on File, 1988.

———. *Honorable Treachery.* New York: Atlantic Monthly Press, 1991.

Page, Bruce, David Leitch, and Phillip Knightley. *The Philby Conspiracy.* New York: Doubleday, 1968.

Persico, Joseph E. *Casey: From OSS to the CIA.* New York: Viking, 1990.

———. *Piercing the Reich: The Penetration of Nazi Germany by American Secret Agents During World War II.* New York: Viking, 1979.

Philby, Kim. *My Silent War.* New York: Grove Press, 1968.

Phillips, David Atlee. *The Night Watch.* New York: Atheneum, 1977.

Powers, Thomas. *The Man Who Kept the Secrets.* New York: Knopf, 1979.

Pruessen, Ronald W. *John Foster Dulles: The Road to Power.* New York: Free Press.

Ranelagh, John. *The Agency: The Rise and Decline of the CIA.* New York: Simon & Schuster, 1986.

Ransom, Harry Howe. *Central Intelligence and National Security.* Cambridge: Harvard University Press, 1958.

Reese, Mary Ellen. *General Reinhard Gehlen.* Washington: George Mason University Press, 1990.

Richelson, Jeffrey T. *The U.S. Intelligence Community.* Cambridge: Ballinger Publishing, 1985.

———. *A Century of Spies.* New York: Oxford University Press, 1995.

Roosevelt, Archie. *For Lust of Knowing.* New York: Little, Brown, 1988.

Roosevelt, Kermit. *The War Report of the OSS.* (two vols.) New York: Walker, 1976.

Rositzke, Harry A. *The CIA's Secret Operations.* Boulder, CO: Westview Press, 1988.

———. *Managing Moscow.* New York: Morrow, 1984.

Rostow, W. W. *Diffusion of Power.* New York: Harper & Bros., 1977.

Schlabrendorff, Fabian von. *They Almost Killed Hitler.* Edited by Gero von Gaevernitz. New York: Macmillan, 1947.

Schlesinger, Arthur M., Jr. *A Thousand Days: John F. Kennedy in the White House*. New York: Houghton Mifflin, 1965.

Schlesinger, Stephen, and Stephen Kinzer. *Bitter Fruit*. New York: Doubleday, 1982.

Sherwood, Robert. *Roosevelt and Hopkins*. New York: Harper Bros., 1950.

Shirer, William L. *Rise and Fall of the Third Reich*. New York: Simon & Schuster, 1960.

Smith, Bradley. *The Shadow Warriors: OSS and the Origins of the CIA*. New York: Basic Books, 1983.

————. *Sharing Secrets with Stalin*. Lawrence, KS: University of Kansas Press, 1996.

Smith, Bradley, and Elena Agarossi. *Operation Sunrise: The Secret Surrender*. New York: Basic Books, 1979.

Smith, Daniel. *Robert Lansing and American Neutrality*. Berkeley: University of California Press, 1958.

Smith, R. Harris. *OSS: The Secret History of America's First Central Intelligence Agency*. Berkeley: University of California Press, 1972.

Sorensen, Theodore C. *Kennedy*. New York: Harper & Row, 1965.

Stevenson, William. *A Man Called Intrepid*. New York: Harcourt Brace Jovanovich, 1977.

Strong, Major General Sir Kenneth. *Intelligence at the Top*. New York: Doubleday & Co., 1969.

Tarrant, V. E. *The Red Orchestra*. New York: John Wiley & Sons, 1996.

Trevor-Roper, Hugh. *The Philby Affair: Espionage, Treason, and Secret Services*. London: William Kimber, 1968.

Troy, Thomas F. *Donovan and the CIA: A History of the Establishment of the Central Intelligence Agency*. Frederick, MD: University Publications of America, 1981.

————. *Wild Bill and Intrepid*. New Haven: Yale University Press, 1996.

Tuchman, Barbara. *The Zimmermann Telegram*. New York: Macmillan, 1958.

Tully, Andrew. *CIA: The Inside Story*. New York: Morrow, 1962.

————. *The Super Spies*. New York: Morrow, 1969.

U.S. Senate, Committee on Foreign Relations, Subcommittee on U.S. Security Agreements and Commitments Abroad. "Church Committee Hearings on Intelligence Oversight." Washington, D.C.: U.S. Government Printing Office, 1972.

U.S. Senate Select Committee. "Study of Government Operations with Respect to Intelligence Activities." Washington, D.C.: U.S. Government Printing Office, 1975.

Visser't Hooft, W. A. *Memoirs*. London: SCM Press, 1973.

Wallach, Erica Glaser. *Light at Midnight*. New York: Doubleday, 1967.

Waller, John H. *The Unseen War in Europe*. New York: Random House, 1996.

West, Nigel. *MI5: British Security Service Operations*. London: Stein & Day, 1981.

————. *MI6: British Secret Intelligence Service Operations*. London: Weidenfeld & Nicolson, 1983.

————, ed. *British Security Coordination*. London: St. Ermin's Press, 1998.

Westerfield, H. Bradford. *Inside CIA's Private World*. New Haven: Yale University Press, 1995.

Whaley, Barton. *Covert German Rearmament, 1919–1939*. Frederick, MD: University Publications of America, 1984.

Winks, Robin. *Cloak and Gown*. New York: Quill, 1987.

Winterbotham, F. W. *The Ultra Secret*. New York: Harper & Row, 1974.

Wise, David. *The Invisible Government.* New York: Vintage Books, 1974.

Wiskemann, Elizabeth. *Europe of the Dictators.* London: Fontana Press, 1966.

————. *The Europe I Saw.* London: Collins, 1968.

Woodhouse, C. M. *Something Ventured.* London: Granada, 1982.

Yardley, Herbert O. *The American Black Chamber.* Indianapolis: Bobbs-Merrill, 1931.

ACKNOWLEDGMENTS

I OWE MUCH to many people who helped along the way.

First there are those who urged the project as long overdue. At the top of that list is Eleanor Lansing Dulles, sister of my subject and a world-class diplomat and economist. She nudged me into this project and sparked my spirit whenever it flagged. At her death at age 101 I lost a good friend. This book redeems my promise to her. I also owe thanks to others of the Dulles clan who were generous with their insights but who left me at liberty to tell the story my way. My appreciation also goes to the late Lawrence Houston and to Garner Ranney, the trustees of Allen Dulles's papers. The mass of Dulles family papers at the Seeley G. Mudd Manuscript Library at Princeton is a researcher's dream of organization, thanks to library archivist Ben Primer and his associates, Nanci A. Young and Jeanne Holiday.

Then there are those who helped me manage to put the story into order. Michael A. Thompson combined the duties of researcher and friend and deserves special praise. He quickly matched my enthusiasm for the document hunt, and he produced prodigious results. He was a good companion. Gail Lewin was in at the early organization, and Charles Bell brought order and method to my files after the whirlwind of writing. German historian Christof Mauch was a generous friend. Scholars Michael and Linda Zaugg undertook a translation that shone a stronger light on the controversial "Bull-Pauls" conversations between Dulles and a representative of Nazi leader Heinrich Himmler. Bradley F. Smith, the American intelligence writer based in London, was a kind guide at the British Public Records Office in Kew. Jane Gelfman went well beyond what a literary agent should have to do.

Spies are supposed to be closed-mouthed by tradition, but I found the men and women of the intelligence community to be generous and forthcoming. For many it was a chance to set their own personal stories straight, and the book was the beneficiary of their candor. Colonel Walter Pforzheimer gave freely of his trenchant advice and his extraordinary book collection. Raymond Rocca, Richard Helms, Ray Cline, William Colby, and Colonel L. K. "Red" White were just a few who gave firsthand accounts of working with Dulles in the OSS-CIA years. Geoffrey Jones opened the OSS archives in his care. J. Kenneth McDonald, the CIA's historian, did all he was asked, without condition. Gervase Cowell, the archival adviser for the files of the British Special Operations Executive, went beyond my requests on many occasions. Samuel Halpern was a wise guide on the bewildering operational maze of the CIA's early years. I am also indebted to M. R. D. Foot, the distinguished British historian, for his tutorials on the history and context of the times.

And finally, a note of gratitude to the best manuscript editor I know, my wife Cecile Srodes. She was rigorous, and she was right every time.

INDEX